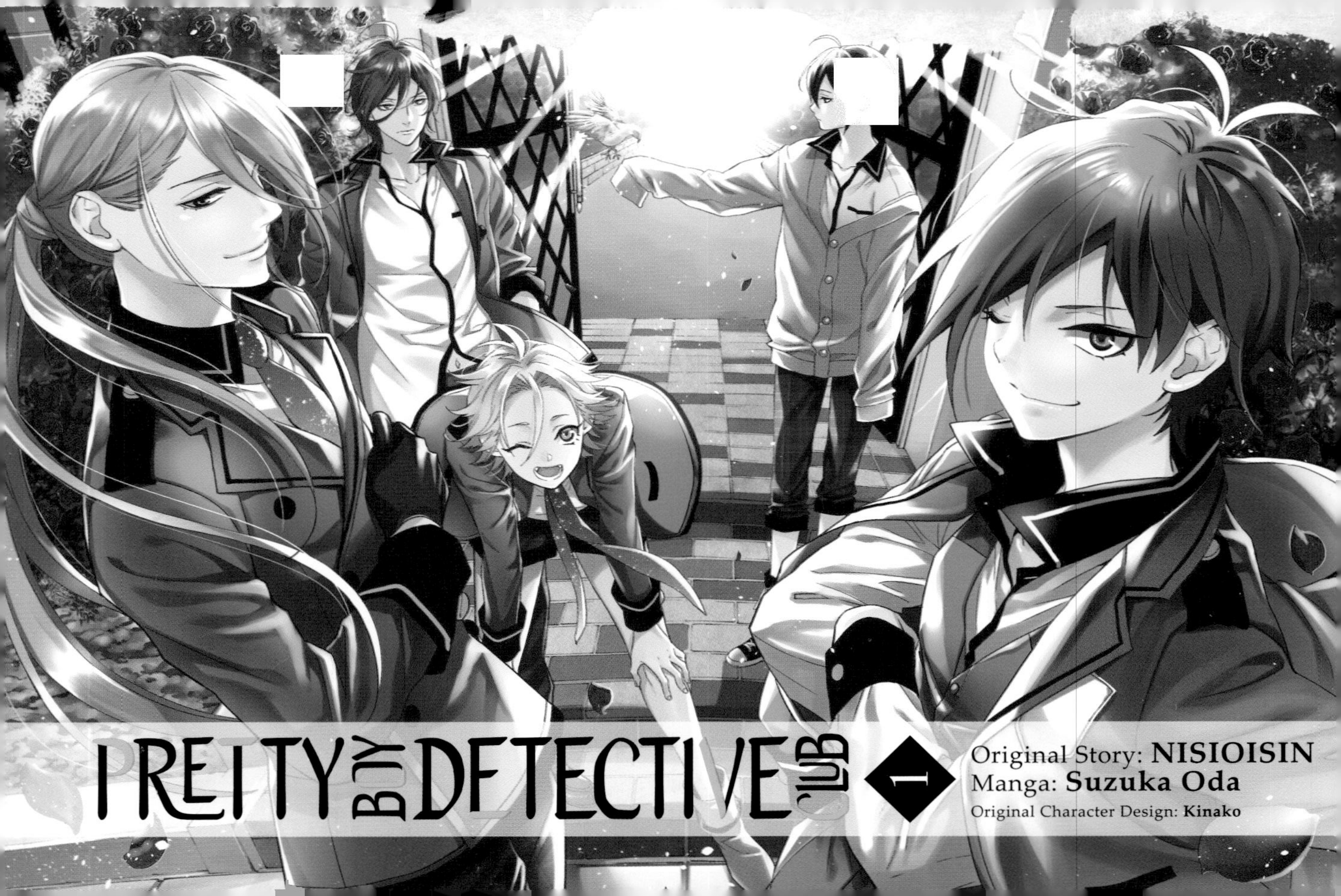
PRETTY BOY DETECTIVE CLUB
1
Original Story: NISIOISIN
Manga: Suzuka Oda
Original Character Design: Kinako

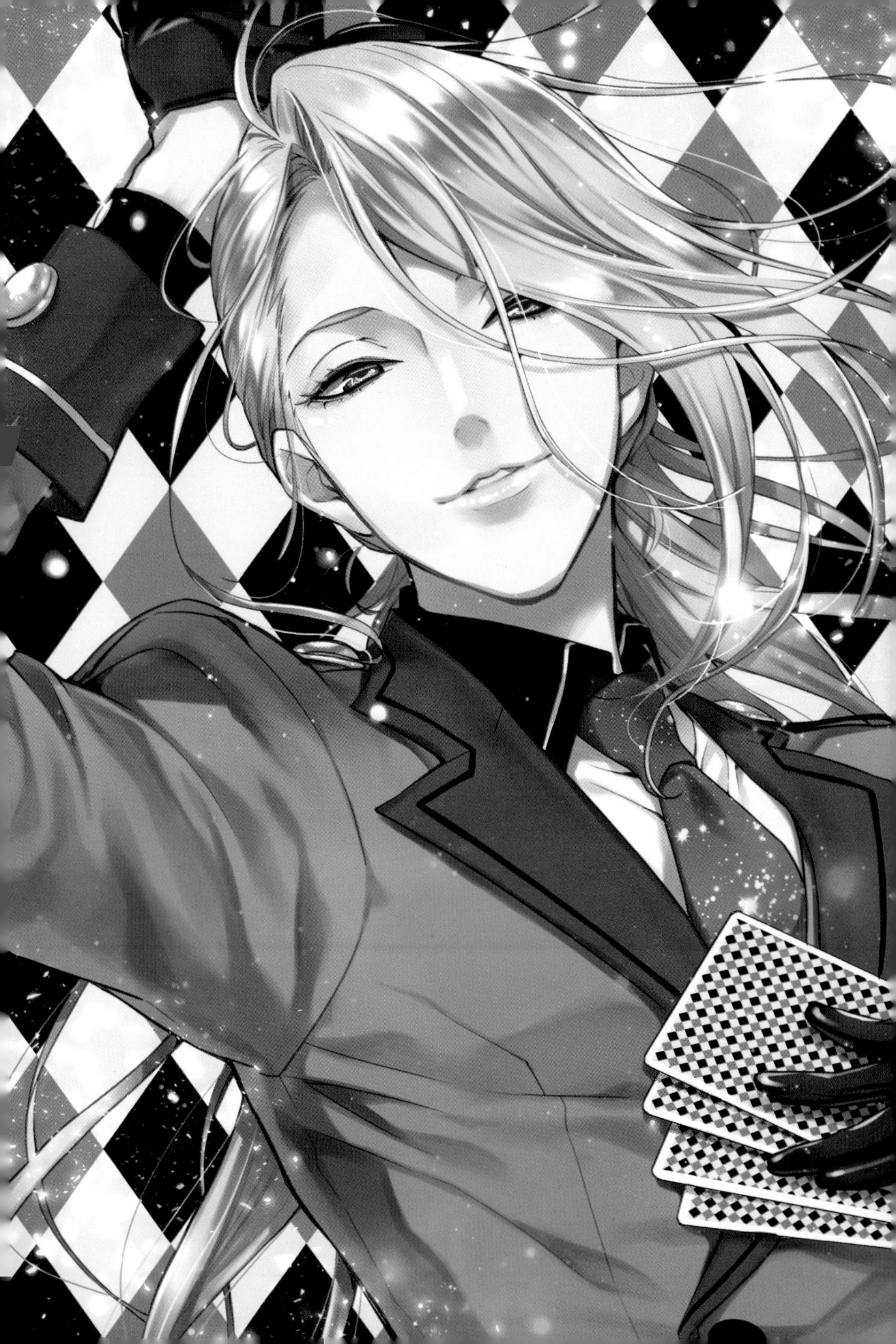

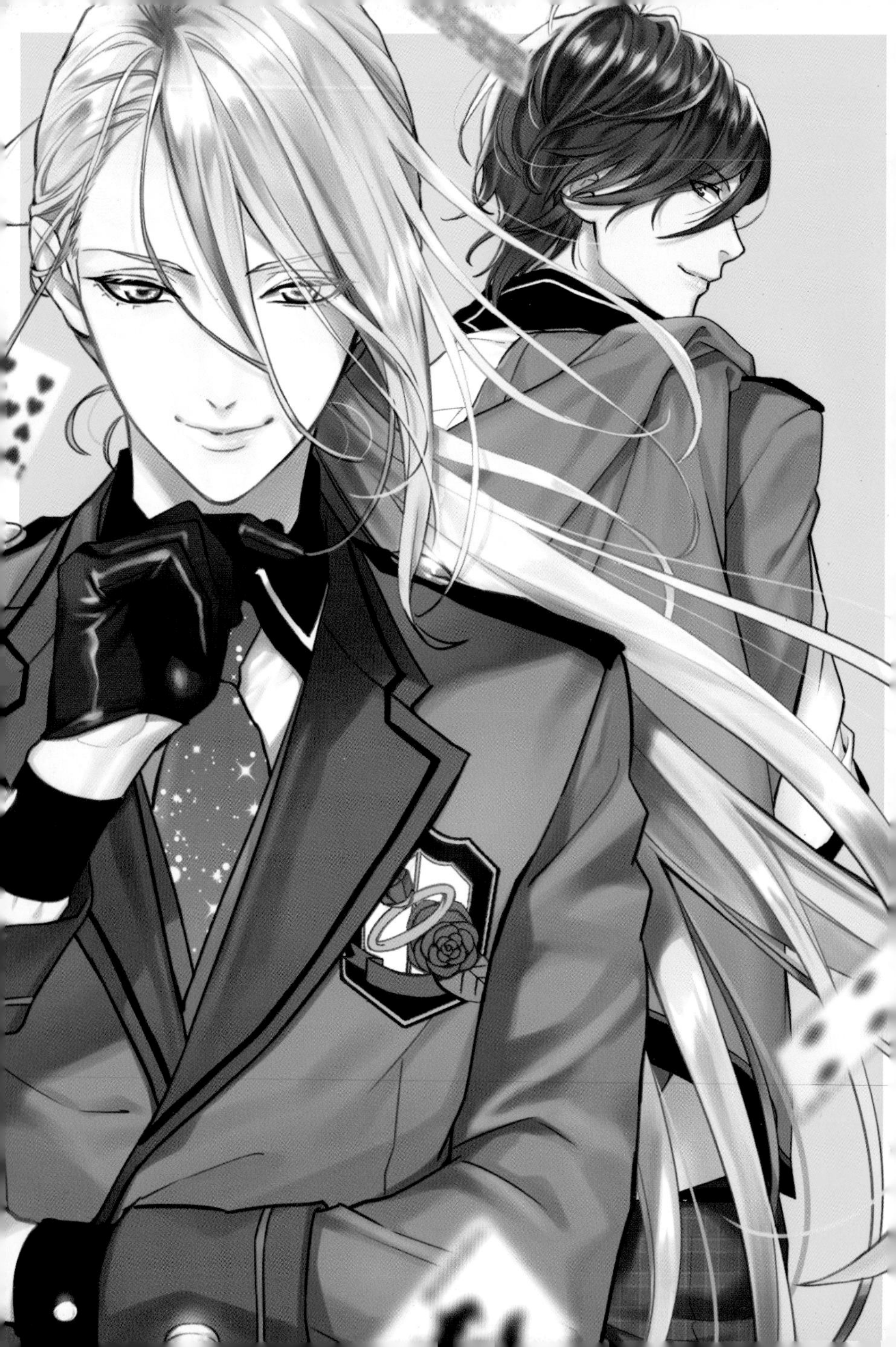

PRETTY BOY DETECTIVE CLUB

1

CONTENTS

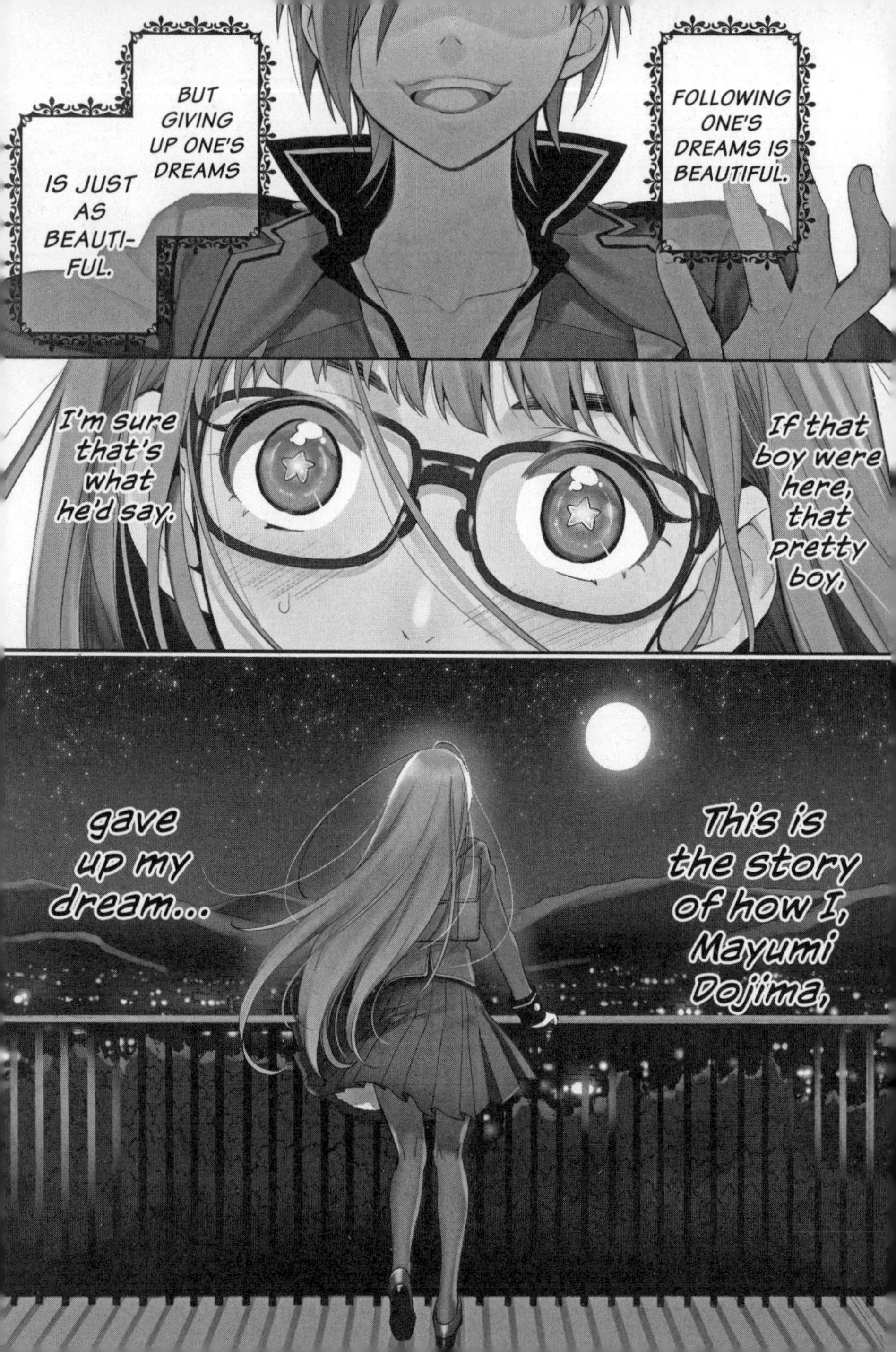
FOLLOWING ONE'S DREAMS IS BEAUTIFUL.
BUT GIVING UP ONE'S DREAMS
IS JUST AS BEAUTI-FUL.
If that boy were here, that pretty boy,
I'm sure that's what he'd say.
This is the story of how I, Mayumi Dojima,
gave up my dream...

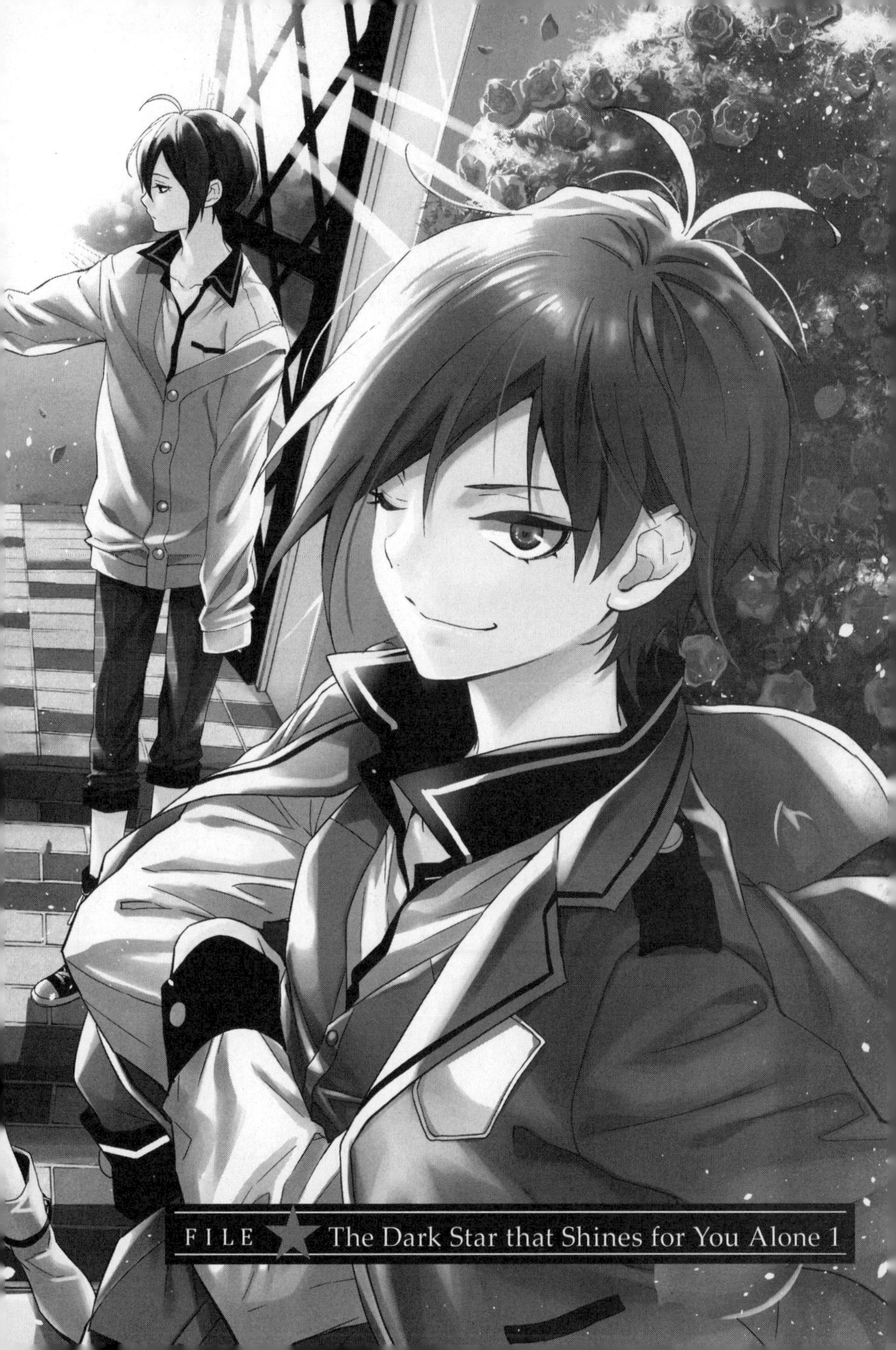
FILE ★ The Dark Star that Shines for You Alone 1

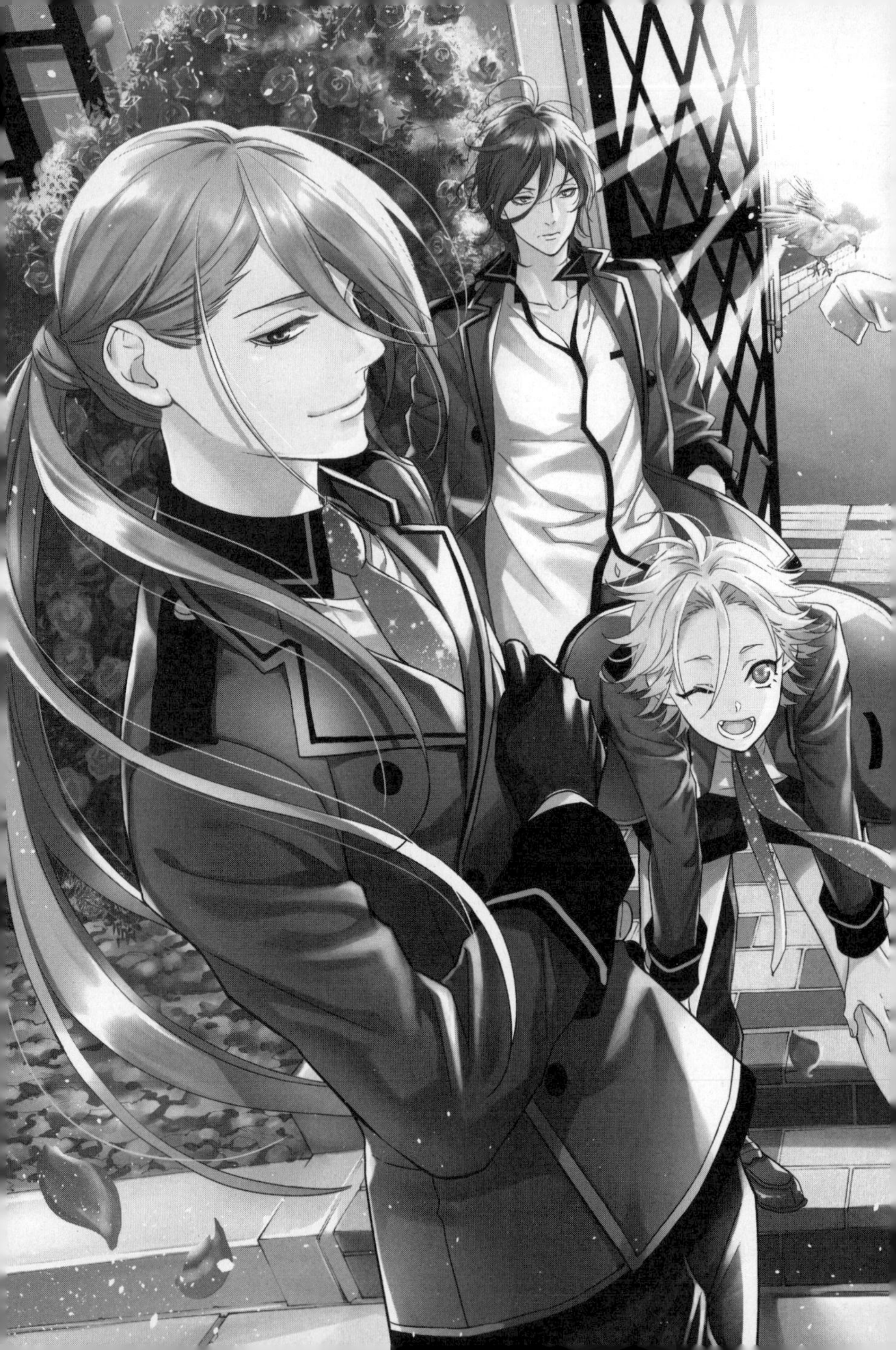

PRETTY BOY

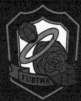

DETECTIVE CLUB!!

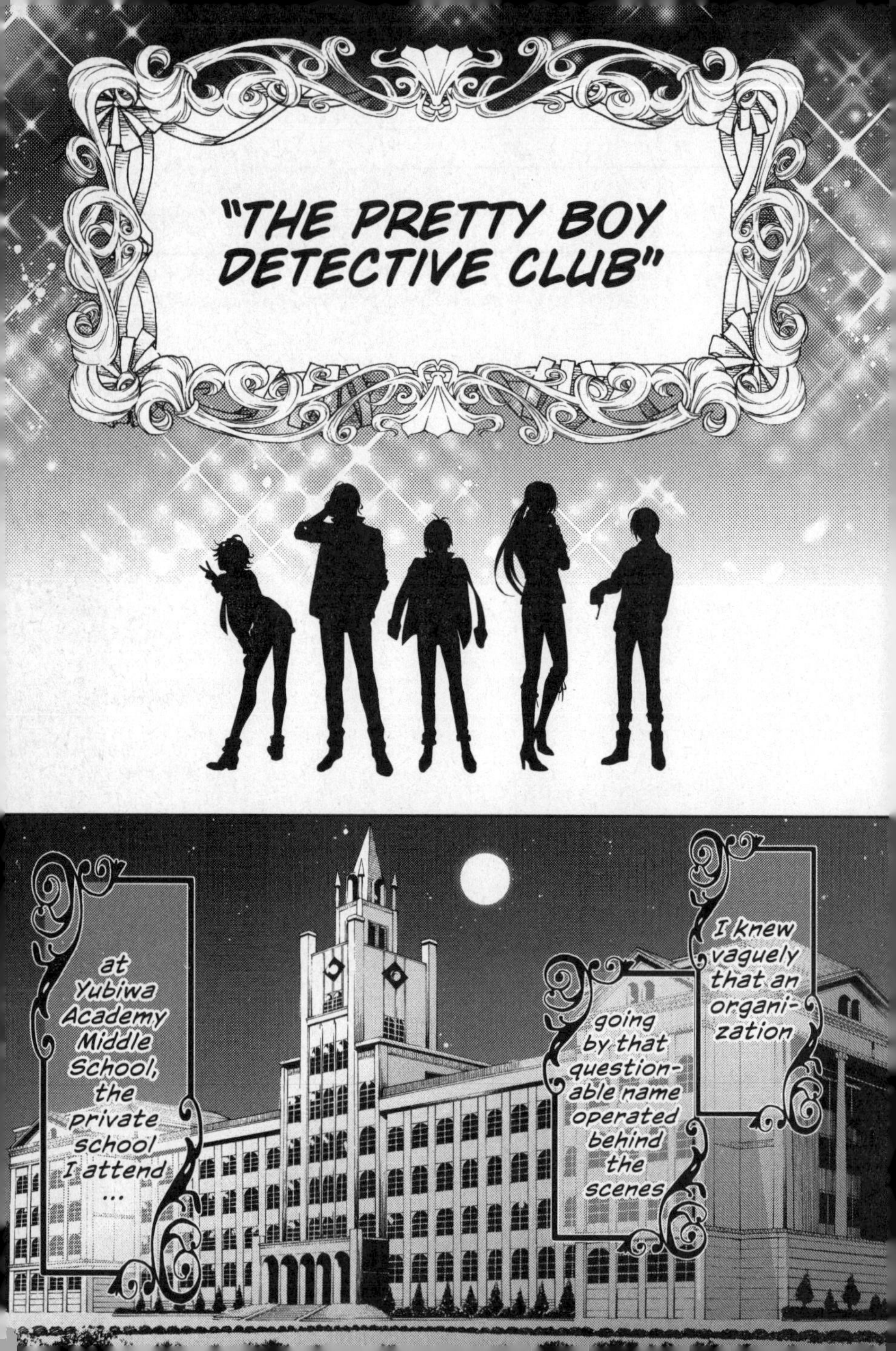
"THE PRETTY BOY DETECTIVE CLUB"
I knew vaguely that an organization
going by that questionable name operated behind the scenes
at Yubiwa Academy Middle School, the private school I attend...

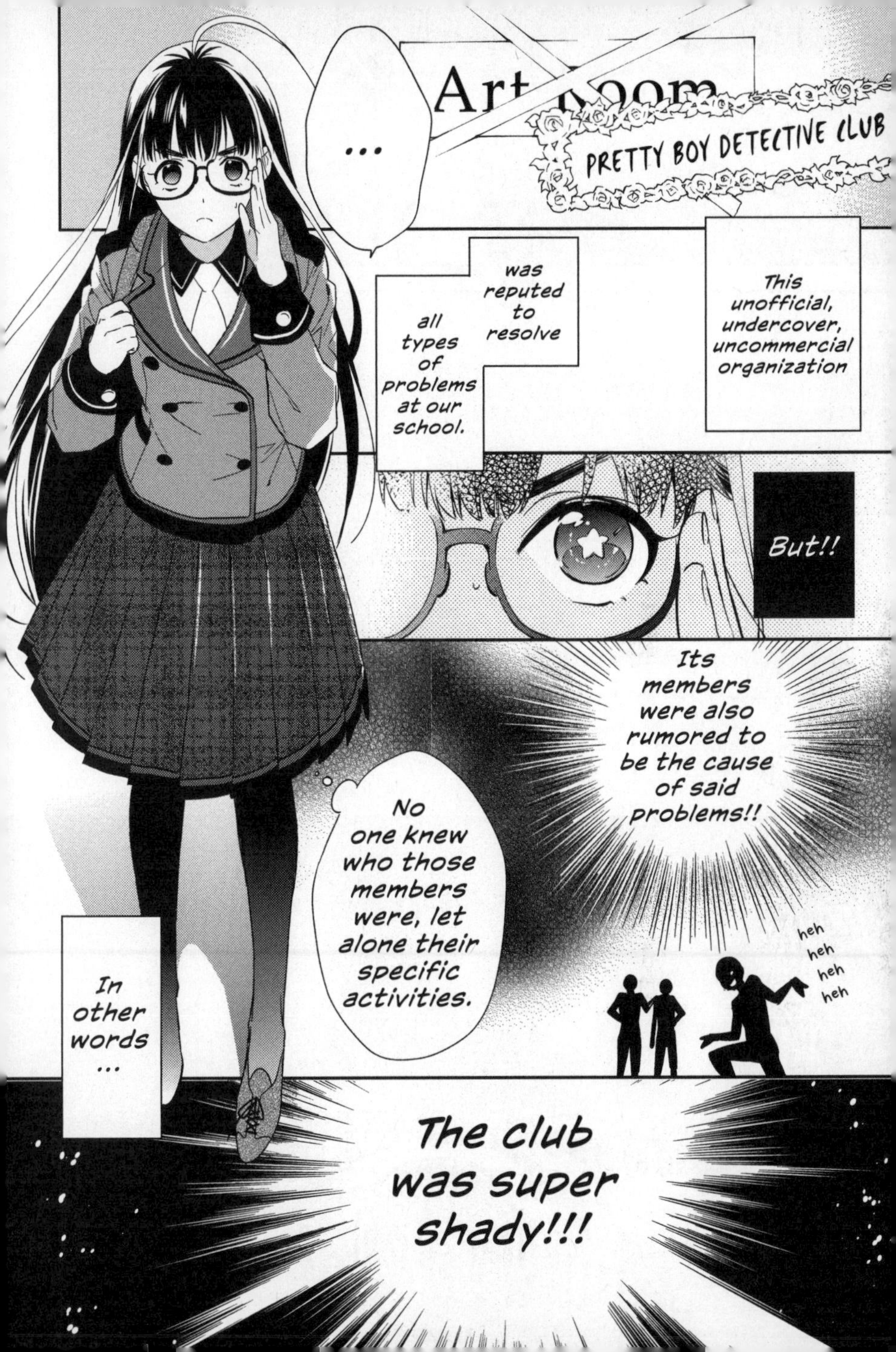

Art Room
PRETTY BOY DETECTIVE CLUB
...
This unofficial, undercover, uncommercial organization
was reputed to resolve
all types of problems at our school.
But!!
Its members were also rumored to be the cause of said problems!!
heh heh heh heh
No one knew who those members were, let alone their specific activities.
In other words...
The club was super shady!!!

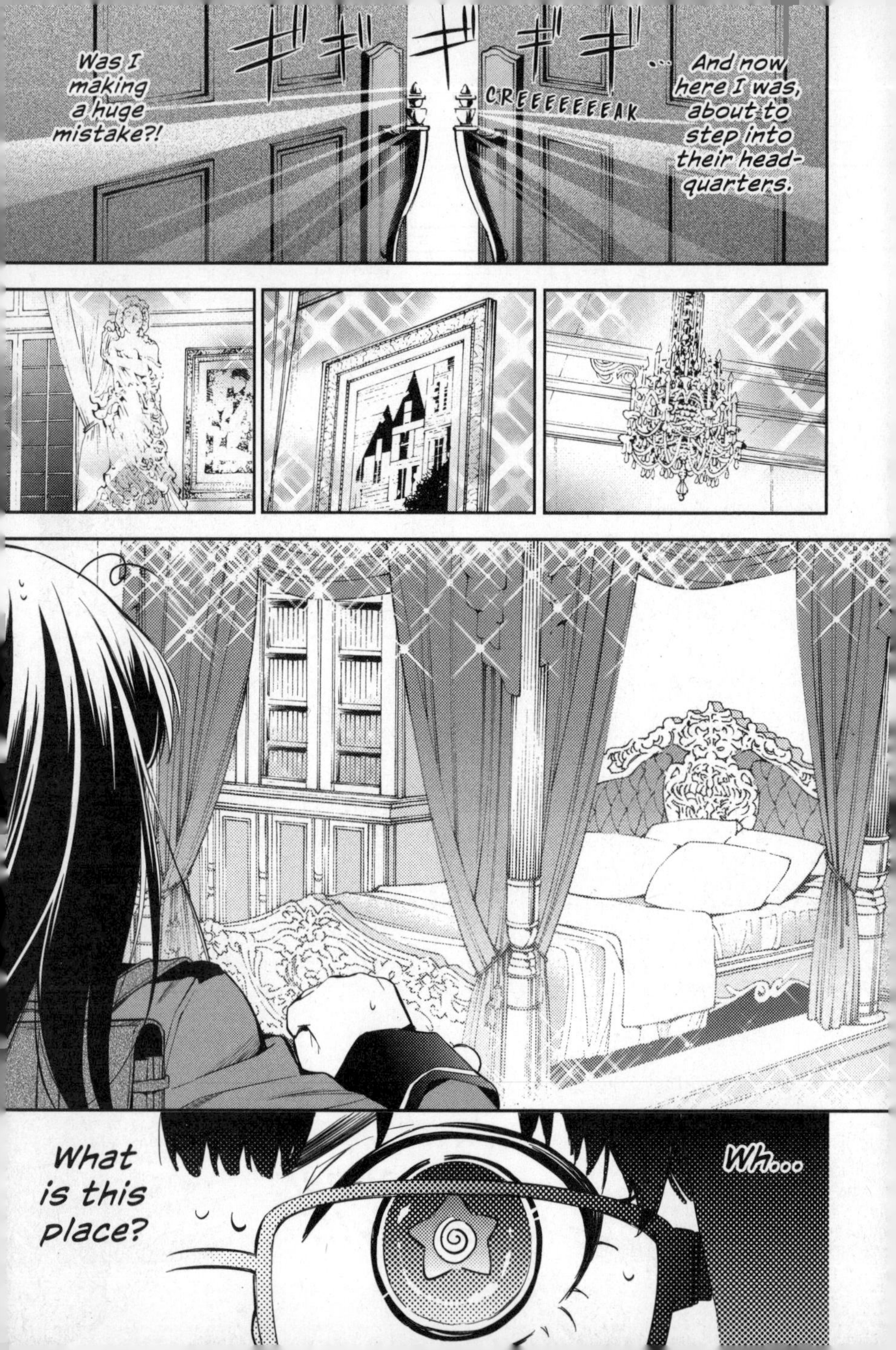
And now here I was, about to step into their headquarters.
ギギギギギ…
CREEEEEEEEAK
Was I making a huge mistake?!
Wh...
What is this place?

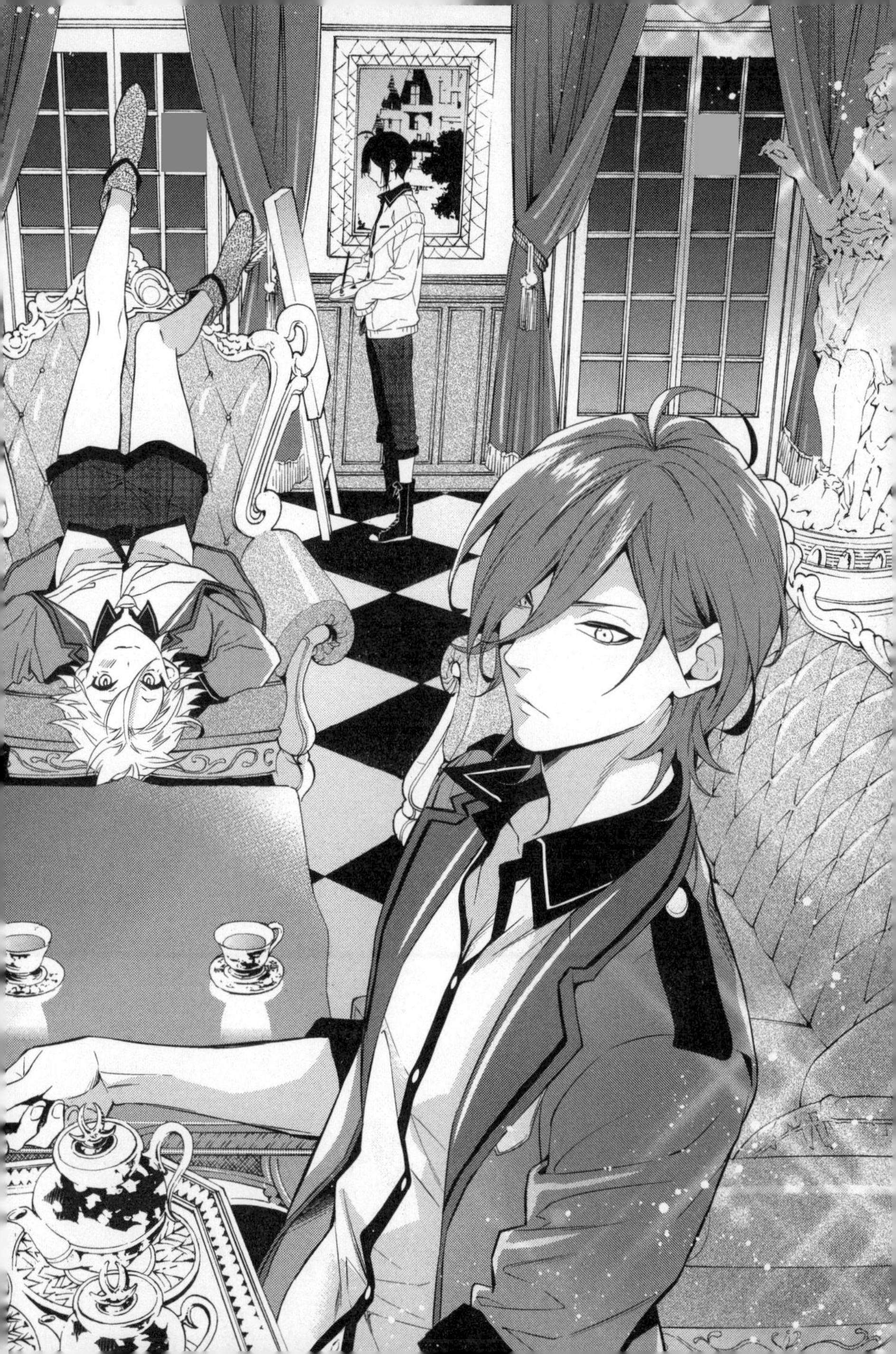

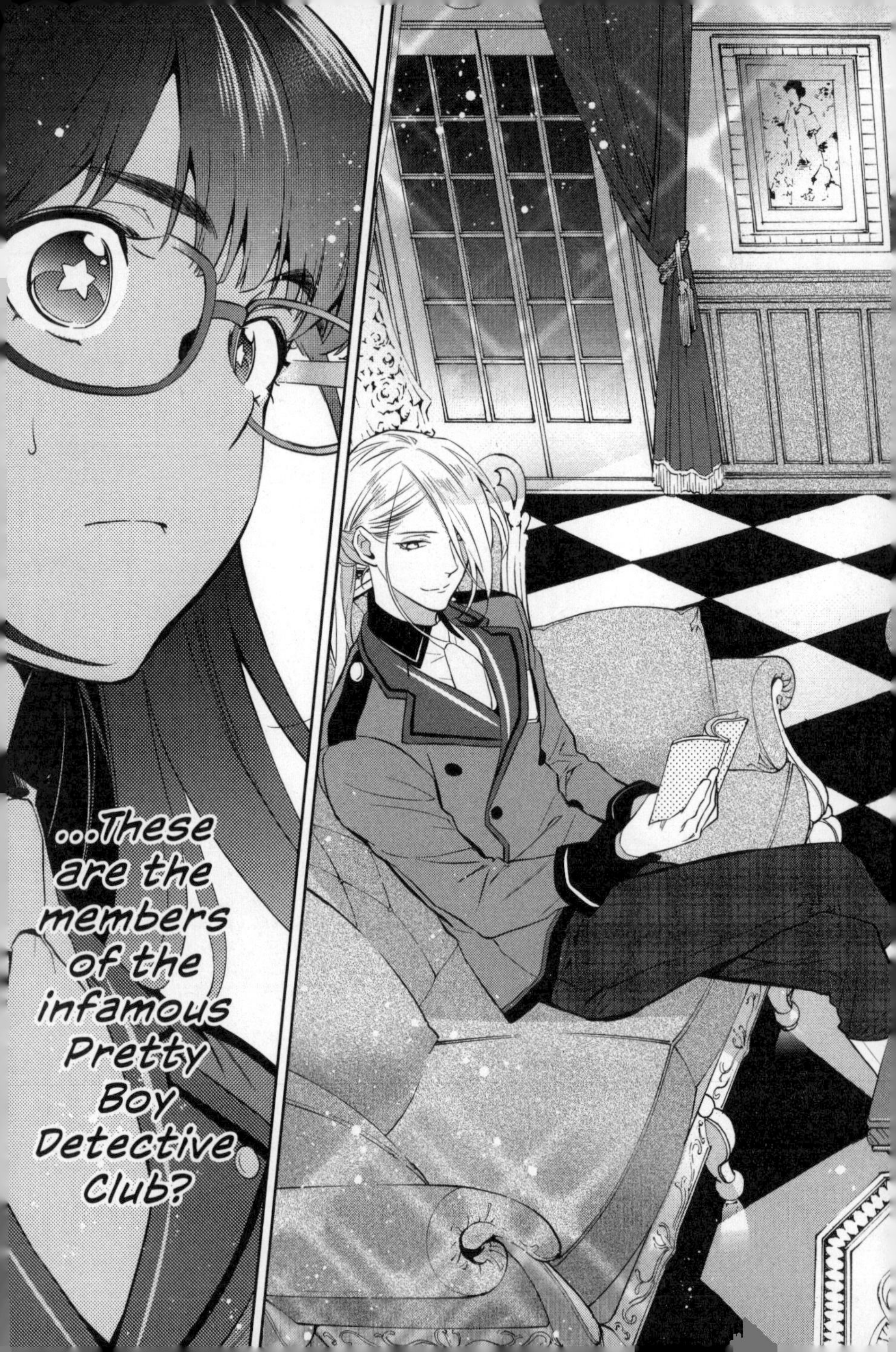
...These are the members of the infamous Pretty Boy Detective Club?

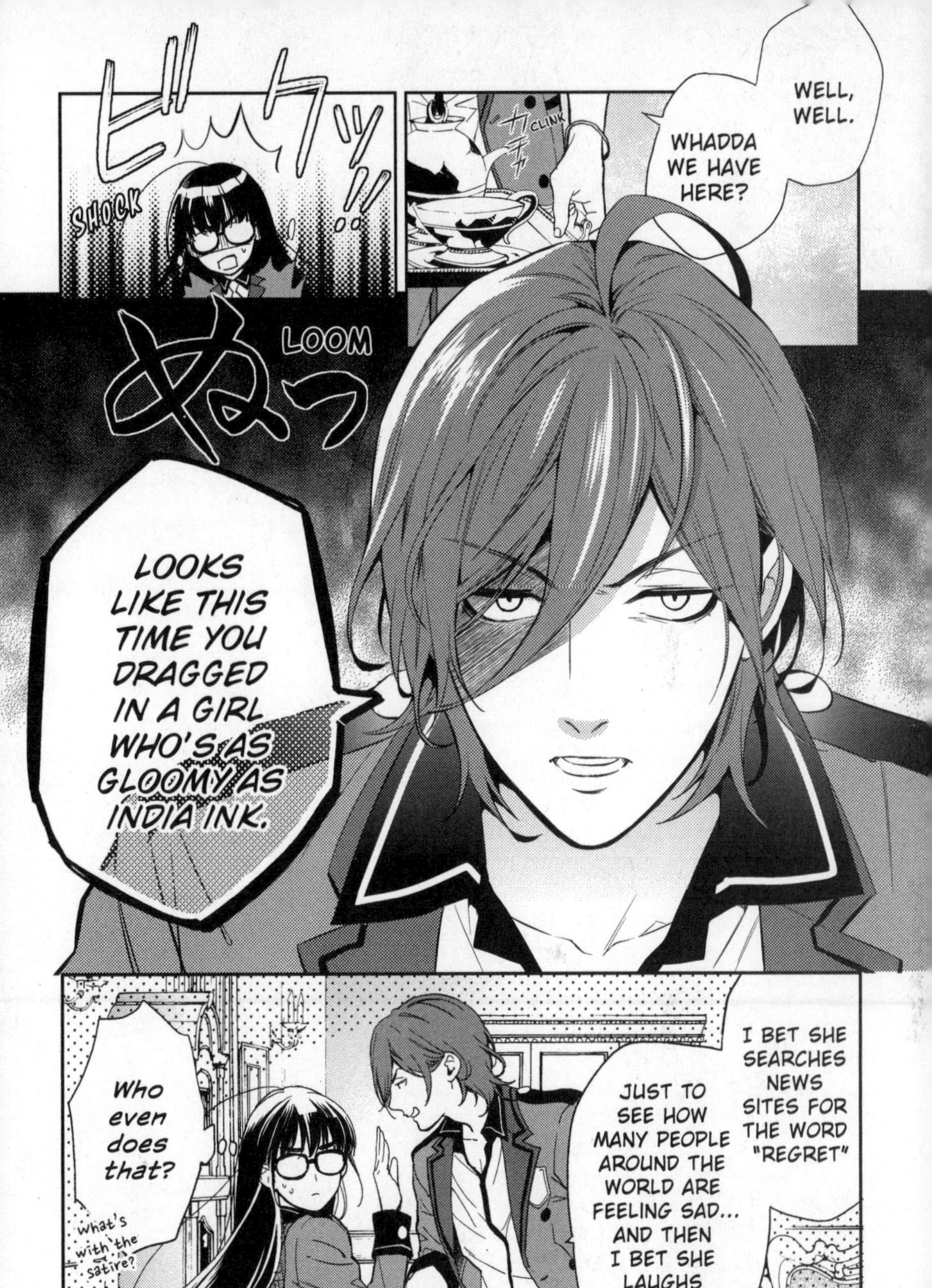
WELL, WELL.
WHADDA WE HAVE HERE?
CLINK
ビクッ!!
SHOCK
ぬっ
LOOM
LOOKS LIKE THIS TIME YOU DRAGGED IN A GIRL WHO'S AS GLOOMY AS INDIA INK.
I BET SHE SEARCHES NEWS SITES FOR THE WORD "REGRET"
JUST TO SEE HOW MANY PEOPLE AROUND THE WORLD ARE FEELING SAD... AND THEN I BET SHE LAUGHS ABOUT IT.
Who even does that?
what's with the satire?

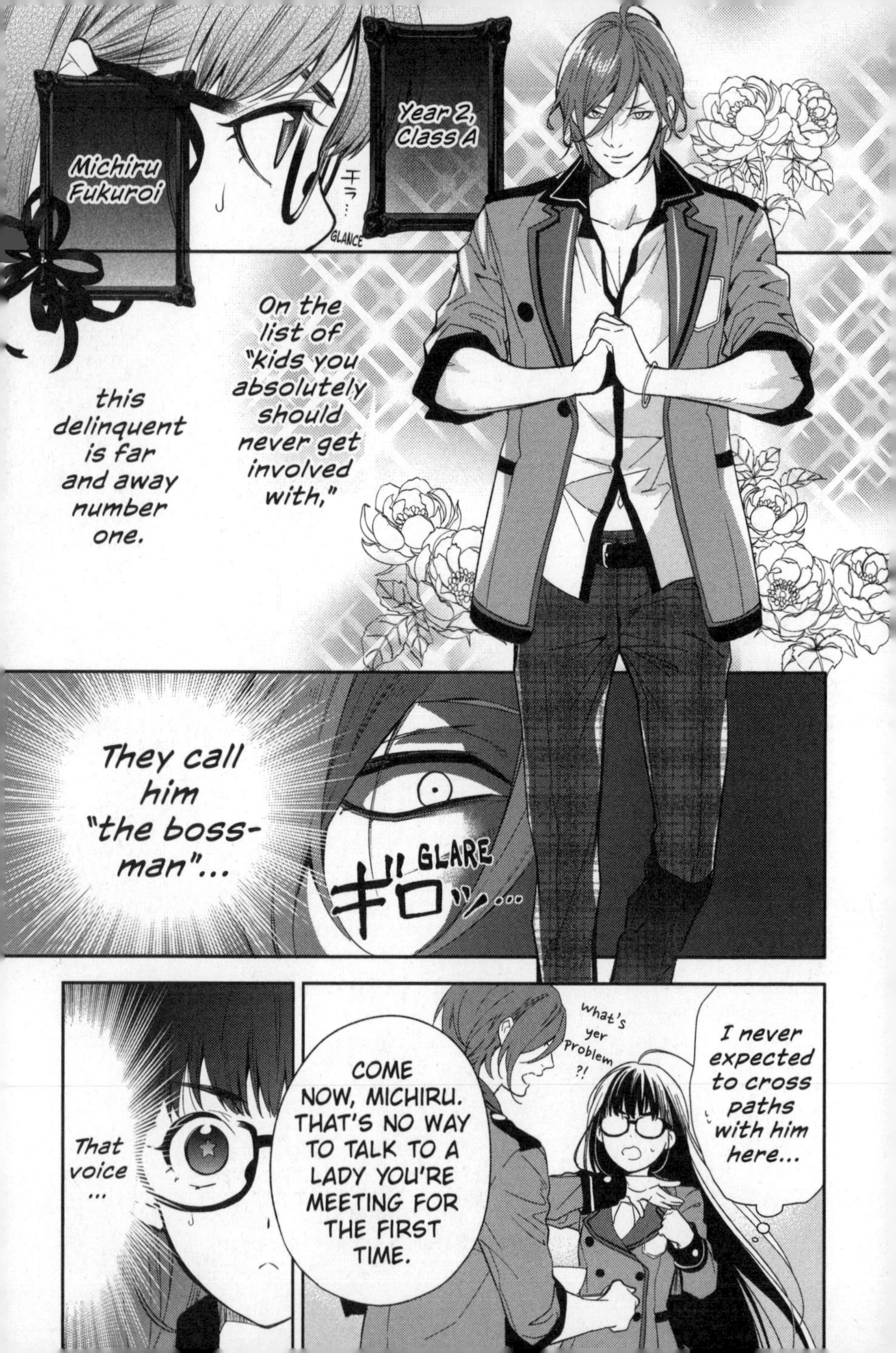
Year 2, Class A
Michiru Fukuroi
チラ…
GLANCE
On the list of "kids you absolutely should never get involved with,"
this delinquent is far and away number one.
They call him "the boss-man"...
ギロッ…
GLARE
I never expected to cross paths with him here...
What's yer problem?!
COME NOW, MICHIRU. THAT'S NO WAY TO TALK TO A LADY YOU'RE MEETING FOR THE FIRST TIME.
That voice ...

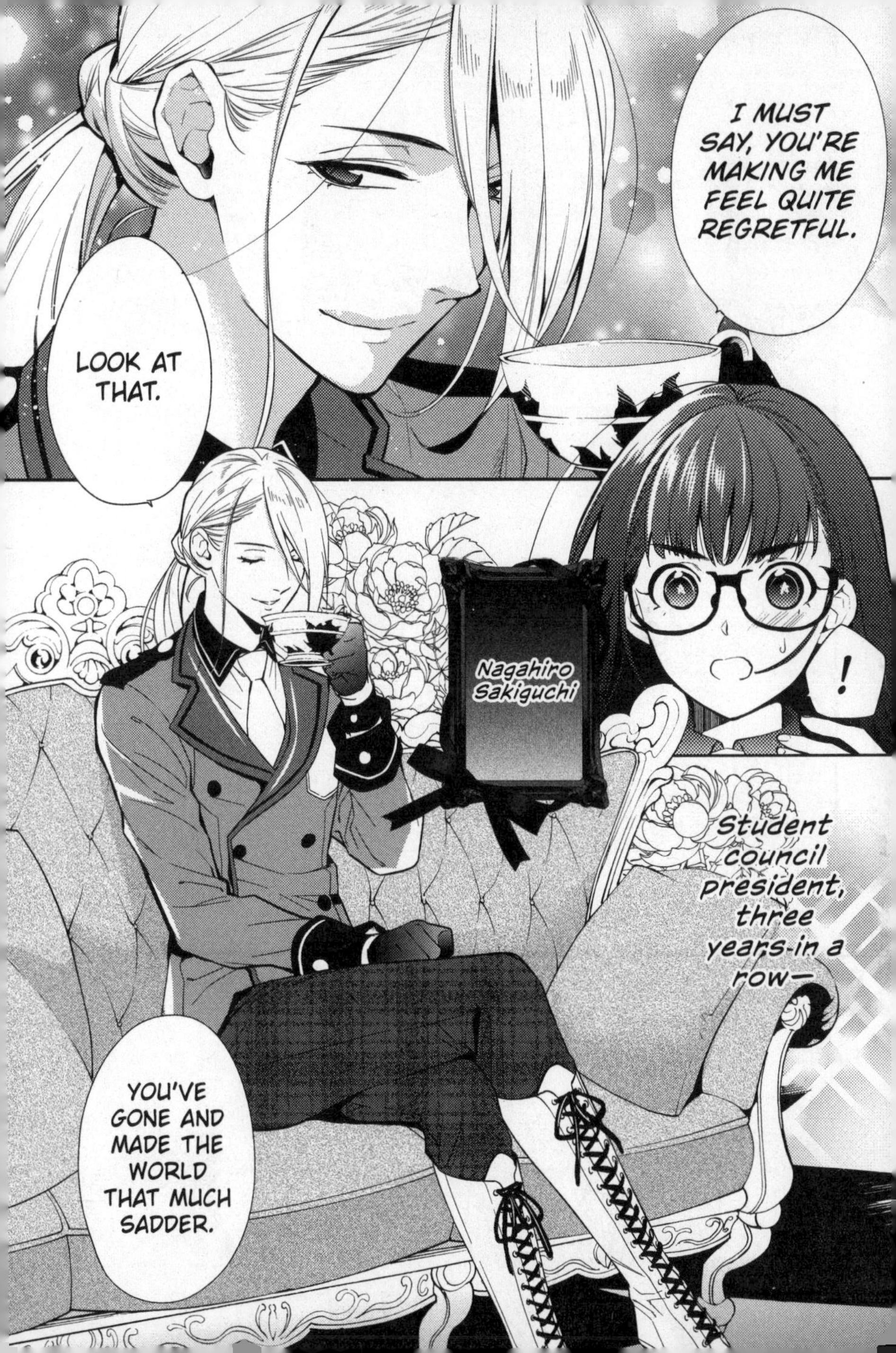
I MUST SAY, YOU'RE MAKING ME FEEL QUITE REGRETFUL.
LOOK AT THAT.
!
Nagahiro Sakiguchi
Student council president, three years in a row—
YOU'VE GONE AND MADE THE WORLD THAT MUCH SADDER.

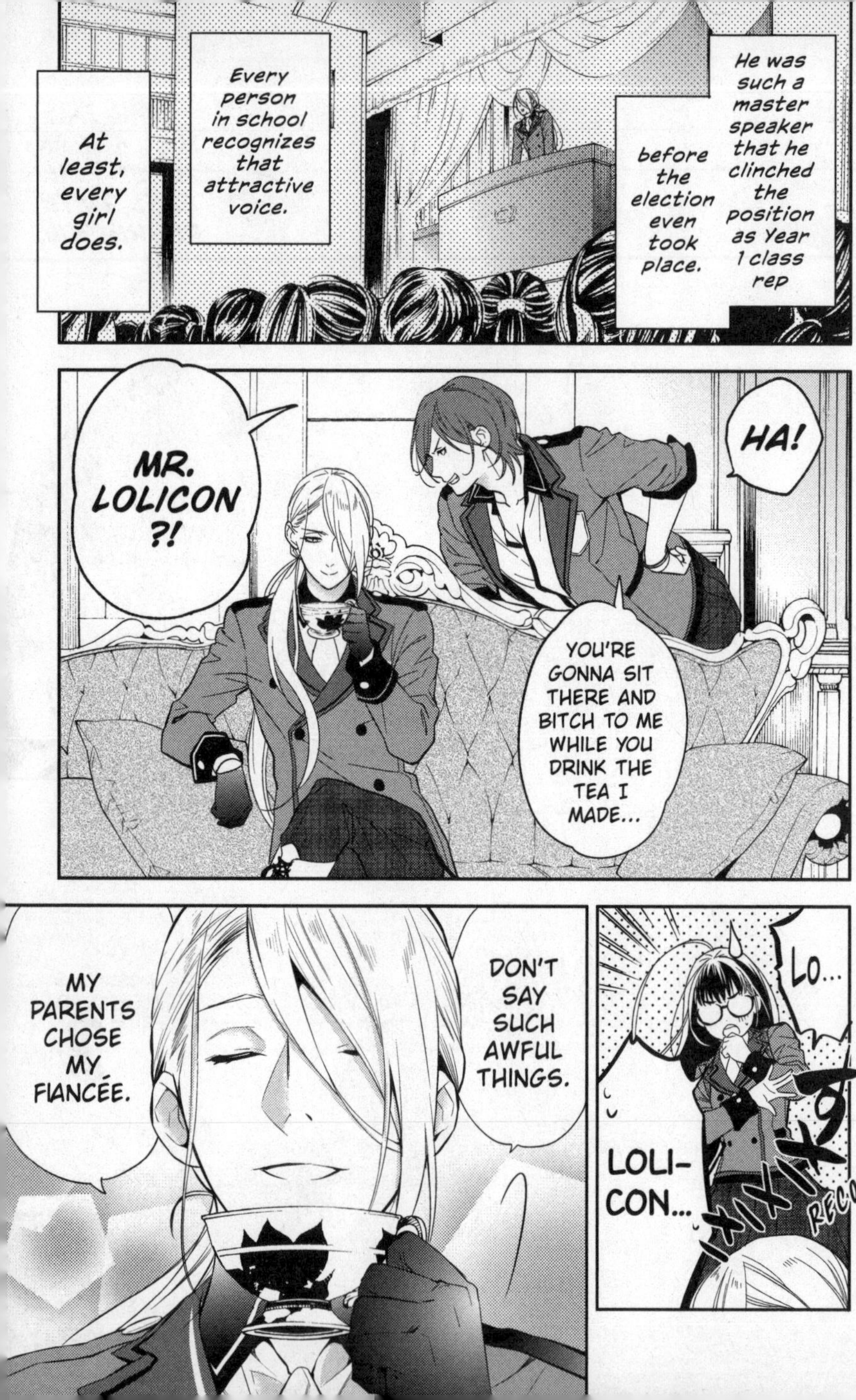
He was such a master speaker that he clinched the position as Year 1 class rep
before the election even took place.
Every person in school recognizes that attractive voice.
At least, every girl does.
HA!
YOU'RE GONNA SIT THERE AND BITCH TO ME WHILE YOU DRINK THE TEA I MADE...
MR. LOLICON?!
LO...
LOLI-CON...
RECOIL
DON'T SAY SUCH AWFUL THINGS.
MY PARENTS CHOSE MY FIANCÉE.

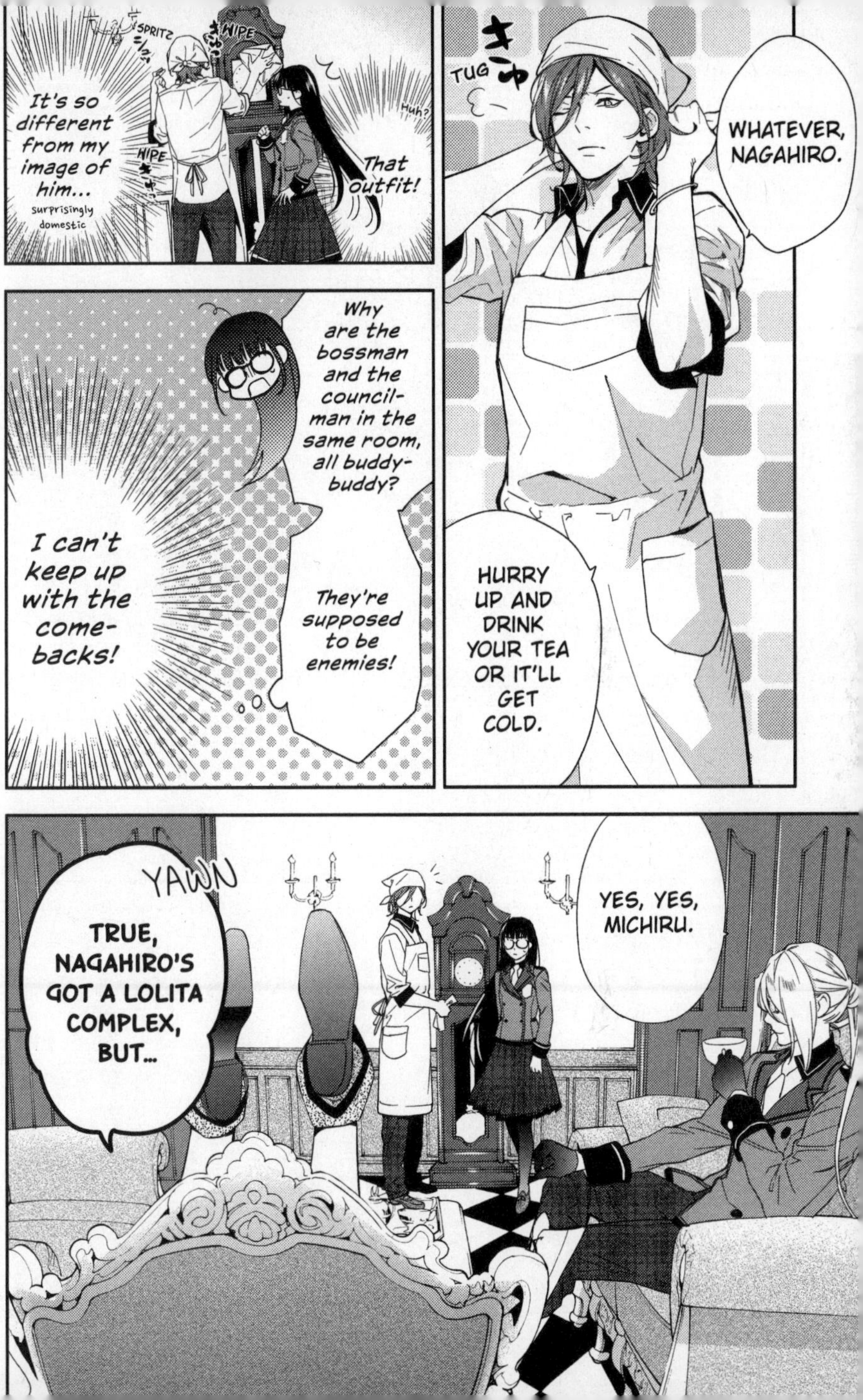

WHATEVER, NAGAHIRO.
TUG
HURRY UP AND DRINK YOUR TEA OR IT'LL GET COLD.
WIPE
SPRITZ
Huh?
That outfit!
WIPE
It's so different from my image of him...
surprisingly domestic
Why are the bossman and the councilman in the same room, all buddy-buddy?
They're supposed to be enemies!
I can't keep up with the comebacks!
YES, YES, MICHIRU.
YAWN
TRUE, NAGAHIRO'S GOT A LOLITA COMPLEX, BUT...

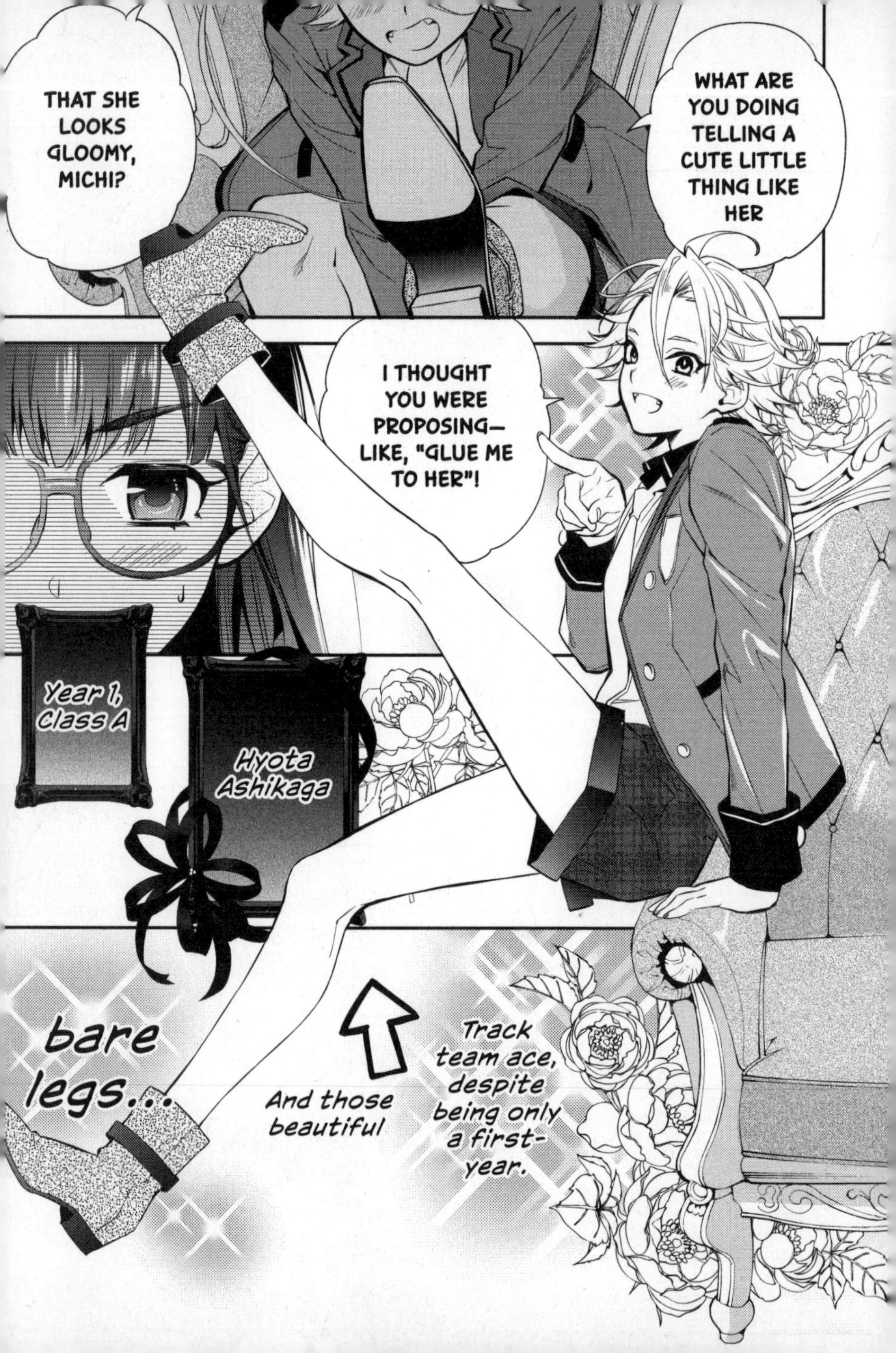
WHAT ARE YOU DOING TELLING A CUTE LITTLE THING LIKE HER
THAT SHE LOOKS GLOOMY, MICHI?
I THOUGHT YOU WERE PROPOSING—LIKE, "GLUE ME TO HER"!
Year 1, Class A
Hyota Ashikaga
Track team ace, despite being only a first-year.
And those beautiful
bare legs...

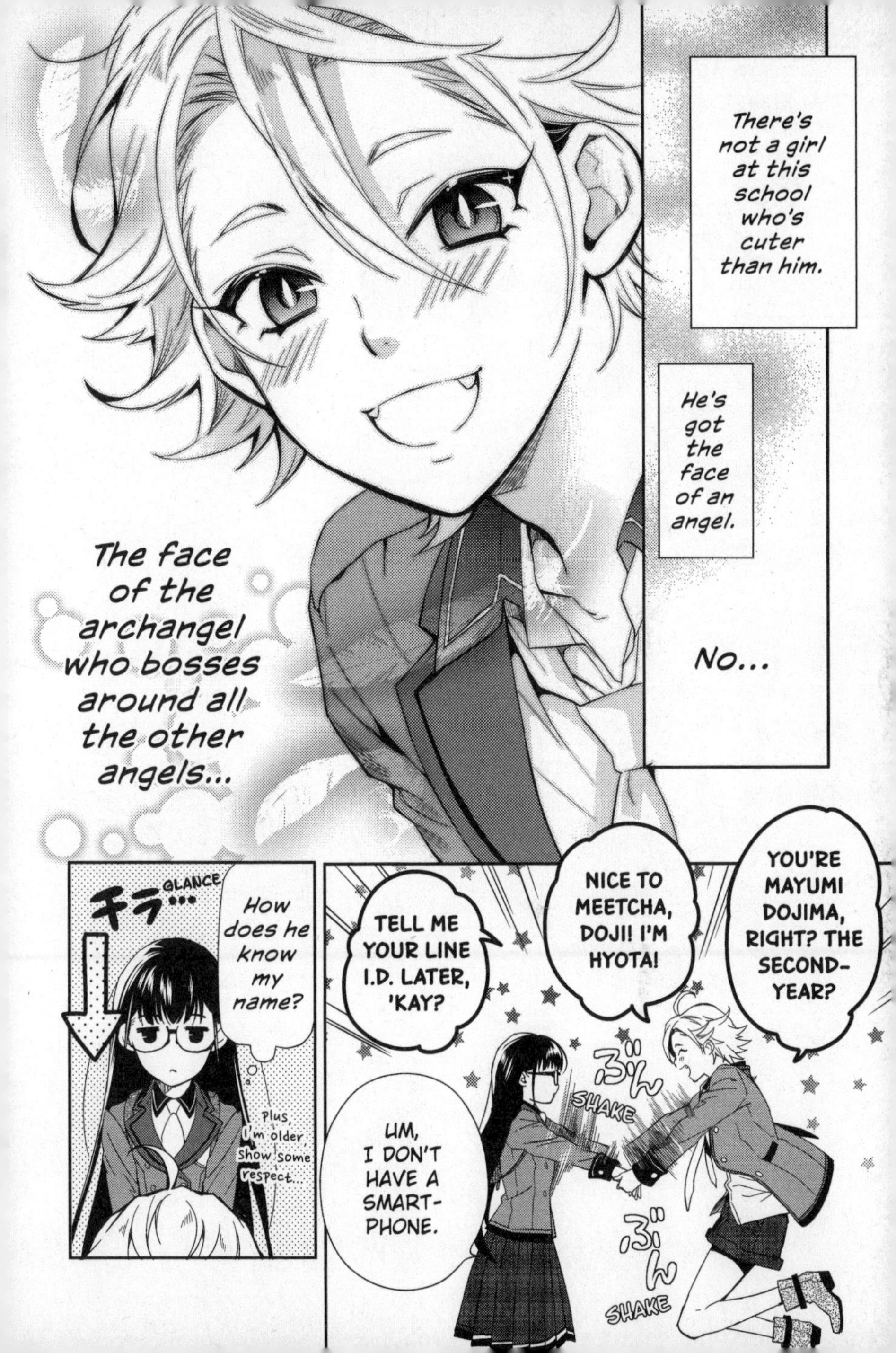
There's not a girl at this school who's cuter than him.
He's got the face of an angel.
No...
The face of the archangel who bosses around all the other angels...
YOU'RE MAYUMI DOJIMA, RIGHT? THE SECOND-YEAR?
NICE TO MEETCHA, DOJI! I'M HYOTA!
TELL ME YOUR LINE I.D. LATER, 'KAY?
ぶん SHAKE
ぶん SHAKE
UM, I DON'T HAVE A SMARTPHONE.
チラ GLANCE
How does he know my name?
Plus, I'm older. Show some respect...

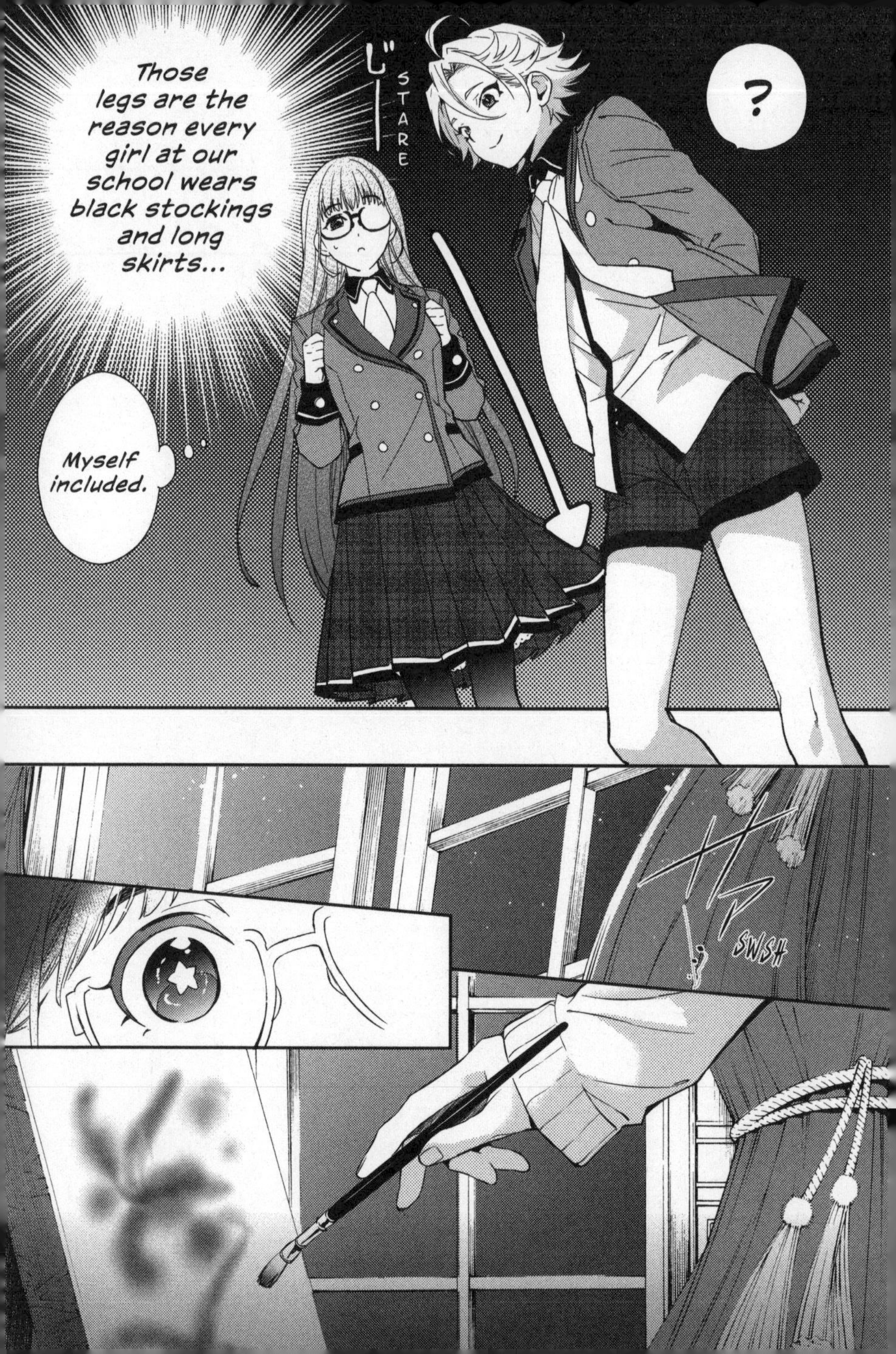
?
じ
STARE
Those legs are the reason every girl at our school wears black stockings and long skirts...
Myself included.
SWSH

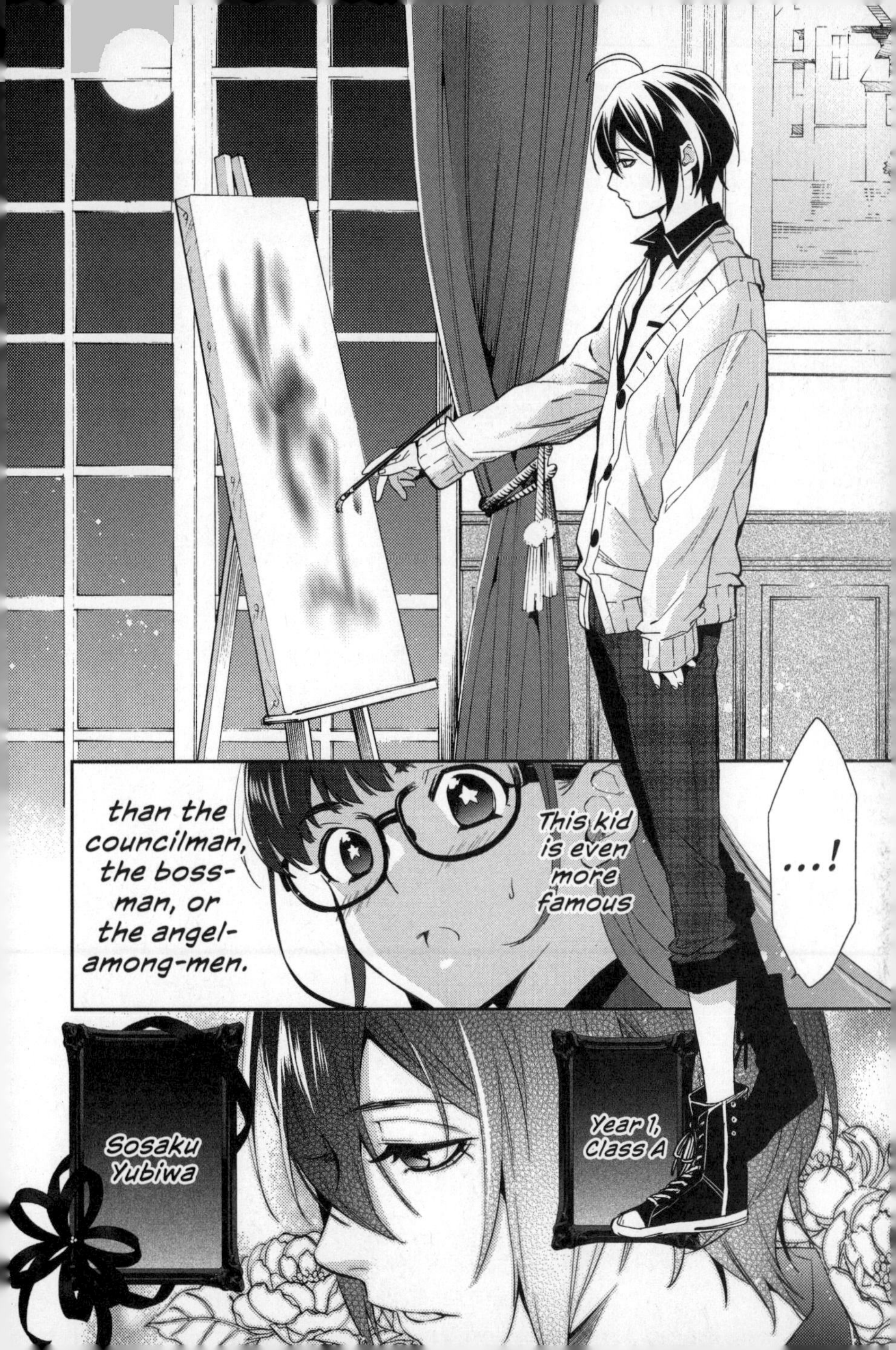
...!
This kid is even more famous
than the councilman, the boss-man, or the angel-among-men.
Year 1, Class A
Sosaku Yubiwa

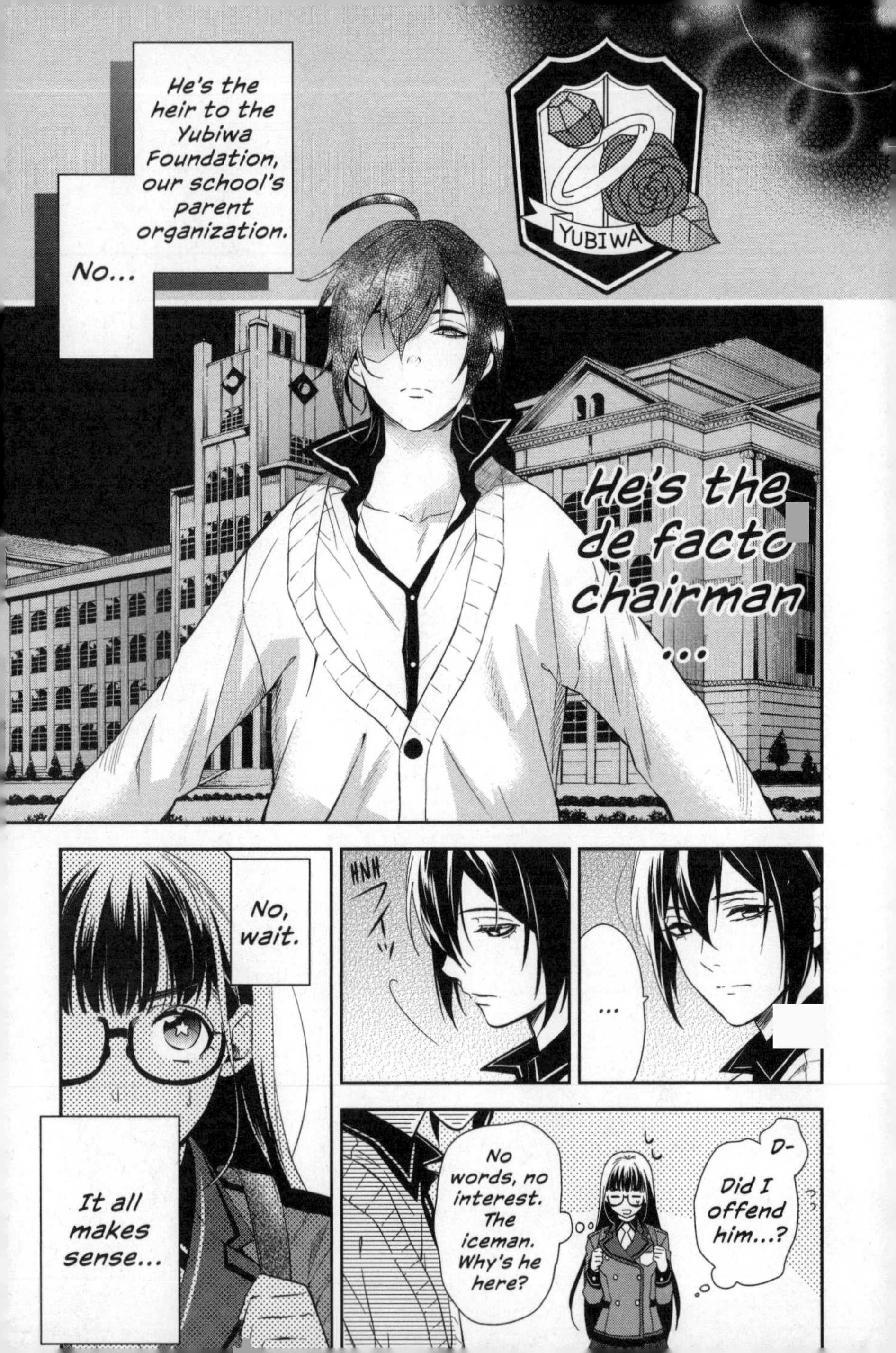
He's the heir to the Yubiwa Foundation, our school's parent organization.
No...
YUBIWA
He's the de facto chairman...
...
HNH
D- Did I offend him...?
No words, no interest. The iceman. Why's he here?
No, wait.
It all makes sense...

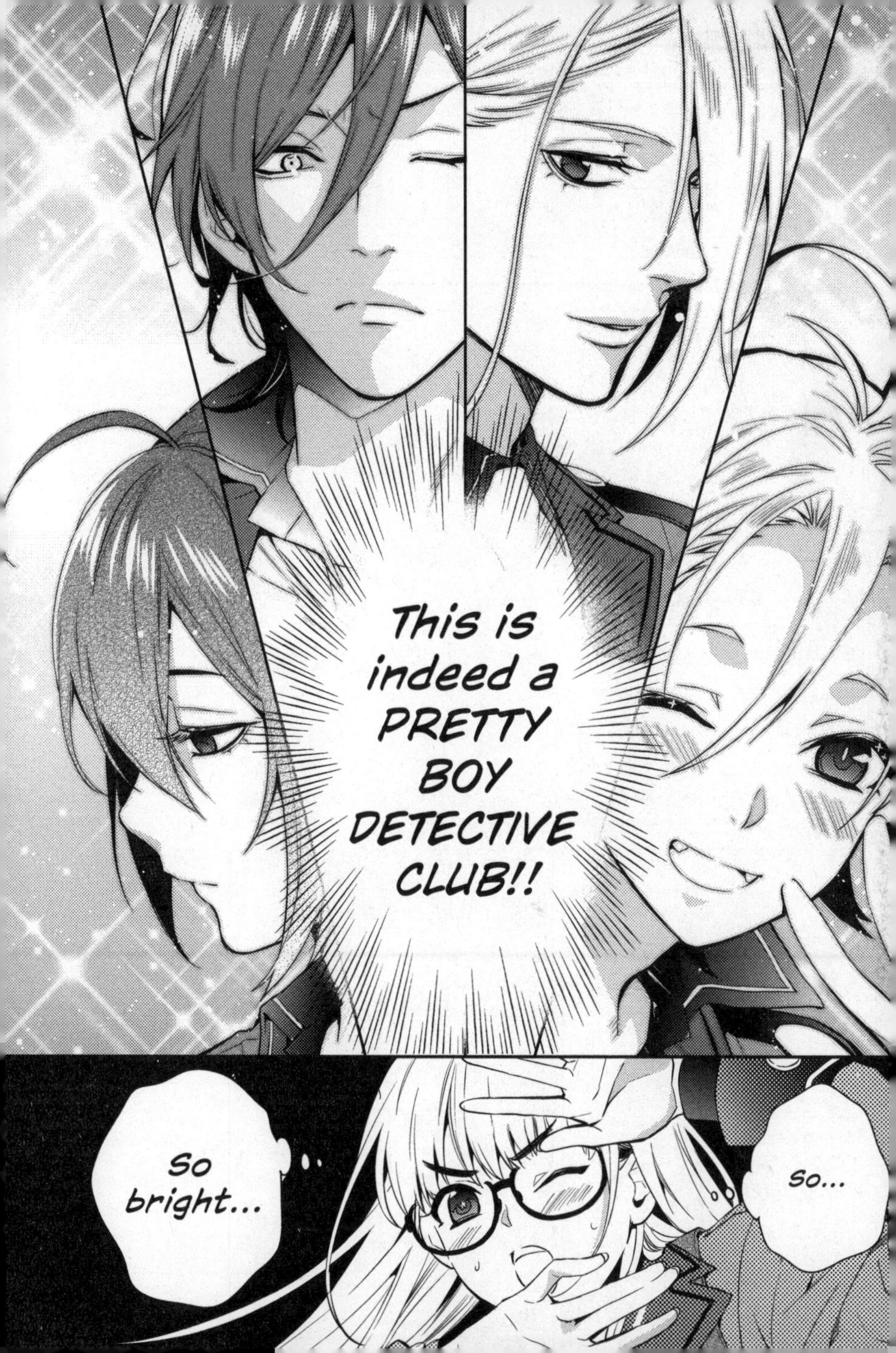
This is indeed a PRETTY BOY DETECTIVE CLUB!!
So...
So bright...

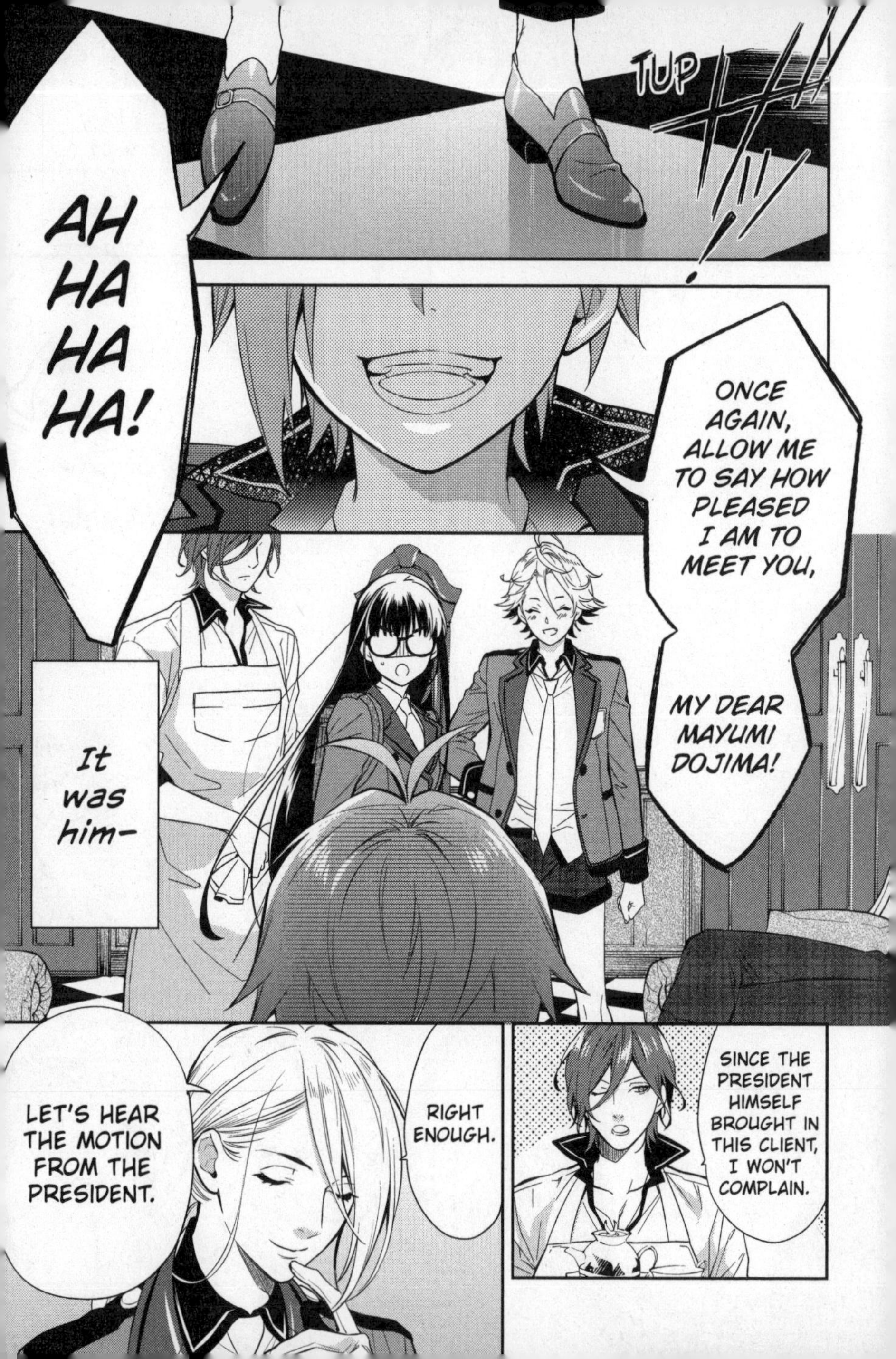
TUP
AH HA HA HA HA!
ONCE AGAIN, ALLOW ME TO SAY HOW PLEASED I AM TO MEET YOU,
MY DEAR MAYUMI DOJIMA!
It was him-
SINCE THE PRESIDENT HIMSELF BROUGHT IN THIS CLIENT, I WON'T COMPLAIN.
RIGHT ENOUGH.
LET'S HEAR THE MOTION FROM THE PRESIDENT.

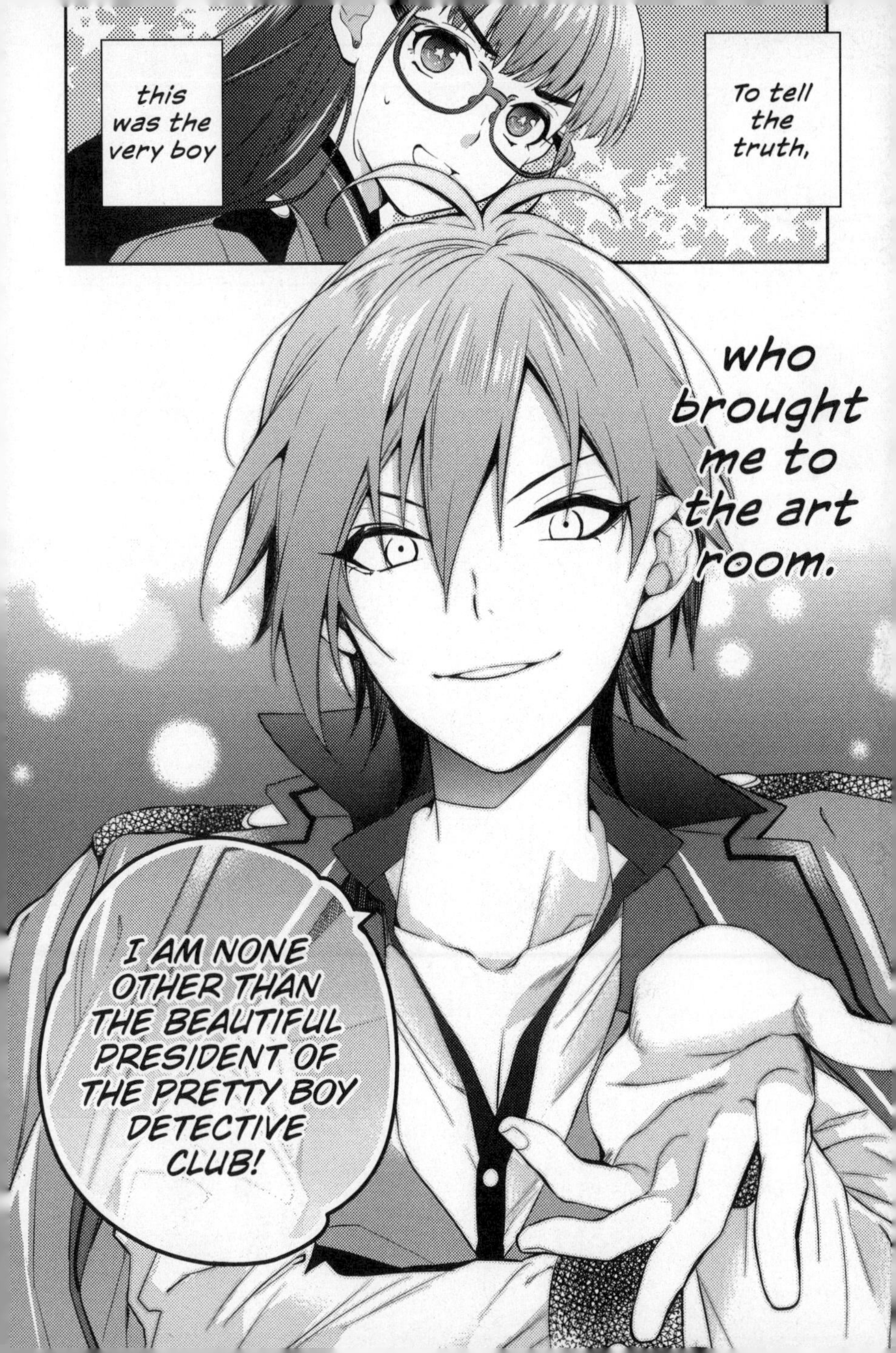
To tell the truth,
this was the very boy
who brought me to the art room.
I AM NONE OTHER THAN THE BEAUTIFUL PRESIDENT OF THE PRETTY BOY DETECTIVE CLUB!

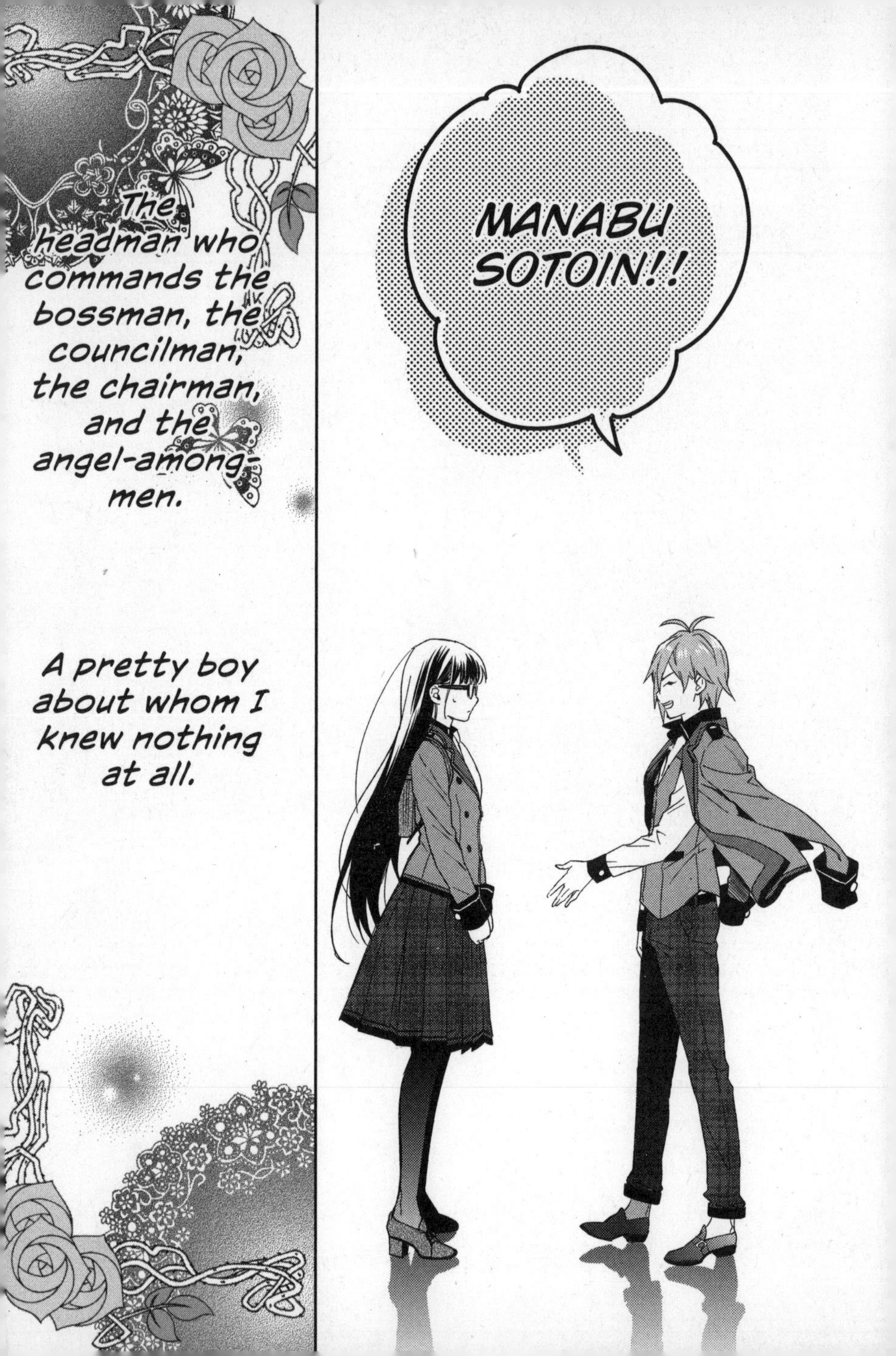
MANABU SOTOIN!!
The headman who commands the bossman, the councilman, the chairman, and the angel-among-men.
A pretty boy about whom I knew nothing at all.

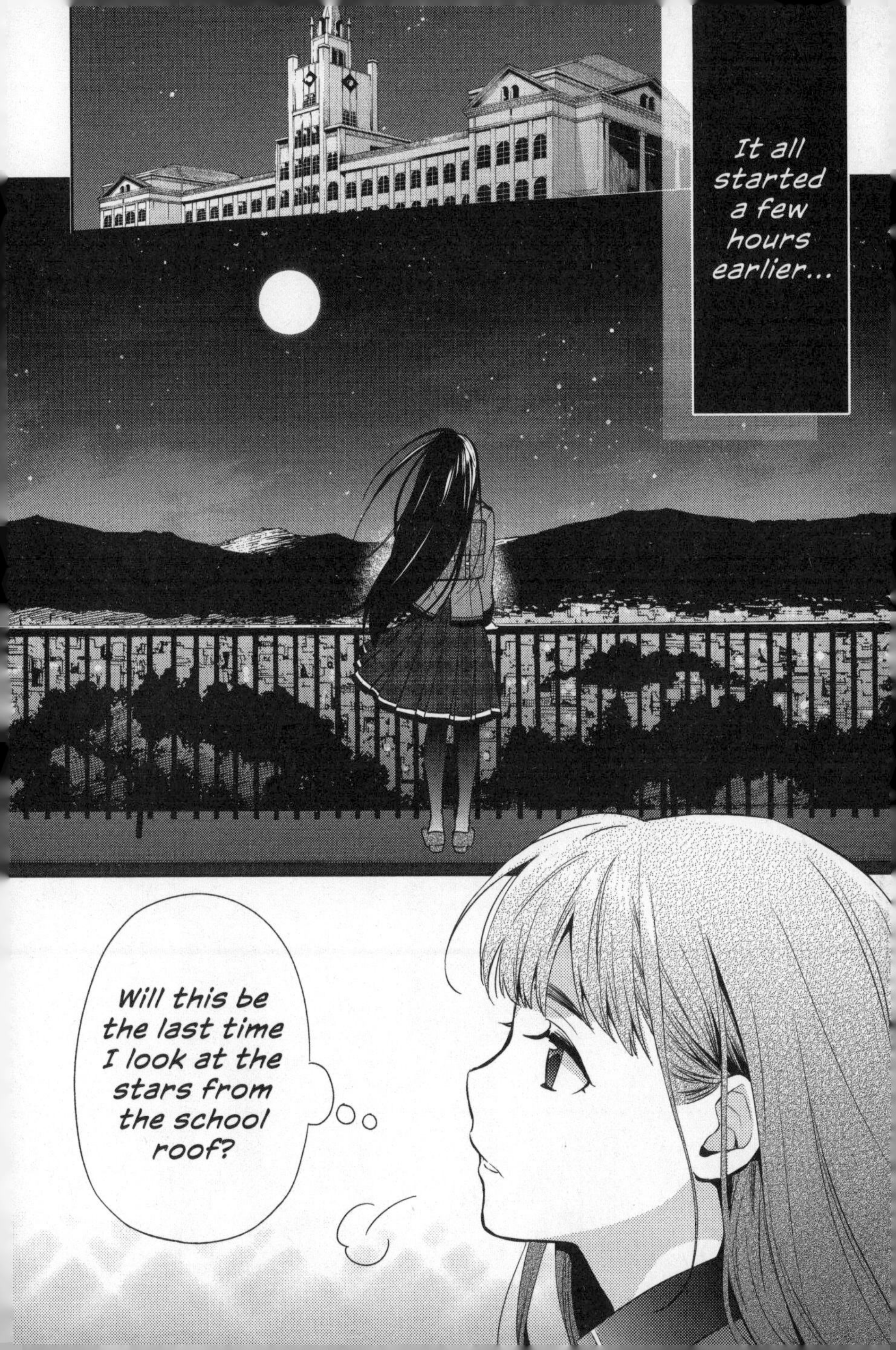
It all started a few hours earlier...
Will this be the last time I look at the stars from the school roof?

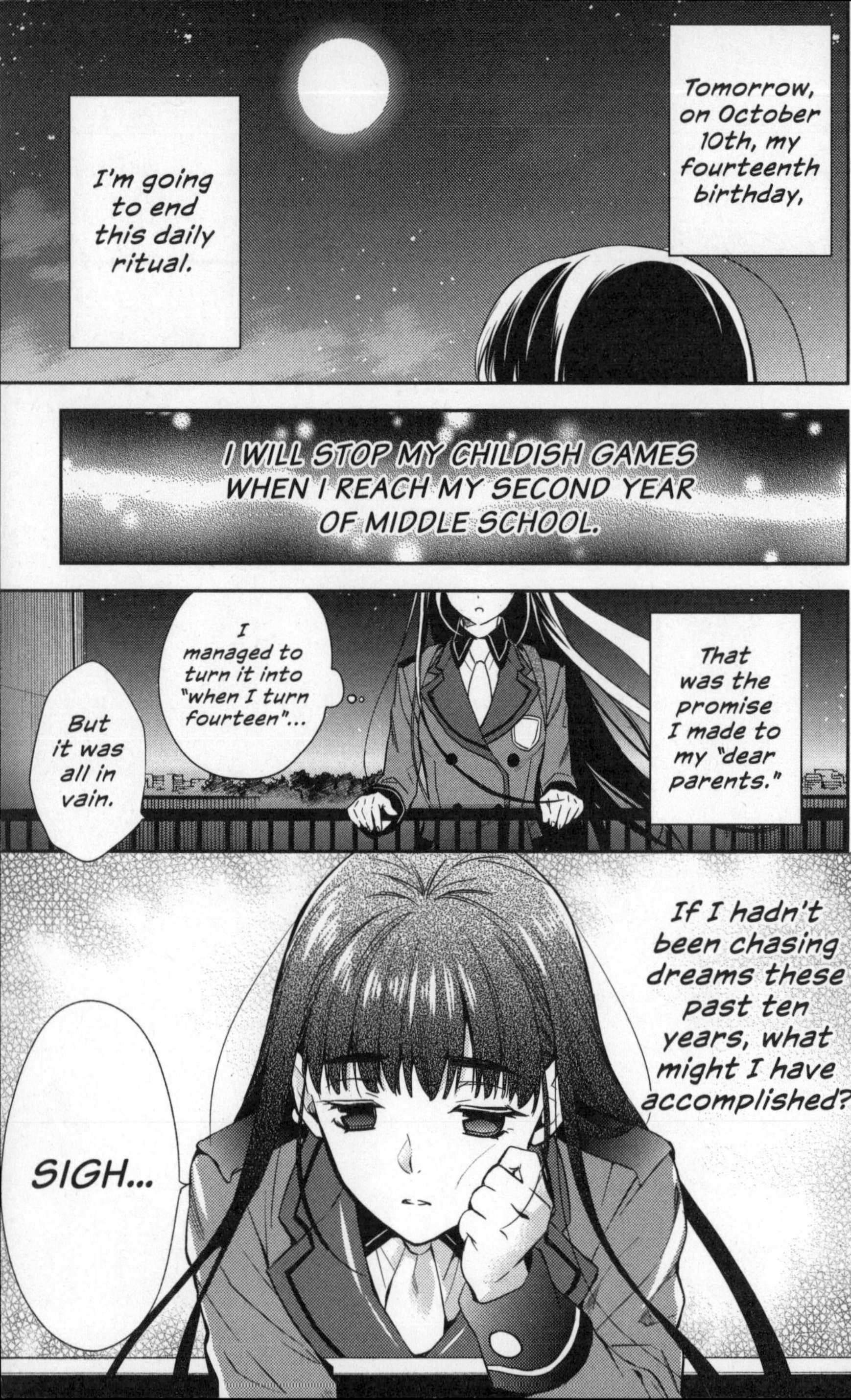
Tomorrow, on October 10th, my fourteenth birthday,
I'm going to end this daily ritual.
I WILL STOP MY CHILDISH GAMES WHEN I REACH MY SECOND YEAR OF MIDDLE SCHOOL.
That was the promise I made to my "dear parents."
I managed to turn it into "when I turn fourteen"...
But it was all in vain.
If I hadn't been chasing dreams these past ten years, what might I have accomplished?
SIGH...

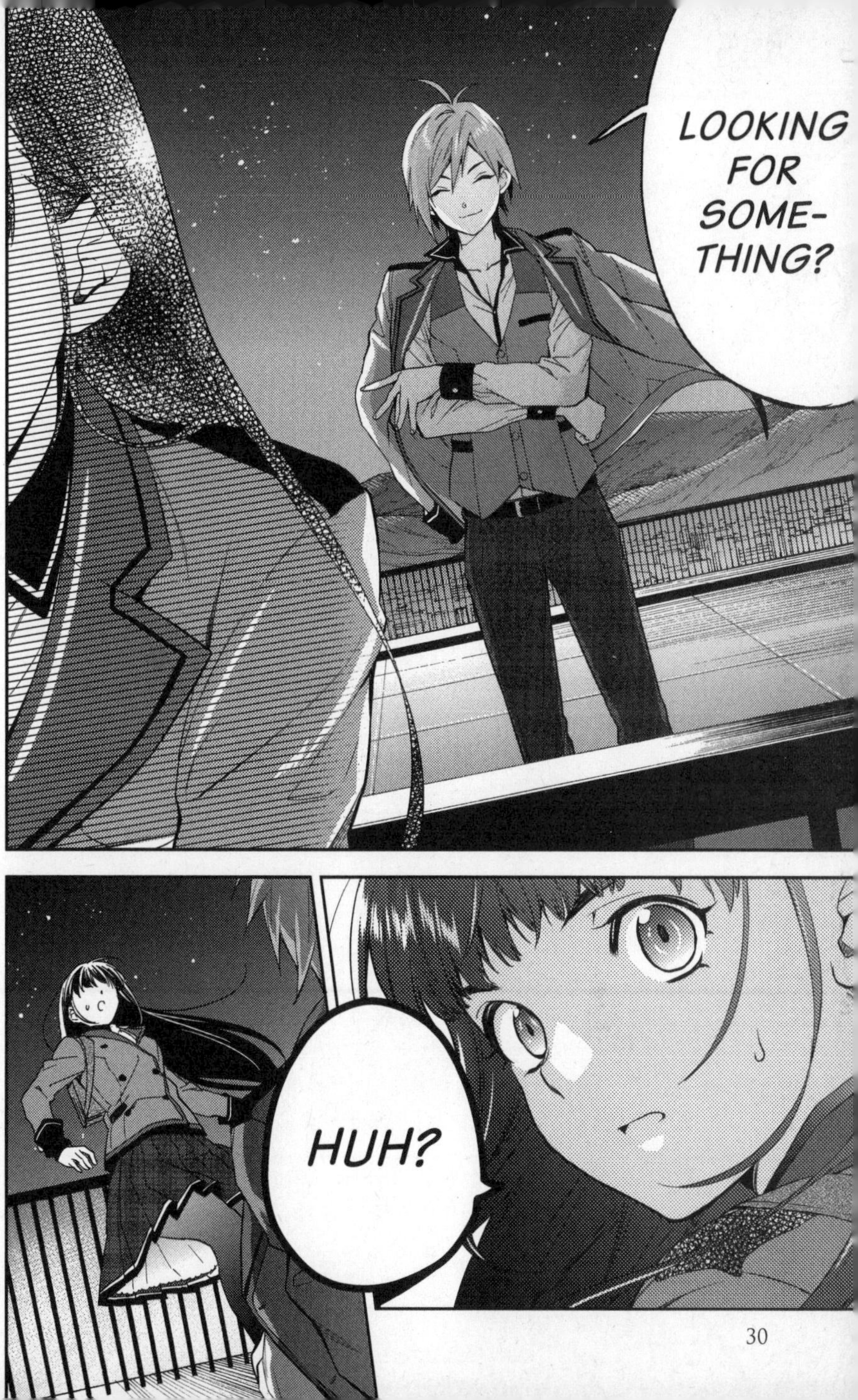
LOOKING FOR SOME-THING?
HUH?

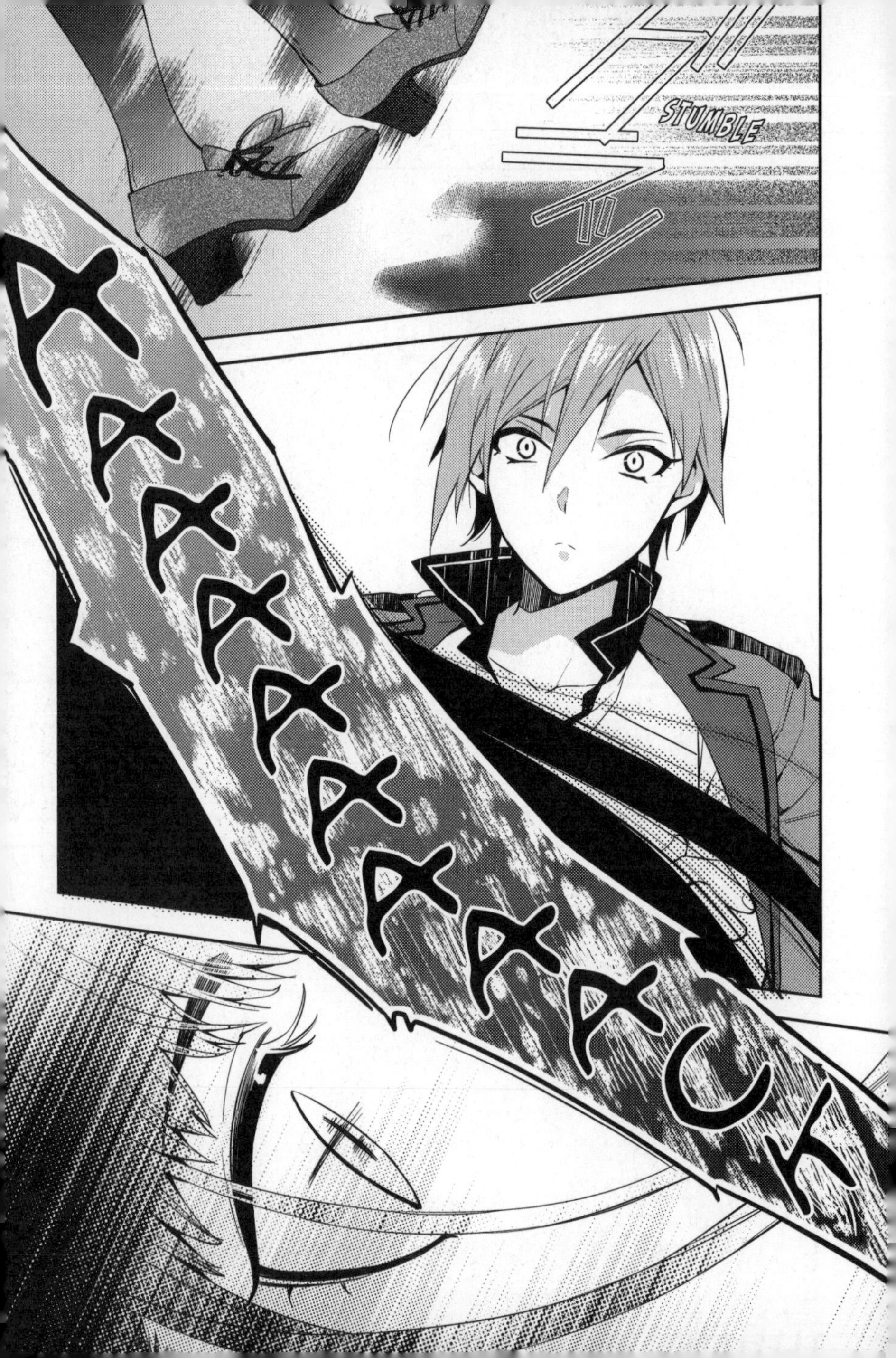

STUMBLE
AAAAAAAAAAACK

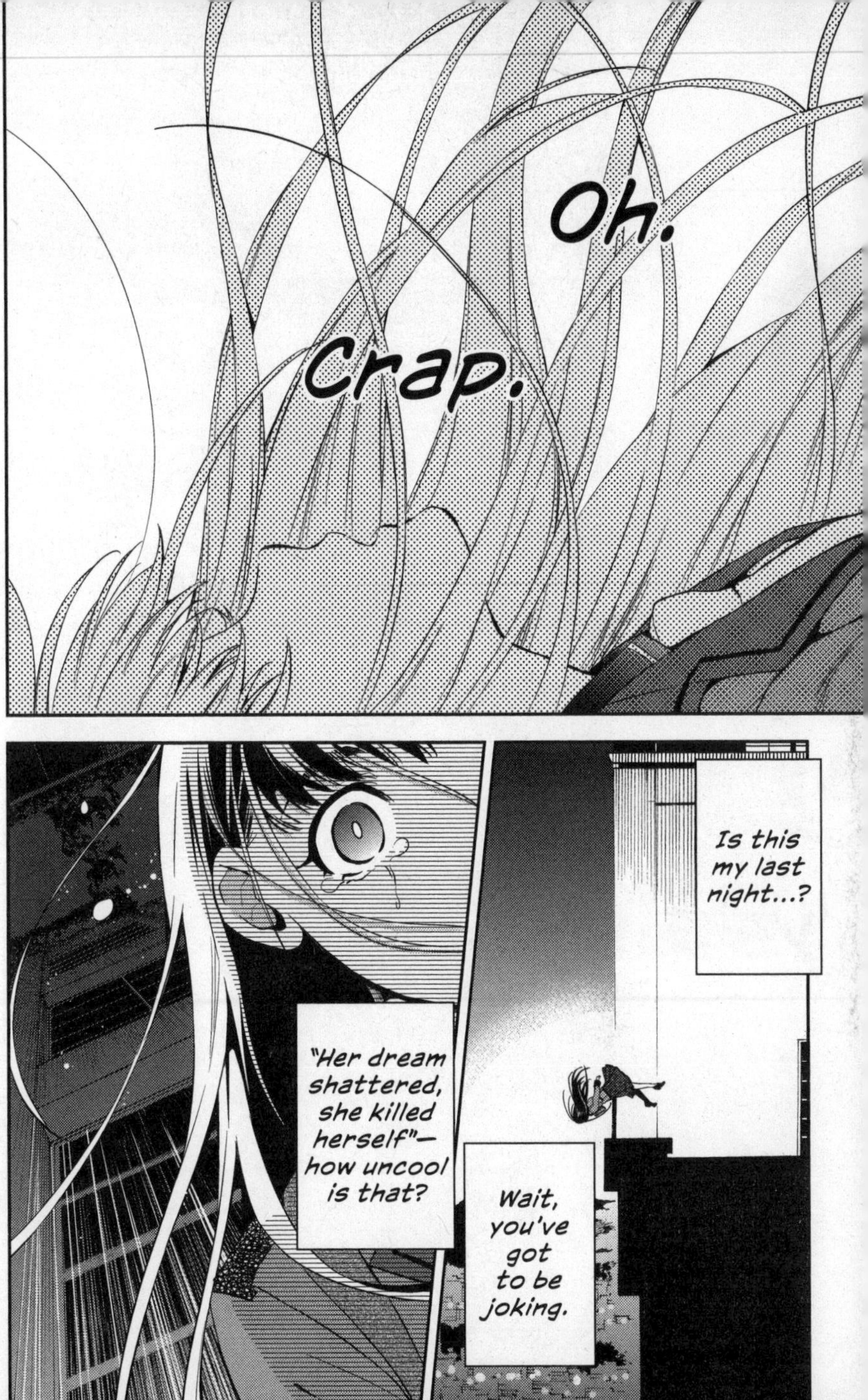
Oh.
Crap.
Is this my last night...?
Wait, you've got to be joking.
"Her dream shattered, she killed herself"—how uncool is that?

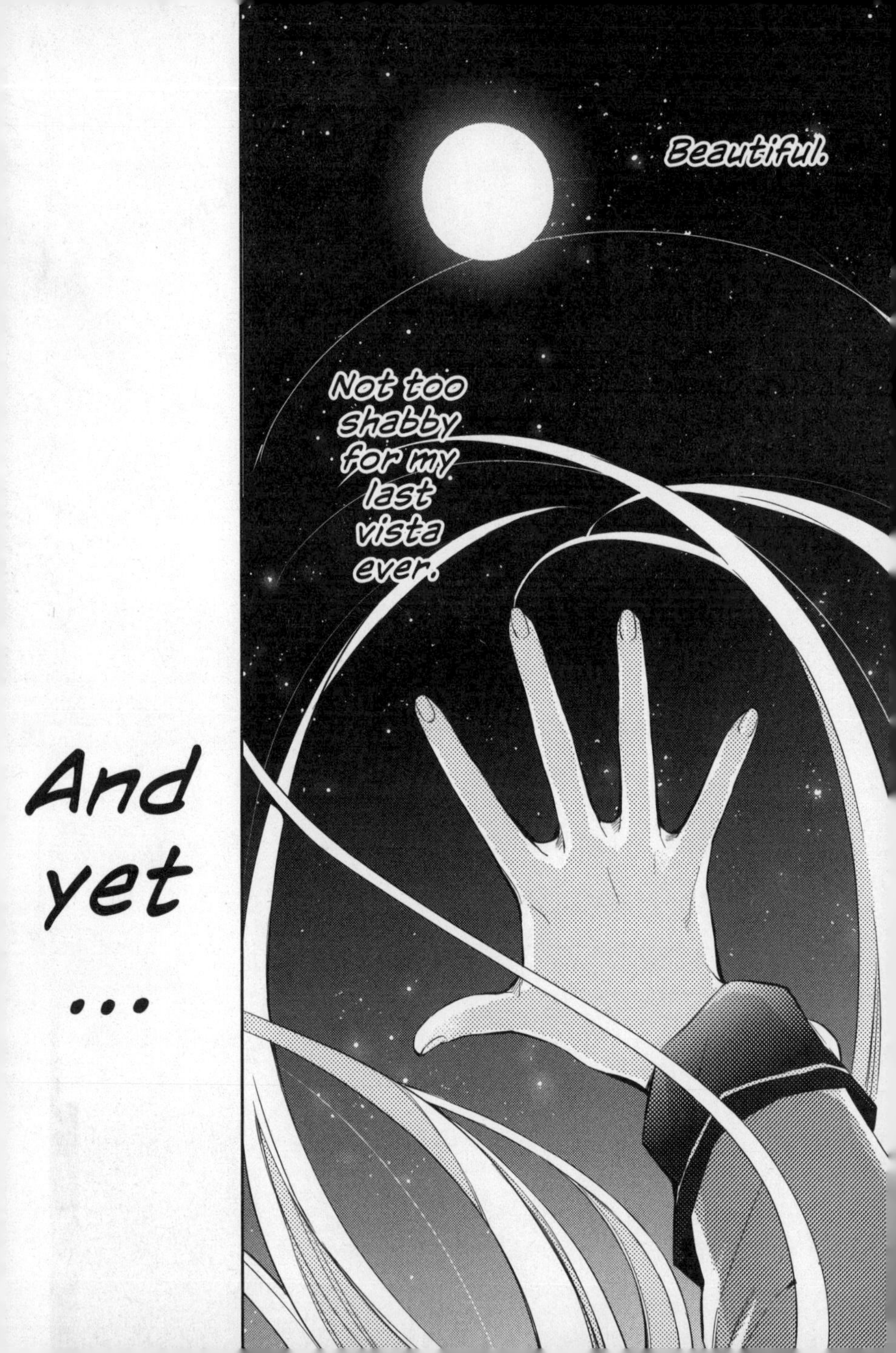
Beautiful.
Not too shabby for my last vista ever.
And yet ...

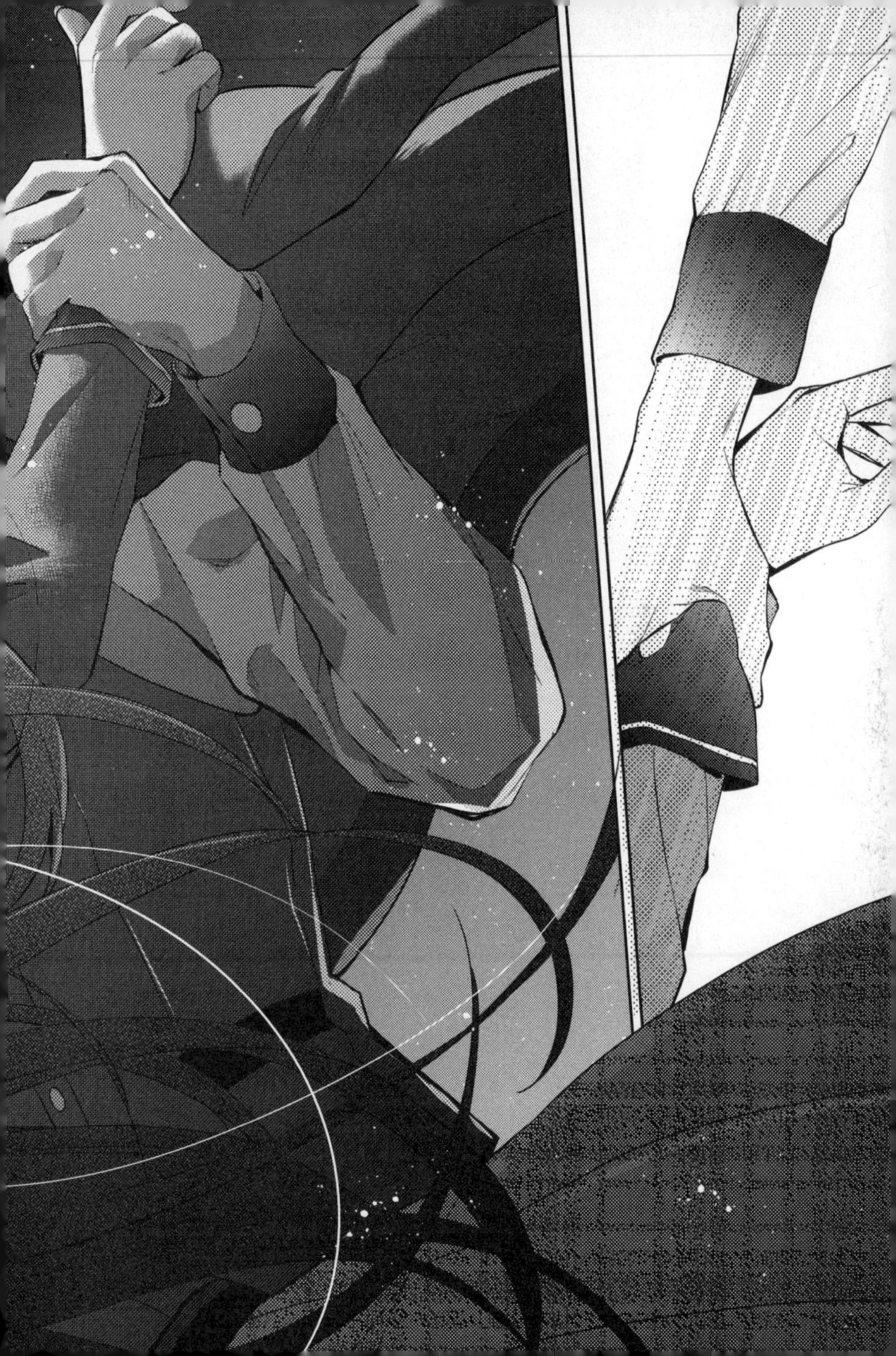

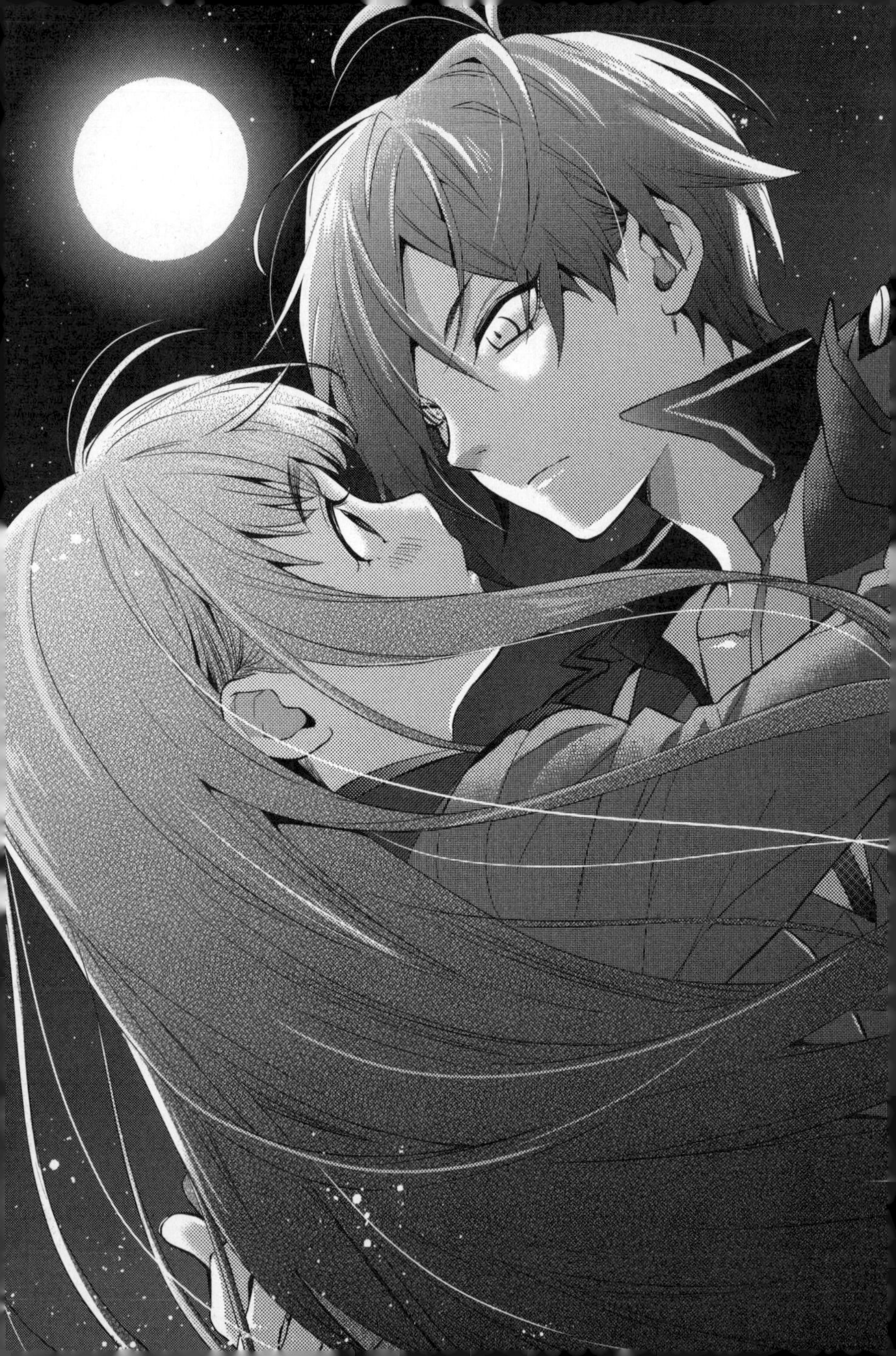

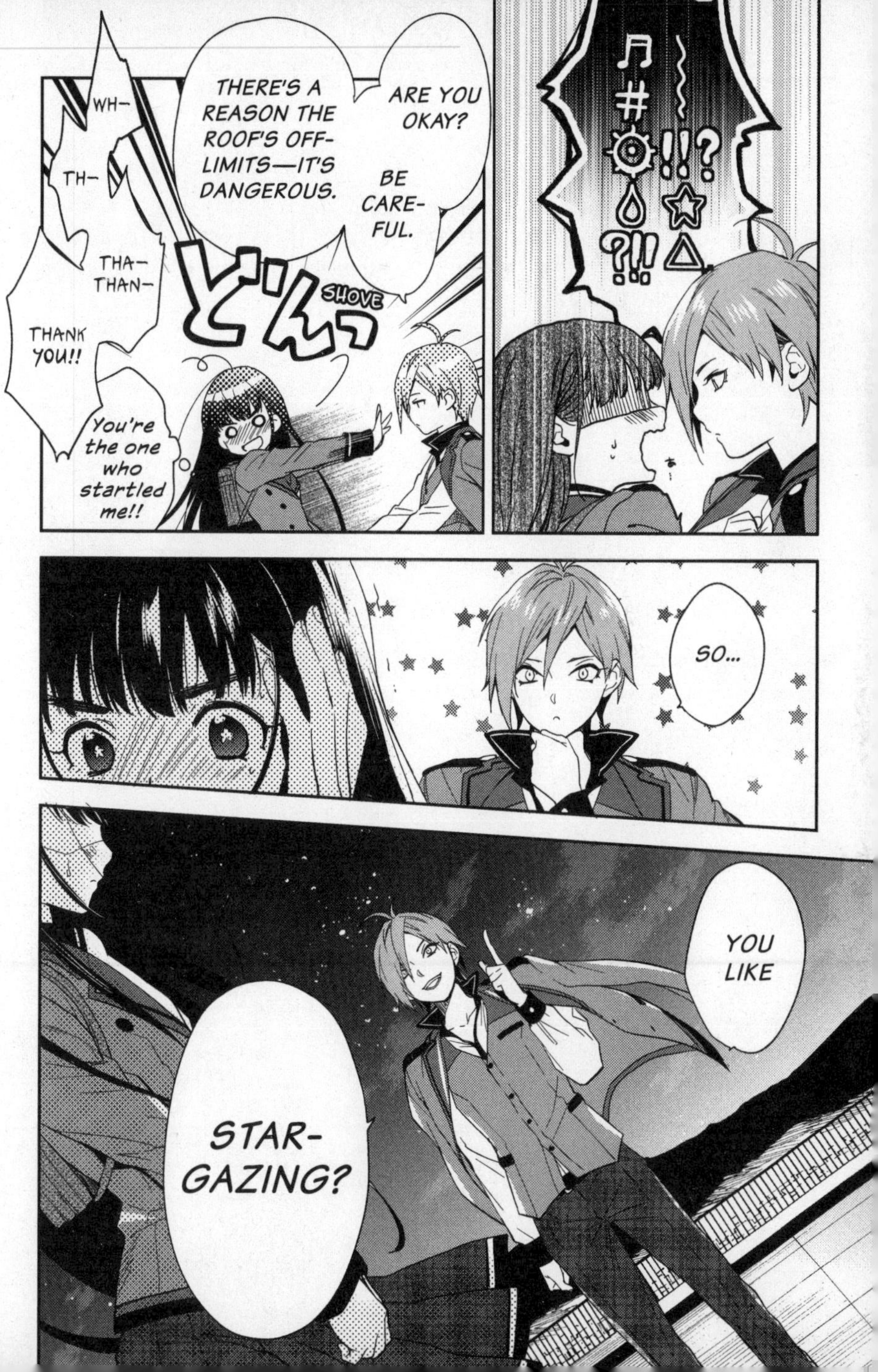
ARE YOU OKAY?
BE CAREFUL.
THERE'S A REASON THE ROOF'S OFF-LIMITS—IT'S DANGEROUS.
どんっ
SHOVE
WH-
TH-
THA-THAN-
THANK YOU!!
You're the one who startled me!!
SO...
YOU LIKE
STARGAZING?

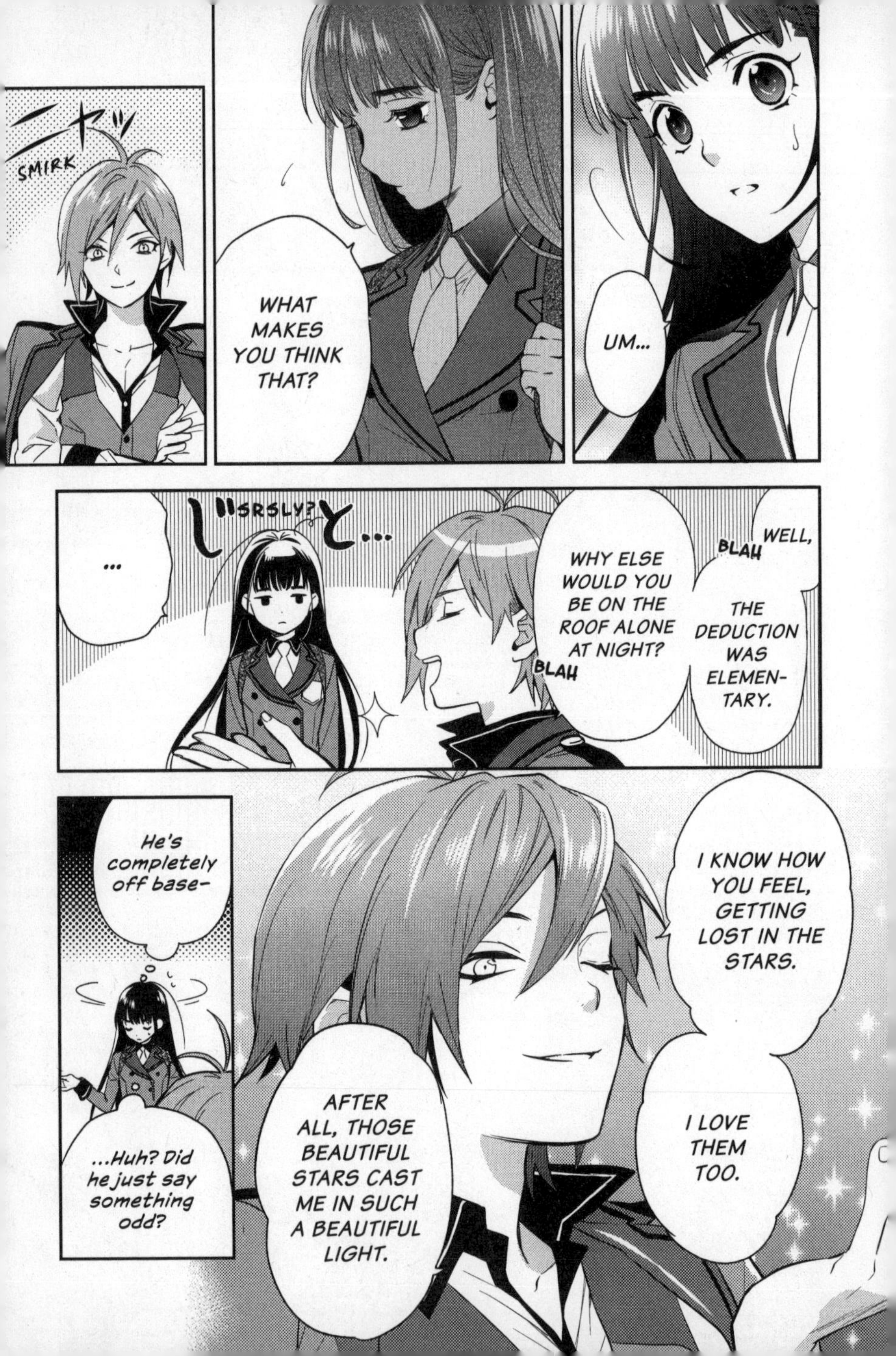
UM...
WHAT MAKES YOU THINK THAT?
ニヤッ
SMIRK
WELL,
THE DEDUCTION WAS ELEMENTARY.
BLAH
WHY ELSE WOULD YOU BE ON THE ROOF ALONE AT NIGHT?
BLAH
SRSLY?
...
I KNOW HOW YOU FEEL, GETTING LOST IN THE STARS.
I LOVE THEM TOO.
AFTER ALL, THOSE BEAUTIFUL STARS CAST ME IN SUCH A BEAUTIFUL LIGHT.
He's completely off base-
...Huh? Did he just say something odd?

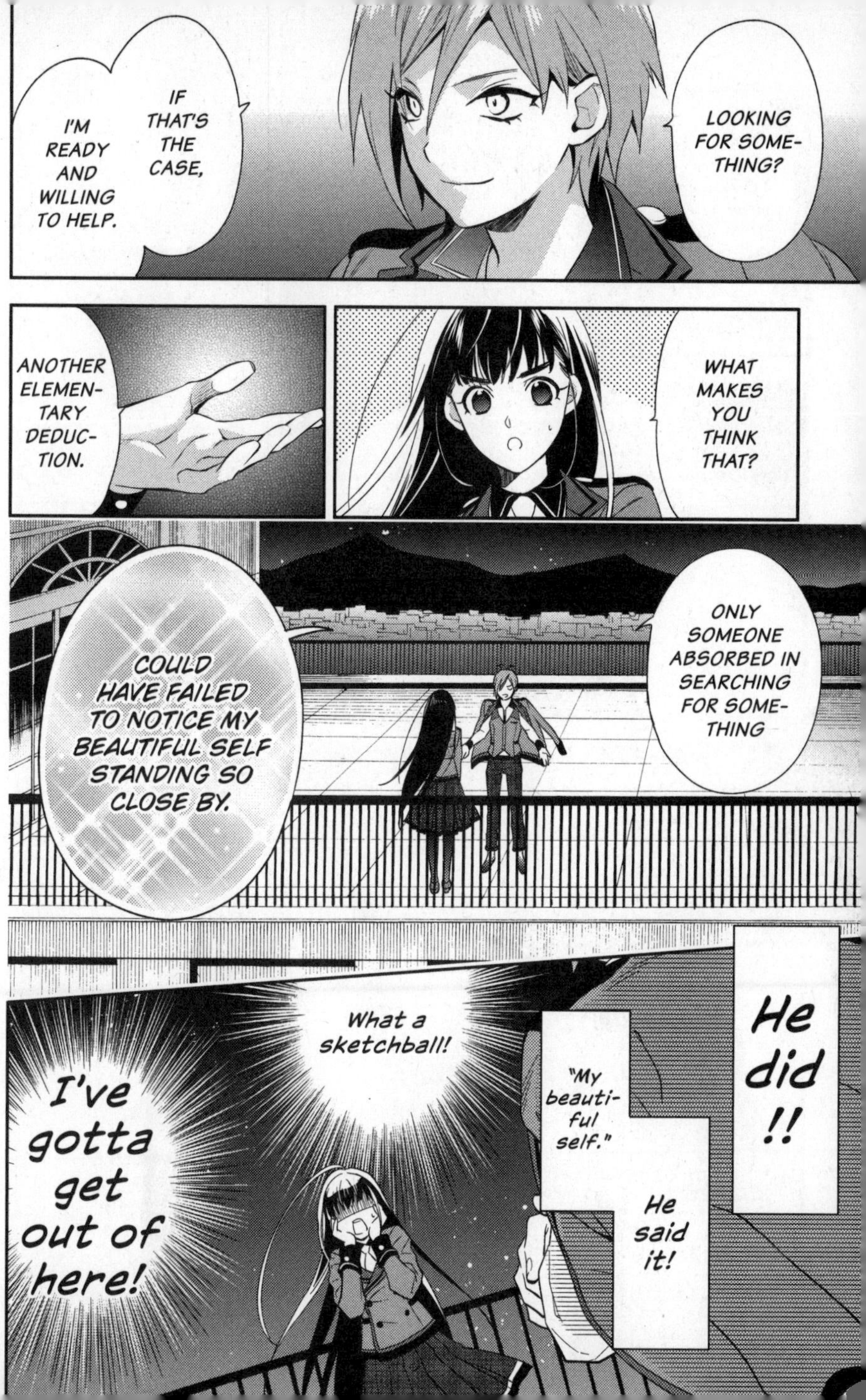
LOOKING FOR SOME-THING?
IF THAT'S THE CASE,
I'M READY AND WILLING TO HELP.
WHAT MAKES YOU THINK THAT?
ANOTHER ELEMENTARY DEDUCTION.
ONLY SOMEONE ABSORBED IN SEARCHING FOR SOME-THING
COULD HAVE FAILED TO NOTICE MY BEAUTIFUL SELF STANDING SO CLOSE BY.
He did!!
"My beauti-ful self."
He said it!
What a sketchball!
I've gotta get out of here!

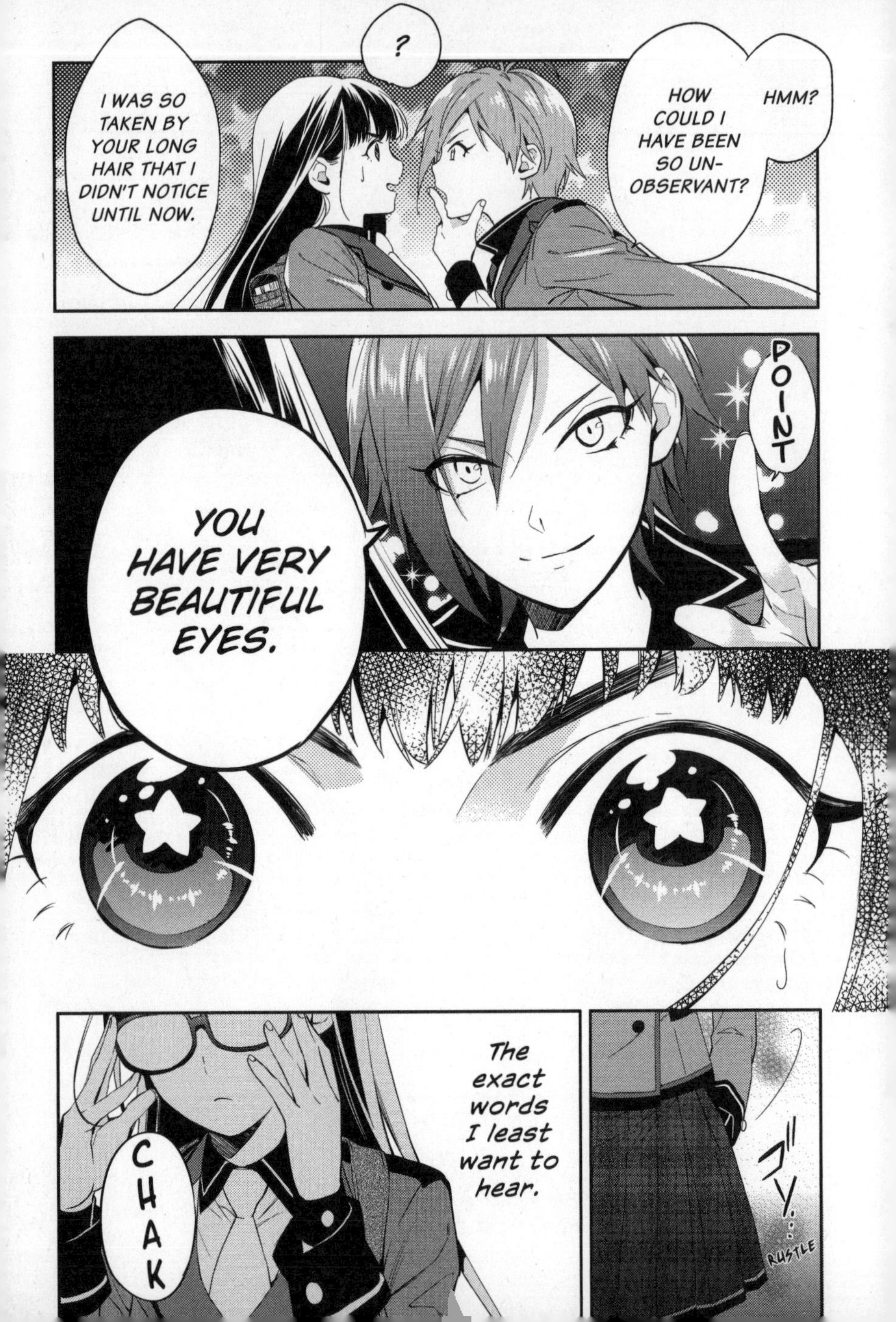
HMM?
HOW COULD I HAVE BEEN SO UN-OBSERVANT?
?
I WAS SO TAKEN BY YOUR LONG HAIR THAT I DIDN'T NOTICE UNTIL NOW.
POINT
YOU HAVE VERY BEAUTIFUL EYES.
RUSTLE
The exact words I least want to hear.
CHAK

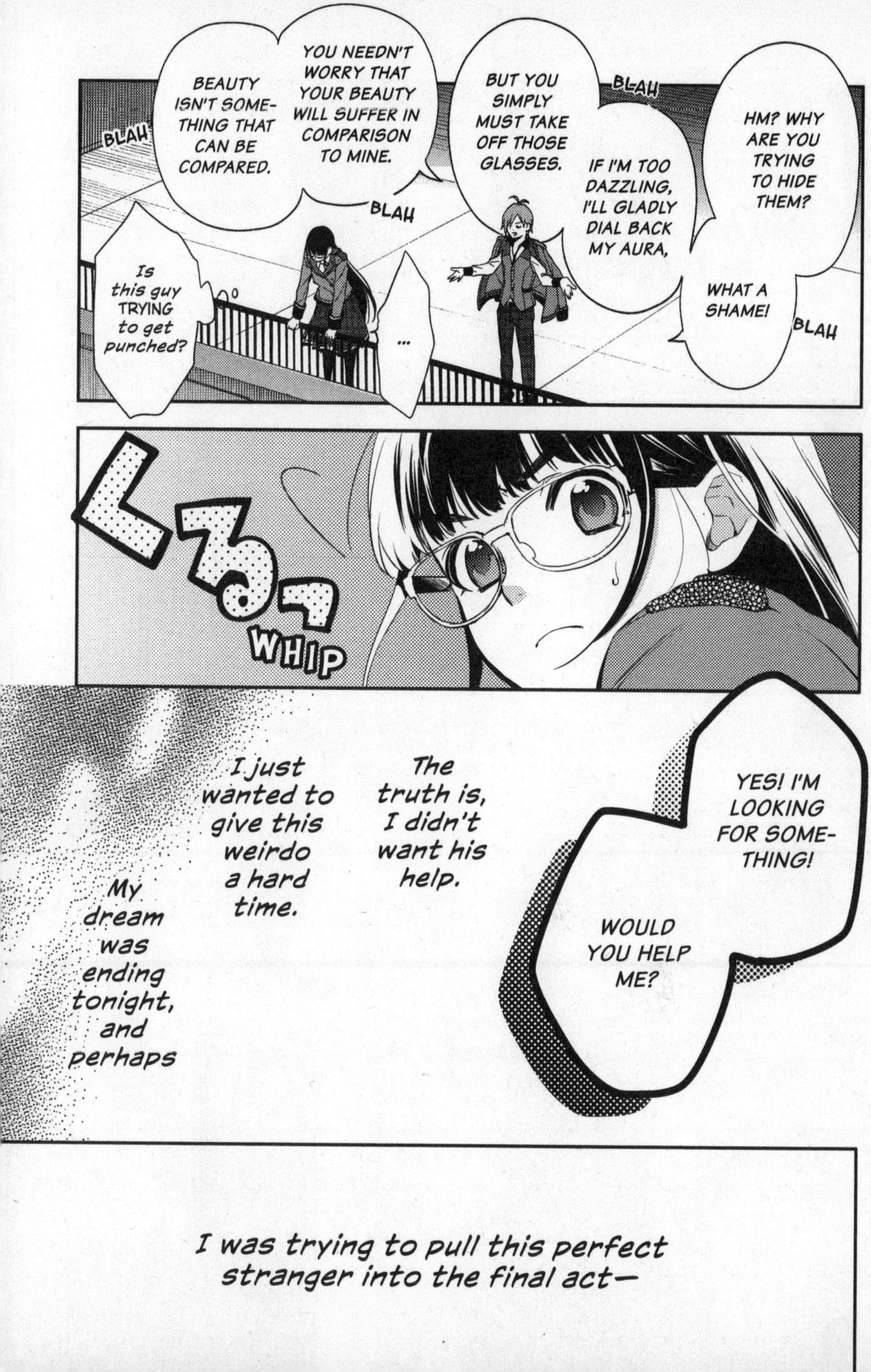
HM? WHY ARE YOU TRYING TO HIDE THEM?
WHAT A SHAME!
BLAH
BLAH
BUT YOU SIMPLY MUST TAKE OFF THOSE GLASSES.
IF I'M TOO DAZZLING, I'LL GLADLY DIAL BACK MY AURA,
YOU NEEDN'T WORRY THAT YOUR BEAUTY WILL SUFFER IN COMPARISON TO MINE.
BLAH
BEAUTY ISN'T SOME-THING THAT CAN BE COMPARED.
BLAH
...
Is this guy TRYING to get punched?
WHIP
YES! I'M LOOKING FOR SOME-THING!
WOULD YOU HELP ME?
The truth is, I didn't want his help.
I just wanted to give this weirdo a hard time.
My dream was ending tonight, and perhaps
I was trying to pull this perfect stranger into the final act—

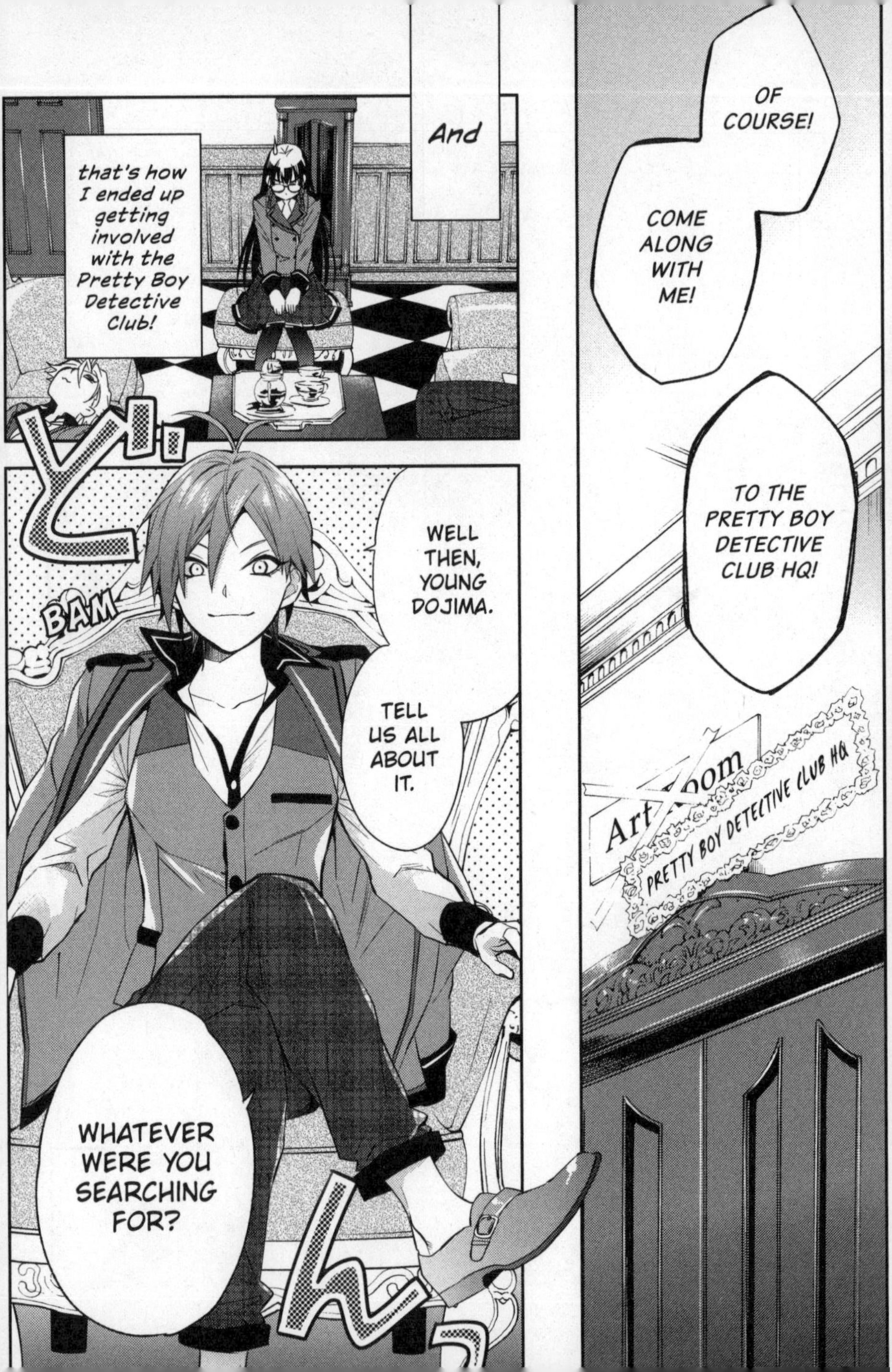
OF COURSE!
COME ALONG WITH ME!
TO THE PRETTY BOY DETECTIVE CLUB HQ!
Art Room
PRETTY BOY DETECTIVE CLUB HQ
And
that's how I ended up getting involved with the Pretty Boy Detective Club!
BAM
WELL THEN, YOUNG DOJIMA.
TELL US ALL ABOUT IT.
WHATEVER WERE YOU SEARCHING FOR?

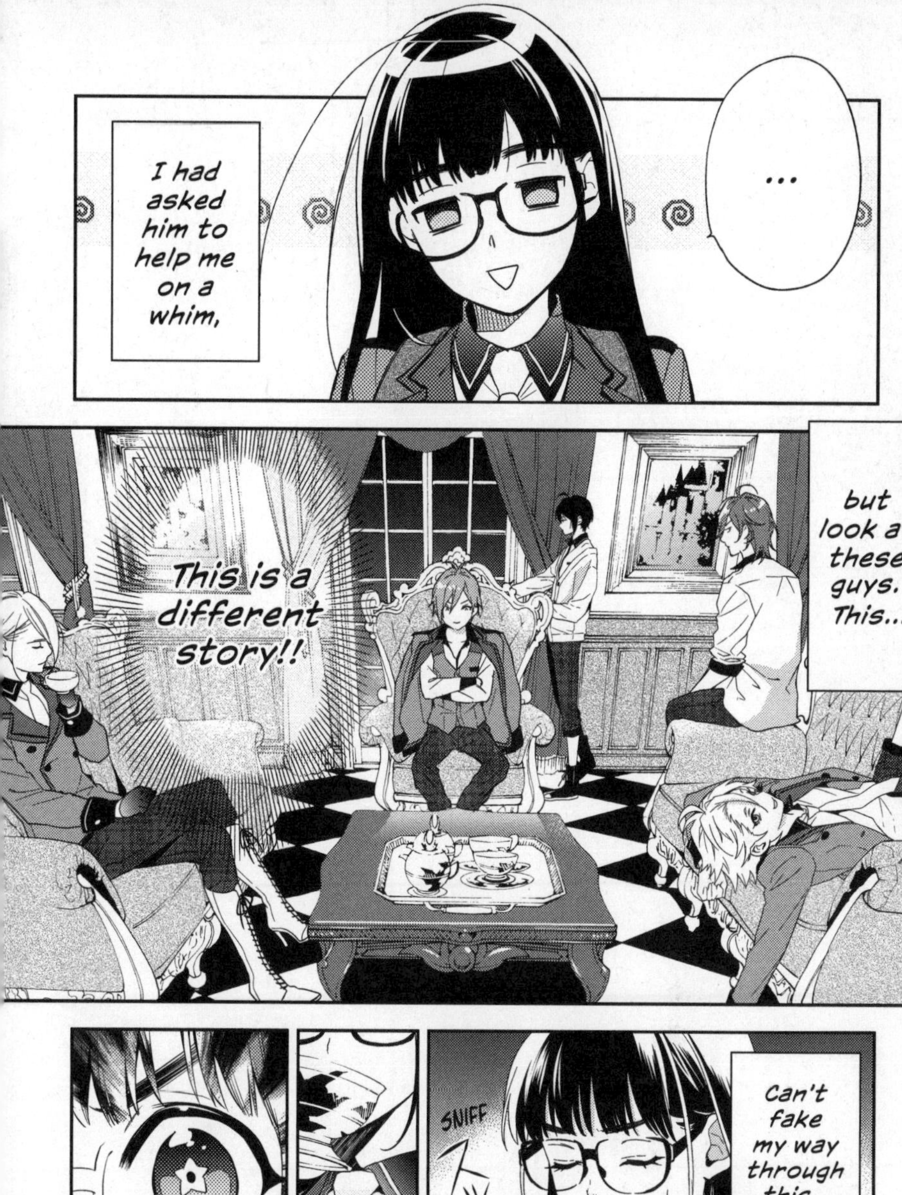
...
I had asked him to help me on a whim,
but look at these guys. This...
This is a different story!!
Can't fake my way through this...
SNIFF
コク... SIP

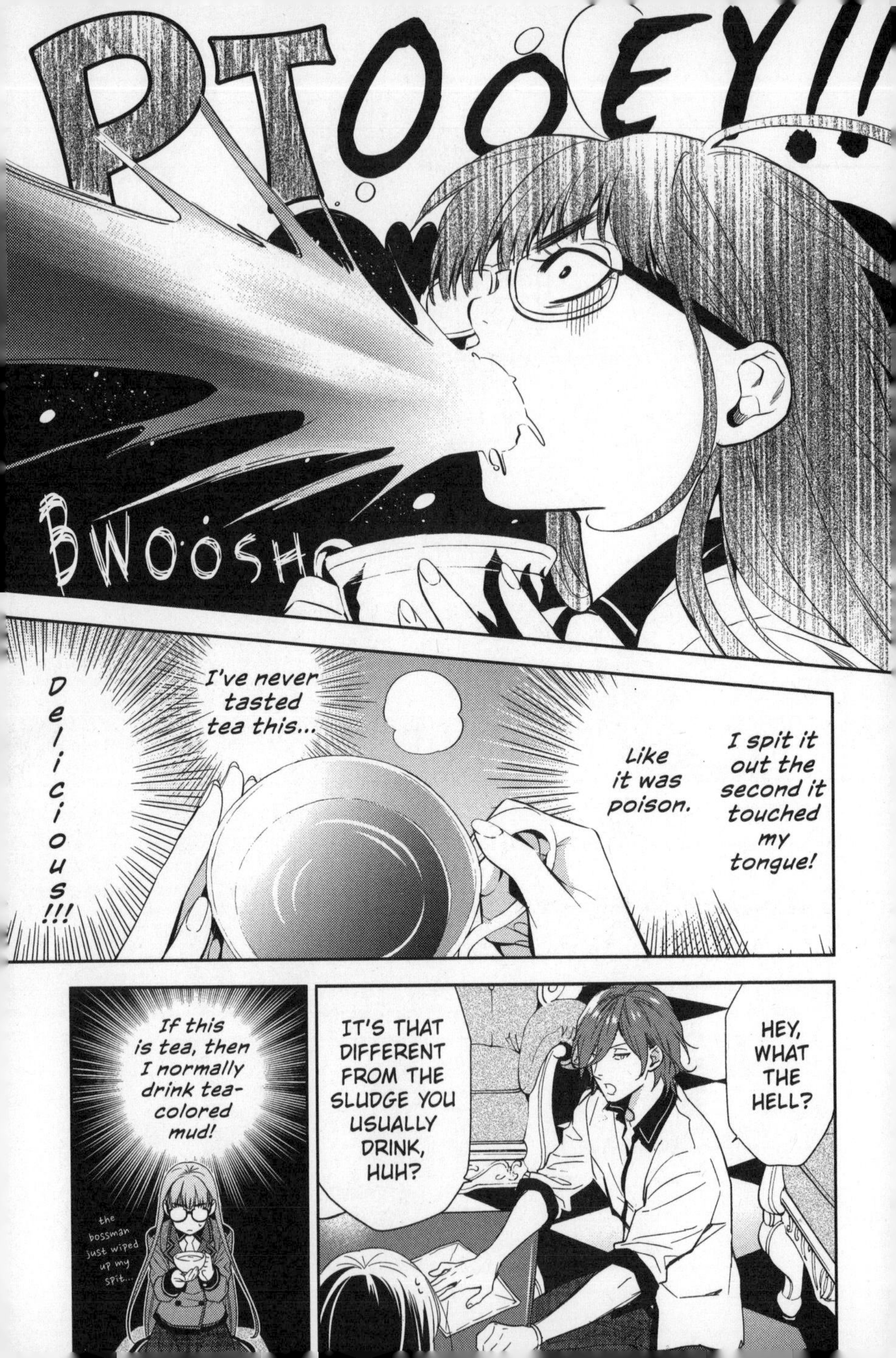
PTOOEY!!
BWOOSH
I spit it out the second it touched my tongue!
Like it was poison.
I've never tasted tea this...
Delicious!!!
HEY, WHAT THE HELL?
IT'S THAT DIFFERENT FROM THE SLUDGE YOU USUALLY DRINK, HUH?
If this is tea, then I normally drink tea-colored mud!
the bossman just wiped up my spit...

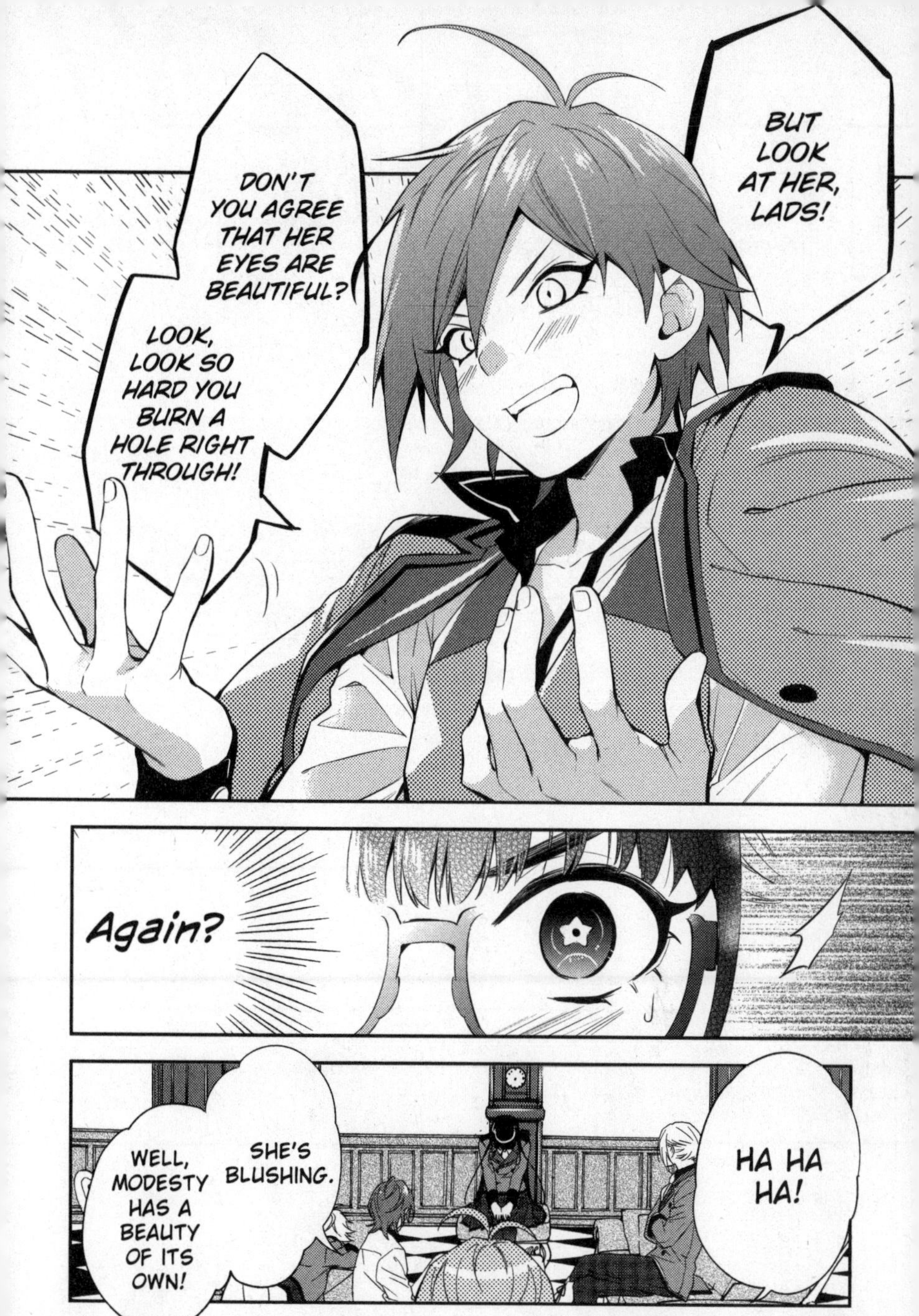
BUT LOOK AT HER, LADS!
DON'T YOU AGREE THAT HER EYES ARE BEAUTIFUL?
LOOK, LOOK SO HARD YOU BURN A HOLE RIGHT THROUGH!
Again?
HA HA HA!
SHE'S BLUSHING.
WELL, MODESTY HAS A BEAUTY OF ITS OWN!

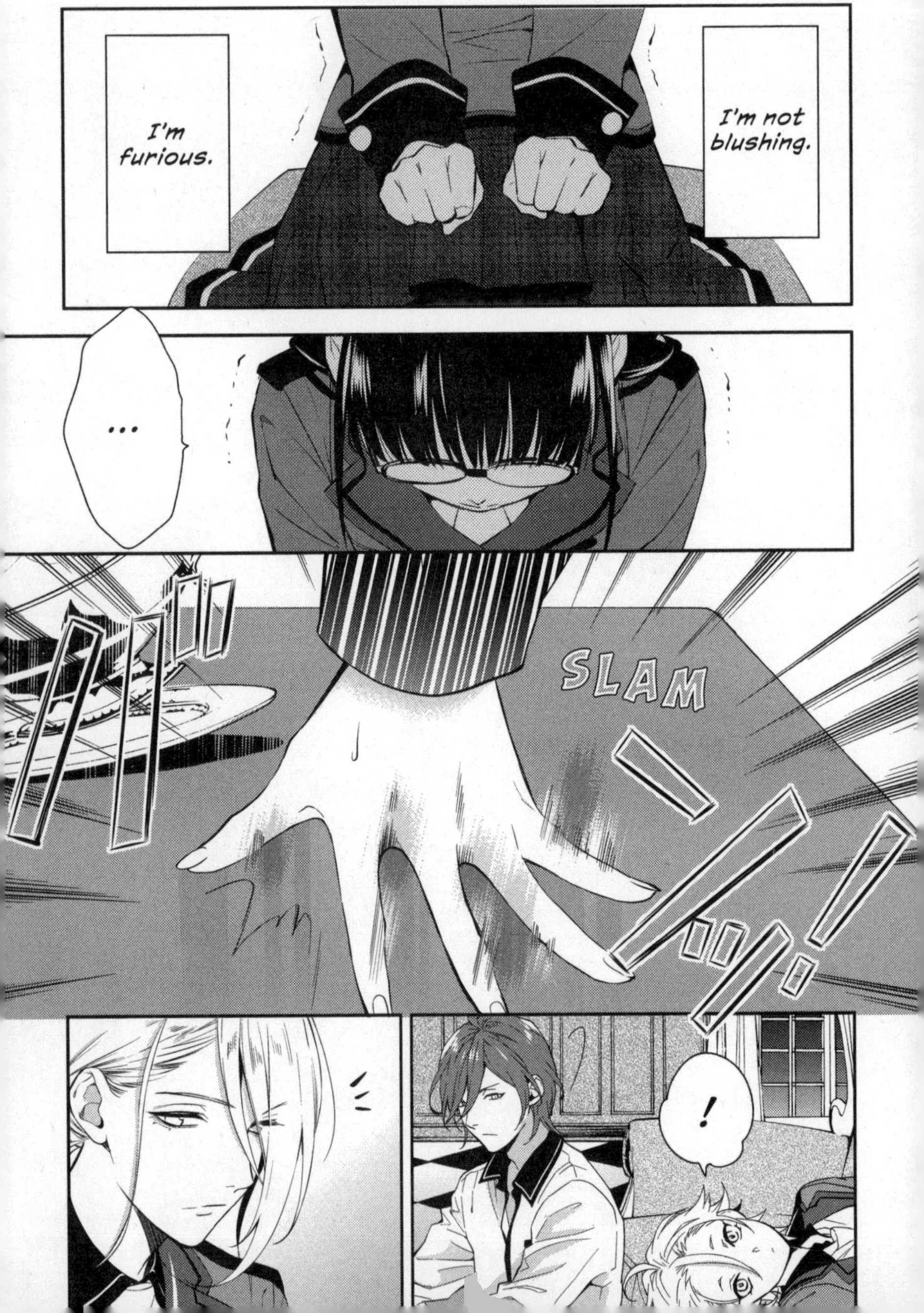
I'm not blushing.
I'm furious.
...
SLAM
!

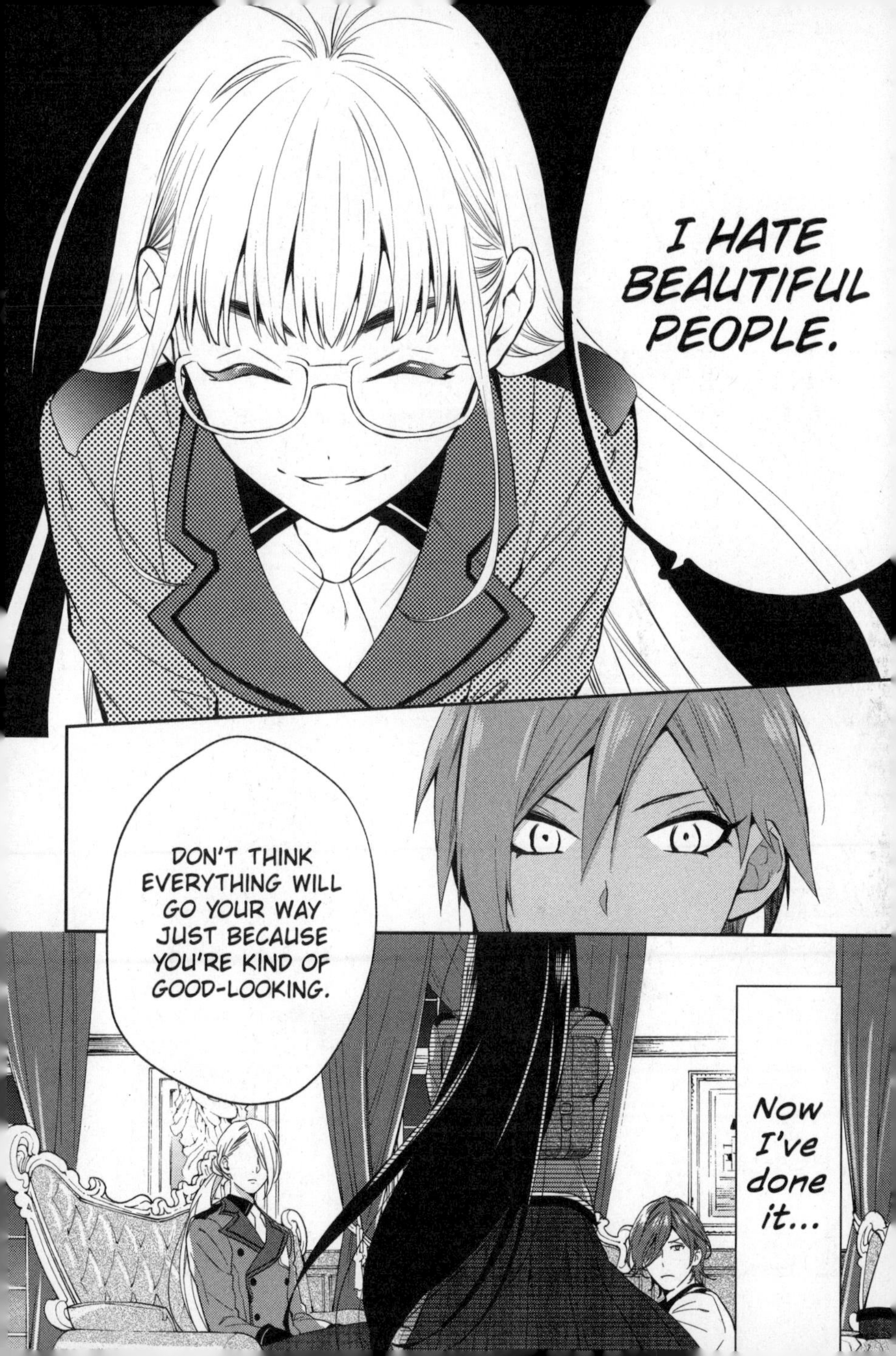
I HATE BEAUTIFUL PEOPLE.
DON'T THINK EVERYTHING WILL GO YOUR WAY JUST BECAUSE YOU'RE KIND OF GOOD-LOOKING.
Now I've done it...

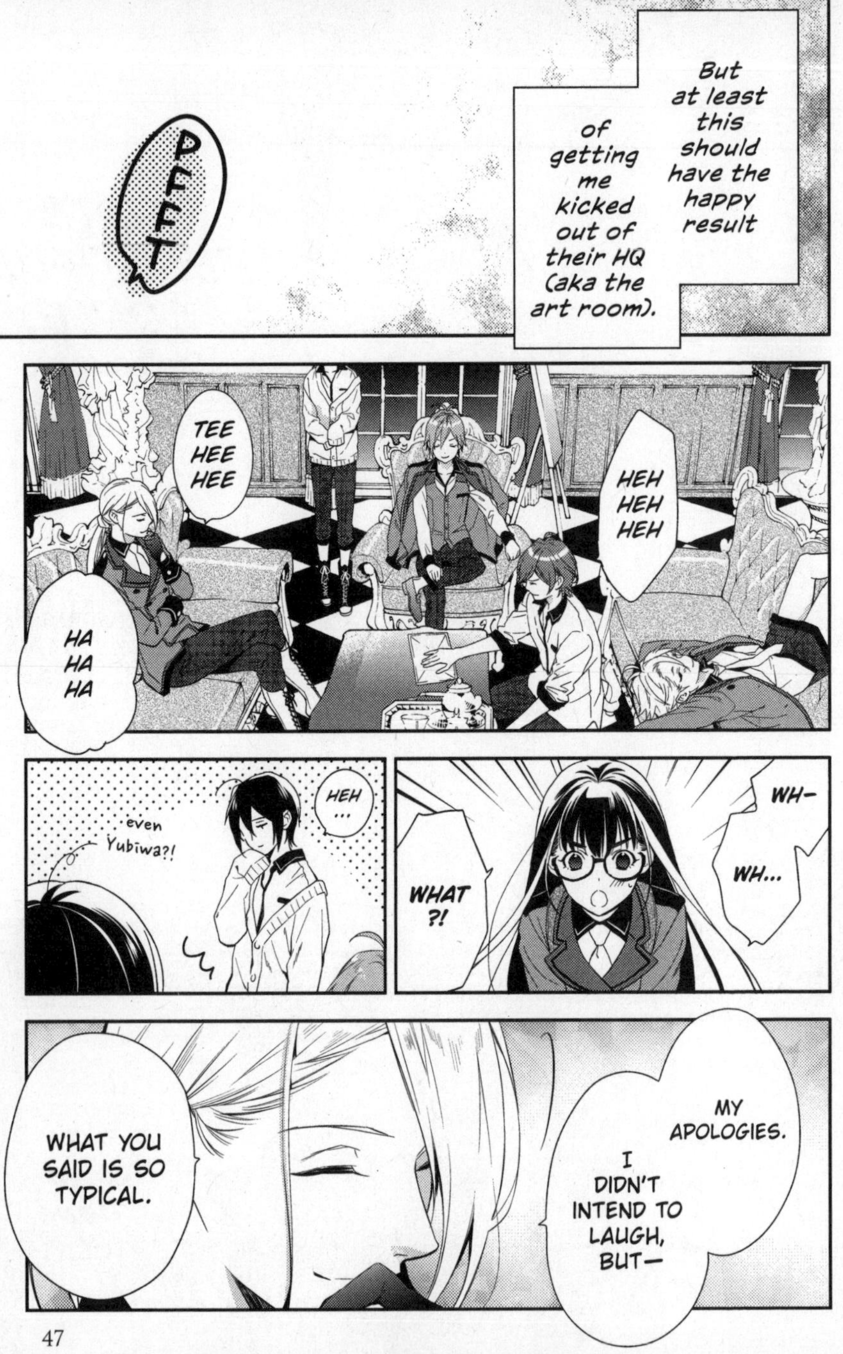

But at least this should have the happy result of getting me kicked out of their HQ (aka the art room).
PFFFT
HEH HEH HEH
TEE HEE HEE
HA HA HA
WH- WH...
WHAT?!
HEH...
even Yubiwa?!
MY APOLOGIES.
I DIDN'T INTEND TO LAUGH, BUT—
WHAT YOU SAID IS SO TYPICAL.

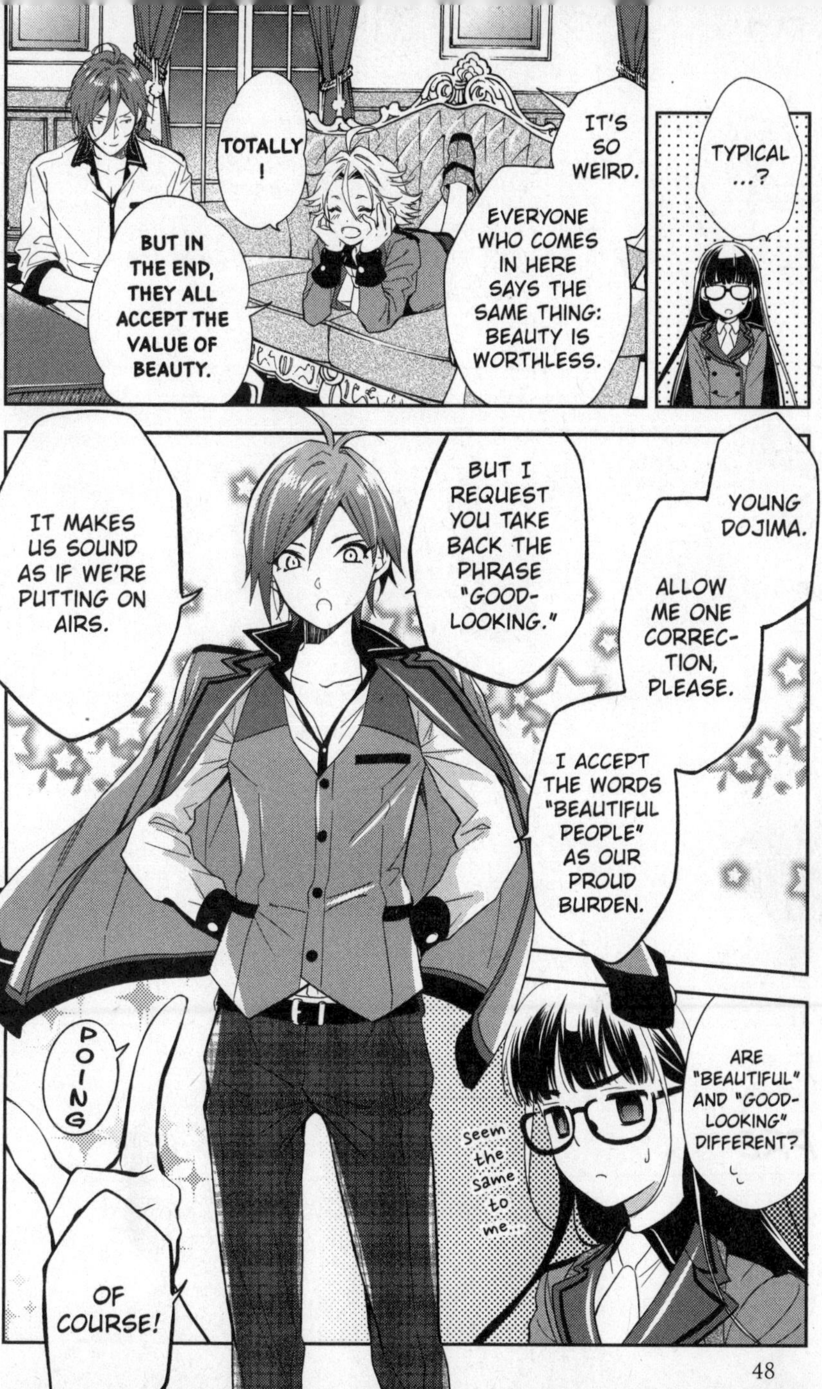
TYPICAL ...?
IT'S SO WEIRD.
EVERYONE WHO COMES IN HERE SAYS THE SAME THING: BEAUTY IS WORTHLESS.
TOTALLY!
BUT IN THE END, THEY ALL ACCEPT THE VALUE OF BEAUTY.
YOUNG DOJIMA.
ALLOW ME ONE CORRECTION, PLEASE.
BUT I REQUEST YOU TAKE BACK THE PHRASE "GOOD-LOOKING."
IT MAKES US SOUND AS IF WE'RE PUTTING ON AIRS.
I ACCEPT THE WORDS "BEAUTIFUL PEOPLE" AS OUR PROUD BURDEN.
ARE "BEAUTIFUL" AND "GOOD-LOOKING" DIFFERENT?
Seem the same to me...
POING
OF COURSE!

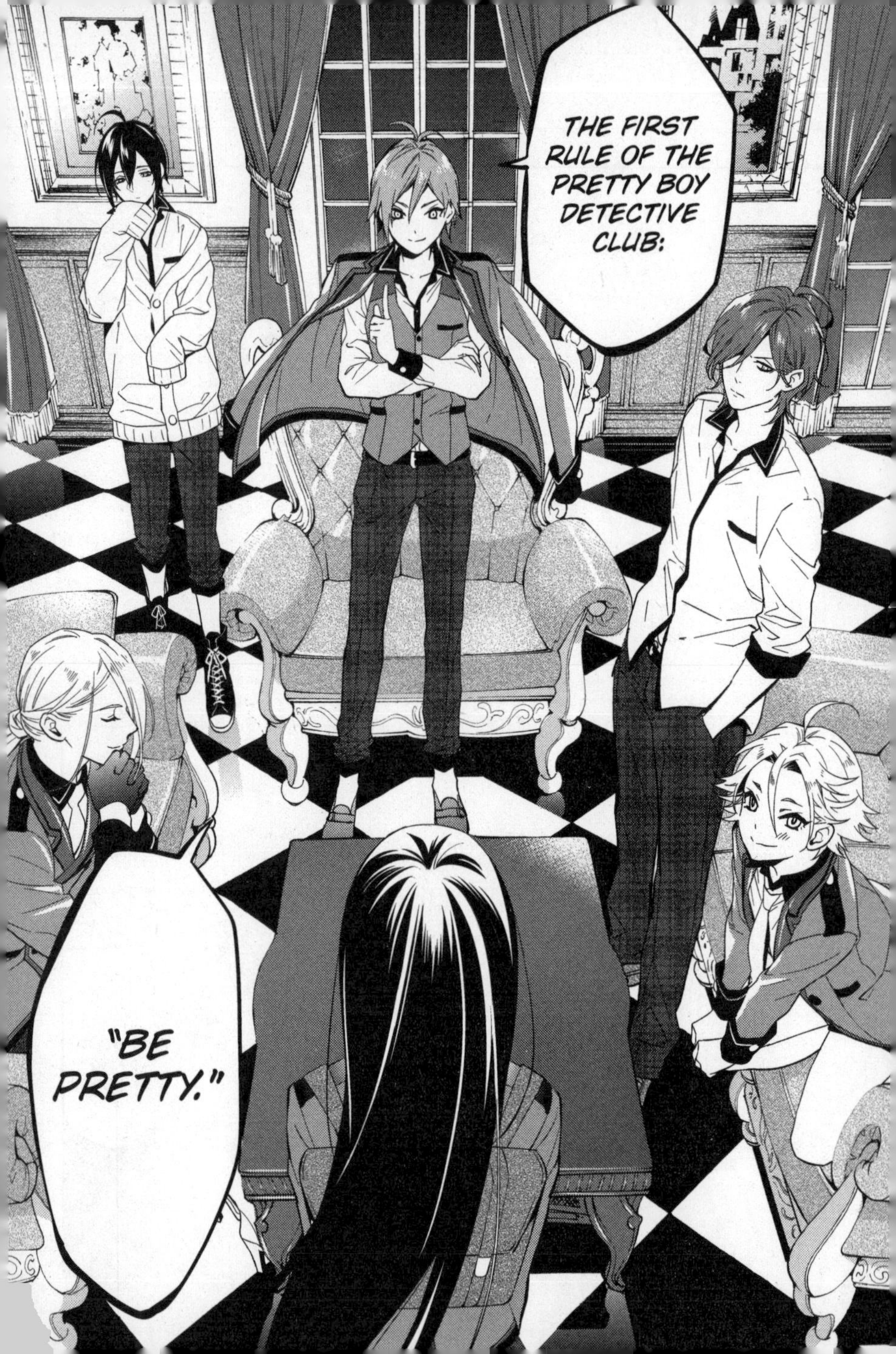
THE FIRST RULE OF THE PRETTY BOY DETECTIVE CLUB:
"BE PRETTY."

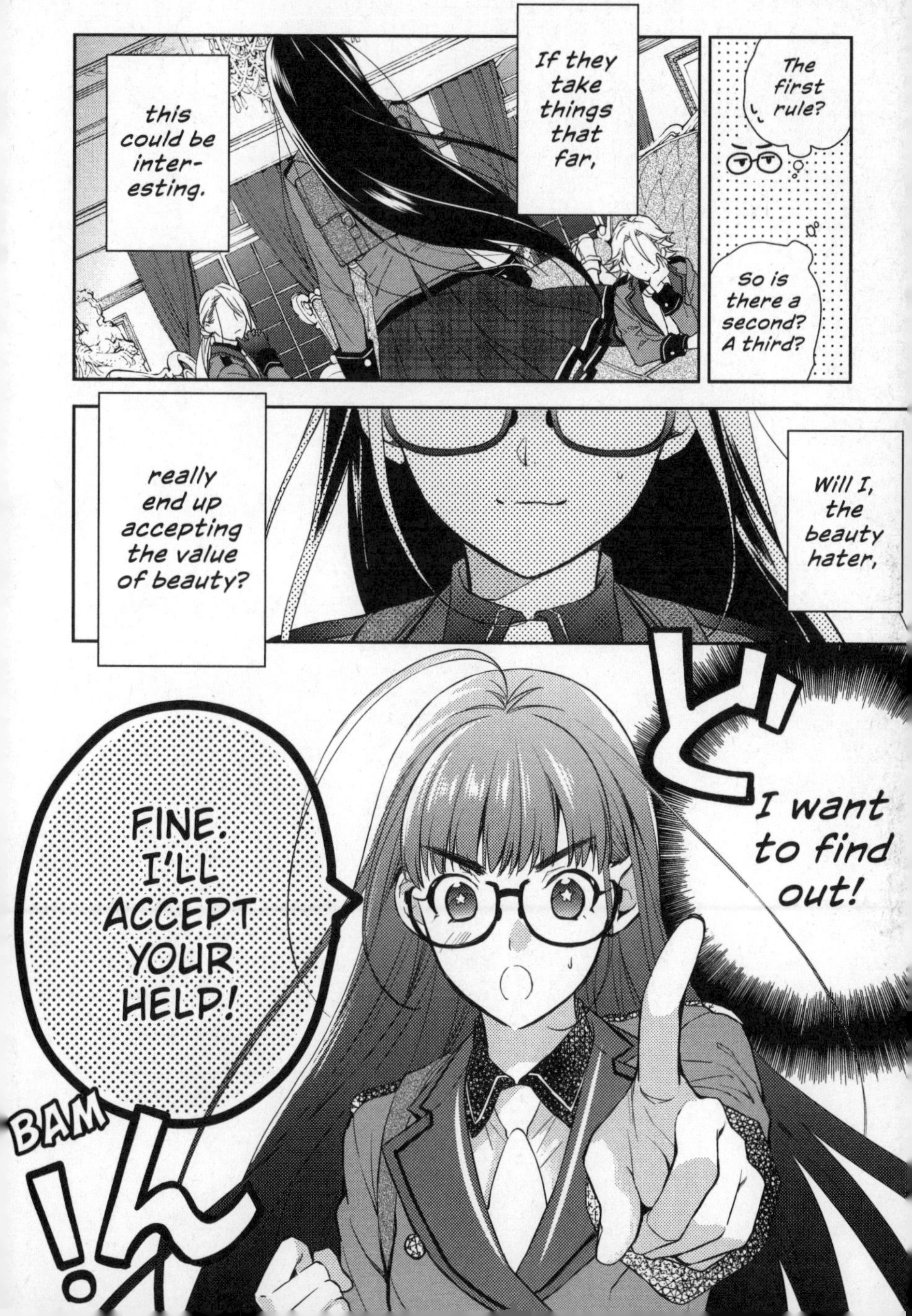
The first rule?
So is there a second? A third?
If they take things that far,
this could be interesting.
Will I, the beauty hater,
really end up accepting the value of beauty?
ど
I want to find out!
FINE. I'LL ACCEPT YOUR HELP!
BAM
ん!

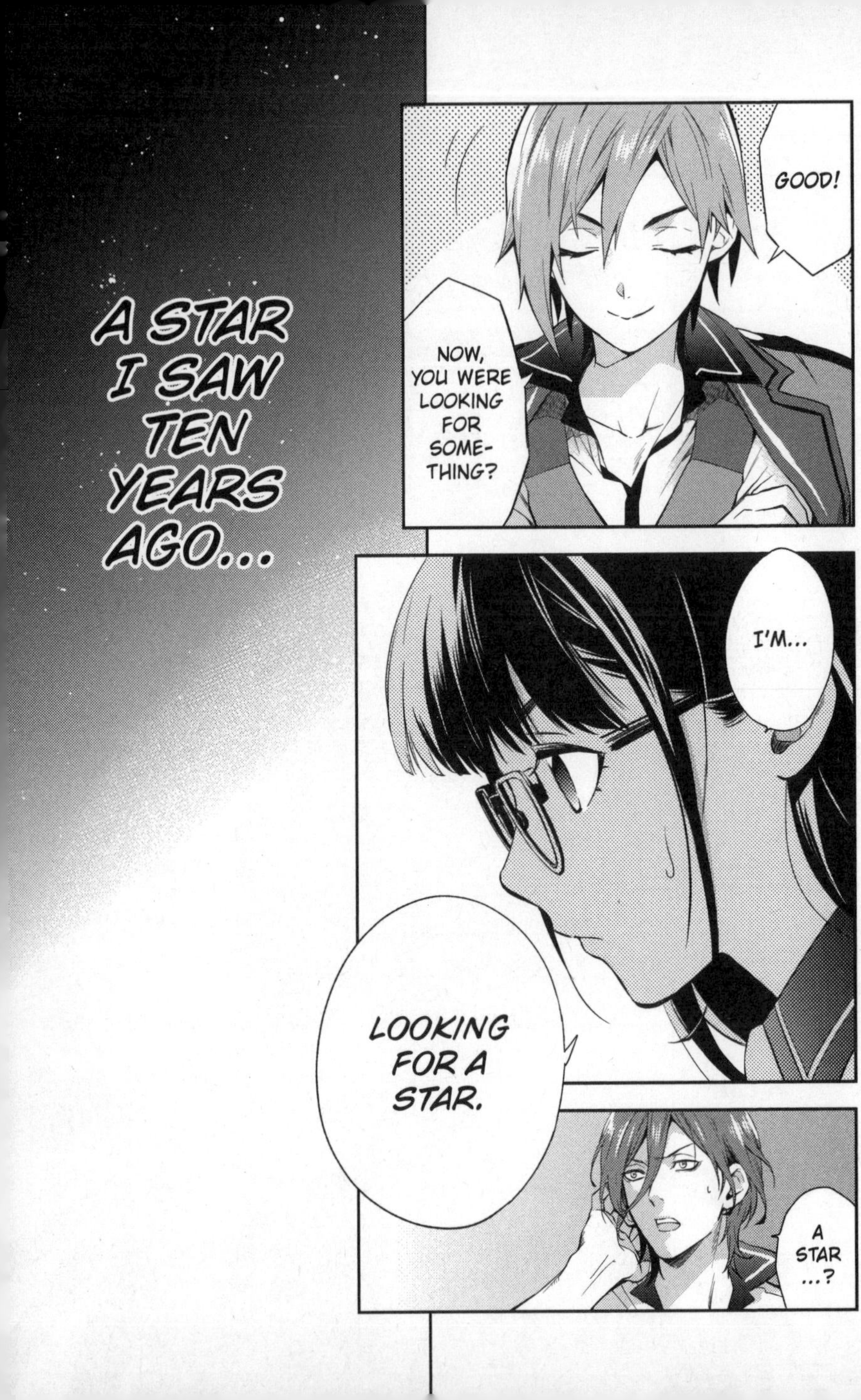
GOOD!
NOW, YOU WERE LOOKING FOR SOME-THING?
I'M...
LOOKING FOR A STAR.
A STAR ...?
A STAR I SAW TEN YEARS AGO...

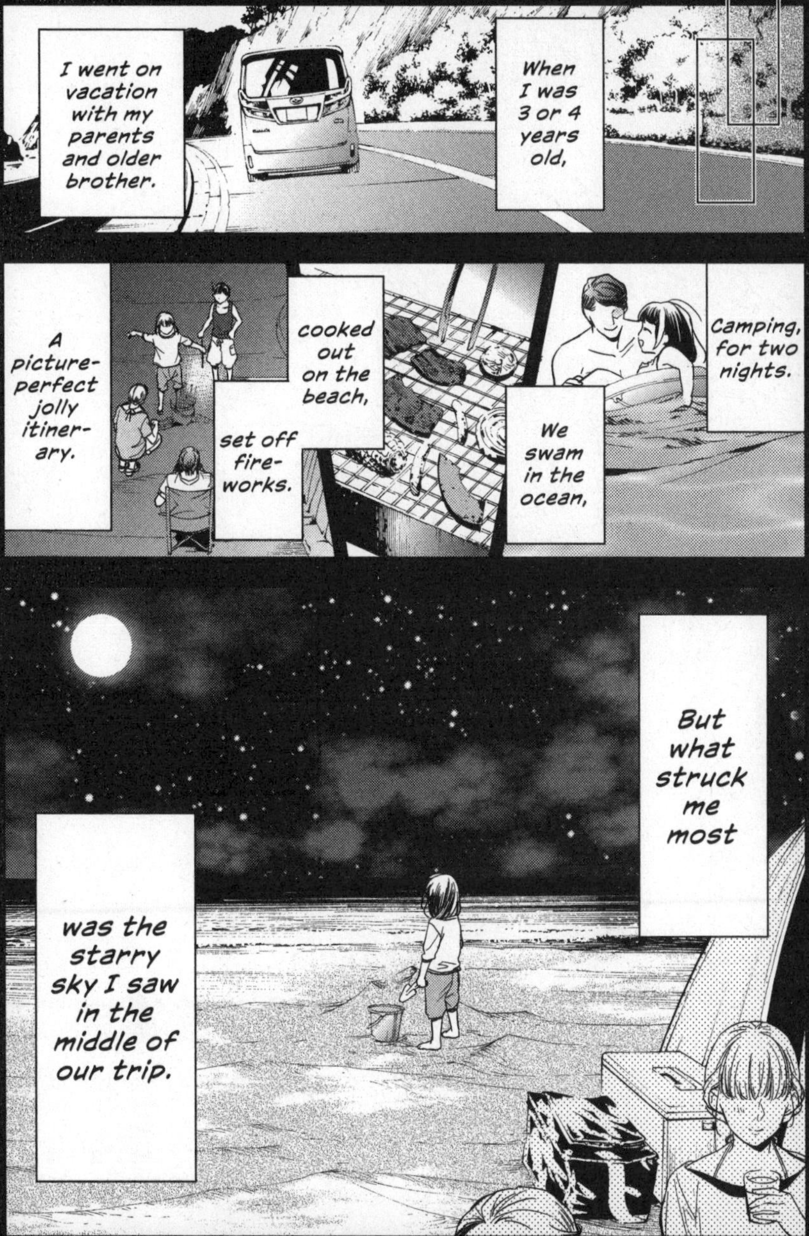
When I was 3 or 4 years old,
I went on vacation with my parents and older brother.
Camping, for two nights.
We swam in the ocean,
cooked out on the beach,
set off fire-works.
A picture-perfect jolly itiner-ary.
But what struck me most
was the starry sky I saw in the middle of our trip.

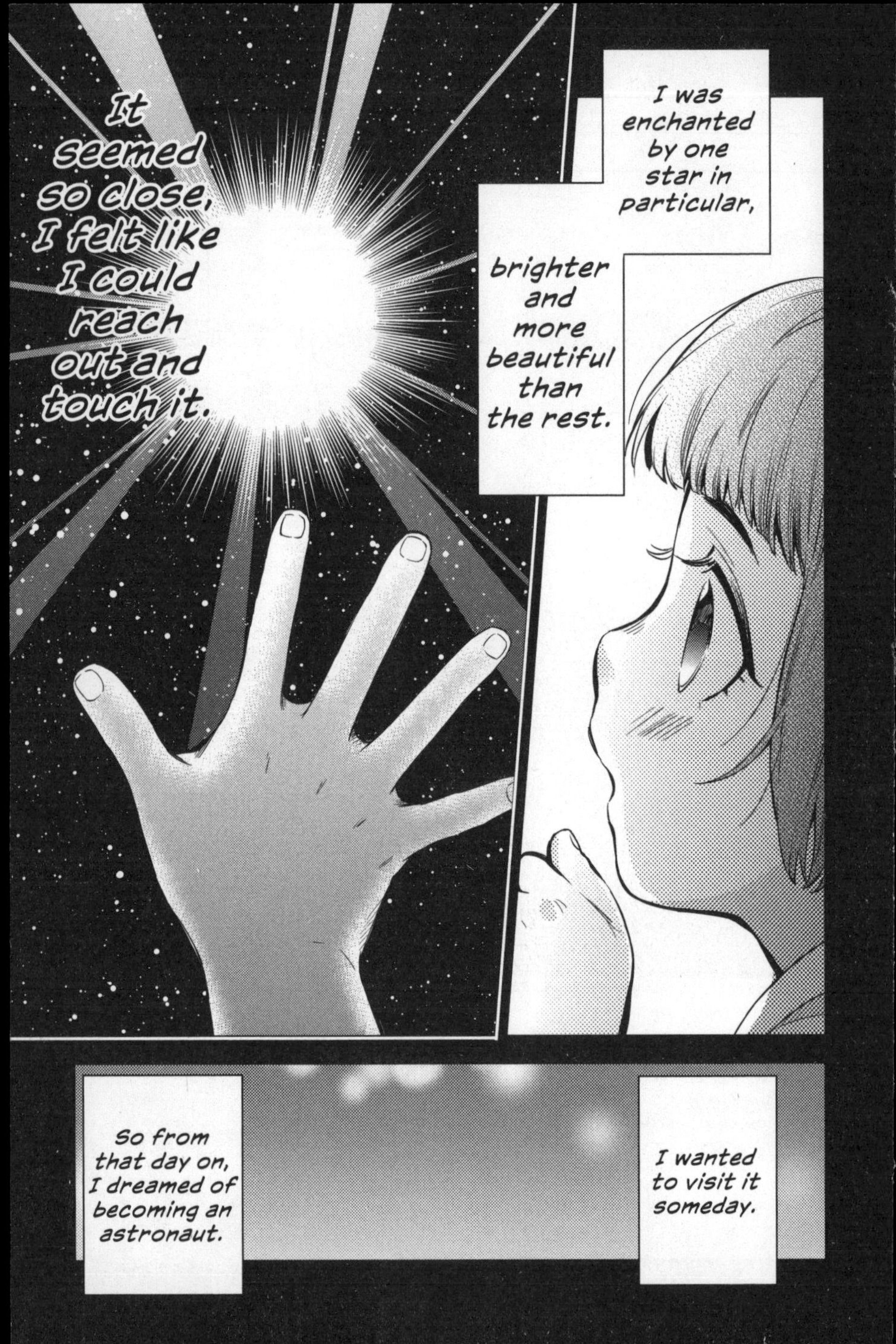
I was enchanted by one star in particular,
brighter and more beautiful than the rest.
It seemed so close, I felt like I could reach out and touch it.
I wanted to visit it someday.
So from that day on, I dreamed of becoming an astronaut.

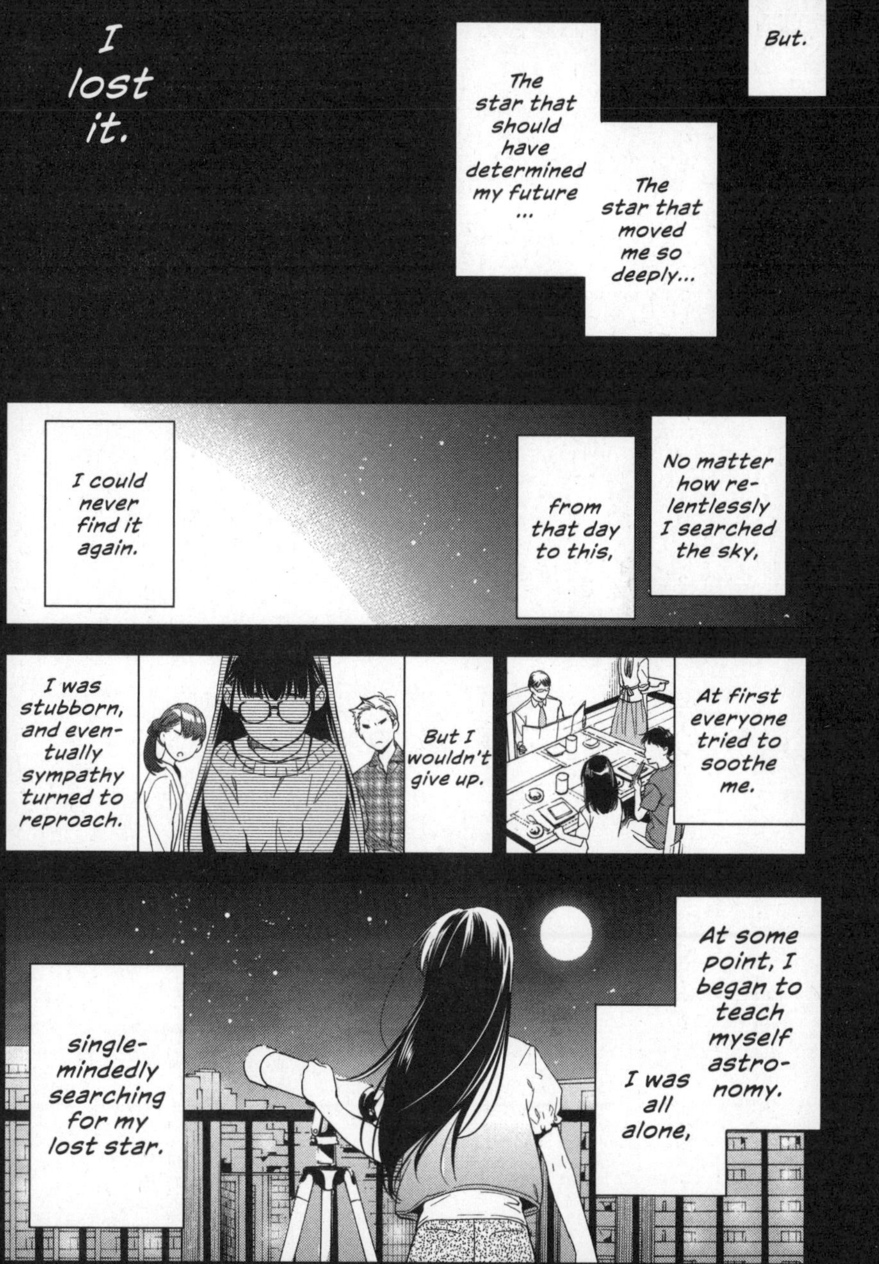
But.
The star that moved me so deeply...
The star that should have determined my future ...
I lost it.
No matter how re-lentlessly I searched the sky,
from that day to this,
I could never find it again.
At first everyone tried to soothe me.
But I wouldn't give up.
I was stubborn, and even-tually sympathy turned to reproach.
At some point, I began to teach myself astro-nomy.
I was all alone,
single-mindedly searching for my lost star.

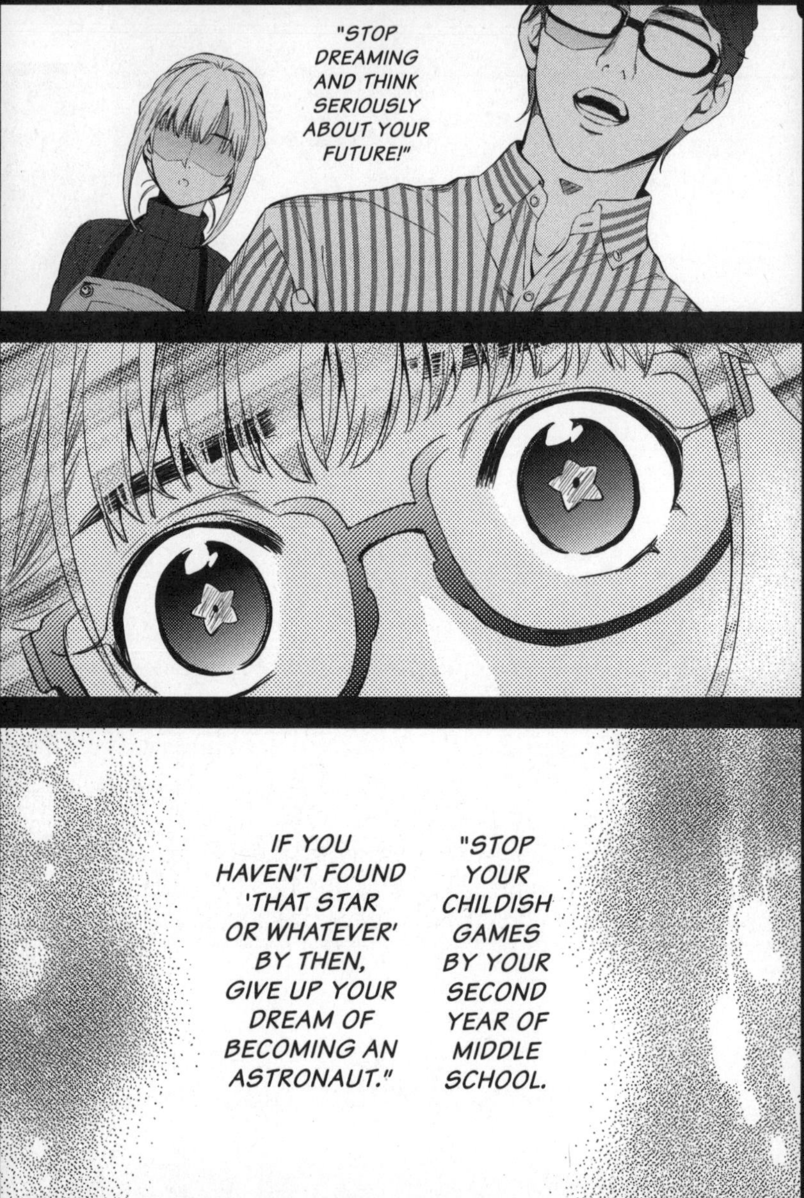
"STOP DREAMING AND THINK SERIOUSLY ABOUT YOUR FUTURE!"
"STOP YOUR CHILDISH GAMES BY YOUR SECOND YEAR OF MIDDLE SCHOOL.
IF YOU HAVEN'T FOUND 'THAT STAR OR WHATEVER' BY THEN, GIVE UP YOUR DREAM OF BECOMING AN ASTRONAUT."

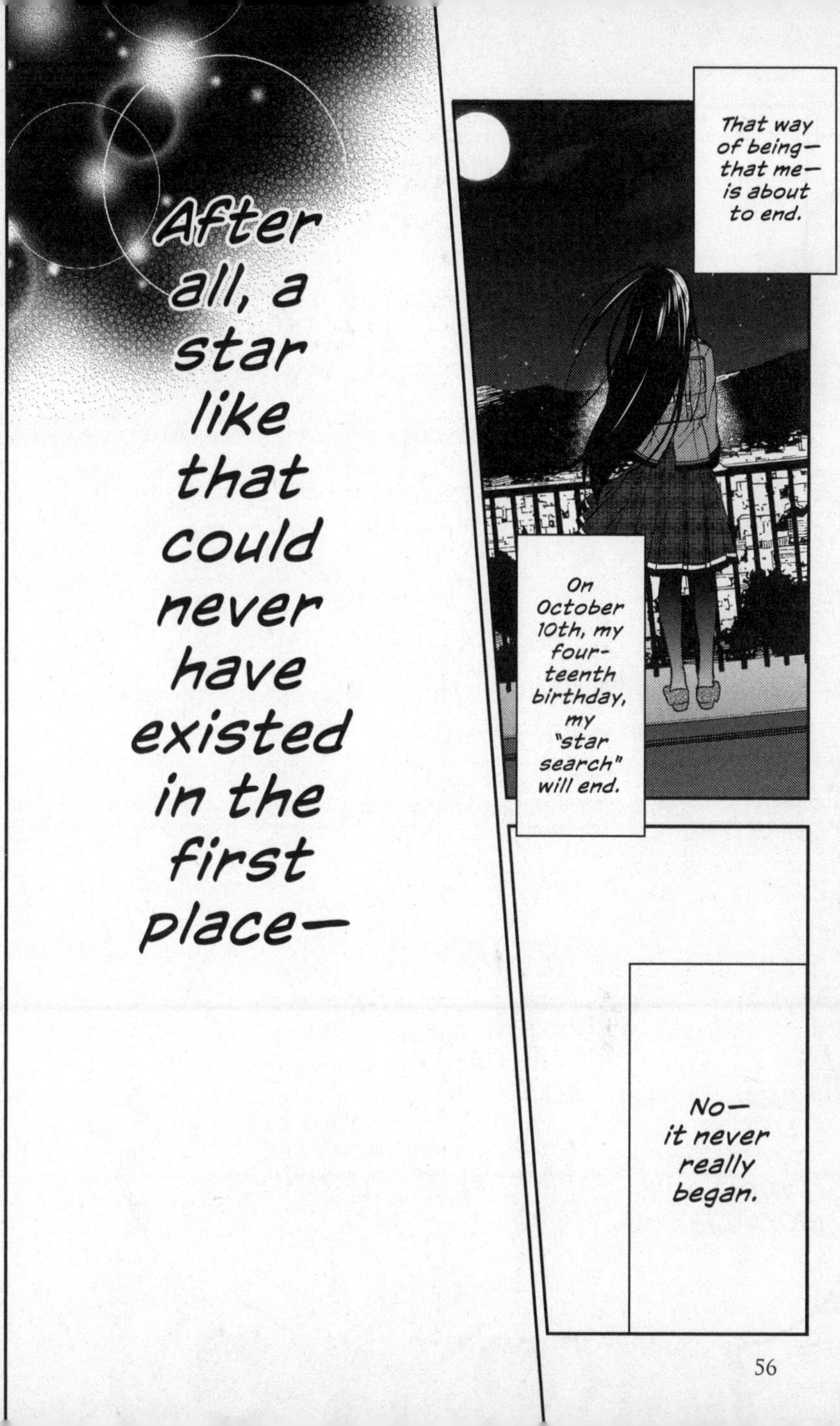
That way of being—that me—is about to end.
On October 10th, my fourteenth birthday, my "star search" will end.
No—it never really began.
After all, a star like that could never have existed in the first place—

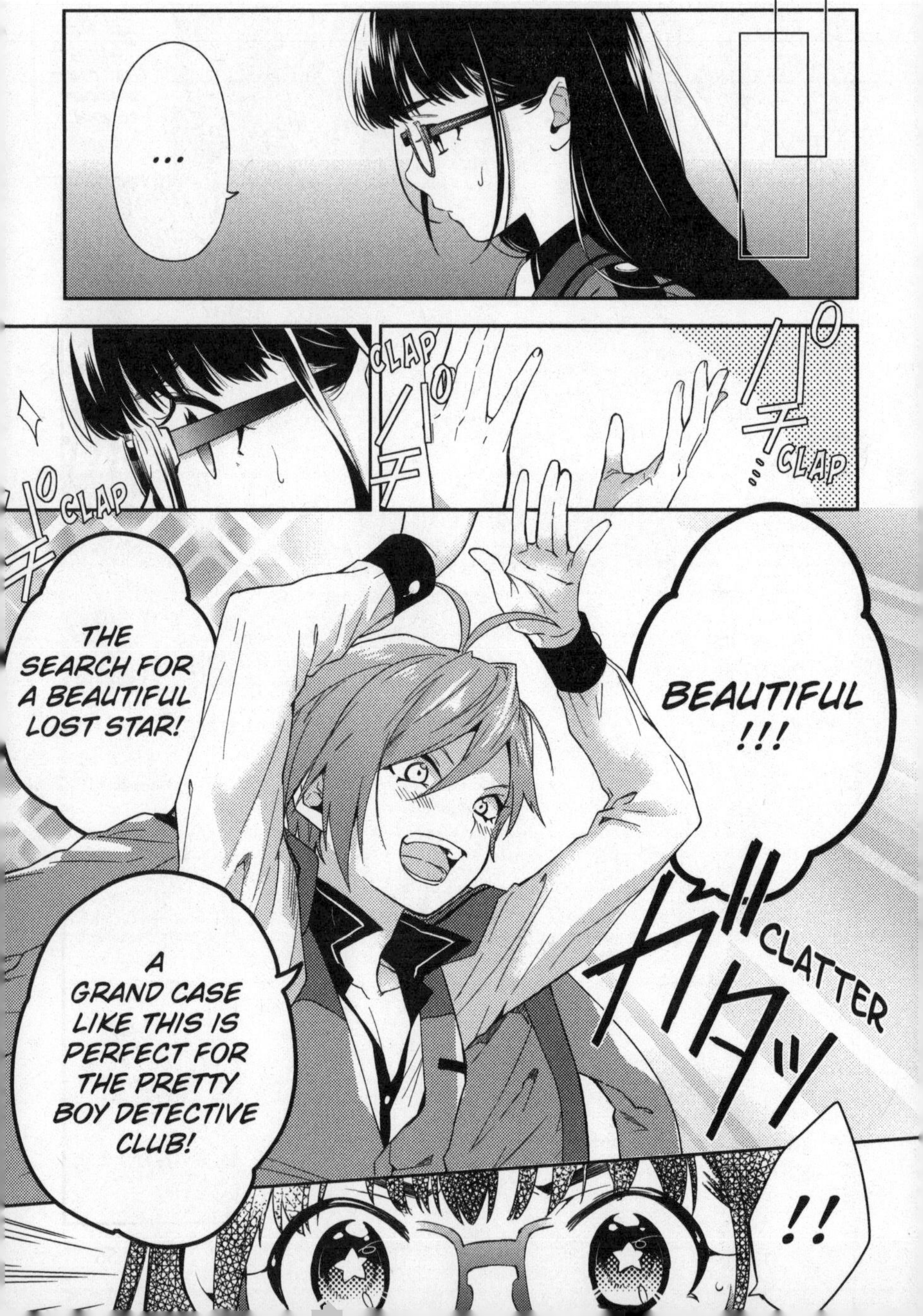
...
CLAP
CLAP
CLAP
BEAUTIFUL !!!
THE SEARCH FOR A BEAUTIFUL LOST STAR!
A GRAND CASE LIKE THIS IS PERFECT FOR THE PRETTY BOY DETECTIVE CLUB!
CLATTER
!!

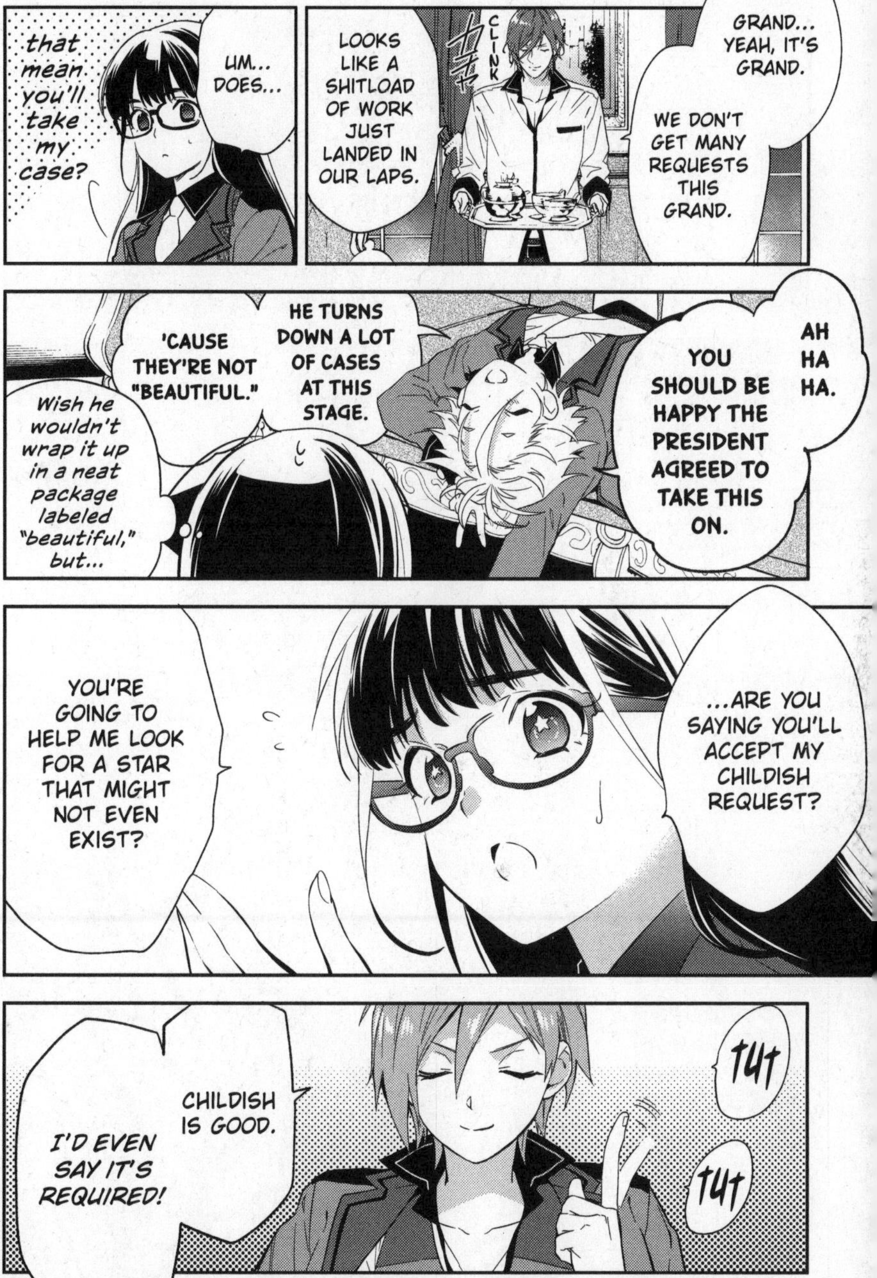
GRAND... YEAH, IT'S GRAND.
WE DON'T GET MANY REQUESTS THIS GRAND.
CLINK
LOOKS LIKE A SHITLOAD OF WORK JUST LANDED IN OUR LAPS.
UM... DOES...
that mean you'll take my case?
AH HA HA.
YOU SHOULD BE HAPPY THE PRESIDENT AGREED TO TAKE THIS ON.
HE TURNS DOWN A LOT OF CASES AT THIS STAGE.
'CAUSE THEY'RE NOT "BEAUTIFUL."
Wish he wouldn't wrap it up in a neat package labeled "beautiful," but...
...ARE YOU SAYING YOU'LL ACCEPT MY CHILDISH REQUEST?
YOU'RE GOING TO HELP ME LOOK FOR A STAR THAT MIGHT NOT EVEN EXIST?
TUT
TUT
CHILDISH IS GOOD.
I'D EVEN SAY IT'S REQUIRED!

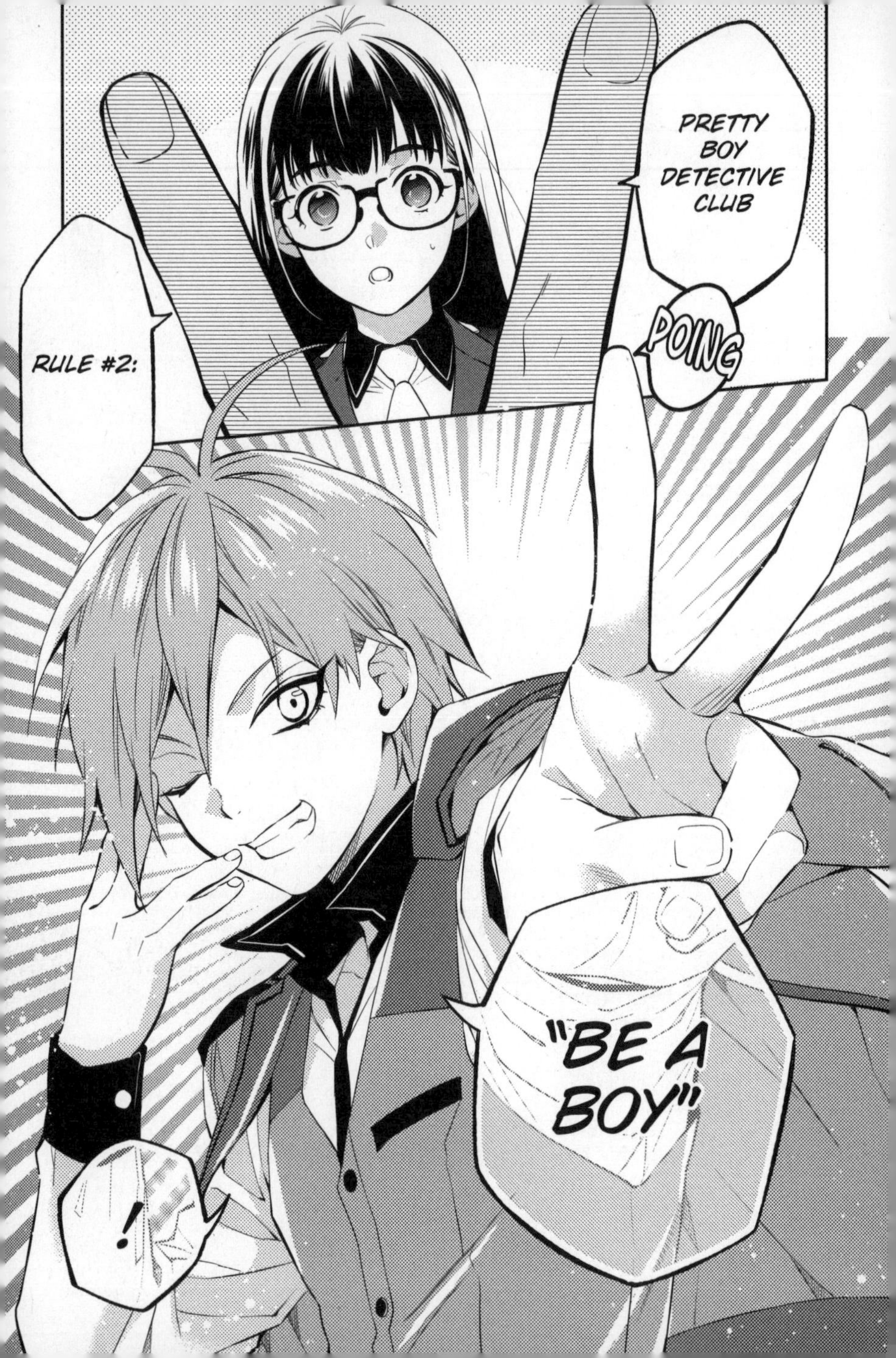
PRETTY BOY DETECTIVE CLUB
POING
RULE #2:
"BE A BOY"
!

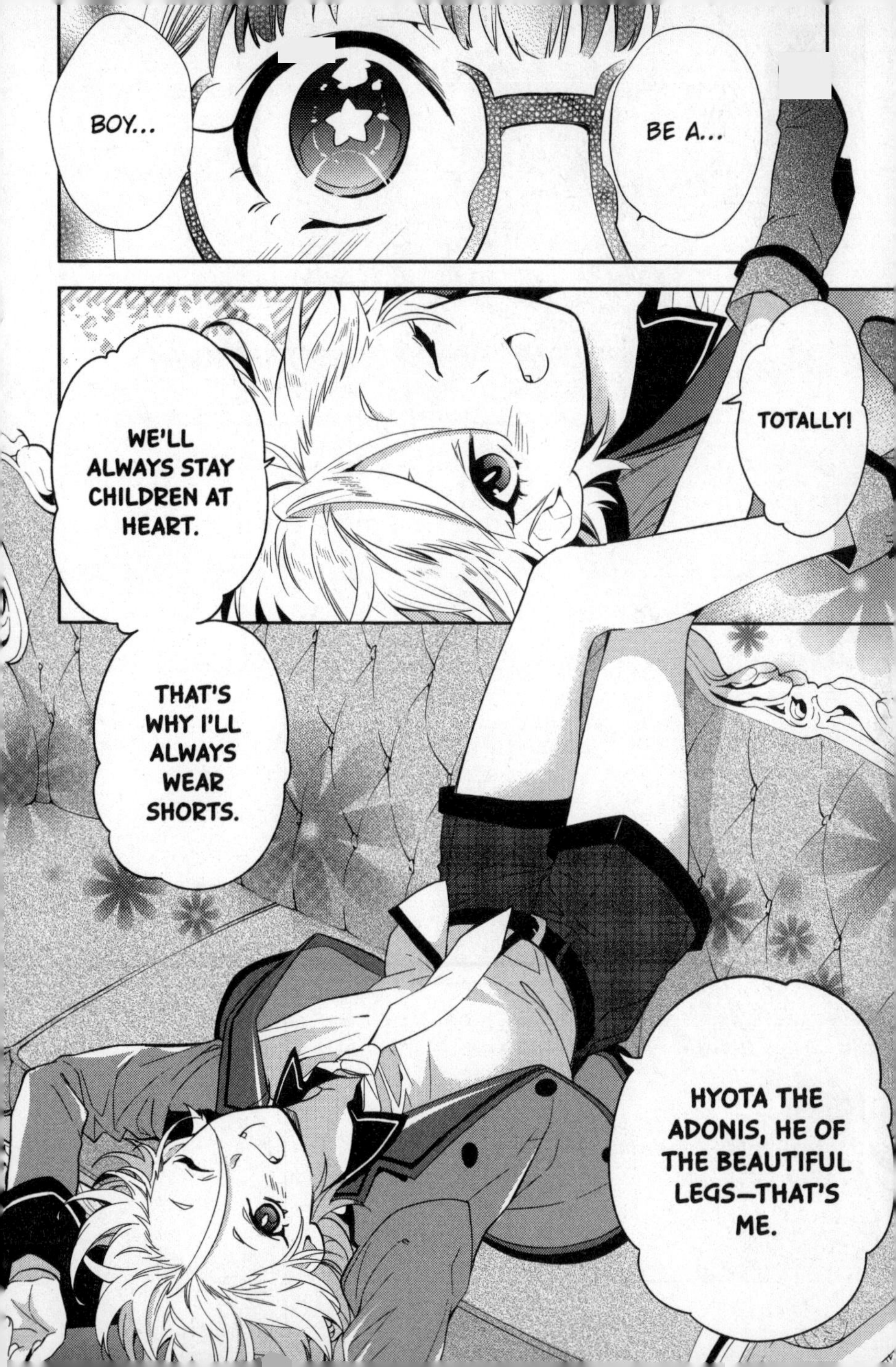
BE A...
BOY...
TOTALLY!
WE'LL ALWAYS STAY CHILDREN AT HEART.
THAT'S WHY I'LL ALWAYS WEAR SHORTS.
HYOTA THE ADONIS, HE OF THE BEAUTIFUL LEGS—THAT'S ME.

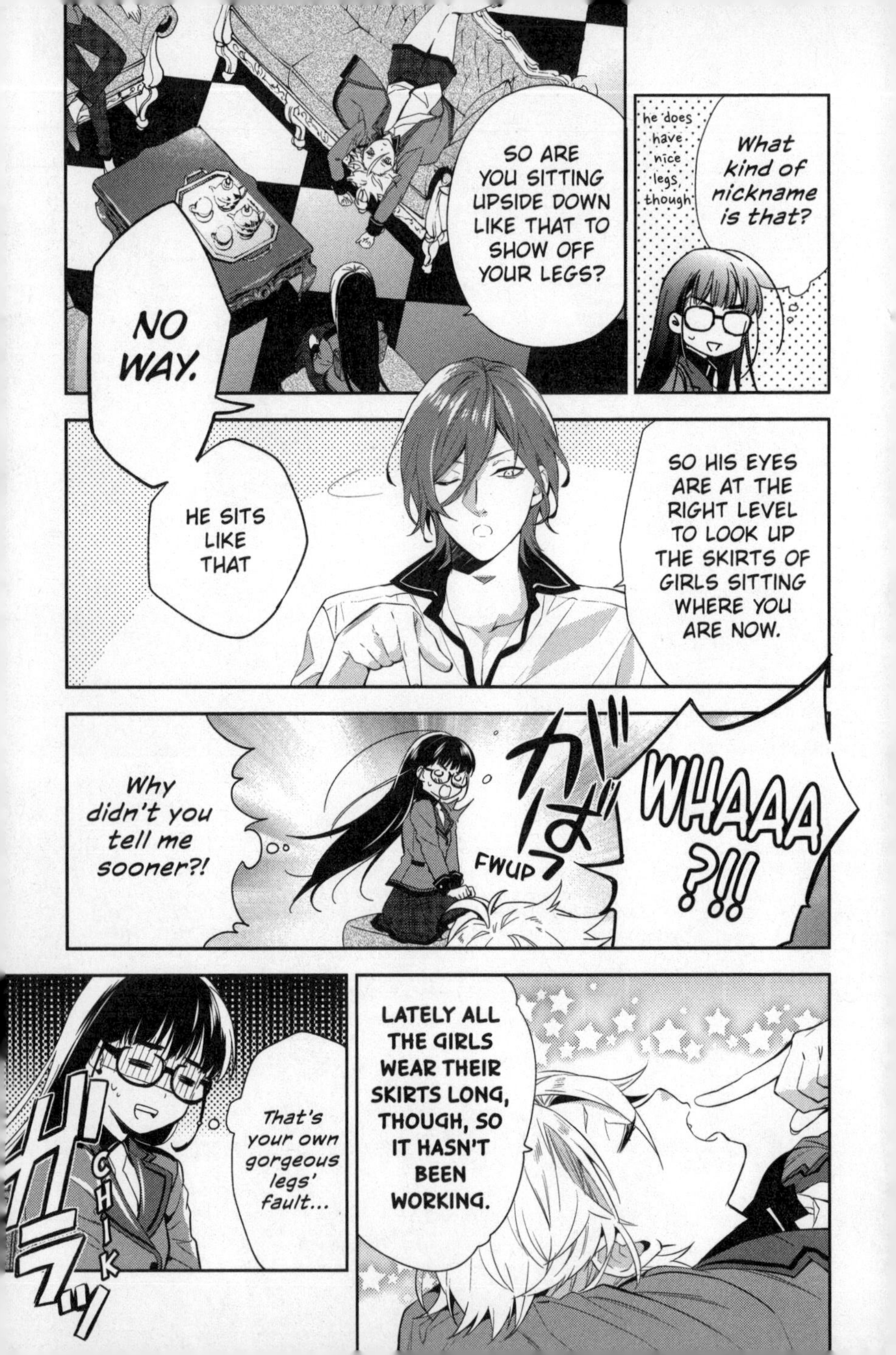
What kind of nickname is that?
he does have nice legs, though
SO ARE YOU SITTING UPSIDE DOWN LIKE THAT TO SHOW OFF YOUR LEGS?
NO WAY.
HE SITS LIKE THAT
SO HIS EYES ARE AT THE RIGHT LEVEL TO LOOK UP THE SKIRTS OF GIRLS SITTING WHERE YOU ARE NOW.
WHAAA ?!!
がばっ
FWUP
Why didn't you tell me sooner?!
LATELY ALL THE GIRLS WEAR THEIR SKIRTS LONG, THOUGH, SO IT HASN'T BEEN WORKING.
That's your own gorgeous legs' fault...
ジャッ
CHIK

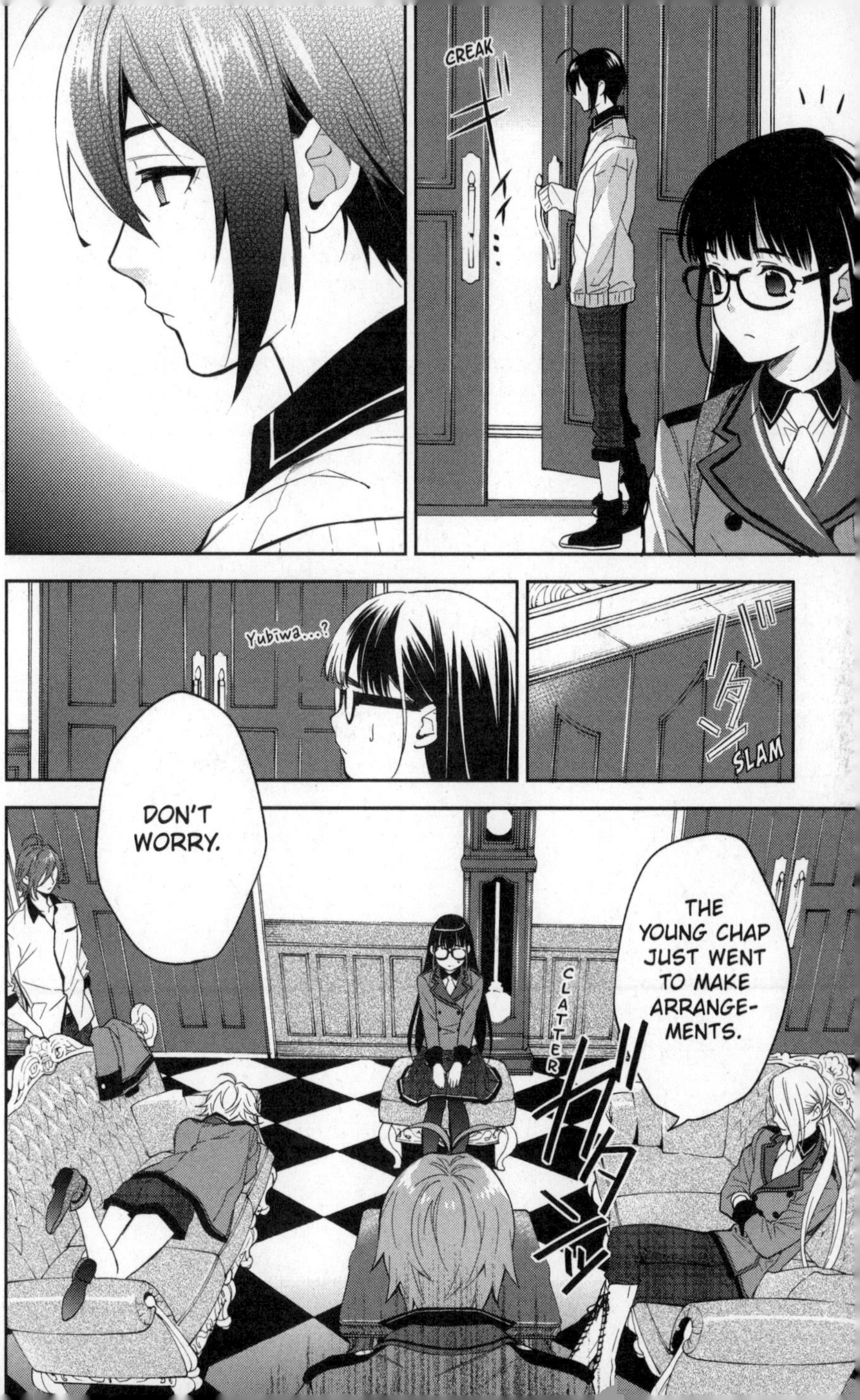
CREAK
SLAM
Yubiwa...?
THE YOUNG CHAP JUST WENT TO MAKE ARRANGE-MENTS.
CLATTER
DON'T WORRY.

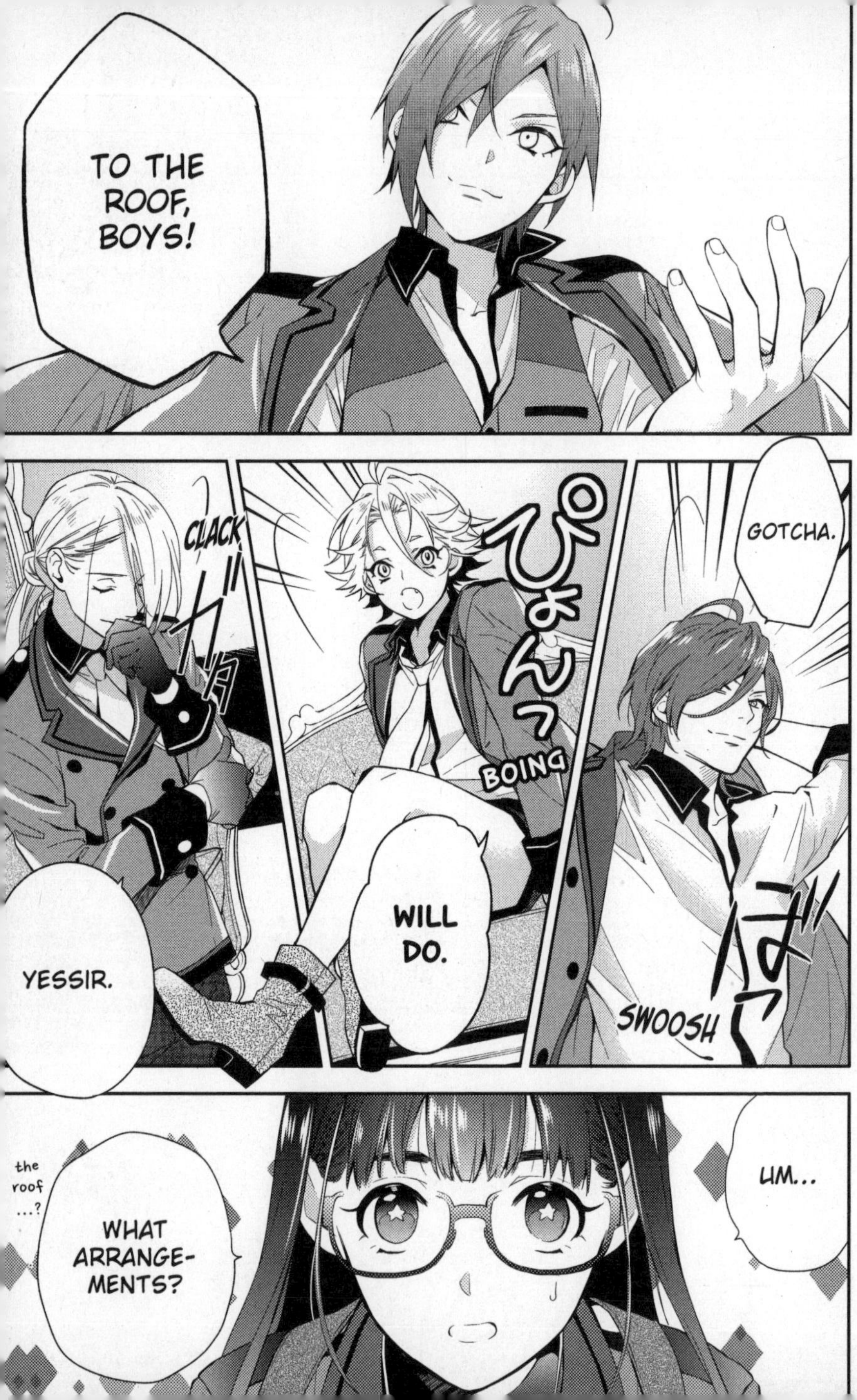
TO THE ROOF, BOYS!
GOTCHA.
ばっ
SWOOSH
ぴょんっ
BOING
WILL DO.
CLACK
YESSIR.
UM...
WHAT ARRANGE-MENTS?
the roof ...?

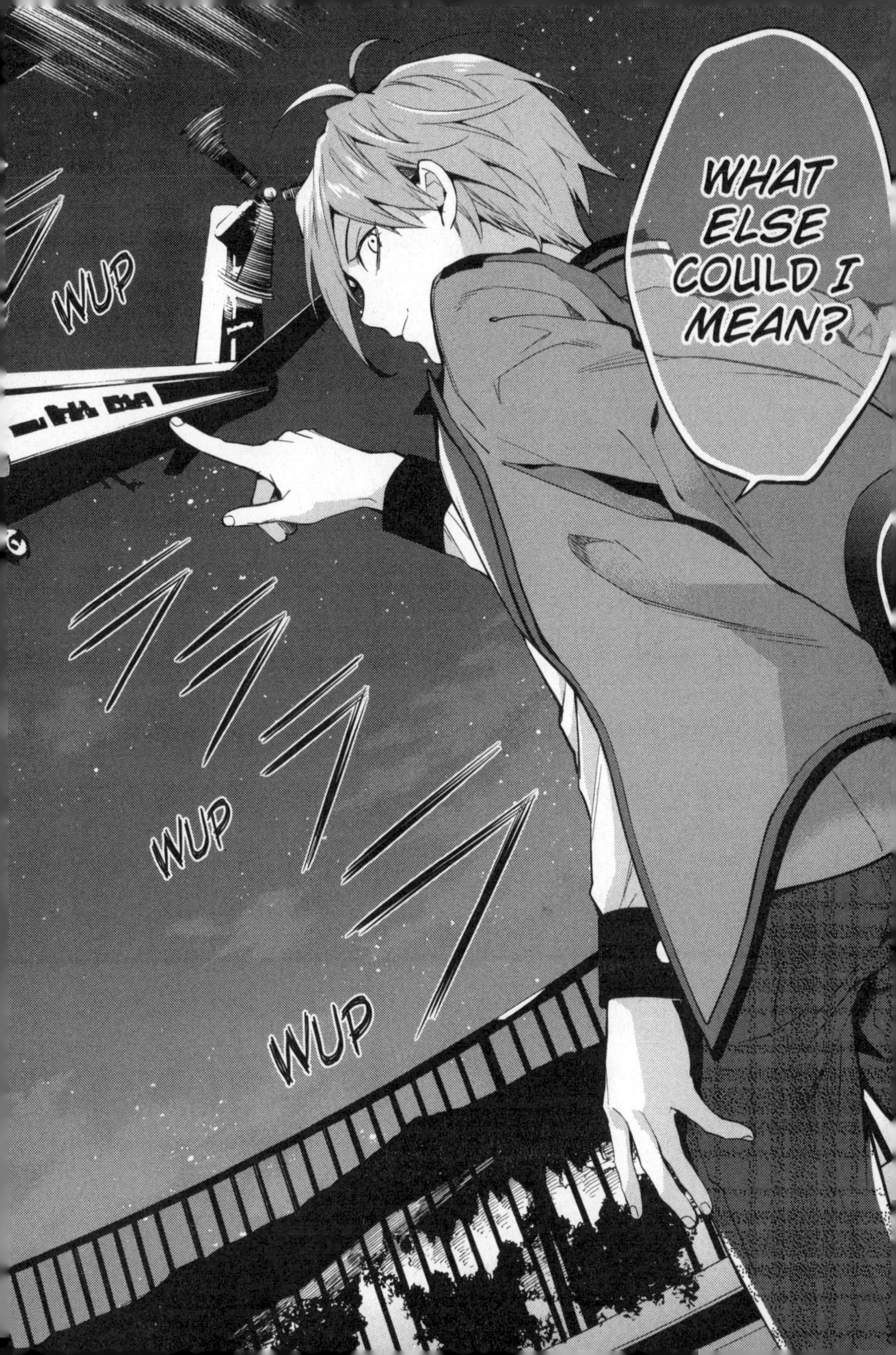
WHAT ELSE COULD I MEAN?
WUP
WUP
WUP

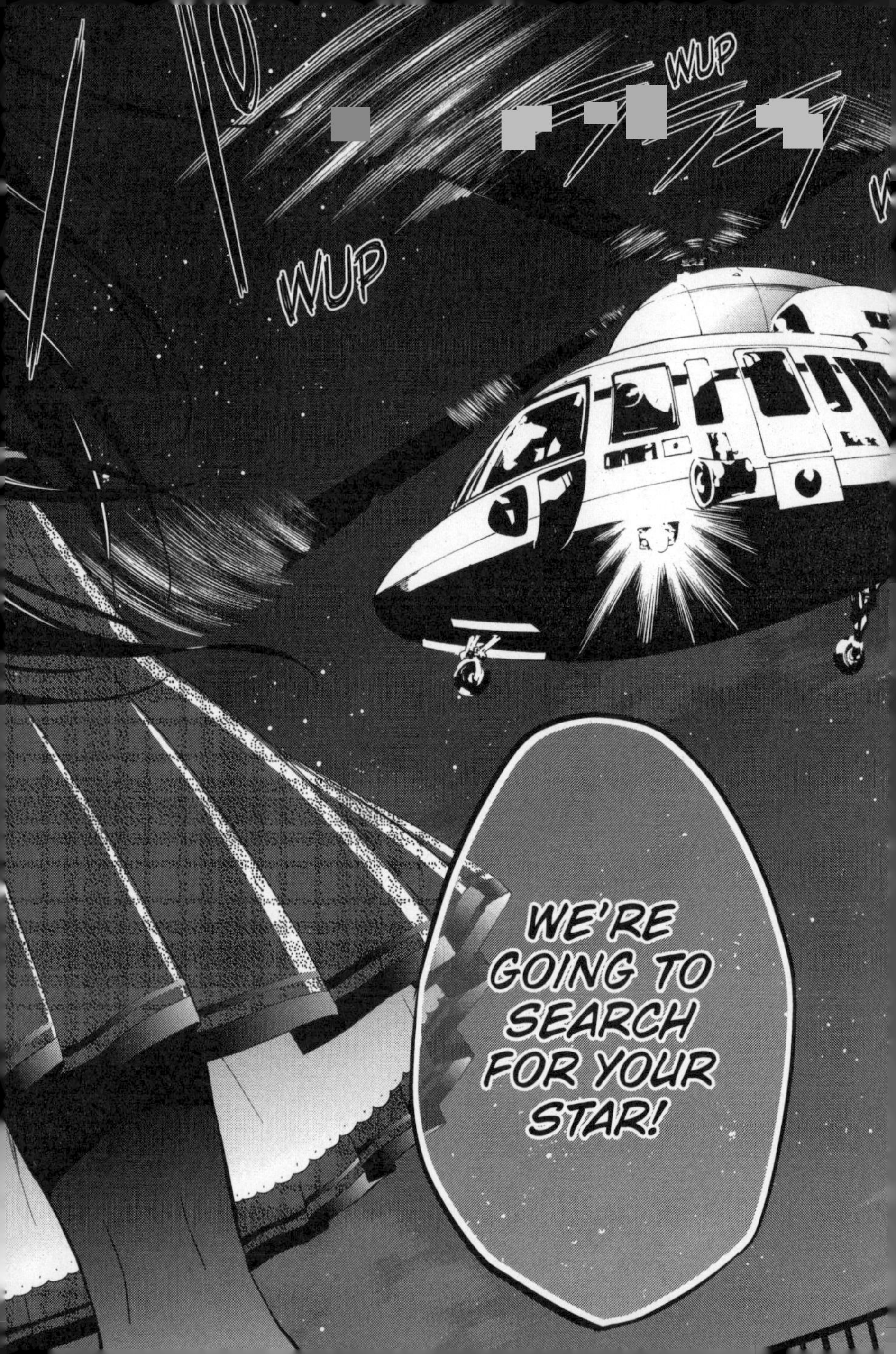
WUP
WUP
WE'RE GOING TO SEARCH FOR YOUR STAR!

PRETTY BOY

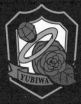

DETECTIVE CLUB!!

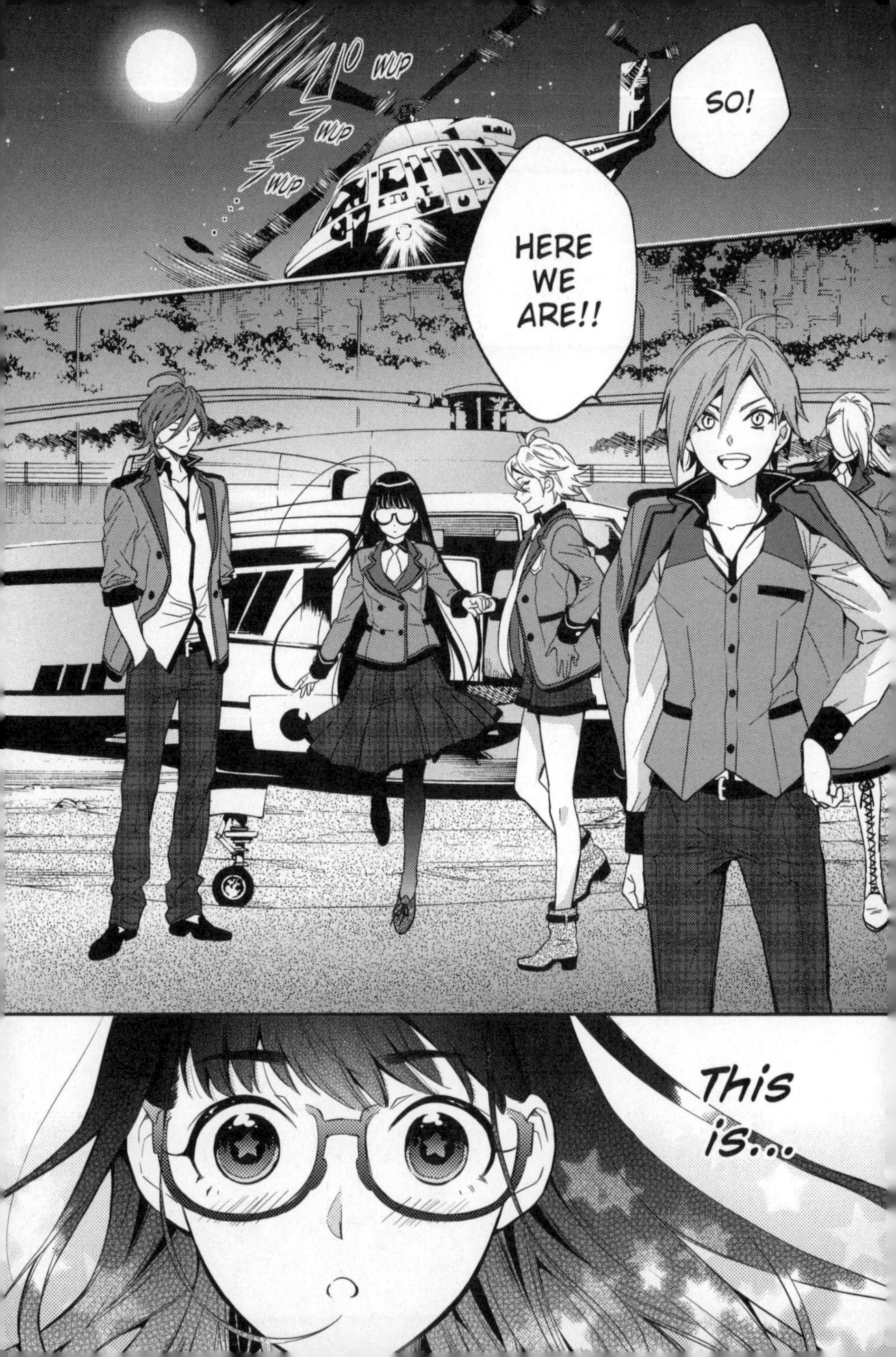
SO!
HERE WE ARE!!
WUP
WUP
WUP
This is...

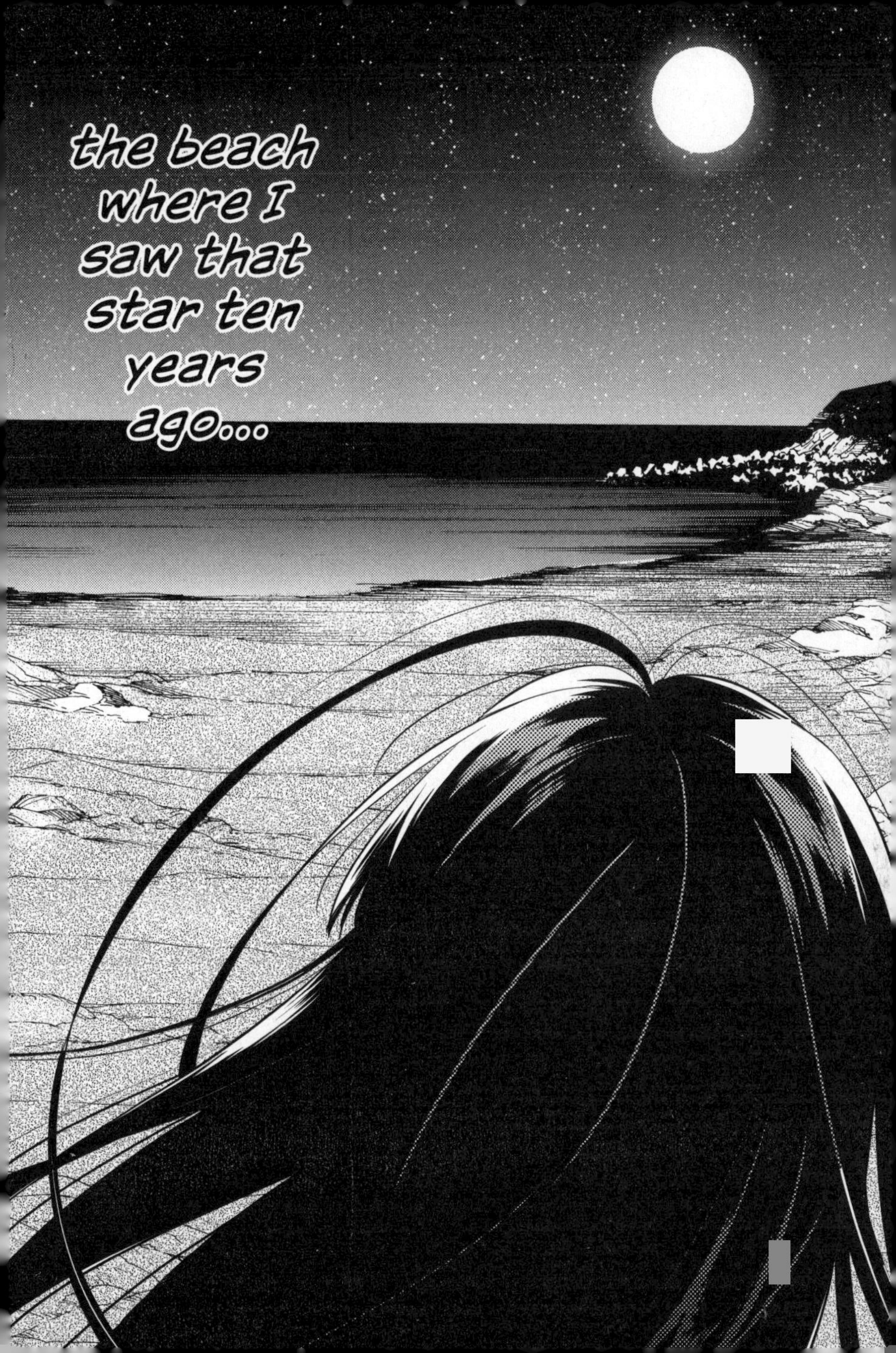
the beach where I saw that star ten years ago...

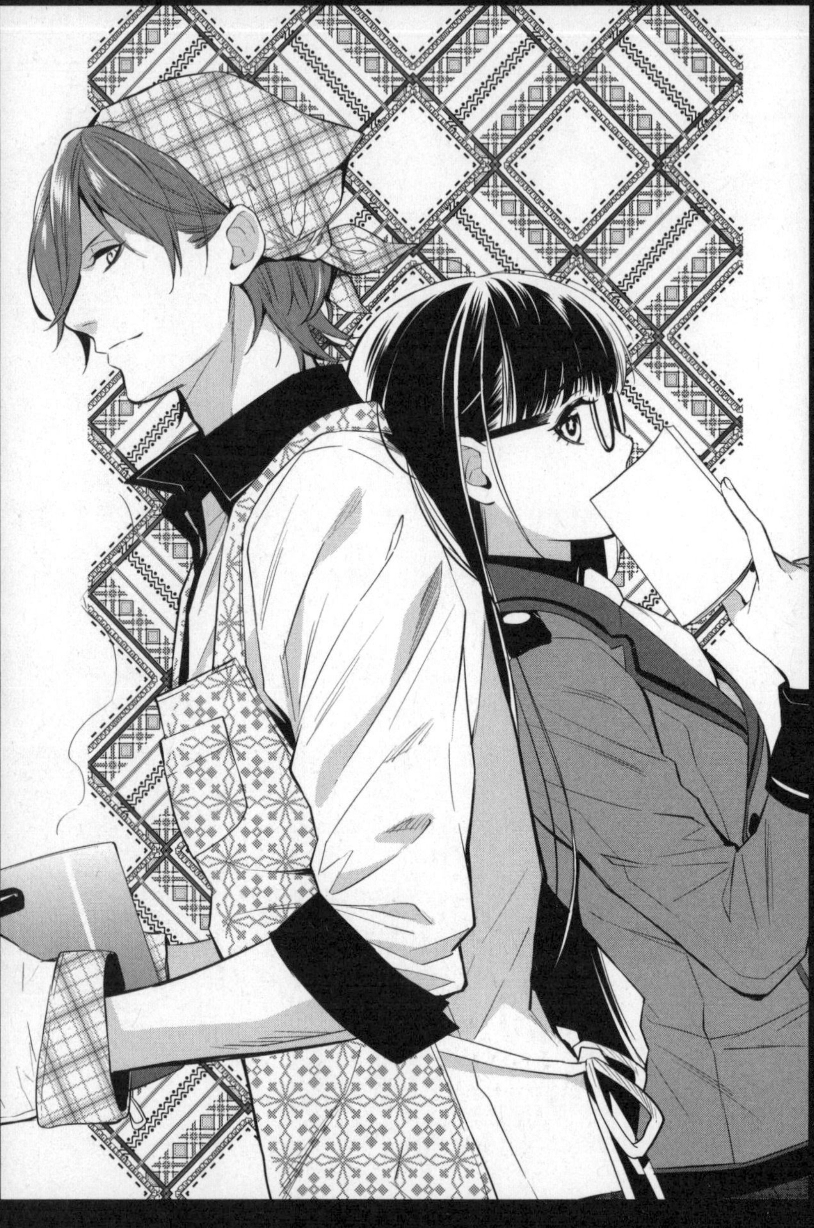

FILE ★ The Dark Star that Shines for You Alone 2

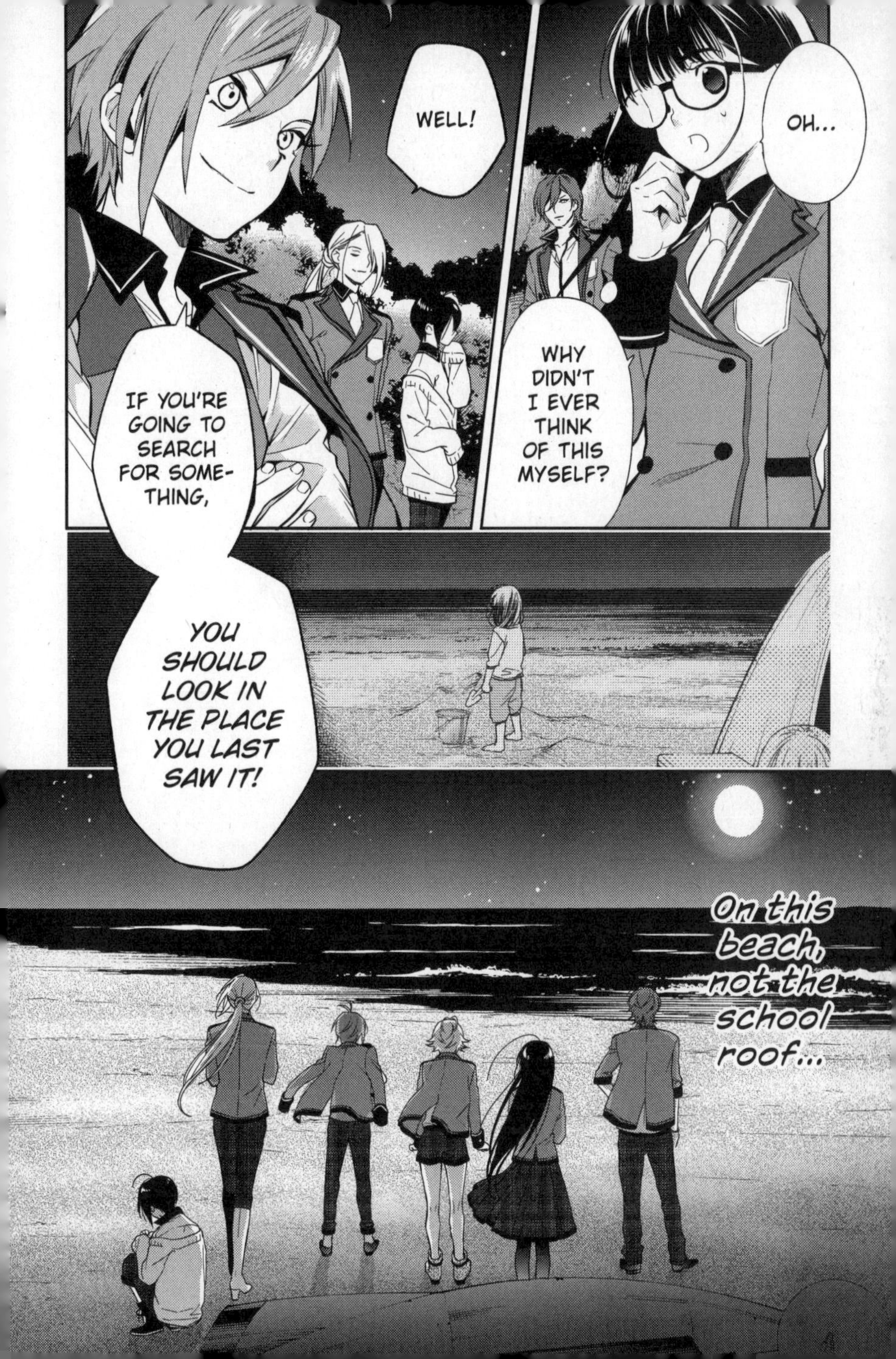
OH...
WHY DIDN'T I EVER THINK OF THIS MYSELF?
WELL!
IF YOU'RE GOING TO SEARCH FOR SOME-THING,
YOU SHOULD LOOK IN THE PLACE YOU LAST SAW IT!
On this beach, not the school roof...

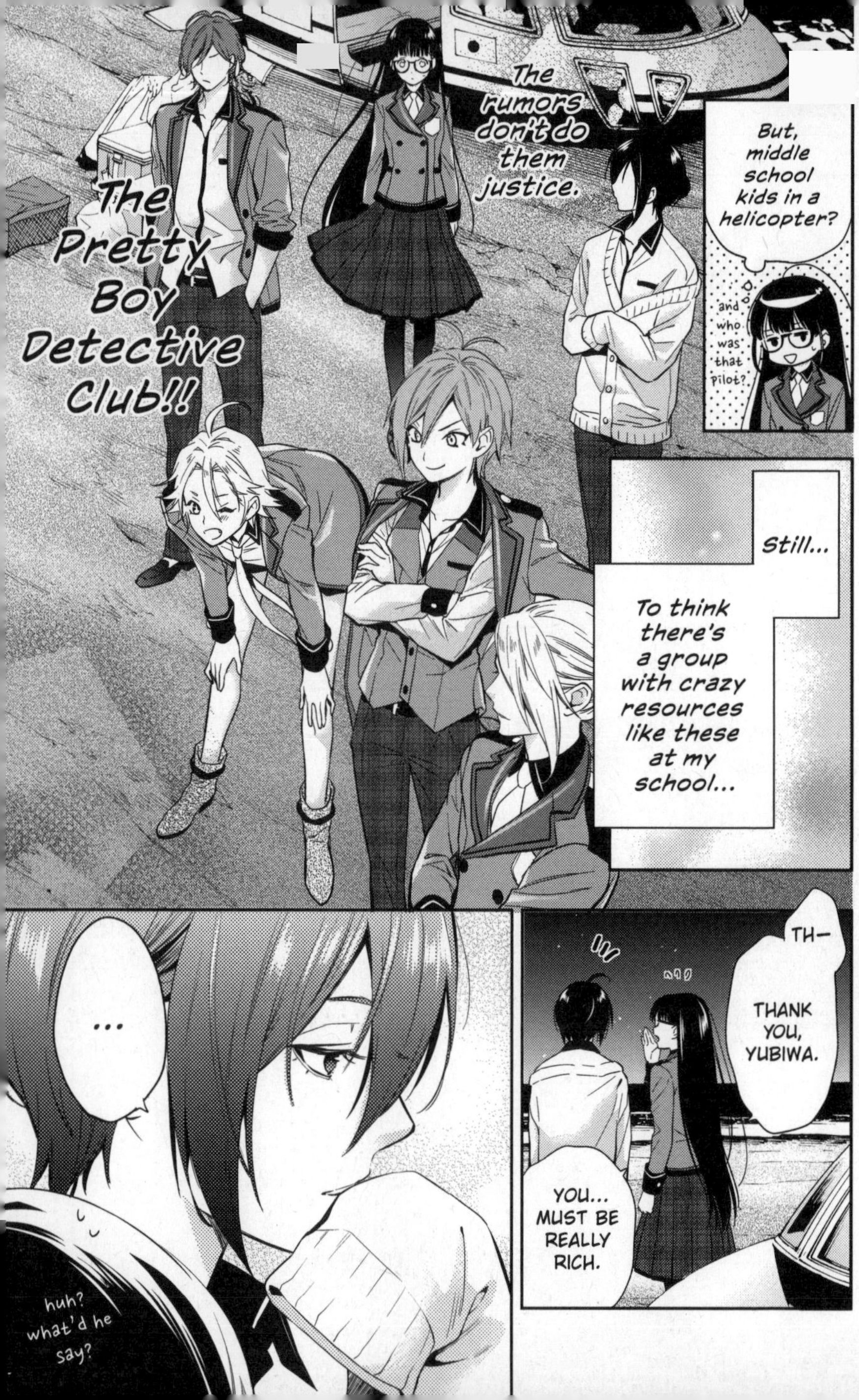
The Pretty Boy Detective Club!!
The rumors don't do them justice.
But, middle school kids in a helicopter?
and who was that pilot?
Still...
To think there's a group with crazy resources like these at my school...
TH—
THANK YOU, YUBIWA.
YOU... MUST BE REALLY RICH.
...
huh? what'd he say?

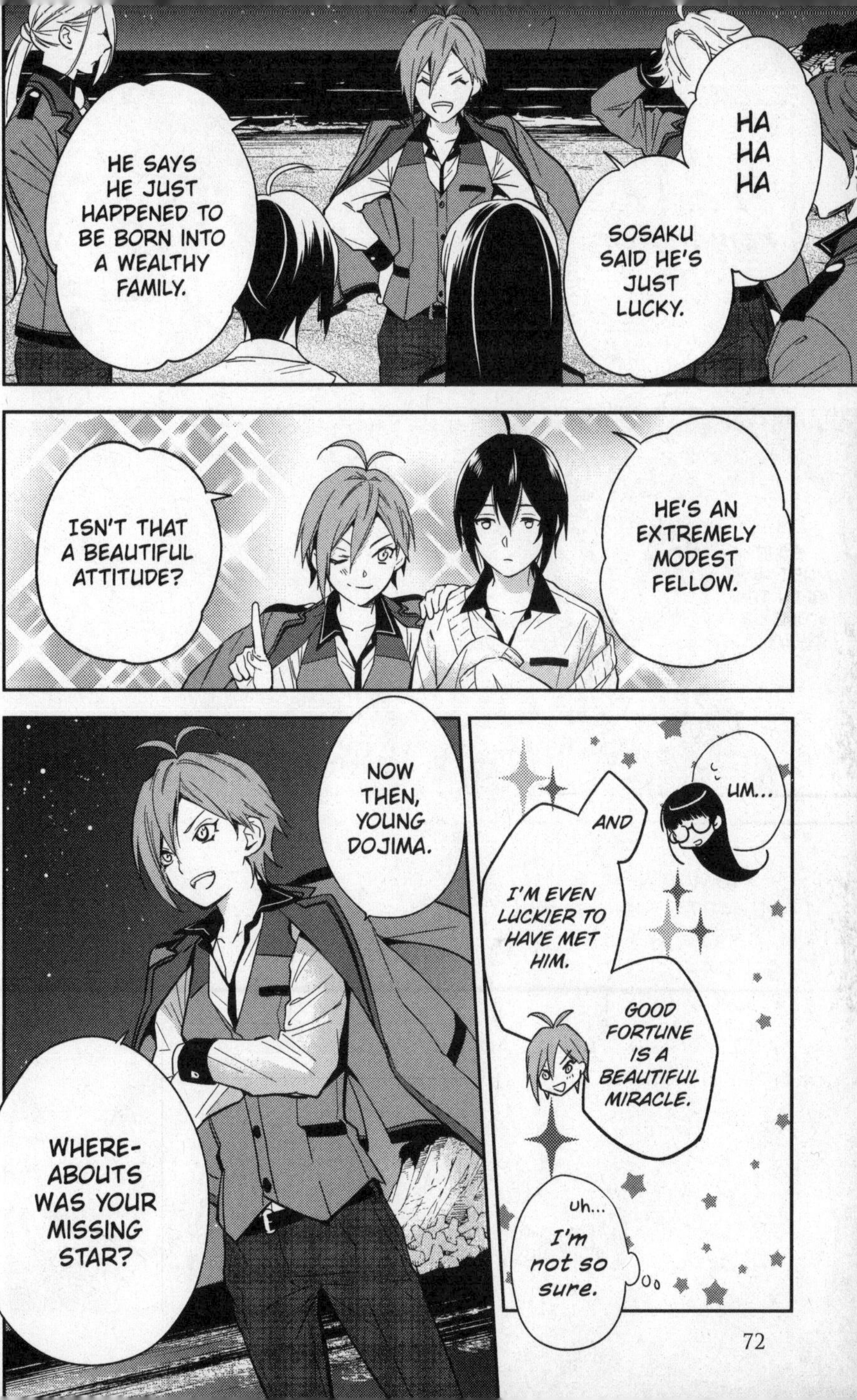
HA HA HA
SOSAKU SAID HE'S JUST LUCKY.
HE SAYS HE JUST HAPPENED TO BE BORN INTO A WEALTHY FAMILY.
HE'S AN EXTREMELY MODEST FELLOW.
ISN'T THAT A BEAUTIFUL ATTITUDE?
UM...
AND I'M EVEN LUCKIER TO HAVE MET HIM.
GOOD FORTUNE IS A BEAUTIFUL MIRACLE.
uh... I'm not so sure.
NOW THEN, YOUNG DOJIMA.
WHERE-ABOUTS WAS YOUR MISSING STAR?

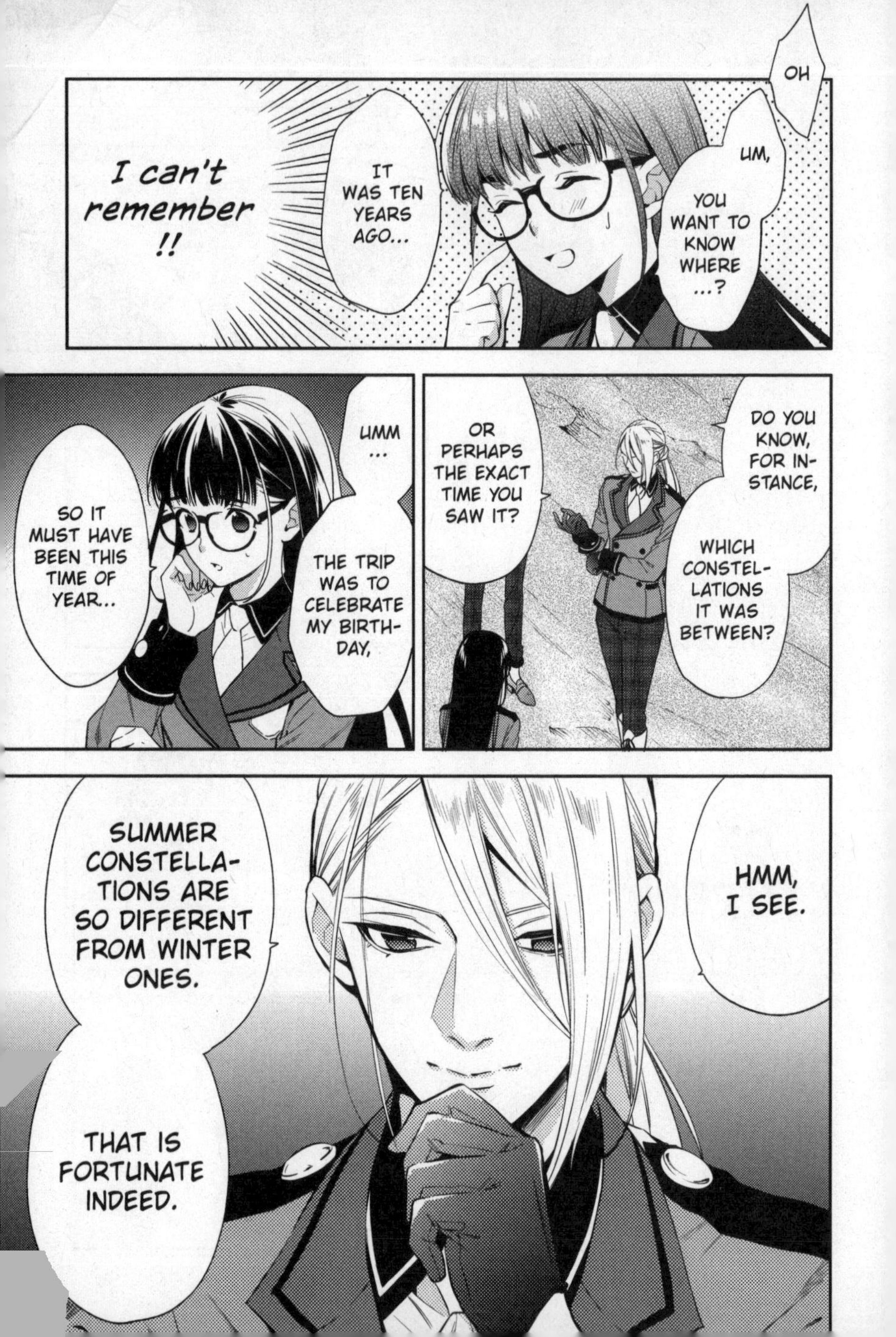
OH
UM,
YOU WANT TO KNOW WHERE ...?
IT WAS TEN YEARS AGO...
I can't remember !!
DO YOU KNOW, FOR INSTANCE,
WHICH CONSTELLATIONS IT WAS BETWEEN?
OR PERHAPS THE EXACT TIME YOU SAW IT?
UMM ...
THE TRIP WAS TO CELEBRATE MY BIRTHDAY,
SO IT MUST HAVE BEEN THIS TIME OF YEAR...
HMM, I SEE.
SUMMER CONSTELLATIONS ARE SO DIFFERENT FROM WINTER ONES.
THAT IS FORTUNATE INDEED.

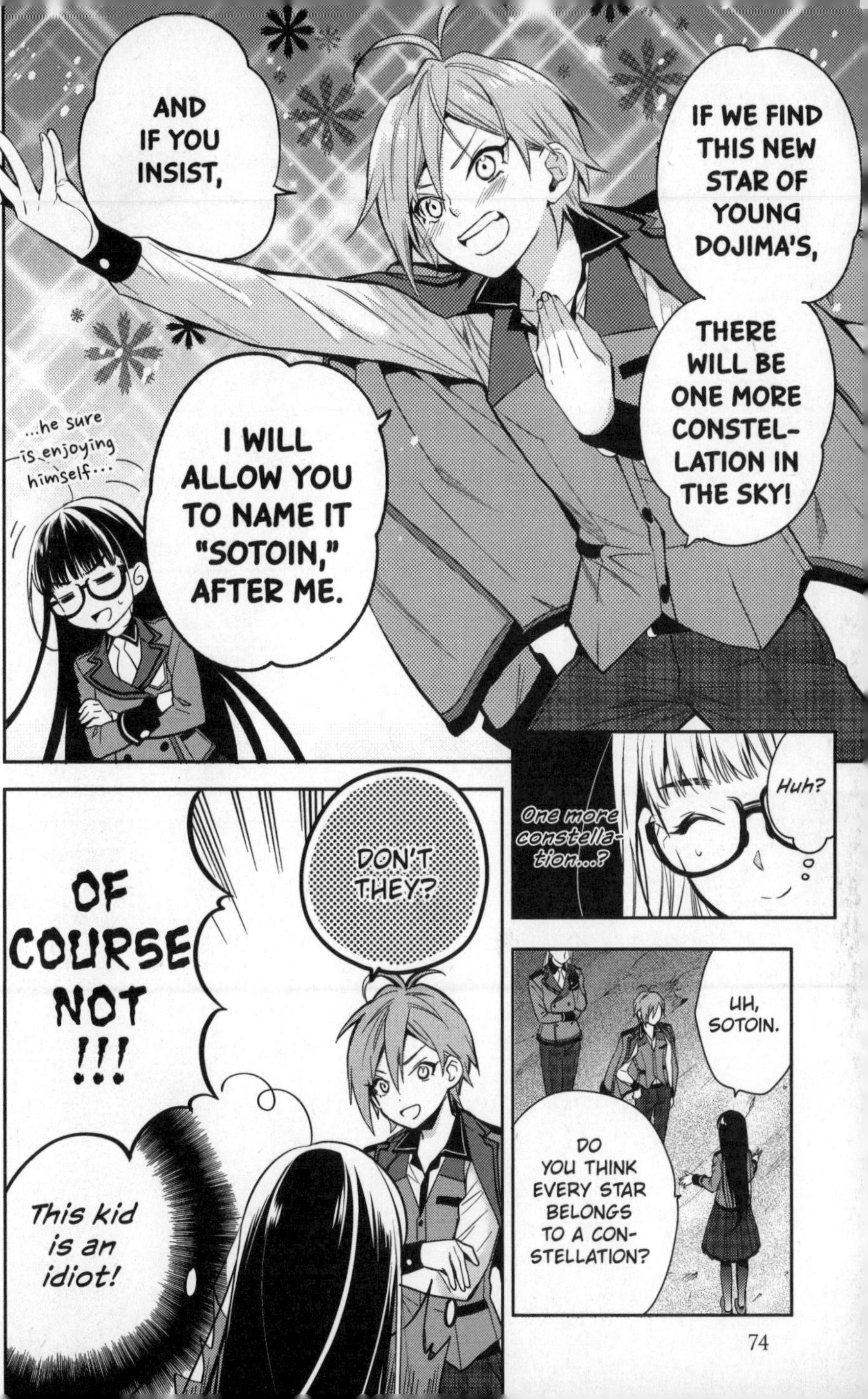
IF WE FIND THIS NEW STAR OF YOUNG DOJIMA'S,
THERE WILL BE ONE MORE CONSTEL-LATION IN THE SKY!
AND IF YOU INSIST,
I WILL ALLOW YOU TO NAME IT "SOTOIN," AFTER ME.
...he sure is enjoying himself...
Huh?
One more constellation...?
UH, SOTOIN.
DO YOU THINK EVERY STAR BELONGS TO A CON-STELLATION?
DON'T THEY?
OF COURSE NOT !!!
This kid is an idiot!

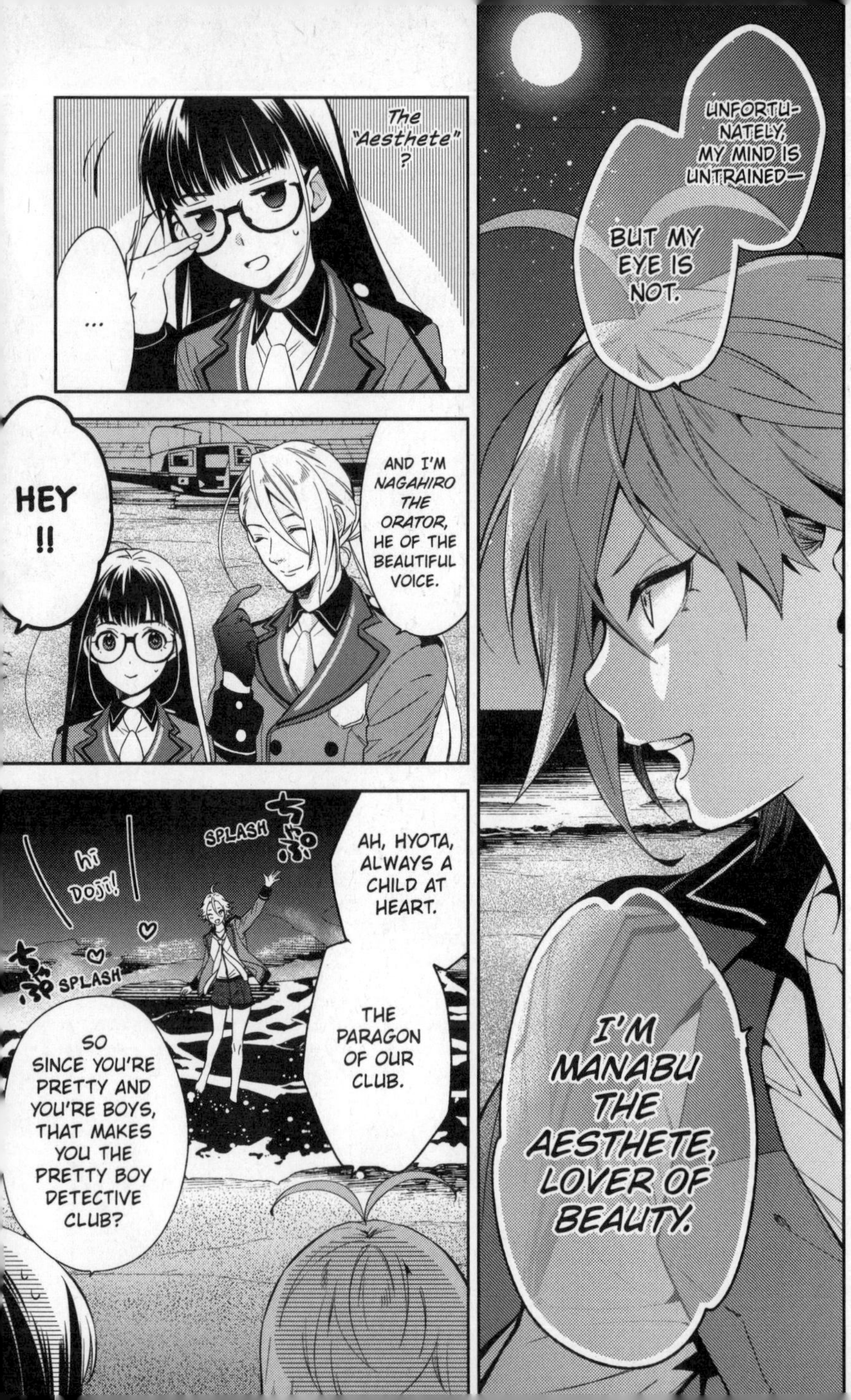
UNFORTU-NATELY, MY MIND IS UNTRAINED—
BUT MY EYE IS NOT.
I'M MANABU THE AESTHETE, LOVER OF BEAUTY.
The "Aesthete"?
...
AND I'M NAGAHIRO THE ORATOR, HE OF THE BEAUTIFUL VOICE.
HEY !!
SPLASH
hi Doji!
SPLASH
AH, HYOTA, ALWAYS A CHILD AT HEART.
THE PARAGON OF OUR CLUB.
SO SINCE YOU'RE PRETTY AND YOU'RE BOYS, THAT MAKES YOU THE PRETTY BOY DETECTIVE CLUB?

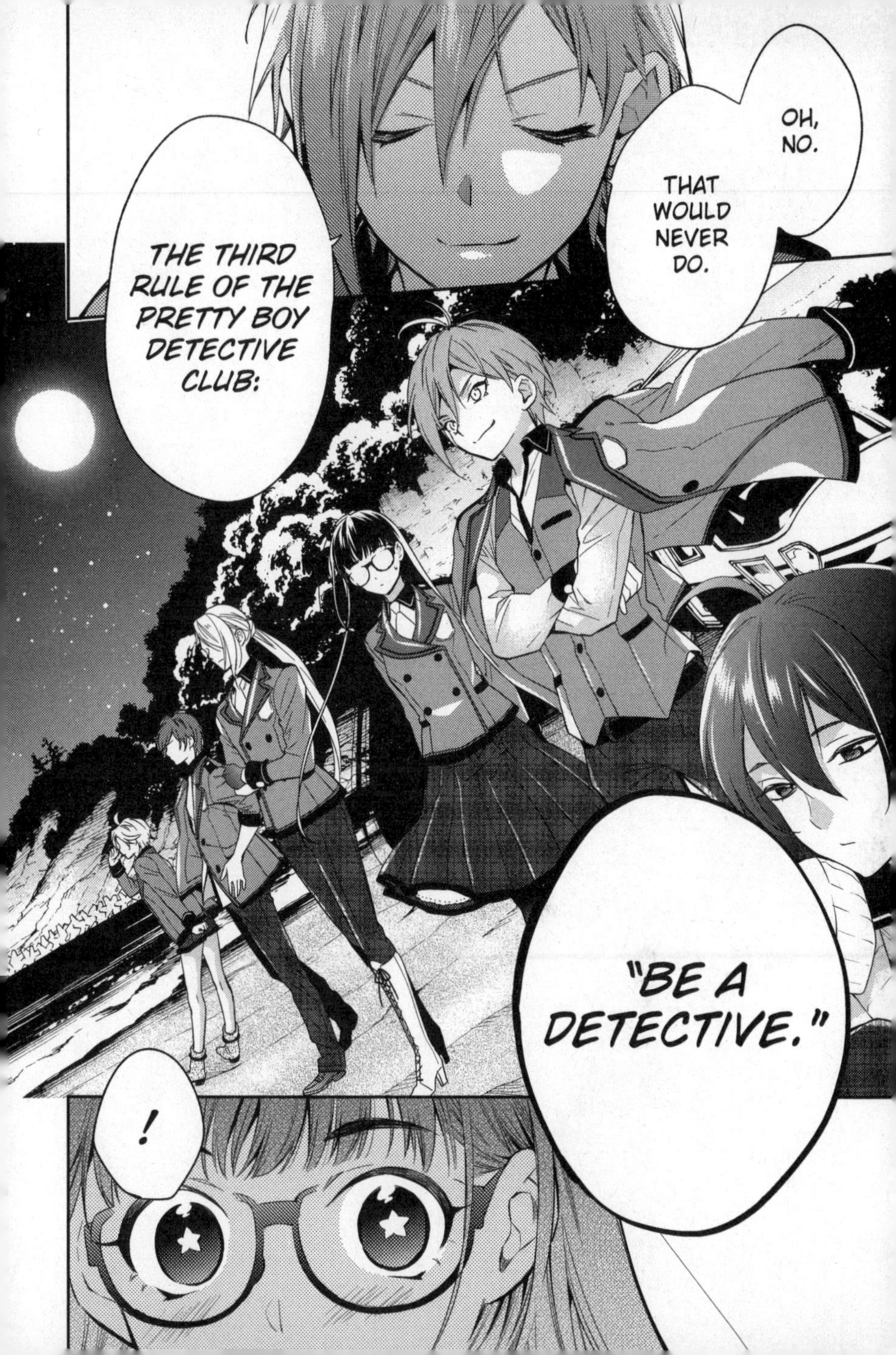
OH, NO.
THAT WOULD NEVER DO.
THE THIRD RULE OF THE PRETTY BOY DETECTIVE CLUB:
"BE A DETECTIVE."
!

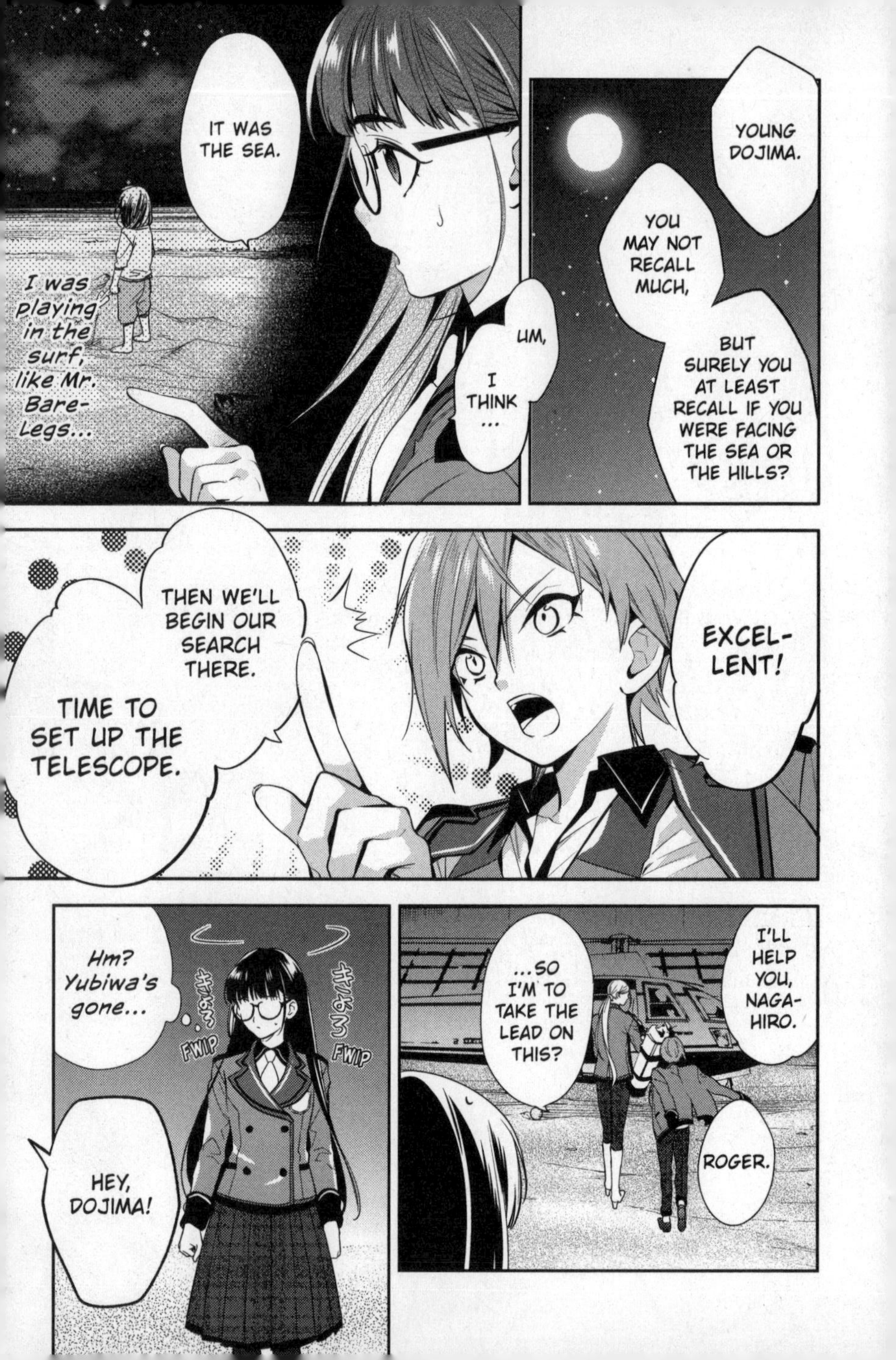
YOUNG DOJIMA.
YOU MAY NOT RECALL MUCH,
BUT SURELY YOU AT LEAST RECALL IF YOU WERE FACING THE SEA OR THE HILLS?
UM,
I THINK...
IT WAS THE SEA.
I was playing in the surf, like Mr. Bare-Legs...
EXCEL-LENT!
THEN WE'LL BEGIN OUR SEARCH THERE.
TIME TO SET UP THE TELESCOPE.
I'LL HELP YOU, NAGA-HIRO.
...SO I'M TO TAKE THE LEAD ON THIS?
ROGER.
Hm? Yubiwa's gone...
きょろ FWIP
きょろ FWIP
HEY, DOJIMA!

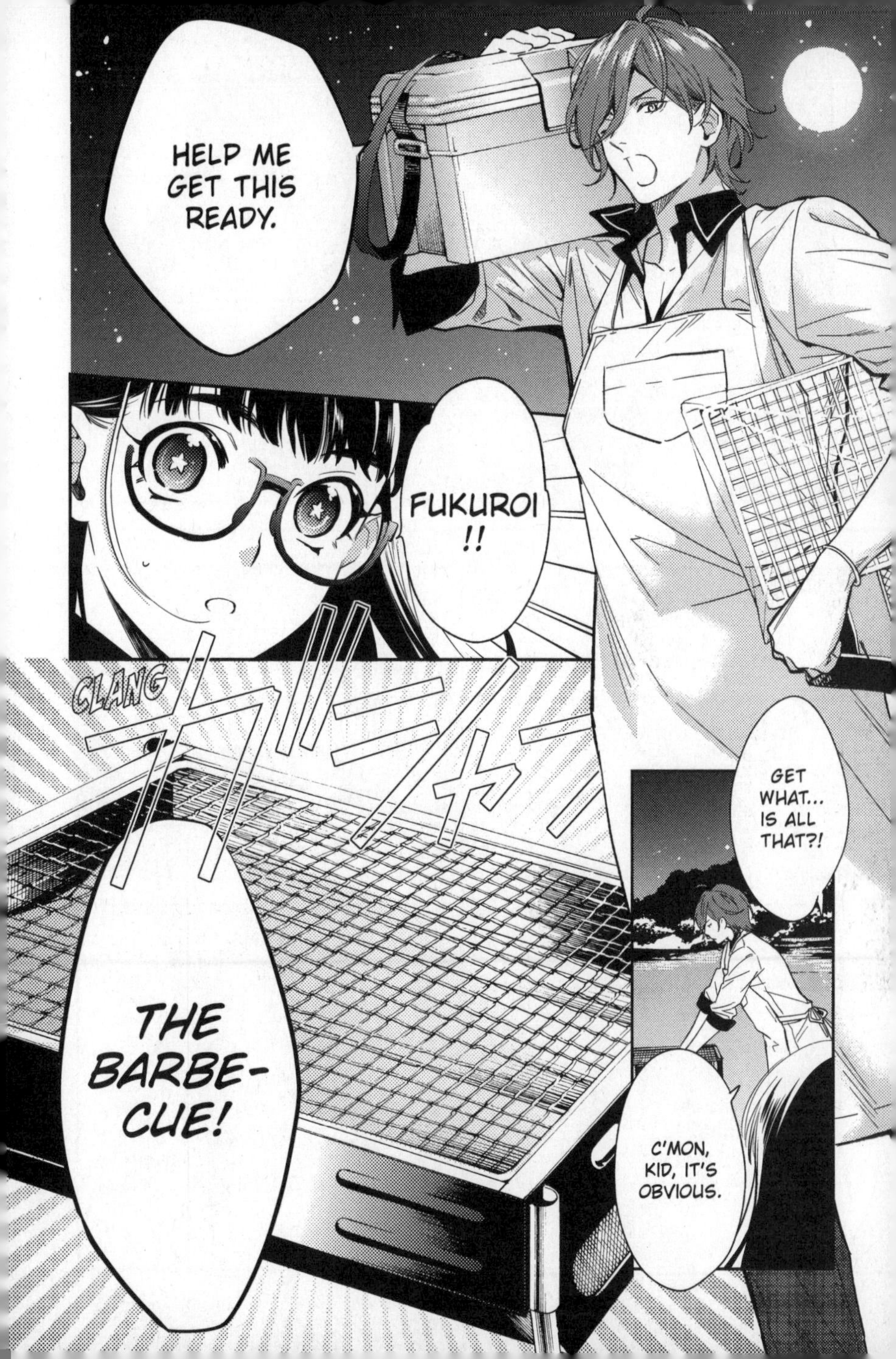
HELP ME GET THIS READY.
FUKUROI !!
GET WHAT... IS ALL THAT?!
C'MON, KID, IT'S OBVIOUS.
CLANG
THE BARBE-CUE!

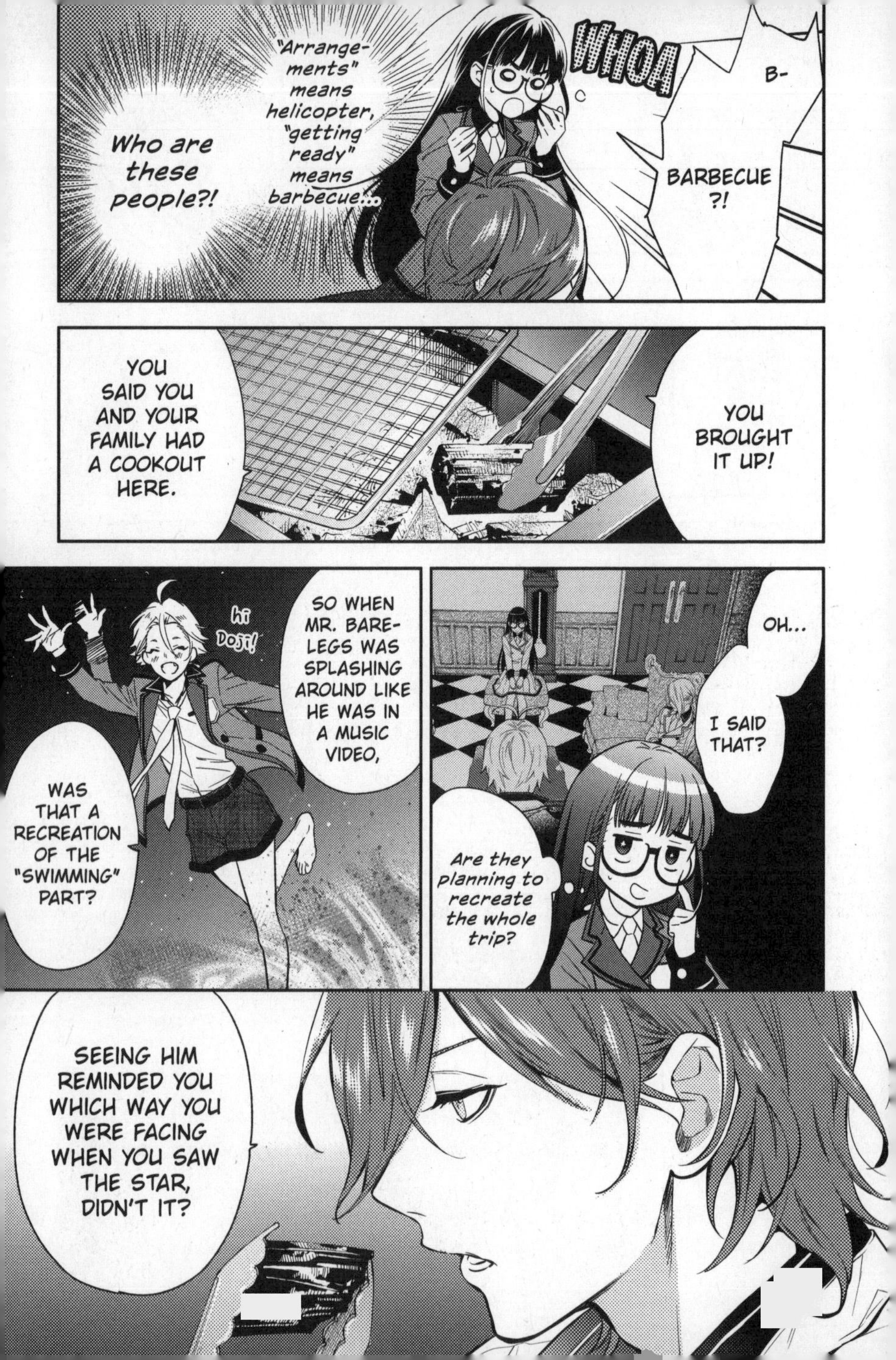
WHOA
B-
BARBECUE ?!
"Arrangements" means helicopter, "getting ready" means barbecue...
Who are these people?!
YOU BROUGHT IT UP!
YOU SAID YOU AND YOUR FAMILY HAD A COOKOUT HERE.
OH...
I SAID THAT?
Are they planning to recreate the whole trip?
SO WHEN MR. BARE-LEGS WAS SPLASHING AROUND LIKE HE WAS IN A MUSIC VIDEO,
WAS THAT A RECREATION OF THE "SWIMMING" PART?
SEEING HIM REMINDED YOU WHICH WAY YOU WERE FACING WHEN YOU SAW THE STAR, DIDN'T IT?

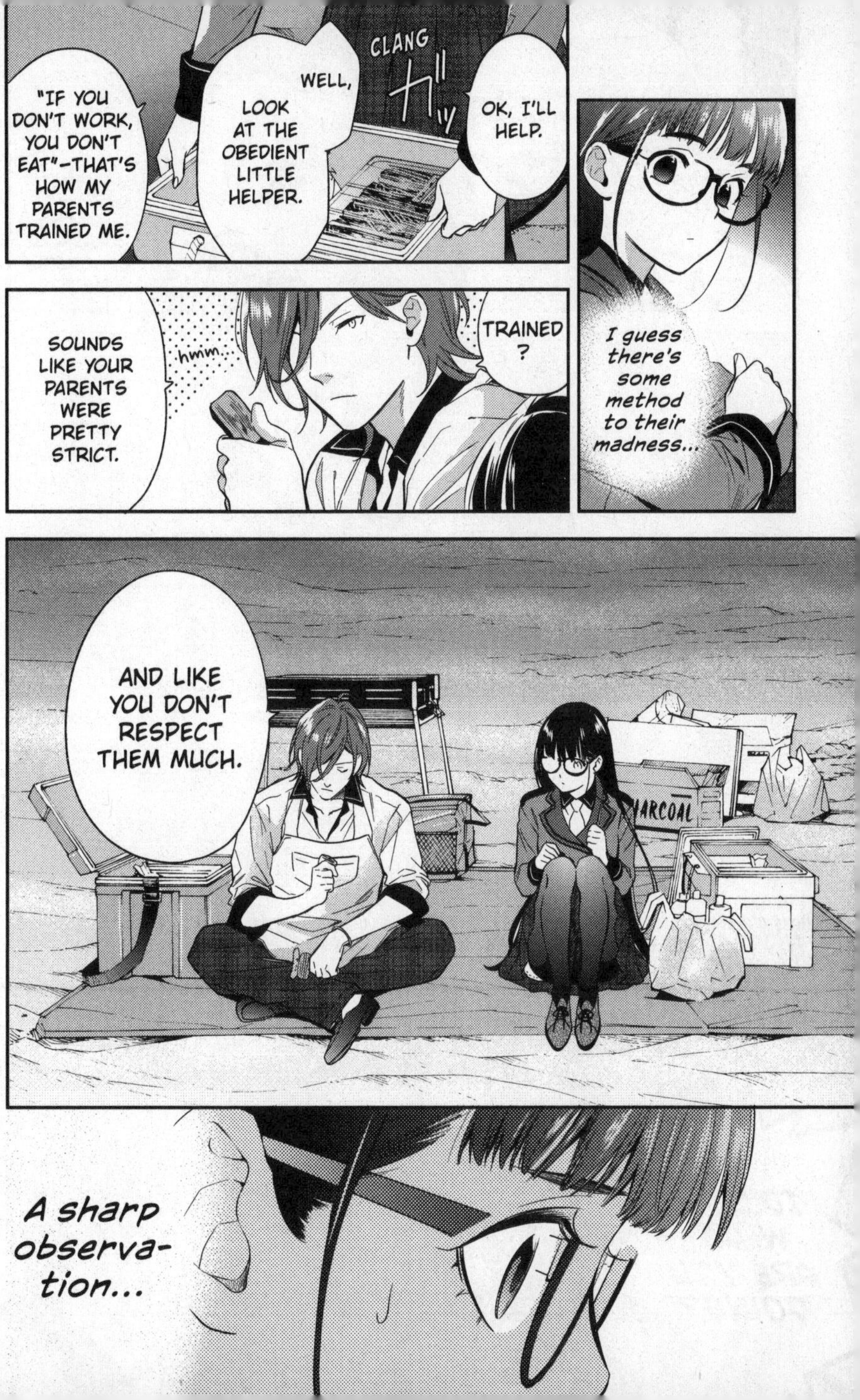
I guess there's some method to their madness...
CLANG
OK, I'LL HELP.
WELL, LOOK AT THE OBEDIENT LITTLE HELPER.
"IF YOU DON'T WORK, YOU DON'T EAT"—THAT'S HOW MY PARENTS TRAINED ME.
TRAINED?
hmm...
SOUNDS LIKE YOUR PARENTS WERE PRETTY STRICT.
AND LIKE YOU DON'T RESPECT THEM MUCH.
CHARCOAL
A sharp observa-tion...

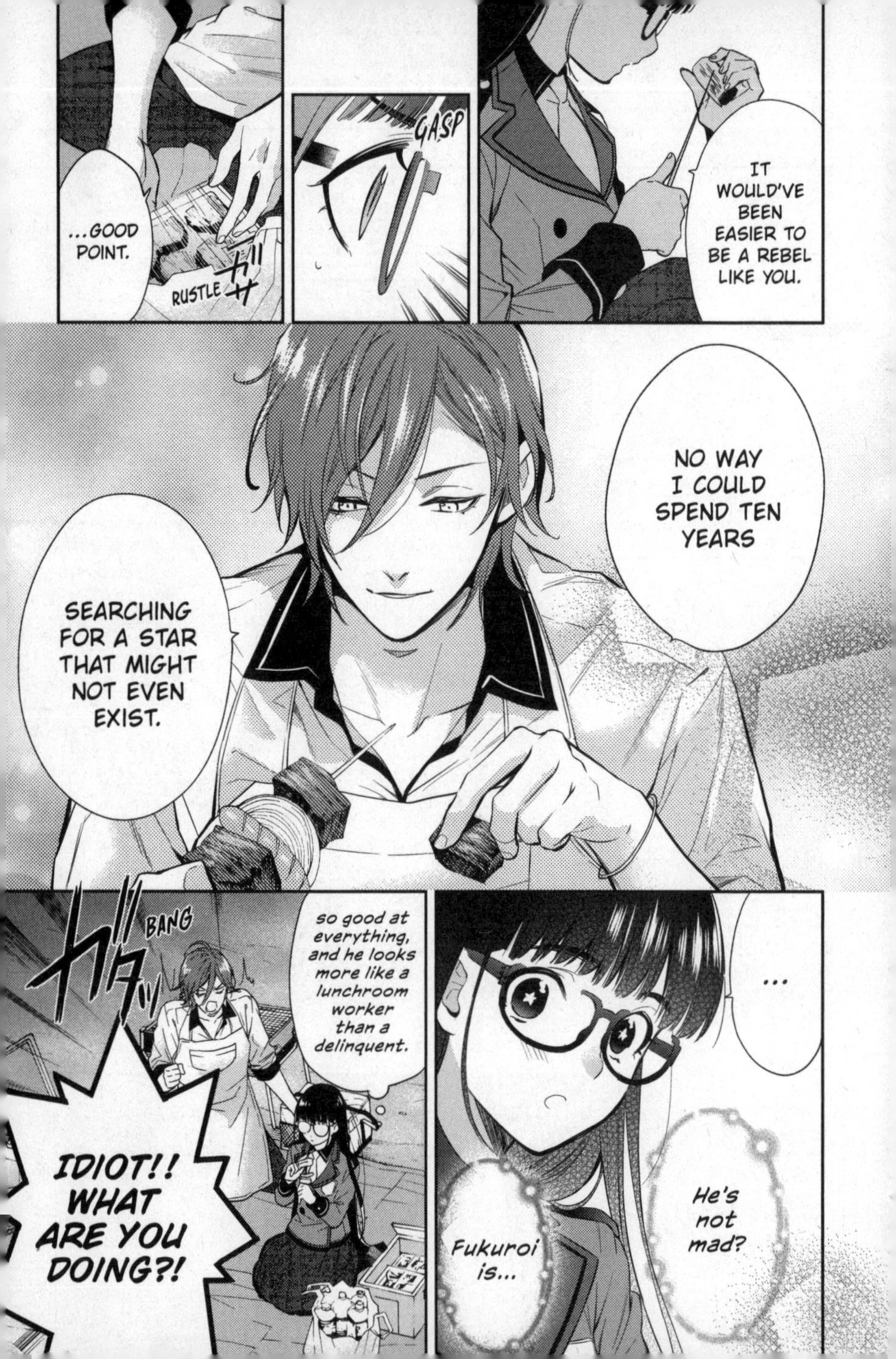

IT WOULD'VE BEEN EASIER TO BE A REBEL LIKE YOU.
GASP
...GOOD POINT.
RUSTLE
NO WAY I COULD SPEND TEN YEARS
SEARCHING FOR A STAR THAT MIGHT NOT EVEN EXIST.
...
He's not mad?
Fukuroi is...
so good at everything, and he looks more like a lunchroom worker than a delinquent.
BANG
IDIOT!! WHAT ARE YOU DOING?!

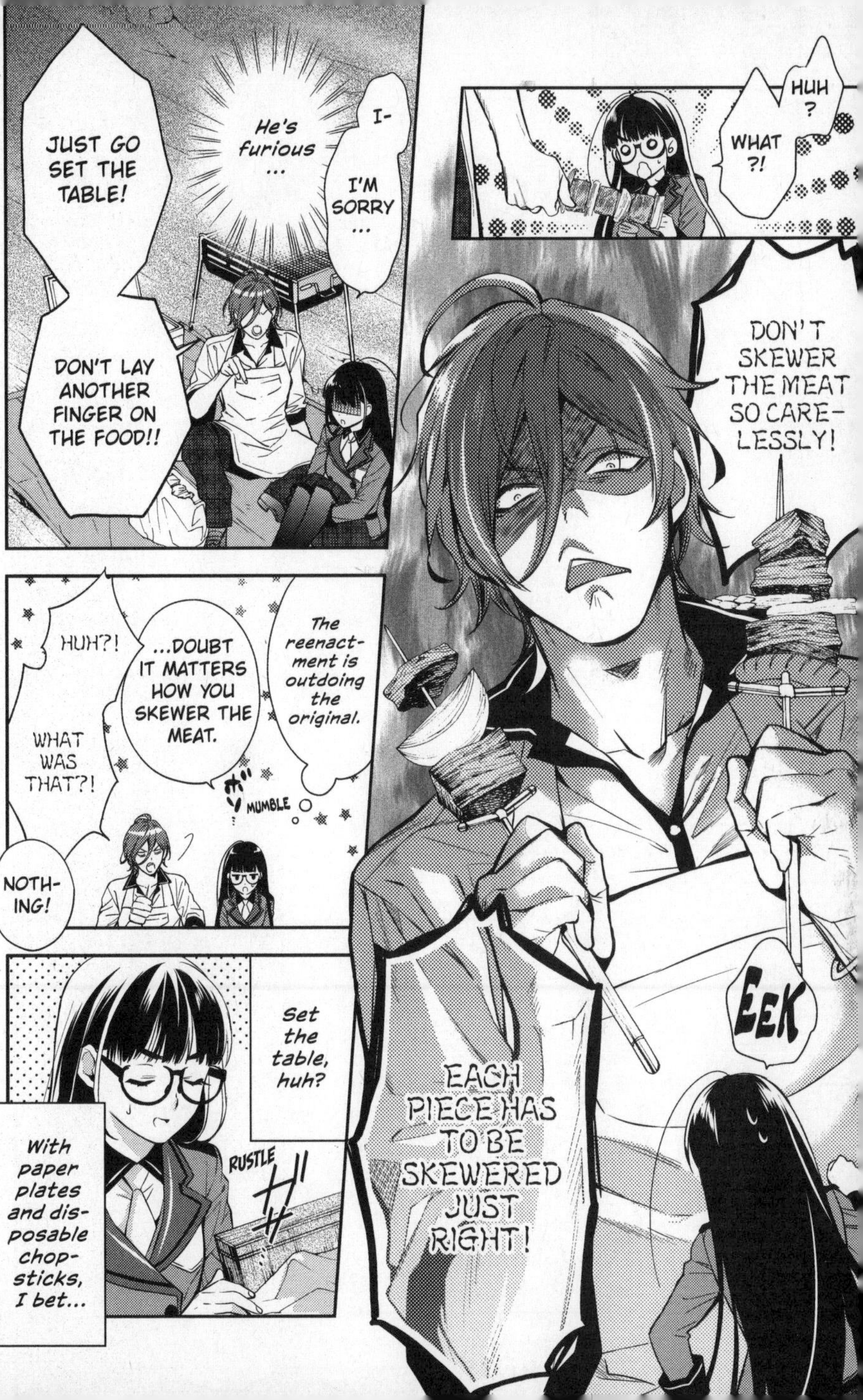
HUH?
WHAT?!
DON'T SKEWER THE MEAT SO CARE-LESSLY!
EACH PIECE HAS TO BE SKEWERED JUST RIGHT!
EEK
I-
I'M SORRY...
He's furious...
JUST GO SET THE TABLE!
DON'T LAY ANOTHER FINGER ON THE FOOD!!
The reenact-ment is outdoing the original.
...DOUBT IT MATTERS HOW YOU SKEWER THE MEAT.
MUMBLE
HUH?!
WHAT WAS THAT?!
NOTH-ING!
Set the table, huh?
RUSTLE
With paper plates and dis-posable chop-sticks, I bet...

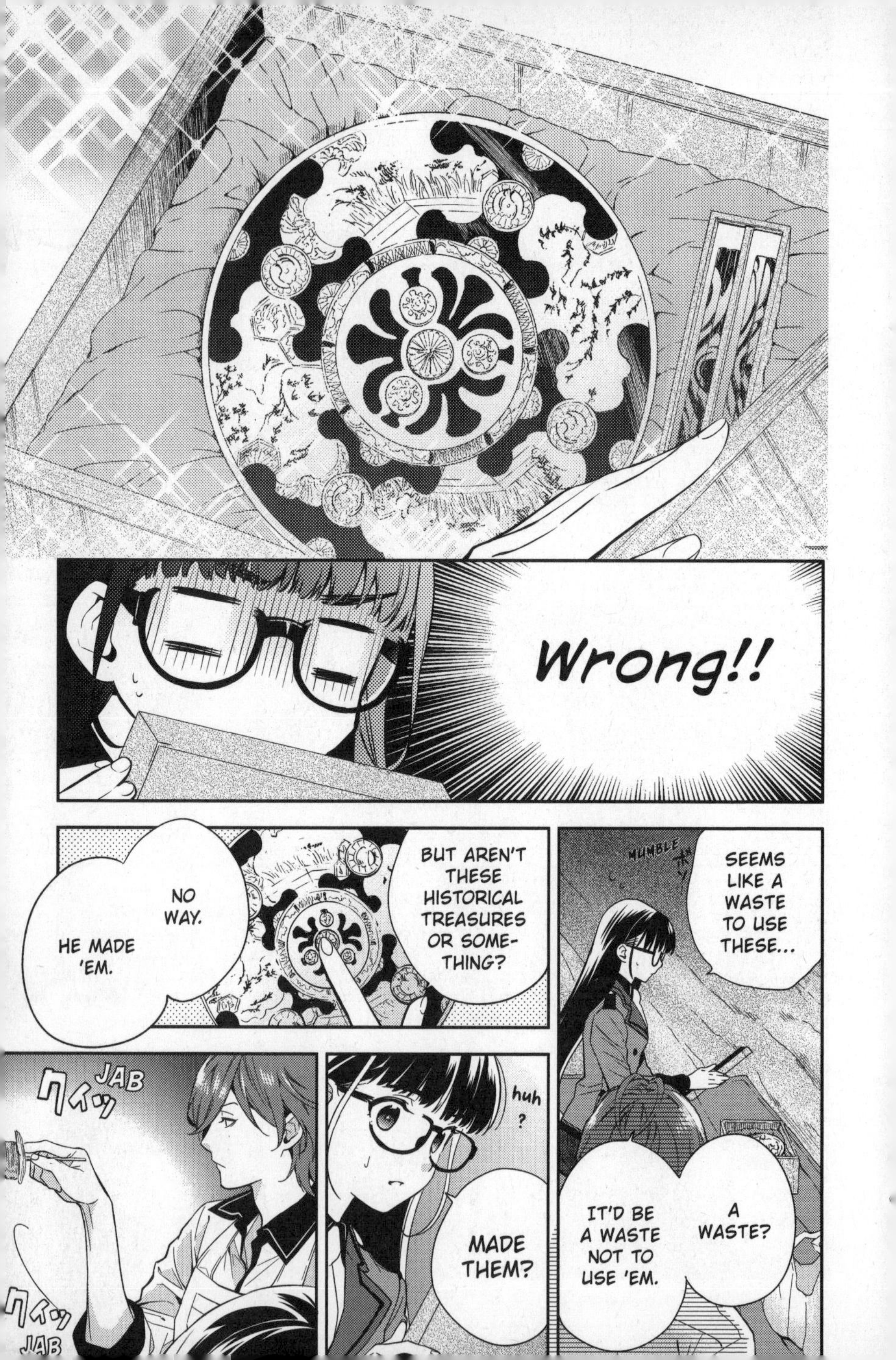

Wrong!!
MUMBLE
SEEMS LIKE A WASTE TO USE THESE...
A WASTE?
IT'D BE A WASTE NOT TO USE 'EM.
BUT AREN'T THESE HISTORICAL TREASURES OR SOME-THING?
NO WAY.
HE MADE 'EM.
huh?
MADE THEM?
クイッ JAB
クイッ JAB

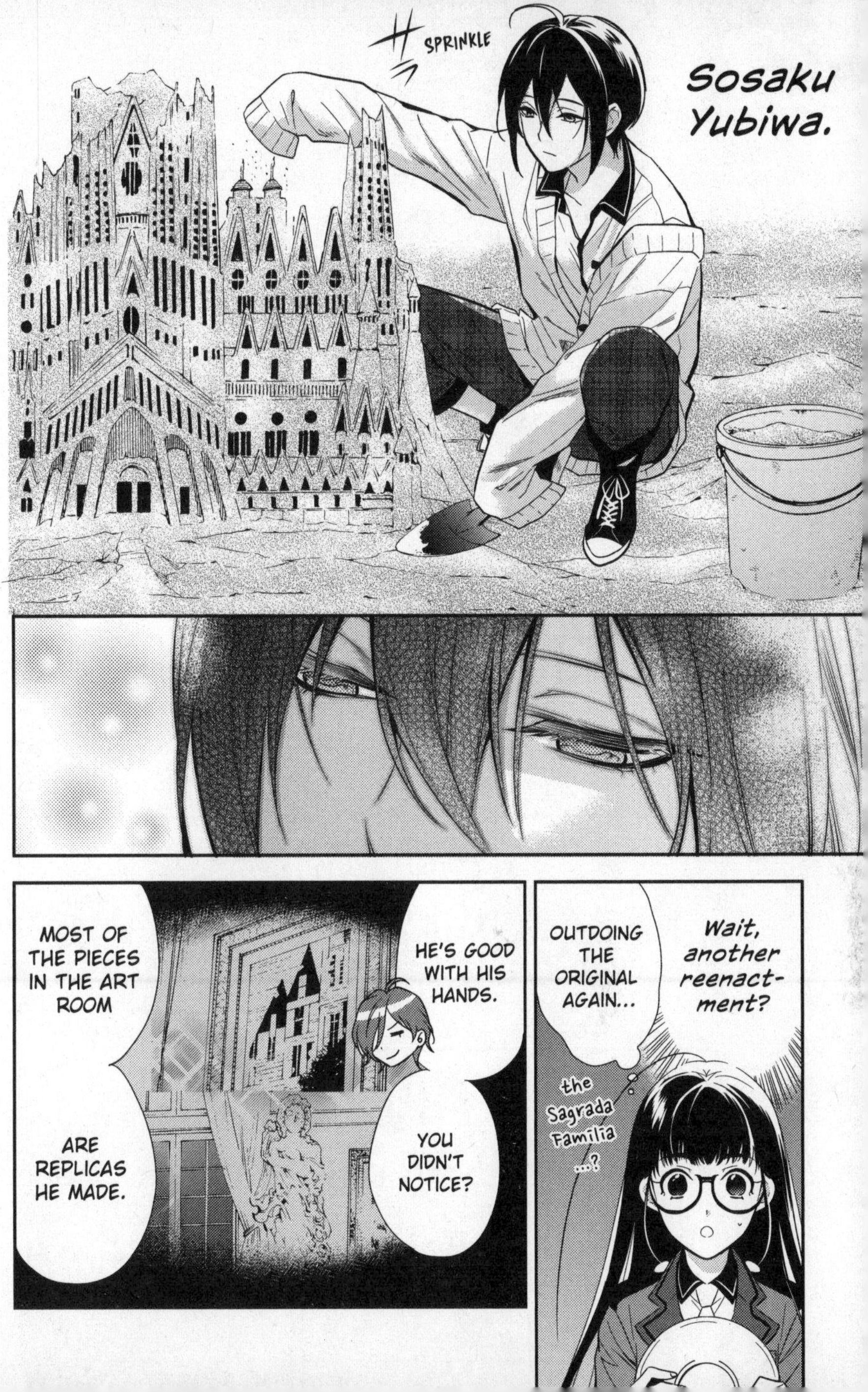
SPRINKLE
Sosaku Yubiwa.
Wait, another reenactment?
OUTDOING THE ORIGINAL AGAIN...
the Sagrada Familia ...?
HE'S GOOD WITH HIS HANDS.
YOU DIDN'T NOTICE?
MOST OF THE PIECES IN THE ART ROOM
ARE REPLICAS HE MADE.

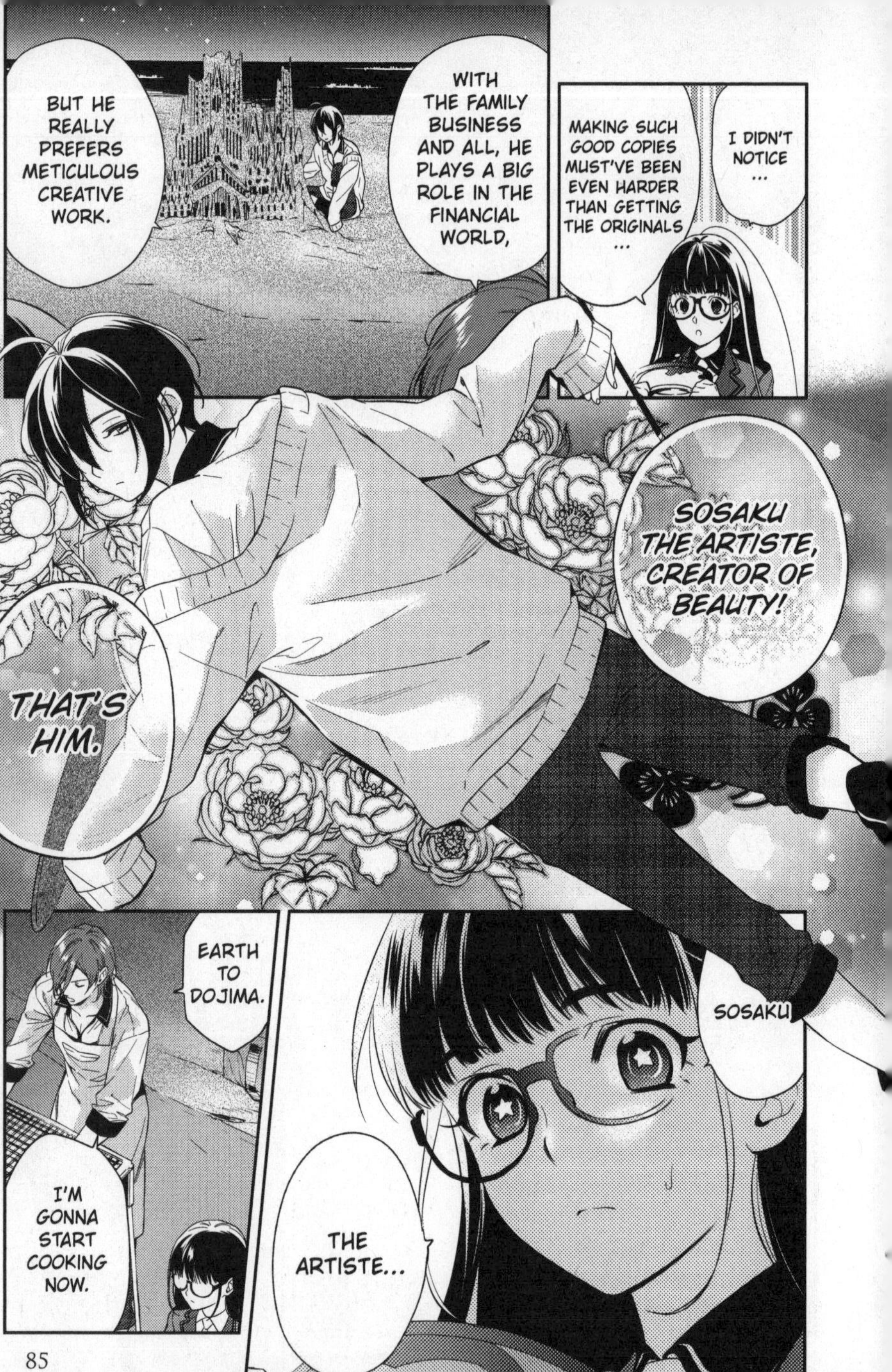
I DIDN'T NOTICE ...
MAKING SUCH GOOD COPIES MUST'VE BEEN EVEN HARDER THAN GETTING THE ORIGINALS ...
WITH THE FAMILY BUSINESS AND ALL, HE PLAYS A BIG ROLE IN THE FINANCIAL WORLD,
BUT HE REALLY PREFERS METICULOUS CREATIVE WORK.
SOSAKU THE ARTISTE, CREATOR OF BEAUTY!
THAT'S HIM.
SOSAKU
THE ARTISTE...
EARTH TO DOJIMA.
I'M GONNA START COOKING NOW.

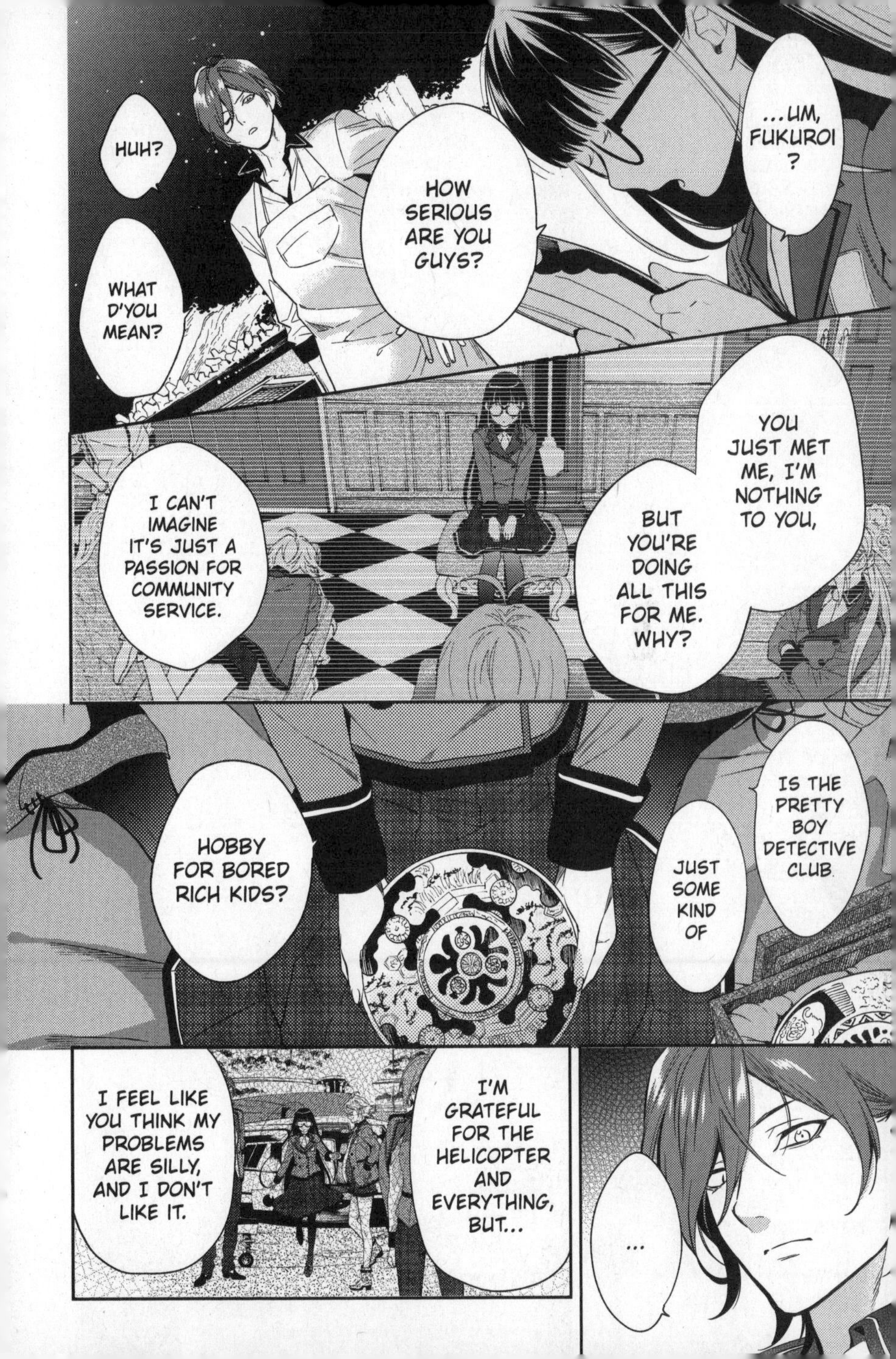
...UM, FUKUROI?
HOW SERIOUS ARE YOU GUYS?
HUH?
WHAT D'YOU MEAN?
YOU JUST MET ME, I'M NOTHING TO YOU,
BUT YOU'RE DOING ALL THIS FOR ME. WHY?
I CAN'T IMAGINE IT'S JUST A PASSION FOR COMMUNITY SERVICE.
IS THE PRETTY BOY DETECTIVE CLUB
JUST SOME KIND OF
HOBBY FOR BORED RICH KIDS?
...
I'M GRATEFUL FOR THE HELICOPTER AND EVERYTHING, BUT...
I FEEL LIKE YOU THINK MY PROBLEMS ARE SILLY, AND I DON'T LIKE IT.

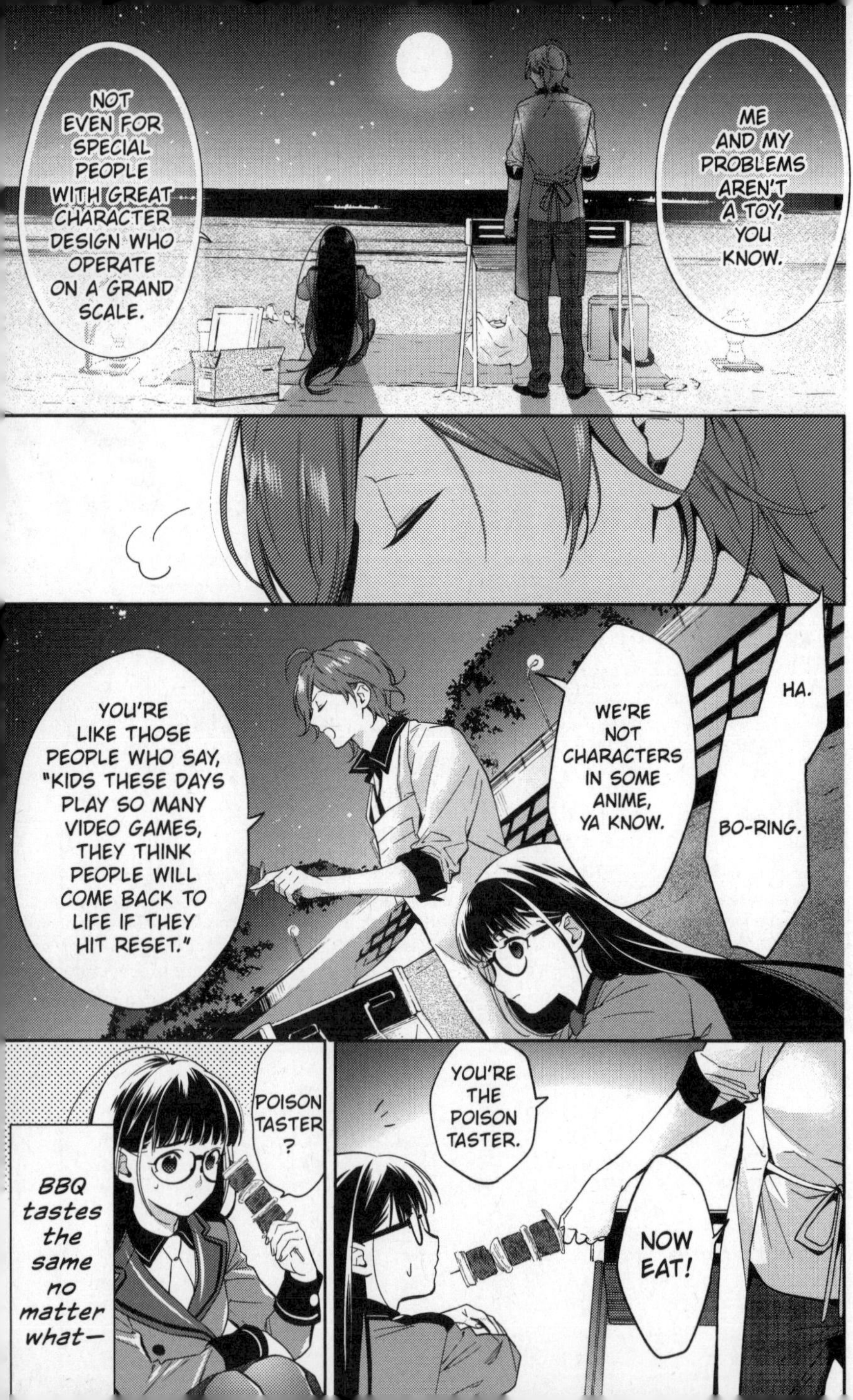
ME AND MY PROBLEMS AREN'T A TOY, YOU KNOW.
NOT EVEN FOR SPECIAL PEOPLE WITH GREAT CHARACTER DESIGN WHO OPERATE ON A GRAND SCALE.
HA. BO-RING.
WE'RE NOT CHARACTERS IN SOME ANIME, YA KNOW.
YOU'RE LIKE THOSE PEOPLE WHO SAY, "KIDS THESE DAYS PLAY SO MANY VIDEO GAMES, THEY THINK PEOPLE WILL COME BACK TO LIFE IF THEY HIT RESET."
YOU'RE THE POISON TASTER.
NOW EAT!
POISON TASTER?
BBQ tastes the same no matter what—

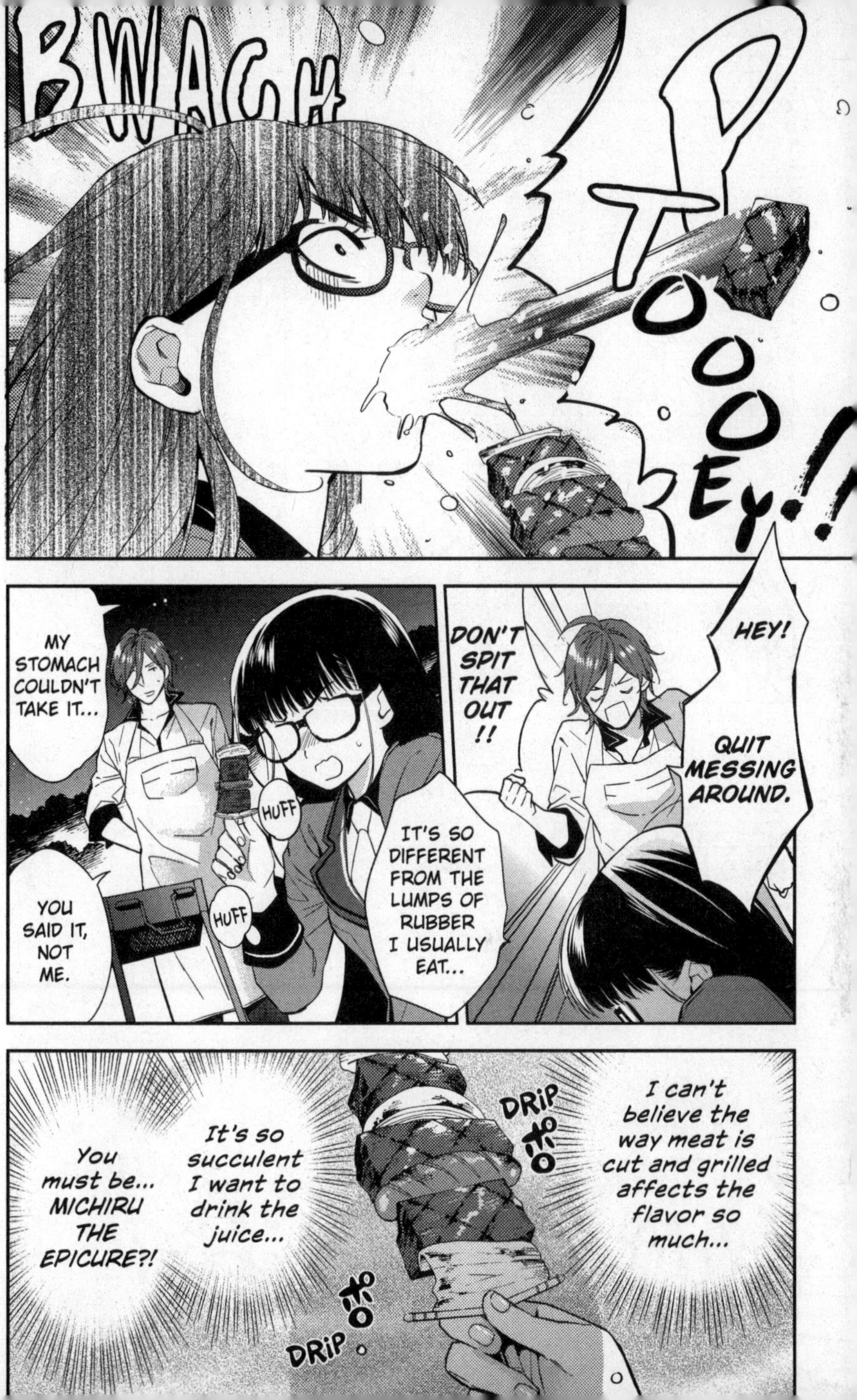
PTOOOOEY!!
BWACH
HEY!
QUIT MESSING AROUND.
DON'T SPIT THAT OUT!!
HUFF
HUFF
IT'S SO DIFFERENT FROM THE LUMPS OF RUBBER I USUALLY EAT...
MY STOMACH COULDN'T TAKE IT...
YOU SAID IT, NOT ME.
I can't believe the way meat is cut and grilled affects the flavor so much...
DRIP
It's so succulent I want to drink the juice...
You must be... MICHIRU THE EPICURE?!
DRIP

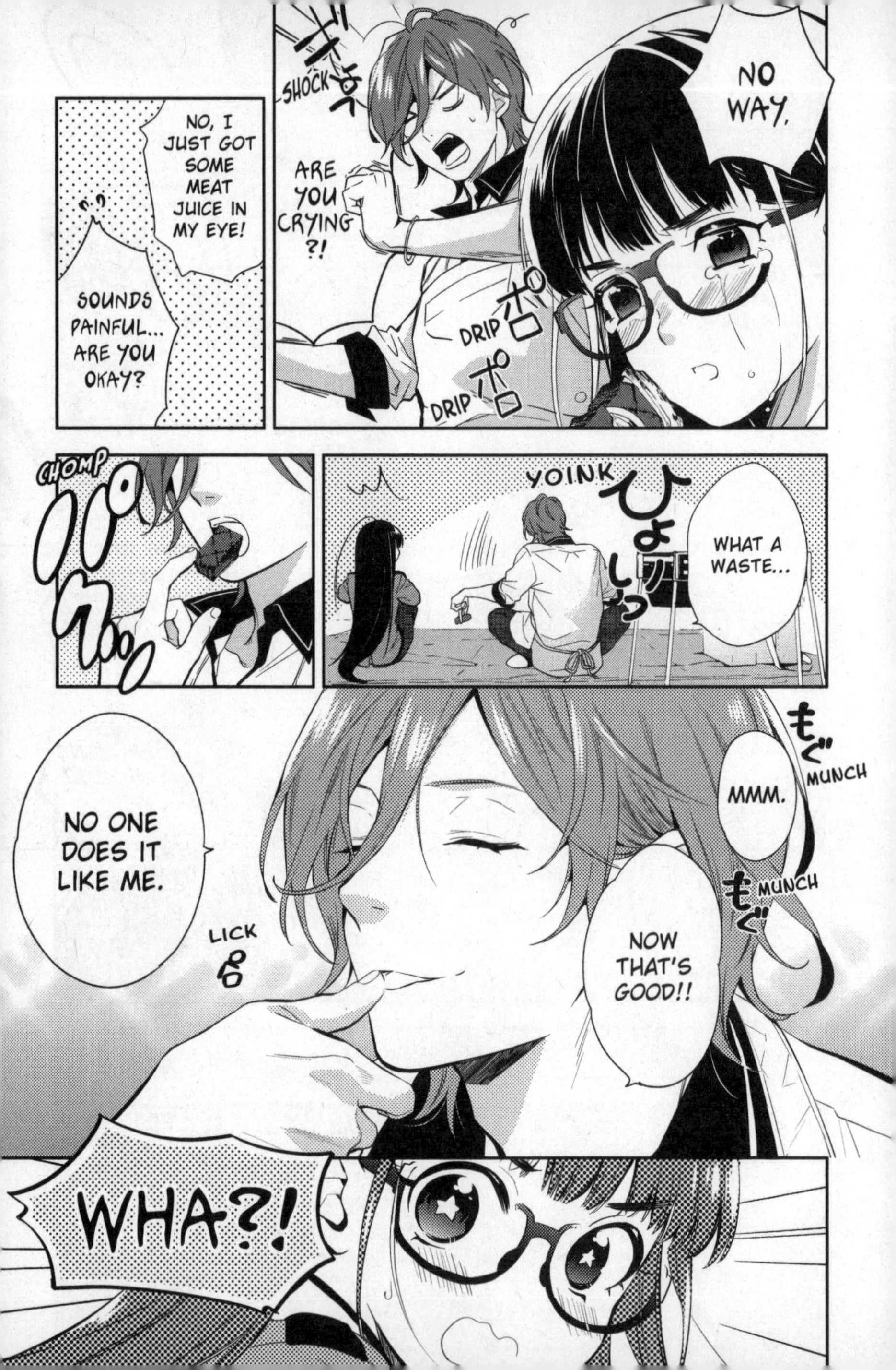
NO WAY.
SHOCK
ARE YOU CRYING?!
DRIP
DRIP
NO, I JUST GOT SOME MEAT JUICE IN MY EYE!
SOUNDS PAINFUL... ARE YOU OKAY?
YOINK
WHAT A WASTE...
CHOMP
MUNCH
MMM.
MUNCH
NOW THAT'S GOOD!!
LICK
NO ONE DOES IT LIKE ME.
WHA?!

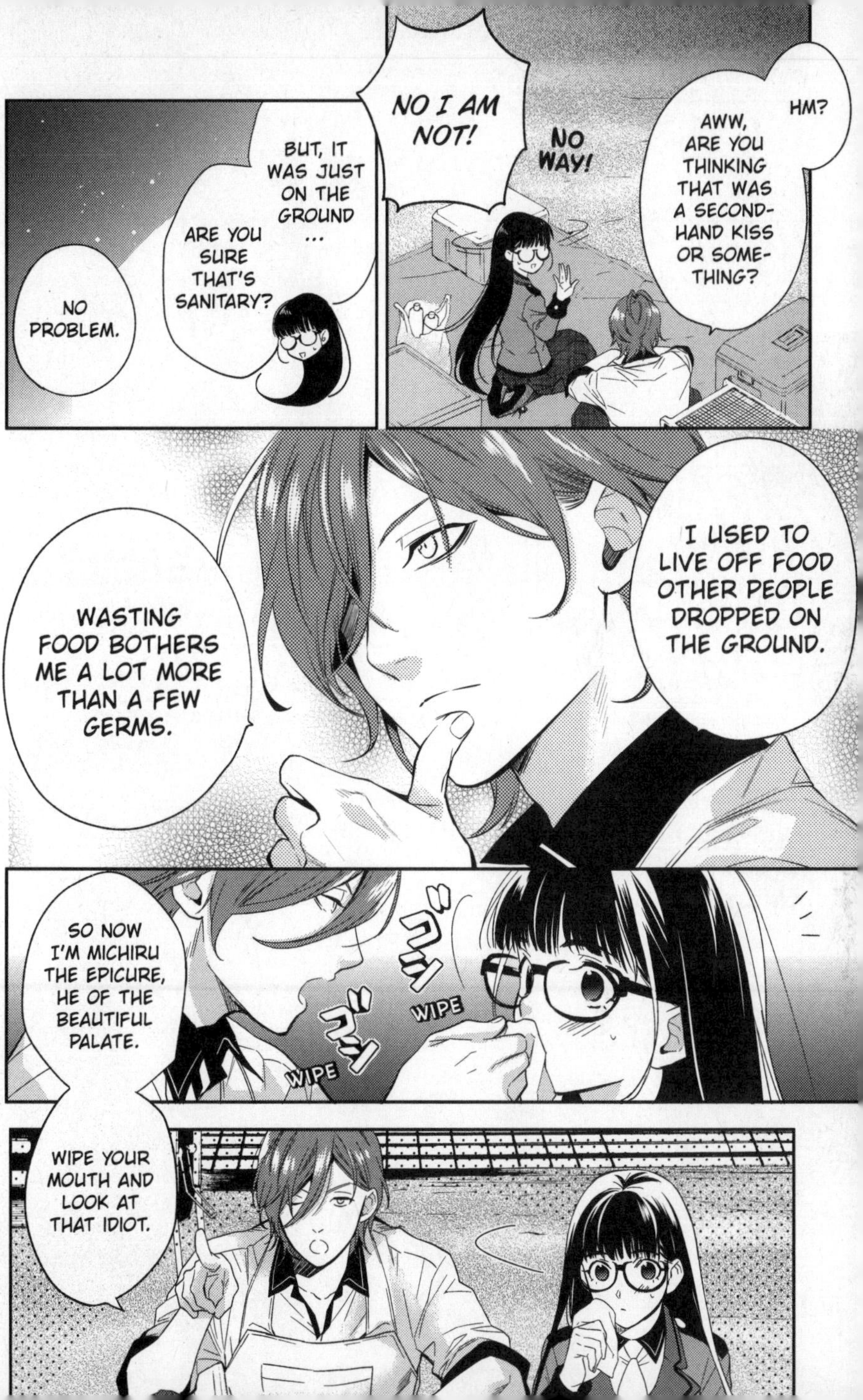
HM?
AWW, ARE YOU THINKING THAT WAS A SECOND-HAND KISS OR SOMETHING?
NO WAY!
NO I AM NOT!
BUT, IT WAS JUST ON THE GROUND ...
ARE YOU SURE THAT'S SANITARY?
NO PROBLEM.
I USED TO LIVE OFF FOOD OTHER PEOPLE DROPPED ON THE GROUND.
WASTING FOOD BOTHERS ME A LOT MORE THAN A FEW GERMS.
WIPE
WIPE
SO NOW I'M MICHIRU THE EPICURE, HE OF THE BEAUTIFUL PALATE.
WIPE YOUR MOUTH AND LOOK AT THAT IDIOT.

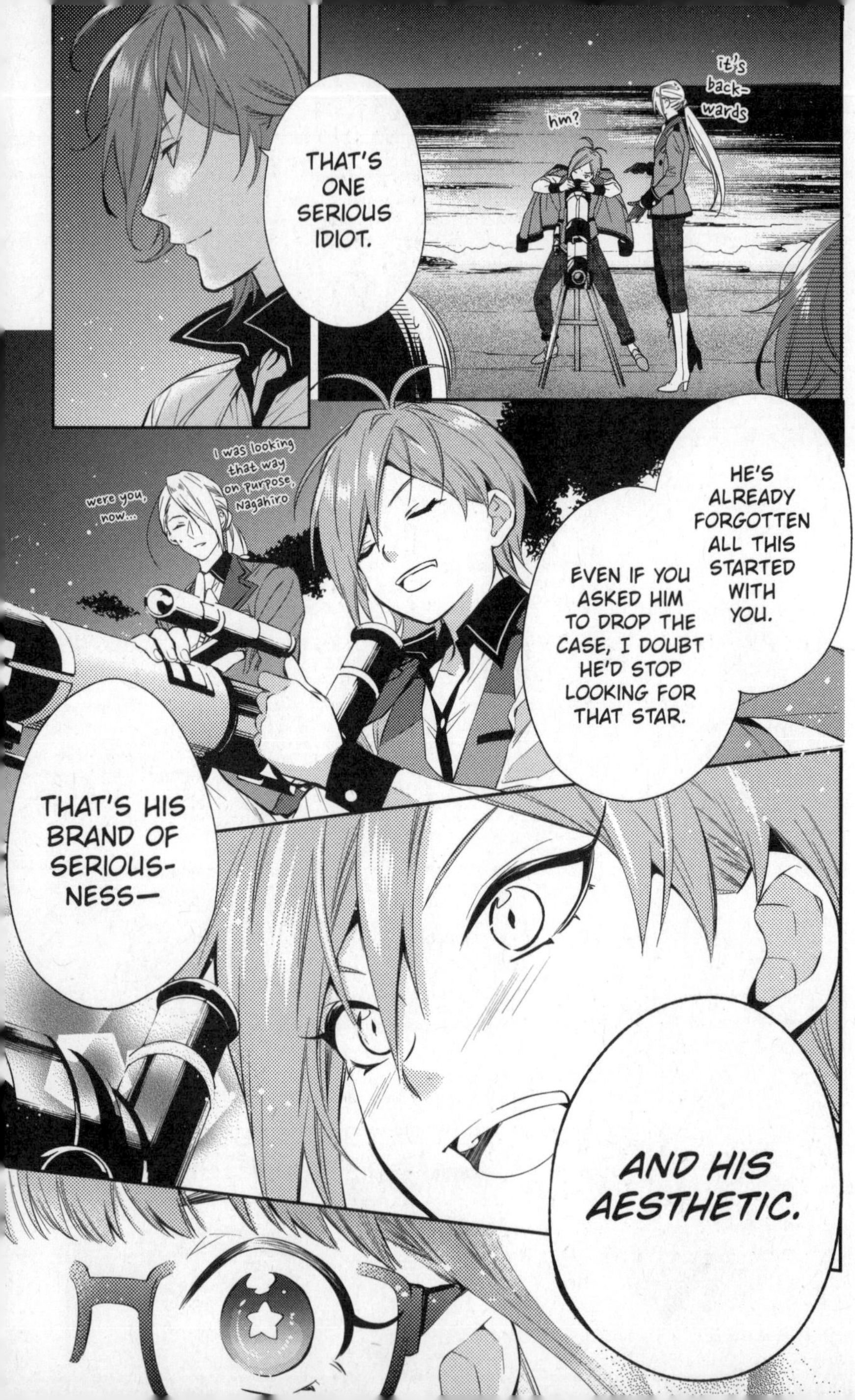

it's back-wards
hm?
THAT'S ONE SERIOUS IDIOT.
HE'S ALREADY FORGOTTEN ALL THIS STARTED WITH YOU.
EVEN IF YOU ASKED HIM TO DROP THE CASE, I DOUBT HE'D STOP LOOKING FOR THAT STAR.
I was looking that way on purpose, Nagahiro
were you, now...
THAT'S HIS BRAND OF SERIOUS-NESS—
AND HIS AESTHETIC.

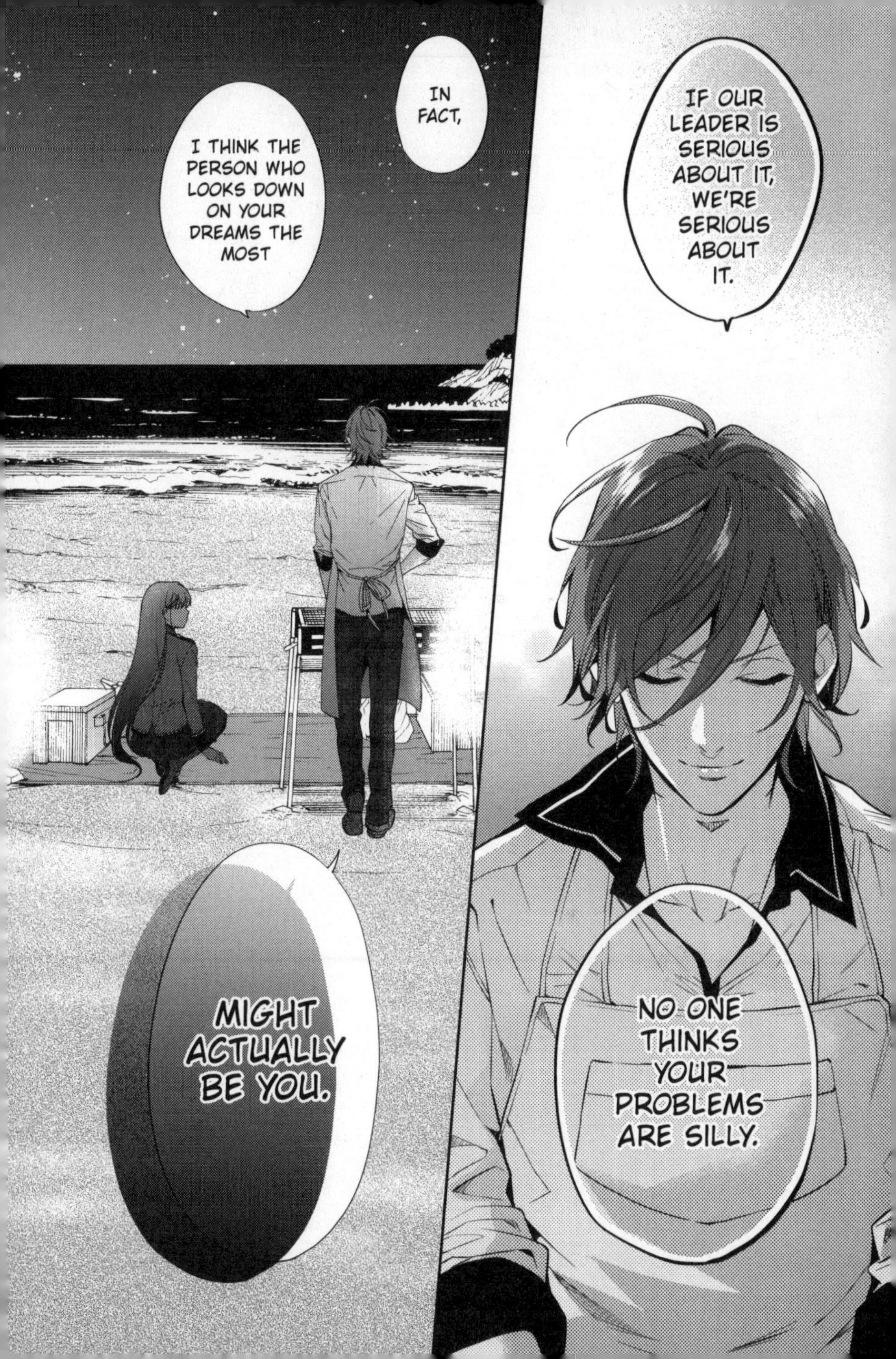
IF OUR LEADER IS SERIOUS ABOUT IT, WE'RE SERIOUS ABOUT IT.
NO ONE THINKS YOUR PROBLEMS ARE SILLY.
IN FACT,
I THINK THE PERSON WHO LOOKS DOWN ON YOUR DREAMS THE MOST
MIGHT ACTUALLY BE YOU.

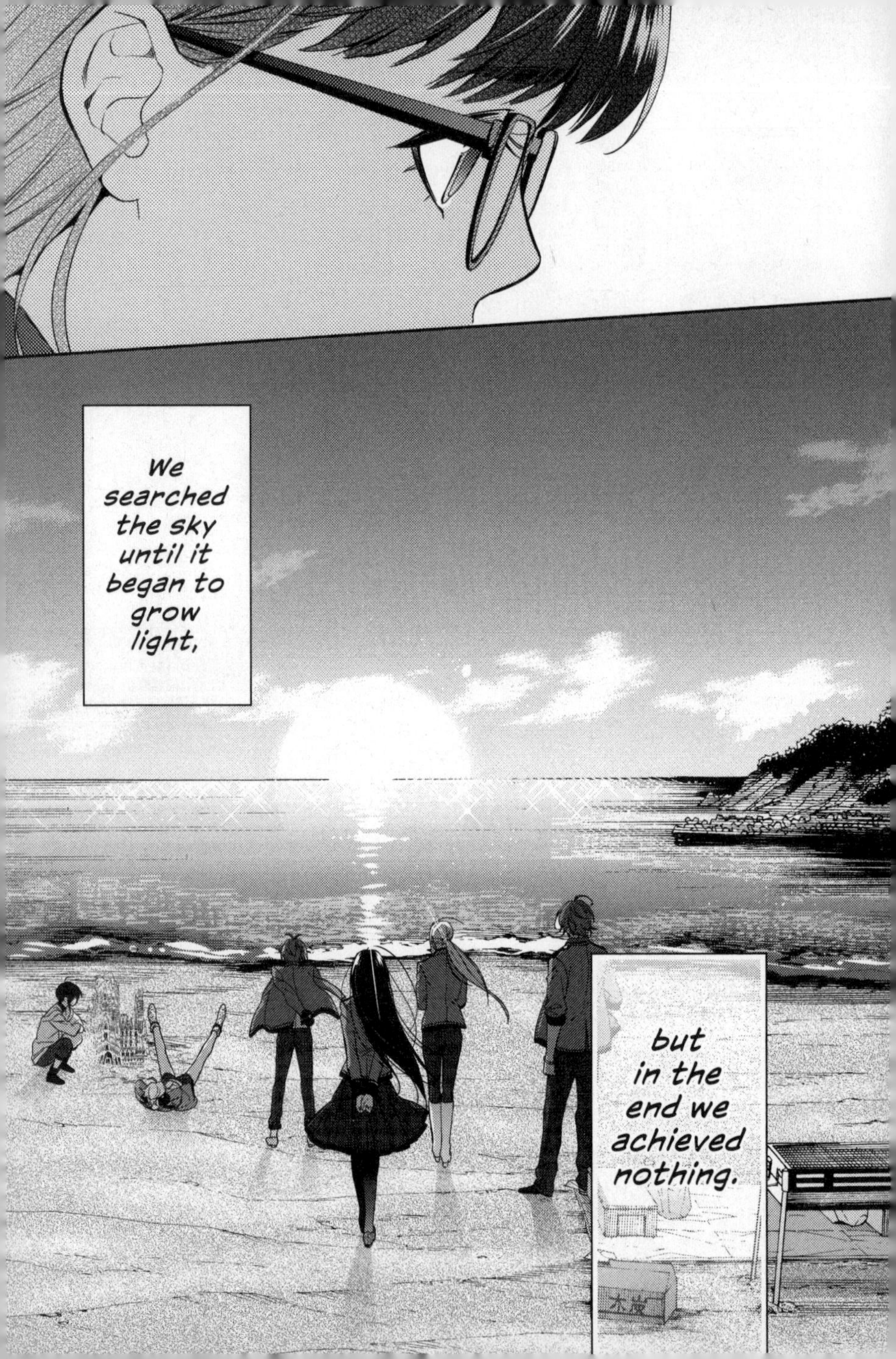
We searched the sky until it began to grow light,
but in the end we achieved nothing.

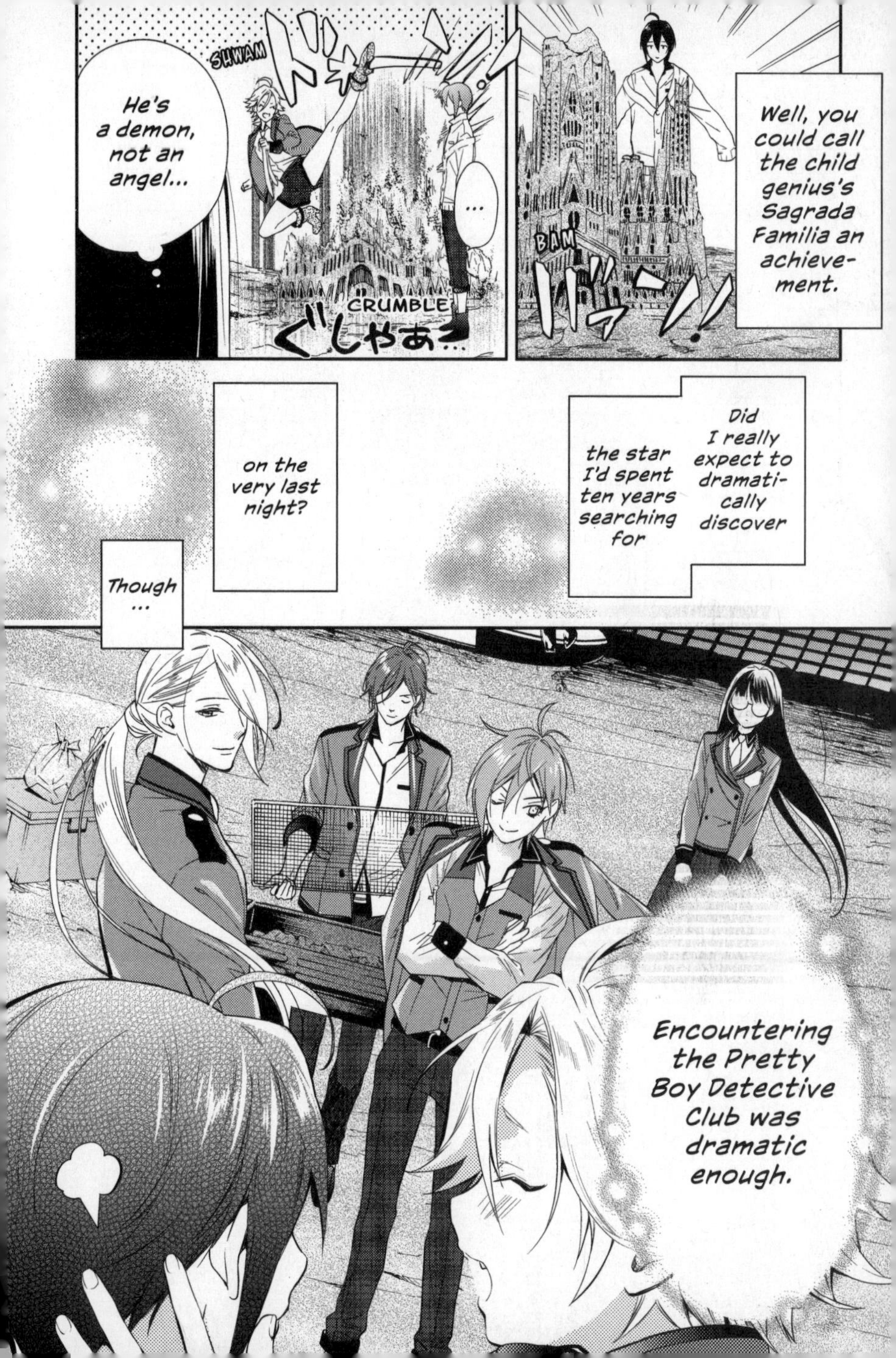

Well, you could call the child genius's Sagrada Familia an achievement.
BAM
SHWAM
He's a demon, not an angel...
...
CRUMBLE
ぐしゃあ
Did I really expect to dramatically discover the star I'd spent ten years searching for
on the very last night?
Though...
Encountering the Pretty Boy Detective Club was dramatic enough.

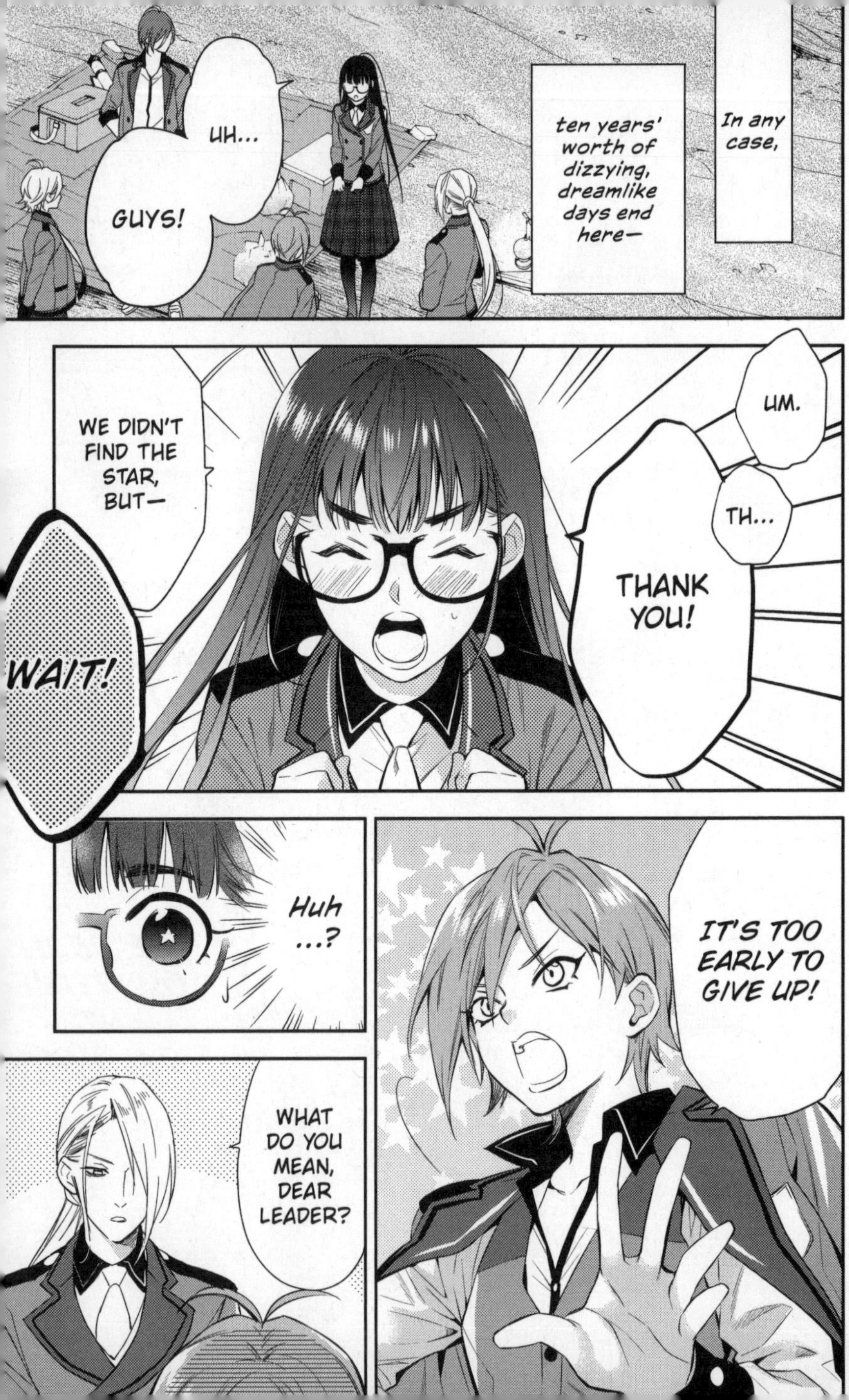
In any case,
ten years' worth of dizzying, dreamlike days end here—
UH...
GUYS!
UM.
TH...
THANK YOU!
WE DIDN'T FIND THE STAR, BUT—
WAIT!
IT'S TOO EARLY TO GIVE UP!
Huh ...?
WHAT DO YOU MEAN, DEAR LEADER?

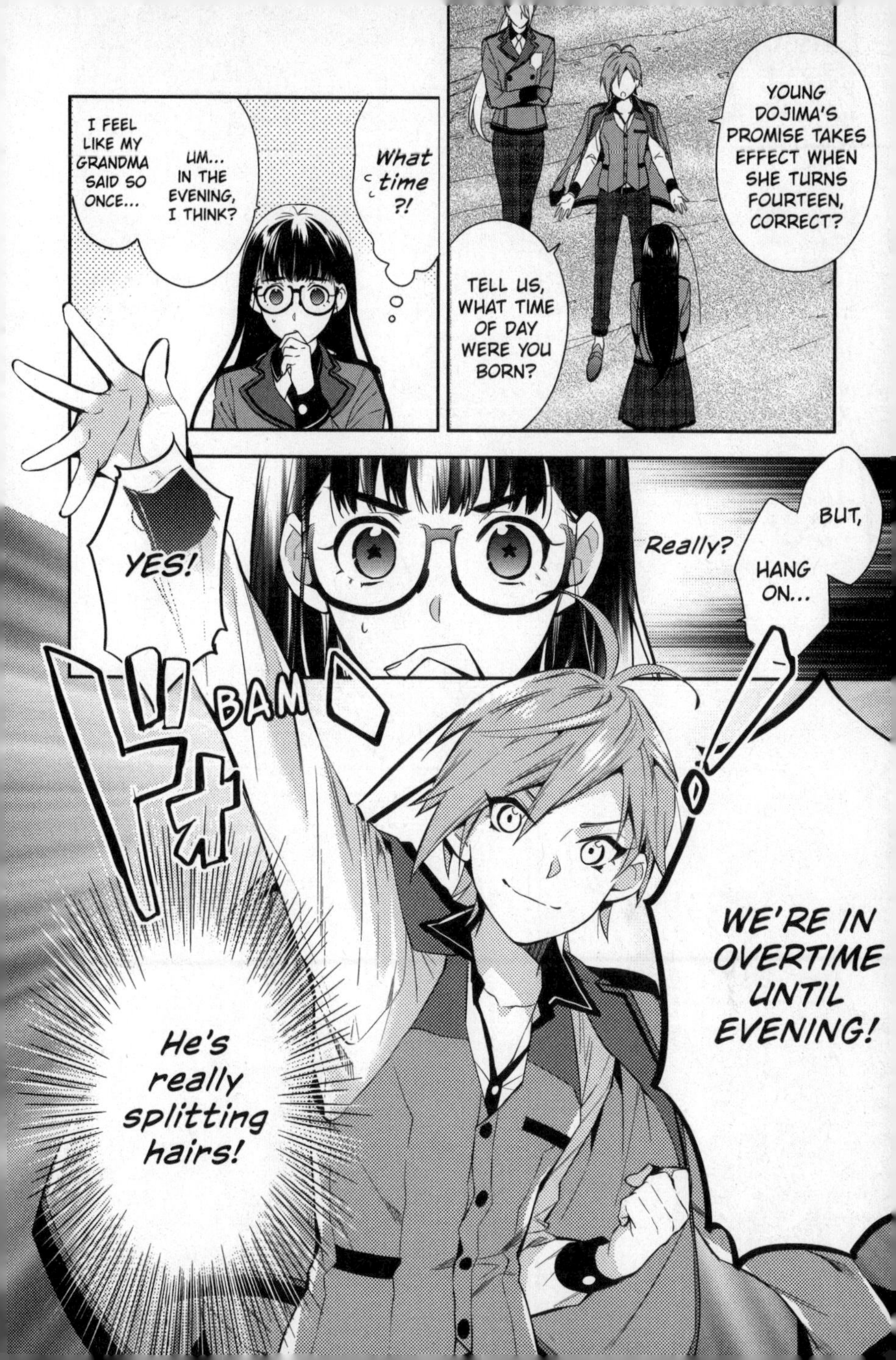
YOUNG DOJIMA'S PROMISE TAKES EFFECT WHEN SHE TURNS FOURTEEN, CORRECT?
TELL US, WHAT TIME OF DAY WERE YOU BORN?
What time ?!
UM... IN THE EVENING, I THINK?
I FEEL LIKE MY GRANDMA SAID SO ONCE...
BUT, HANG ON...
Really?
YES!
BAM
WE'RE IN OVERTIME UNTIL EVENING!
He's really splitting hairs!

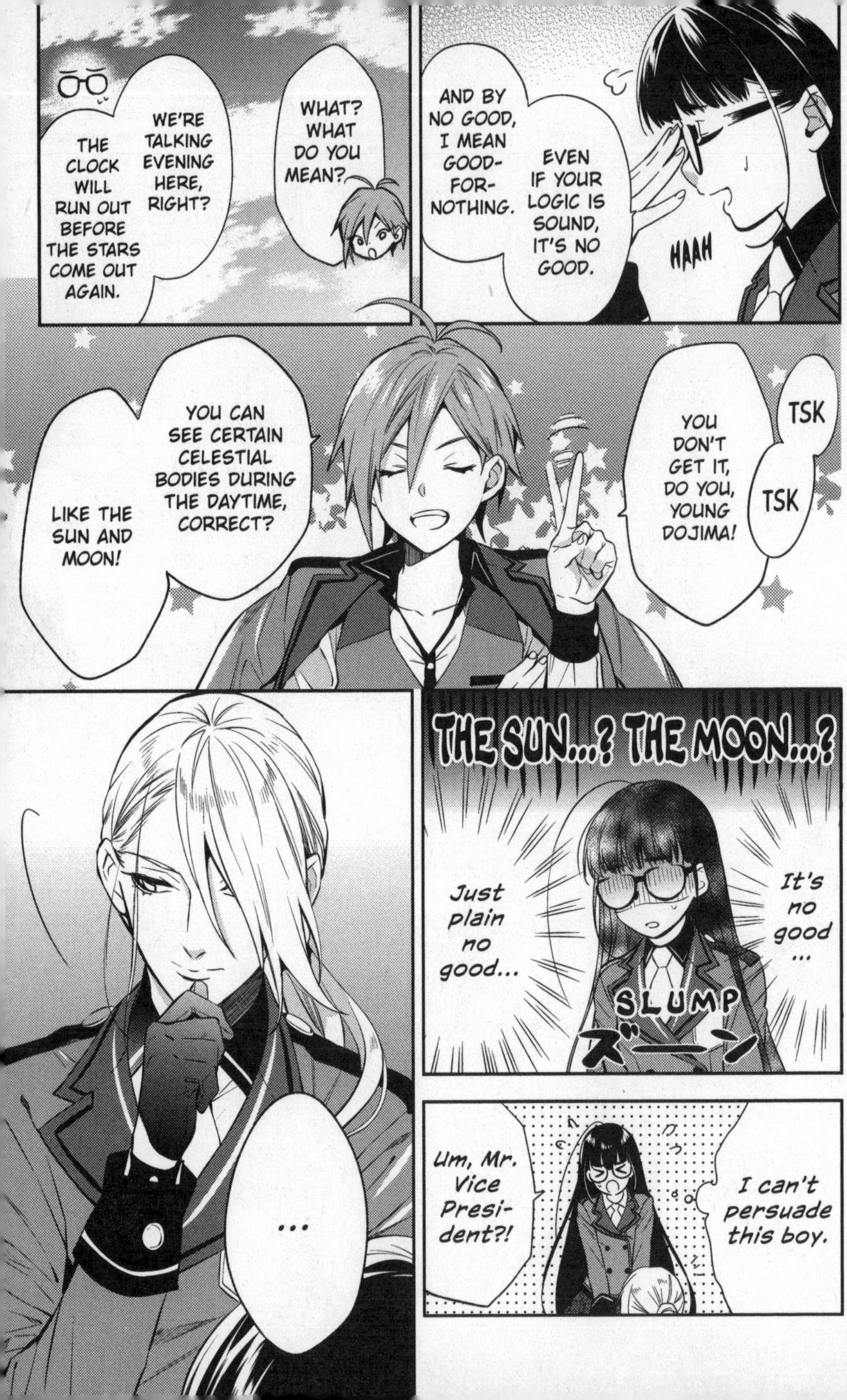
HAAH
EVEN IF YOUR LOGIC IS SOUND, IT'S NO GOOD.
AND BY NO GOOD, I MEAN GOOD-FOR-NOTHING.
WHAT? WHAT DO YOU MEAN?
WE'RE TALKING EVENING HERE, RIGHT?
THE CLOCK WILL RUN OUT BEFORE THE STARS COME OUT AGAIN.
TSK
TSK
YOU DON'T GET IT, DO YOU, YOUNG DOJIMA!
YOU CAN SEE CERTAIN CELESTIAL BODIES DURING THE DAYTIME, CORRECT?
LIKE THE SUN AND MOON!
THE SUN...? THE MOON...?
It's no good ...
Just plain no good...
SLUMP
ズーン
I can't persuade this boy.
Um, Mr. Vice President?!
...

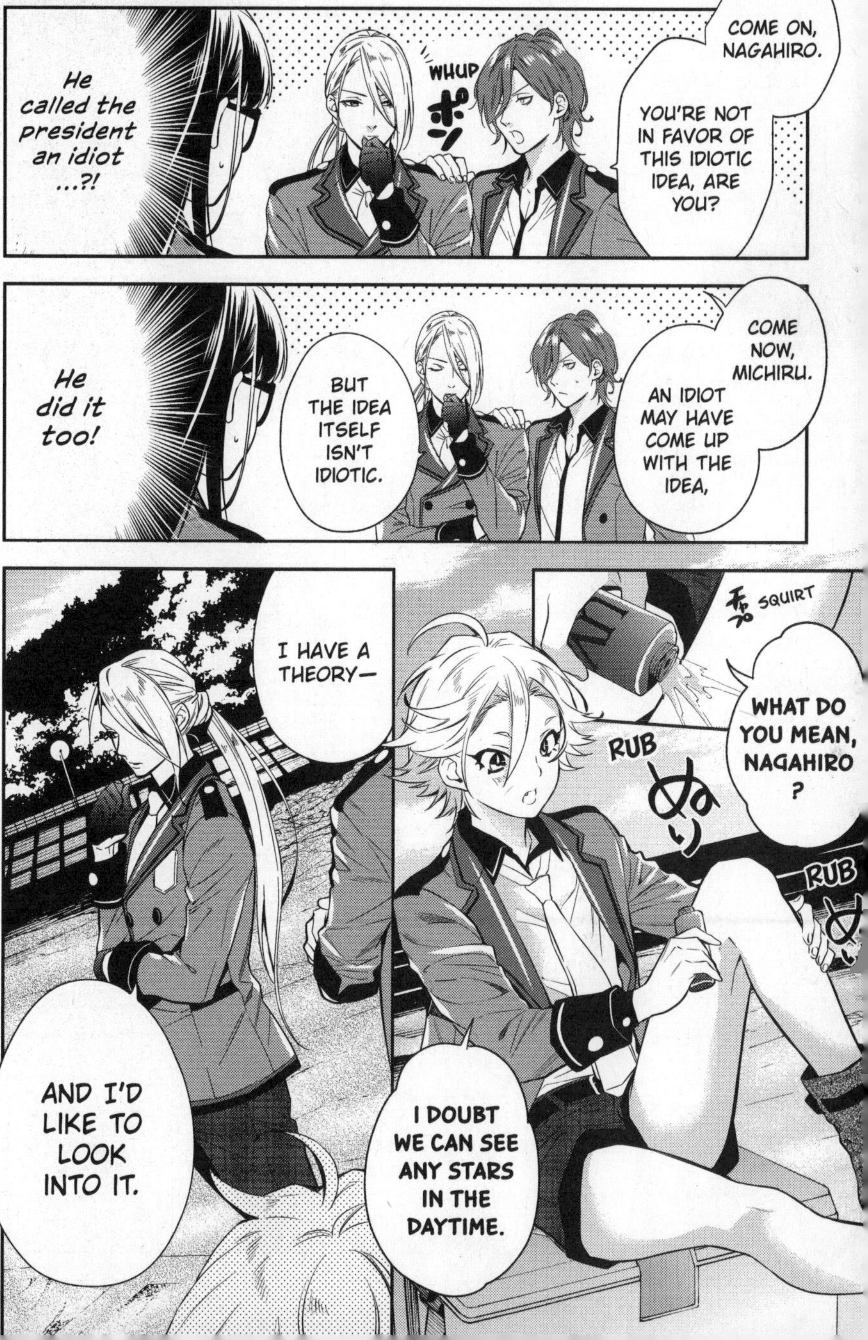
COME ON, NAGAHIRO.
YOU'RE NOT IN FAVOR OF THIS IDIOTIC IDEA, ARE YOU?
WHUP
ポン
He called the president an idiot ...?!
COME NOW, MICHIRU.
AN IDIOT MAY HAVE COME UP WITH THE IDEA,
BUT THE IDEA ITSELF ISN'T IDIOTIC.
He did it too!
SQUIRT
WHAT DO YOU MEAN, NAGAHIRO?
RUB
ぬり
RUB
ぬり
I DOUBT WE CAN SEE ANY STARS IN THE DAYTIME.
I HAVE A THEORY—
AND I'D LIKE TO LOOK INTO IT.

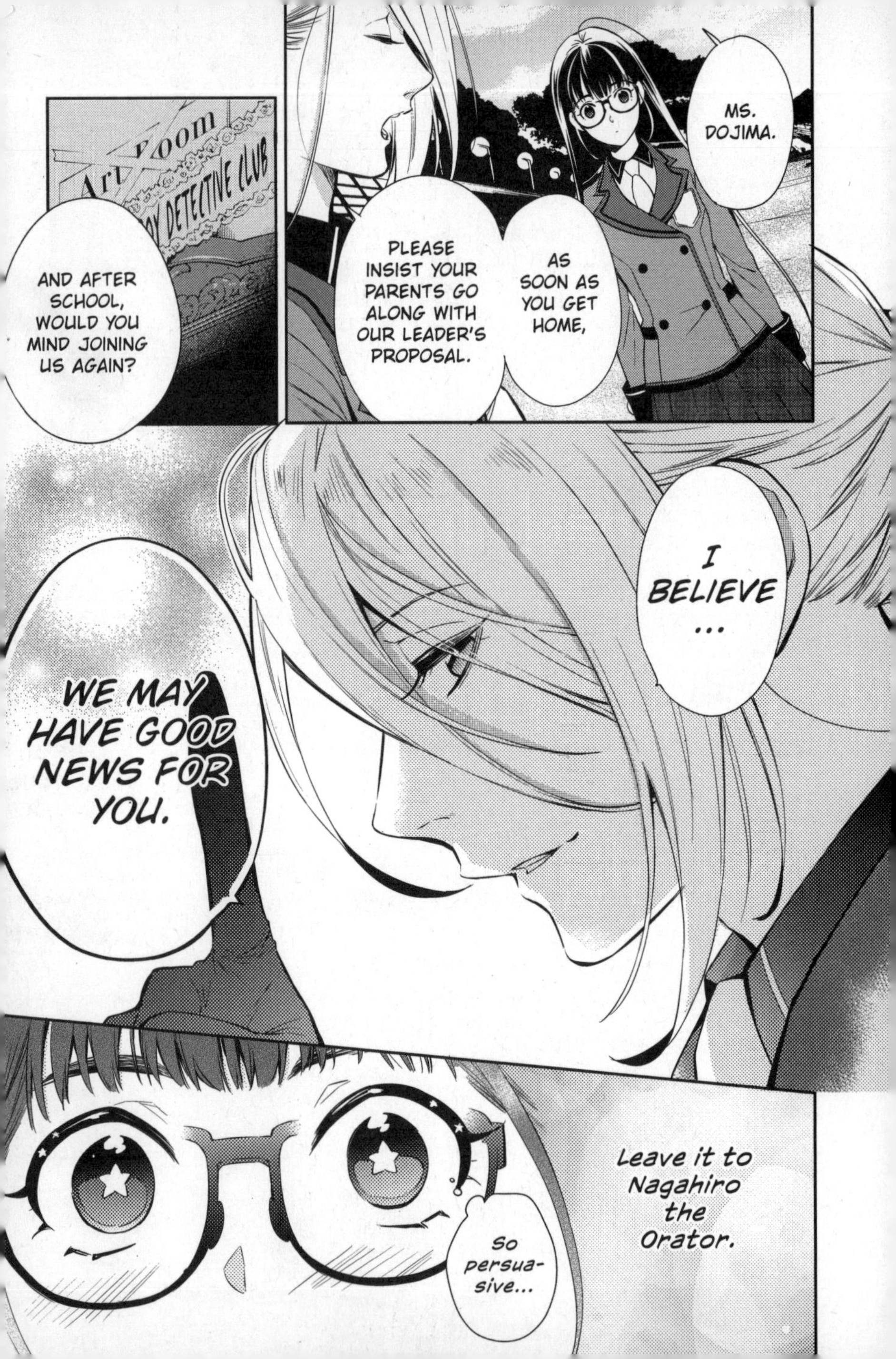

MS. DOJIMA.
AS SOON AS YOU GET HOME,
PLEASE INSIST YOUR PARENTS GO ALONG WITH OUR LEADER'S PROPOSAL.
Art Room
DETECTIVE CLUB
AND AFTER SCHOOL, WOULD YOU MIND JOINING US AGAIN?
I BELIEVE...
WE MAY HAVE GOOD NEWS FOR YOU.
Leave it to Nagahiro the Orator.
So persua-sive...

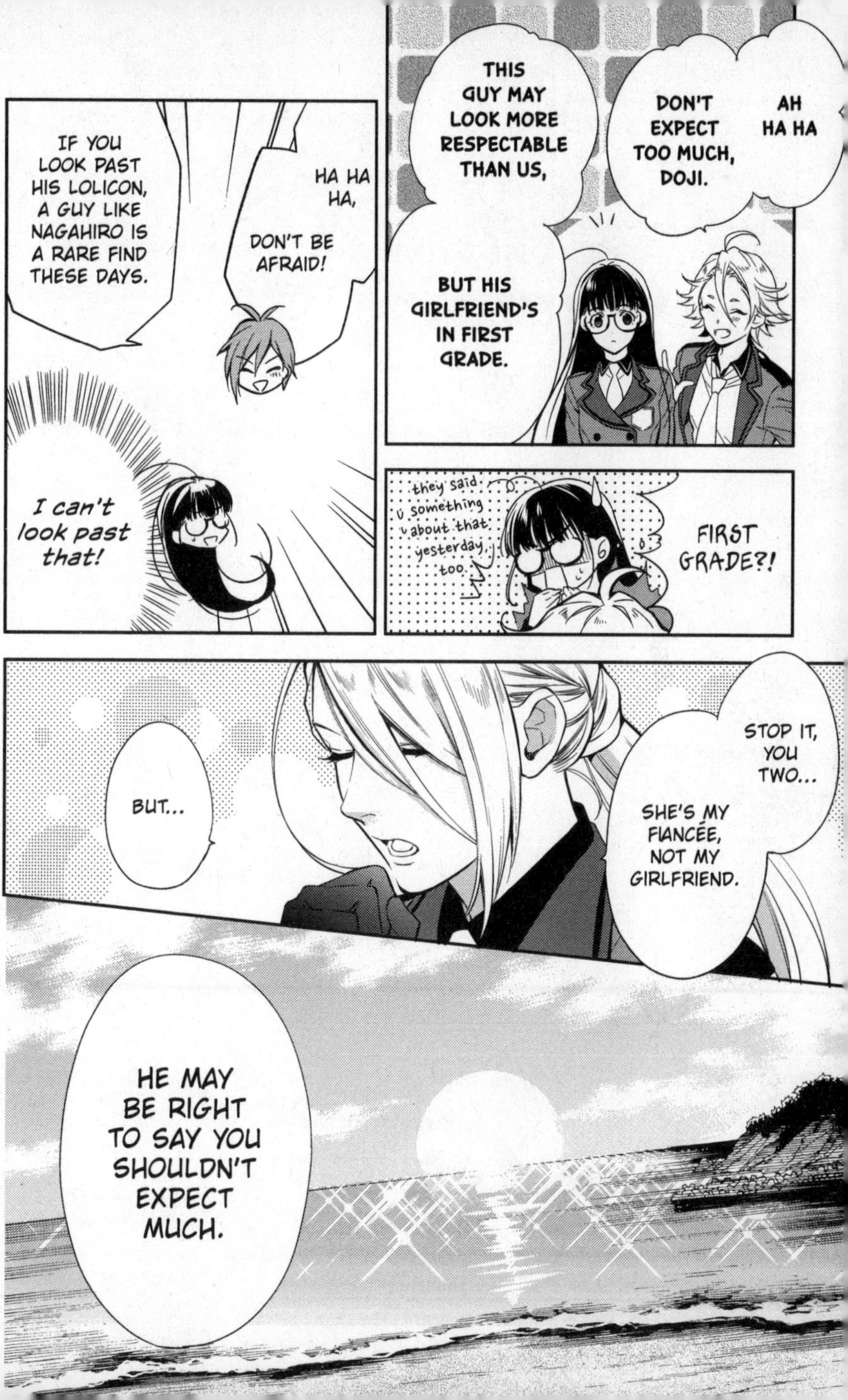
AH HA HA
DON'T EXPECT TOO MUCH, DOJI.
THIS GUY MAY LOOK MORE RESPECTABLE THAN US,
BUT HIS GIRLFRIEND'S IN FIRST GRADE.
FIRST GRADE?!
they said something about that yesterday, too.
HA HA HA,
DON'T BE AFRAID!
IF YOU LOOK PAST HIS LOLICON, A GUY LIKE NAGAHIRO IS A RARE FIND THESE DAYS.
I can't look past that!
STOP IT, YOU TWO...
SHE'S MY FIANCÉE, NOT MY GIRLFRIEND.
BUT...
HE MAY BE RIGHT TO SAY YOU SHOULDN'T EXPECT MUCH.

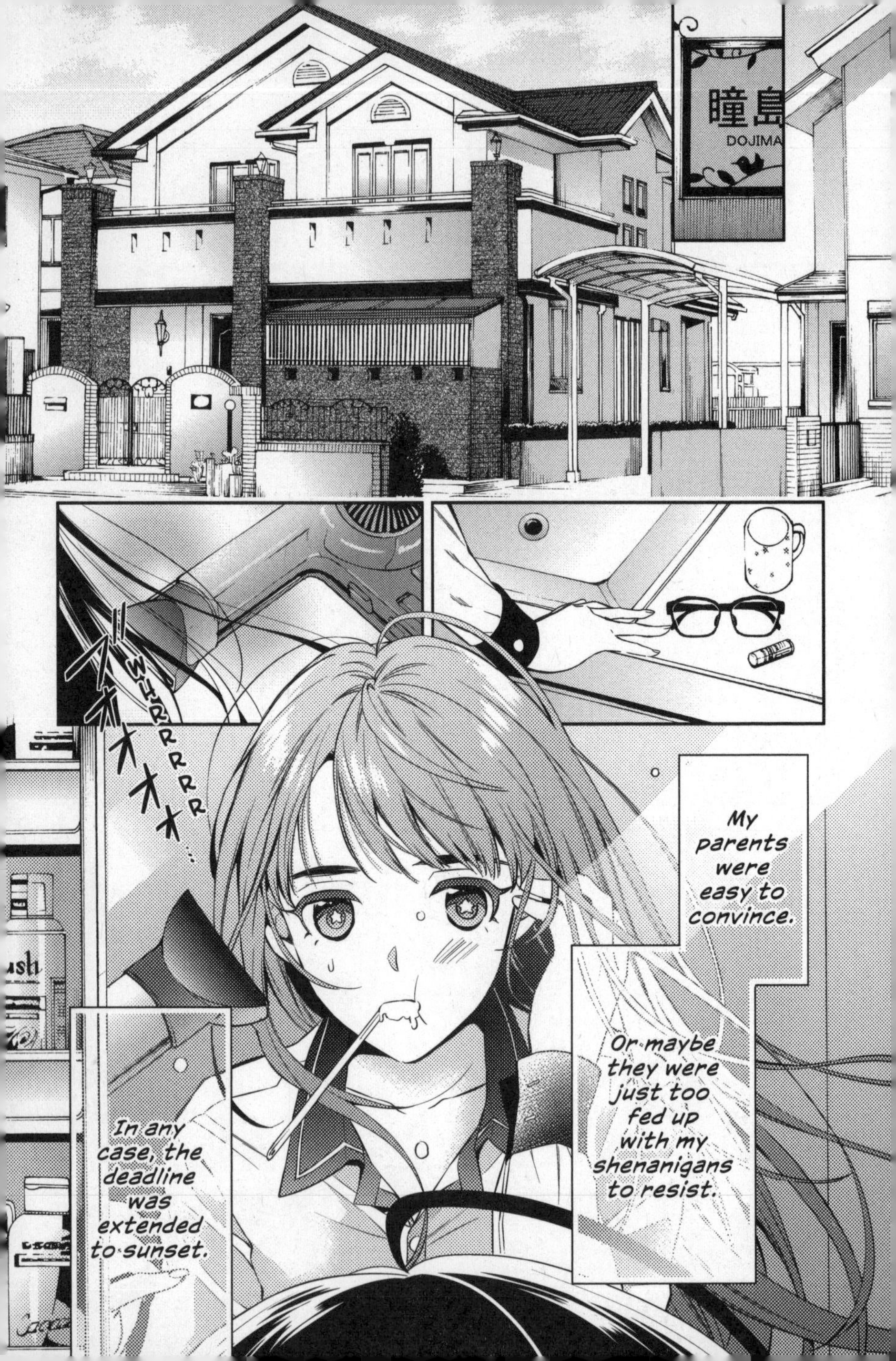
瞳島
DOJIMA
WHRRRRR...
My parents were easy to convince.
Or maybe they were just too fed up with my shenanigans to resist.
In any case, the deadline was extended to sunset.

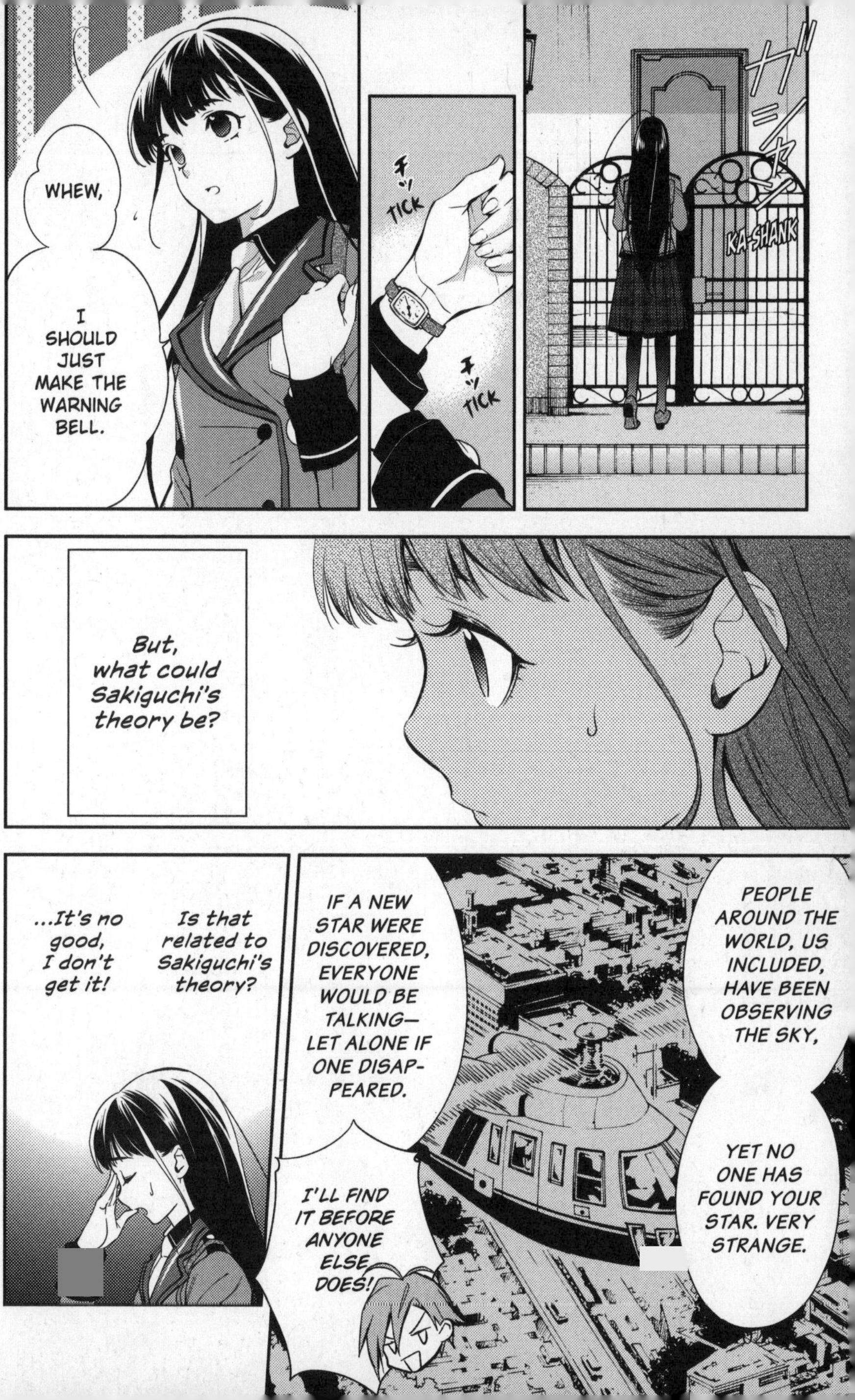
KA-SHANK
TICK
TICK
WHEW,
I SHOULD JUST MAKE THE WARNING BELL.
But, what could Sakiguchi's theory be?
PEOPLE AROUND THE WORLD, US INCLUDED, HAVE BEEN OBSERVING THE SKY,
YET NO ONE HAS FOUND YOUR STAR. VERY STRANGE.
IF A NEW STAR WERE DISCOVERED, EVERYONE WOULD BE TALKING— LET ALONE IF ONE DISAP-PEARED.
I'LL FIND IT BEFORE ANYONE ELSE DOES!
Is that related to Sakiguchi's theory?
...It's no good, I don't get it!

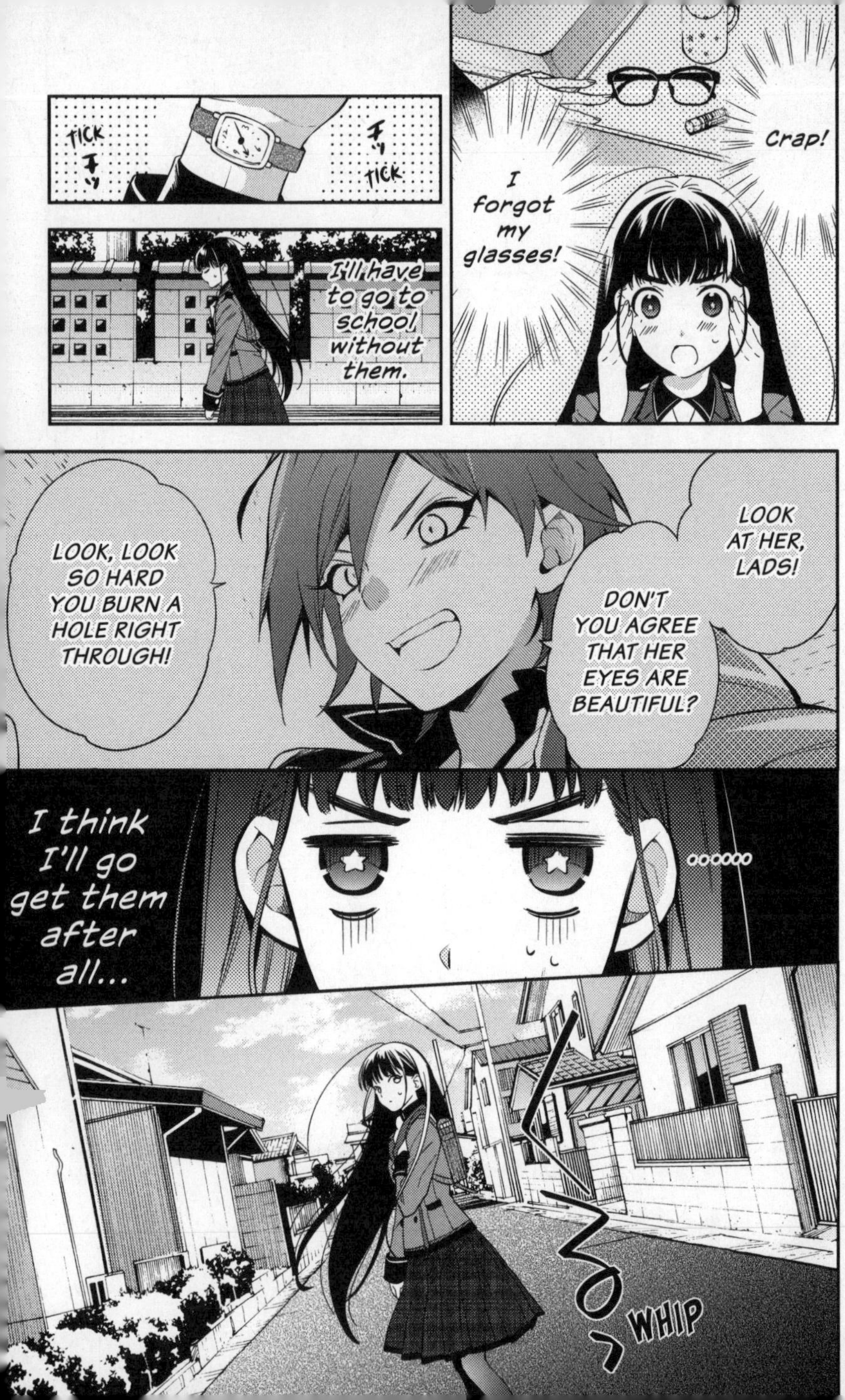
Crap!
I forgot my glasses!
TICK
チッ
チッ
TICK
I'll have to go to school without them.
LOOK AT HER, LADS!
DON'T YOU AGREE THAT HER EYES ARE BEAUTIFUL?
LOOK, LOOK SO HARD YOU BURN A HOLE RIGHT THROUGH!
......
I think I'll go get them after all...
WHIP

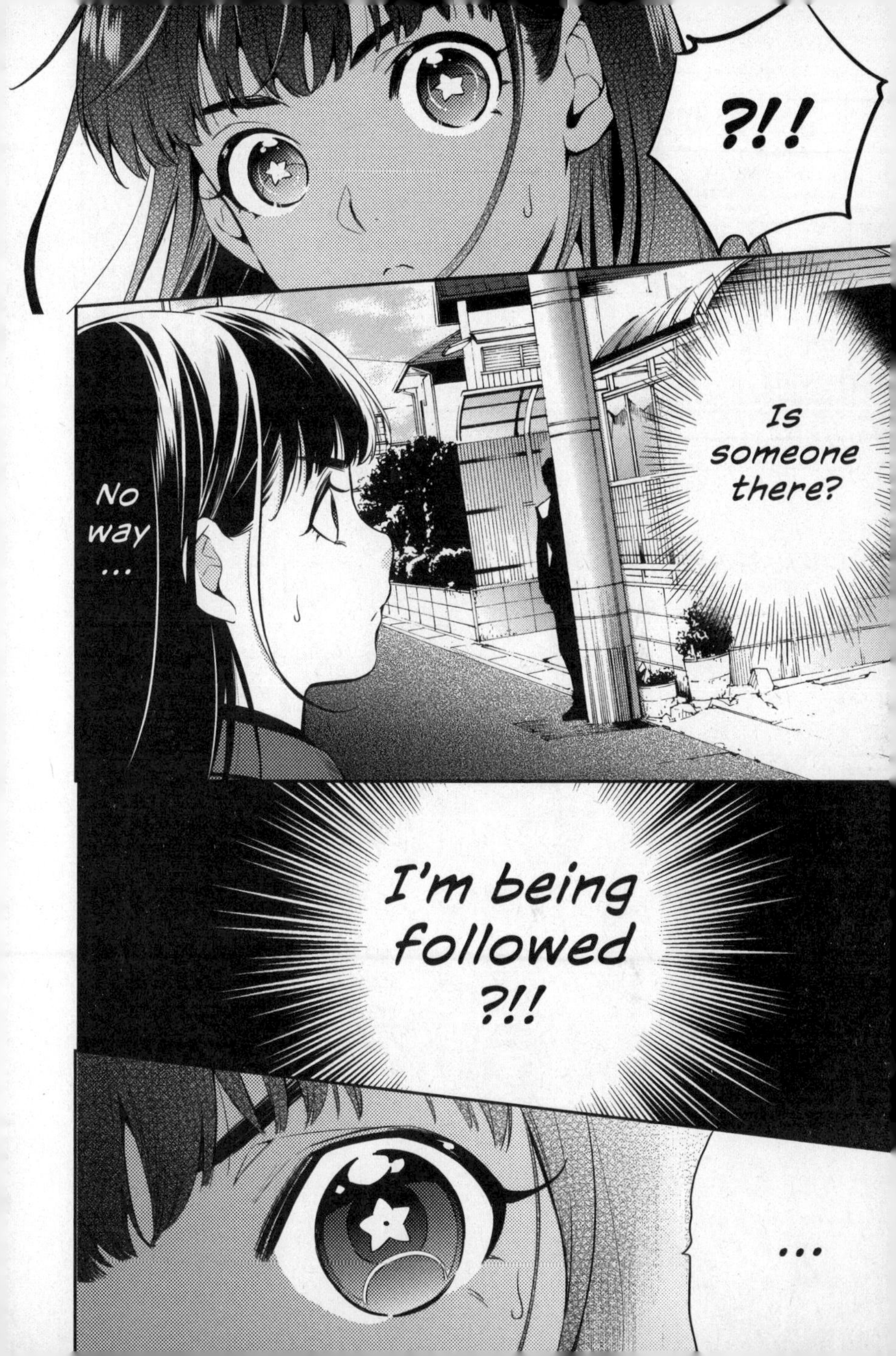

?!!
Is someone there?
No way ...
I'm being followed ?!!
...

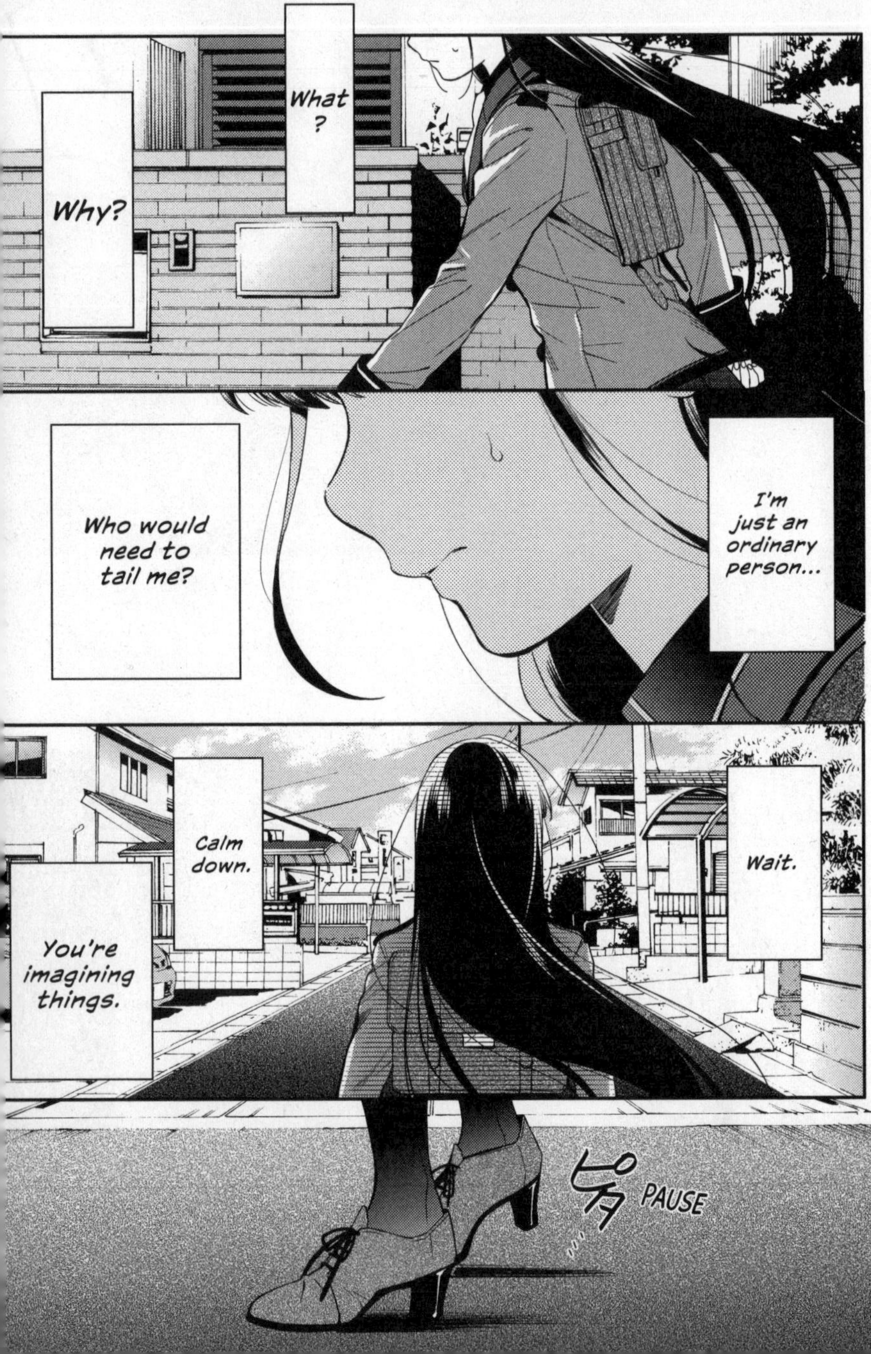
What?
Why?
I'm just an ordinary person...
Who would need to tail me?
Wait.
Calm down.
You're imagining things.
ピク
PAUSE

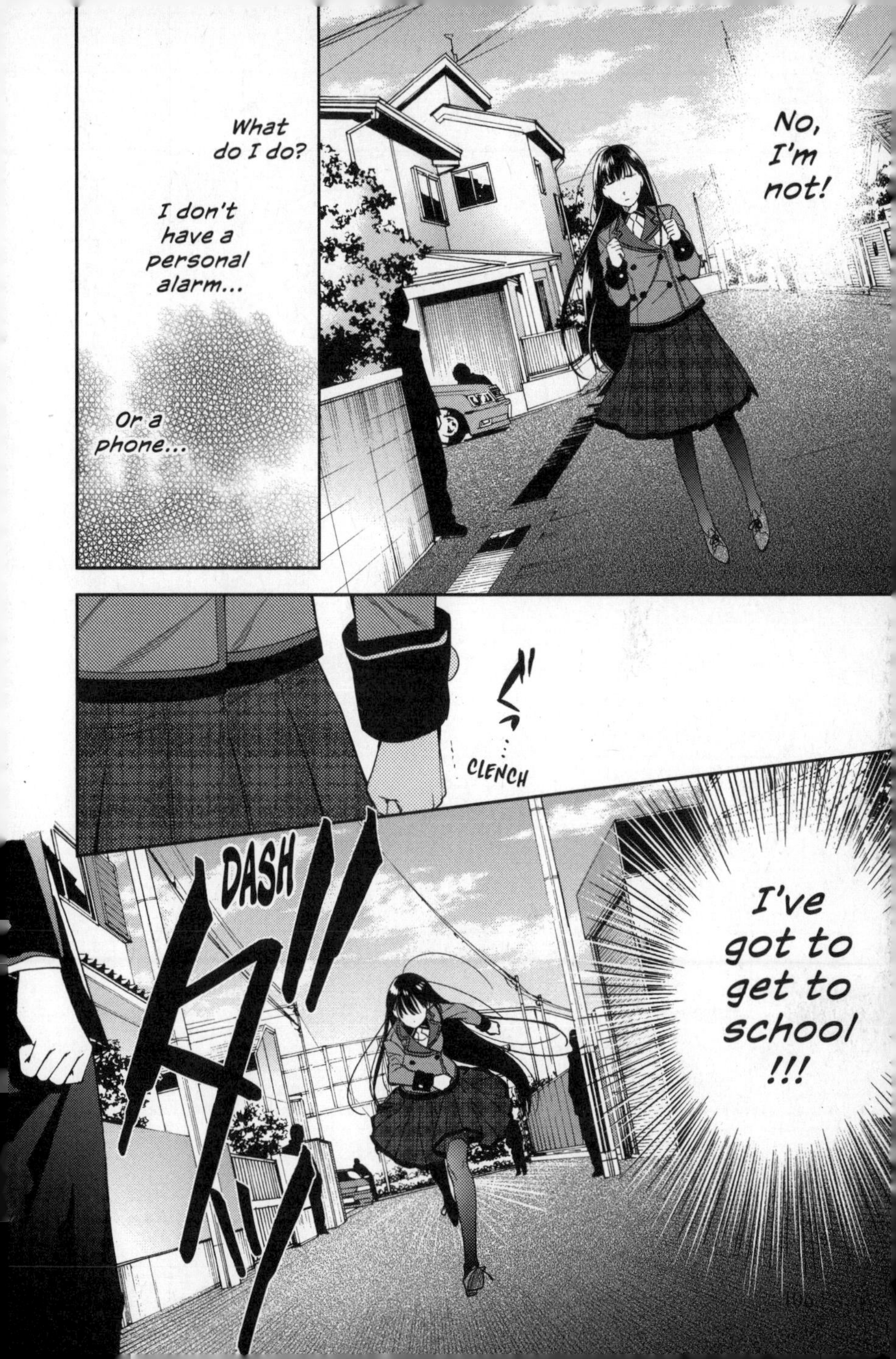
No, I'm not!
What do I do?
I don't have a personal alarm...
Or a phone...
CLENCH
I've got to get to school!!!
DASH

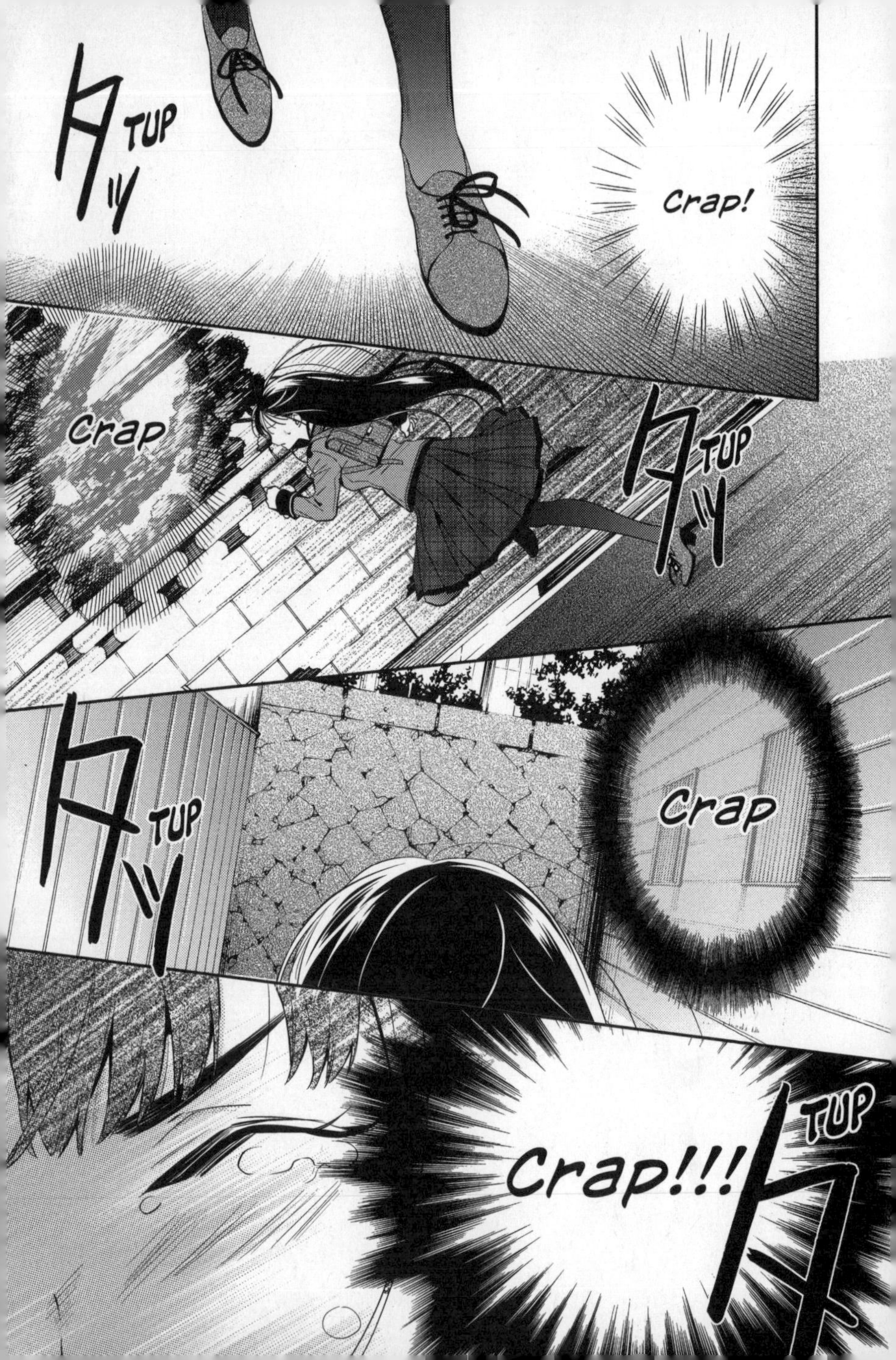
Crap!
タッ TUP
タッ TUP
Crap
Crap
タッ TUP
TUP
Crap!!!

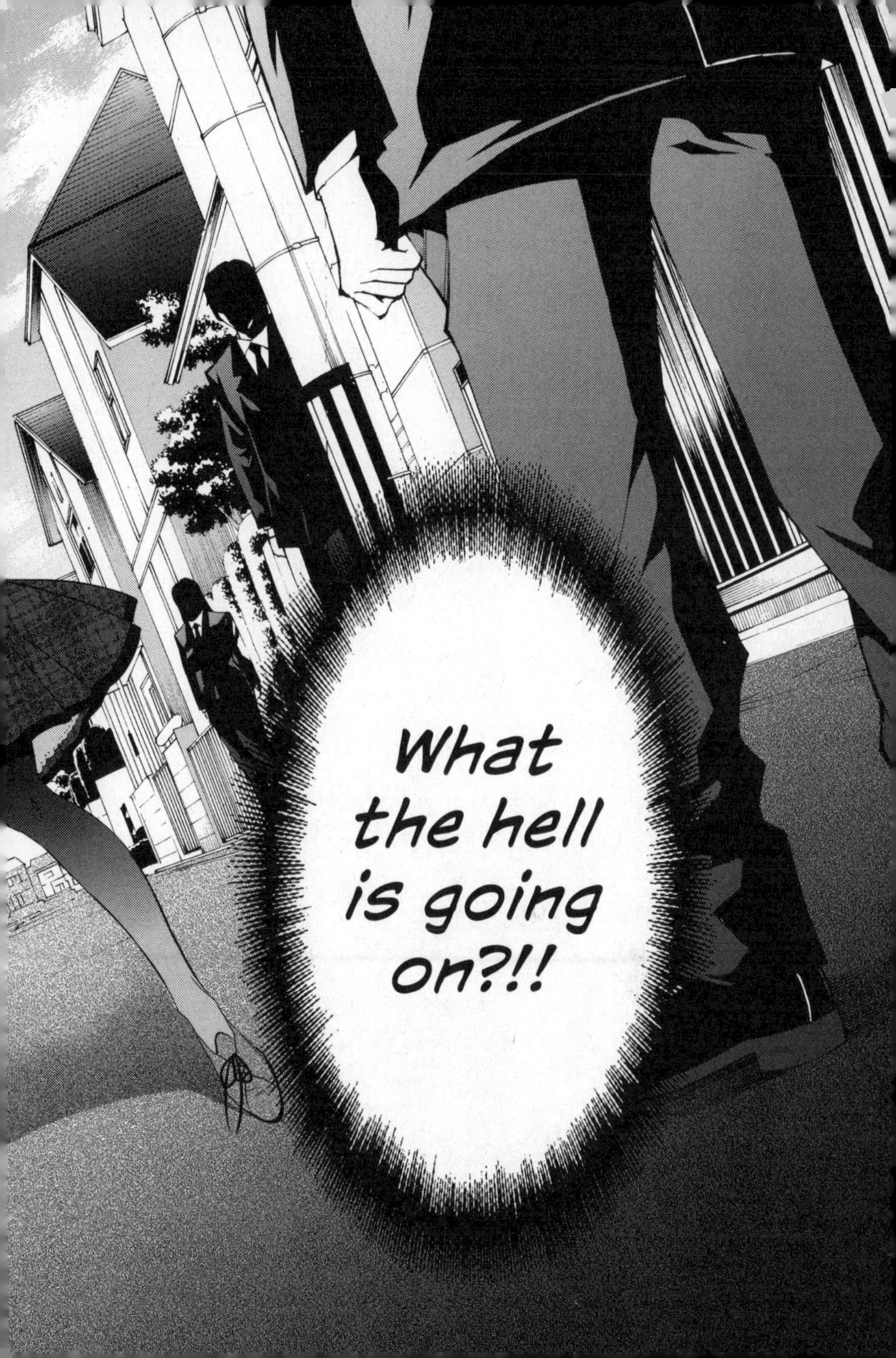
What the hell is going on?!!

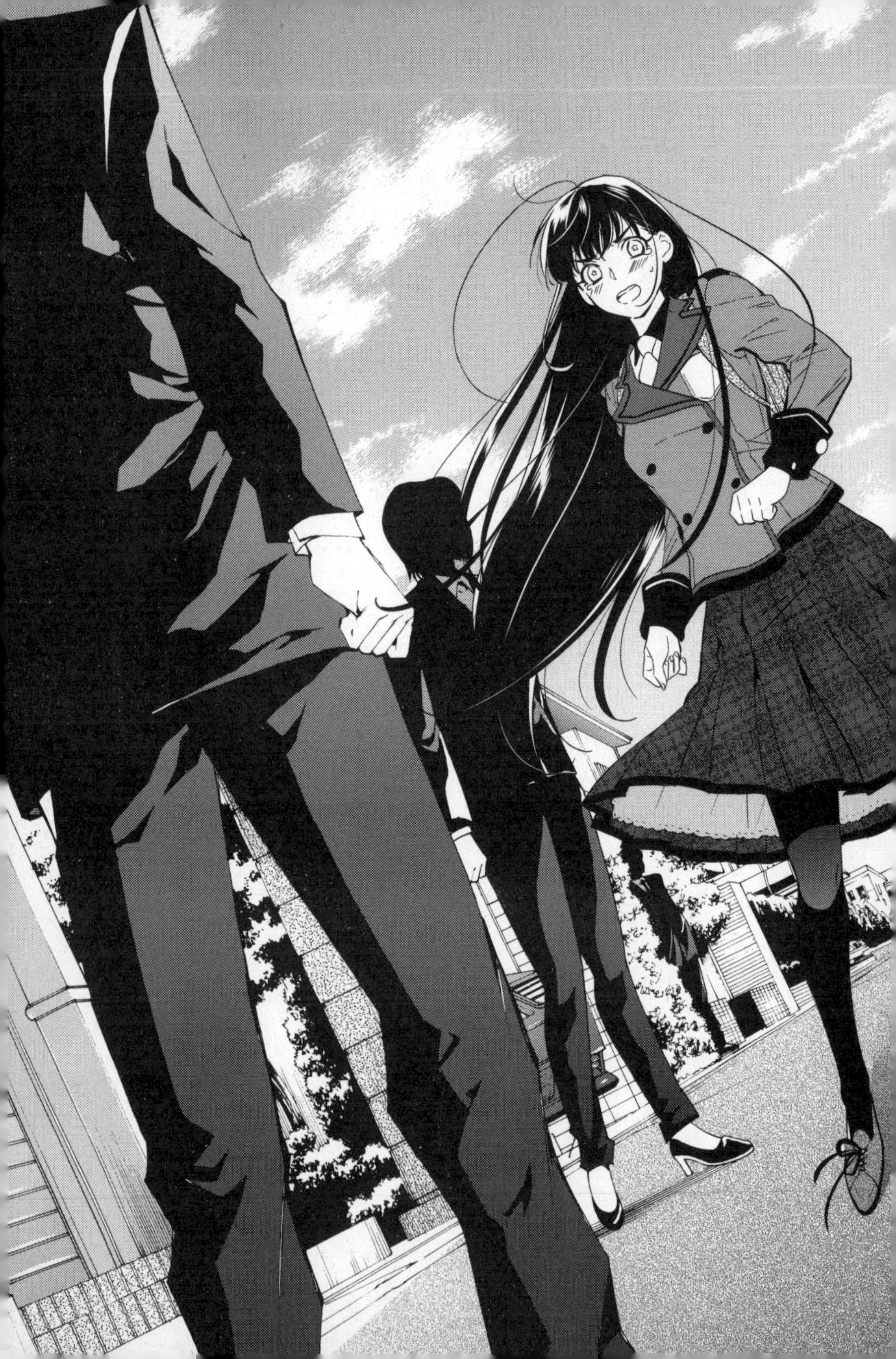

PRETTY BOY

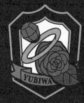

DETECTIVE CLUB!!

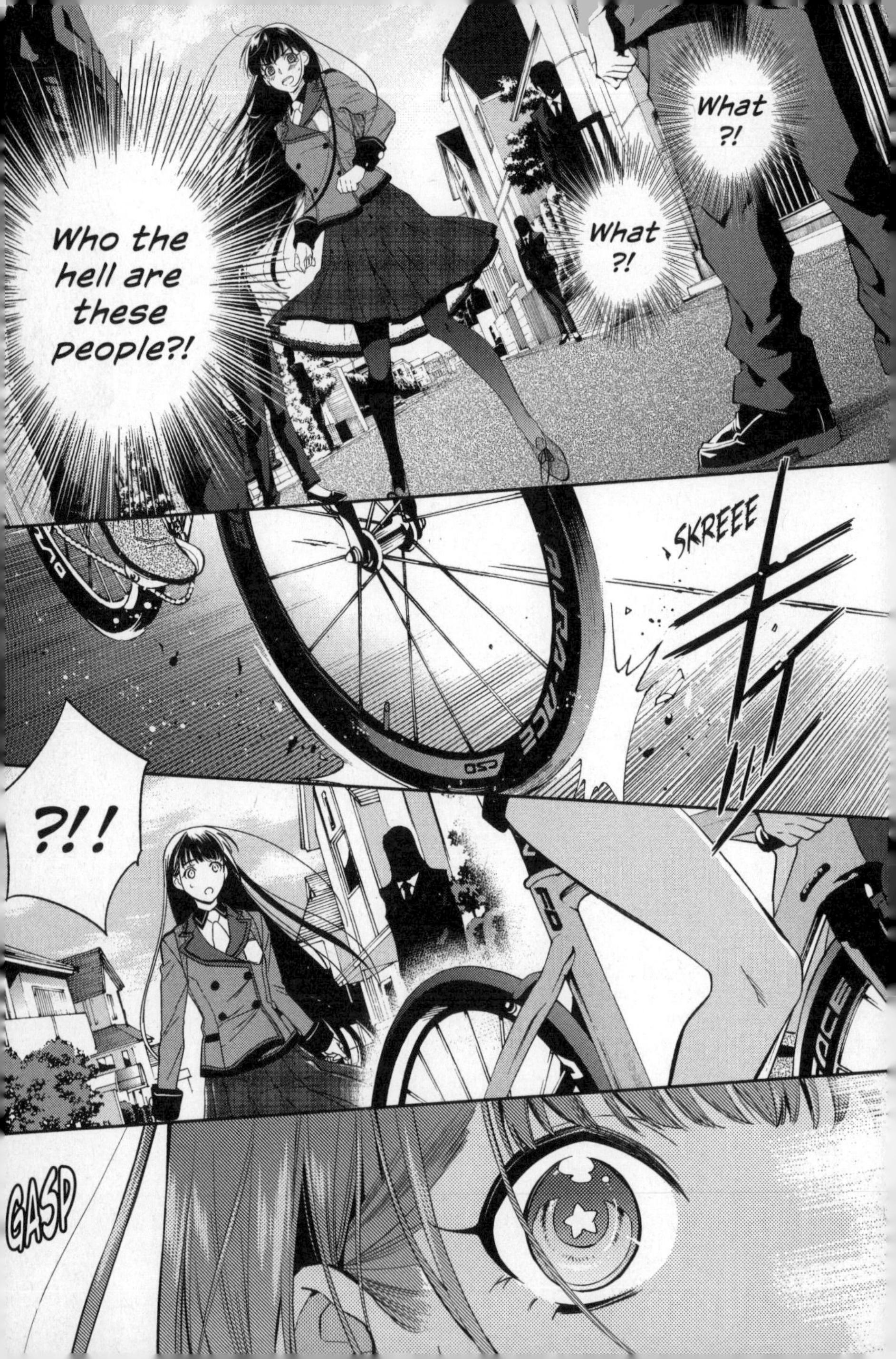
What ?!
What ?!
Who the hell are these people?!
SKREEE
?!!
GASP

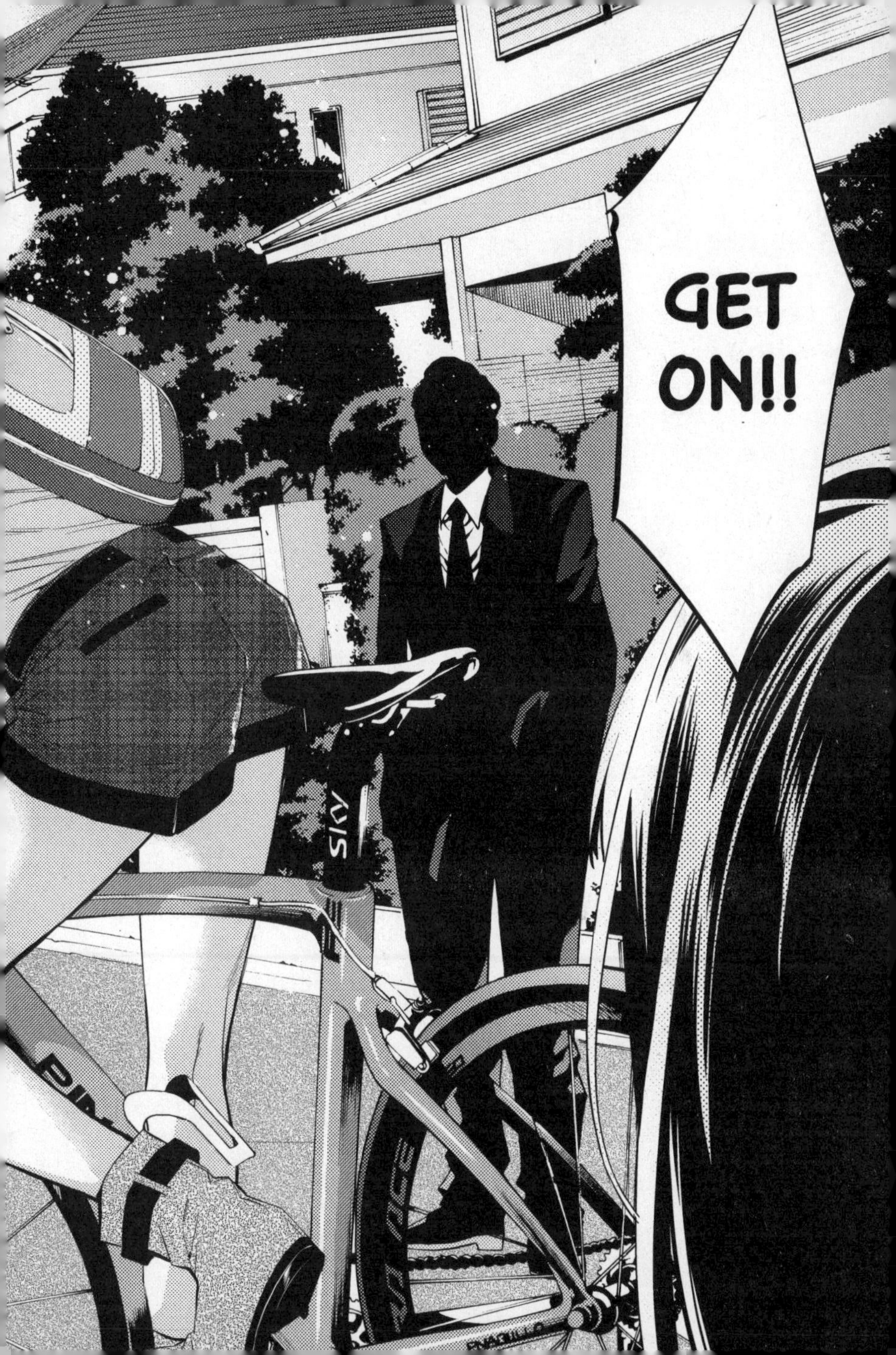
GET ON!!
SKY

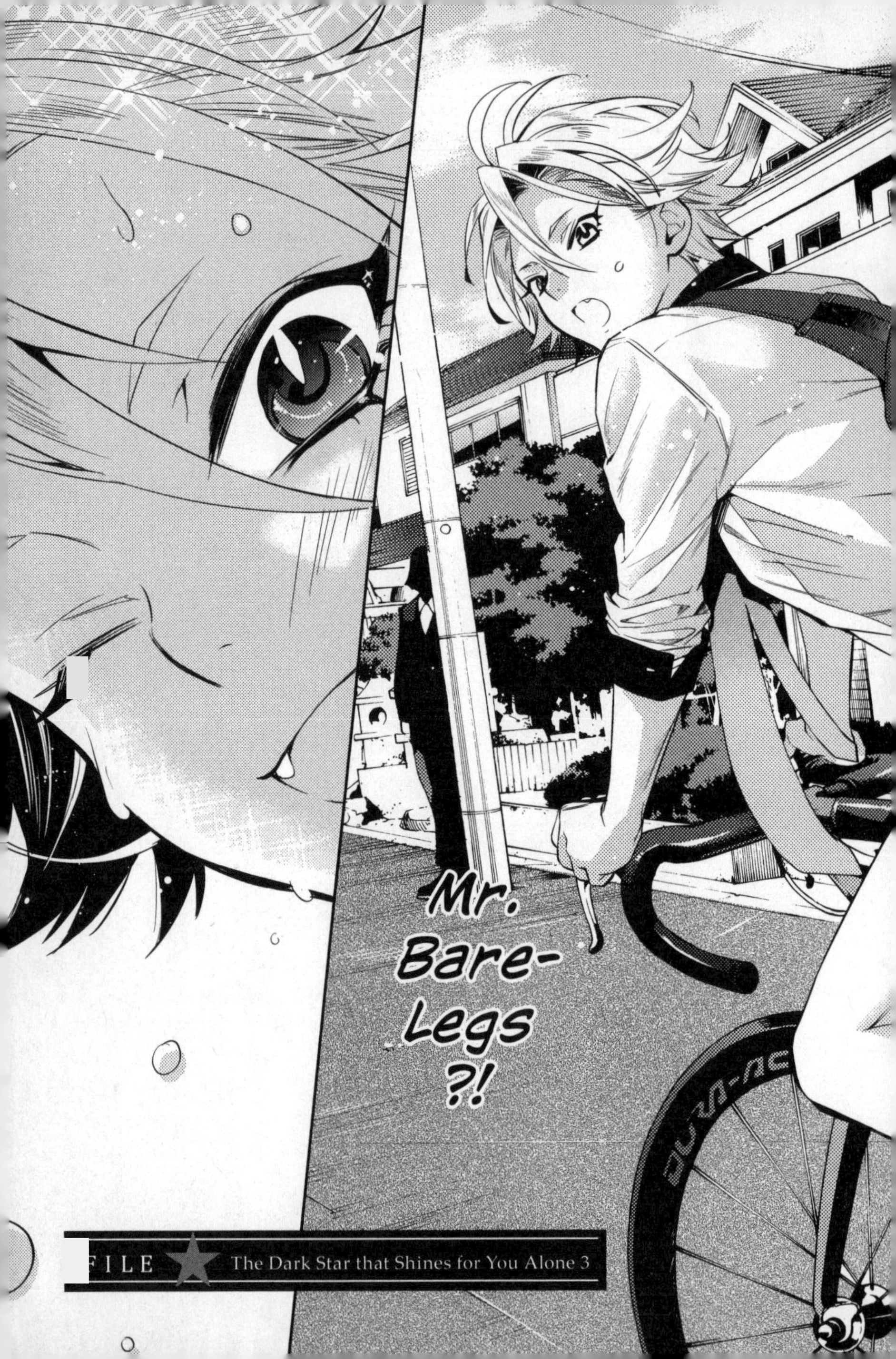
Mr. Bare-Legs ?!
FILE The Dark Star that Shines for You Alone 3

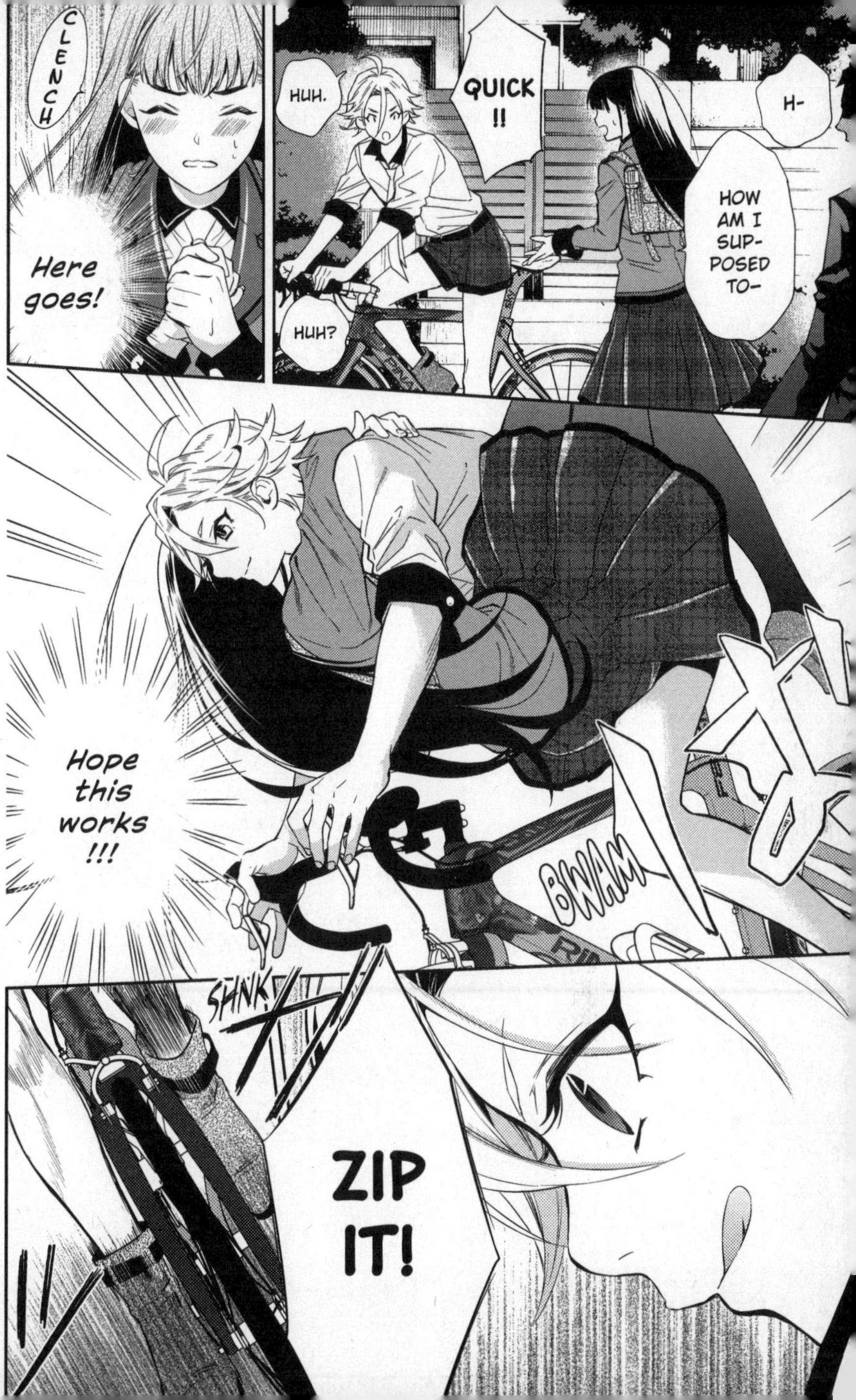
H-
HOW AM I SUPPOSED TO-
QUICK !!
HUH.
HUH?
CLENCH
Here goes!
Hope this works !!!
BWAM
SHNK
ZIP IT!

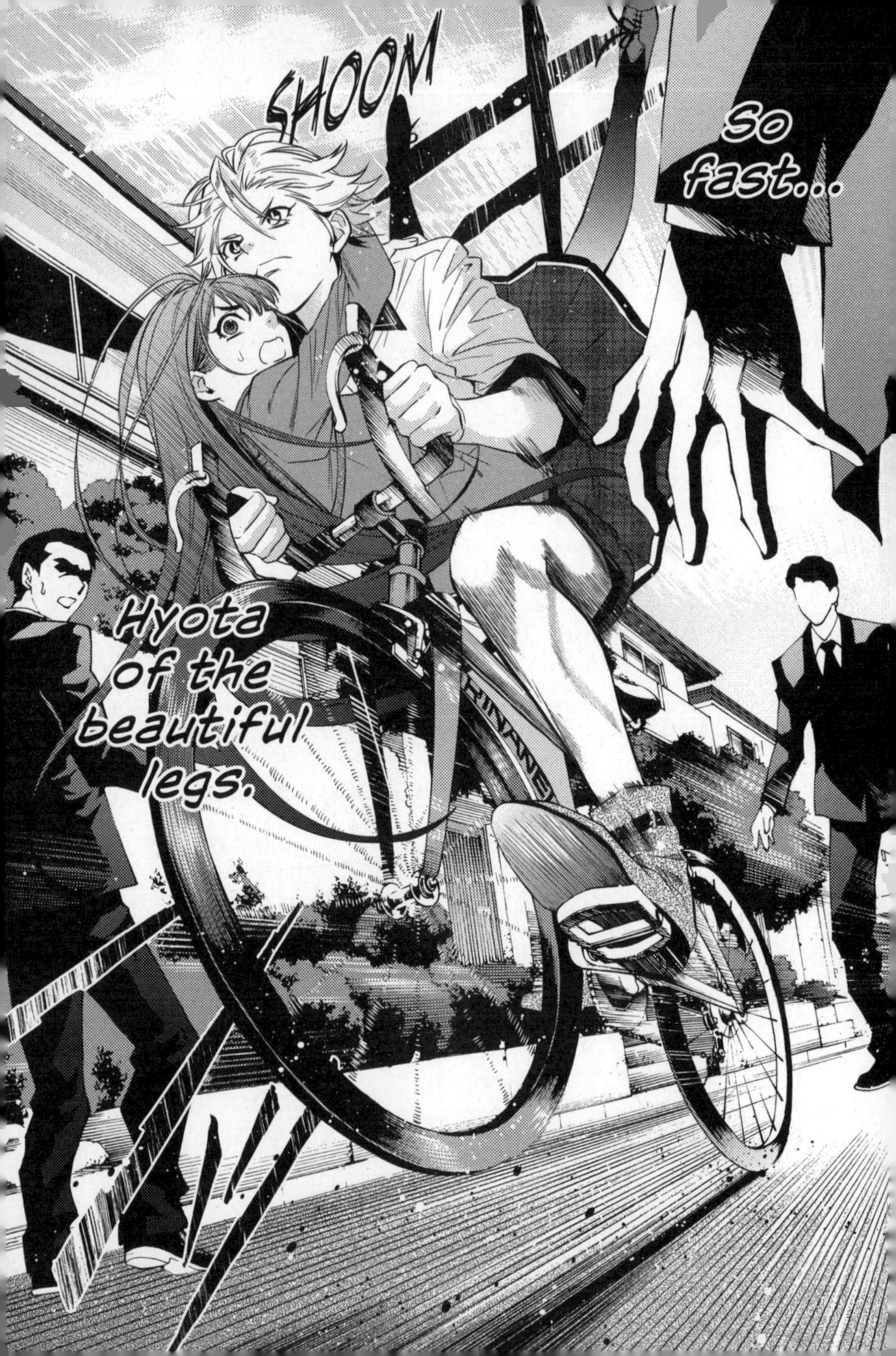

So fast...
SHOOM
Hyota of the beautiful legs.

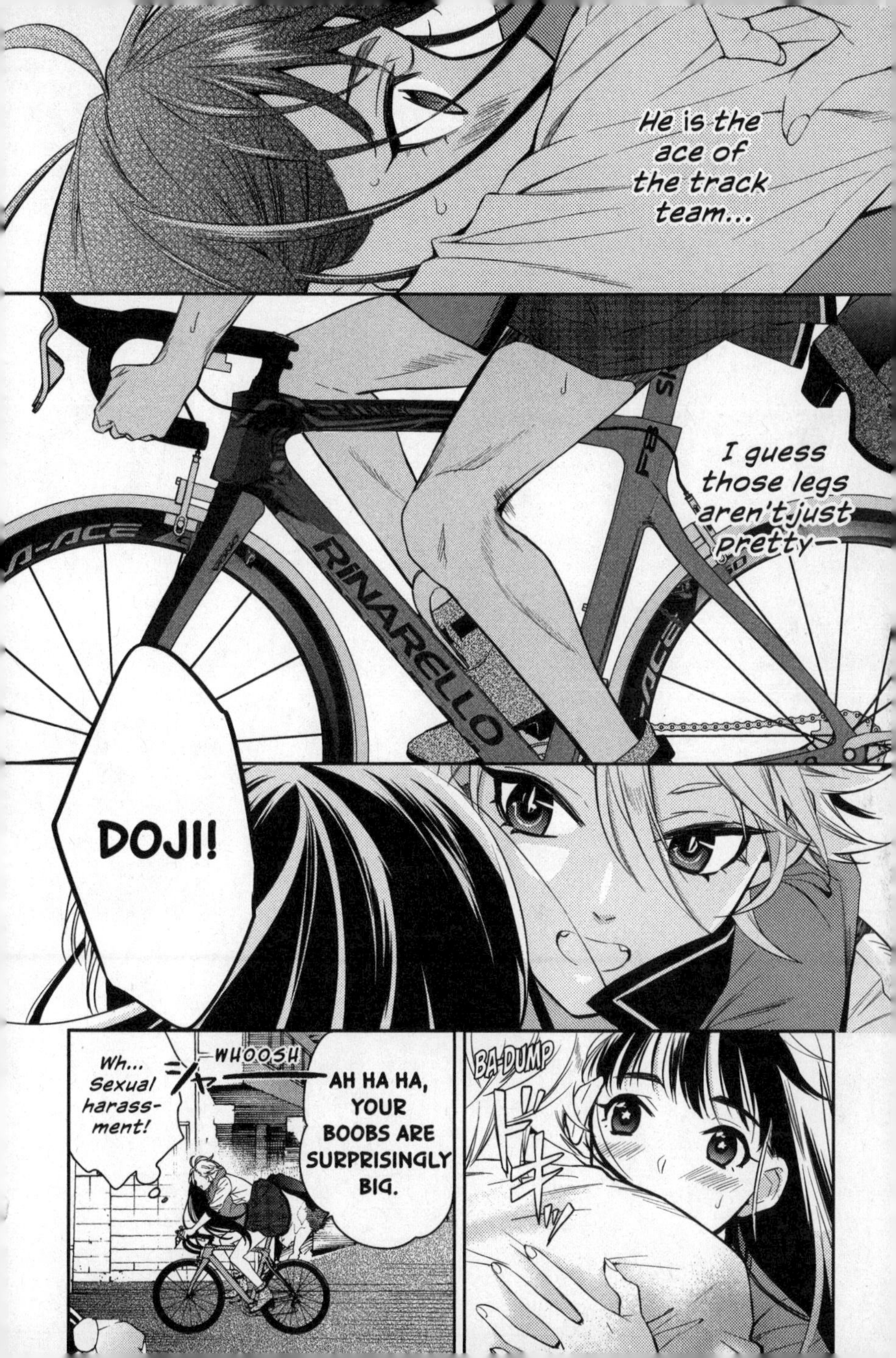

He is the ace of the track team...
I guess those legs aren't just pretty—
RINARELLO
DOJI!
BA-DUMP
ドキッ
WHOOSH
AH HA HA, YOUR BOOBS ARE SURPRISINGLY BIG.
Wh... Sexual harass-ment!

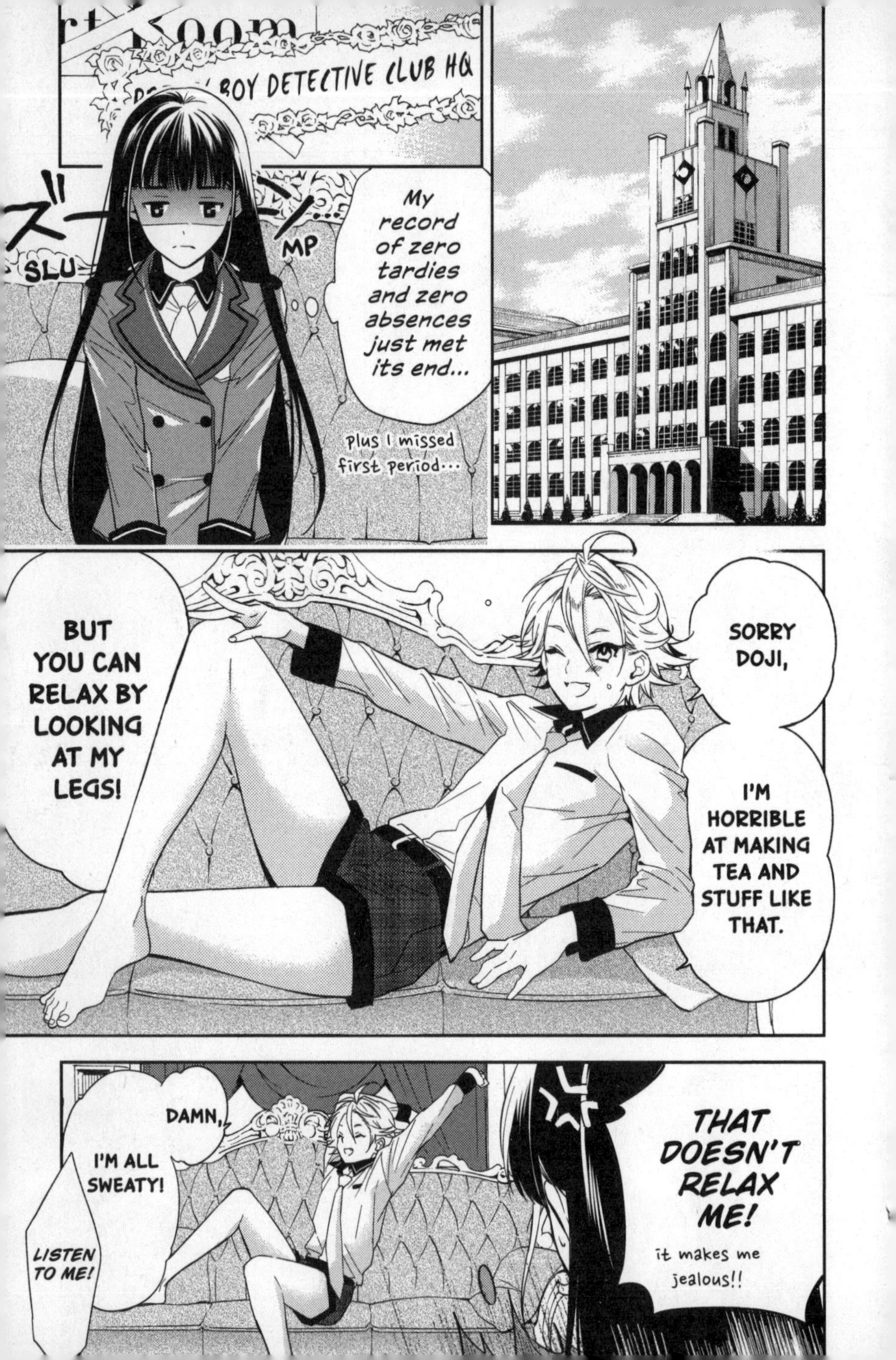
BOY DETECTIVE CLUB HQ
SLU
MP
My record of zero tardies and zero absences just met its end...
Plus I missed first period...
SORRY DOJI,
I'M HORRIBLE AT MAKING TEA AND STUFF LIKE THAT.
BUT YOU CAN RELAX BY LOOKING AT MY LEGS!
THAT DOESN'T RELAX ME!
it makes me jealous!!
DAMN,
I'M ALL SWEATY!
LISTEN TO ME!

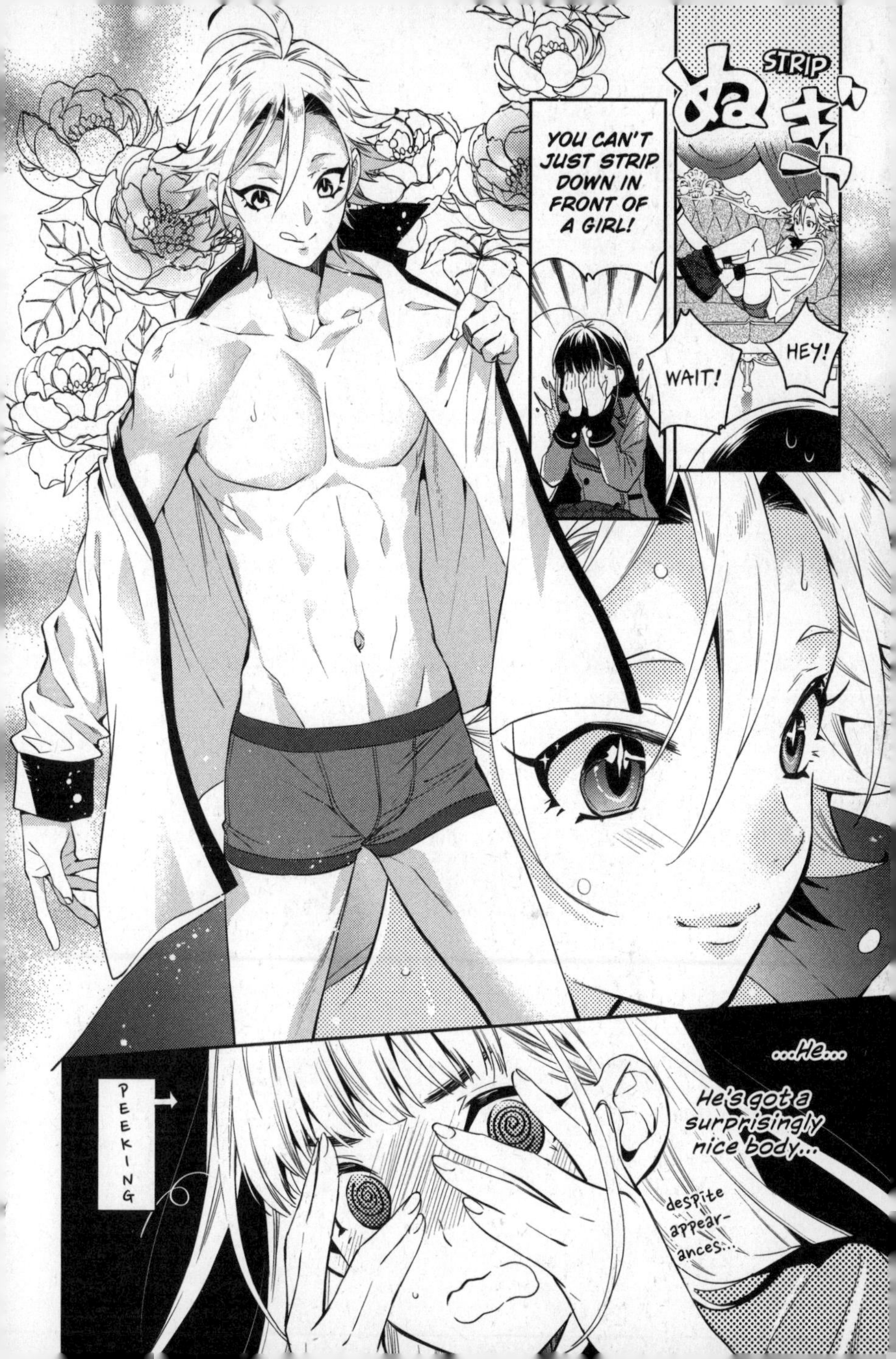
ぬぎ
STRIP
HEY!
WAIT!
YOU CAN'T JUST STRIP DOWN IN FRONT OF A GIRL!
...He...
He's got a surprisingly nice body...
despite appearances...
PEEKING

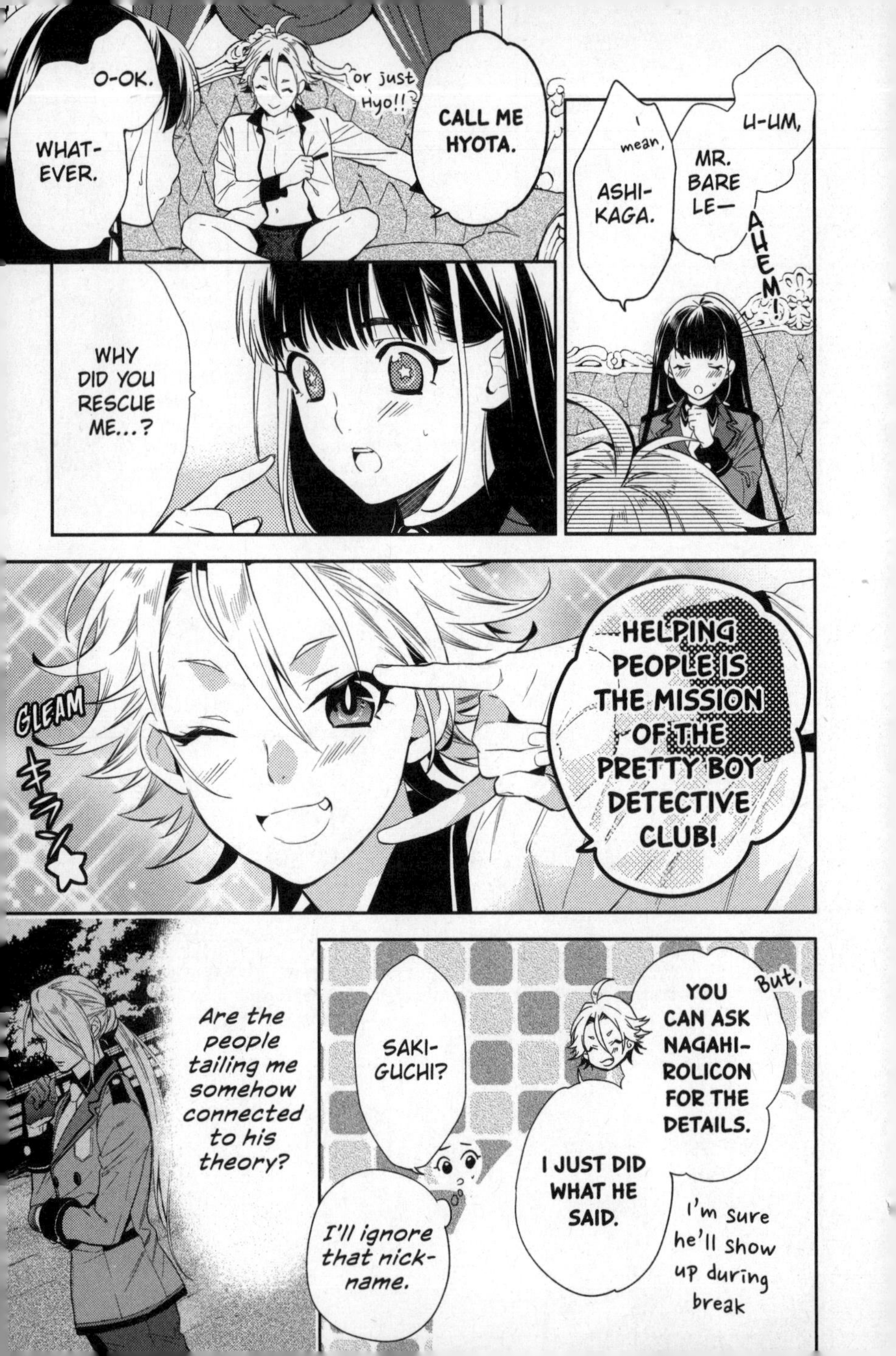
U-UM,
MR. BARE LE—
AHEM!
I mean,
ASHI-KAGA.
CALL ME HYOTA.
or just Hyo!!
O-OK.
WHAT-EVER.
WHY DID YOU RESCUE ME...?
HELPING PEOPLE IS THE MISSION OF THE PRETTY BOY DETECTIVE CLUB!
GLEAM
But,
YOU CAN ASK NAGAHI-ROLICON FOR THE DETAILS.
SAKI-GUCHI?
I JUST DID WHAT HE SAID.
I'm sure he'll show up during break
I'll ignore that nick-name.
Are the people tailing me somehow connected to his theory?

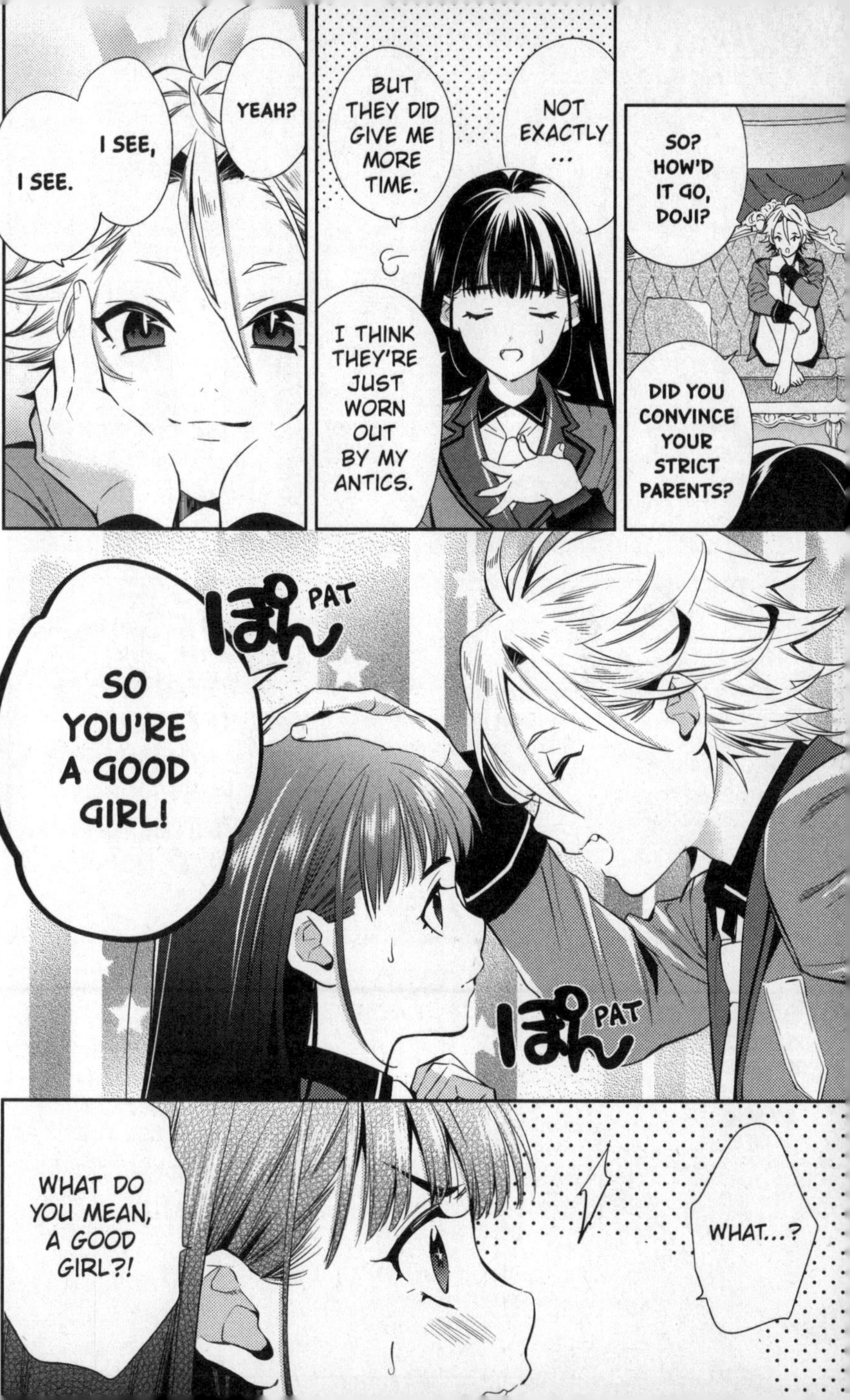
SO? HOW'D IT GO, DOJI?
DID YOU CONVINCE YOUR STRICT PARENTS?
NOT EXACTLY ...
BUT THEY DID GIVE ME MORE TIME.
I THINK THEY'RE JUST WORN OUT BY MY ANTICS.
YEAH?
I SEE, I SEE.
ぽん PAT
SO YOU'RE A GOOD GIRL!
ぽん PAT
WHAT...?
WHAT DO YOU MEAN, A GOOD GIRL?!

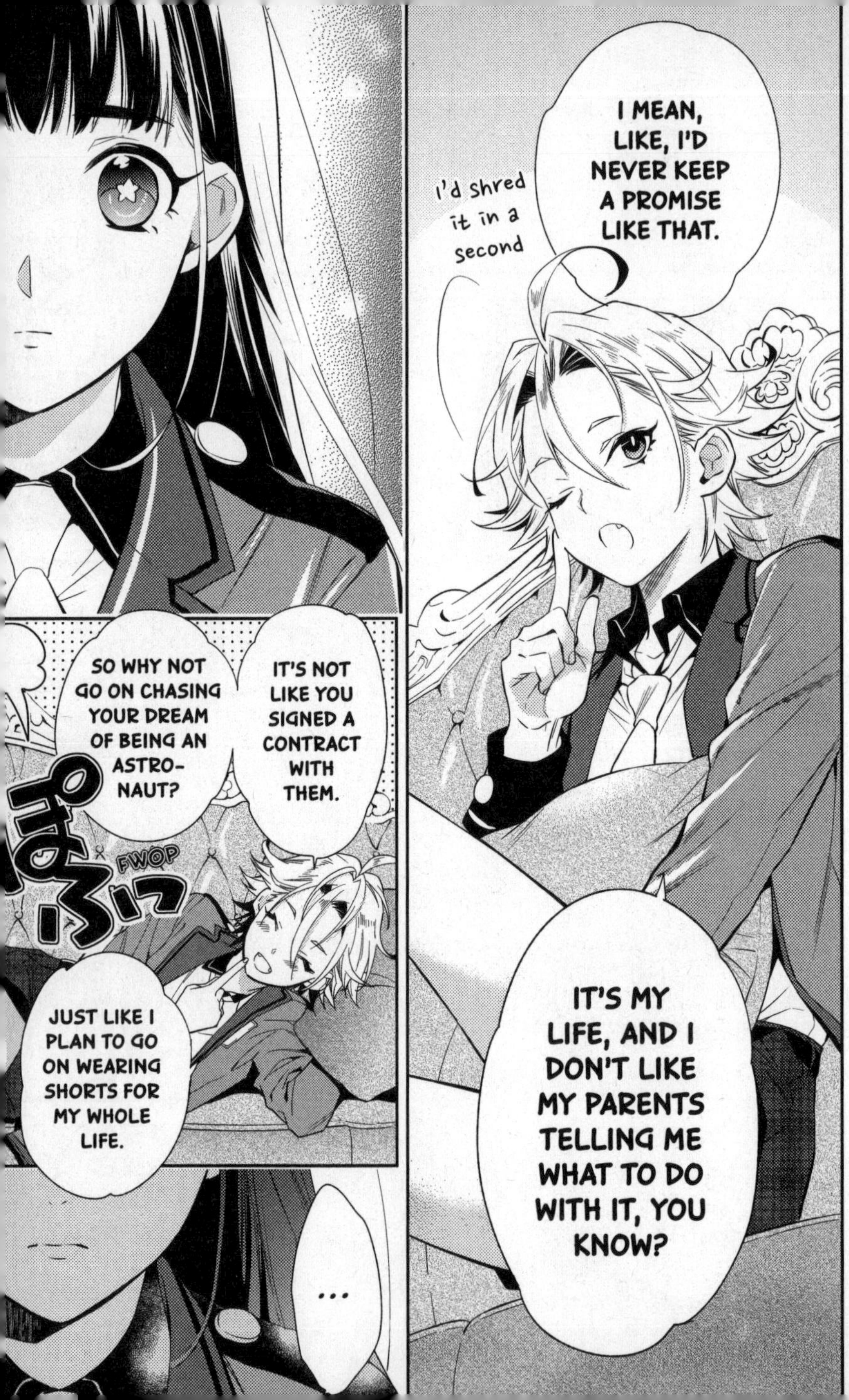
I MEAN, LIKE, I'D NEVER KEEP A PROMISE LIKE THAT.
I'd shred it in a second
IT'S MY LIFE, AND I DON'T LIKE MY PARENTS TELLING ME WHAT TO DO WITH IT, YOU KNOW?
IT'S NOT LIKE YOU SIGNED A CONTRACT WITH THEM.
SO WHY NOT GO ON CHASING YOUR DREAM OF BEING AN ASTRO-NAUT?
FWOP
JUST LIKE I PLAN TO GO ON WEARING SHORTS FOR MY WHOLE LIFE.
...

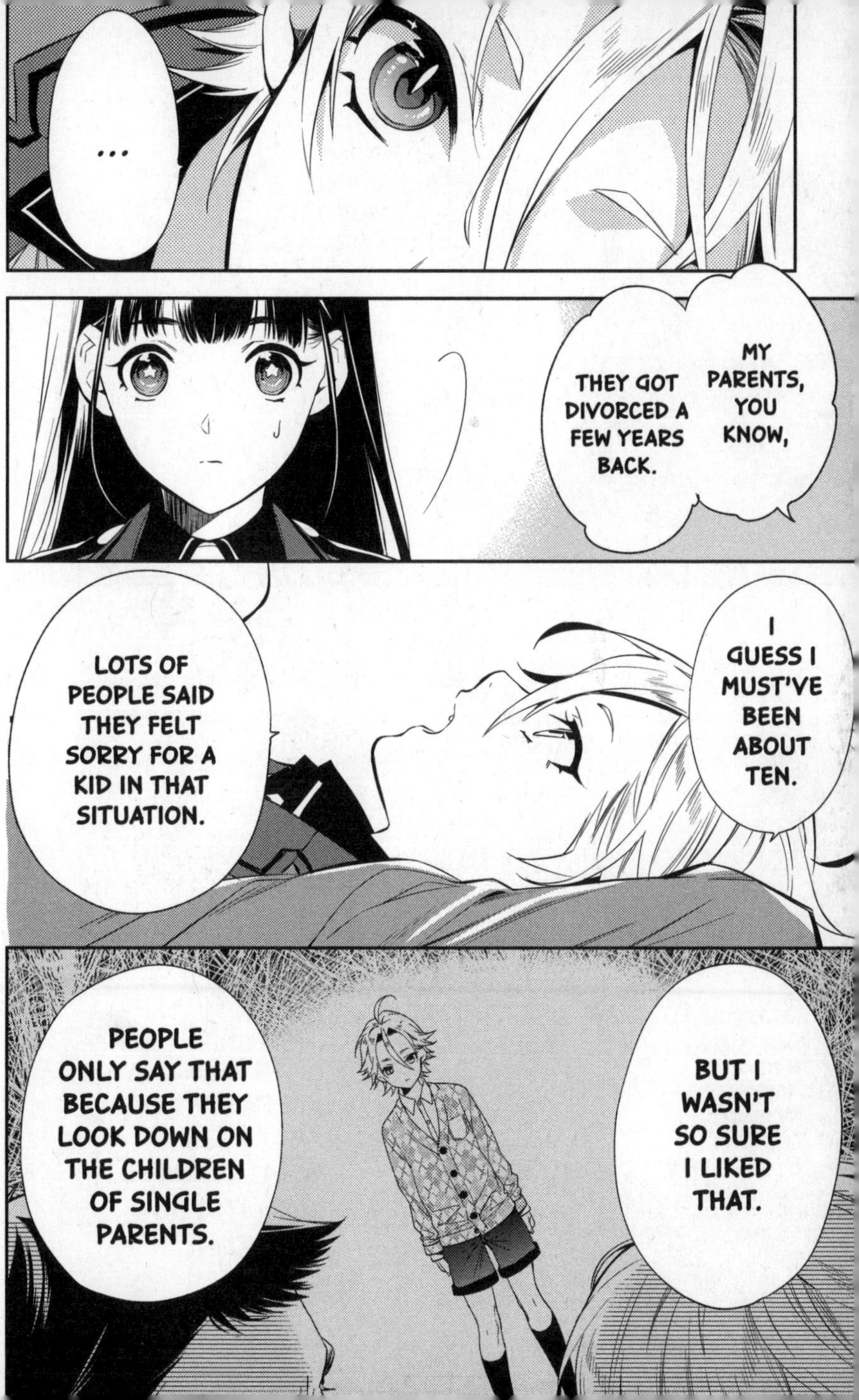
...
MY PARENTS, YOU KNOW,
THEY GOT DIVORCED A FEW YEARS BACK.
I GUESS I MUST'VE BEEN ABOUT TEN.
LOTS OF PEOPLE SAID THEY FELT SORRY FOR A KID IN THAT SITUATION.
BUT I WASN'T SO SURE I LIKED THAT.
PEOPLE ONLY SAY THAT BECAUSE THEY LOOK DOWN ON THE CHILDREN OF SINGLE PARENTS.

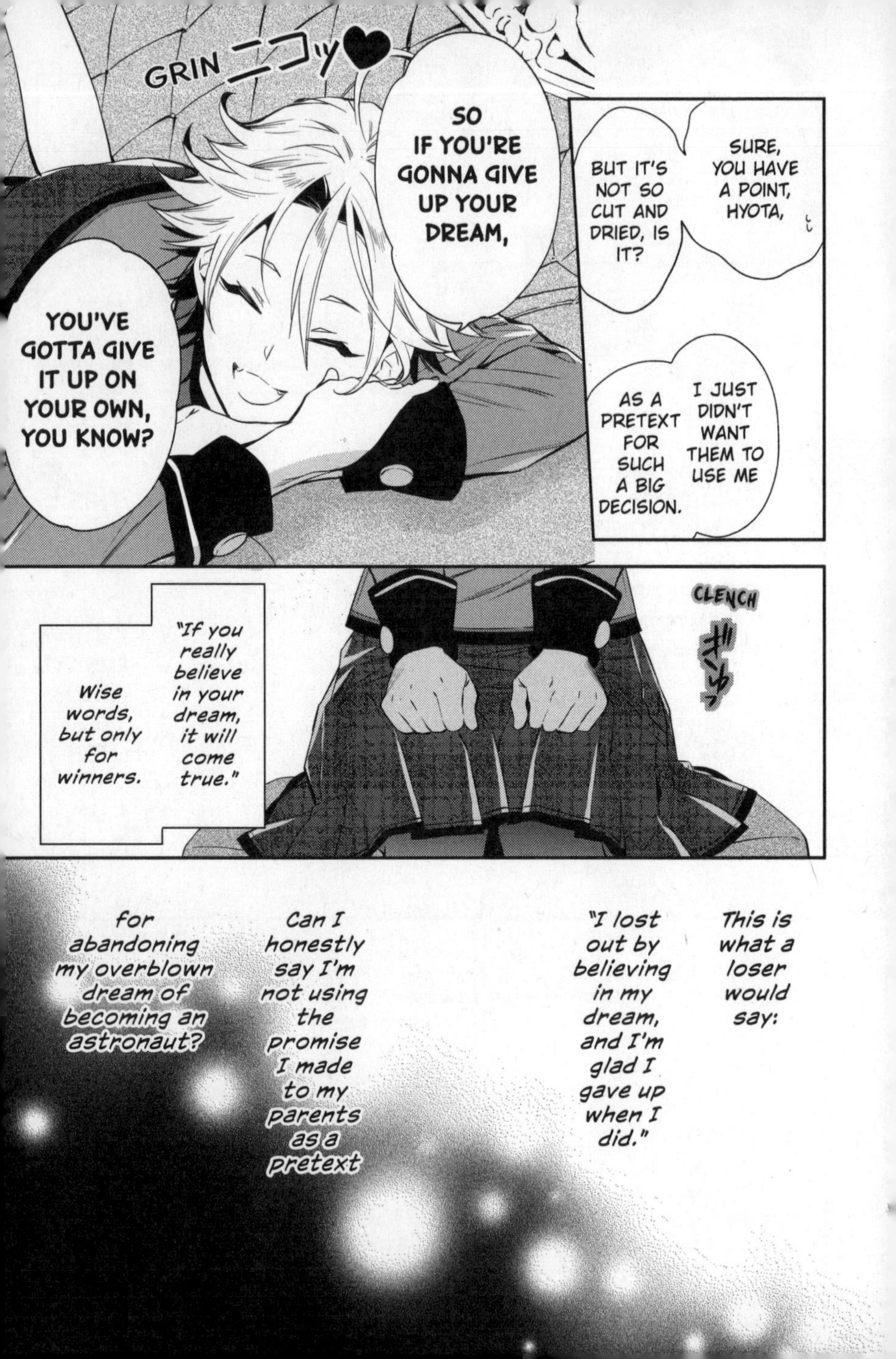
GRIN ニコッ♥
SO IF YOU'RE GONNA GIVE UP YOUR DREAM,
YOU'VE GOTTA GIVE IT UP ON YOUR OWN, YOU KNOW?
SURE, YOU HAVE A POINT, HYOTA,
BUT IT'S NOT SO CUT AND DRIED, IS IT?
I JUST DIDN'T WANT THEM TO USE ME
AS A PRETEXT FOR SUCH A BIG DECISION.
CLENCH ギュッ
"If you really believe in your dream, it will come true."
Wise words, but only for winners.
This is what a loser would say:
"I lost out by believing in my dream, and I'm glad I gave up when I did."
Can I honestly say I'm not using the promise I made to my parents as a pretext
for abandoning my overblown dream of becoming an astronaut?

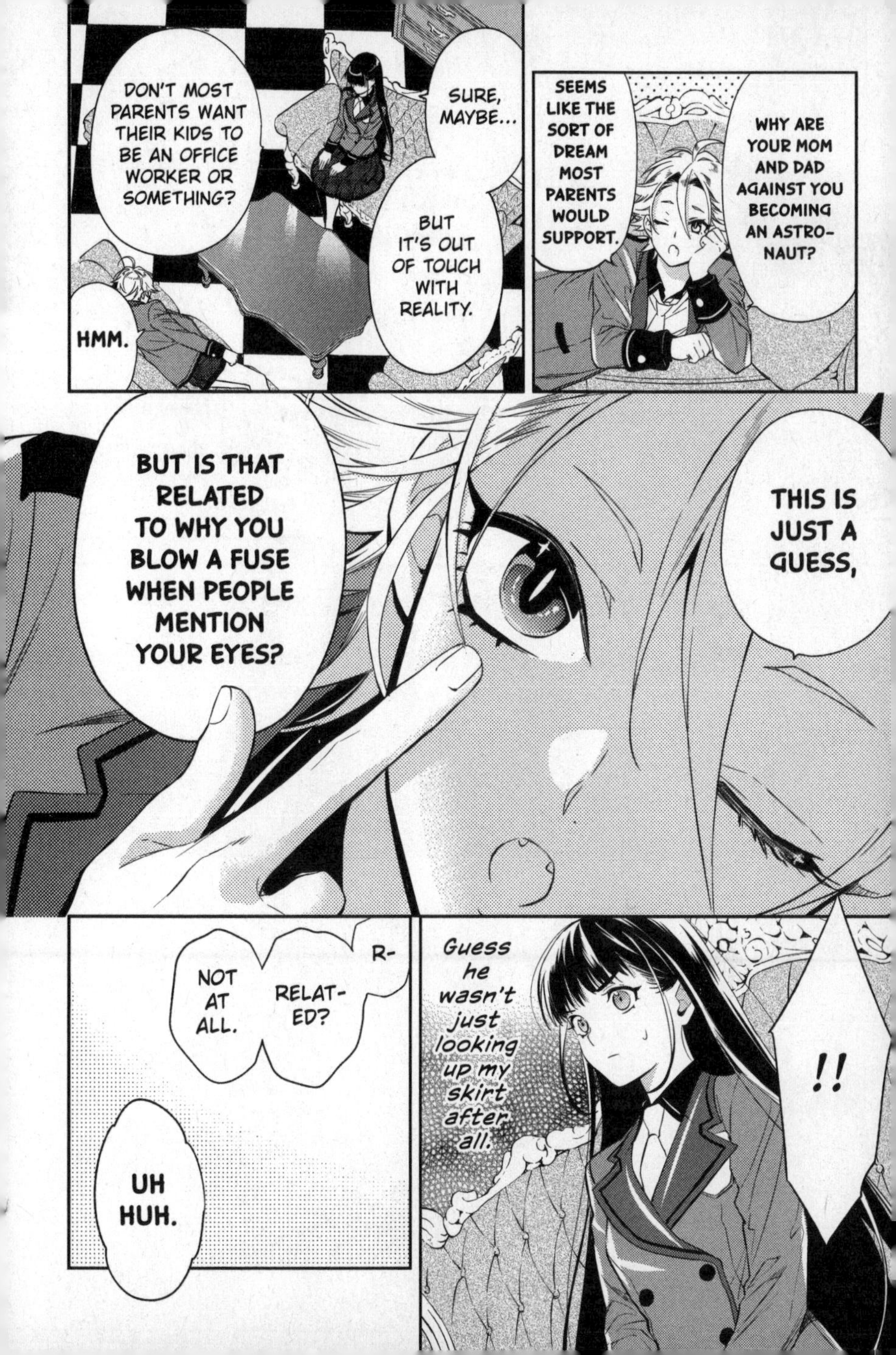
WHY ARE YOUR MOM AND DAD AGAINST YOU BECOMING AN ASTRO-NAUT?
SEEMS LIKE THE SORT OF DREAM MOST PARENTS WOULD SUPPORT.
SURE, MAYBE...
BUT IT'S OUT OF TOUCH WITH REALITY.
DON'T MOST PARENTS WANT THEIR KIDS TO BE AN OFFICE WORKER OR SOMETHING?
HMM.
THIS IS JUST A GUESS,
BUT IS THAT RELATED TO WHY YOU BLOW A FUSE WHEN PEOPLE MENTION YOUR EYES?
!!
Guess he wasn't just looking up my skirt after all.
R-
RELAT-ED?
NOT AT ALL.
UH HUH.

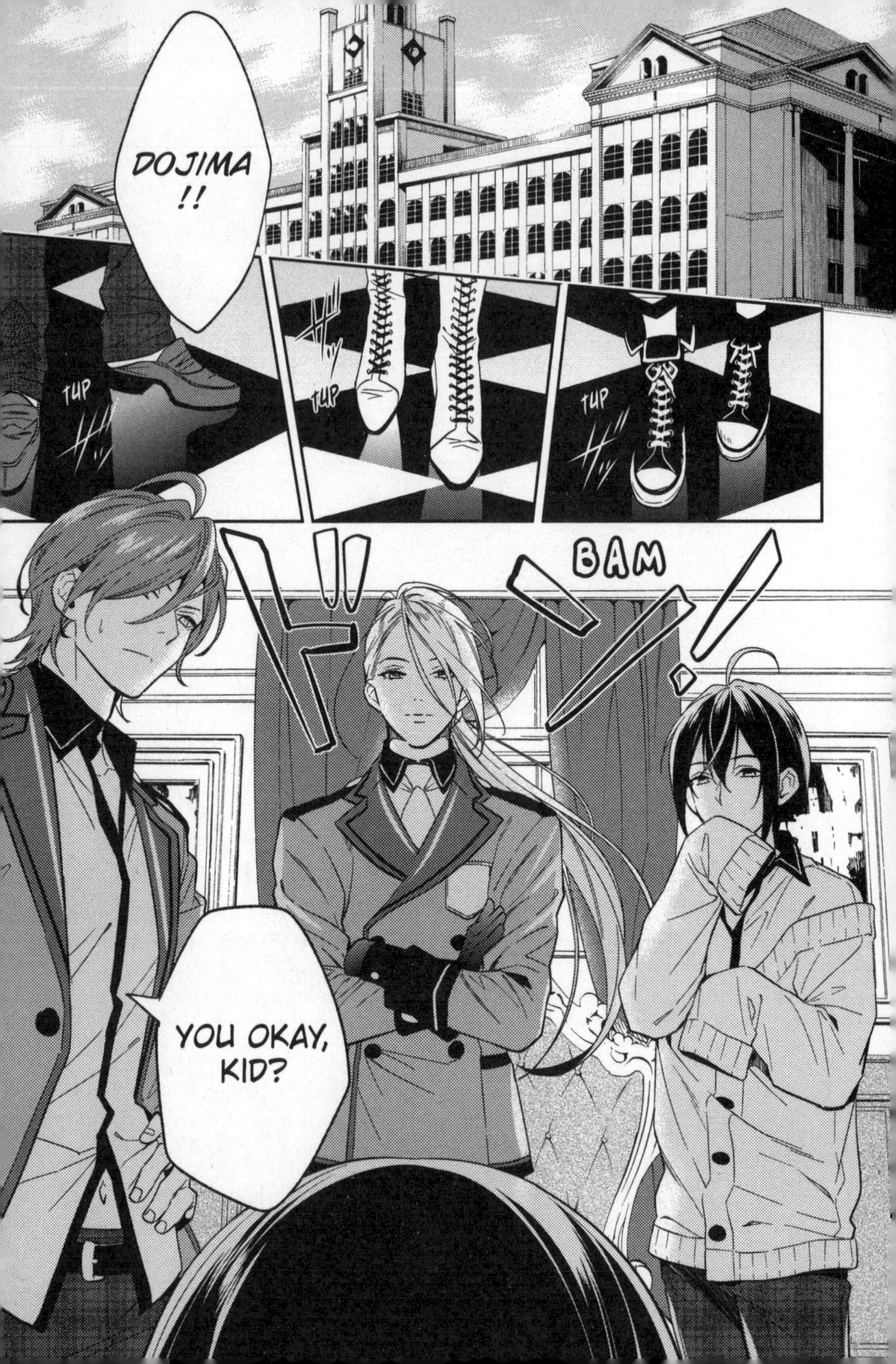
DOJIMA !!
TUP
TUP
TUP
BAM
YOU OKAY, KID?

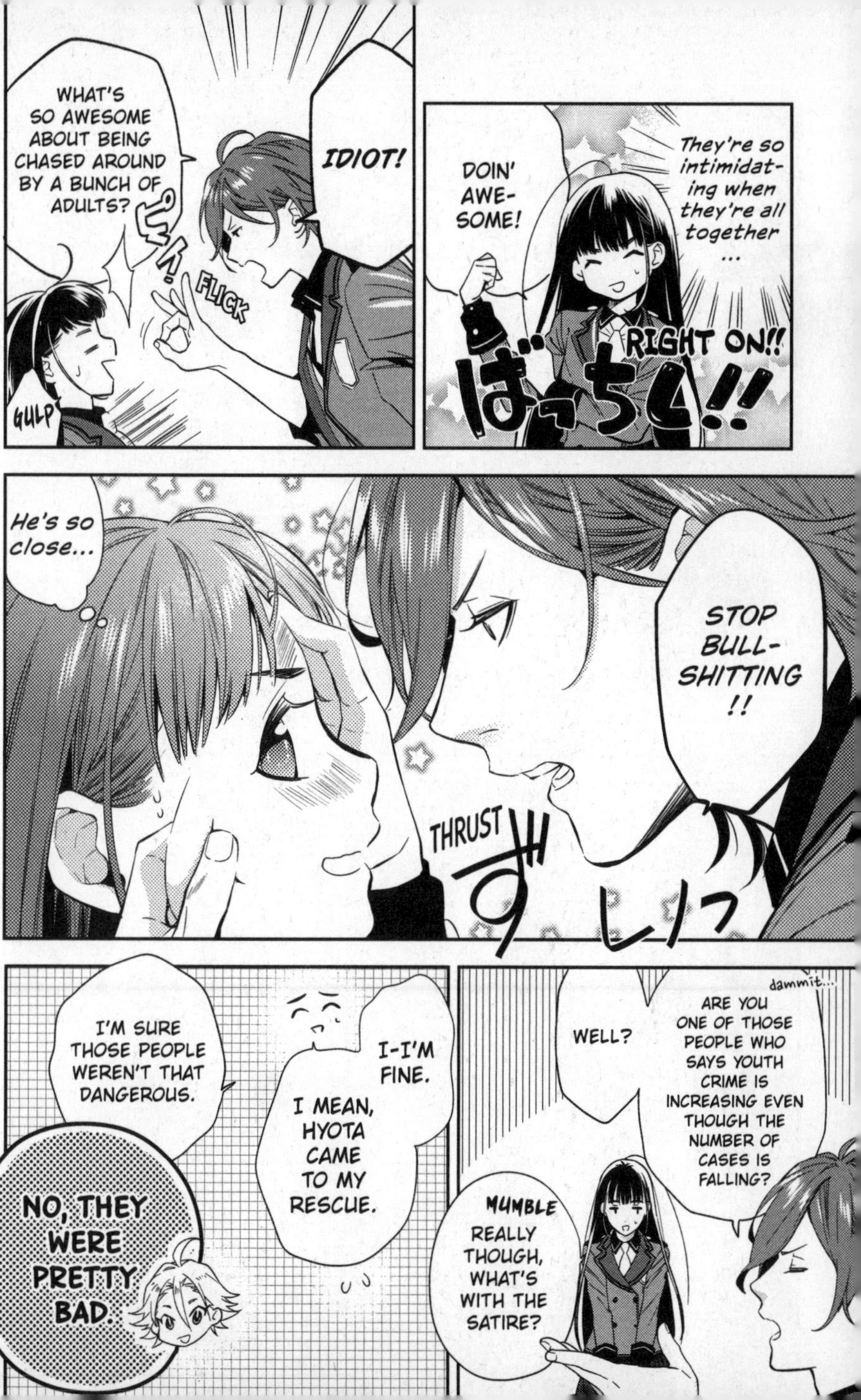
They're so intimidating when they're all together ...
DOIN' AWESOME!
RIGHT ON!!
ばっちし!!
IDIOT!
WHAT'S SO AWESOME ABOUT BEING CHASED AROUND BY A BUNCH OF ADULTS?
FLICK
GULP
STOP BULLSHITTING !!
THRUST
ずいっ
He's so close...
dammit...
ARE YOU ONE OF THOSE PEOPLE WHO SAYS YOUTH CRIME IS INCREASING EVEN THOUGH THE NUMBER OF CASES IS FALLING?
WELL?
MUMBLE
REALLY THOUGH, WHAT'S WITH THE SATIRE?
I-I'M FINE.
I MEAN, HYOTA CAME TO MY RESCUE.
I'M SURE THOSE PEOPLE WEREN'T THAT DANGEROUS.
NO, THEY WERE PRETTY BAD.

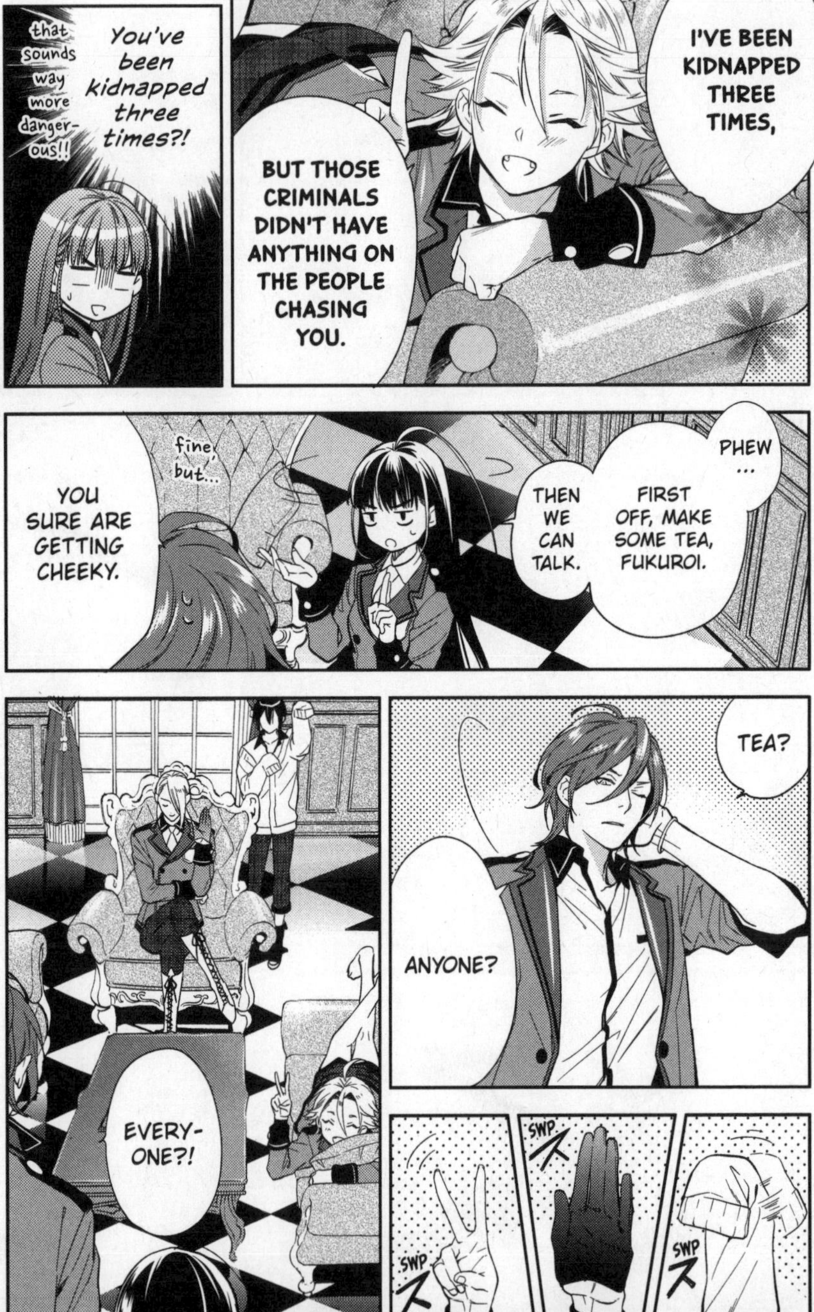
I'VE BEEN KIDNAPPED THREE TIMES,
BUT THOSE CRIMINALS DIDN'T HAVE ANYTHING ON THE PEOPLE CHASING YOU.
You've been kidnapped three times?!
that sounds way more danger-ous!!
PHEW ...
FIRST OFF, MAKE SOME TEA, FUKUROI.
THEN WE CAN TALK.
fine, but...
YOU SURE ARE GETTING CHEEKY.
TEA?
ANYONE?
SWP
SWP
SWP
EVERY-ONE?!

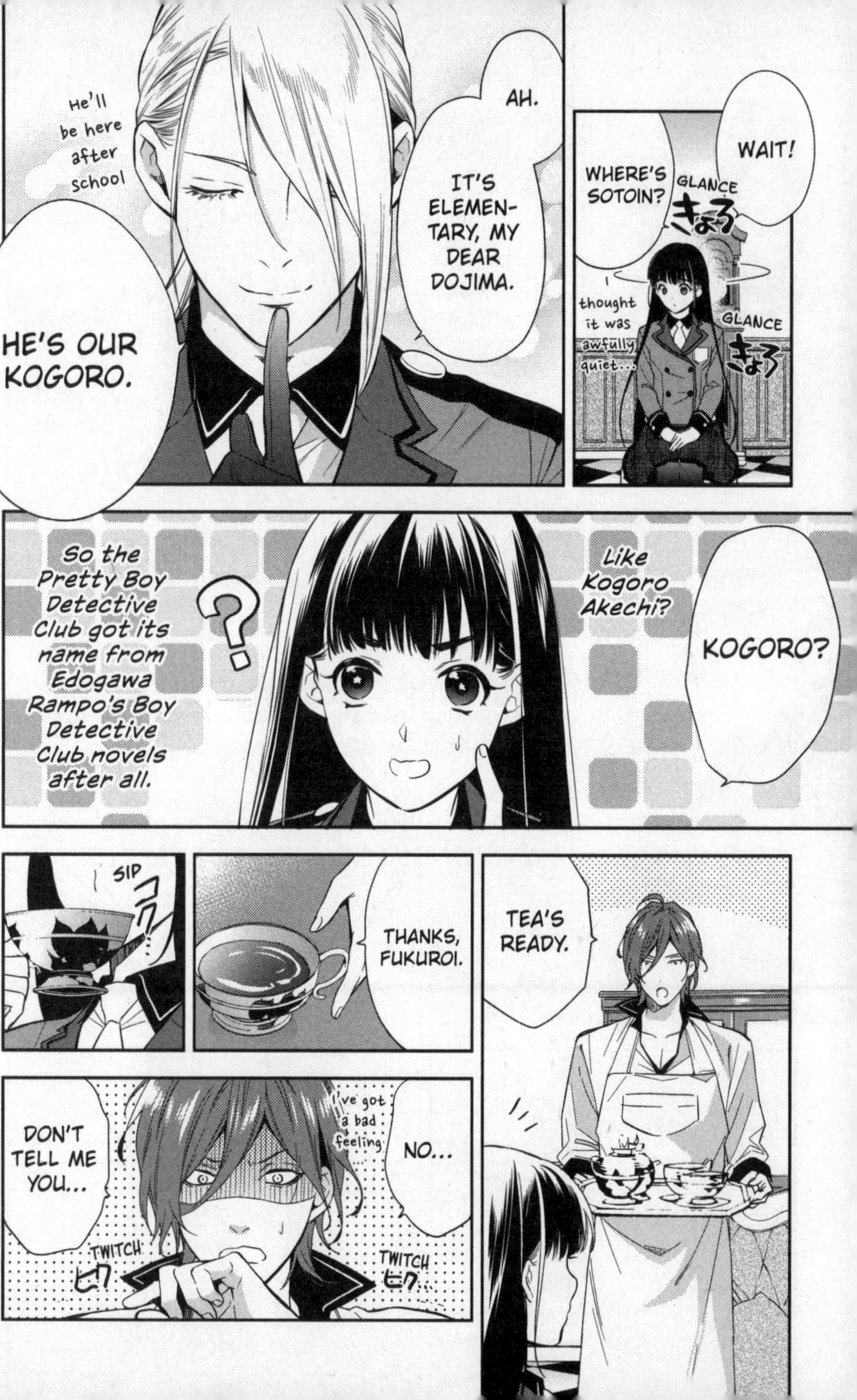
WAIT!
WHERE'S SOTOIN?
GLANCE
きょろ
I thought it was awfully quiet...
GLANCE
きょろ
AH.
IT'S ELEMENTARY, MY DEAR DOJIMA.
He'll be here after school
HE'S OUR KOGORO.
KOGORO?
Like Kogoro Akechi?
So the Pretty Boy Detective Club got its name from Edogawa Rampo's Boy Detective Club novels after all.
TEA'S READY.
THANKS, FUKUROI.
SIP
コク
NO...
I've got a bad feeling
DON'T TELL ME YOU...
TWITCH
ピク
TWITCH
ピク

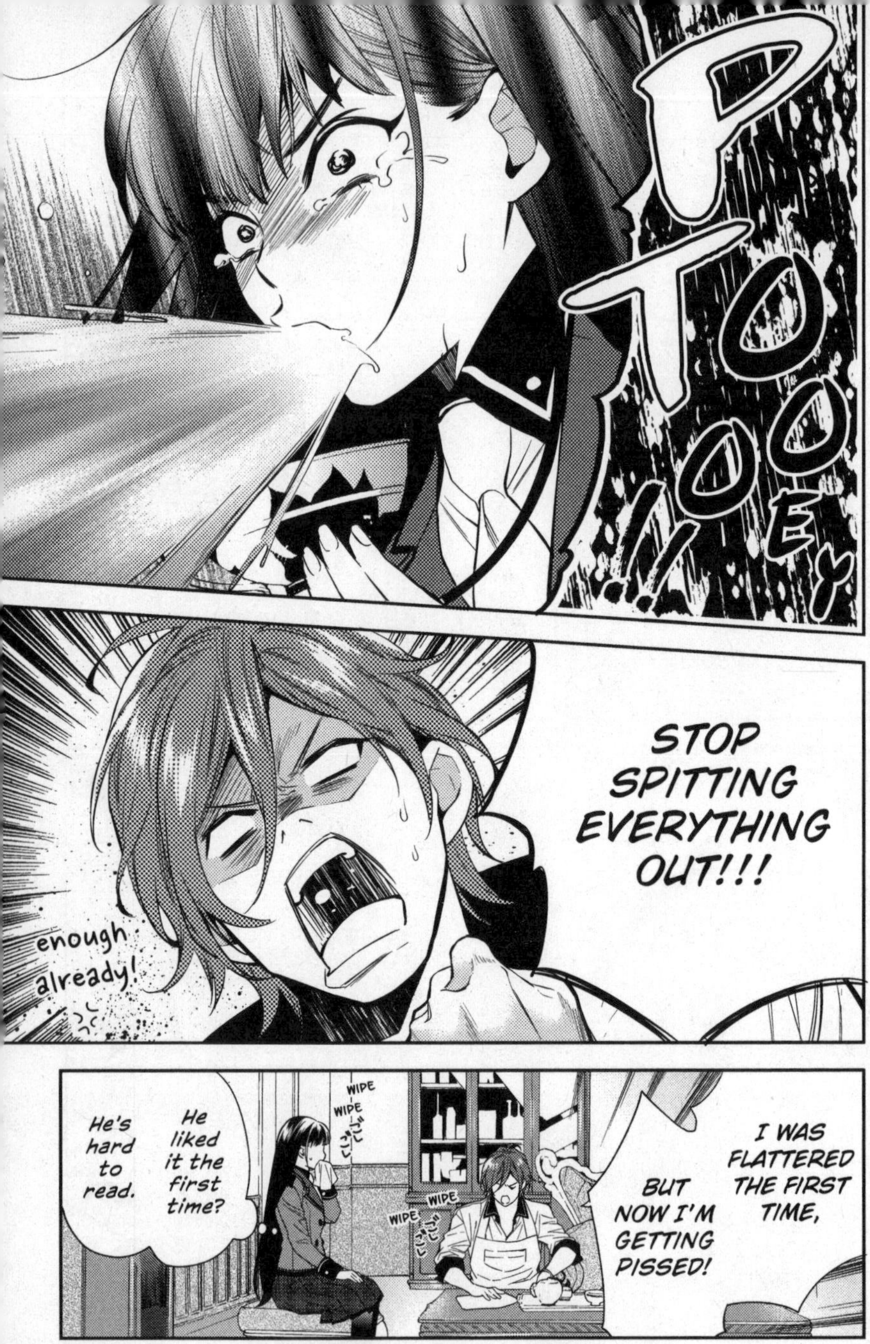
PTOOEY!!!
STOP SPITTING EVERYTHING OUT!!!
enough already!
I WAS FLATTERED THE FIRST TIME,
BUT NOW I'M GETTING PISSED!
WIPE WIPE
WIPE WIPE
He liked it the first time?
He's hard to read.

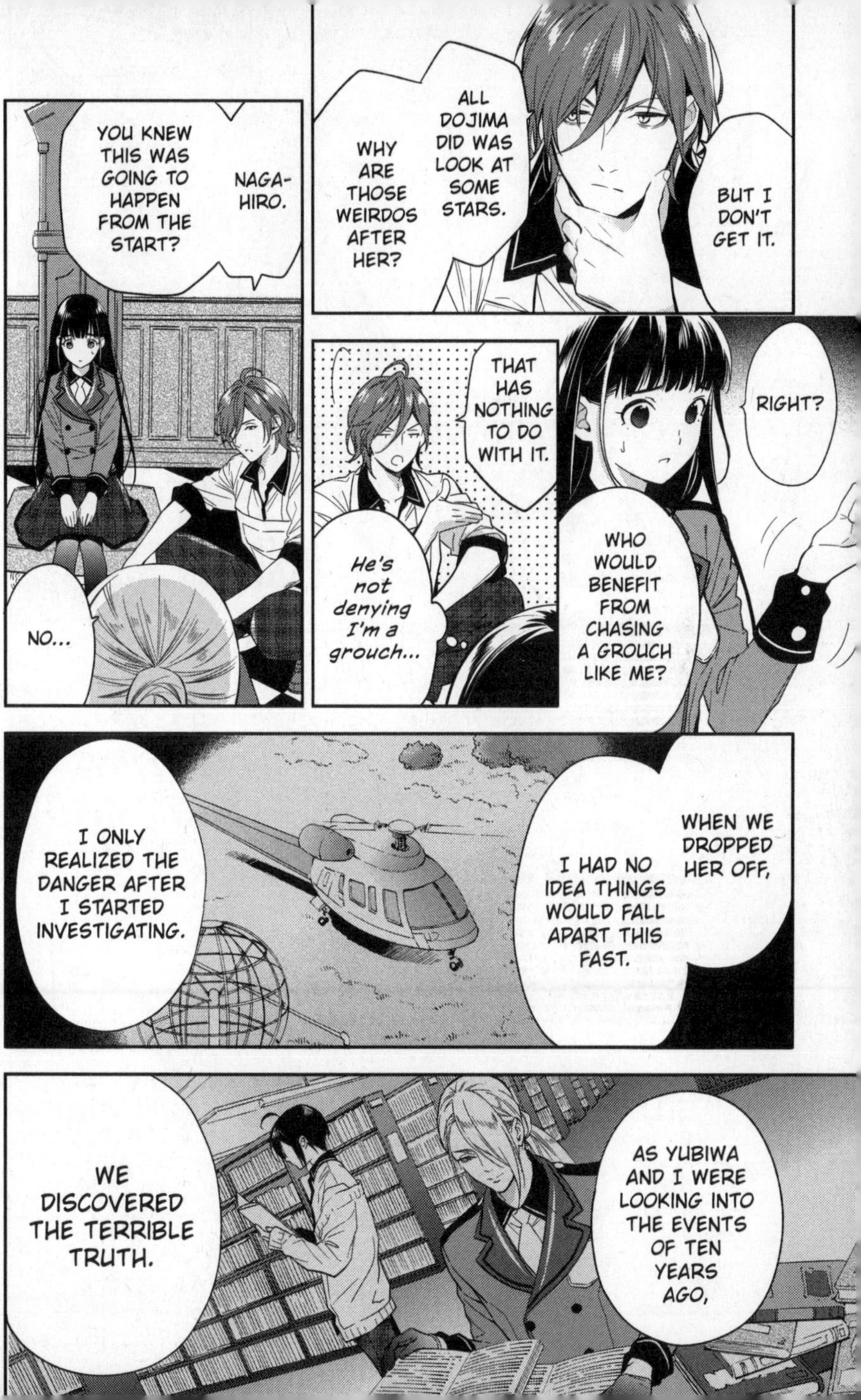
BUT I DON'T GET IT.
ALL DOJIMA DID WAS LOOK AT SOME STARS.
WHY ARE THOSE WEIRDOS AFTER HER?
RIGHT?
WHO WOULD BENEFIT FROM CHASING A GROUCH LIKE ME?
THAT HAS NOTHING TO DO WITH IT.
He's not denying I'm a grouch...
NAGA-HIRO.
YOU KNEW THIS WAS GOING TO HAPPEN FROM THE START?
NO...
WHEN WE DROPPED HER OFF,
I HAD NO IDEA THINGS WOULD FALL APART THIS FAST.
I ONLY REALIZED THE DANGER AFTER I STARTED INVESTIGATING.
AS YUBIWA AND I WERE LOOKING INTO THE EVENTS OF TEN YEARS AGO,
WE DISCOVERED THE TERRIBLE TRUTH.

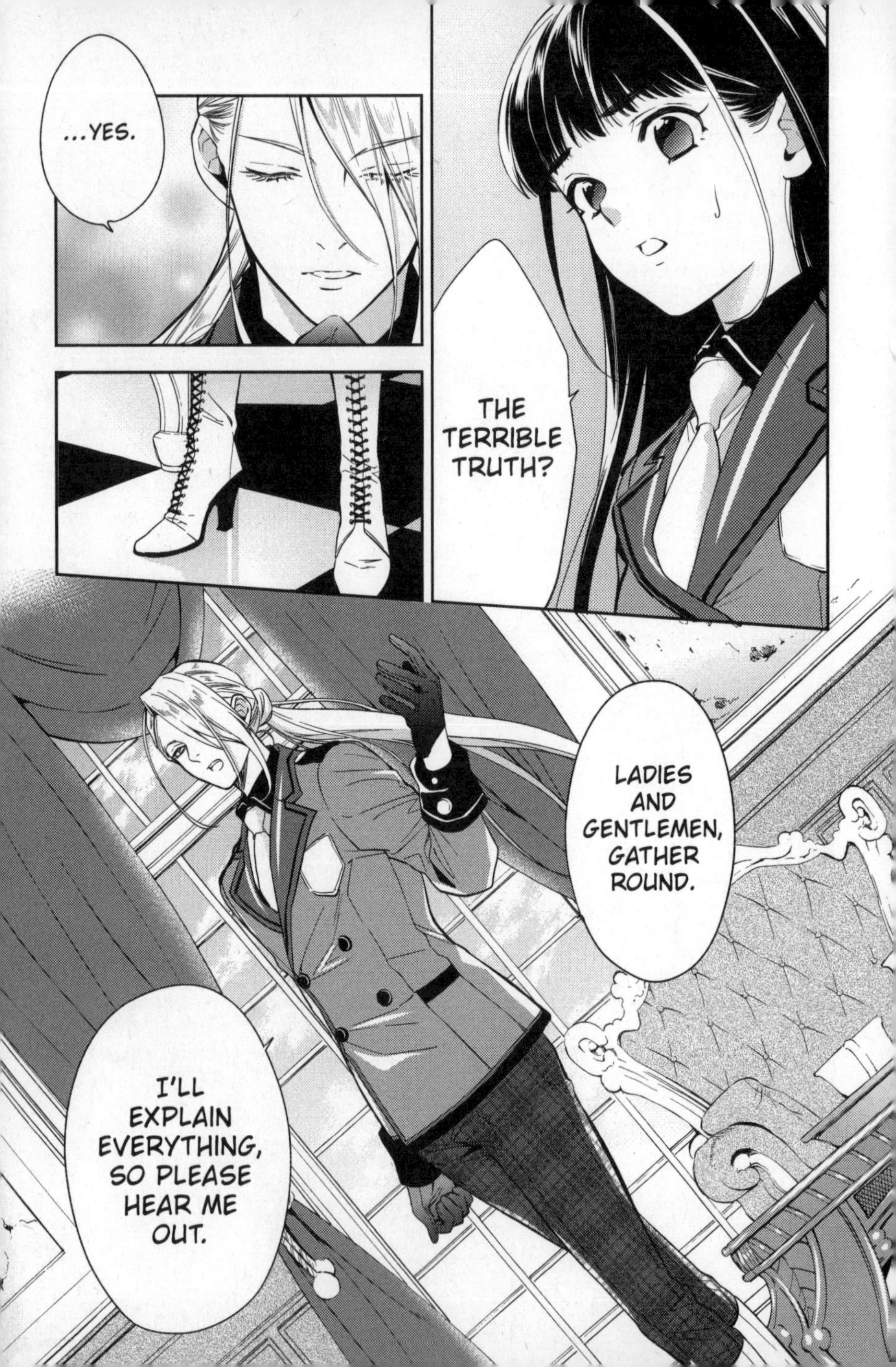
THE TERRIBLE TRUTH?
...YES.
LADIES AND GENTLEMEN, GATHER ROUND.
I'LL EXPLAIN EVERYTHING, SO PLEASE HEAR ME OUT.

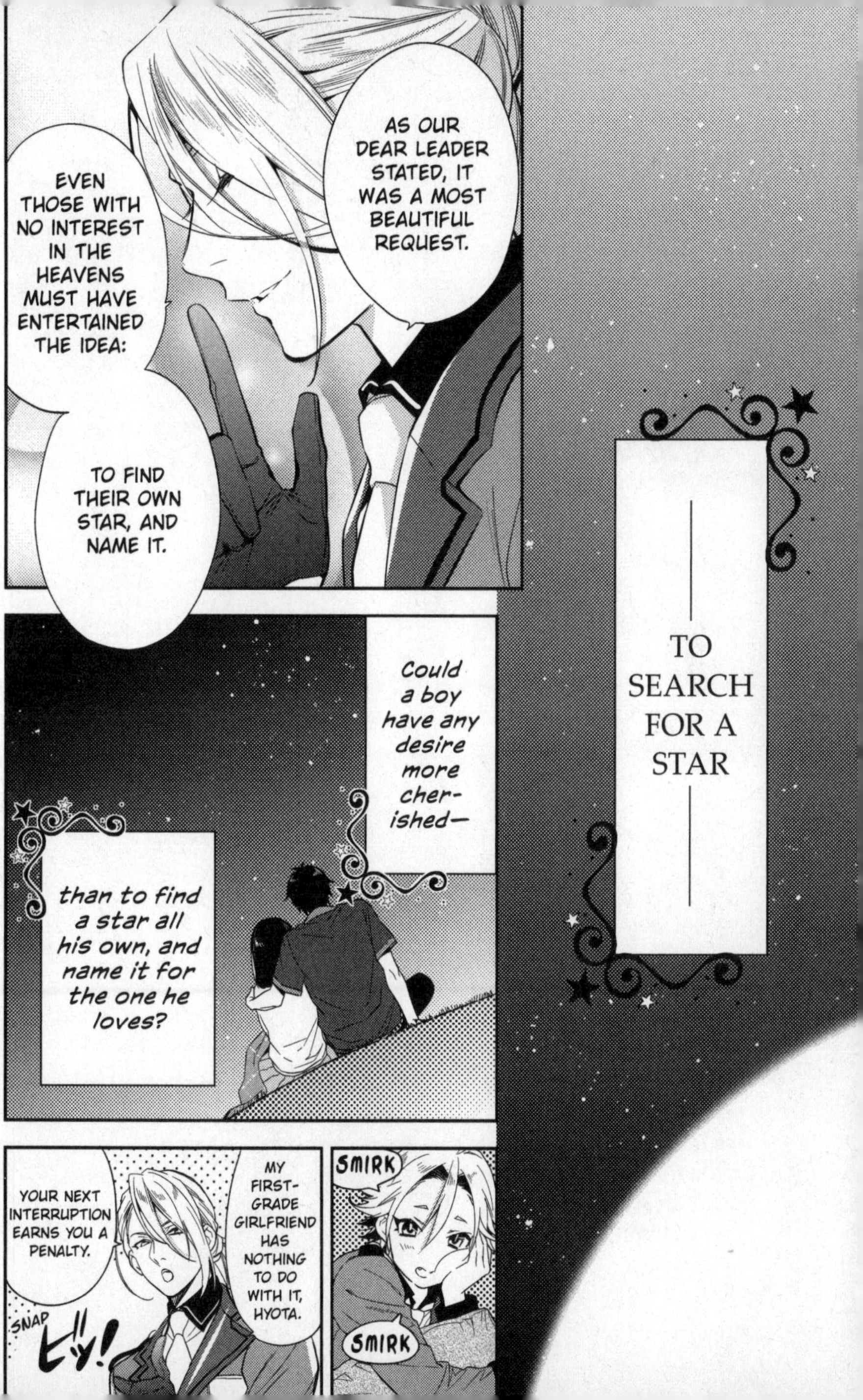
TO SEARCH FOR A STAR
AS OUR DEAR LEADER STATED, IT WAS A MOST BEAUTIFUL REQUEST.
EVEN THOSE WITH NO INTEREST IN THE HEAVENS MUST HAVE ENTERTAINED THE IDEA:
TO FIND THEIR OWN STAR, AND NAME IT.
Could a boy have any desire more cher-ished—
than to find a star all his own, and name it for the one he loves?
SMIRK
SMIRK
MY FIRST-GRADE GIRLFRIEND HAS NOTHING TO DO WITH IT, HYOTA.
YOUR NEXT INTERRUPTION EARNS YOU A PENALTY.
SNAP
ピッ!

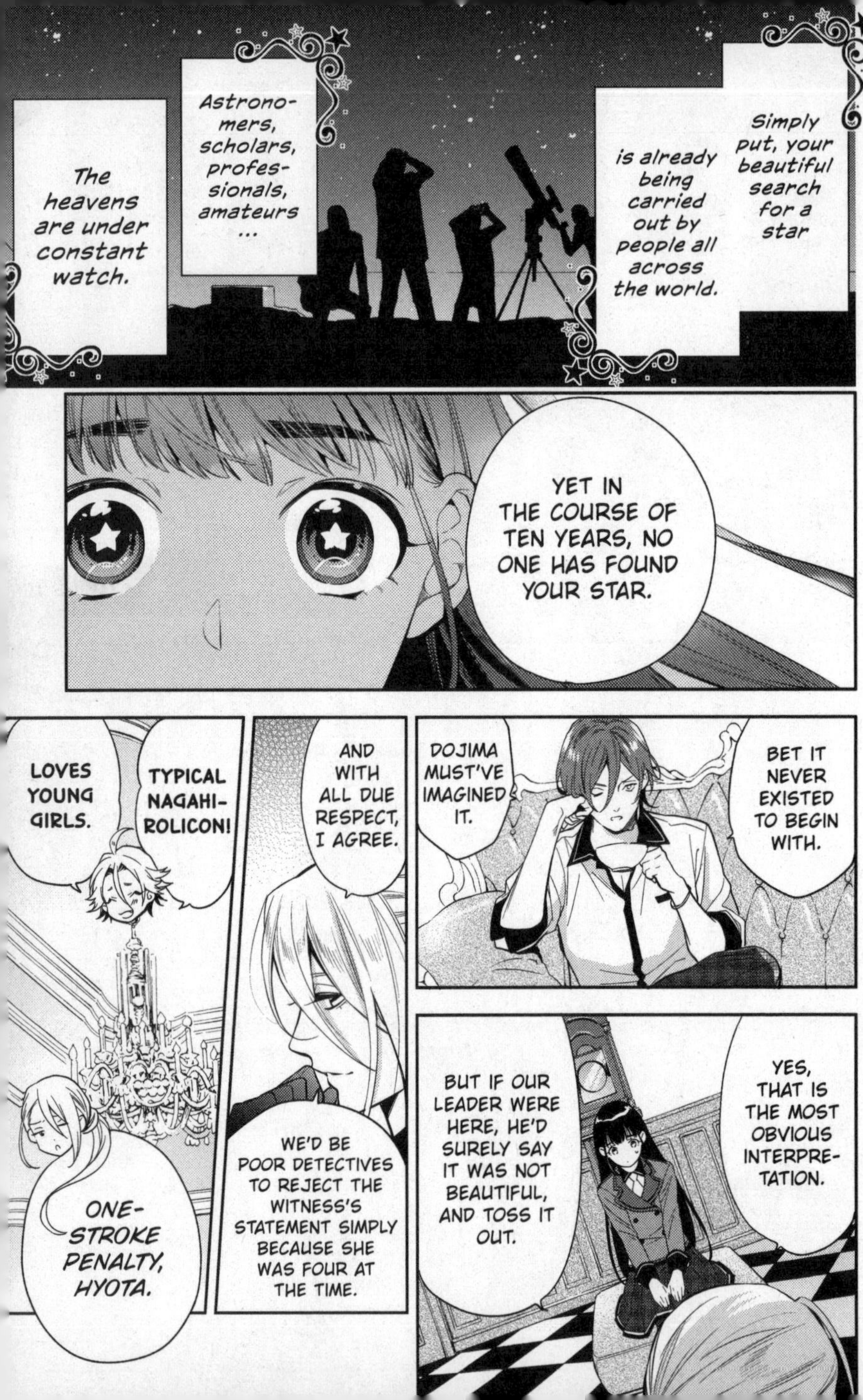
Simply put, your beautiful search for a star
is already being carried out by people all across the world.
Astronomers, scholars, professionals, amateurs ...
The heavens are under constant watch.
YET IN THE COURSE OF TEN YEARS, NO ONE HAS FOUND YOUR STAR.
BET IT NEVER EXISTED TO BEGIN WITH.
DOJIMA MUST'VE IMAGINED IT.
YES, THAT IS THE MOST OBVIOUS INTERPRETATION.
BUT IF OUR LEADER WERE HERE, HE'D SURELY SAY IT WAS NOT BEAUTIFUL, AND TOSS IT OUT.
AND WITH ALL DUE RESPECT, I AGREE.
WE'D BE POOR DETECTIVES TO REJECT THE WITNESS'S STATEMENT SIMPLY BECAUSE SHE WAS FOUR AT THE TIME.
TYPICAL NAGAHI-ROLICON!
LOVES YOUNG GIRLS.
ONE-STROKE PENALTY, HYOTA.

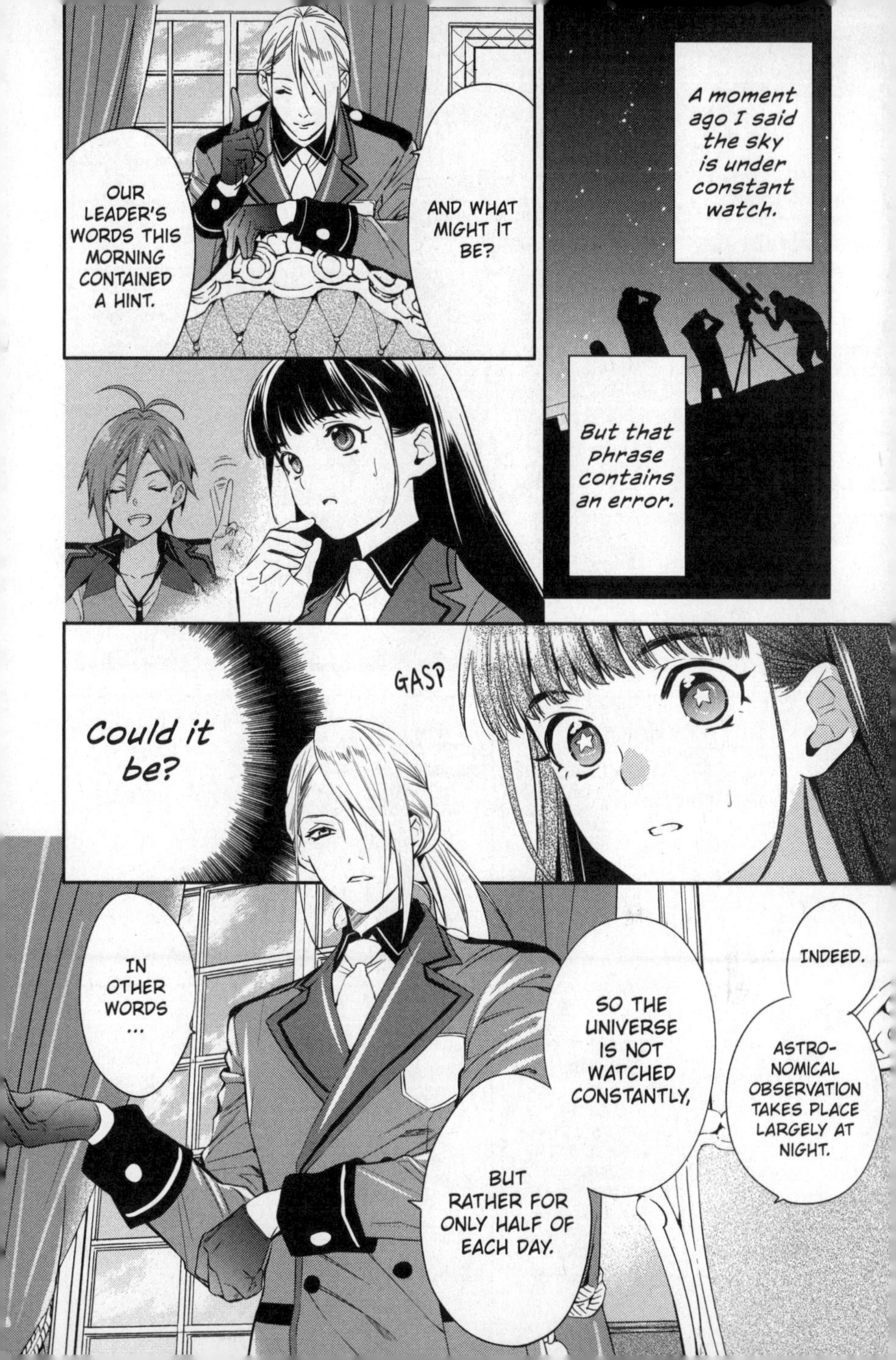

A moment ago I said the sky is under constant watch.
But that phrase contains an error.
AND WHAT MIGHT IT BE?
OUR LEADER'S WORDS THIS MORNING CONTAINED A HINT.
GASP
Could it be?
INDEED.
ASTRO-NOMICAL OBSERVATION TAKES PLACE LARGELY AT NIGHT.
SO THE UNIVERSE IS NOT WATCHED CONSTANTLY,
BUT RATHER FOR ONLY HALF OF EACH DAY.
IN OTHER WORDS ...

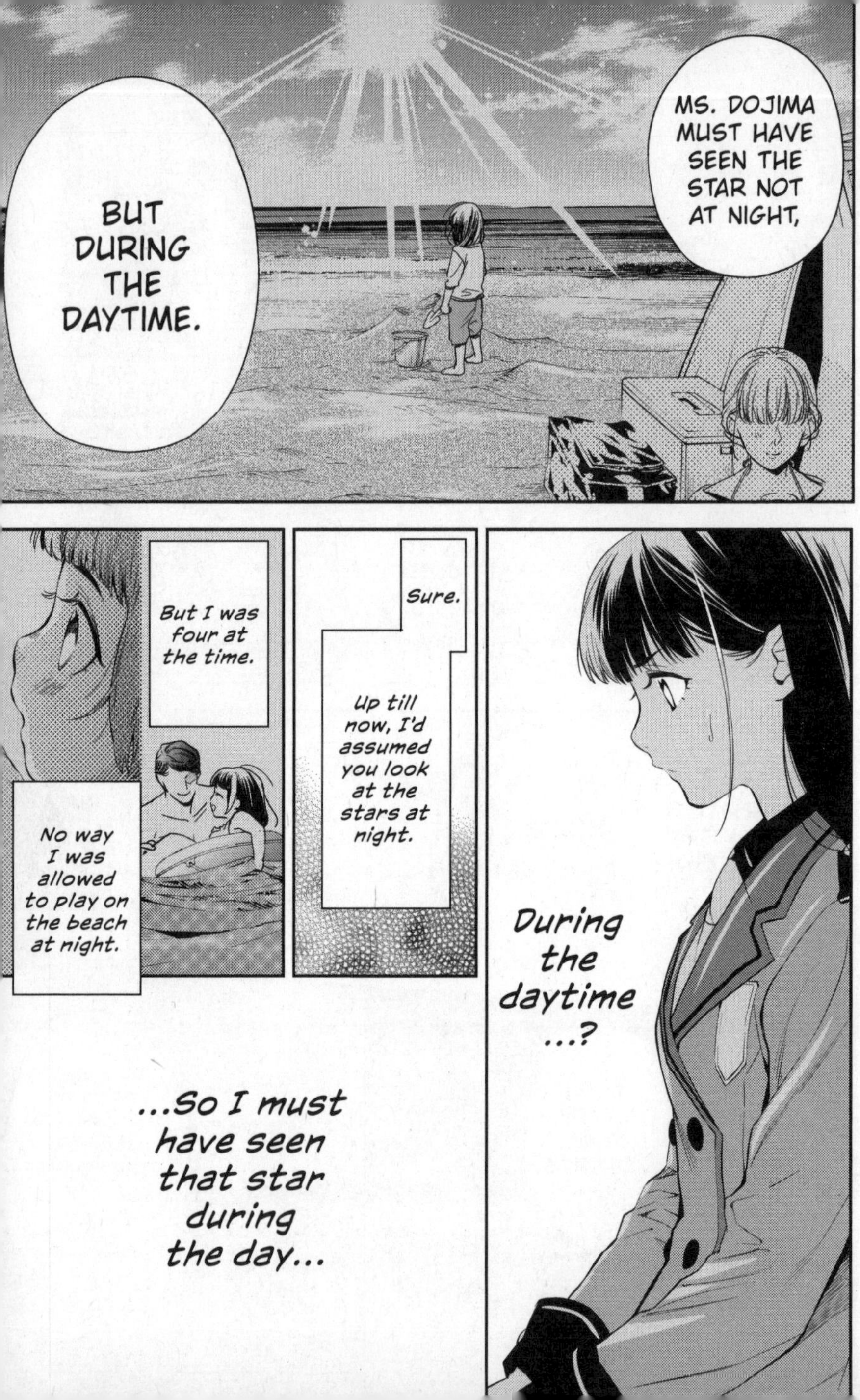
MS. DOJIMA MUST HAVE SEEN THE STAR NOT AT NIGHT,
BUT DURING THE DAYTIME.
During the daytime ...?
Sure.
Up till now, I'd assumed you look at the stars at night.
But I was four at the time.
No way I was allowed to play on the beach at night.
...So I must have seen that star during the day...

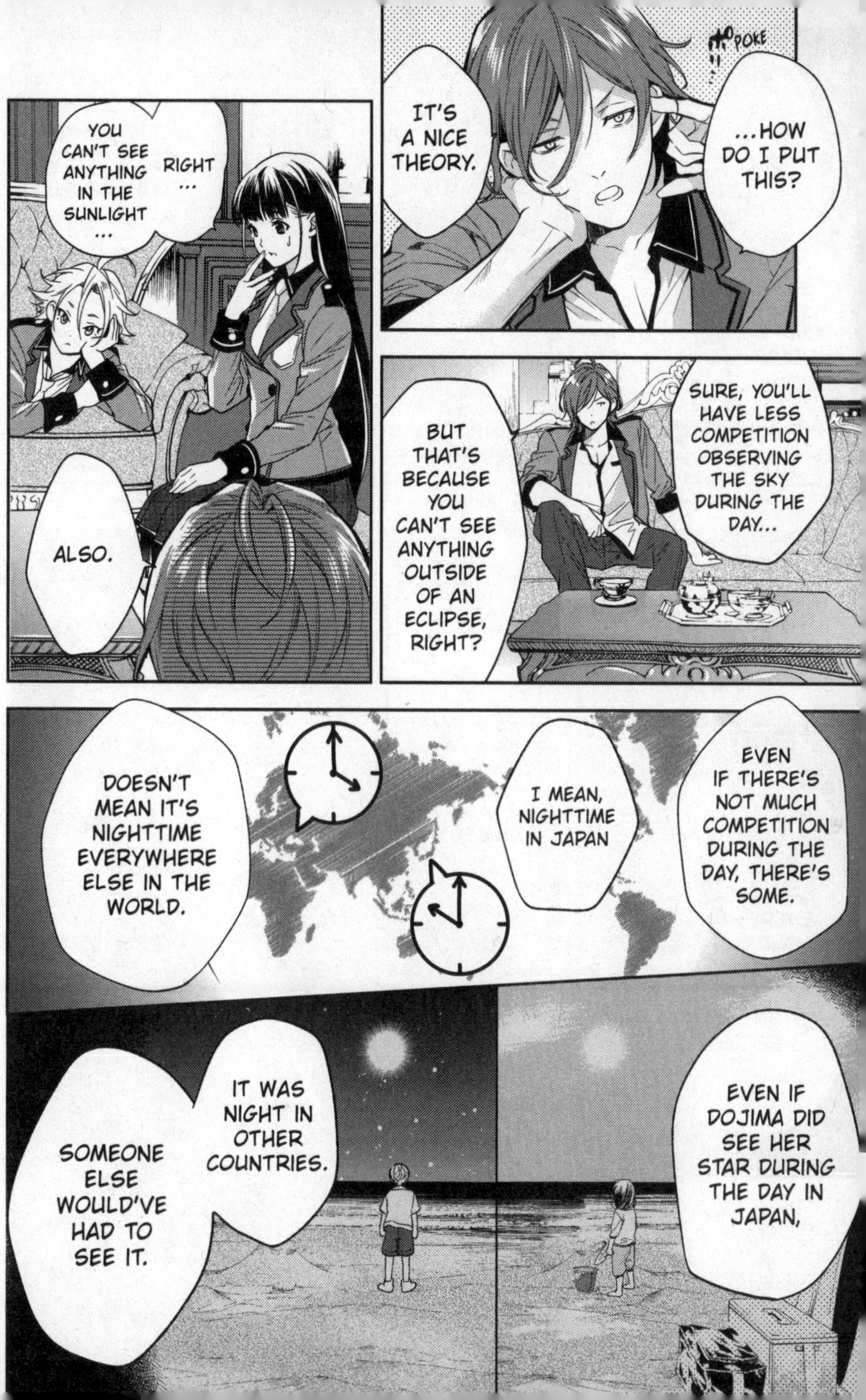
POKE
...HOW DO I PUT THIS?
IT'S A NICE THEORY.
SURE, YOU'LL HAVE LESS COMPETITION OBSERVING THE SKY DURING THE DAY...
BUT THAT'S BECAUSE YOU CAN'T SEE ANYTHING OUTSIDE OF AN ECLIPSE, RIGHT?
YOU CAN'T SEE ANYTHING IN THE SUNLIGHT ...
RIGHT ...
ALSO.
EVEN IF THERE'S NOT MUCH COMPETITION DURING THE DAY, THERE'S SOME.
I MEAN, NIGHTTIME IN JAPAN
DOESN'T MEAN IT'S NIGHTTIME EVERYWHERE ELSE IN THE WORLD.
EVEN IF DOJIMA DID SEE HER STAR DURING THE DAY IN JAPAN,
IT WAS NIGHT IN OTHER COUNTRIES.
SOMEONE ELSE WOULD'VE HAD TO SEE IT.

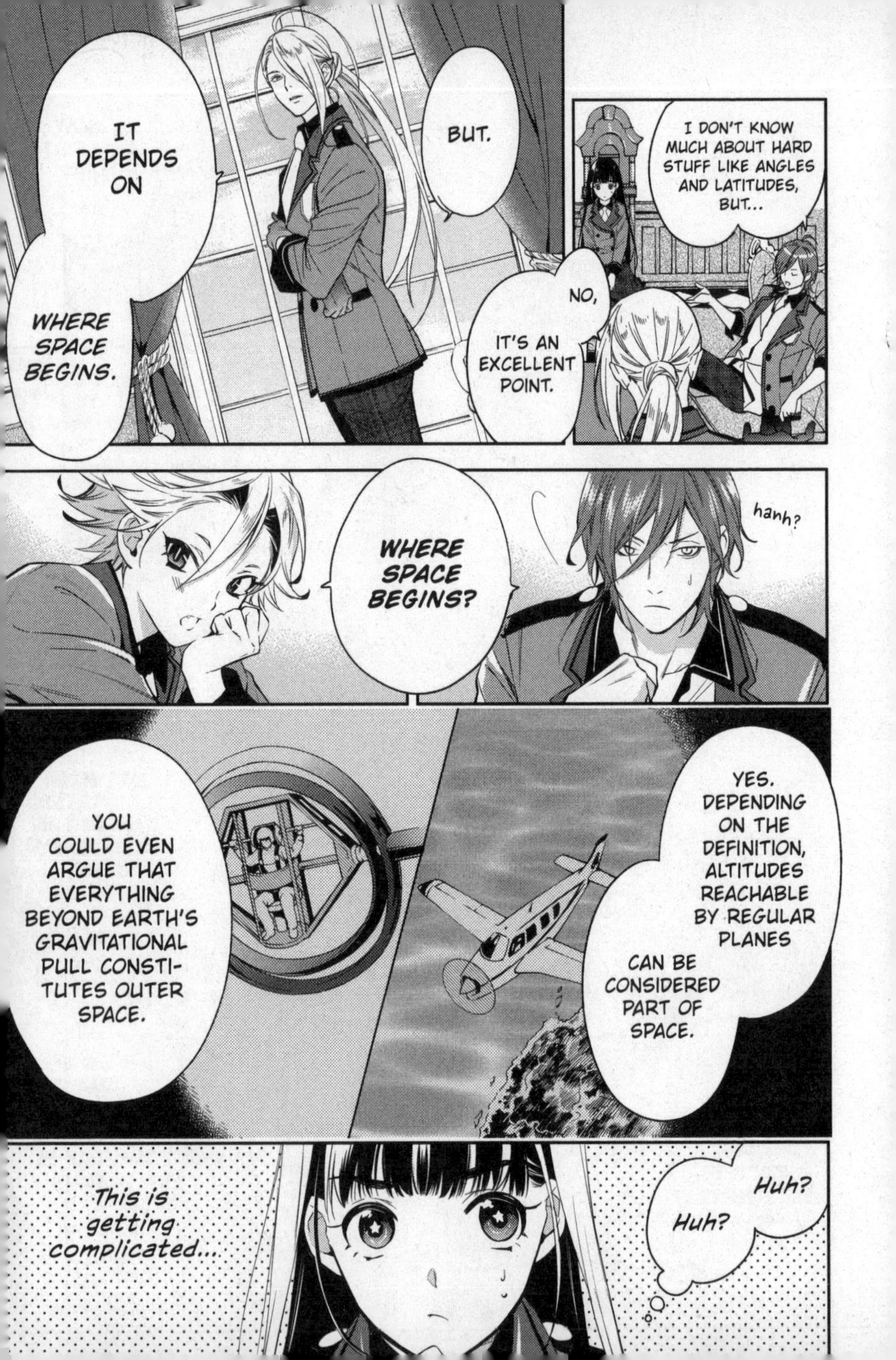
I DON'T KNOW MUCH ABOUT HARD STUFF LIKE ANGLES AND LATITUDES, BUT...
NO,
IT'S AN EXCELLENT POINT.
BUT.
IT DEPENDS ON
WHERE SPACE BEGINS.
hanh?
WHERE SPACE BEGINS?
YES. DEPENDING ON THE DEFINITION, ALTITUDES REACHABLE BY REGULAR PLANES
CAN BE CONSIDERED PART OF SPACE.
YOU COULD EVEN ARGUE THAT EVERYTHING BEYOND EARTH'S GRAVITATIONAL PULL CONSTI-TUTES OUTER SPACE.
Huh?
Huh?
This is getting complicated...

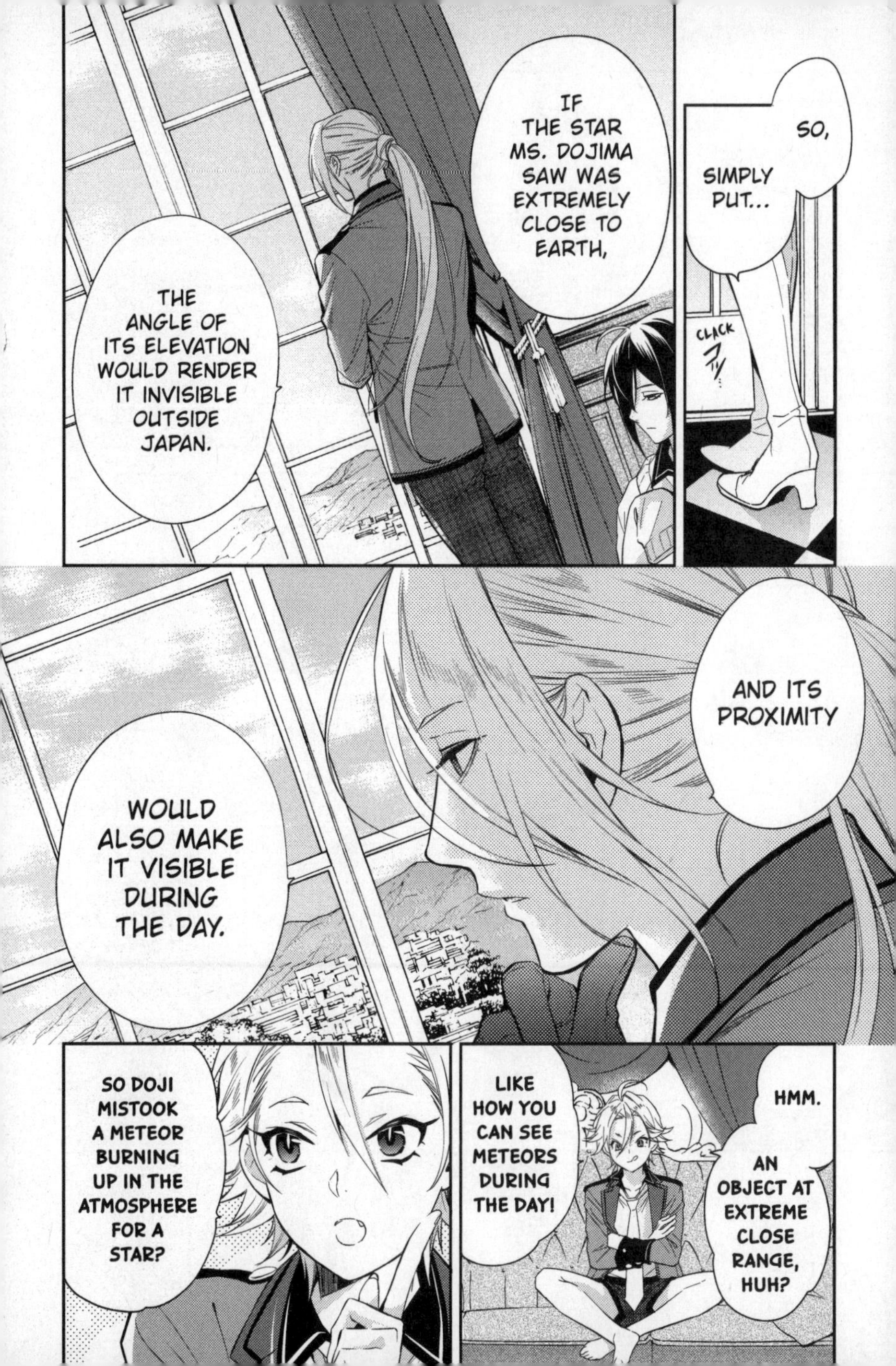

SO,
SIMPLY PUT...
CLACK
IF THE STAR MS. DOJIMA SAW WAS EXTREMELY CLOSE TO EARTH,
THE ANGLE OF ITS ELEVATION WOULD RENDER IT INVISIBLE OUTSIDE JAPAN.
AND ITS PROXIMITY
WOULD ALSO MAKE IT VISIBLE DURING THE DAY.
HMM.
AN OBJECT AT EXTREME CLOSE RANGE, HUH?
LIKE HOW YOU CAN SEE METEORS DURING THE DAY!
SO DOJI MISTOOK A METEOR BURNING UP IN THE ATMOSPHERE FOR A STAR?

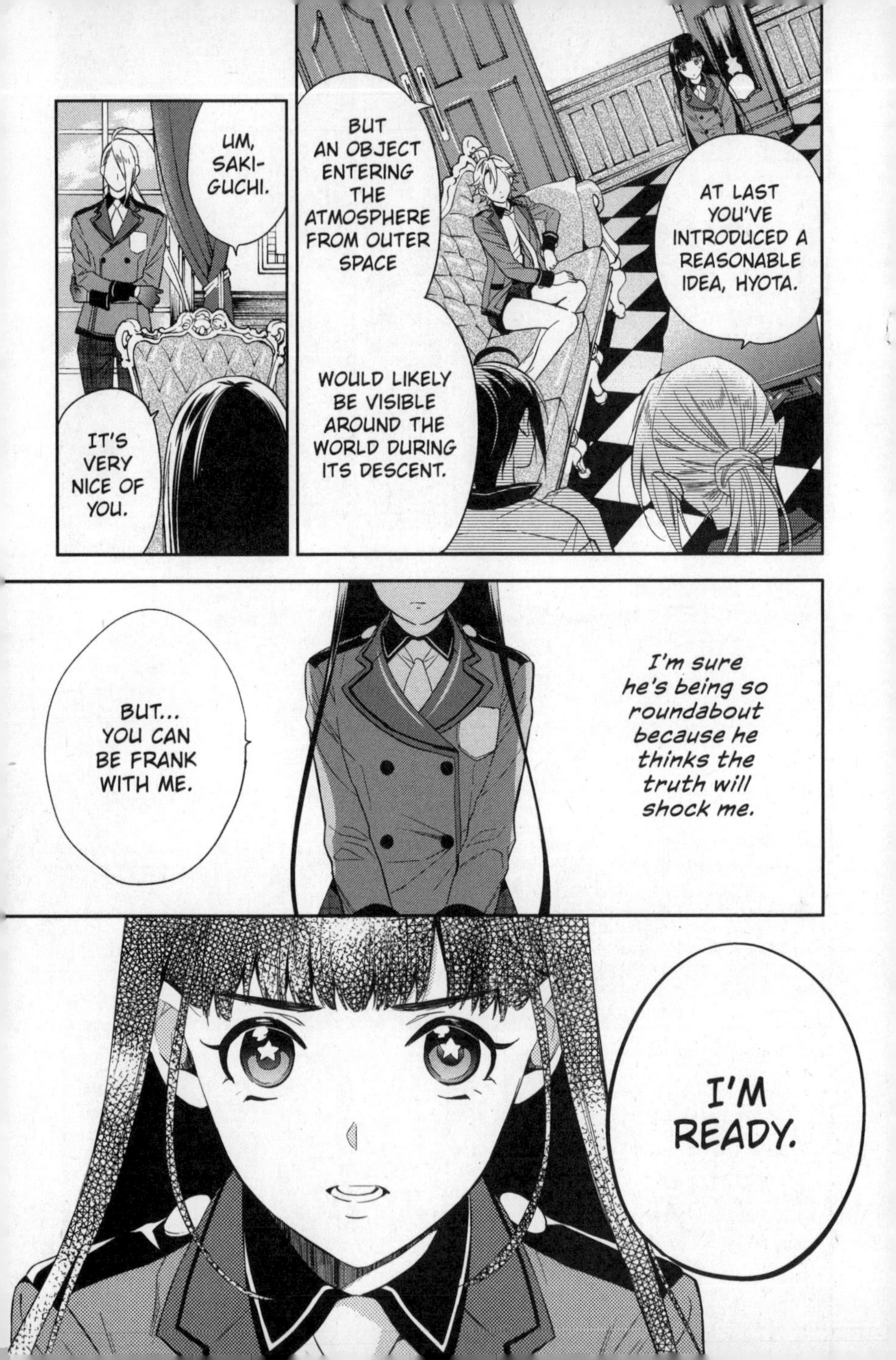
AT LAST YOU'VE INTRODUCED A REASONABLE IDEA, HYOTA.
BUT AN OBJECT ENTERING THE ATMOSPHERE FROM OUTER SPACE
WOULD LIKELY BE VISIBLE AROUND THE WORLD DURING ITS DESCENT.
UM, SAKI-GUCHI.
IT'S VERY NICE OF YOU.
I'm sure he's being so roundabout because he thinks the truth will shock me.
BUT... YOU CAN BE FRANK WITH ME.
I'M READY.

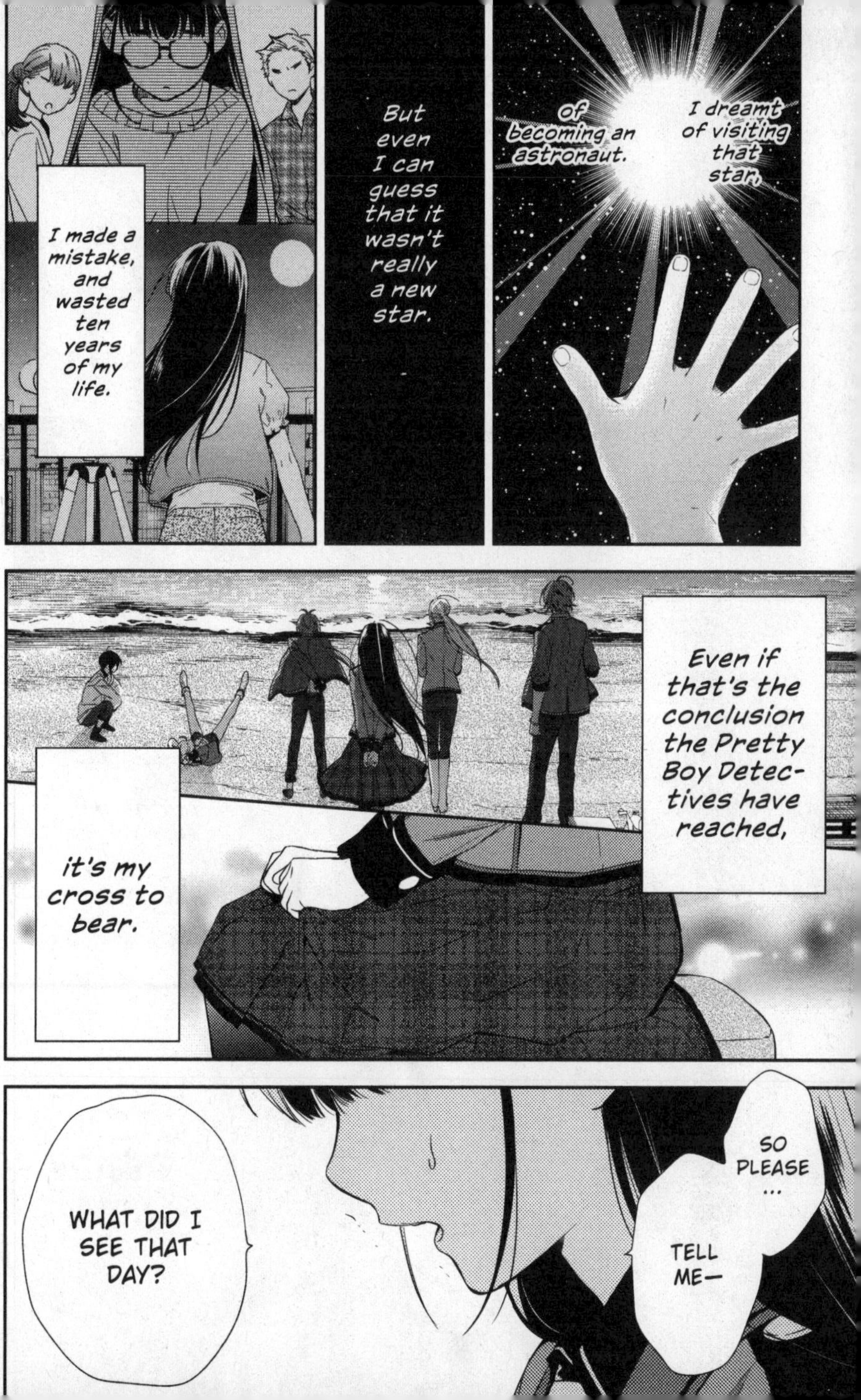
I dreamt of visiting that star,
of becoming an astronaut.
But even I can guess that it wasn't really a new star.
I made a mistake, and wasted ten years of my life.
Even if that's the conclusion the Pretty Boy Detectives have reached,
it's my cross to bear.
SO PLEASE ...
TELL ME—
WHAT DID I SEE THAT DAY?

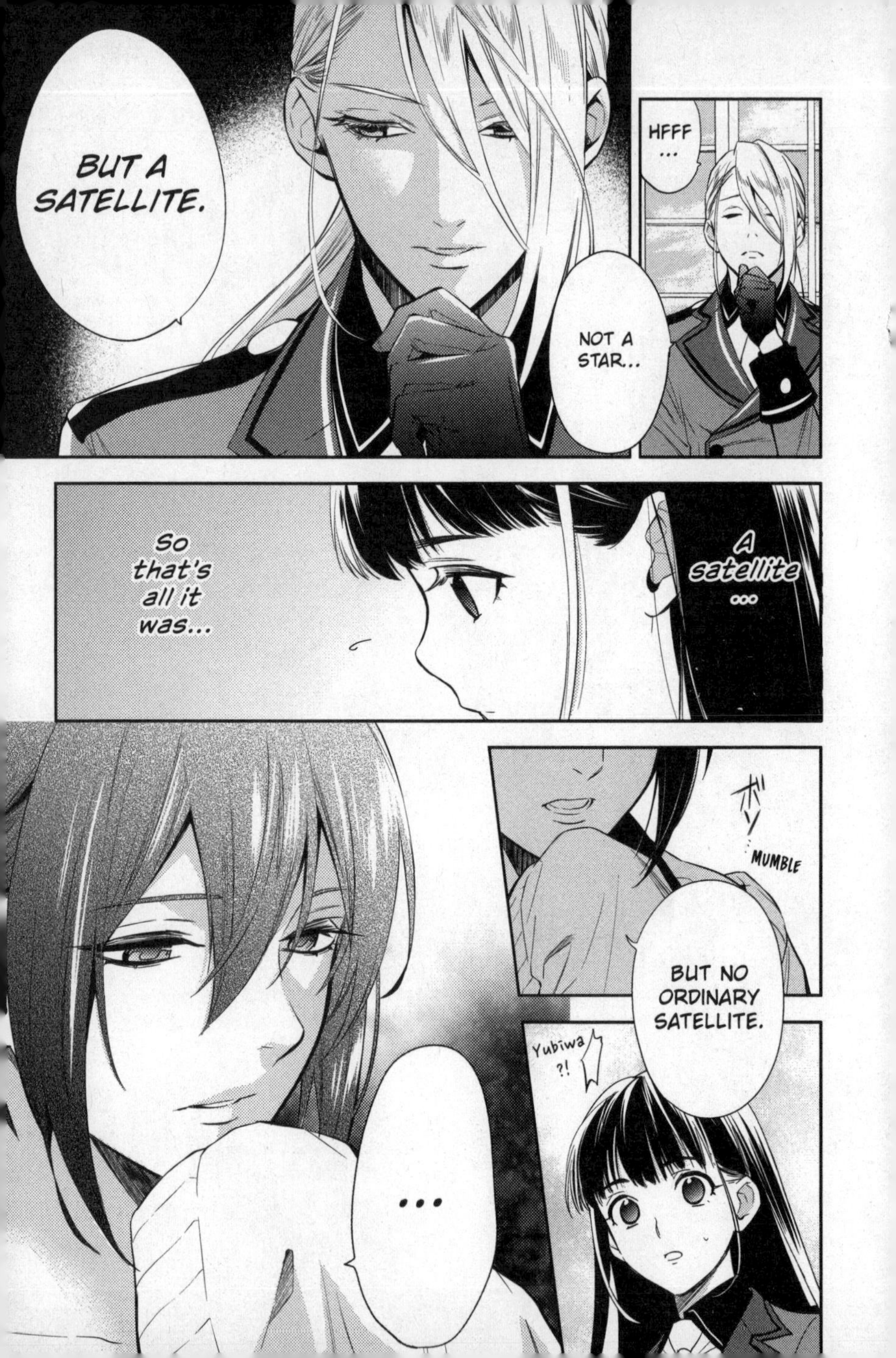
HFFF...
NOT A STAR...
BUT A SATELLITE.
A satellite...
So that's all it was...
ボソ
MUMBLE
BUT NO ORDINARY SATELLITE.
Yubiwa?!
...

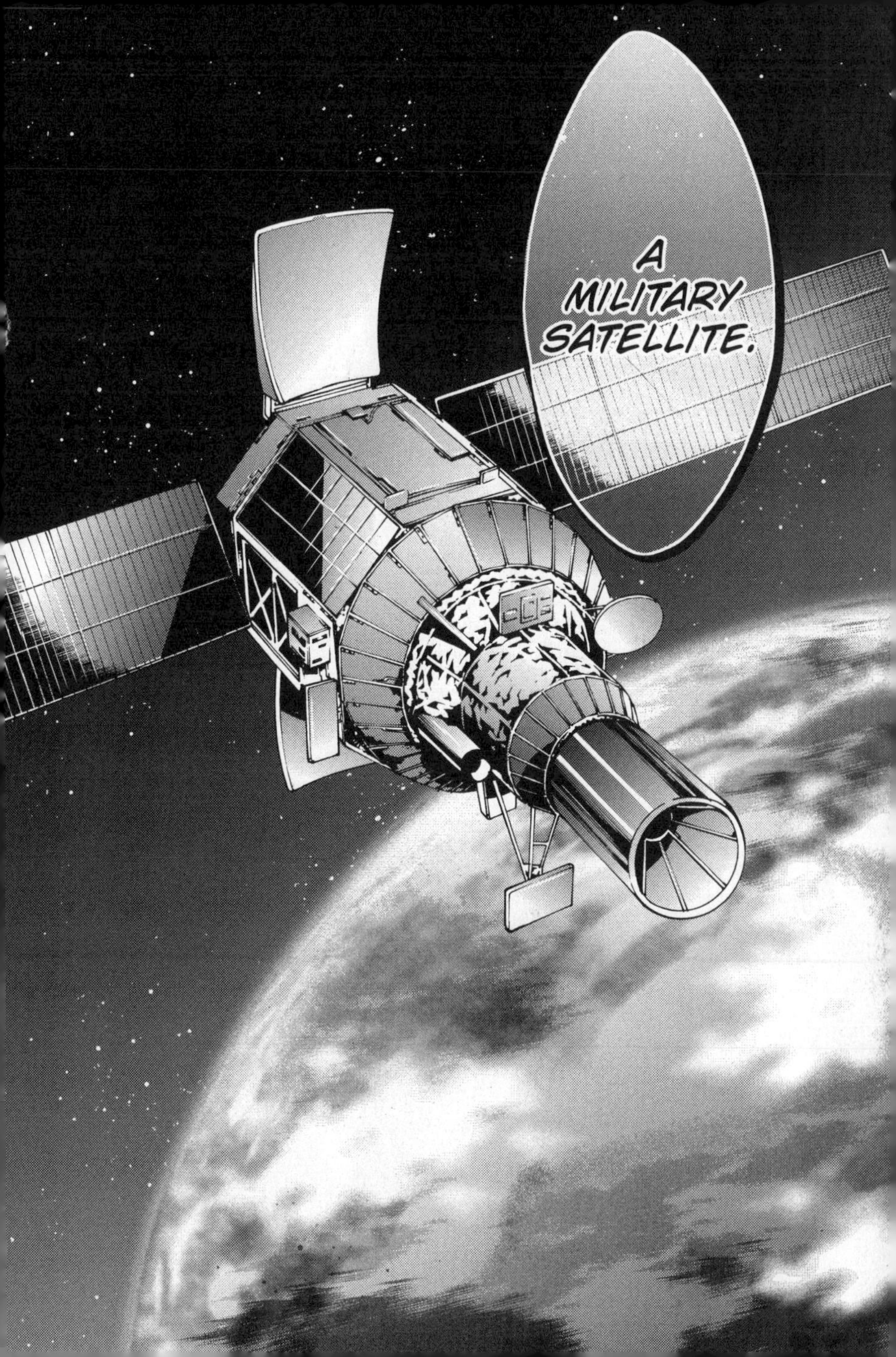
A MILITARY SATELLITE.

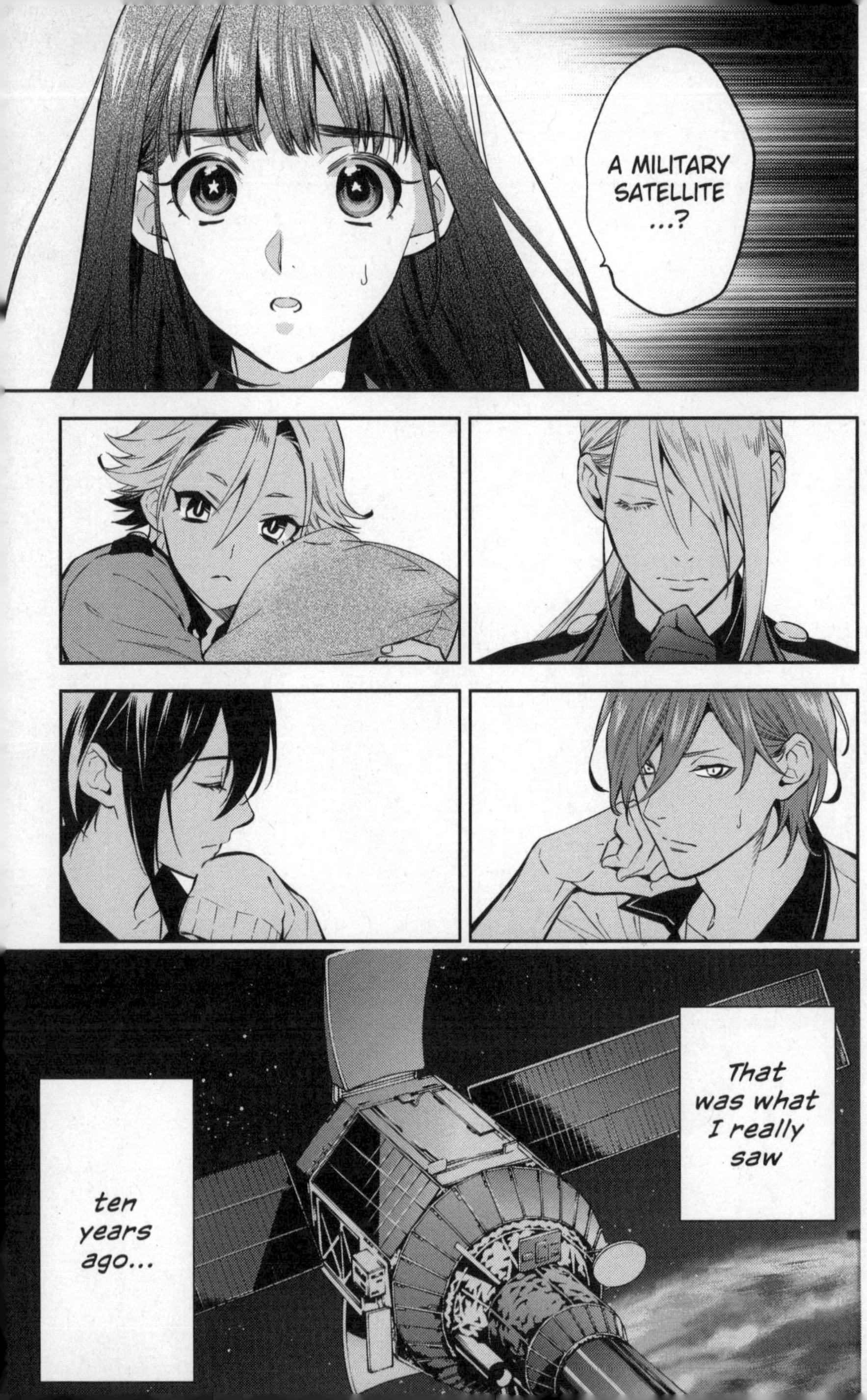
A MILITARY SATELLITE ...?
That was what I really saw
ten years ago...

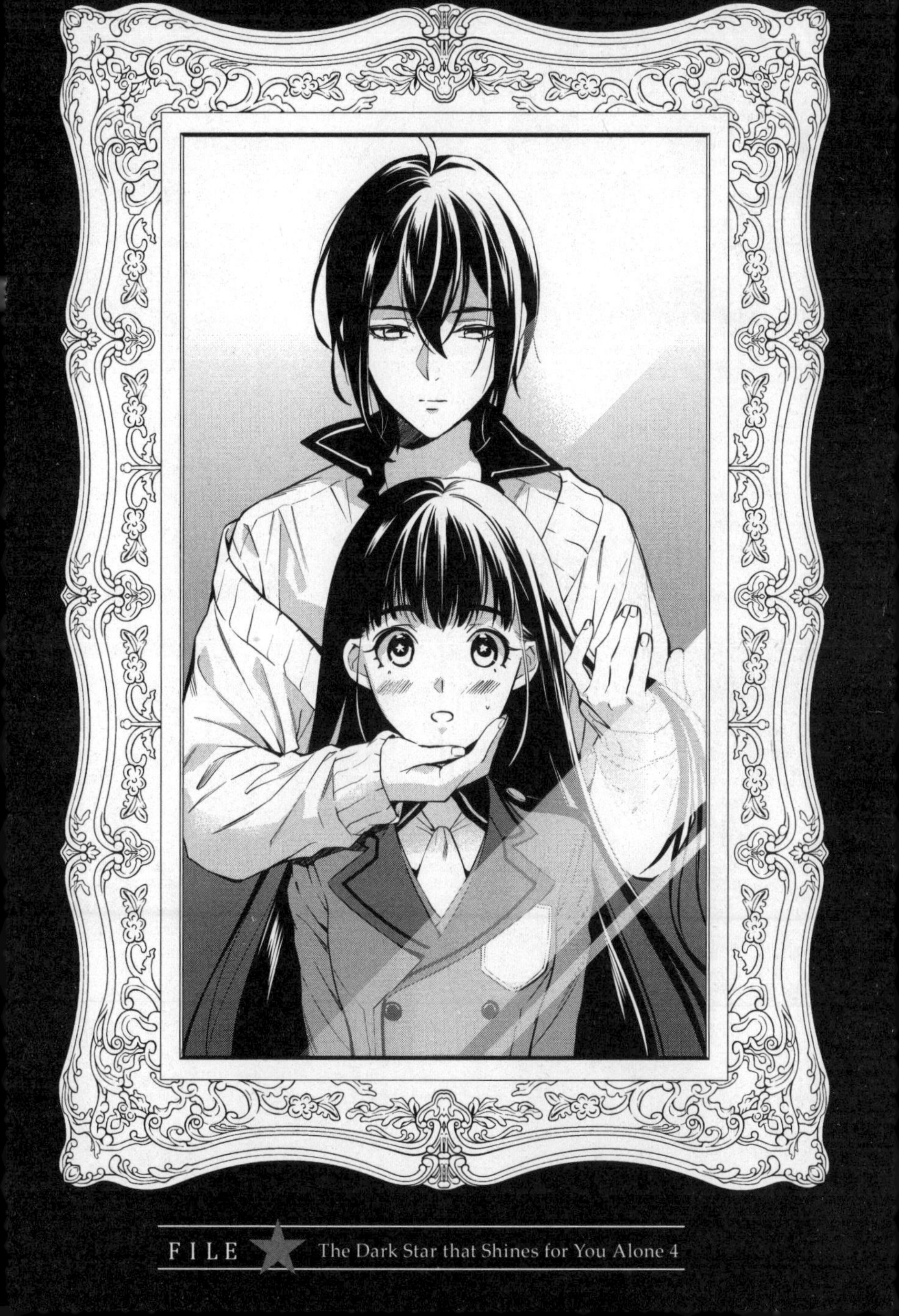

FILE ★ The Dark Star that Shines for You Alone 4

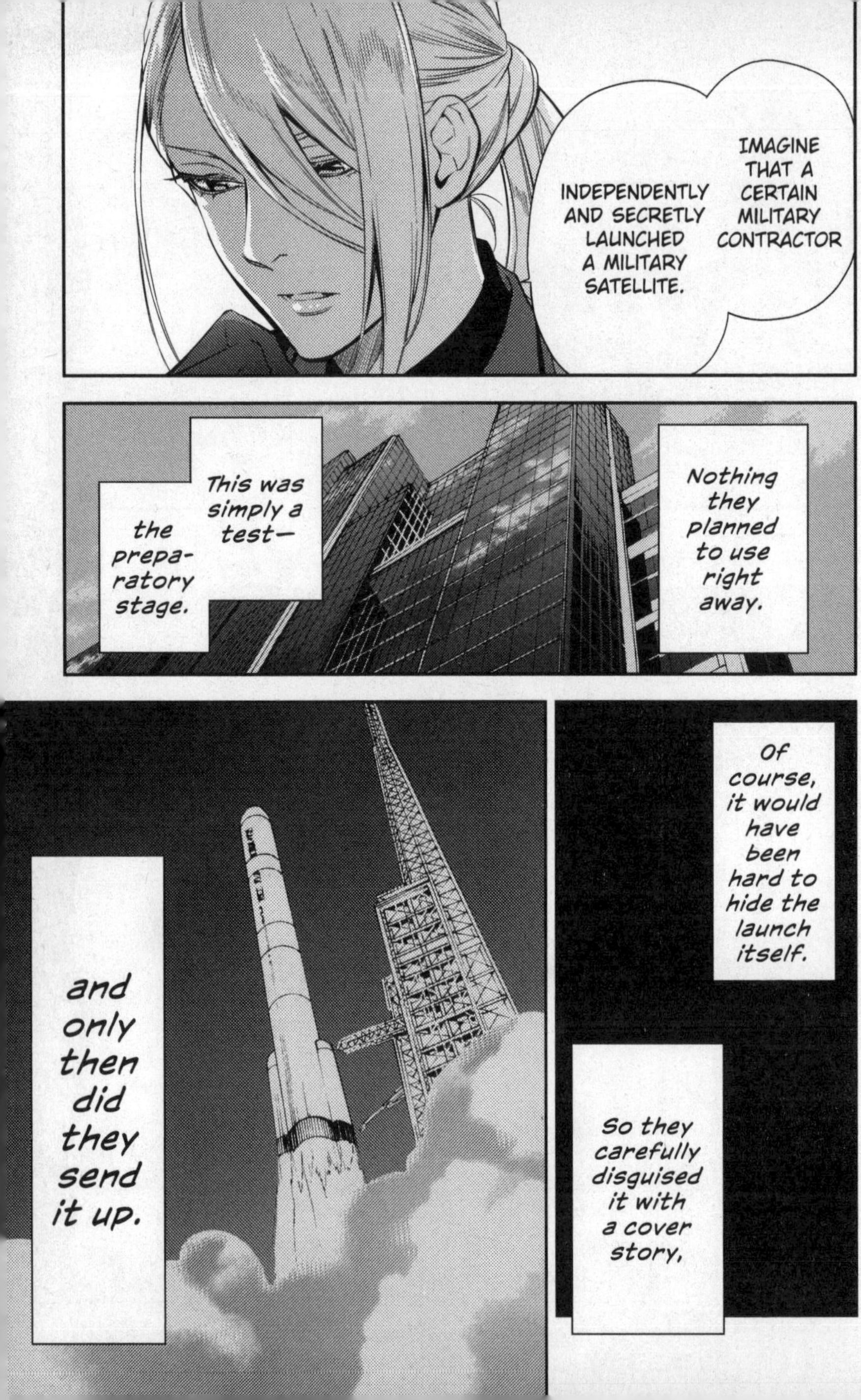
IMAGINE THAT A CERTAIN MILITARY CONTRACTOR
INDEPENDENTLY AND SECRETLY LAUNCHED A MILITARY SATELLITE.
Nothing they planned to use right away.
This was simply a test—
the prepa-ratory stage.
Of course, it would have been hard to hide the launch itself.
So they carefully disguised it with a cover story,
and only then did they send it up.

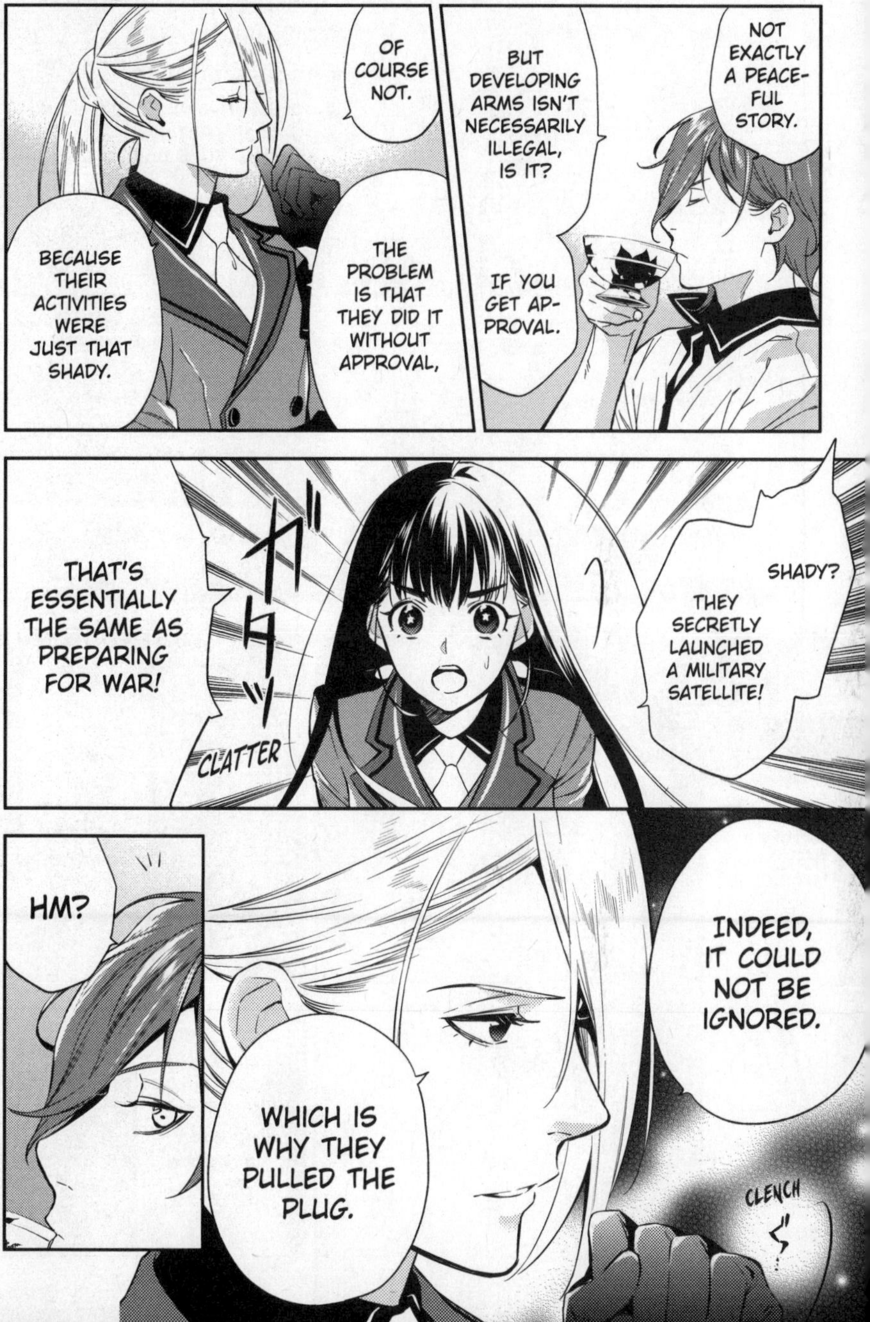
NOT EXACTLY A PEACEFUL STORY.
BUT DEVELOPING ARMS ISN'T NECESSARILY ILLEGAL, IS IT?
IF YOU GET APPROVAL.
OF COURSE NOT.
THE PROBLEM IS THAT THEY DID IT WITHOUT APPROVAL,
BECAUSE THEIR ACTIVITIES WERE JUST THAT SHADY.
SHADY?
THEY SECRETLY LAUNCHED A MILITARY SATELLITE!
THAT'S ESSENTIALLY THE SAME AS PREPARING FOR WAR!
ガタッ
CLATTER
INDEED, IT COULD NOT BE IGNORED.
WHICH IS WHY THEY PULLED THE PLUG.
CLENCH
ぐ…
HM?

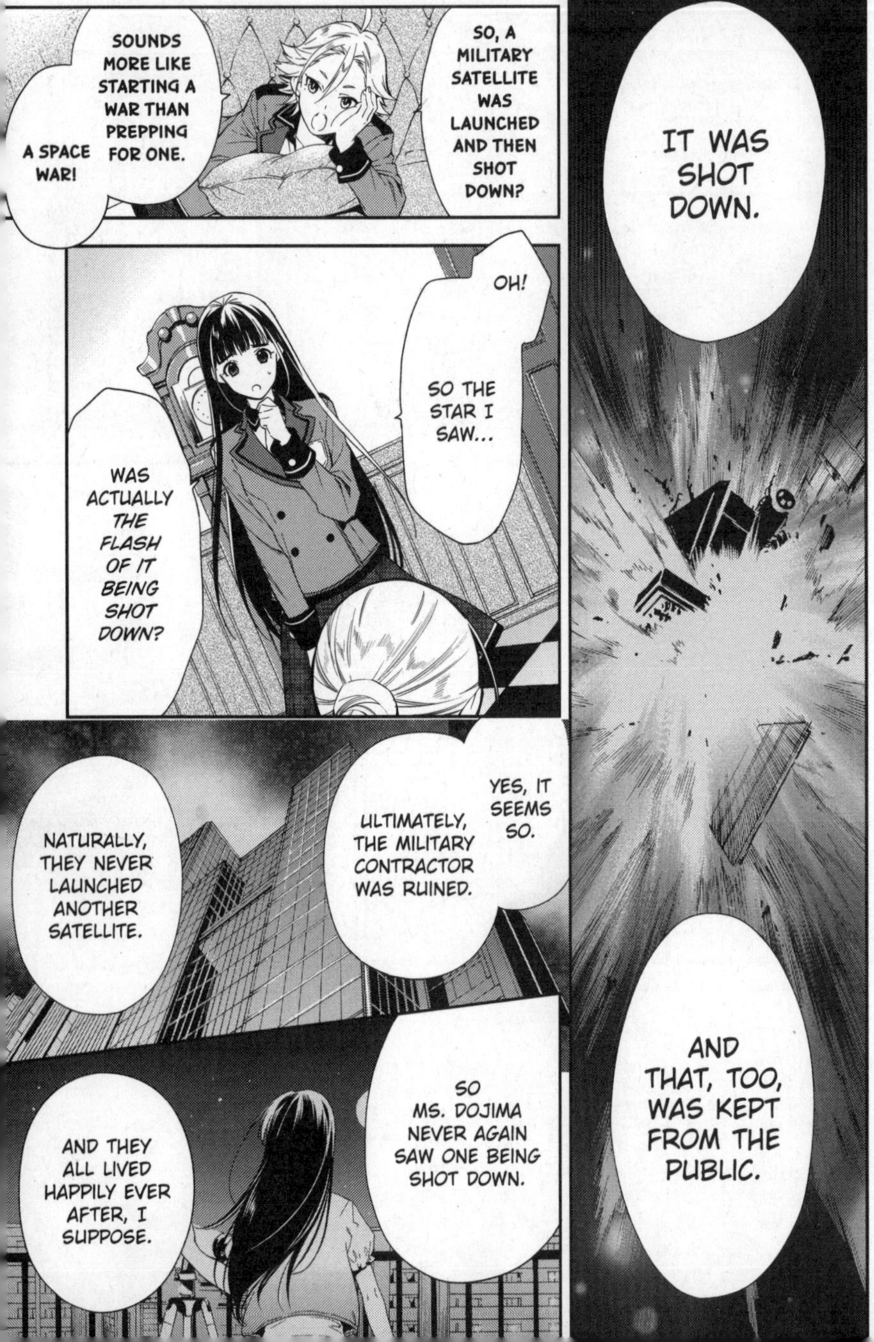
IT WAS SHOT DOWN.
AND THAT, TOO, WAS KEPT FROM THE PUBLIC.
SO, A MILITARY SATELLITE WAS LAUNCHED AND THEN SHOT DOWN?
SOUNDS MORE LIKE STARTING A WAR THAN PREPPING FOR ONE.
A SPACE WAR!
OH!
SO THE STAR I SAW...
WAS ACTUALLY *THE FLASH OF IT BEING SHOT DOWN?*
YES, IT SEEMS SO.
ULTIMATELY, THE MILITARY CONTRACTOR WAS RUINED.
NATURALLY, THEY NEVER LAUNCHED ANOTHER SATELLITE.
SO MS. DOJIMA NEVER AGAIN SAW ONE BEING SHOT DOWN.
AND THEY ALL LIVED HAPPILY EVER AFTER, I SUPPOSE.

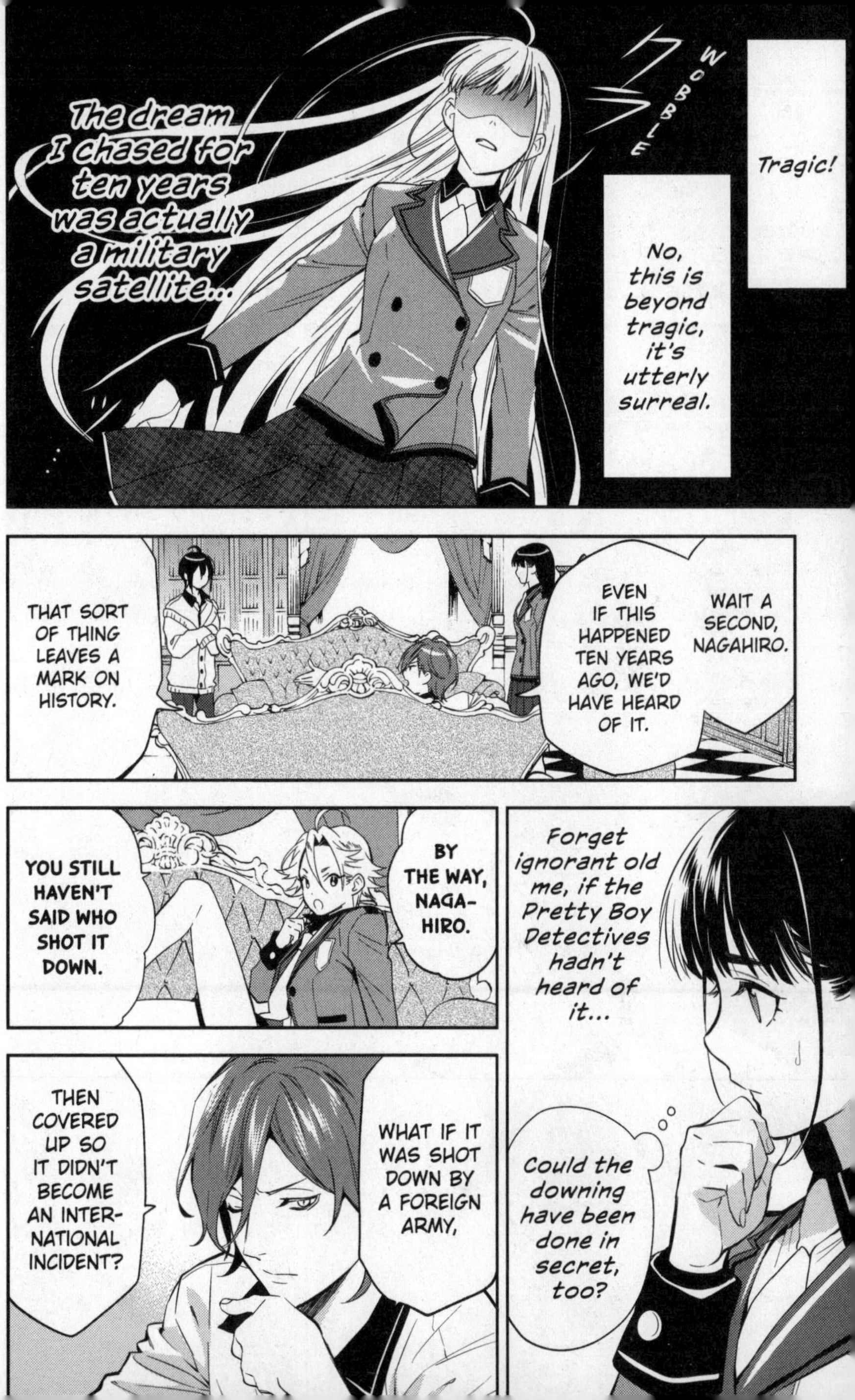
Tragic!
No, this is beyond tragic, it's utterly surreal.
WOBBLE
The dream I chased for ten years was actually a military satellite...
WAIT A SECOND, NAGAHIRO.
EVEN IF THIS HAPPENED TEN YEARS AGO, WE'D HAVE HEARD OF IT.
THAT SORT OF THING LEAVES A MARK ON HISTORY.
Forget ignorant old me, if the Pretty Boy Detectives hadn't heard of it...
Could the downing have been done in secret, too?
BY THE WAY, NAGA-HIRO.
YOU STILL HAVEN'T SAID WHO SHOT IT DOWN.
WHAT IF IT WAS SHOT DOWN BY A FOREIGN ARMY,
THEN COVERED UP SO IT DIDN'T BECOME AN INTER-NATIONAL INCIDENT?

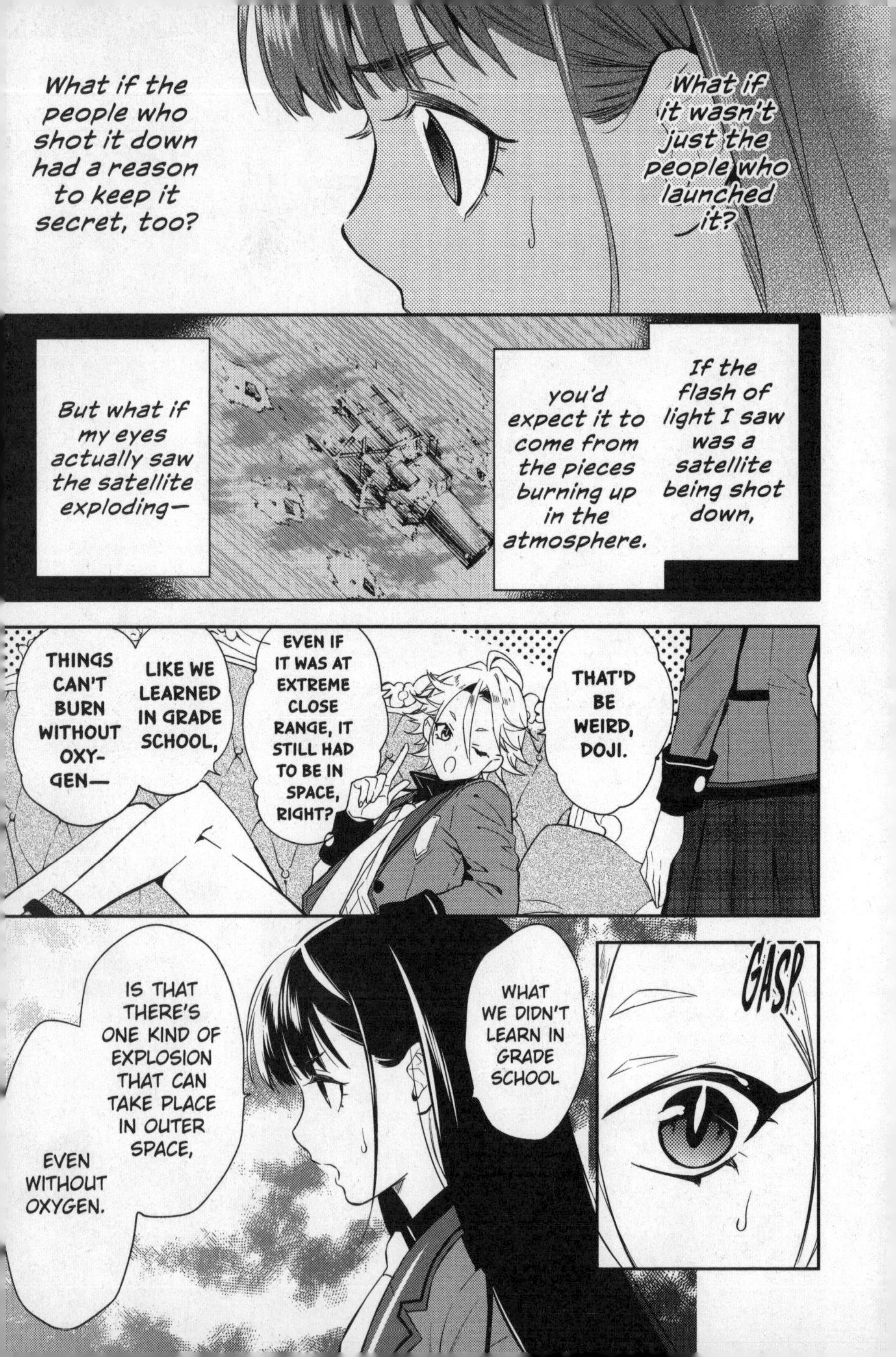
What if it wasn't just the people who launched it?
What if the people who shot it down had a reason to keep it secret, too?
If the flash of light I saw was a satellite being shot down,
you'd expect it to come from the pieces burning up in the atmosphere.
But what if my eyes actually saw the satellite exploding—
THAT'D BE WEIRD, DOJI.
EVEN IF IT WAS AT EXTREME CLOSE RANGE, IT STILL HAD TO BE IN SPACE, RIGHT?
LIKE WE LEARNED IN GRADE SCHOOL,
THINGS CAN'T BURN WITHOUT OXY-GEN—
GASP
WHAT WE DIDN'T LEARN IN GRADE SCHOOL
IS THAT THERE'S ONE KIND OF EXPLOSION THAT CAN TAKE PLACE IN OUTER SPACE,
EVEN WITHOUT OXYGEN.

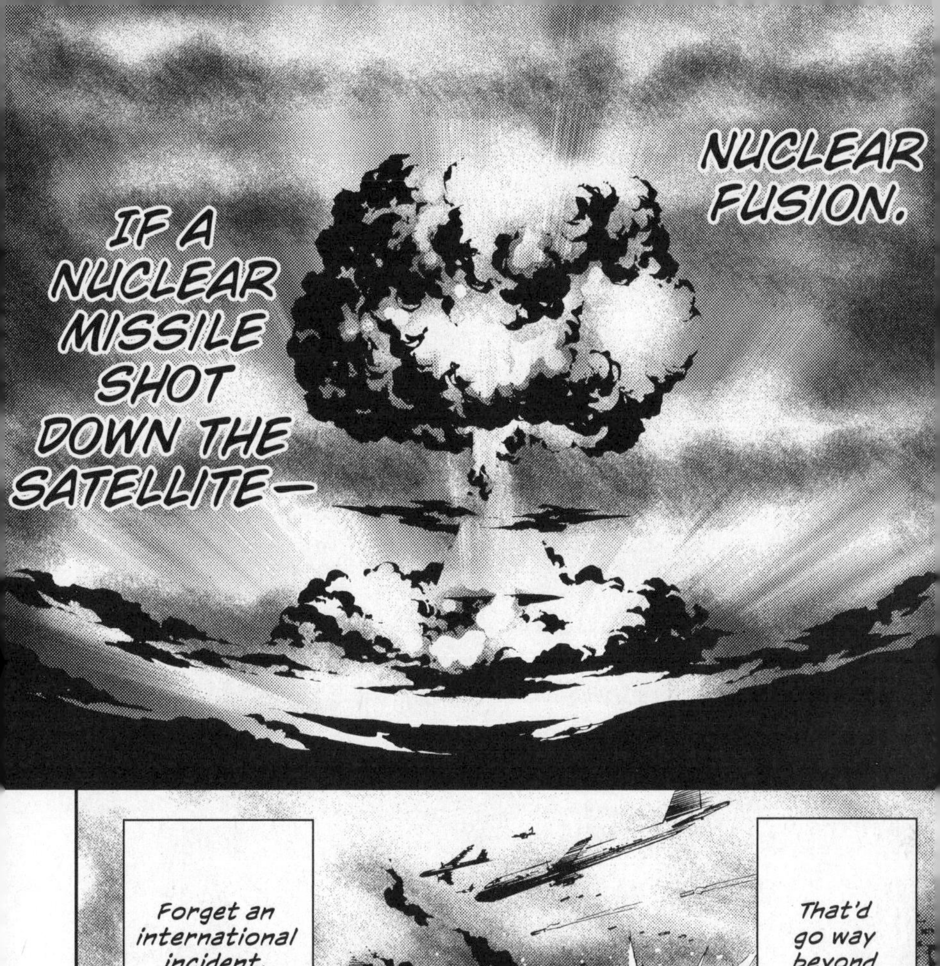
NUCLEAR FUSION.
IF A NUCLEAR MISSILE SHOT DOWN THE SATELLITE—

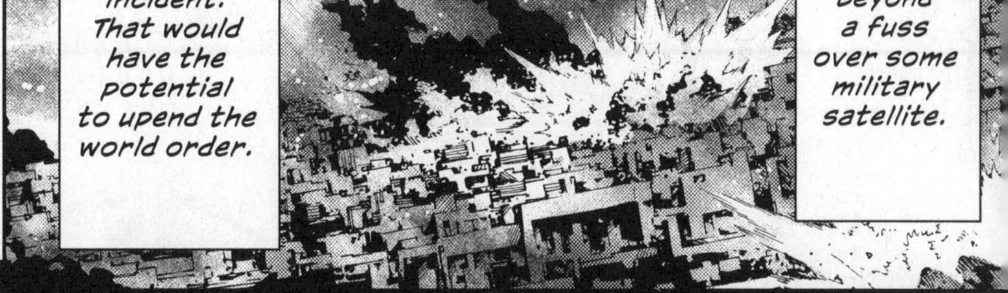
That'd go way beyond a fuss over some military satellite.
Forget an international incident. That would have the potential to upend the world order.

It couldn't be made public.

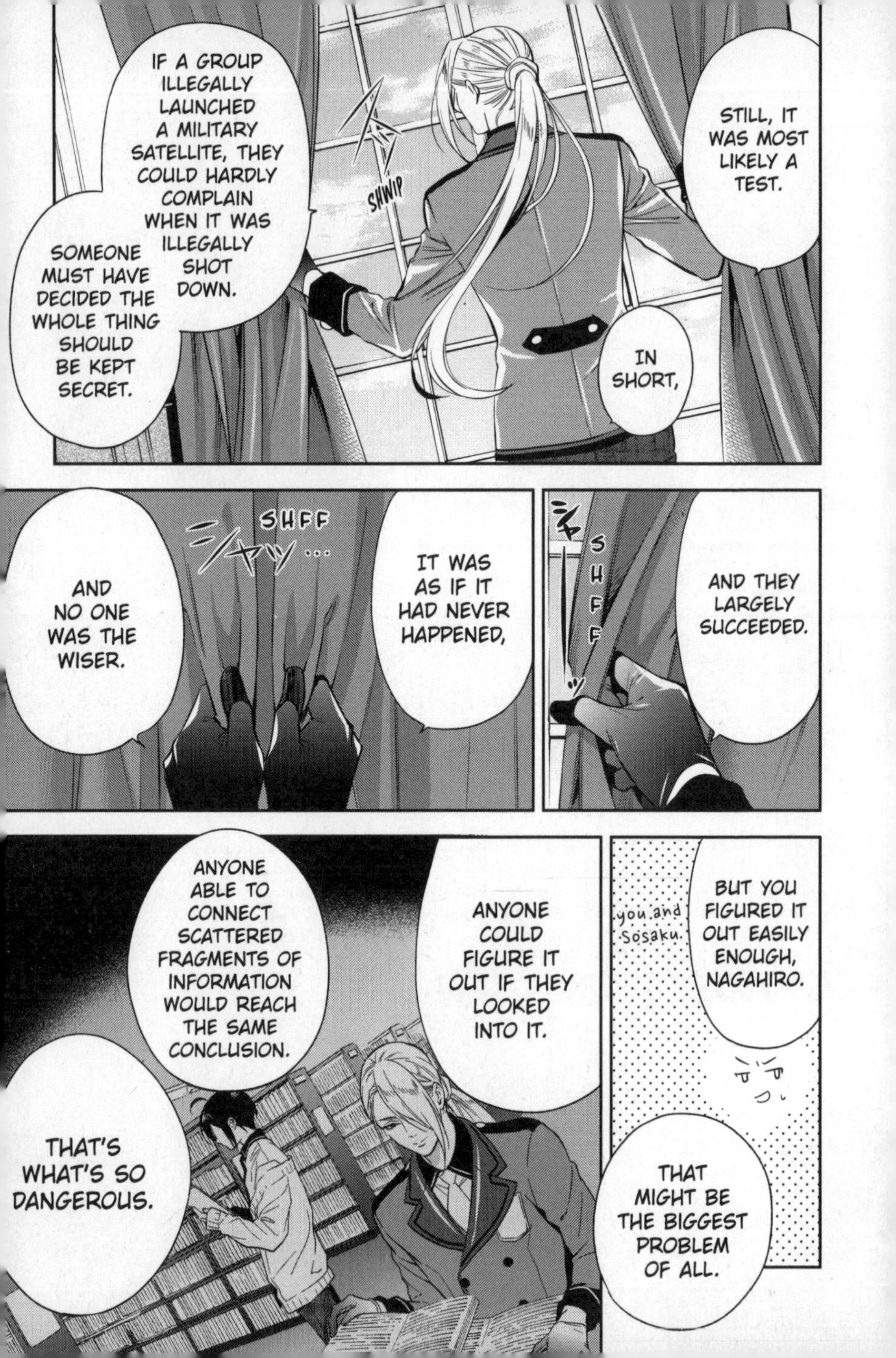
STILL, IT WAS MOST LIKELY A TEST.
IN SHORT,
SHWIP
IF A GROUP ILLEGALLY LAUNCHED A MILITARY SATELLITE, THEY COULD HARDLY COMPLAIN WHEN IT WAS ILLEGALLY SHOT DOWN.
SOMEONE MUST HAVE DECIDED THE WHOLE THING SHOULD BE KEPT SECRET.
SHFF
AND THEY LARGELY SUCCEEDED.
SHFF
IT WAS AS IF IT HAD NEVER HAPPENED,
AND NO ONE WAS THE WISER.
BUT YOU FIGURED IT OUT EASILY ENOUGH, NAGAHIRO.
you and Sosaku.
THAT MIGHT BE THE BIGGEST PROBLEM OF ALL.
ANYONE COULD FIGURE IT OUT IF THEY LOOKED INTO IT.
ANYONE ABLE TO CONNECT SCATTERED FRAGMENTS OF INFORMATION WOULD REACH THE SAME CONCLUSION.
THAT'S WHAT'S SO DANGEROUS.

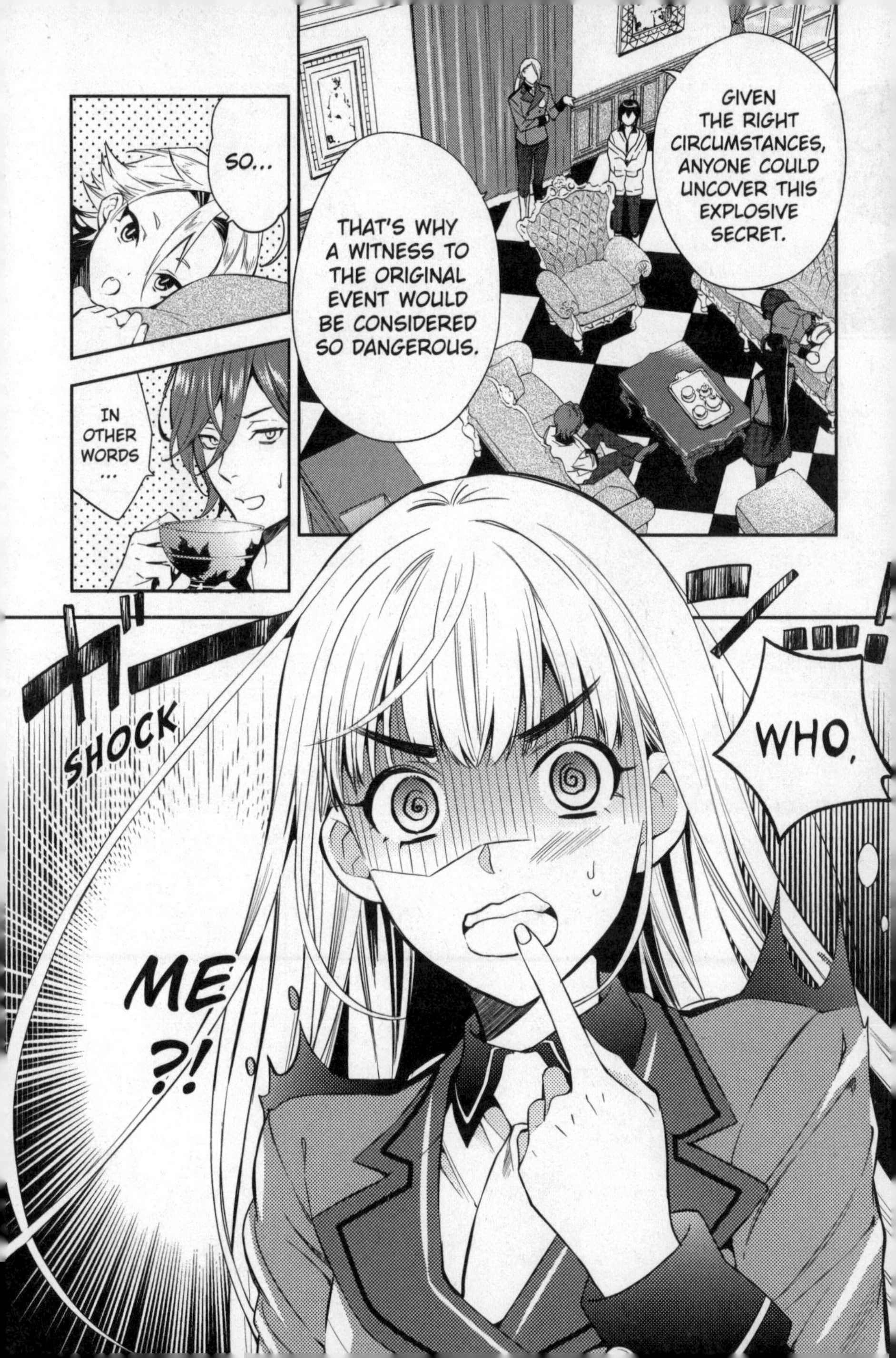
GIVEN THE RIGHT CIRCUMSTANCES, ANYONE COULD UNCOVER THIS EXPLOSIVE SECRET.
THAT'S WHY A WITNESS TO THE ORIGINAL EVENT WOULD BE CONSIDERED SO DANGEROUS.
SO...
IN OTHER WORDS...
WHO,
SHOCK
ME?!

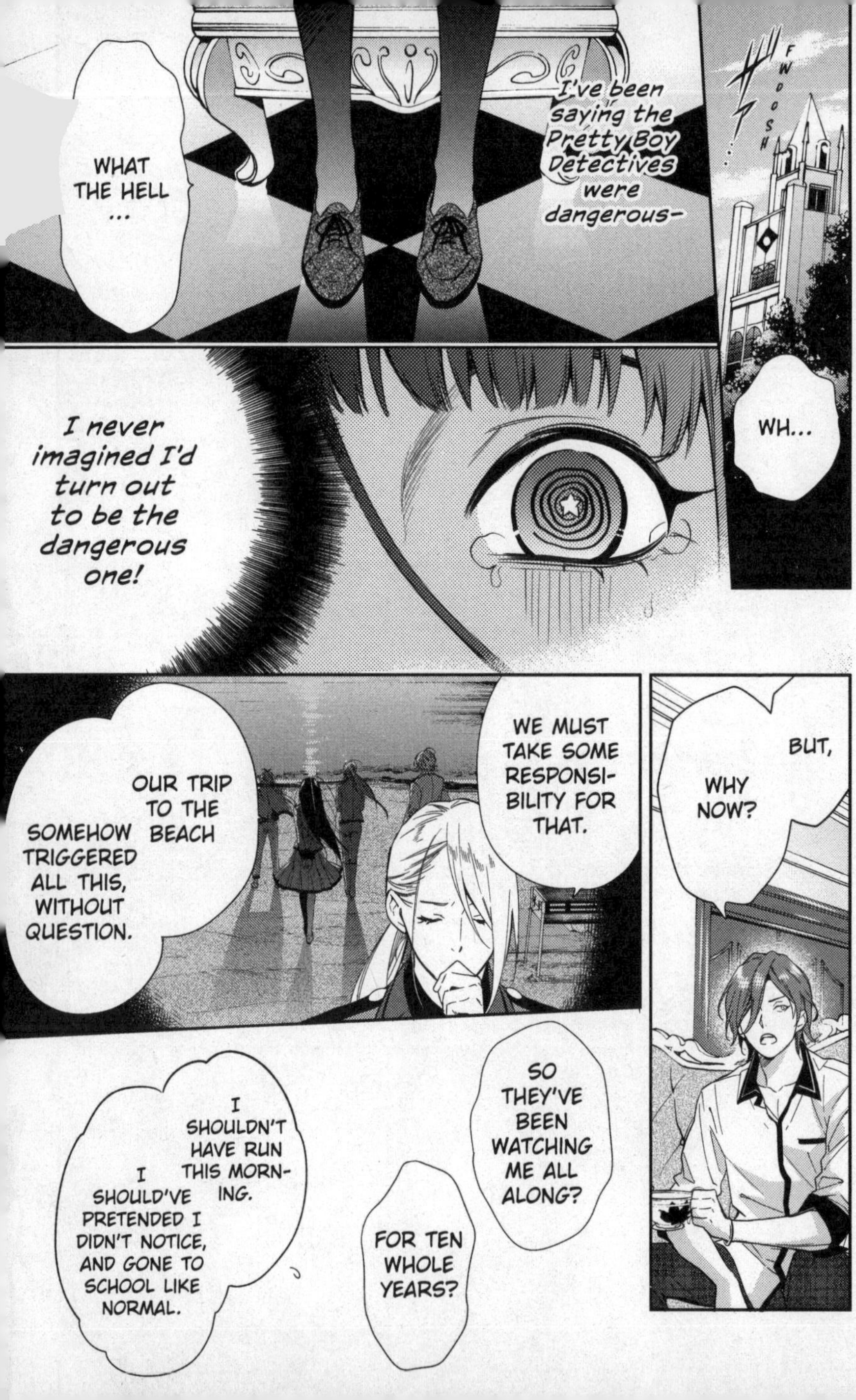
FWOOSH
WH...
I've been saying the Pretty Boy Detectives were dangerous-
WHAT THE HELL ...
I never imagined I'd turn out to be the dangerous one!
BUT, WHY NOW?
WE MUST TAKE SOME RESPONSIBILITY FOR THAT.
OUR TRIP TO THE BEACH SOMEHOW TRIGGERED ALL THIS, WITHOUT QUESTION.
SO THEY'VE BEEN WATCHING ME ALL ALONG?
FOR TEN WHOLE YEARS?
I SHOULDN'T HAVE RUN THIS MORNING. I SHOULD'VE PRETENDED I DIDN'T NOTICE, AND GONE TO SCHOOL LIKE NORMAL.

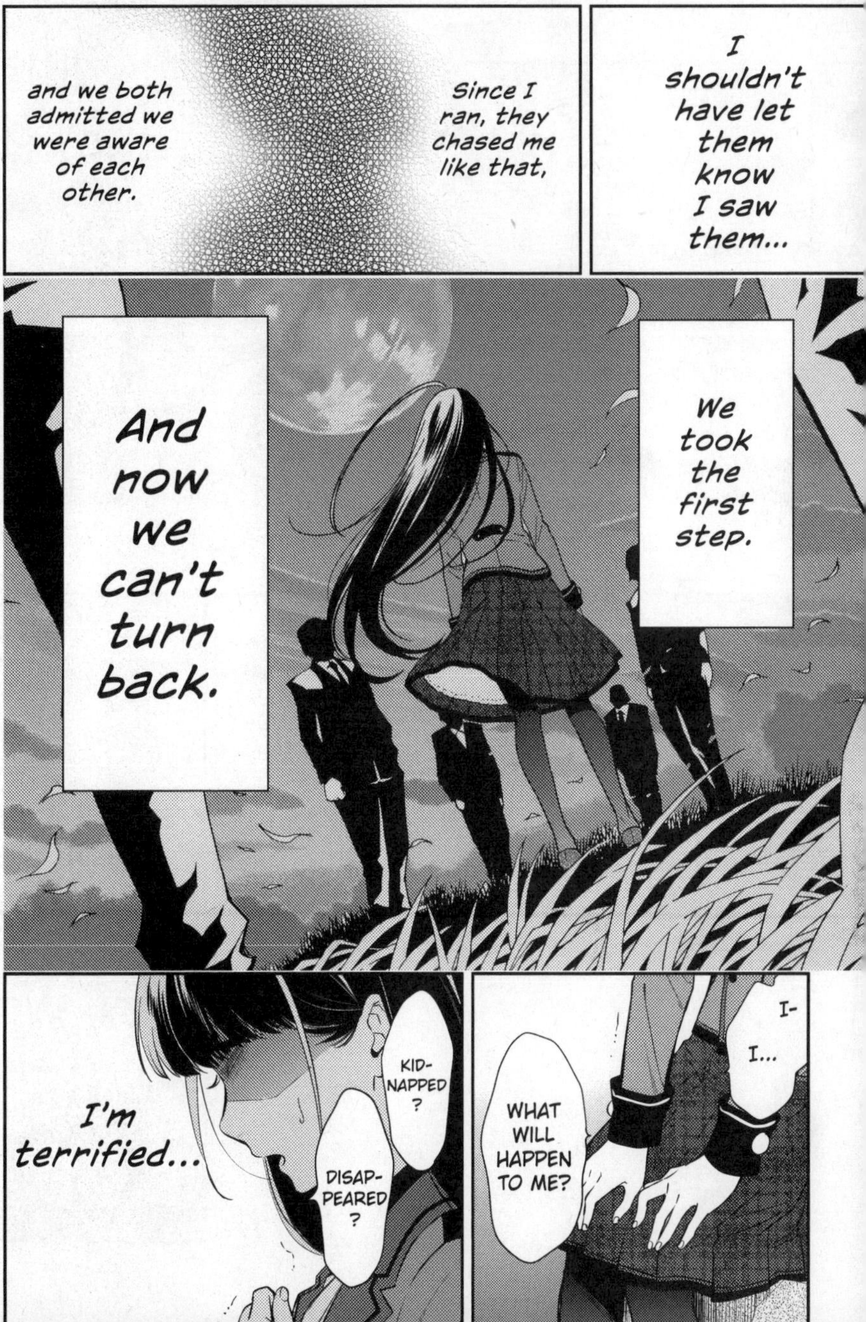
I shouldn't have let them know I saw them...
Since I ran, they chased me like that,
and we both admitted we were aware of each other.
We took the first step.
And now we can't turn back.
I-
I...
WHAT WILL HAPPEN TO ME?
KID-NAPPED?
DISAP-PEARED?
I'm terrified...

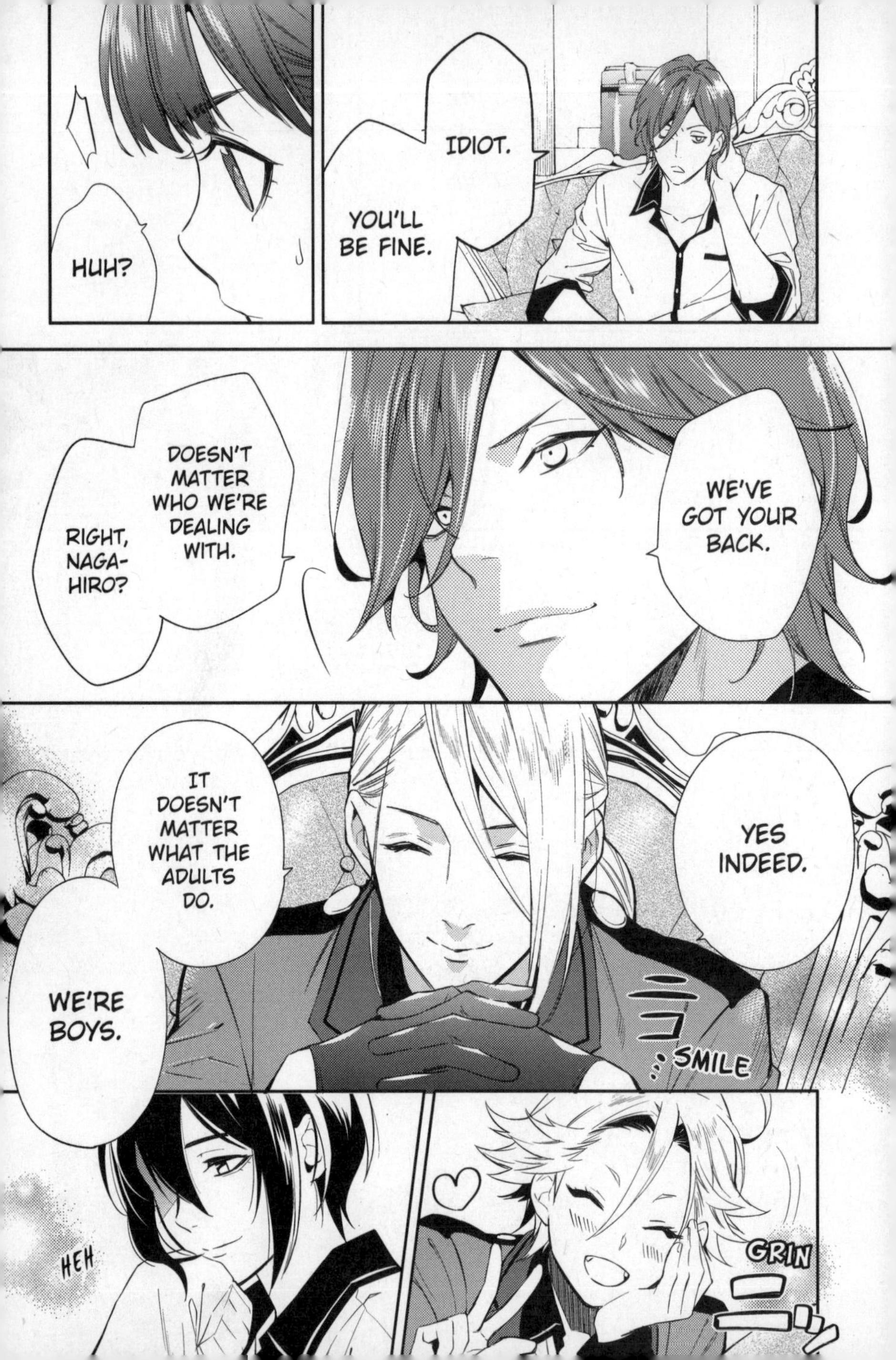
IDIOT.
YOU'LL BE FINE.
HUH?
WE'VE GOT YOUR BACK.
DOESN'T MATTER WHO WE'RE DEALING WITH.
RIGHT, NAGA-HIRO?
YES INDEED.
IT DOESN'T MATTER WHAT THE ADULTS DO.
SMILE
WE'RE BOYS.
GRIN
HEH

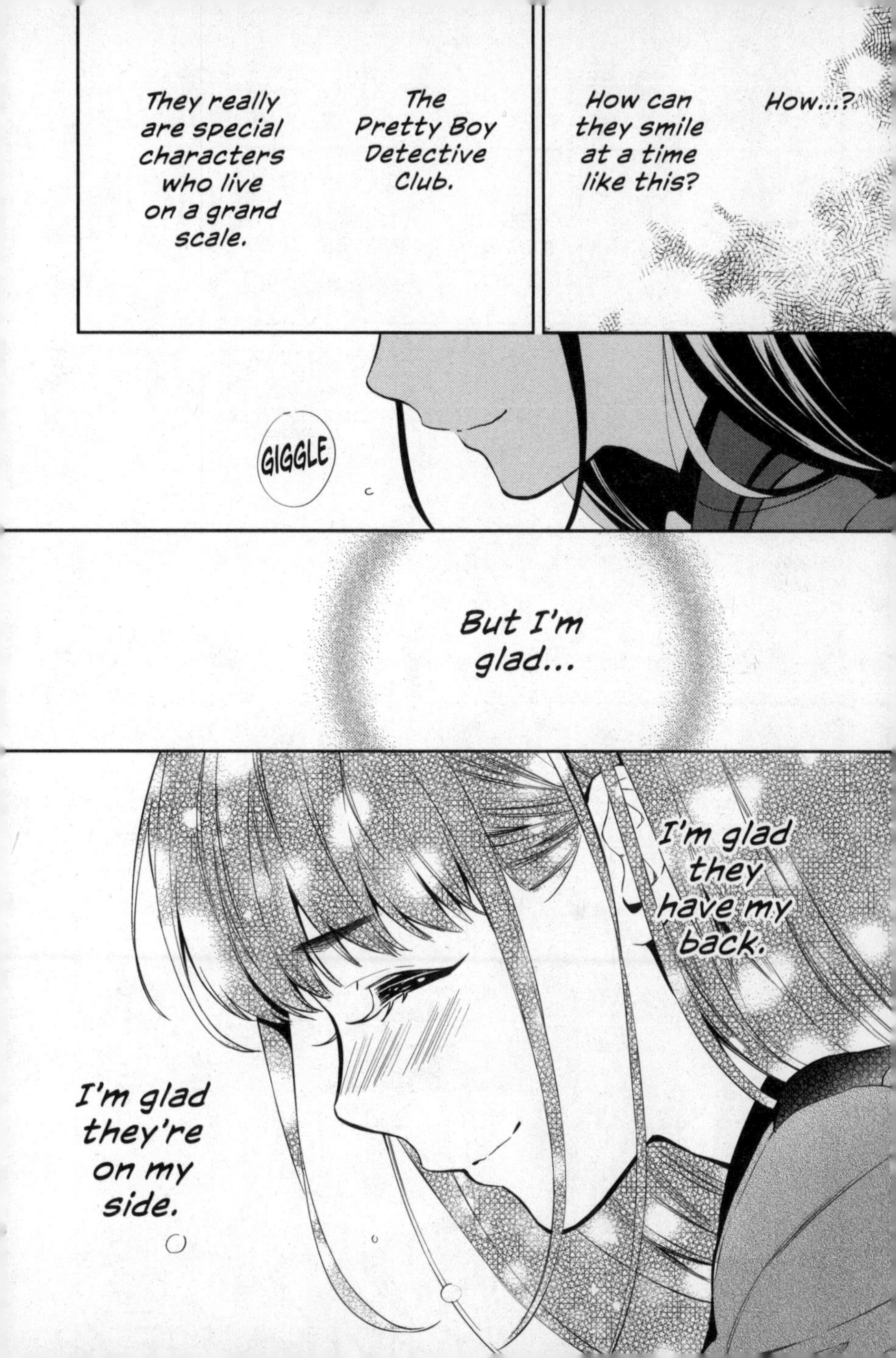
How...?
How can they smile at a time like this?
The Pretty Boy Detective Club.
They really are special characters who live on a grand scale.
GIGGLE
But I'm glad...
I'm glad they have my back.
I'm glad they're on my side.

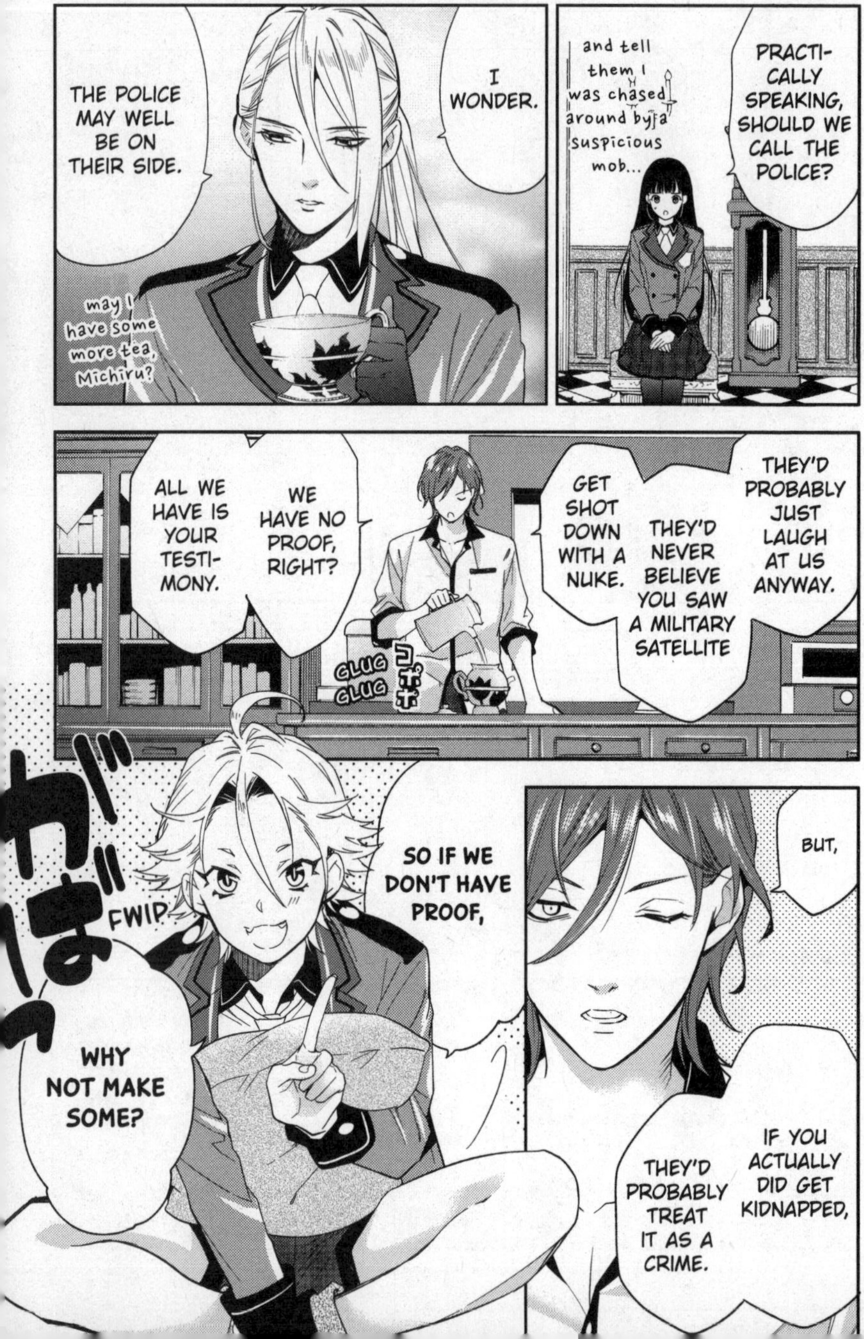
PRACTI-CALLY SPEAKING, SHOULD WE CALL THE POLICE?
and tell them I was chased around by a suspicious mob...
I WONDER.
THE POLICE MAY WELL BE ON THEIR SIDE.
may I have some more tea, Michiru?
THEY'D PROBABLY JUST LAUGH AT US ANYWAY.
THEY'D NEVER BELIEVE YOU SAW A MILITARY SATELLITE
GET SHOT DOWN WITH A NUKE.
WE HAVE NO PROOF, RIGHT?
ALL WE HAVE IS YOUR TESTIMONY.
GLUG GLUG
コポポ
BUT,
IF YOU ACTUALLY DID GET KIDNAPPED,
THEY'D PROBABLY TREAT IT AS A CRIME.
SO IF WE DON'T HAVE PROOF,
WHY NOT MAKE SOME?
FWIP
がばっ

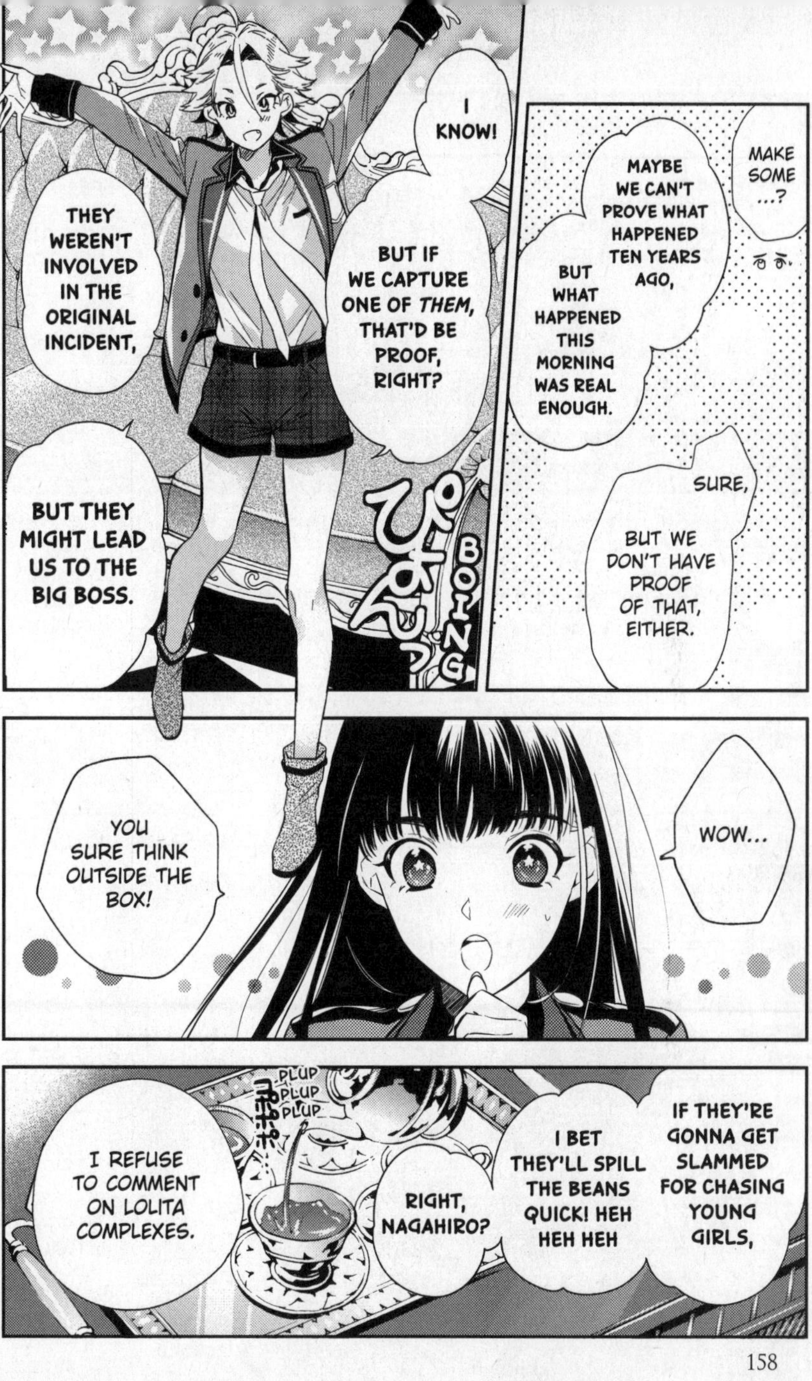
MAKE SOME ...?
MAYBE WE CAN'T PROVE WHAT HAPPENED TEN YEARS AGO,
BUT WHAT HAPPENED THIS MORNING WAS REAL ENOUGH.
SURE,
BUT WE DON'T HAVE PROOF OF THAT, EITHER.
I KNOW!
BUT IF WE CAPTURE ONE OF *THEM*, THAT'D BE PROOF, RIGHT?
THEY WEREN'T INVOLVED IN THE ORIGINAL INCIDENT,
BUT THEY MIGHT LEAD US TO THE BIG BOSS.
BOING
WOW...
YOU SURE THINK OUTSIDE THE BOX!
IF THEY'RE GONNA GET SLAMMED FOR CHASING YOUNG GIRLS,
I BET THEY'LL SPILL THE BEANS QUICK! HEH HEH HEH
RIGHT, NAGAHIRO?
PLUP PLUP PLUP
I REFUSE TO COMMENT ON LOLITA COMPLEXES.

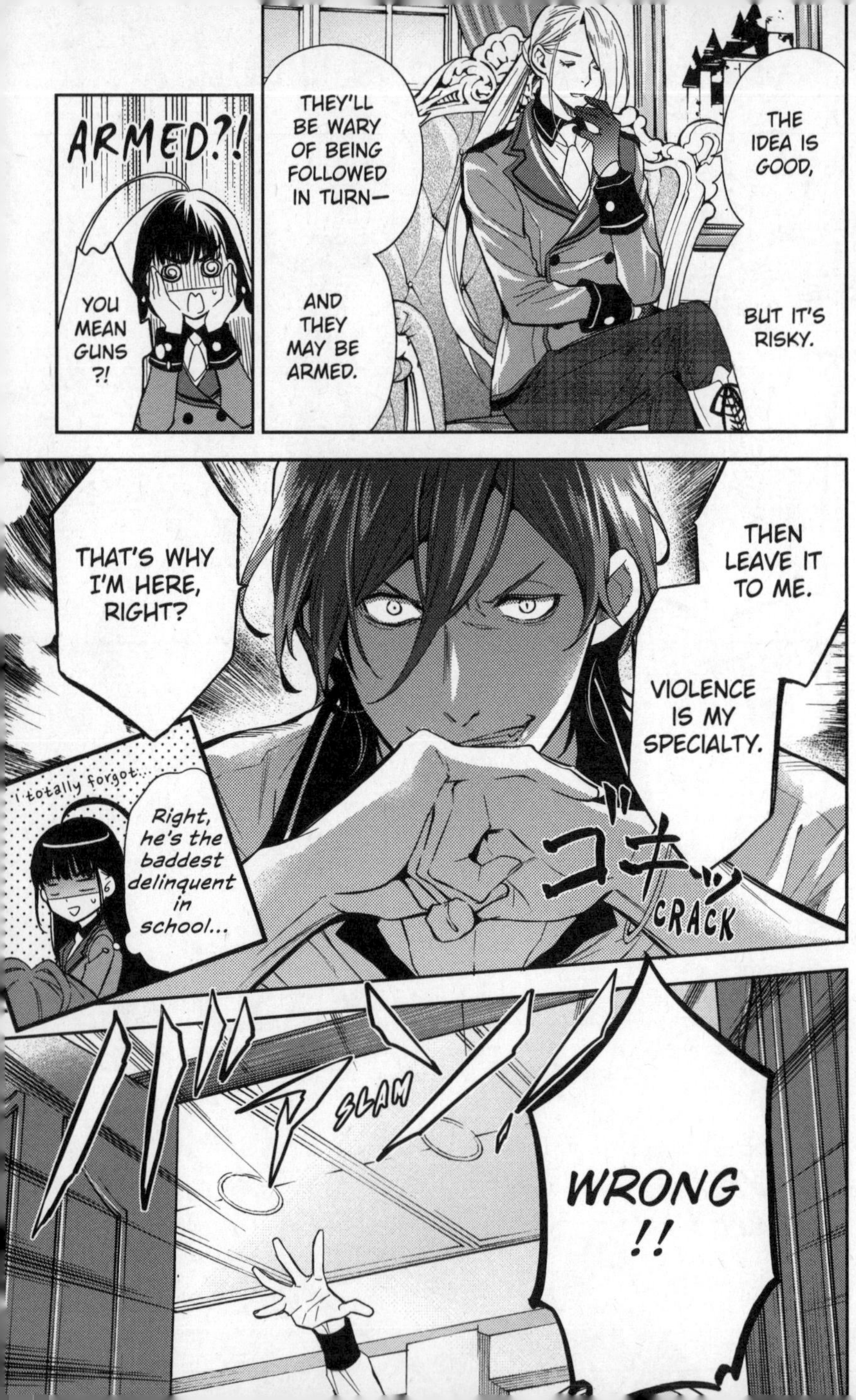
THE IDEA IS GOOD,
BUT IT'S RISKY.
THEY'LL BE WARY OF BEING FOLLOWED IN TURN—
AND THEY MAY BE ARMED.
ARMED?!
YOU MEAN GUNS?!
THEN LEAVE IT TO ME.
VIOLENCE IS MY SPECIALTY.
THAT'S WHY I'M HERE, RIGHT?
ゴキッ
CRACK
I totally forgot...
Right, he's the baddest delinquent in school...
WRONG!!
SLAM

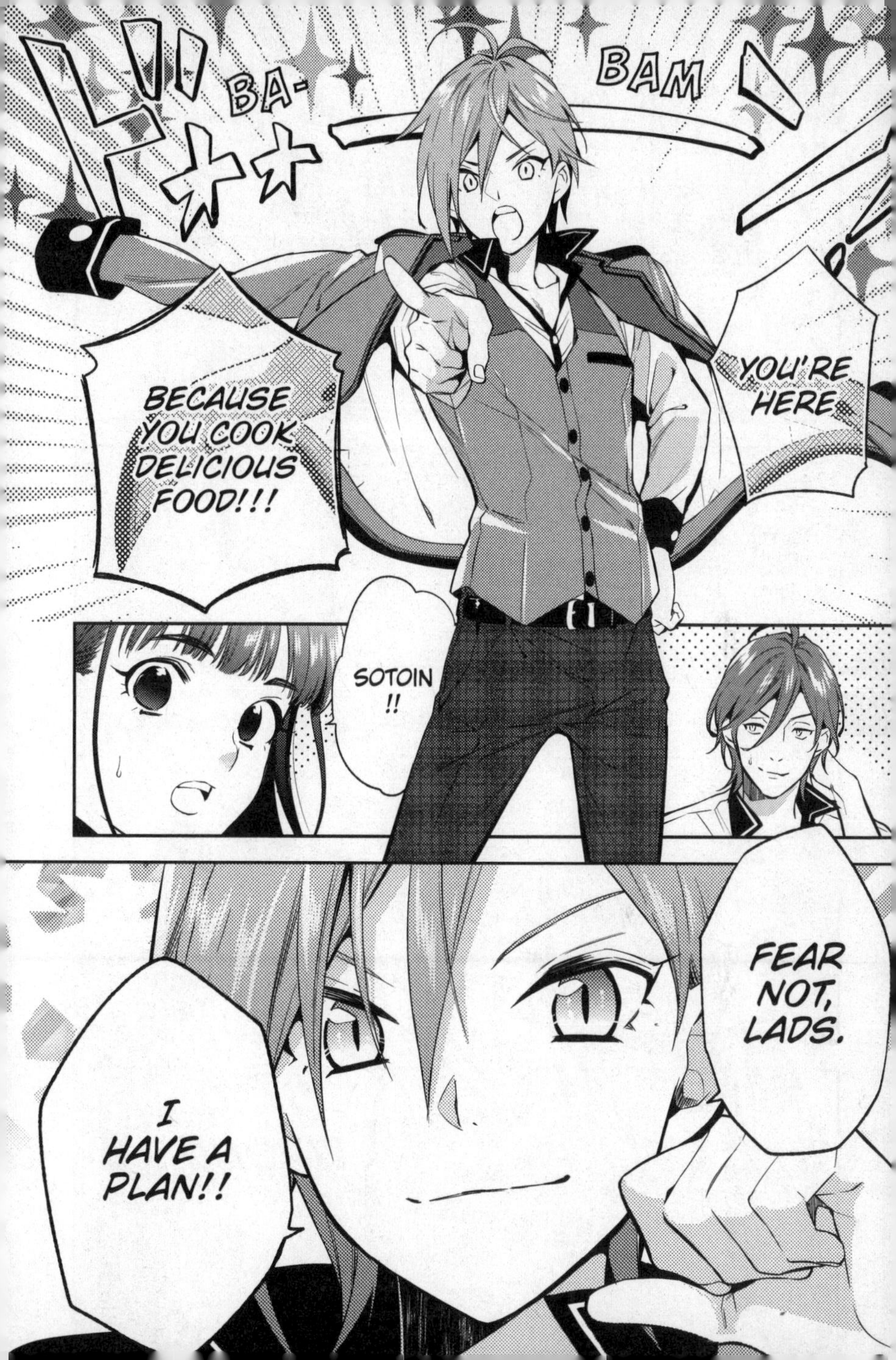
BA- BAM
YOU'RE HERE
BECAUSE YOU COOK DELICIOUS FOOD!!!
SOTOIN !!
FEAR NOT, LADS.
I HAVE A PLAN!!

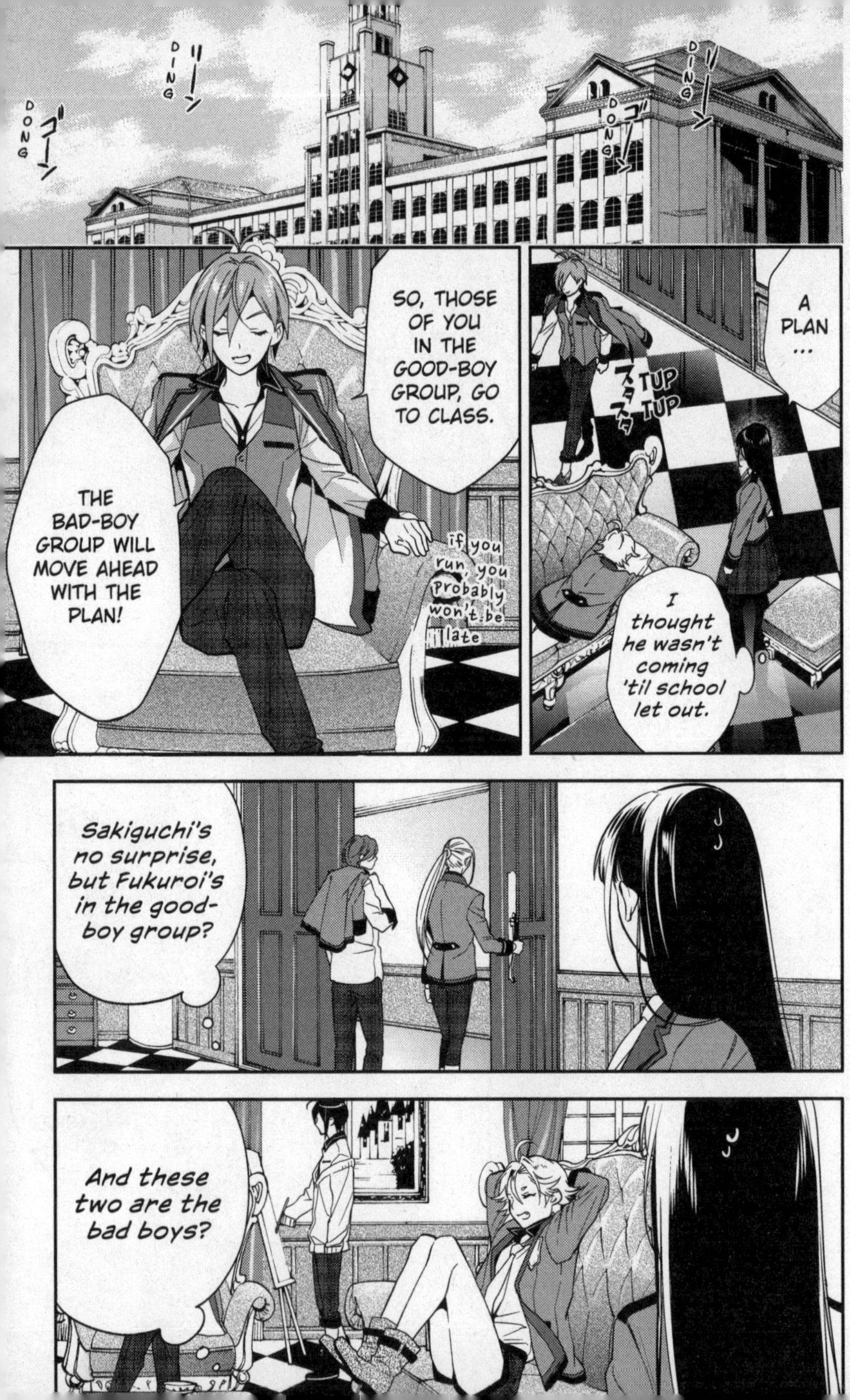
DING
DONG
DING
DONG
SO, THOSE OF YOU IN THE GOOD-BOY GROUP, GO TO CLASS.
THE BAD-BOY GROUP WILL MOVE AHEAD WITH THE PLAN!
if you run, you probably won't be late
TUP TUP
A PLAN ...
I thought he wasn't coming 'til school let out.
Sakiguchi's no surprise, but Fukuroi's in the good-boy group?
And these two are the bad boys?

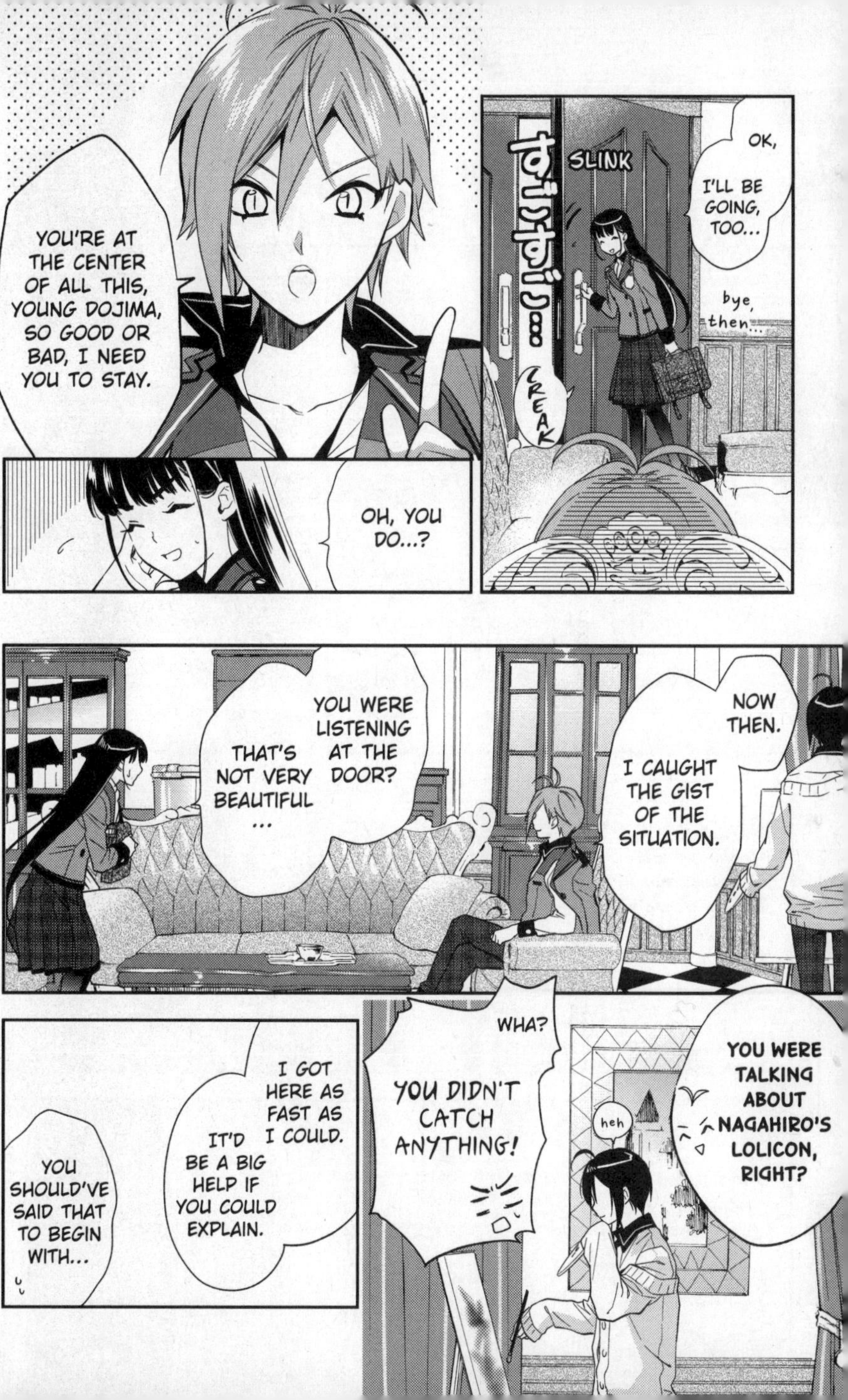
OK, I'LL BE GOING, TOO...
bye, then...
すごすご...
SLINK
CREAK
YOU'RE AT THE CENTER OF ALL THIS, YOUNG DOJIMA, SO GOOD OR BAD, I NEED YOU TO STAY.
OH, YOU DO...?
NOW THEN.
I CAUGHT THE GIST OF THE SITUATION.
YOU WERE LISTENING AT THE DOOR?
THAT'S NOT VERY BEAUTIFUL...
YOU WERE TALKING ABOUT NAGAHIRO'S LOLICON, RIGHT?
heh
WHA?
YOU DIDN'T CATCH ANYTHING!
I GOT HERE AS FAST AS I COULD.
IT'D BE A BIG HELP IF YOU COULD EXPLAIN.
YOU SHOULD'VE SAID THAT TO BEGIN WITH...

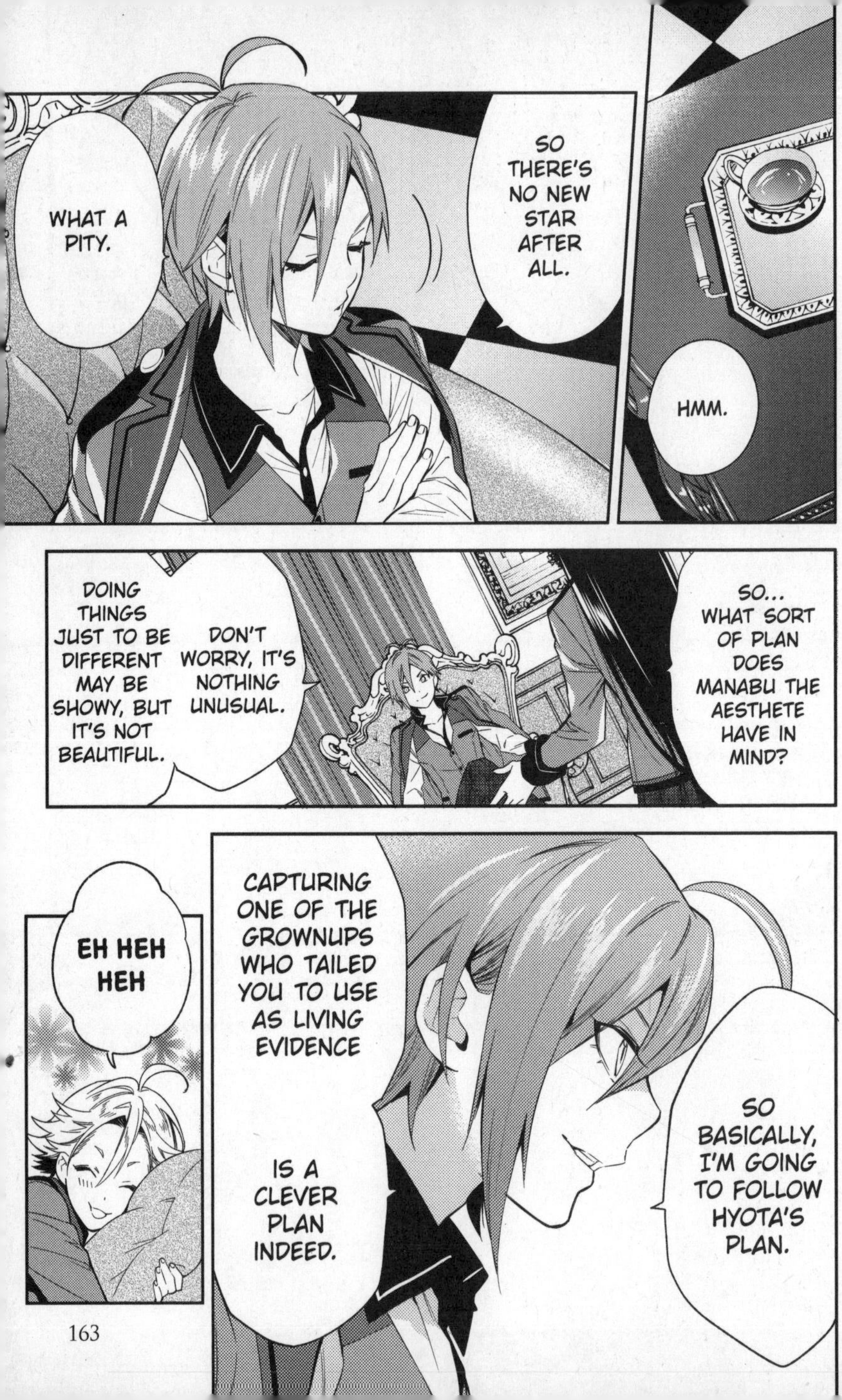
HMM.
SO THERE'S NO NEW STAR AFTER ALL.
WHAT A PITY.
SO... WHAT SORT OF PLAN DOES MANABU THE AESTHETE HAVE IN MIND?
DON'T WORRY, IT'S NOTHING UNUSUAL.
DOING THINGS JUST TO BE DIFFERENT MAY BE SHOWY, BUT IT'S NOT BEAUTIFUL.
SO BASICALLY, I'M GOING TO FOLLOW HYOTA'S PLAN.
CAPTURING ONE OF THE GROWNUPS WHO TAILED YOU TO USE AS LIVING EVIDENCE
IS A CLEVER PLAN INDEED.
EH HEH HEH

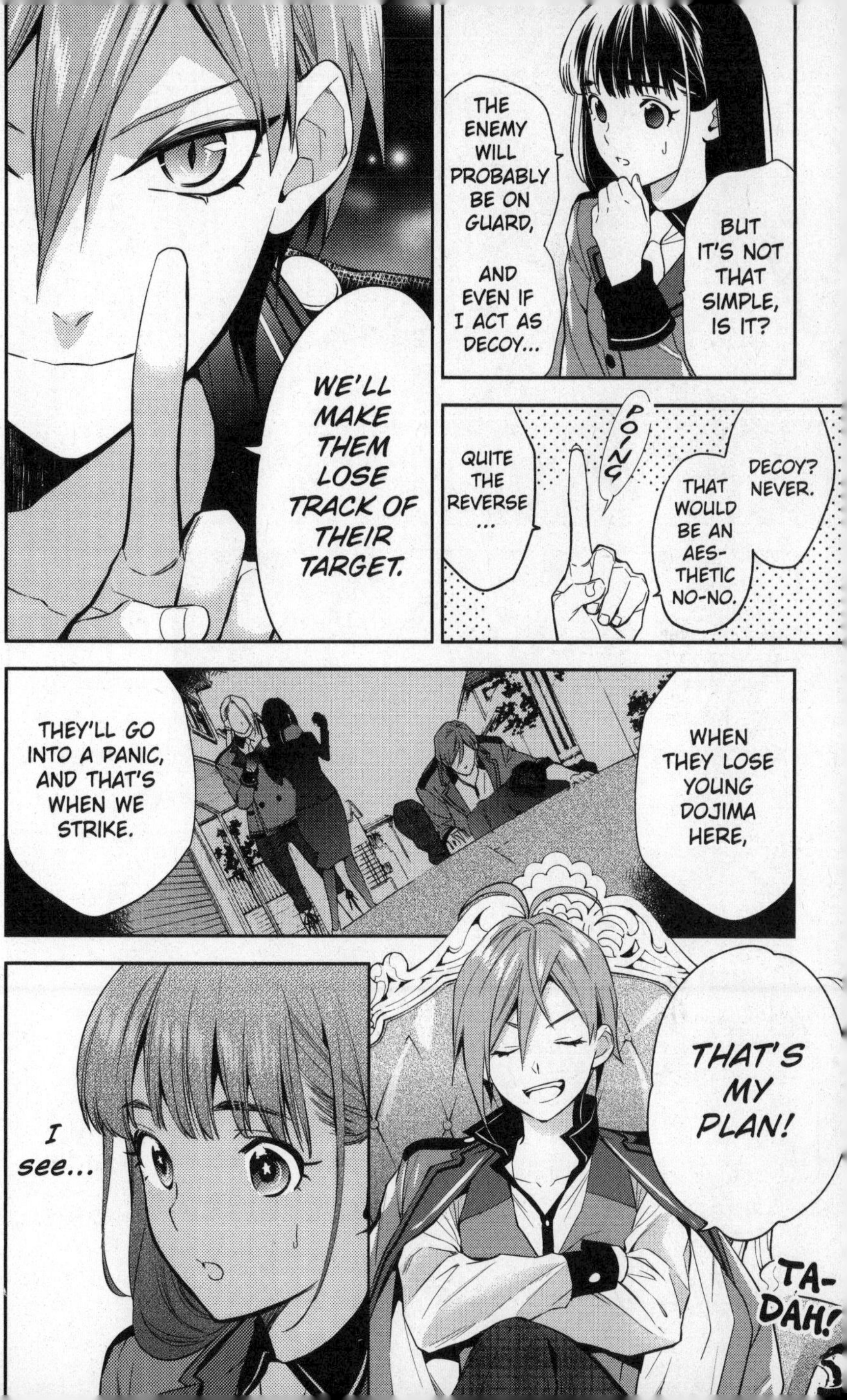
THE ENEMY WILL PROBABLY BE ON GUARD,
AND EVEN IF I ACT AS DECOY...
BUT IT'S NOT THAT SIMPLE, IS IT?
DECOY? NEVER.
THAT WOULD BE AN AES-THETIC NO-NO.
POING
QUITE THE REVERSE...
WE'LL MAKE THEM LOSE TRACK OF THEIR TARGET.
WHEN THEY LOSE YOUNG DOJIMA HERE,
THEY'LL GO INTO A PANIC, AND THAT'S WHEN WE STRIKE.
THAT'S MY PLAN!
TA-DAH!
I see...

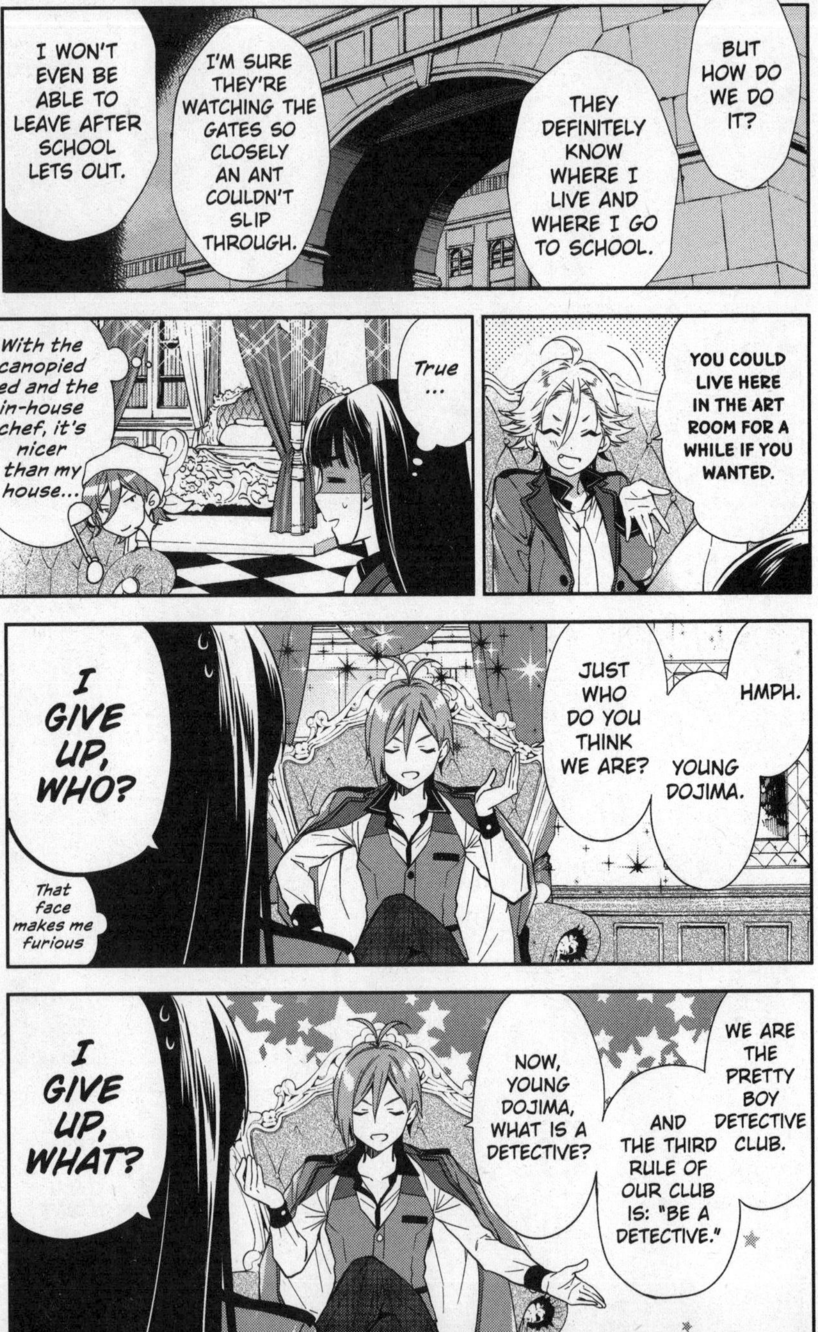
BUT HOW DO WE DO IT?
THEY DEFINITELY KNOW WHERE I LIVE AND WHERE I GO TO SCHOOL.
I'M SURE THEY'RE WATCHING THE GATES SO CLOSELY AN ANT COULDN'T SLIP THROUGH.
I WON'T EVEN BE ABLE TO LEAVE AFTER SCHOOL LETS OUT.
YOU COULD LIVE HERE IN THE ART ROOM FOR A WHILE IF YOU WANTED.
True ...
With the canopied bed and the in-house chef, it's nicer than my house...
HMPH.
YOUNG DOJIMA.
JUST WHO DO YOU THINK WE ARE?
I GIVE UP, WHO?
That face makes me furious
WE ARE THE PRETTY BOY DETECTIVE CLUB.
AND THE THIRD RULE OF OUR CLUB IS: "BE A DETECTIVE."
NOW, YOUNG DOJIMA, WHAT IS A DETECTIVE?
I GIVE UP, WHAT?

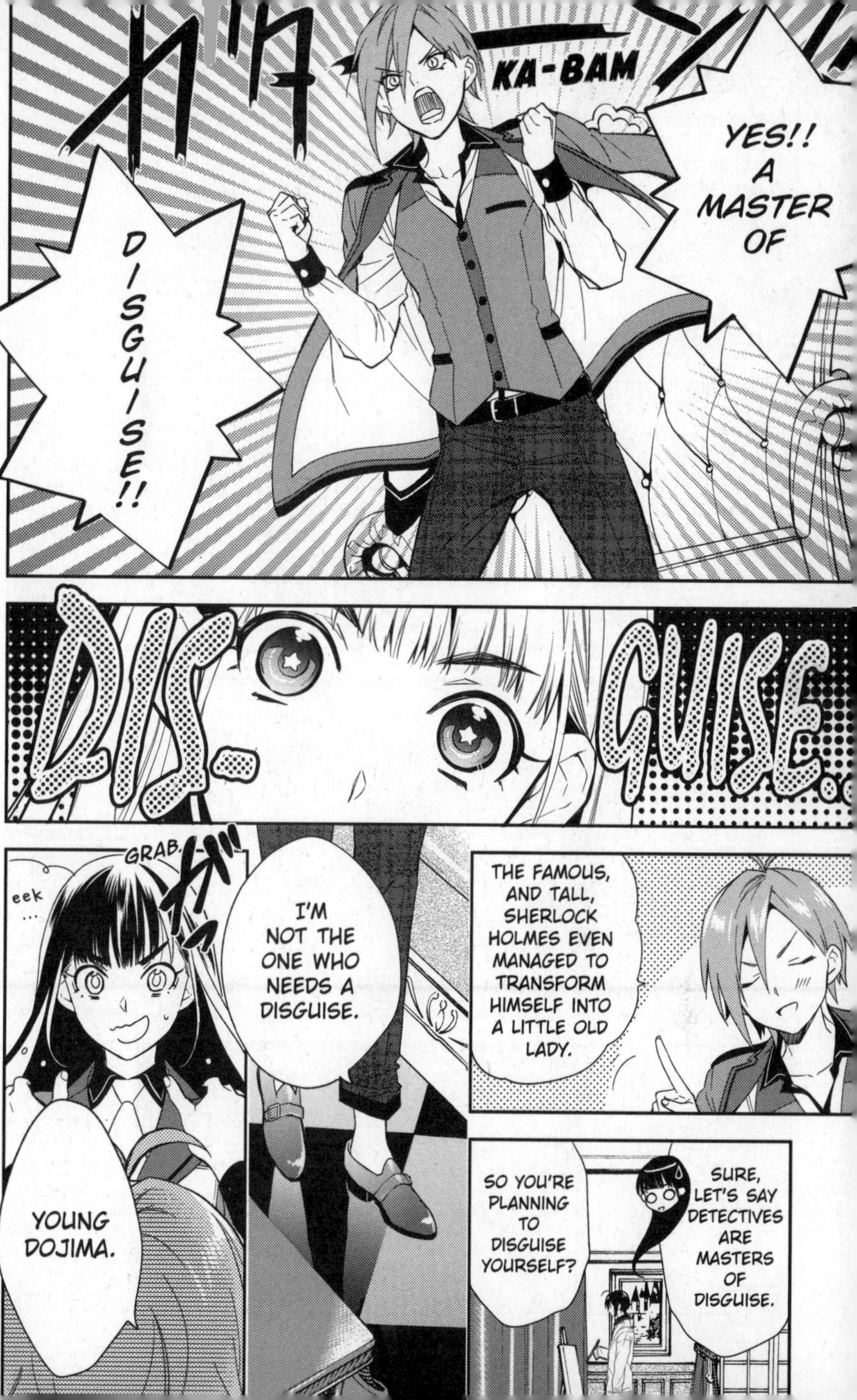
カッ
KA-BAM
YES!! A MASTER OF
DISGUISE!!
DIS- GUISE..
THE FAMOUS, AND TALL, SHERLOCK HOLMES EVEN MANAGED TO TRANSFORM HIMSELF INTO A LITTLE OLD LADY.
SURE, LET'S SAY DETECTIVES ARE MASTERS OF DISGUISE.
SO YOU'RE PLANNING TO DISGUISE YOURSELF?
I'M NOT THE ONE WHO NEEDS A DISGUISE.
GRAB.
eek ...
YOUNG DOJIMA.

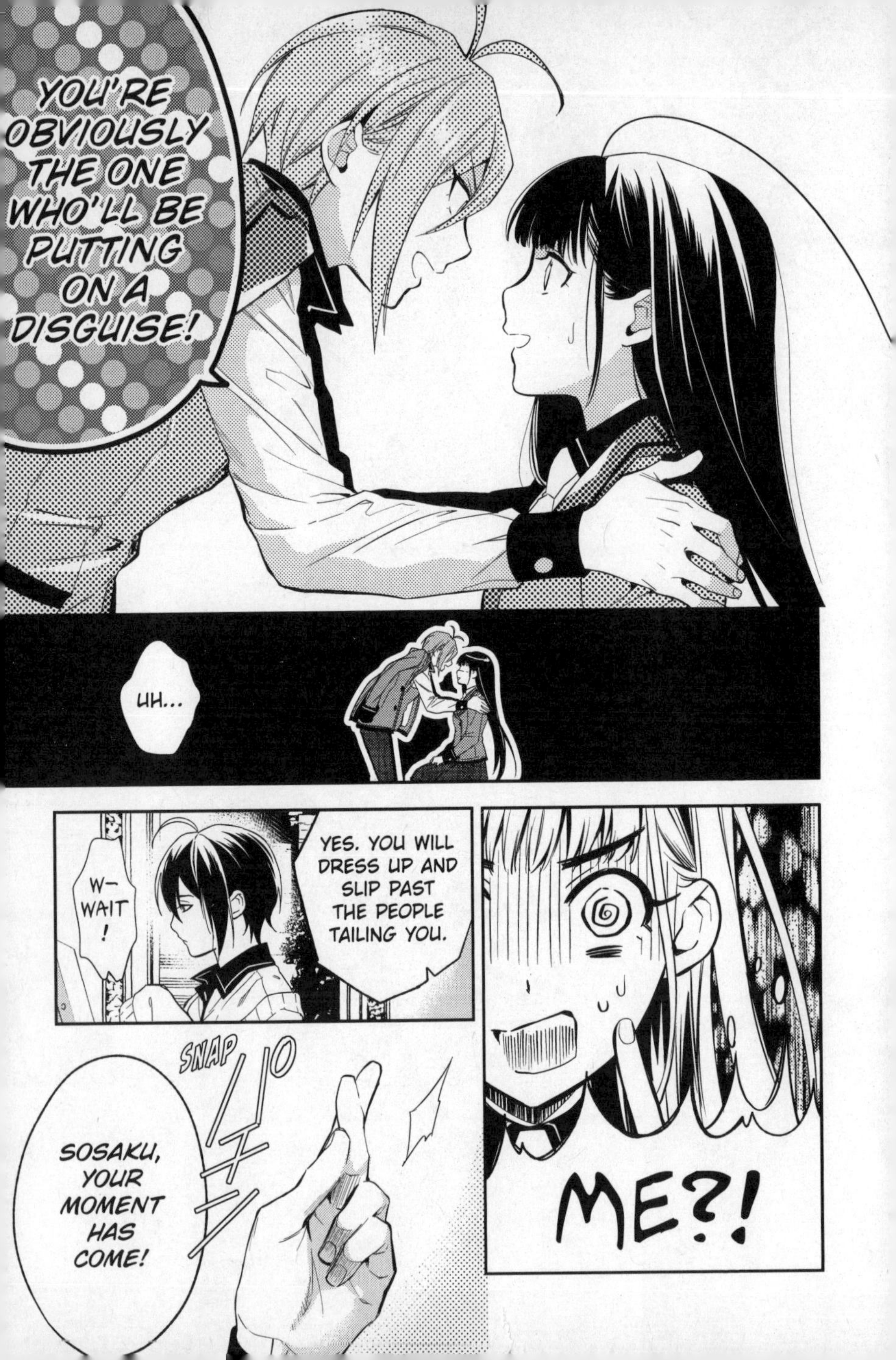
YOU'RE OBVIOUSLY THE ONE WHO'LL BE PUTTING ON A DISGUISE!
UH...
ME?!
YES. YOU WILL DRESS UP AND SLIP PAST THE PEOPLE TAILING YOU.
W— WAIT !
SNAP
SOSAKU, YOUR MOMENT HAS COME!

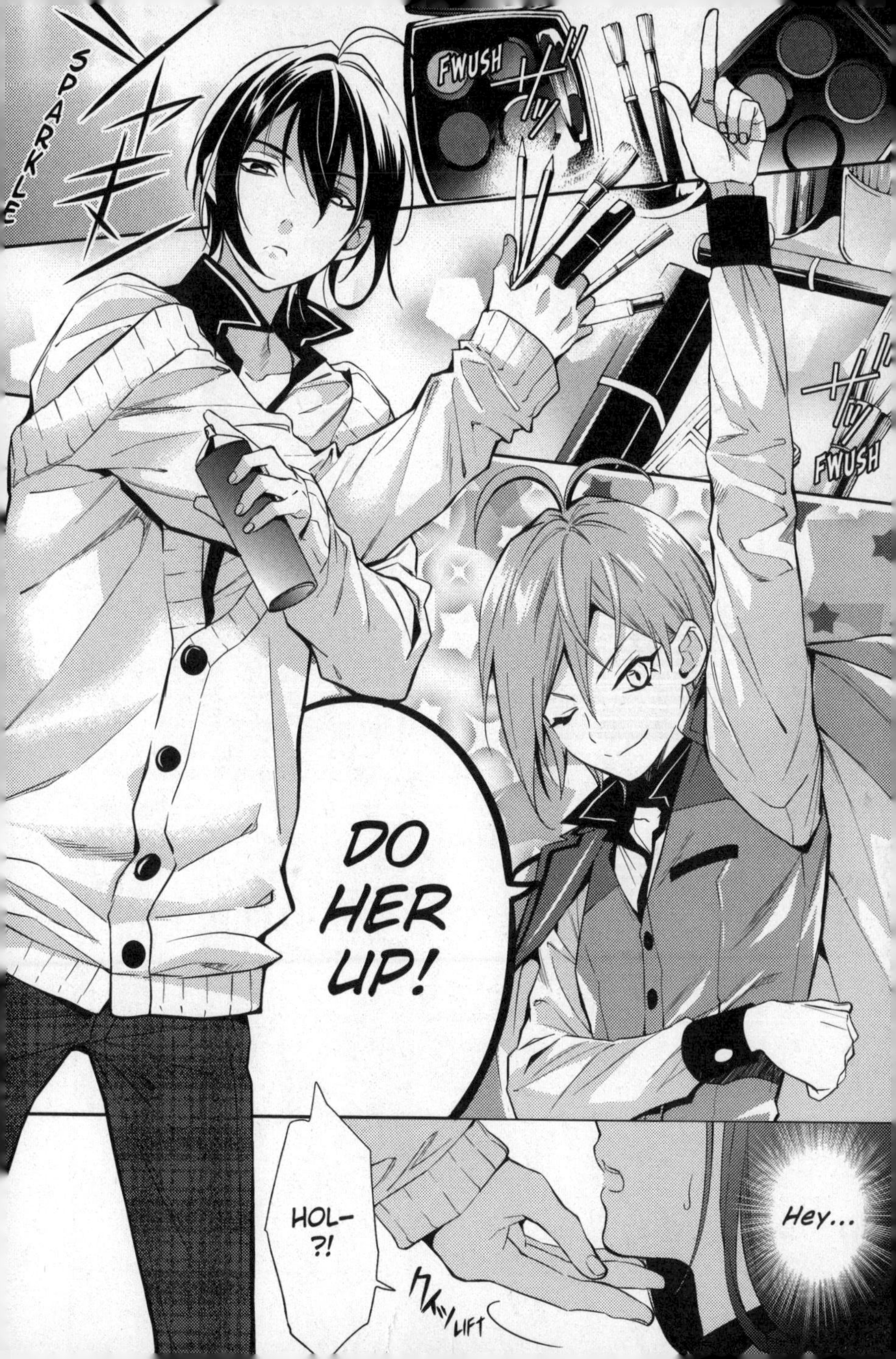
FWUSH
FWUSH
DO HER UP!
SPARKLE
Hey...
HOL- ?!
LIFT

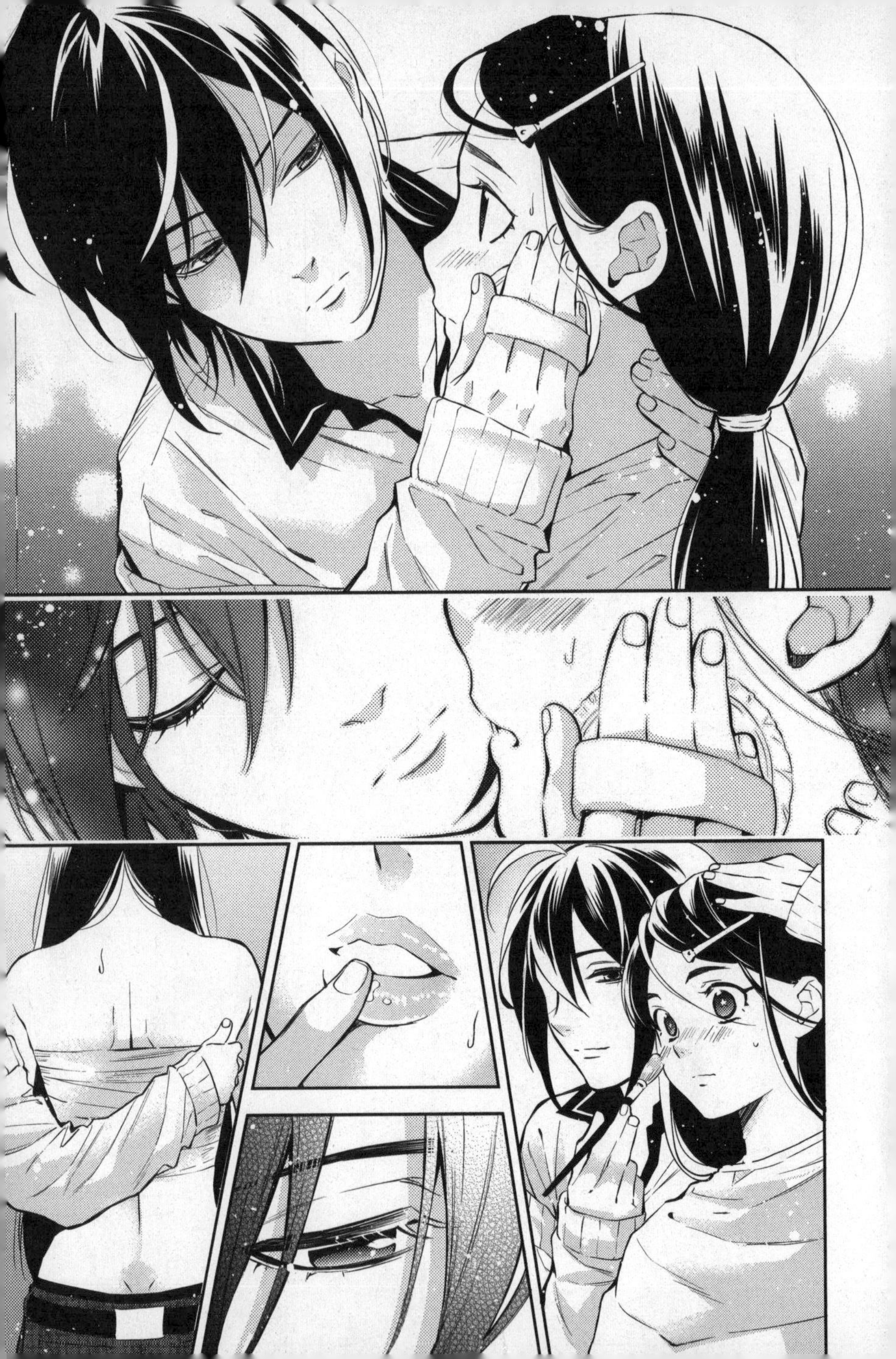

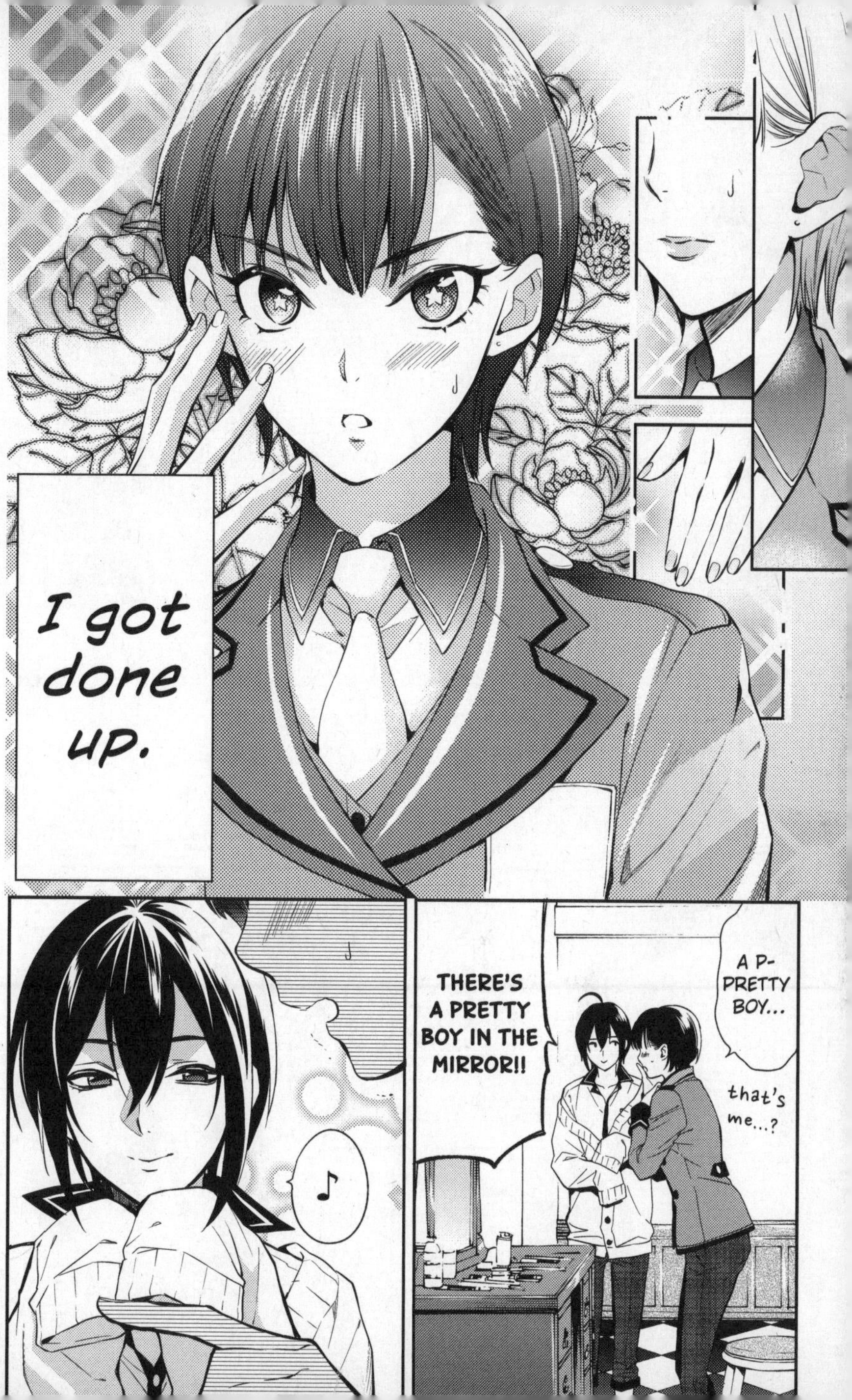
I got done up.
A P-PRETTY BOY...
that's me...?
THERE'S A PRETTY BOY IN THE MIRROR!!
♪

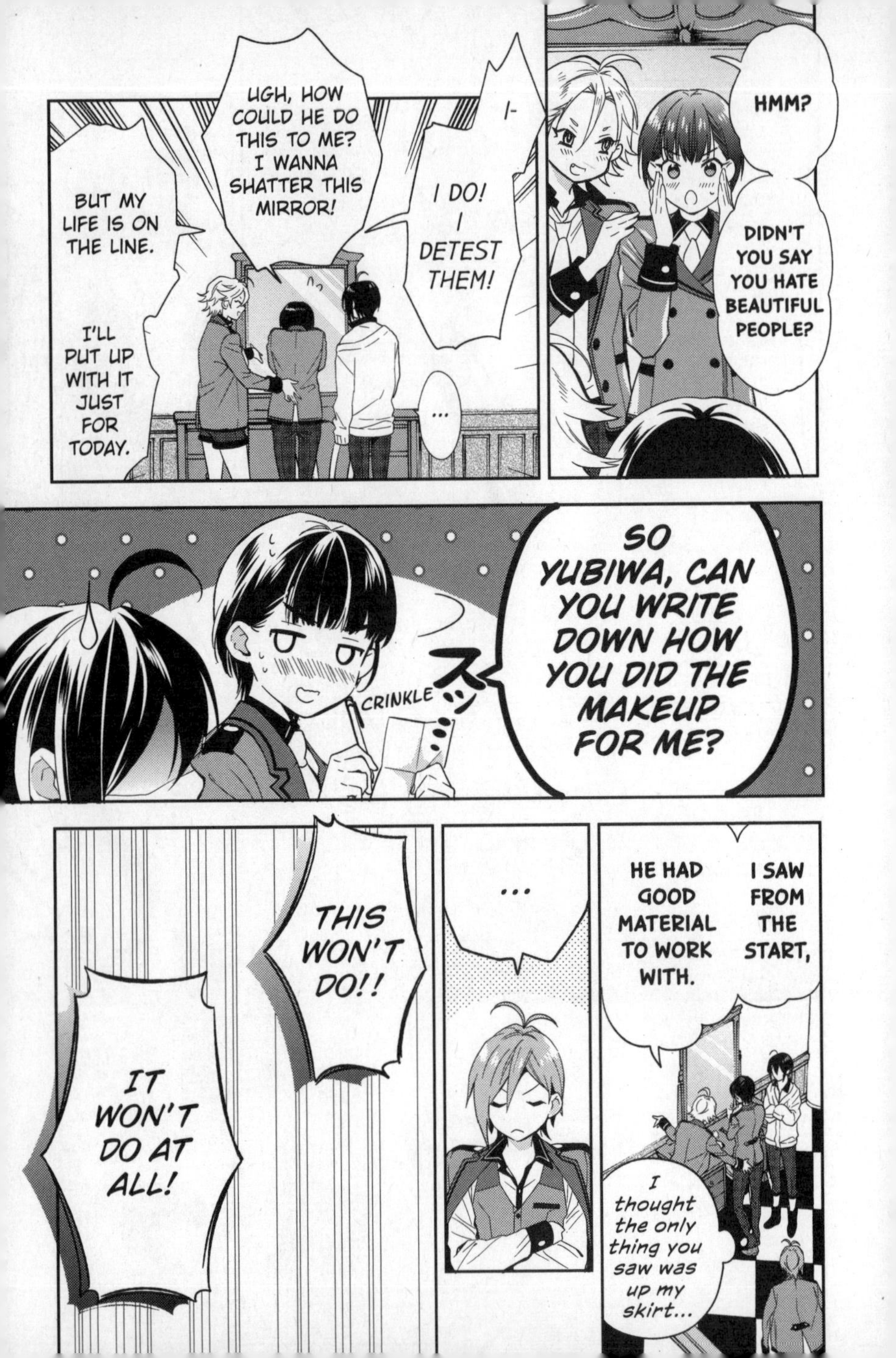
HMM?
DIDN'T YOU SAY YOU HATE BEAUTIFUL PEOPLE?
I-
UGH, HOW COULD HE DO THIS TO ME? I WANNA SHATTER THIS MIRROR!
I DO! I DETEST THEM!
BUT MY LIFE IS ON THE LINE.
...
I'LL PUT UP WITH IT JUST FOR TODAY.
SO YUBIWA, CAN YOU WRITE DOWN HOW YOU DID THE MAKEUP FOR ME?
スッ
CRINKLE
I SAW FROM THE START,
HE HAD GOOD MATERIAL TO WORK WITH.
I thought the only thing you saw was up my skirt...
...
THIS WON'T DO!!
IT WON'T DO AT ALL!

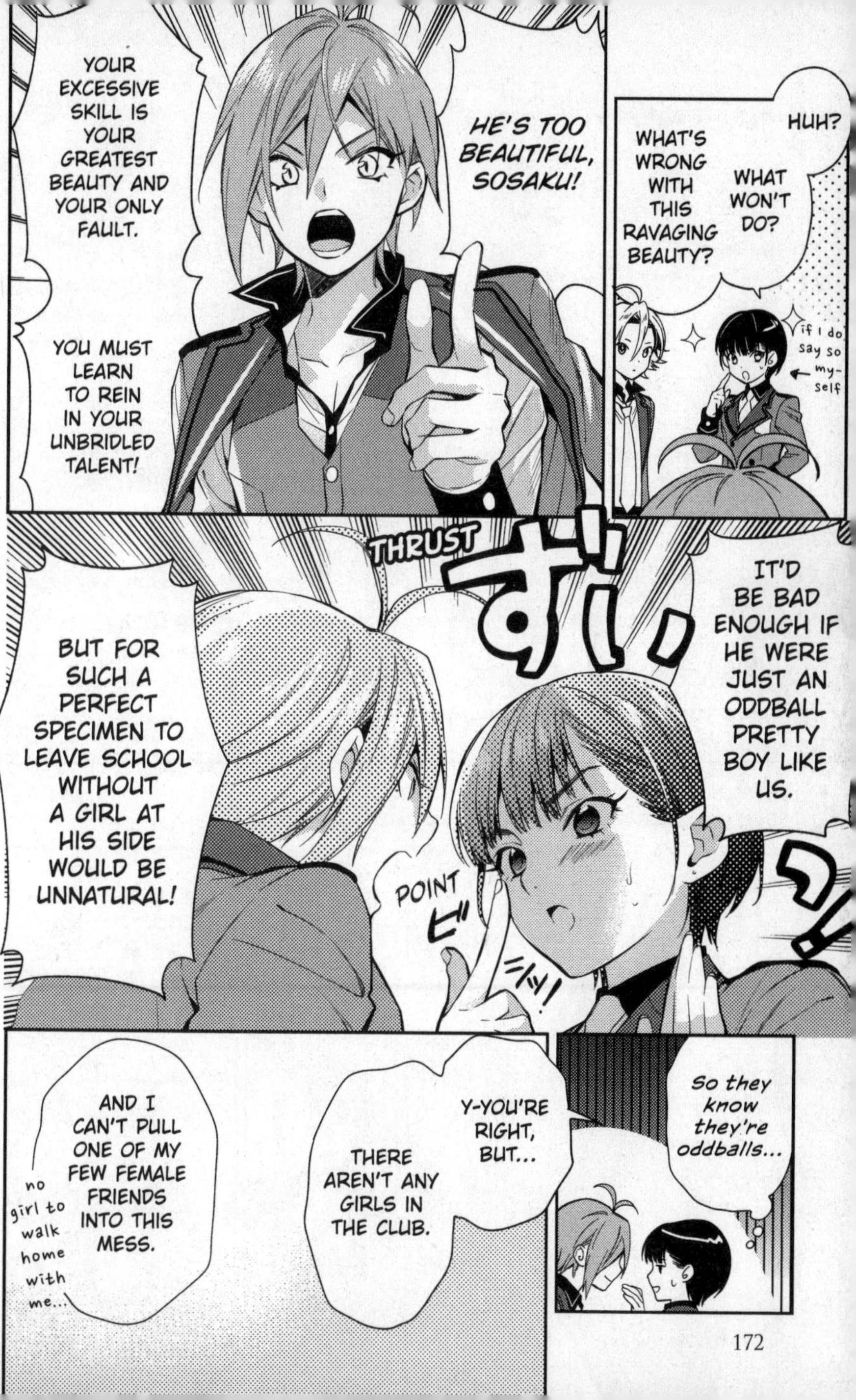
HUH?
WHAT WON'T DO?
WHAT'S WRONG WITH THIS RAVAGING BEAUTY?
if I do say so my-self
HE'S TOO BEAUTIFUL, SOSAKU!
YOUR EXCESSIVE SKILL IS YOUR GREATEST BEAUTY AND YOUR ONLY FAULT.
YOU MUST LEARN TO REIN IN YOUR UNBRIDLED TALENT!
THRUST
ずい
IT'D BE BAD ENOUGH IF HE WERE JUST AN ODDBALL PRETTY BOY LIKE US.
BUT FOR SUCH A PERFECT SPECIMEN TO LEAVE SCHOOL WITHOUT A GIRL AT HIS SIDE WOULD BE UNNATURAL!
POINT
ビ
シッ!
So they know they're oddballs...
Y-YOU'RE RIGHT, BUT...
THERE AREN'T ANY GIRLS IN THE CLUB.
AND I CAN'T PULL ONE OF MY FEW FEMALE FRIENDS INTO THIS MESS.
no girl to walk home with me...

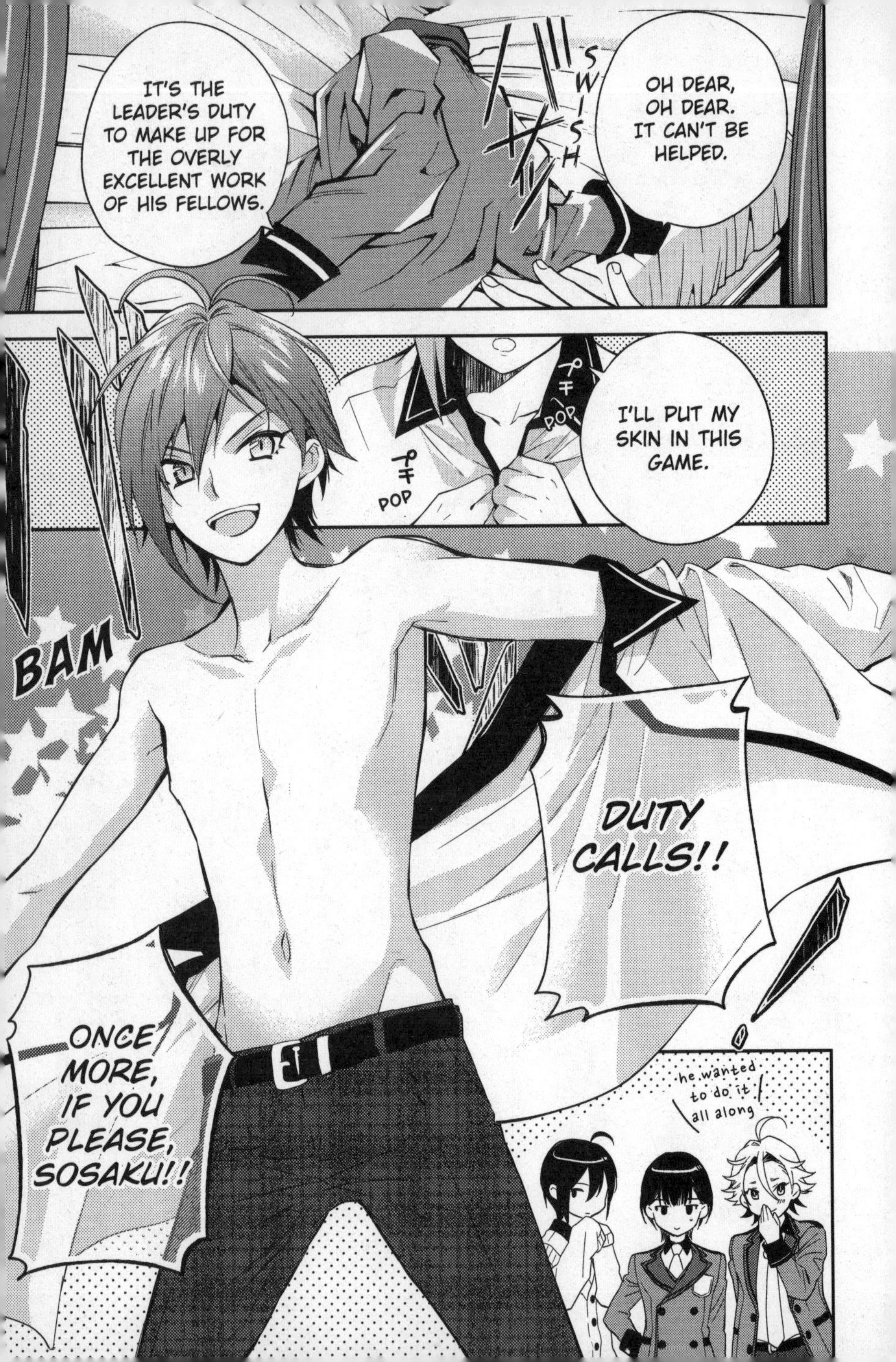
OH DEAR, OH DEAR. IT CAN'T BE HELPED.
SWISH
IT'S THE LEADER'S DUTY TO MAKE UP FOR THE OVERLY EXCELLENT WORK OF HIS FELLOWS.
I'LL PUT MY SKIN IN THIS GAME.
POP
POP
DUTY CALLS!!
BAM
ONCE MORE, IF YOU PLEASE, SOSAKU!!
he wanted to do it all along

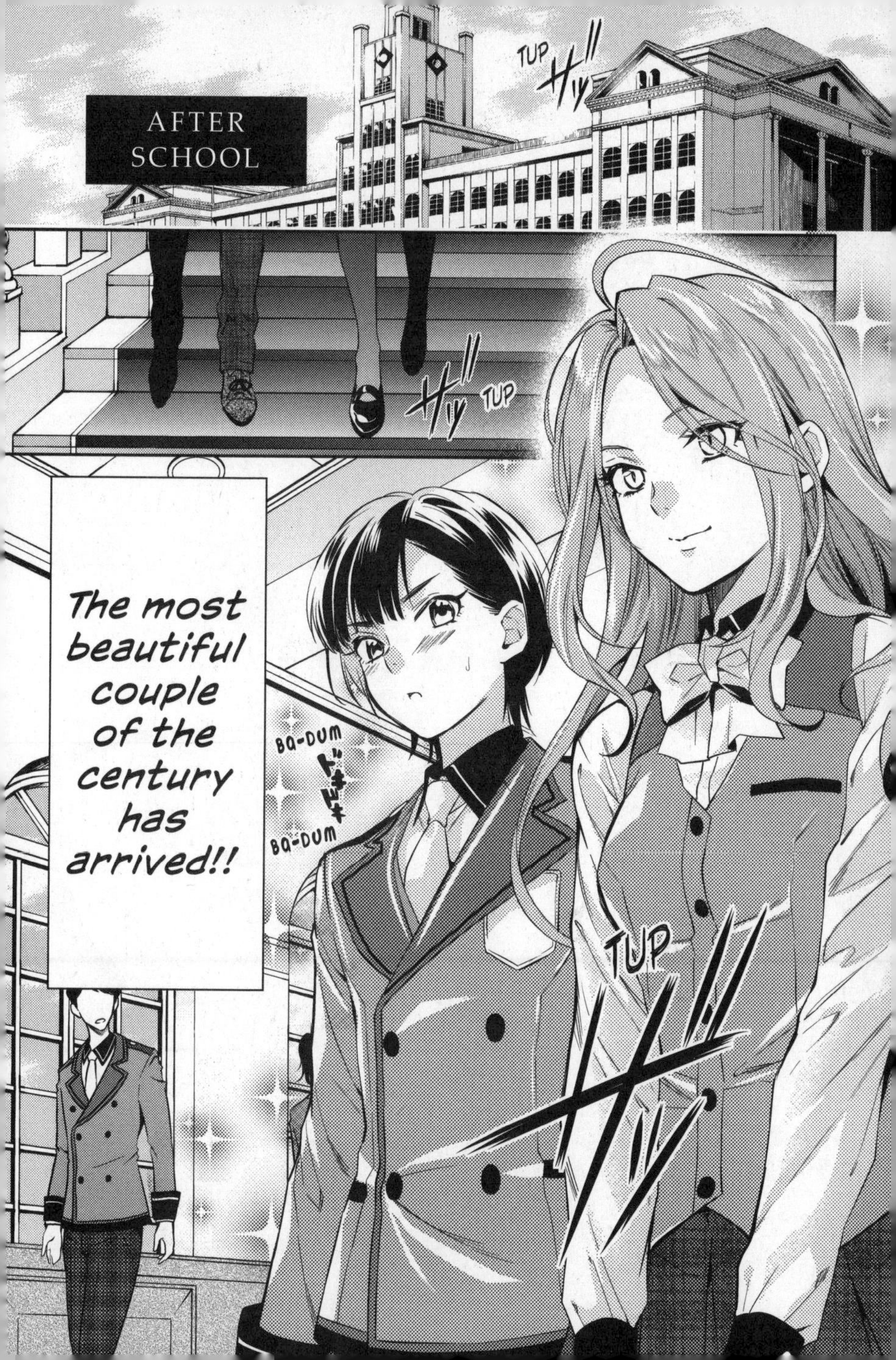
TUP
AFTER SCHOOL
TUP
TUP
BA-DUM
BA-DUM
The most beautiful couple of the century has arrived!!

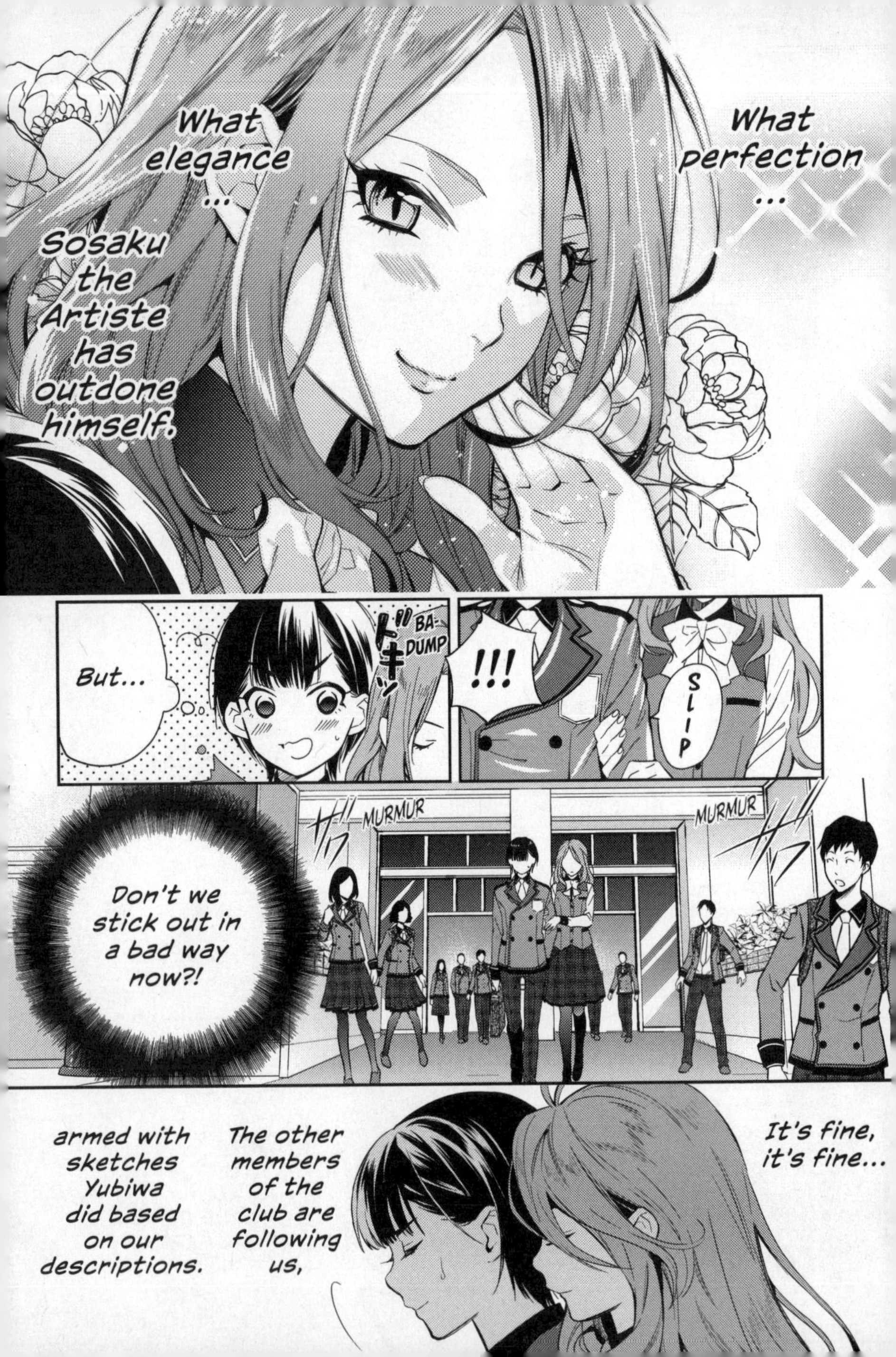

What perfection...
What elegance...
Sosaku the Artiste has outdone himself.
!!!
SLIP
BA-DUMP
But...
MURMUR
MURMUR
Don't we stick out in a bad way now?!
It's fine, it's fine...
The other members of the club are following us,
armed with sketches Yubiwa did based on our descriptions.

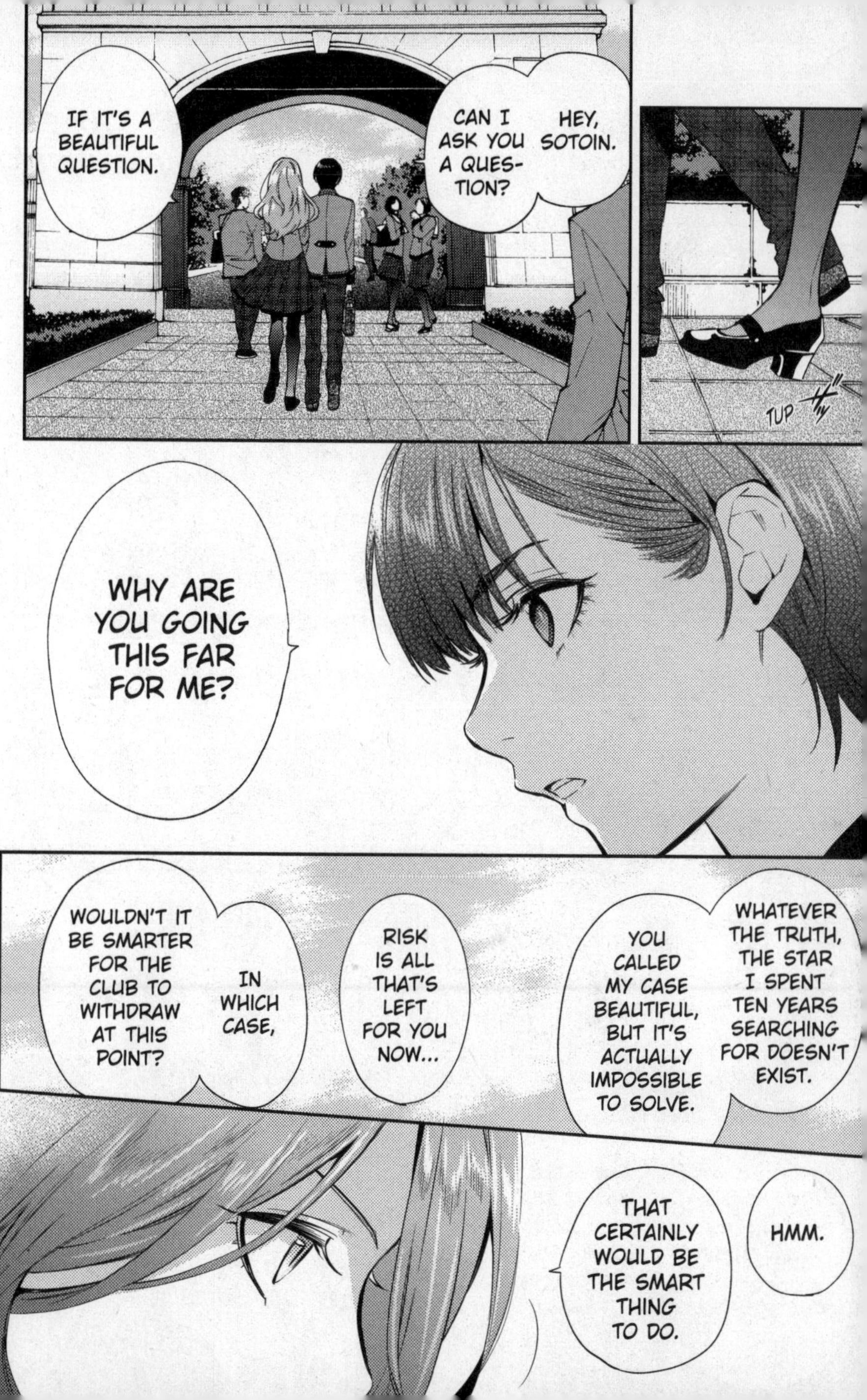
TUP
HEY, SOTOIN.
CAN I ASK YOU A QUESTION?
IF IT'S A BEAUTIFUL QUESTION.
WHY ARE YOU GOING THIS FAR FOR ME?
WHATEVER THE TRUTH, THE STAR I SPENT TEN YEARS SEARCHING FOR DOESN'T EXIST.
YOU CALLED MY CASE BEAUTIFUL, BUT IT'S ACTUALLY IMPOSSIBLE TO SOLVE.
RISK IS ALL THAT'S LEFT FOR YOU NOW...
IN WHICH CASE,
WOULDN'T IT BE SMARTER FOR THE CLUB TO WITHDRAW AT THIS POINT?
HMM.
THAT CERTAINLY WOULD BE THE SMART THING TO DO.

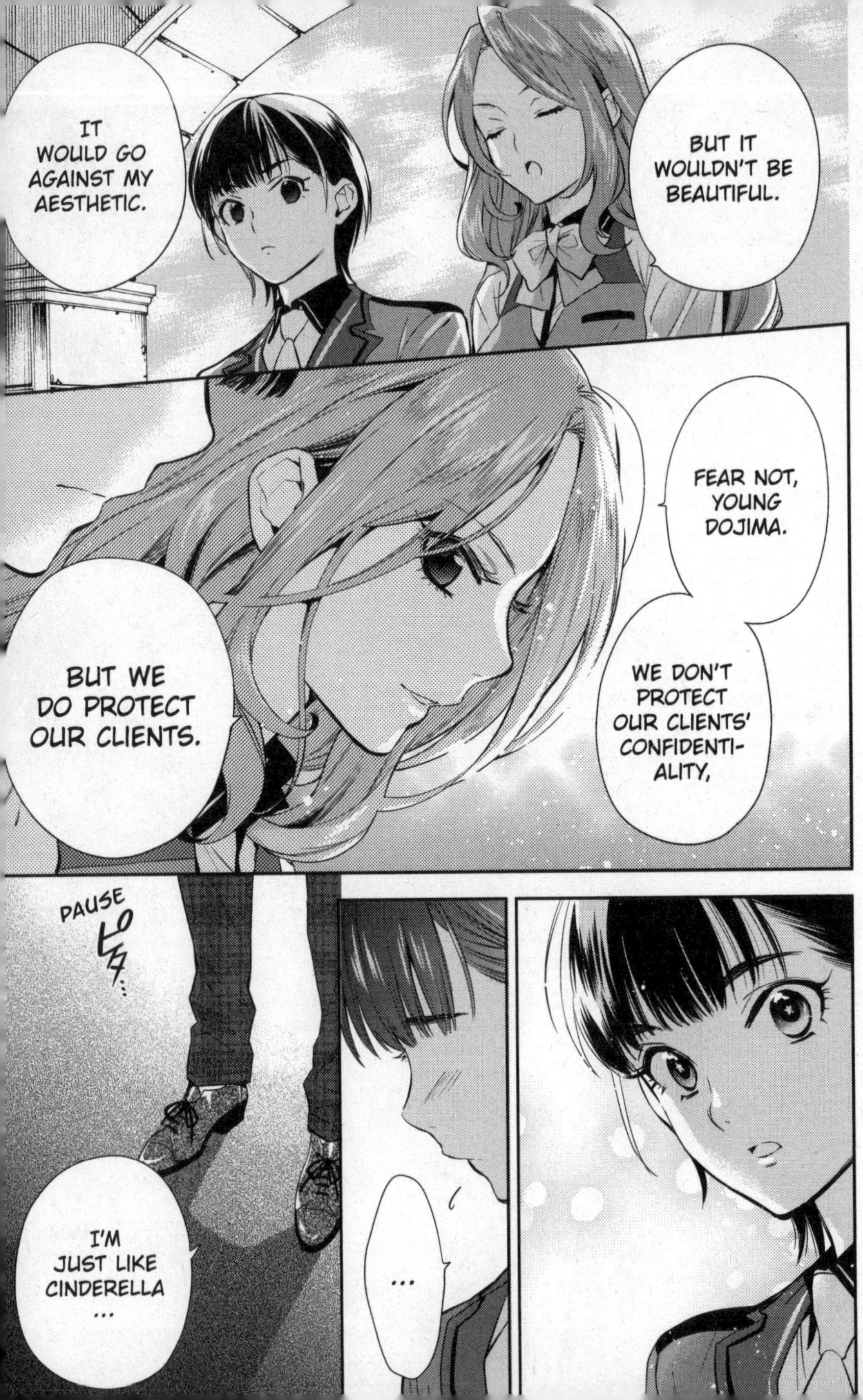
BUT IT WOULDN'T BE BEAUTIFUL.
IT WOULD GO AGAINST MY AESTHETIC.
FEAR NOT, YOUNG DOJIMA.
WE DON'T PROTECT OUR CLIENTS' CONFIDENTIALITY,
BUT WE DO PROTECT OUR CLIENTS.
...
PAUSE
ピク…
I'M JUST LIKE CINDERELLA ...

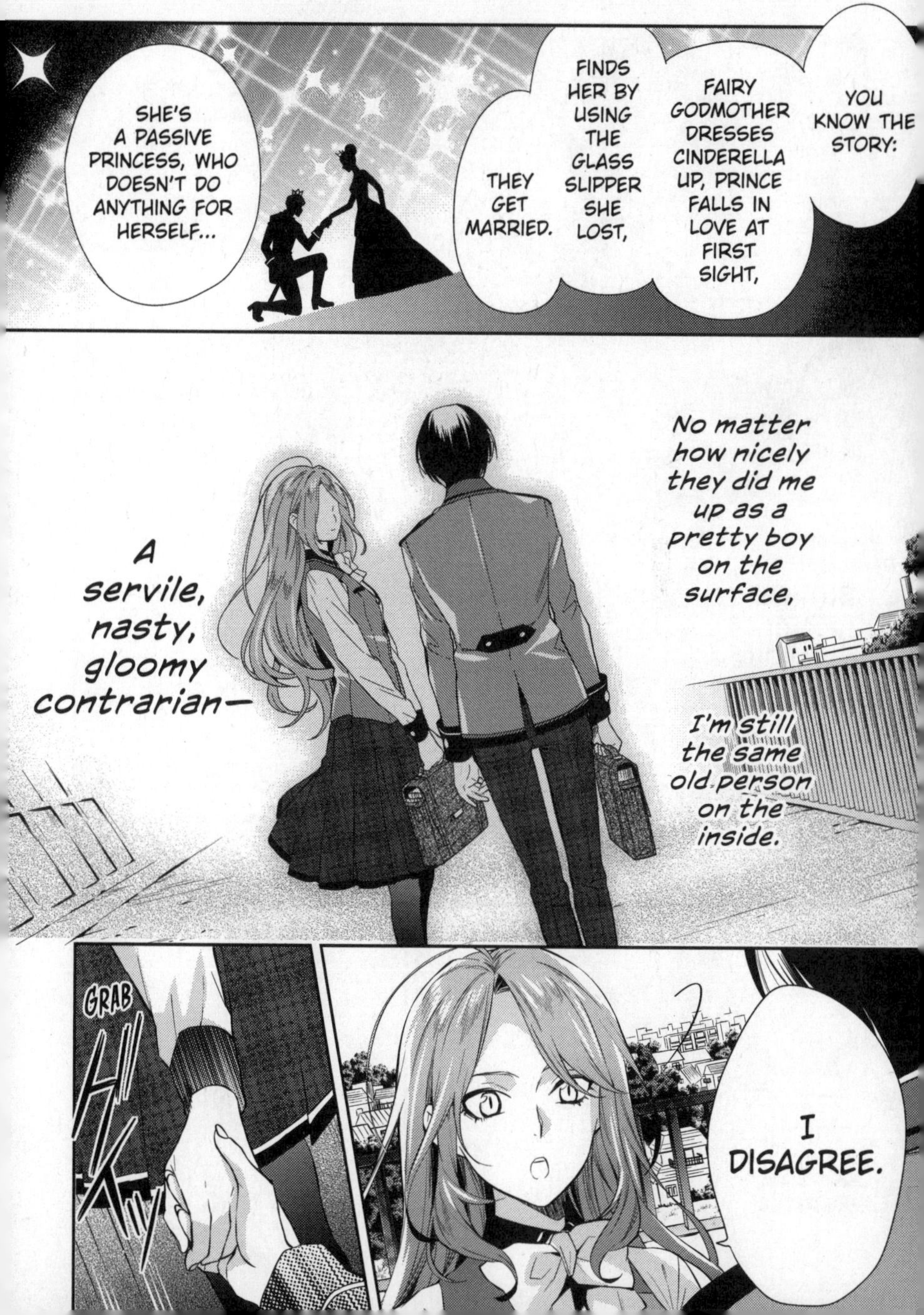
YOU KNOW THE STORY:
FAIRY GODMOTHER DRESSES CINDERELLA UP, PRINCE FALLS IN LOVE AT FIRST SIGHT,
FINDS HER BY USING THE GLASS SLIPPER SHE LOST,
THEY GET MARRIED.
SHE'S A PASSIVE PRINCESS, WHO DOESN'T DO ANYTHING FOR HERSELF...
No matter how nicely they did me up as a pretty boy on the surface,
I'm still the same old person on the inside.
A servile, nasty, gloomy contrarian—
I DISAGREE.
GRAB

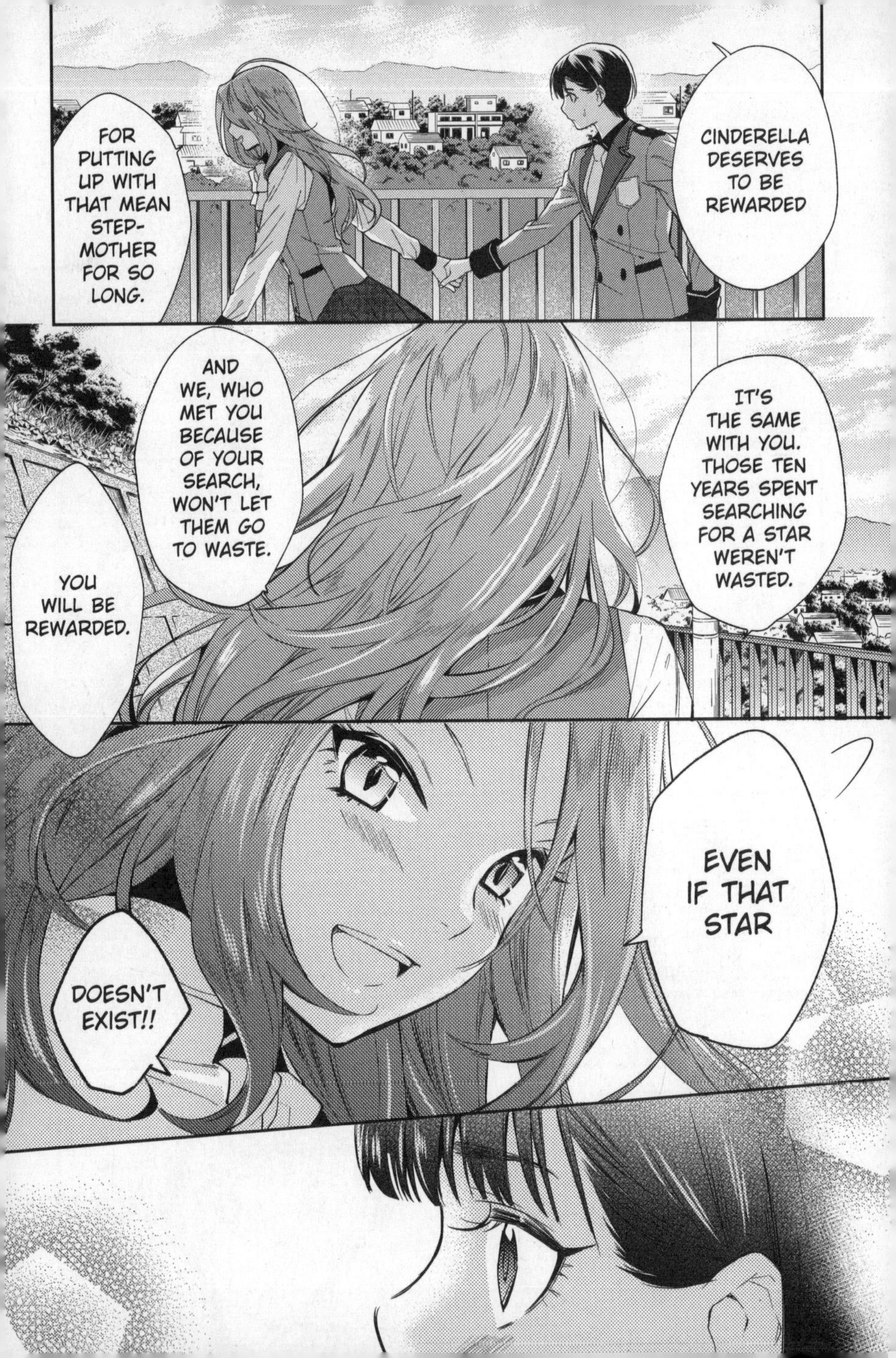
CINDERELLA DESERVES TO BE REWARDED
FOR PUTTING UP WITH THAT MEAN STEP-MOTHER FOR SO LONG.
IT'S THE SAME WITH YOU. THOSE TEN YEARS SPENT SEARCHING FOR A STAR WEREN'T WASTED.
AND WE, WHO MET YOU BECAUSE OF YOUR SEARCH, WON'T LET THEM GO TO WASTE.
YOU WILL BE REWARDED.
EVEN IF THAT STAR
DOESN'T EXIST!!

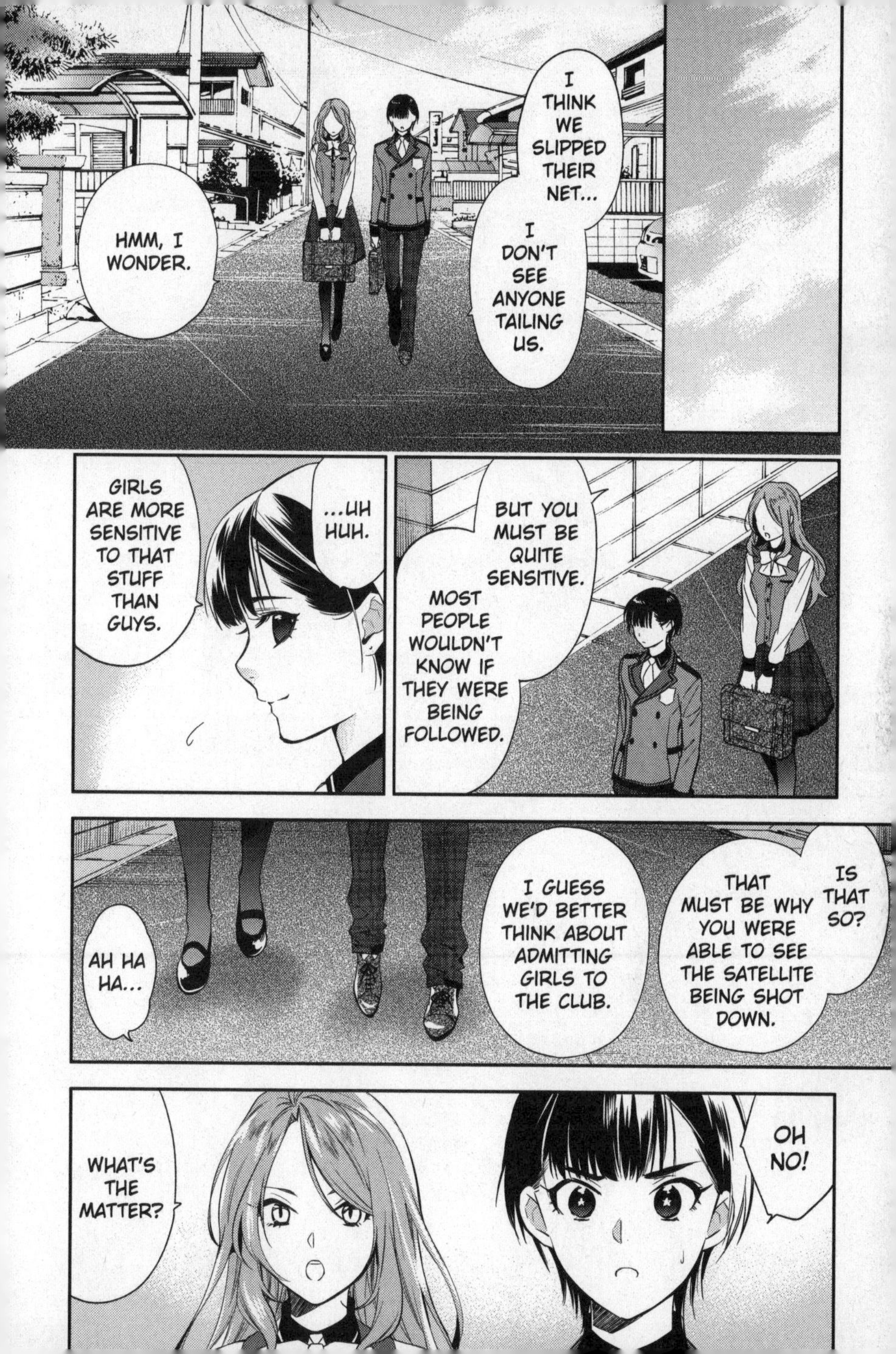

I THINK WE SLIPPED THEIR NET...
I DON'T SEE ANYONE TAILING US.
HMM, I WONDER.
BUT YOU MUST BE QUITE SENSITIVE.
MOST PEOPLE WOULDN'T KNOW IF THEY WERE BEING FOLLOWED.
...UH HUH.
GIRLS ARE MORE SENSITIVE TO THAT STUFF THAN GUYS.
IS THAT SO?
THAT MUST BE WHY YOU WERE ABLE TO SEE THE SATELLITE BEING SHOT DOWN.
I GUESS WE'D BETTER THINK ABOUT ADMITTING GIRLS TO THE CLUB.
AH HA HA...
OH NO!
WHAT'S THE MATTER?

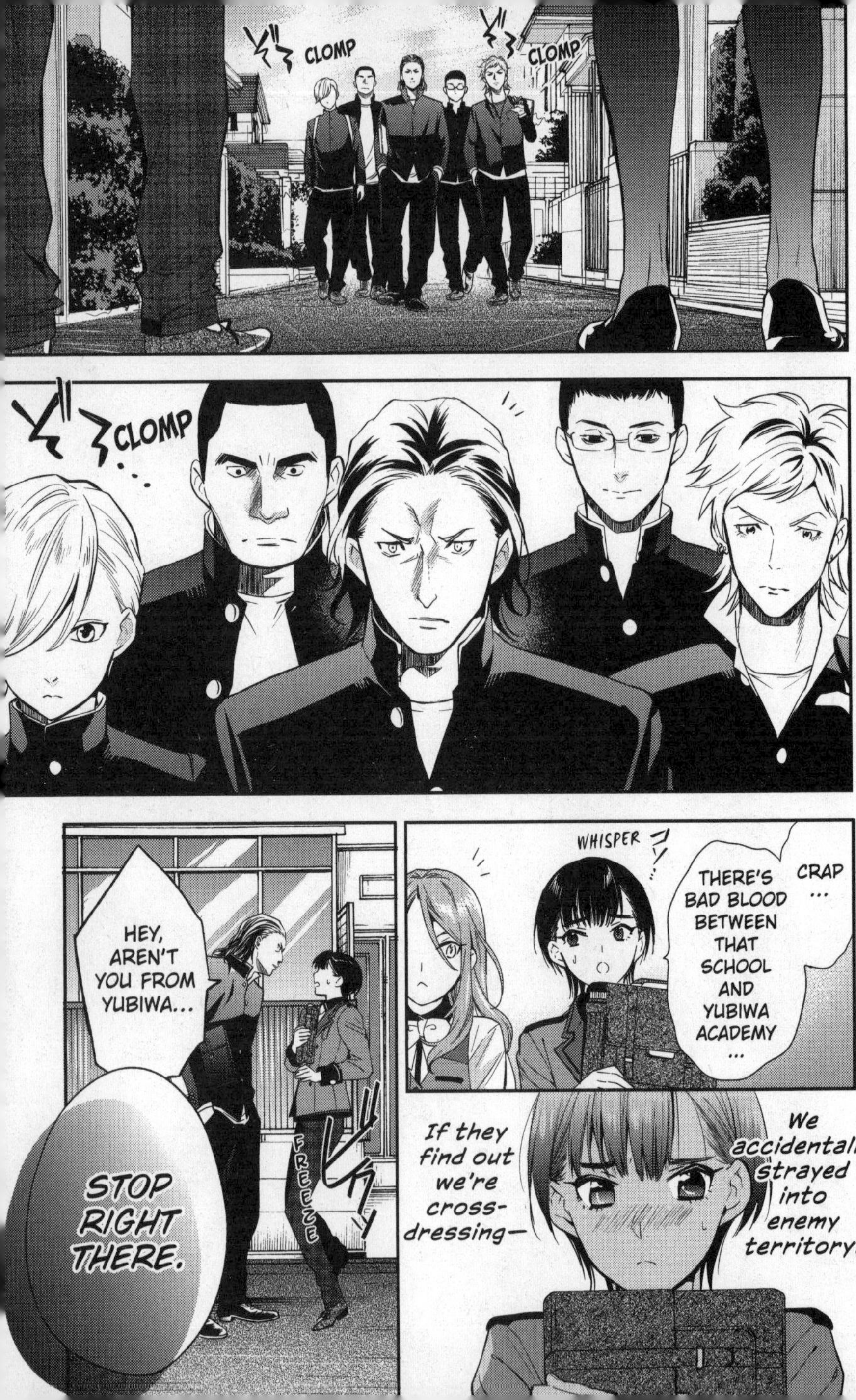

CLOMP
CLOMP
CLOMP
WHISPER
CRAP ...
THERE'S BAD BLOOD BETWEEN THAT SCHOOL AND YUBIWA ACADEMY ...
We accidentally strayed into enemy territory.
If they find out we're cross-dressing—
HEY, AREN'T YOU FROM YUBIWA...
FREEZE
STOP RIGHT THERE.

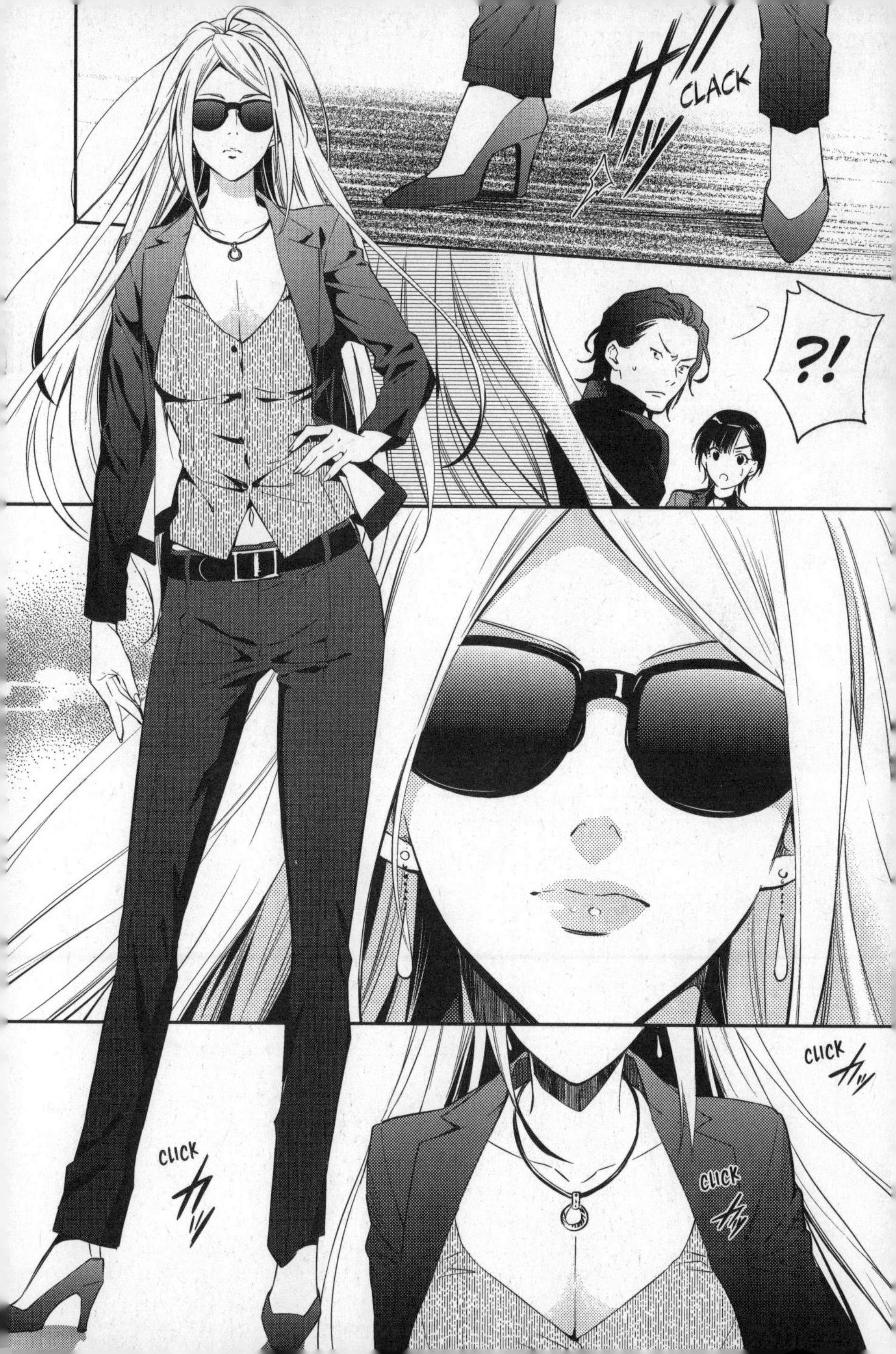
CLACK
?!
CLICK
CLICK
CLICK

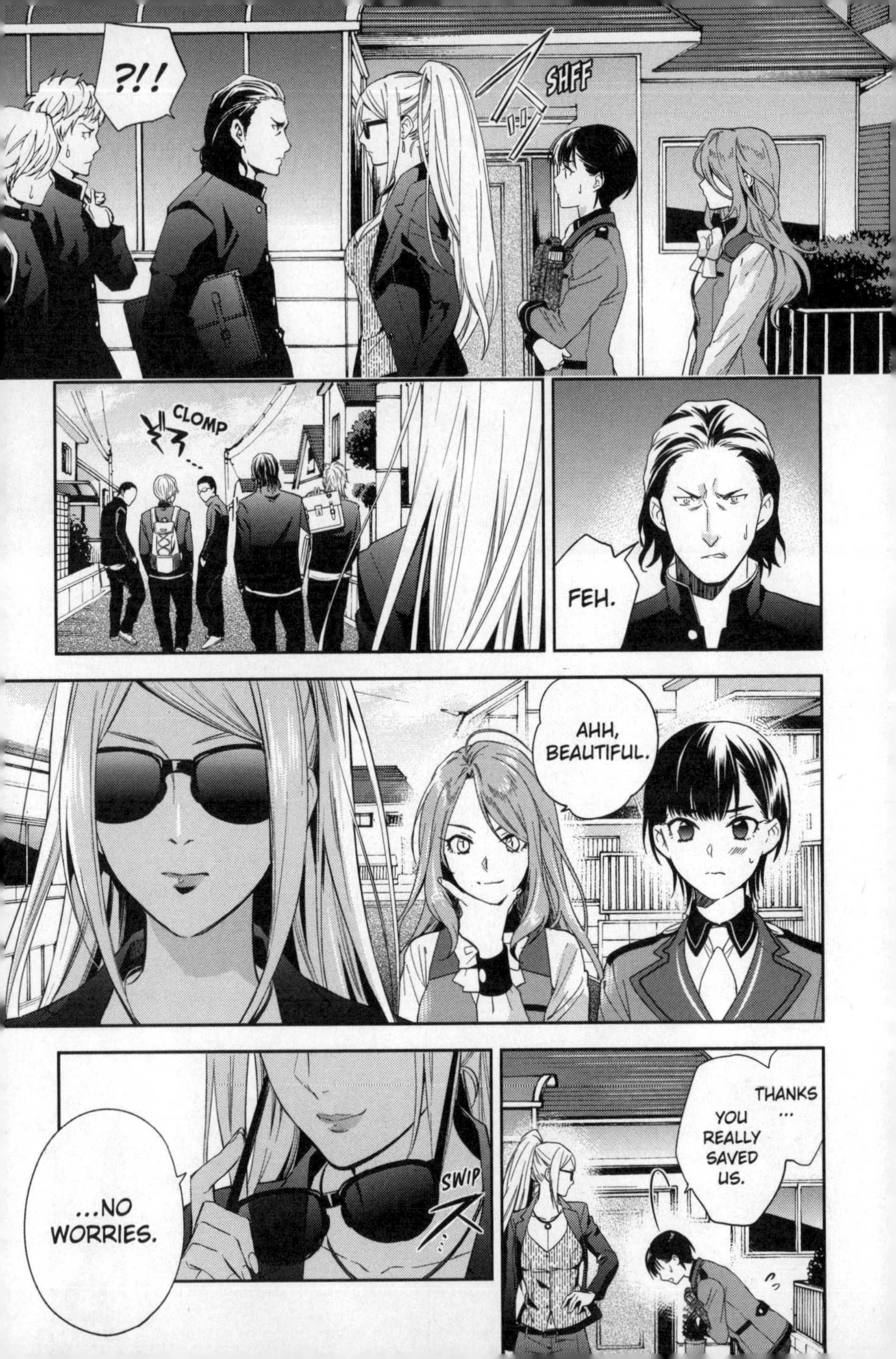
SHFF
?!!
FEH.
CLOMP
AHH, BEAUTIFUL.
THANKS...
YOU REALLY SAVED US.
SWIP
...NO WORRIES.

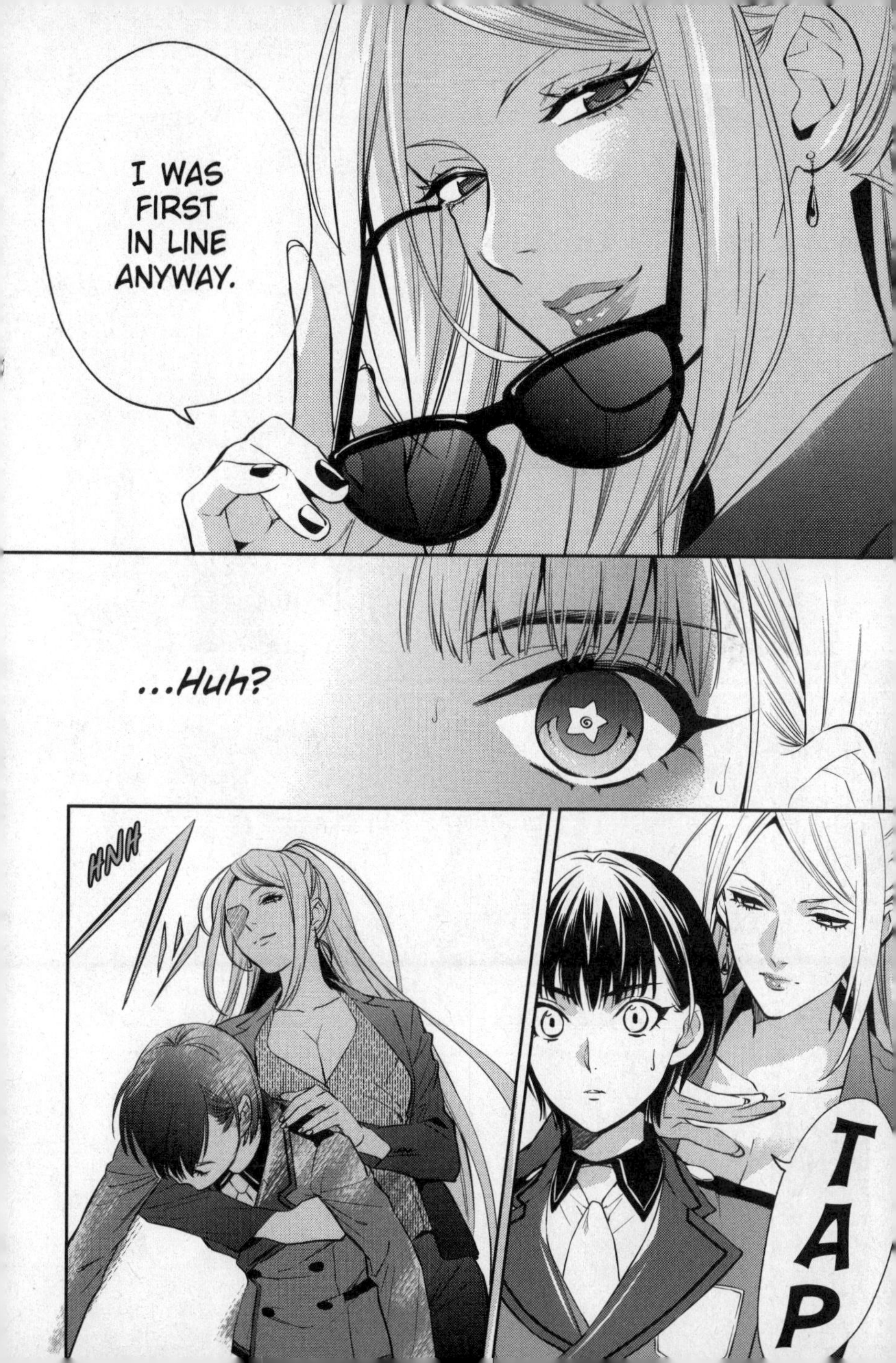
I WAS FIRST IN LINE ANYWAY.
...Huh?
TAP
HNH

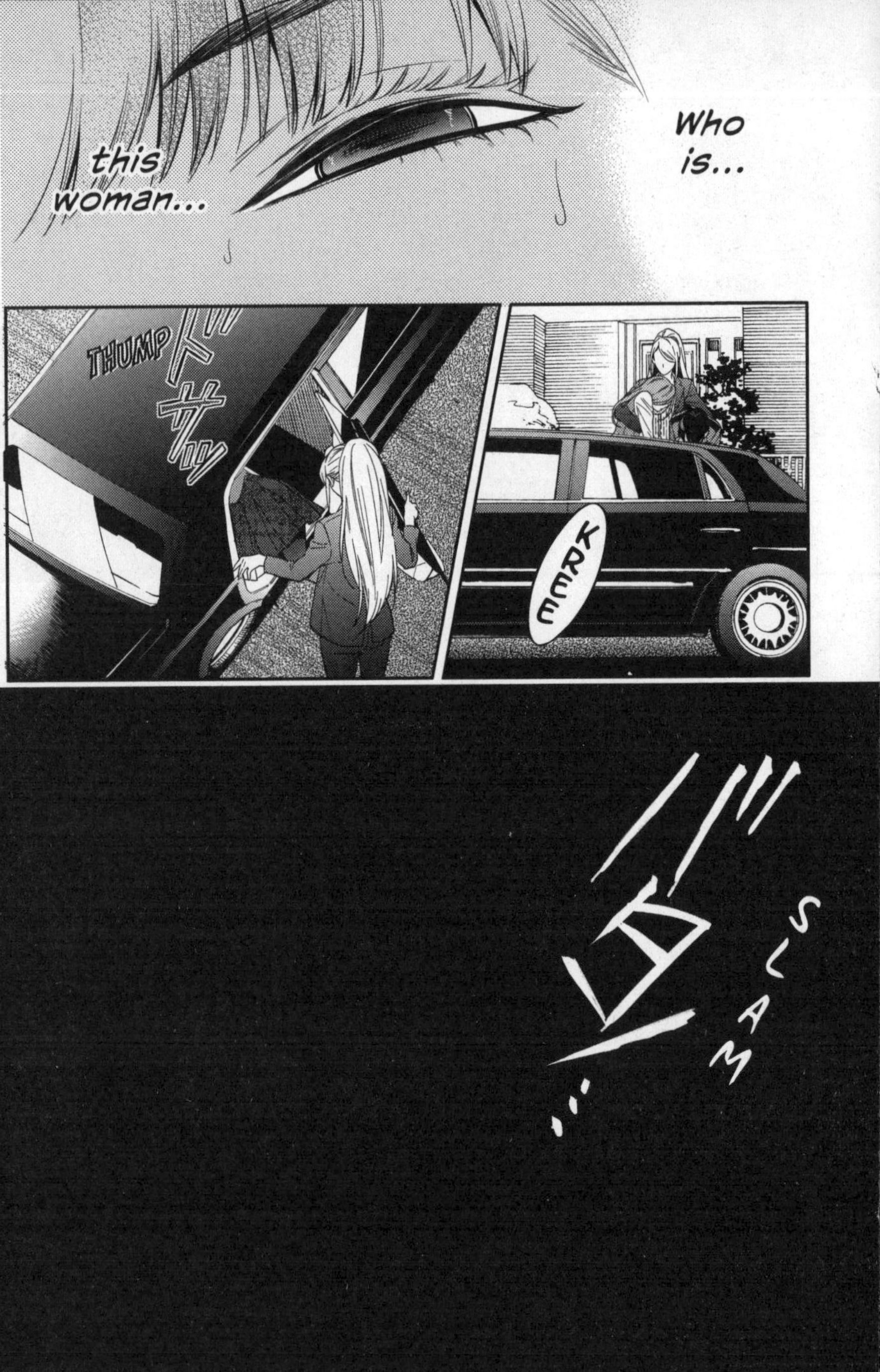
Who is...
this woman...
KREE
THUMP
SLAM

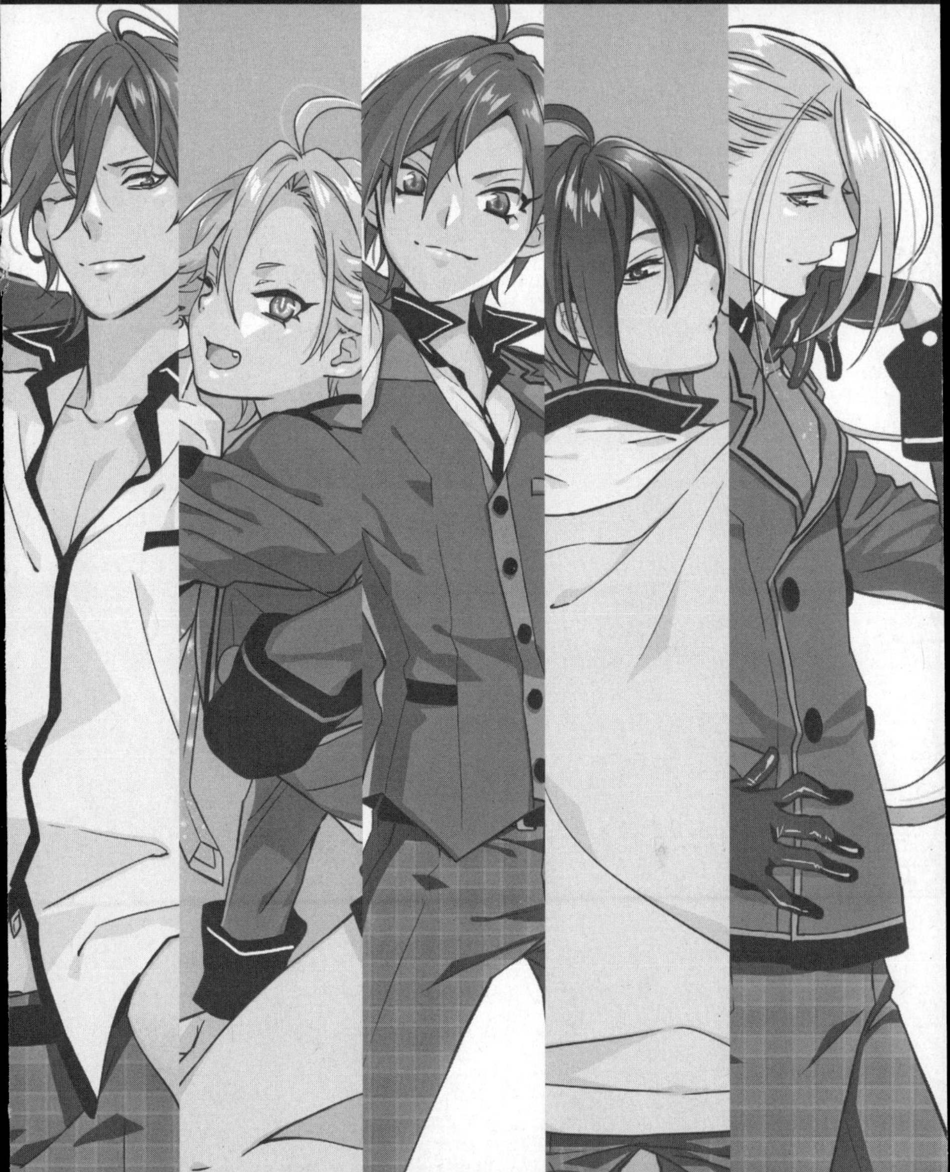

FILE ★ The Dark Star that Shines for You Alone 5

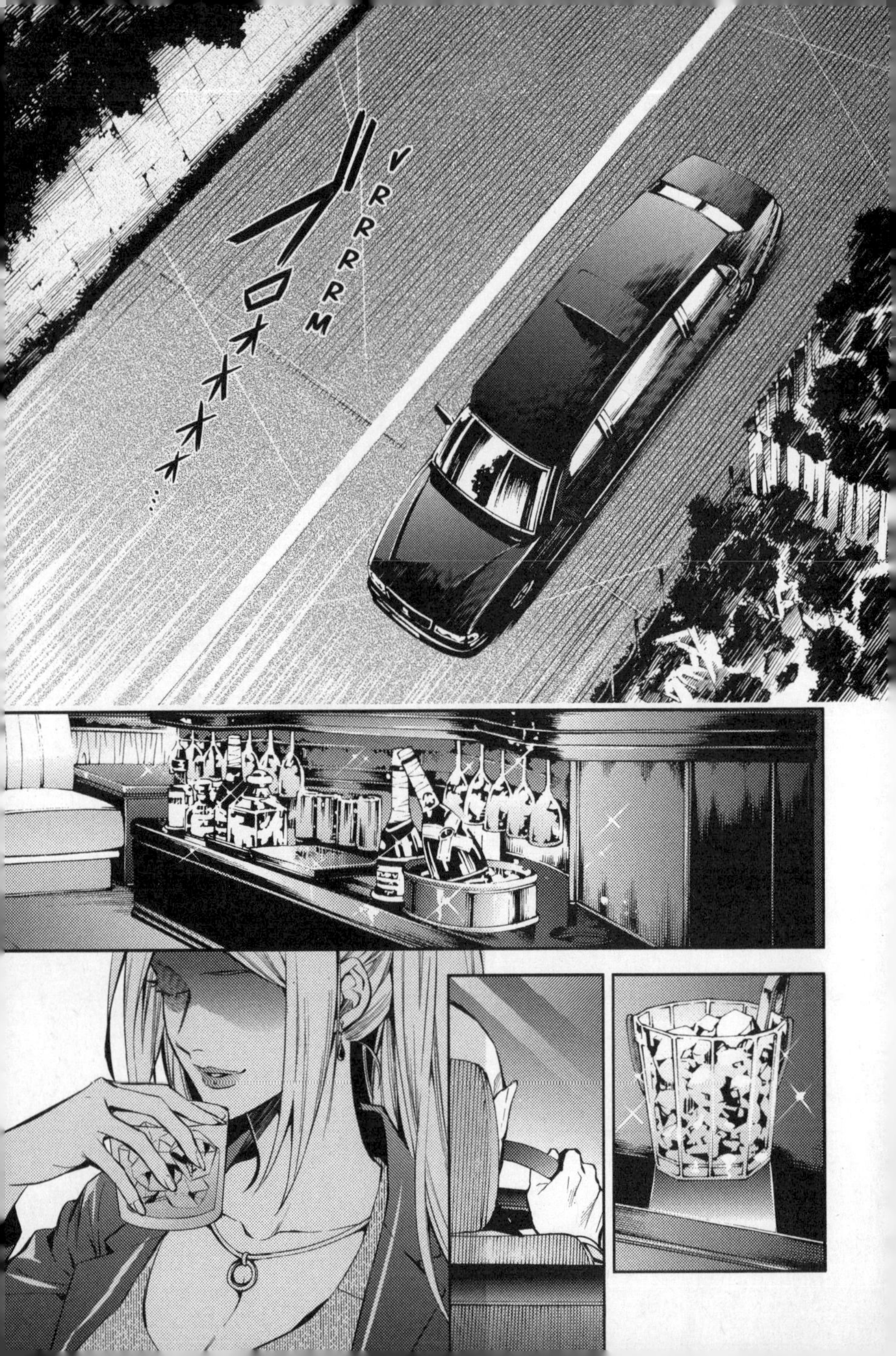
VRRRRRM

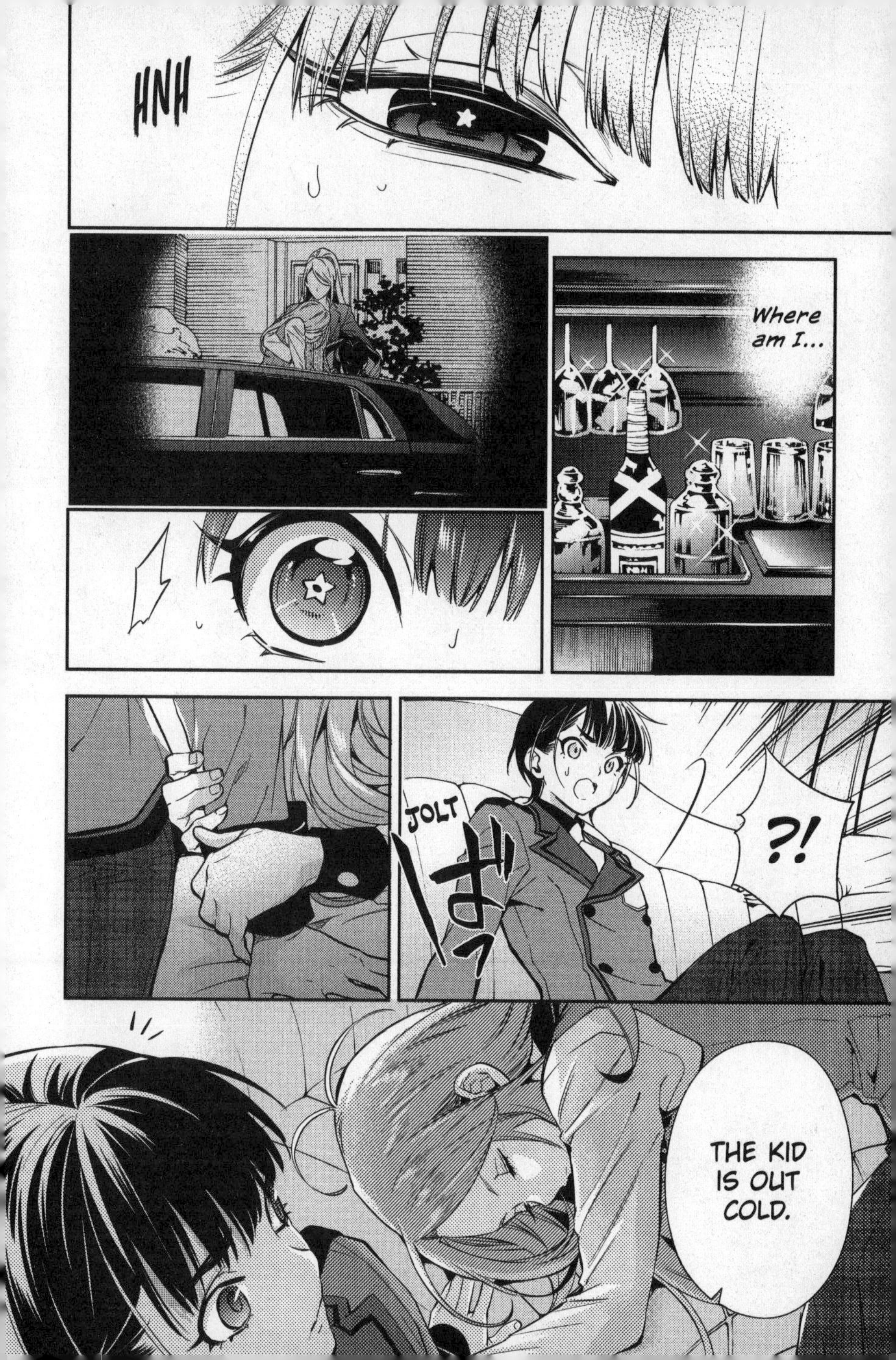
HNH
Where am I...
?!
JOLT
THE KID IS OUT COLD.

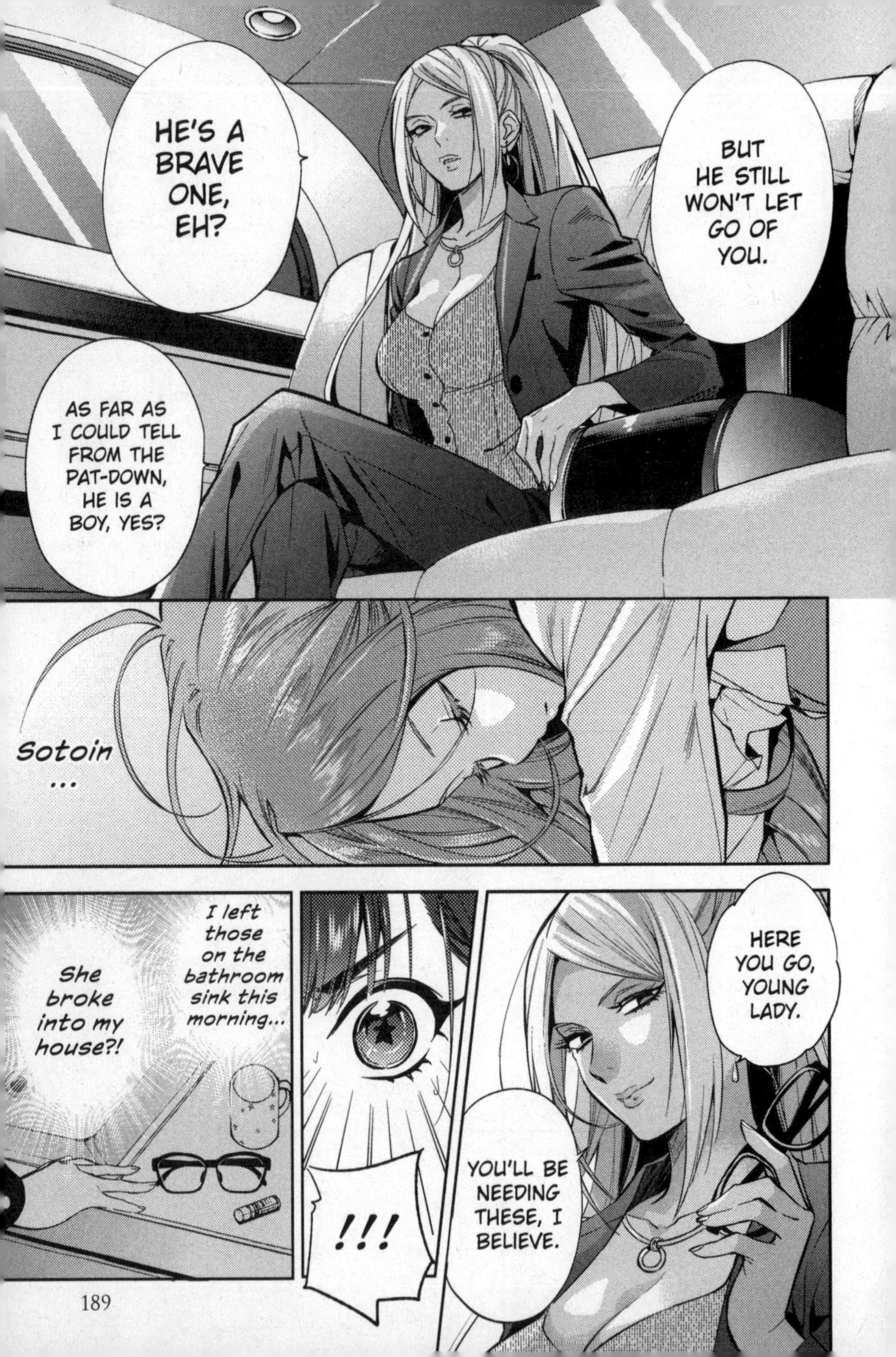
HE'S A BRAVE ONE, EH?
BUT HE STILL WON'T LET GO OF YOU.
AS FAR AS I COULD TELL FROM THE PAT-DOWN, HE IS A BOY, YES?
Sotoin ...
HERE YOU GO, YOUNG LADY.
YOU'LL BE NEEDING THESE, I BELIEVE.
!!!
I left those on the bathroom sink this morning...
She broke into my house?!

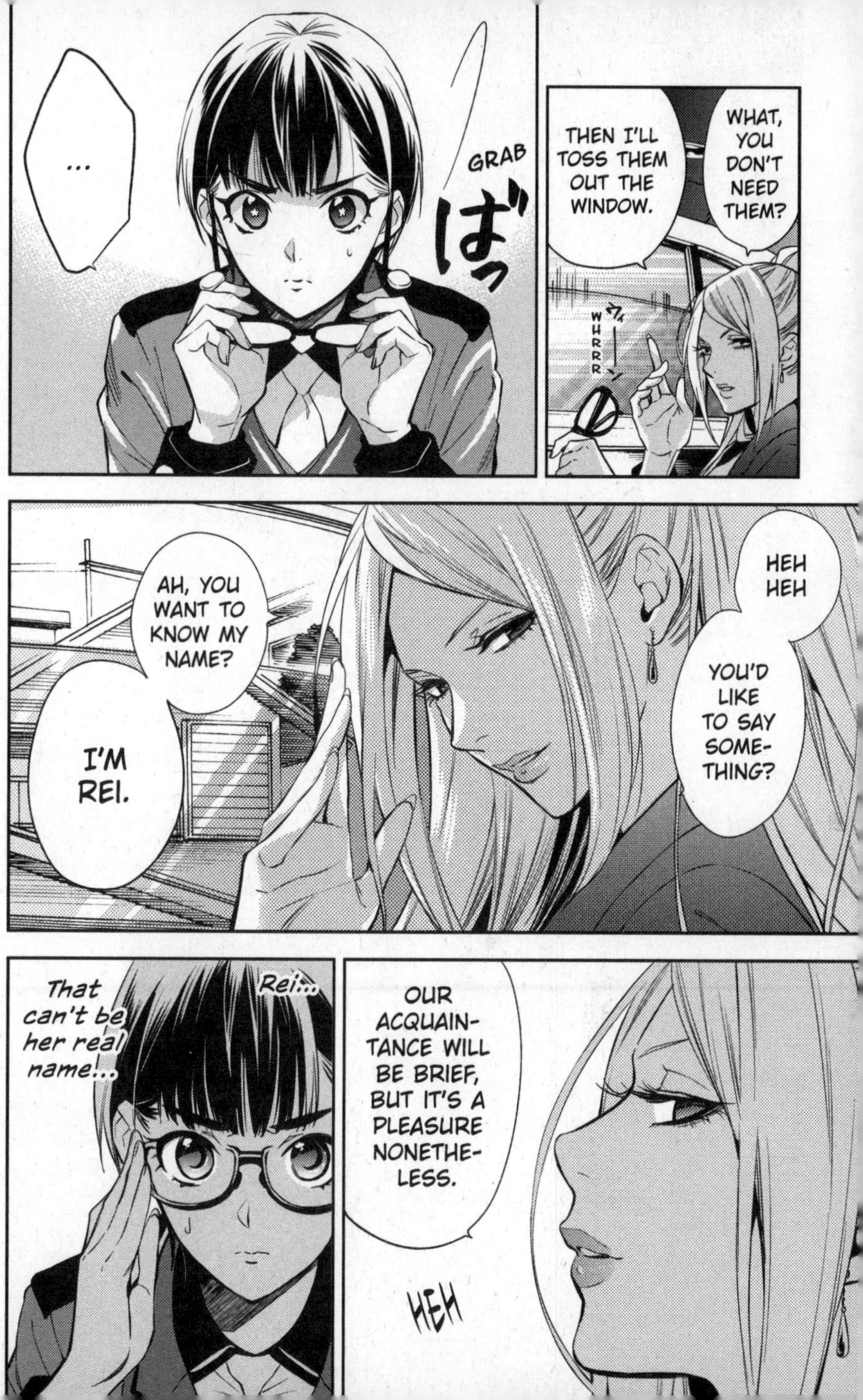
WHAT, YOU DON'T NEED THEM?
THEN I'LL TOSS THEM OUT THE WINDOW.
WHRRR
GRAB
ばっ
...
HEH HEH
YOU'D LIKE TO SAY SOME-THING?
AH, YOU WANT TO KNOW MY NAME?
I'M REI.
OUR ACQUAIN-TANCE WILL BE BRIEF, BUT IT'S A PLEASURE NONETHE-LESS.
HEH
Rei...
That can't be her real name...

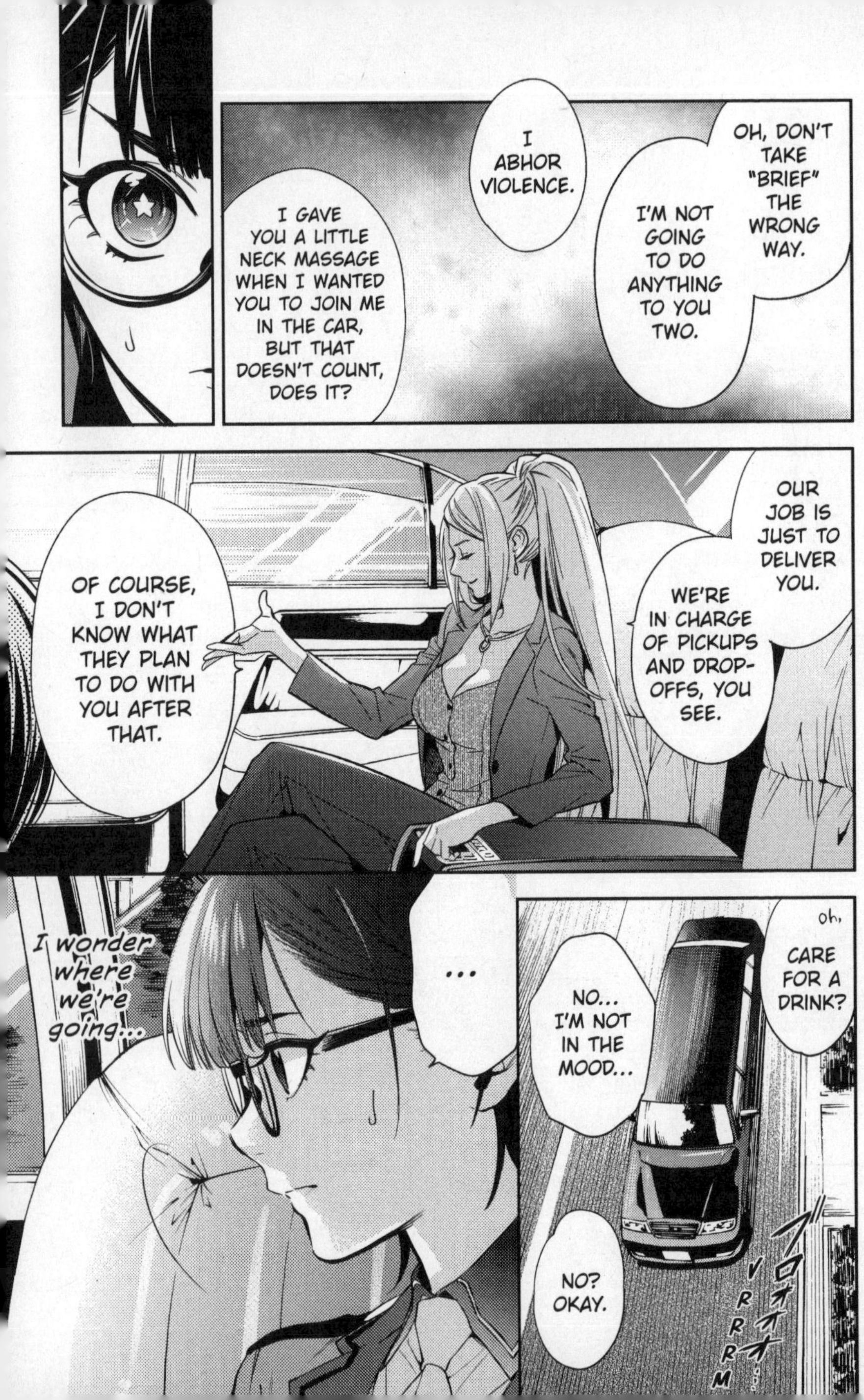
OH, DON'T TAKE "BRIEF" THE WRONG WAY.
I'M NOT GOING TO DO ANYTHING TO YOU TWO.
I ABHOR VIOLENCE.
I GAVE YOU A LITTLE NECK MASSAGE WHEN I WANTED YOU TO JOIN ME IN THE CAR, BUT THAT DOESN'T COUNT, DOES IT?
OUR JOB IS JUST TO DELIVER YOU.
WE'RE IN CHARGE OF PICKUPS AND DROP-OFFS, YOU SEE.
OF COURSE, I DON'T KNOW WHAT THEY PLAN TO DO WITH YOU AFTER THAT.
Oh, CARE FOR A DRINK?
NO... I'M NOT IN THE MOOD...
NO? OKAY.
VRRRRM
...
I wonder where we're going...

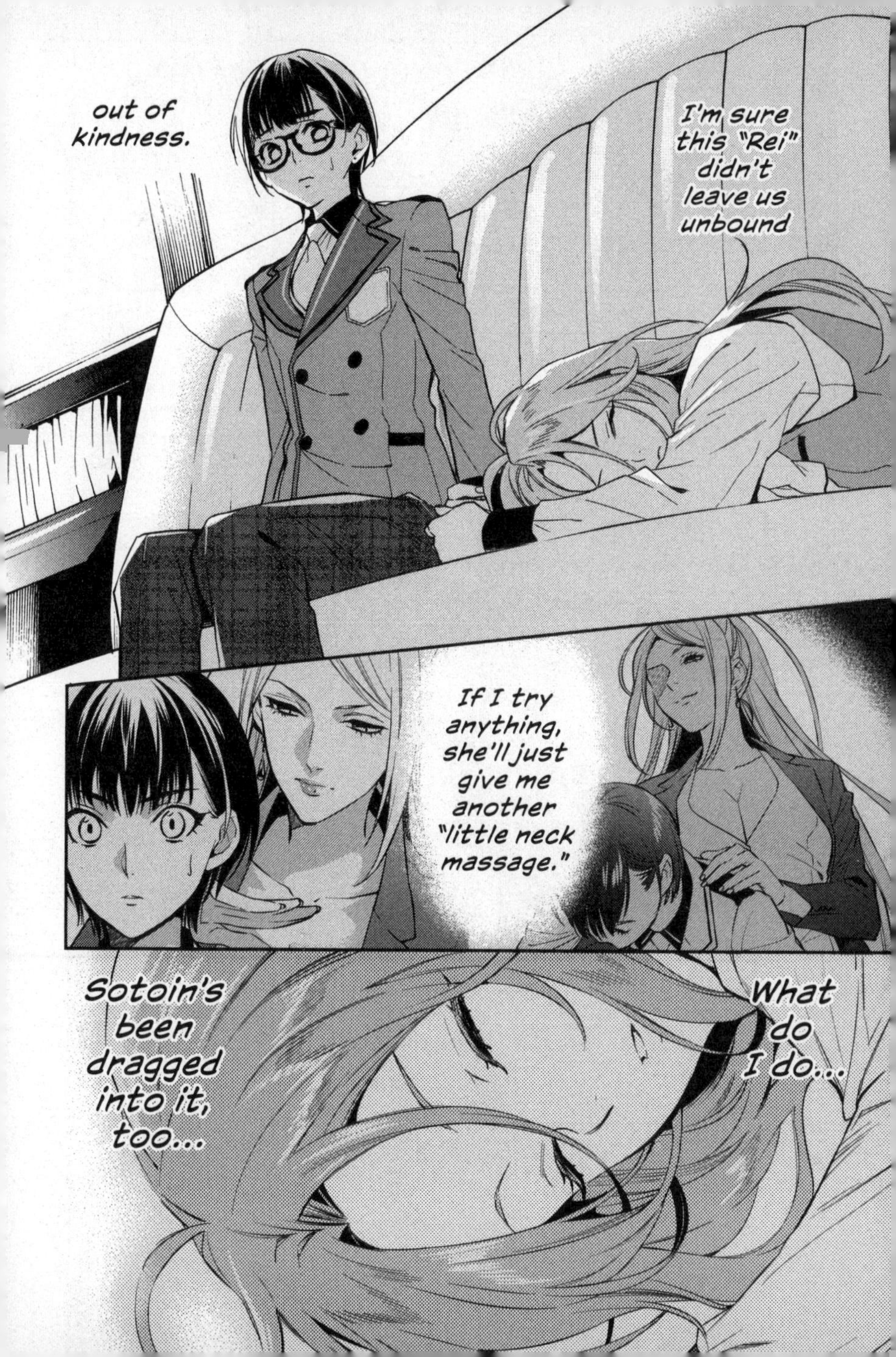
I'm sure this "Rei" didn't leave us unbound
out of kindness.
If I try anything, she'll just give me another "little neck massage."
What do I do...
Sotoin's been dragged into it, too...

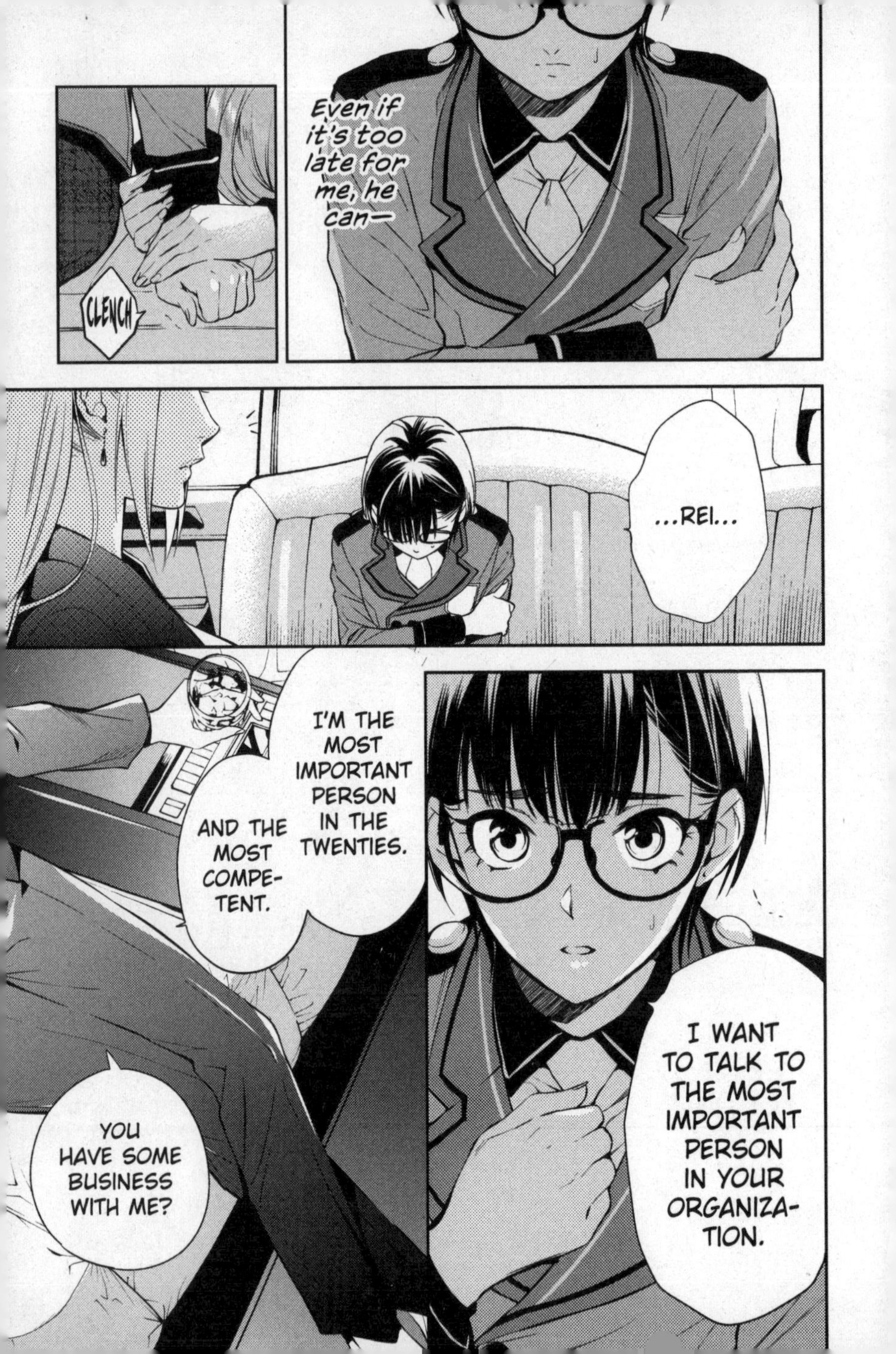
Even if it's too late for me, he can—
CLENCH
...REI...
I WANT TO TALK TO THE MOST IMPORTANT PERSON IN YOUR ORGANIZATION.
I'M THE MOST IMPORTANT PERSON IN THE TWENTIES.
AND THE MOST COMPETENT.
YOU HAVE SOME BUSINESS WITH ME?

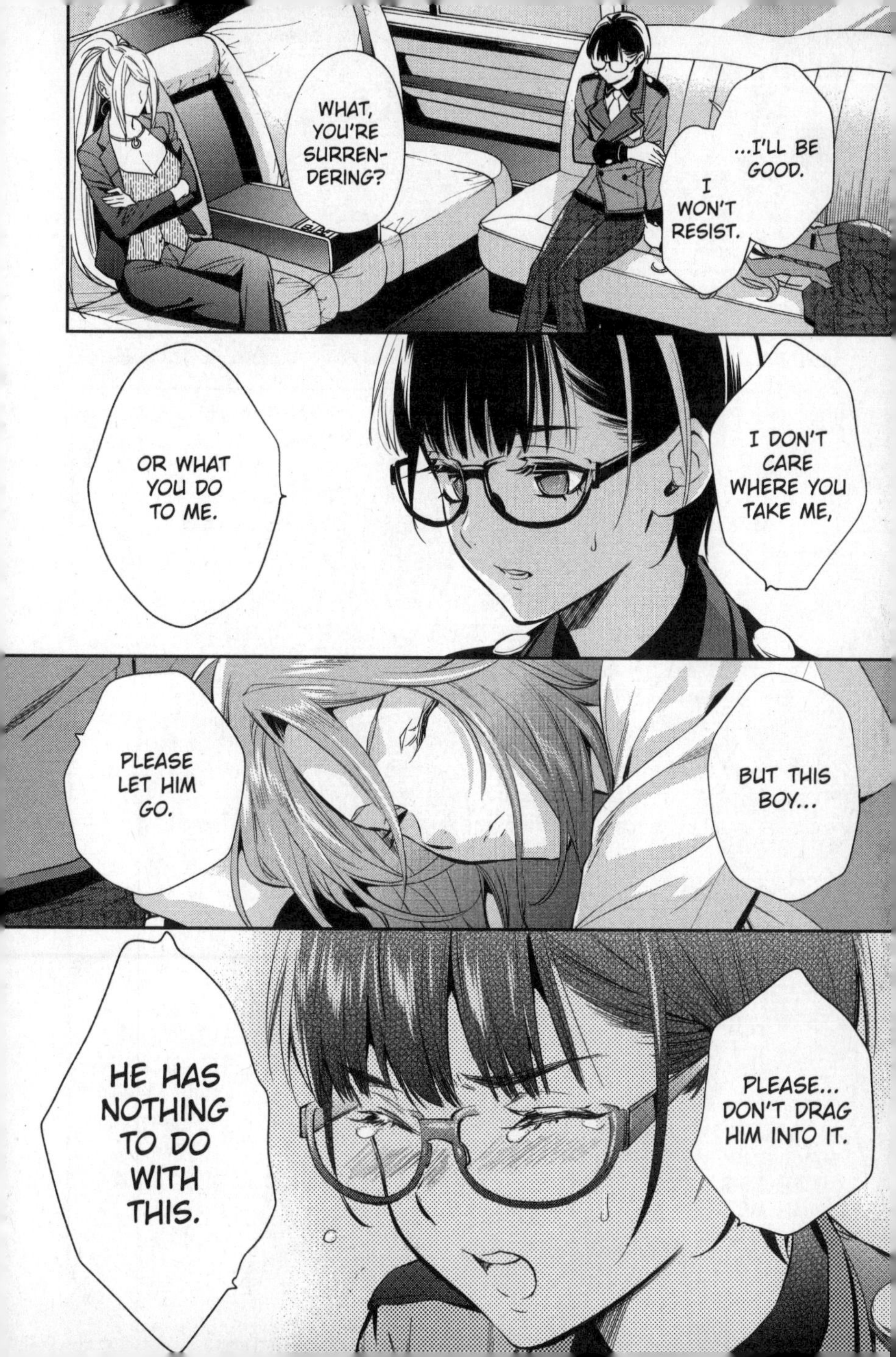
...I'LL BE GOOD. I WON'T RESIST.
WHAT, YOU'RE SURREN-DERING?
I DON'T CARE WHERE YOU TAKE ME,
OR WHAT YOU DO TO ME.
BUT THIS BOY...
PLEASE LET HIM GO.
PLEASE... DON'T DRAG HIM INTO IT.
HE HAS NOTHING TO DO WITH THIS.

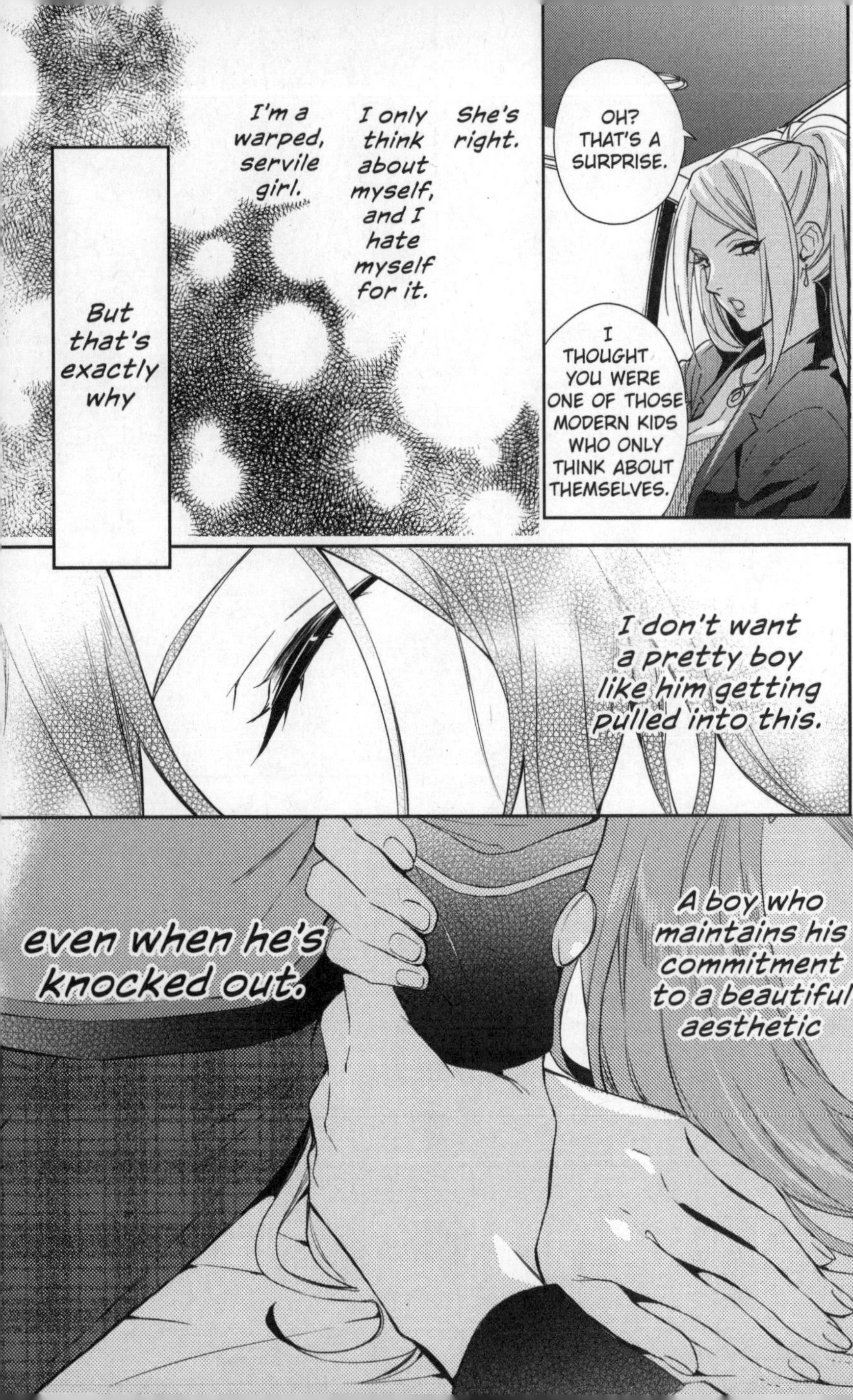
OH? THAT'S A SURPRISE.
I THOUGHT YOU WERE ONE OF THOSE MODERN KIDS WHO ONLY THINK ABOUT THEMSELVES.
She's right.
I only think about myself, and I hate myself for it.
I'm a warped, servile girl.
But that's exactly why
I don't want a pretty boy like him getting pulled into this.
A boy who maintains his commitment to a beautiful aesthetic
even when he's knocked out.

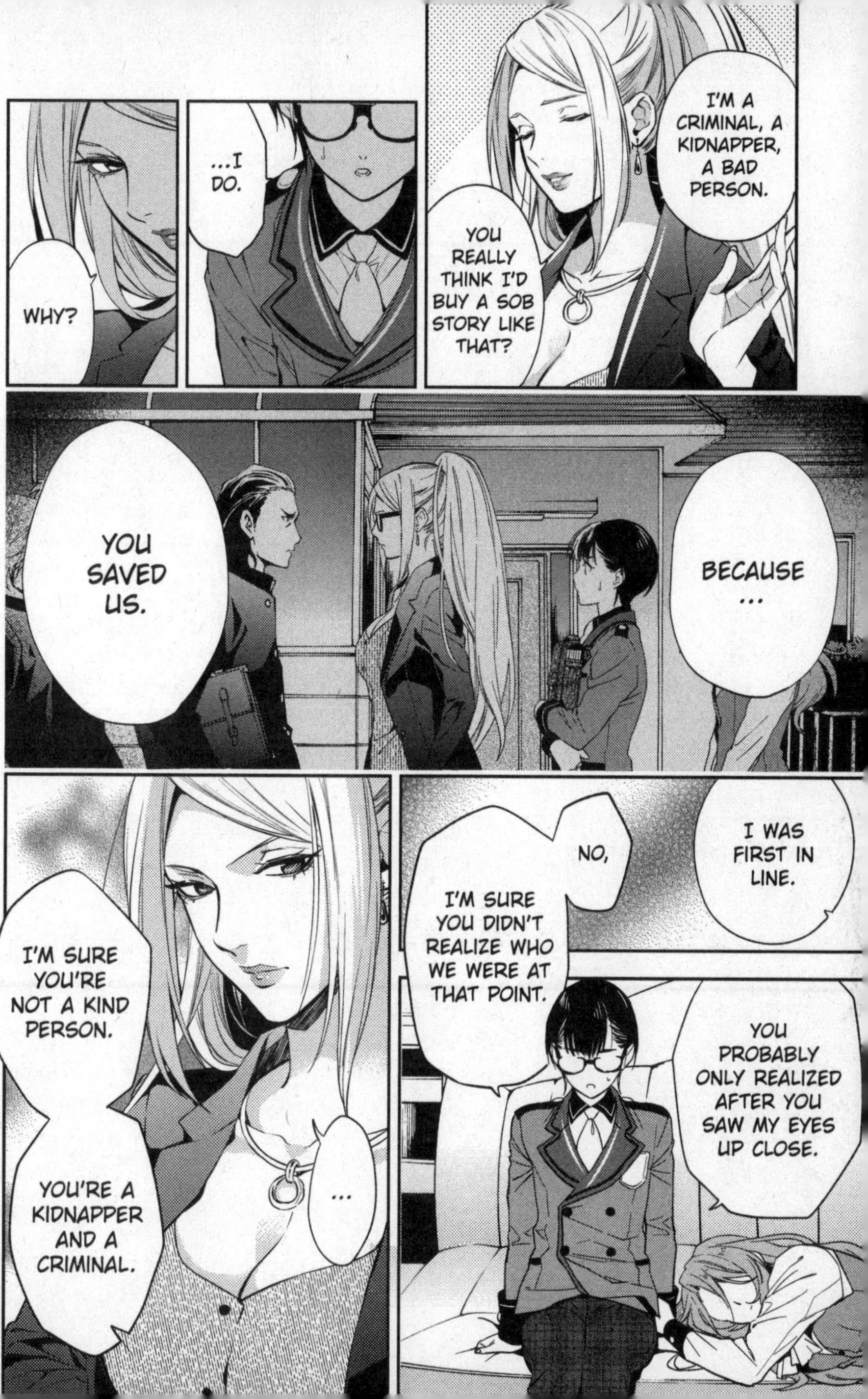
I'M A CRIMINAL, A KIDNAPPER, A BAD PERSON.
YOU REALLY THINK I'D BUY A SOB STORY LIKE THAT?
...I DO.
WHY?
BECAUSE ...
YOU SAVED US.
I WAS FIRST IN LINE.
NO,
I'M SURE YOU DIDN'T REALIZE WHO WE WERE AT THAT POINT.
YOU PROBABLY ONLY REALIZED AFTER YOU SAW MY EYES UP CLOSE.
I'M SURE YOU'RE NOT A KIND PERSON.
...
YOU'RE A KIDNAPPER AND A CRIMINAL.

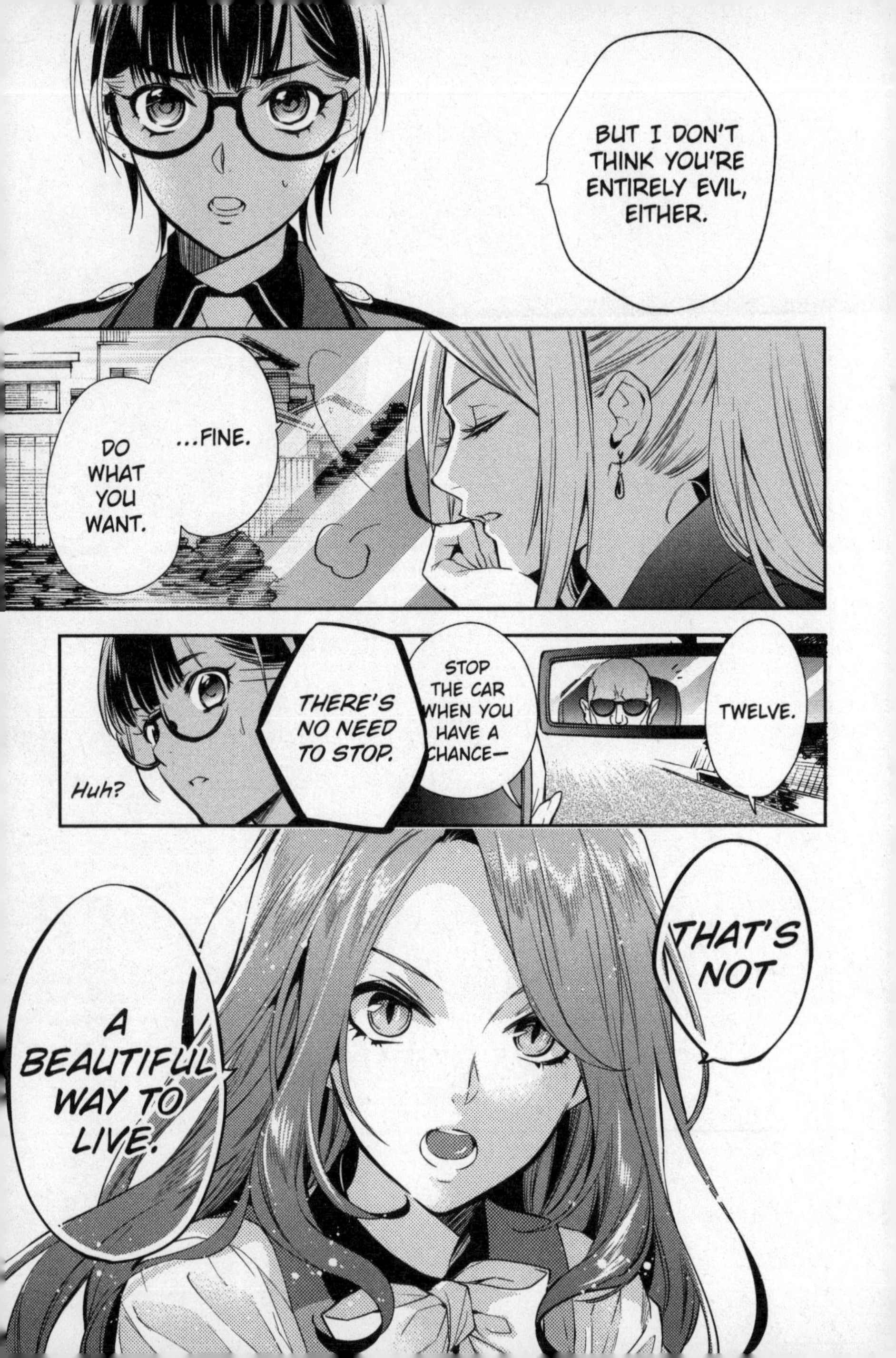
BUT I DON'T THINK YOU'RE ENTIRELY EVIL, EITHER.
...FINE.
DO WHAT YOU WANT.
TWELVE.
STOP THE CAR WHEN YOU HAVE A CHANCE—
THERE'S NO NEED TO STOP.
Huh?
THAT'S NOT
A BEAUTIFUL WAY TO LIVE.

MANABU SOTOIN IS A GENUINE IDIOT.

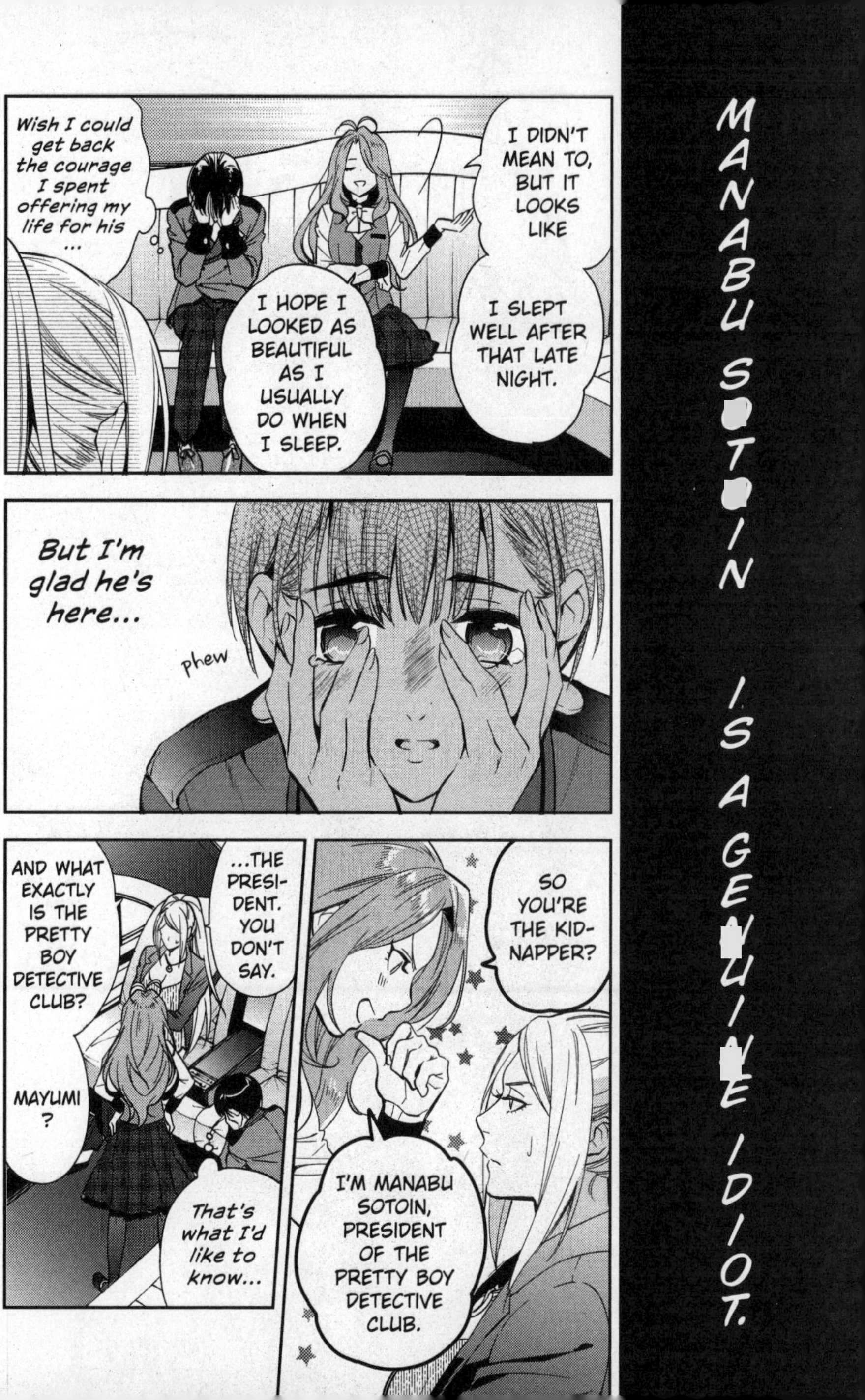
I DIDN'T MEAN TO, BUT IT LOOKS LIKE
I SLEPT WELL AFTER THAT LATE NIGHT.
I HOPE I LOOKED AS BEAUTIFUL AS I USUALLY DO WHEN I SLEEP.
Wish I could get back the courage I spent offering my life for his ...
But I'm glad he's here...
phew
SO YOU'RE THE KID-NAPPER?
I'M MANABU SOTOIN, PRESIDENT OF THE PRETTY BOY DETECTIVE CLUB.
...THE PRESI-DENT. YOU DON'T SAY.
AND WHAT EXACTLY IS THE PRETTY BOY DETECTIVE CLUB?
MAYUMI ?
That's what I'd like to know...

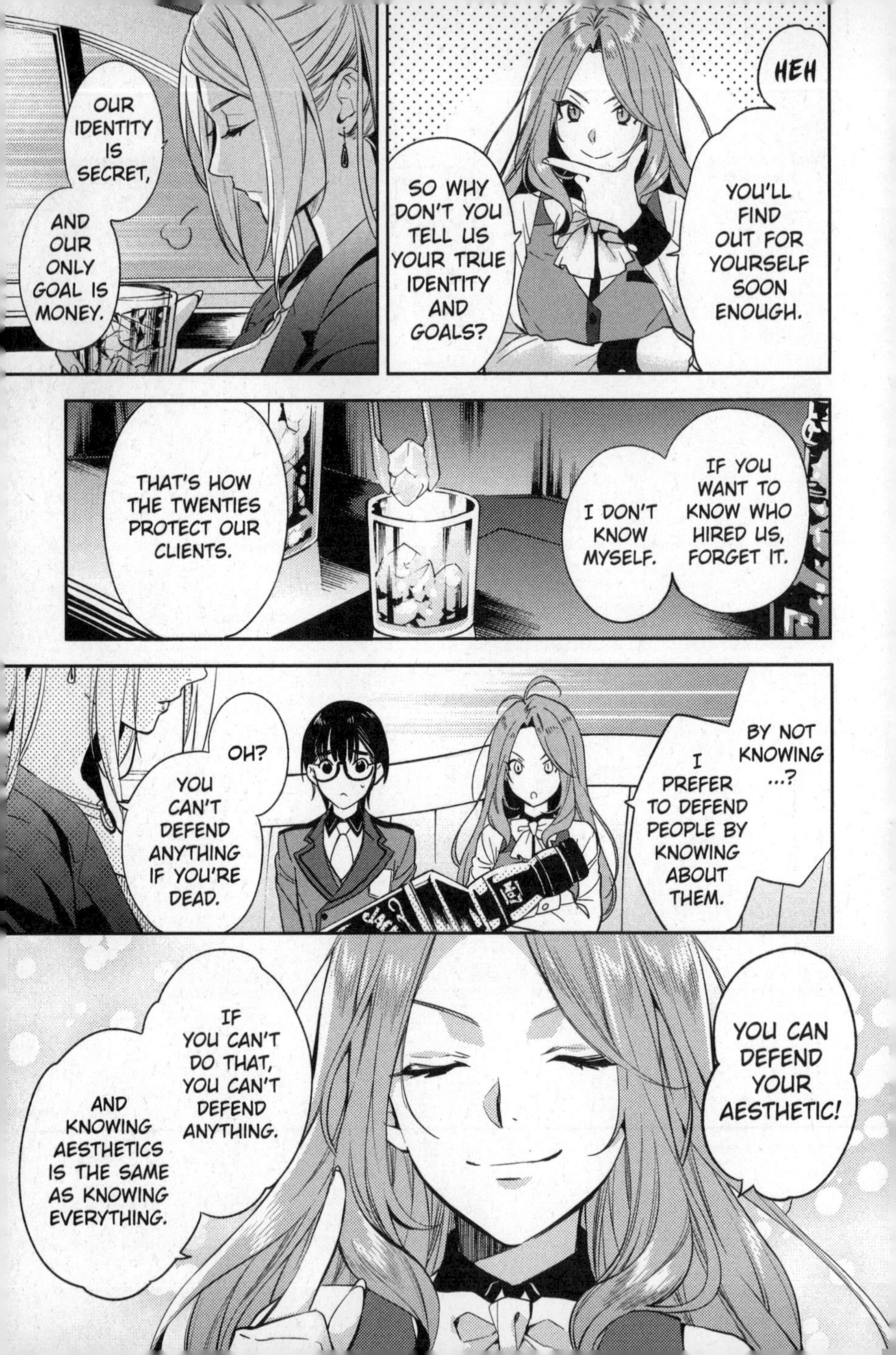
HEH
YOU'LL FIND OUT FOR YOURSELF SOON ENOUGH.
SO WHY DON'T YOU TELL US YOUR TRUE IDENTITY AND GOALS?
OUR IDENTITY IS SECRET,
AND OUR ONLY GOAL IS MONEY.
IF YOU WANT TO KNOW WHO HIRED US, FORGET IT.
I DON'T KNOW MYSELF.
THAT'S HOW THE TWENTIES PROTECT OUR CLIENTS.
BY NOT KNOWING ...?
I PREFER TO DEFEND PEOPLE BY KNOWING ABOUT THEM.
OH?
YOU CAN'T DEFEND ANYTHING IF YOU'RE DEAD.
YOU CAN DEFEND YOUR AESTHETIC!
IF YOU CAN'T DO THAT, YOU CAN'T DEFEND ANYTHING.
AND KNOWING AESTHETICS IS THE SAME AS KNOWING EVERYTHING.

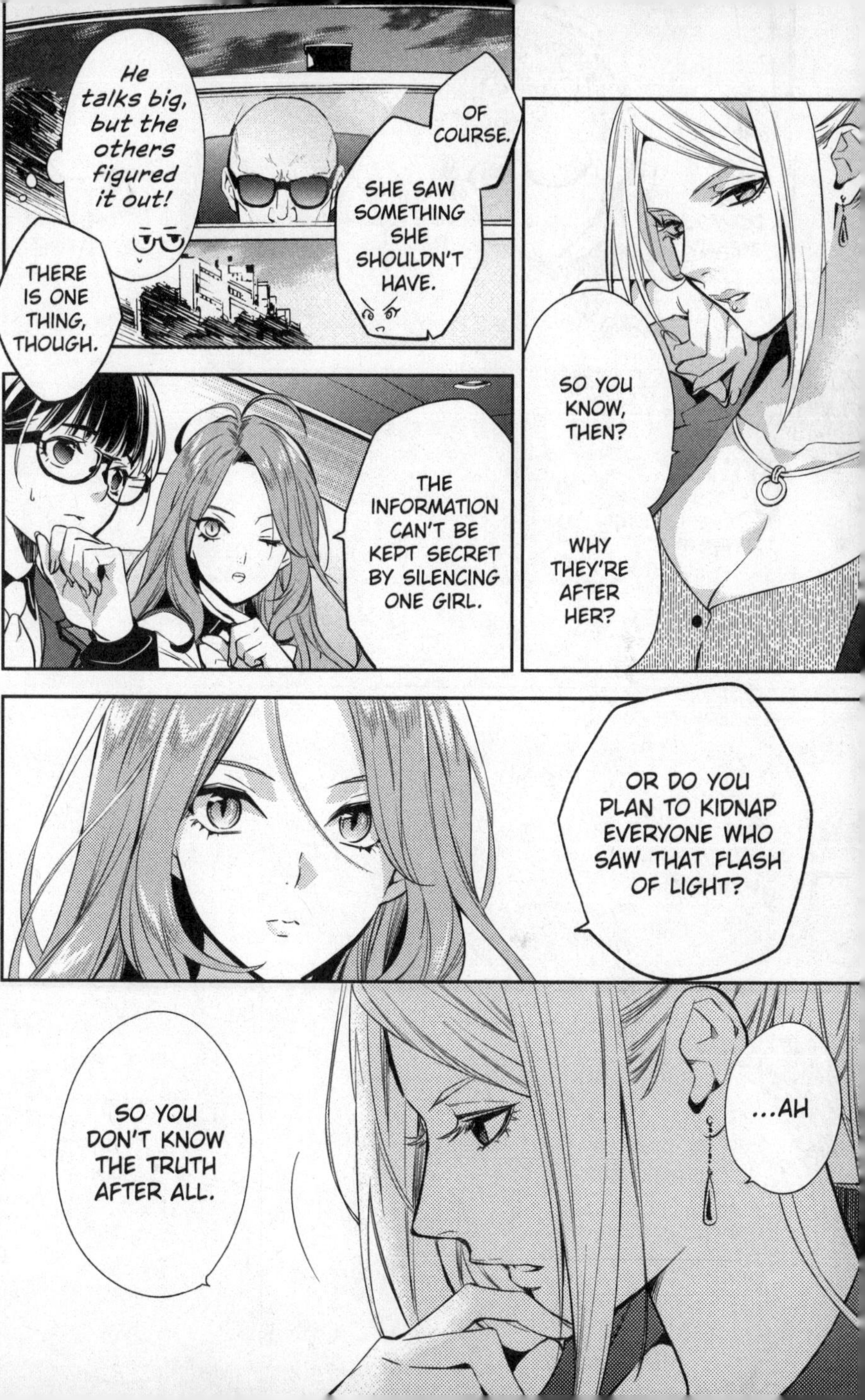
SO YOU KNOW, THEN?
WHY THEY'RE AFTER HER?
OF COURSE.
SHE SAW SOMETHING SHE SHOULDN'T HAVE.
He talks big, but the others figured it out!
THERE IS ONE THING, THOUGH.
THE INFORMATION CAN'T BE KEPT SECRET BY SILENCING ONE GIRL.
OR DO YOU PLAN TO KIDNAP EVERYONE WHO SAW THAT FLASH OF LIGHT?
...AH
SO YOU DON'T KNOW THE TRUTH AFTER ALL.

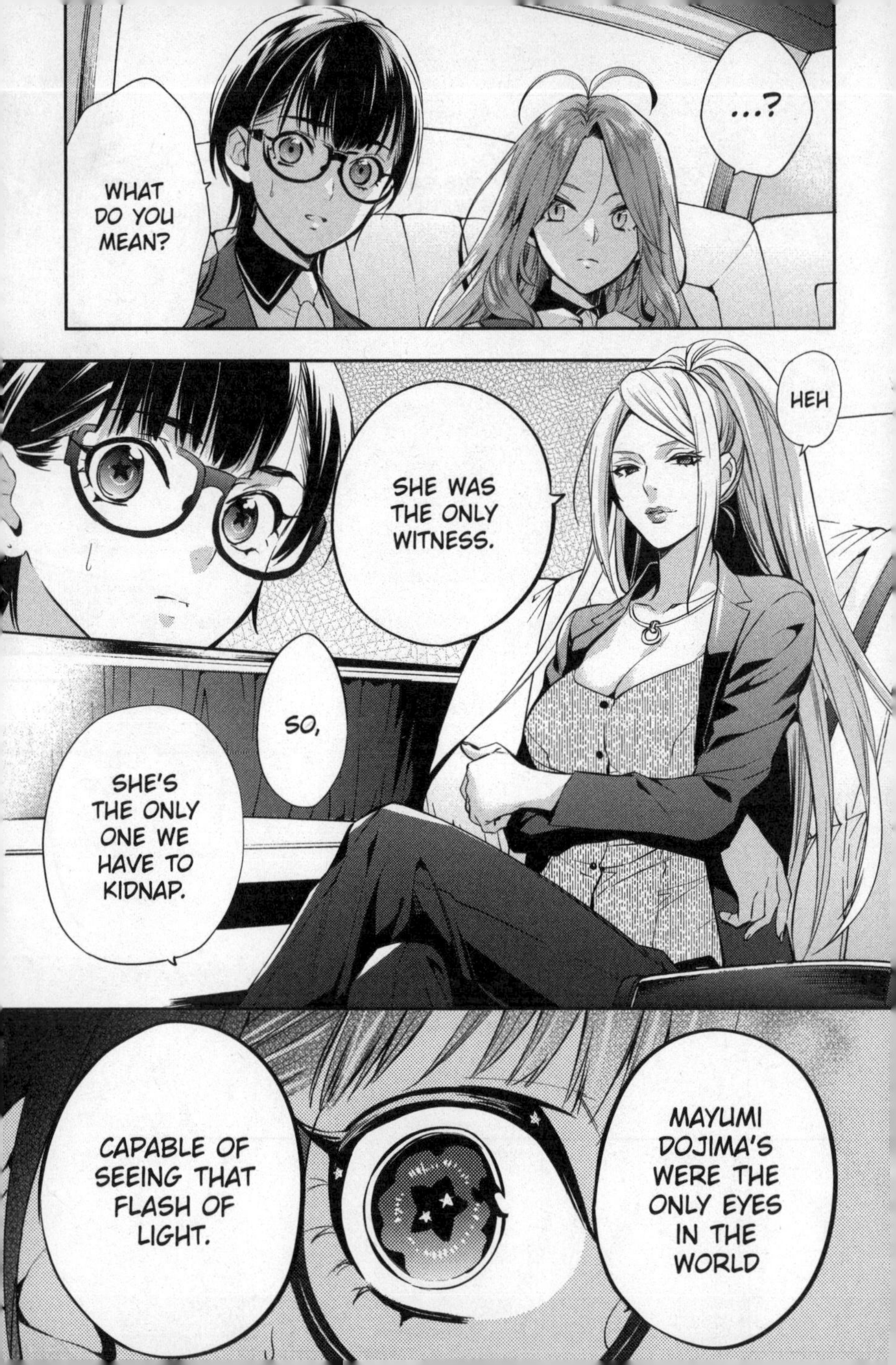
...?
WHAT DO YOU MEAN?
HEH
SHE WAS THE ONLY WITNESS.
SO,
SHE'S THE ONLY ONE WE HAVE TO KIDNAP.
MAYUMI DOJIMA'S WERE THE ONLY EYES IN THE WORLD
CAPABLE OF SEEING THAT FLASH OF LIGHT.

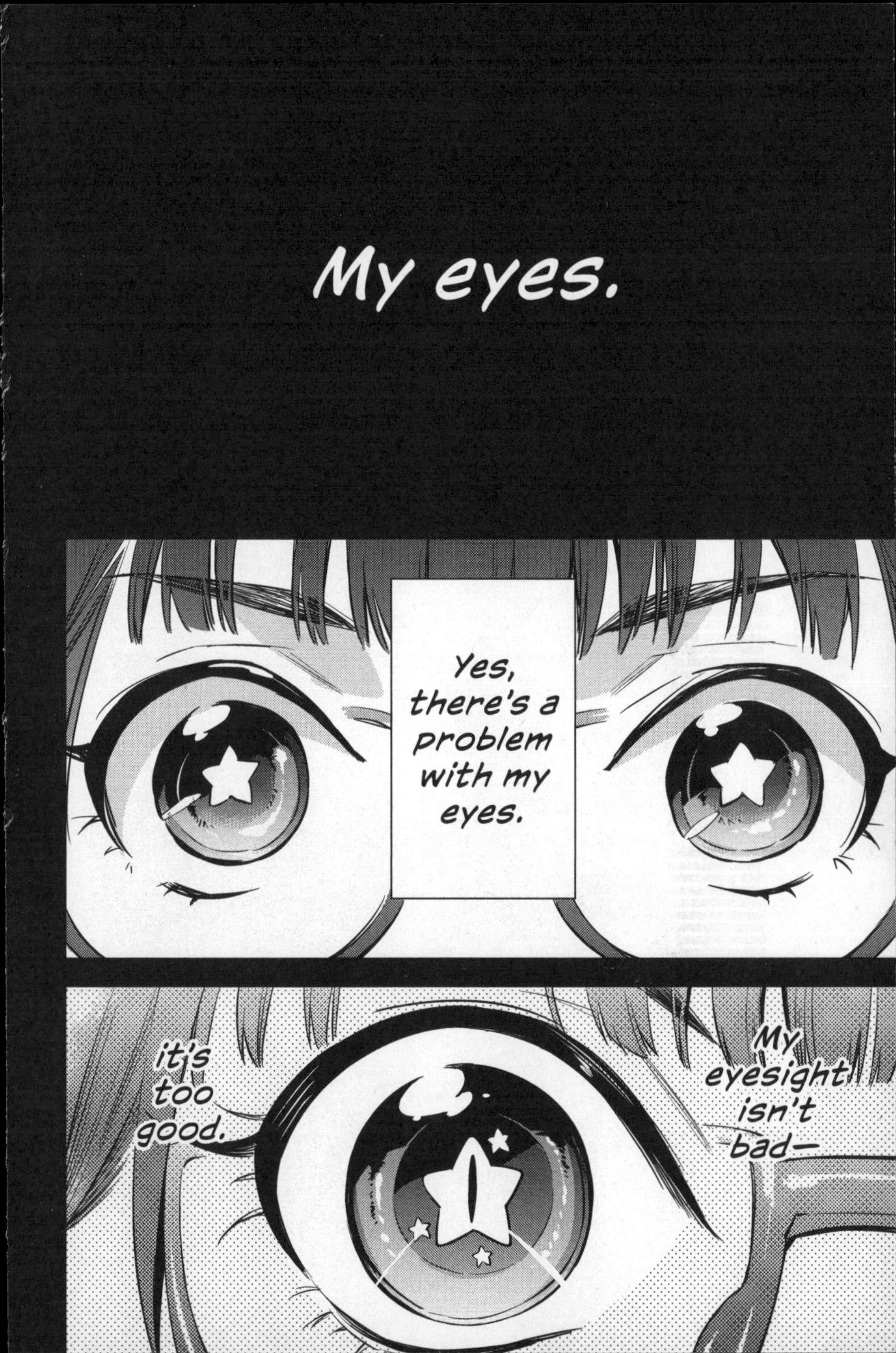
My eyes.
Yes, there's a problem with my eyes.
My eyesight isn't bad—
it's too good.

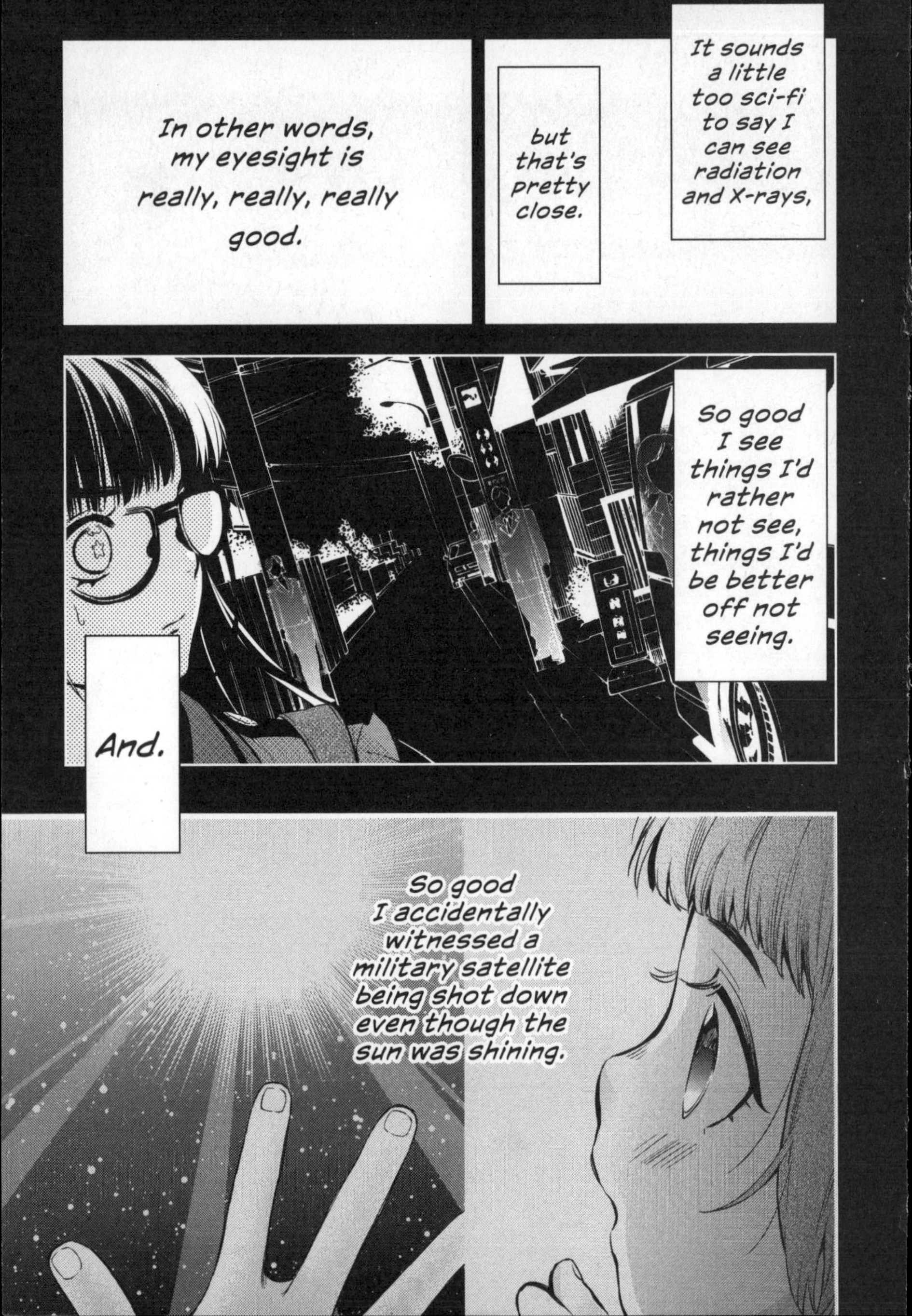
It sounds a little too sci-fi to say I can see radiation and X-rays,
but that's pretty close.
In other words, my eyesight is really, really, really good.
So good I see things I'd rather not see, things I'd be better off not seeing.
And.
So good I accidentally witnessed a military satellite being shot down even though the sun was shining.

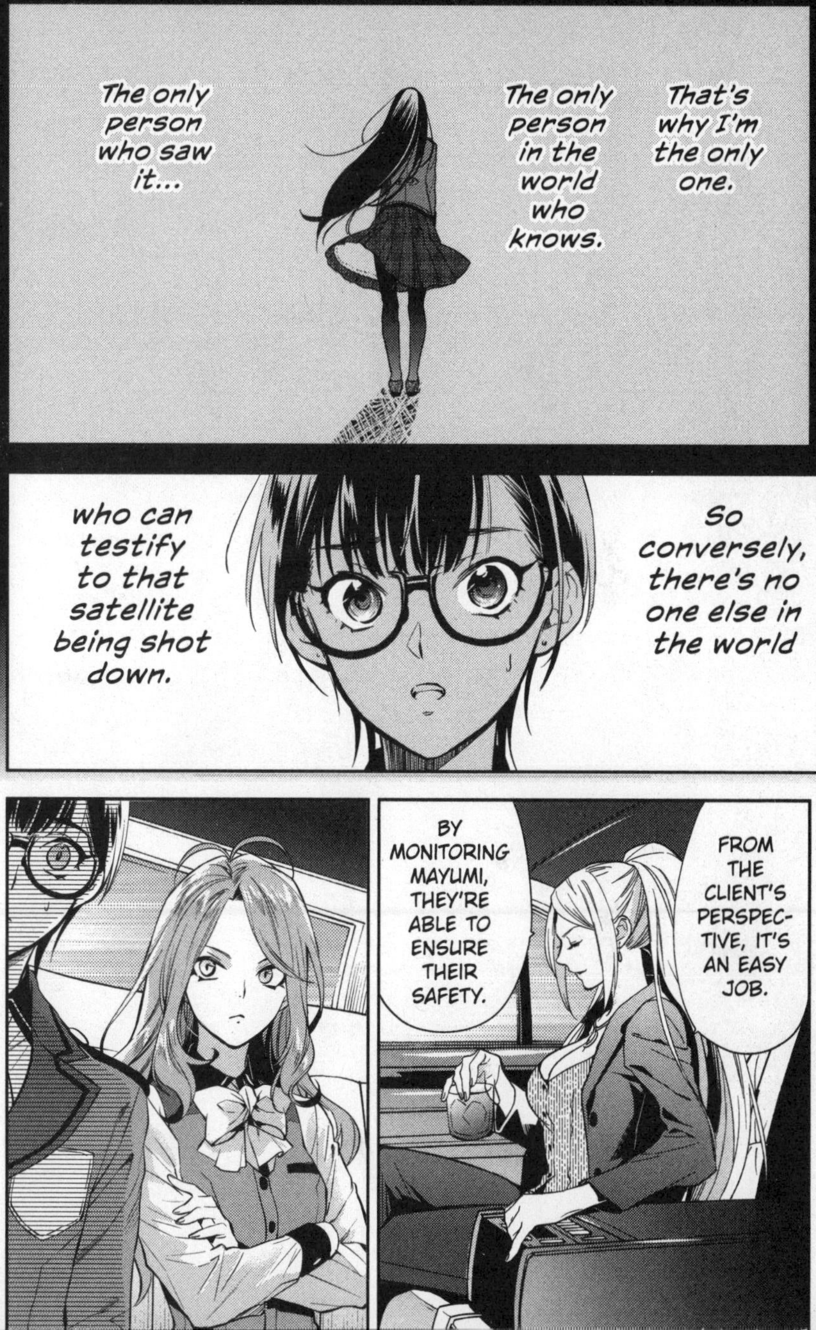
That's why I'm the only one.
The only person in the world who knows.
The only person who saw it...
So conversely, there's no one else in the world
who can testify to that satellite being shot down.
FROM THE CLIENT'S PERSPEC-TIVE, IT'S AN EASY JOB.
BY MONITORING MAYUMI, THEY'RE ABLE TO ENSURE THEIR SAFETY.

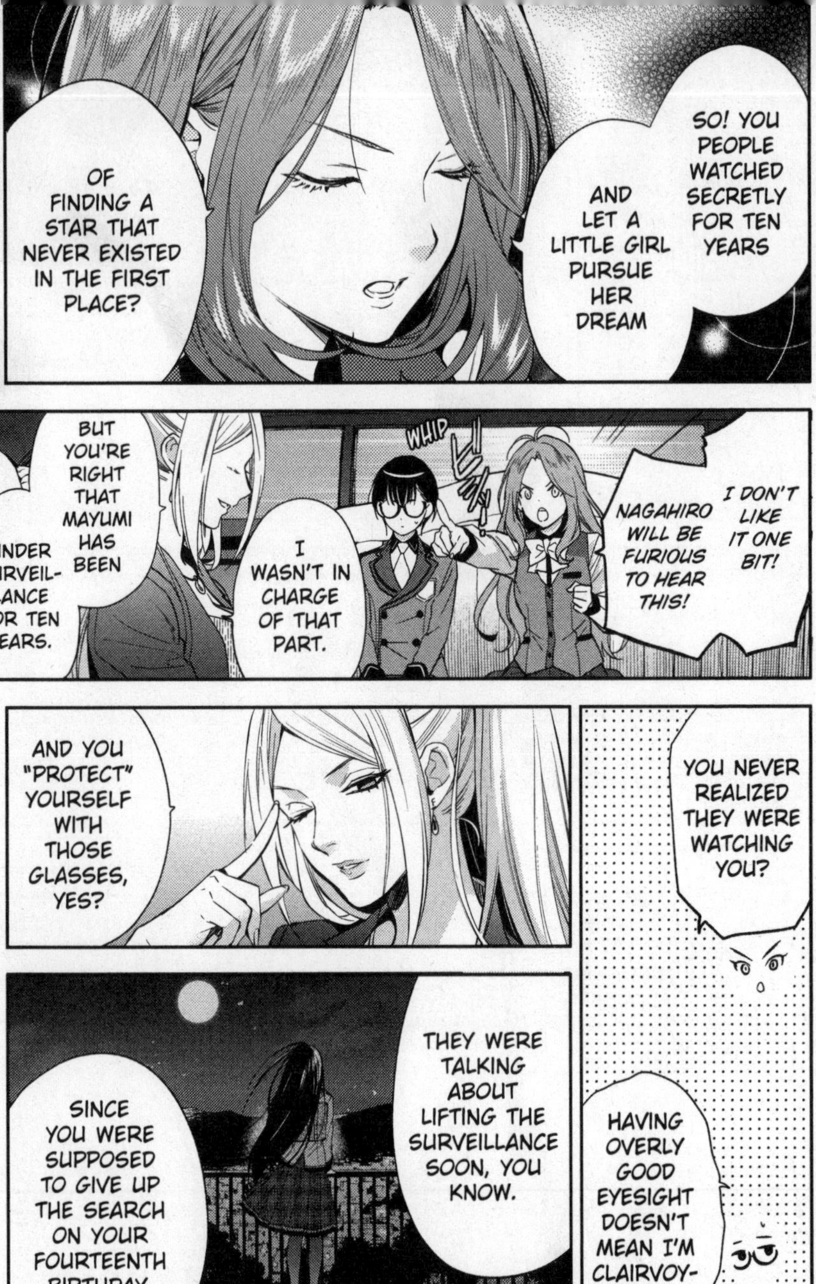
SO! YOU PEOPLE WATCHED SECRETLY FOR TEN YEARS
AND LET A LITTLE GIRL PURSUE HER DREAM
OF FINDING A STAR THAT NEVER EXISTED IN THE FIRST PLACE?
I DON'T LIKE IT ONE BIT!
NAGAHIRO WILL BE FURIOUS TO HEAR THIS!
WHIP
I WASN'T IN CHARGE OF THAT PART.
BUT YOU'RE RIGHT THAT MAYUMI HAS BEEN
UNDER SURVEIL-LANCE FOR TEN YEARS.
YOU NEVER REALIZED THEY WERE WATCHING YOU?
HAVING OVERLY GOOD EYESIGHT DOESN'T MEAN I'M CLAIRVOY-ANT!
AND YOU "PROTECT" YOURSELF WITH THOSE GLASSES, YES?
THEY WERE TALKING ABOUT LIFTING THE SURVEILLANCE SOON, YOU KNOW.
SINCE YOU WERE SUPPOSED TO GIVE UP THE SEARCH ON YOUR FOURTEENTH BIRTHDAY.

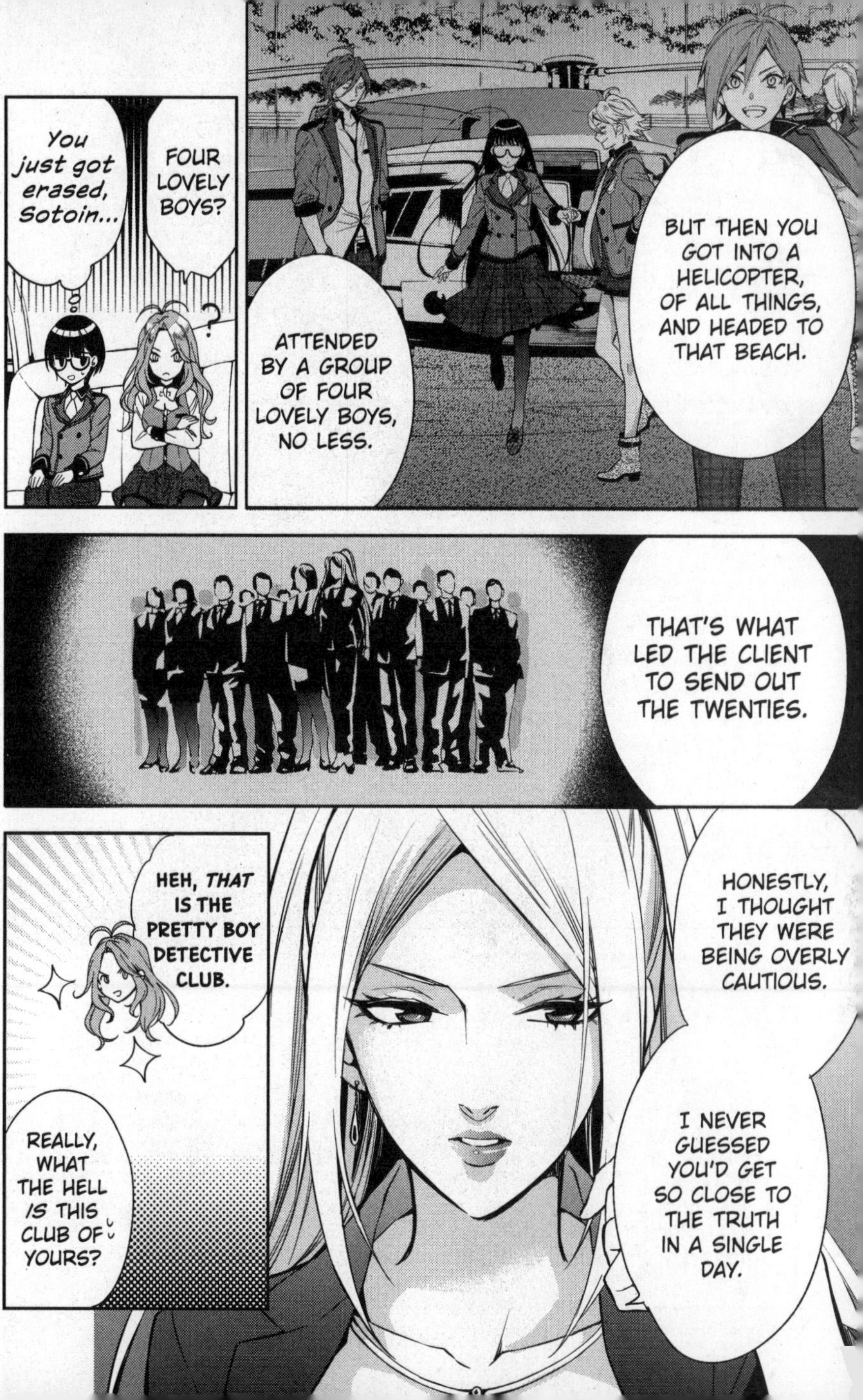

BUT THEN YOU GOT INTO A HELICOPTER, OF ALL THINGS, AND HEADED TO THAT BEACH.
ATTENDED BY A GROUP OF FOUR LOVELY BOYS, NO LESS.
FOUR LOVELY BOYS?
You just got erased, Sotoin...
THAT'S WHAT LED THE CLIENT TO SEND OUT THE TWENTIES.
HONESTLY, I THOUGHT THEY WERE BEING OVERLY CAUTIOUS.
I NEVER GUESSED YOU'D GET SO CLOSE TO THE TRUTH IN A SINGLE DAY.
HEH, *THAT* IS THE PRETTY BOY DETECTIVE CLUB.
REALLY, WHAT THE HELL *IS* THIS CLUB OF YOURS?

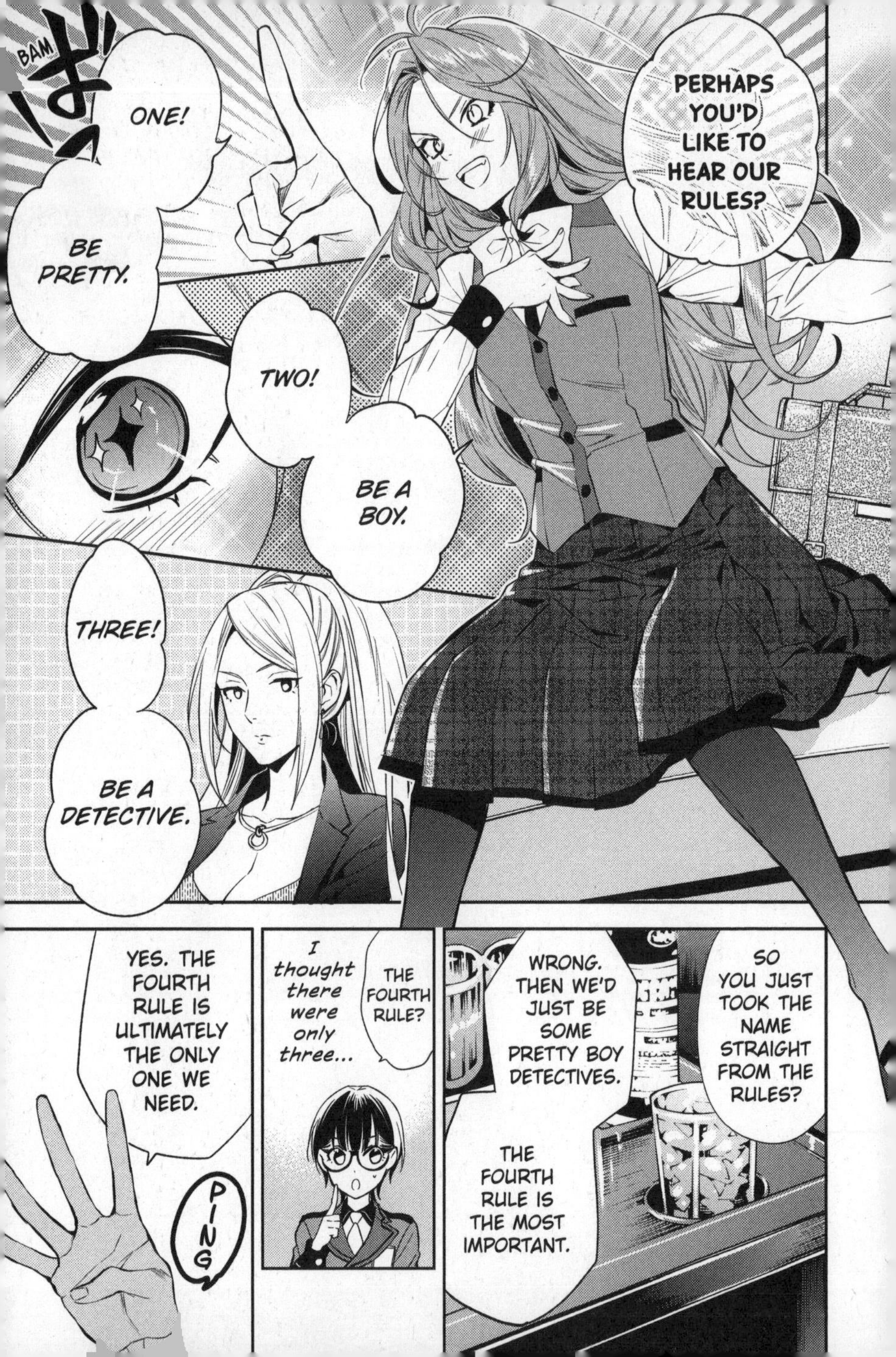
PERHAPS YOU'D LIKE TO HEAR OUR RULES?
BAM
ONE!
BE PRETTY.
TWO!
BE A BOY.
THREE!
BE A DETECTIVE.
SO YOU JUST TOOK THE NAME STRAIGHT FROM THE RULES?
WRONG. THEN WE'D JUST BE SOME PRETTY BOY DETECTIVES.
THE FOURTH RULE IS THE MOST IMPORTANT.
THE FOURTH RULE?
I thought there were only three...
YES. THE FOURTH RULE IS ULTIMATELY THE ONLY ONE WE NEED.
PING

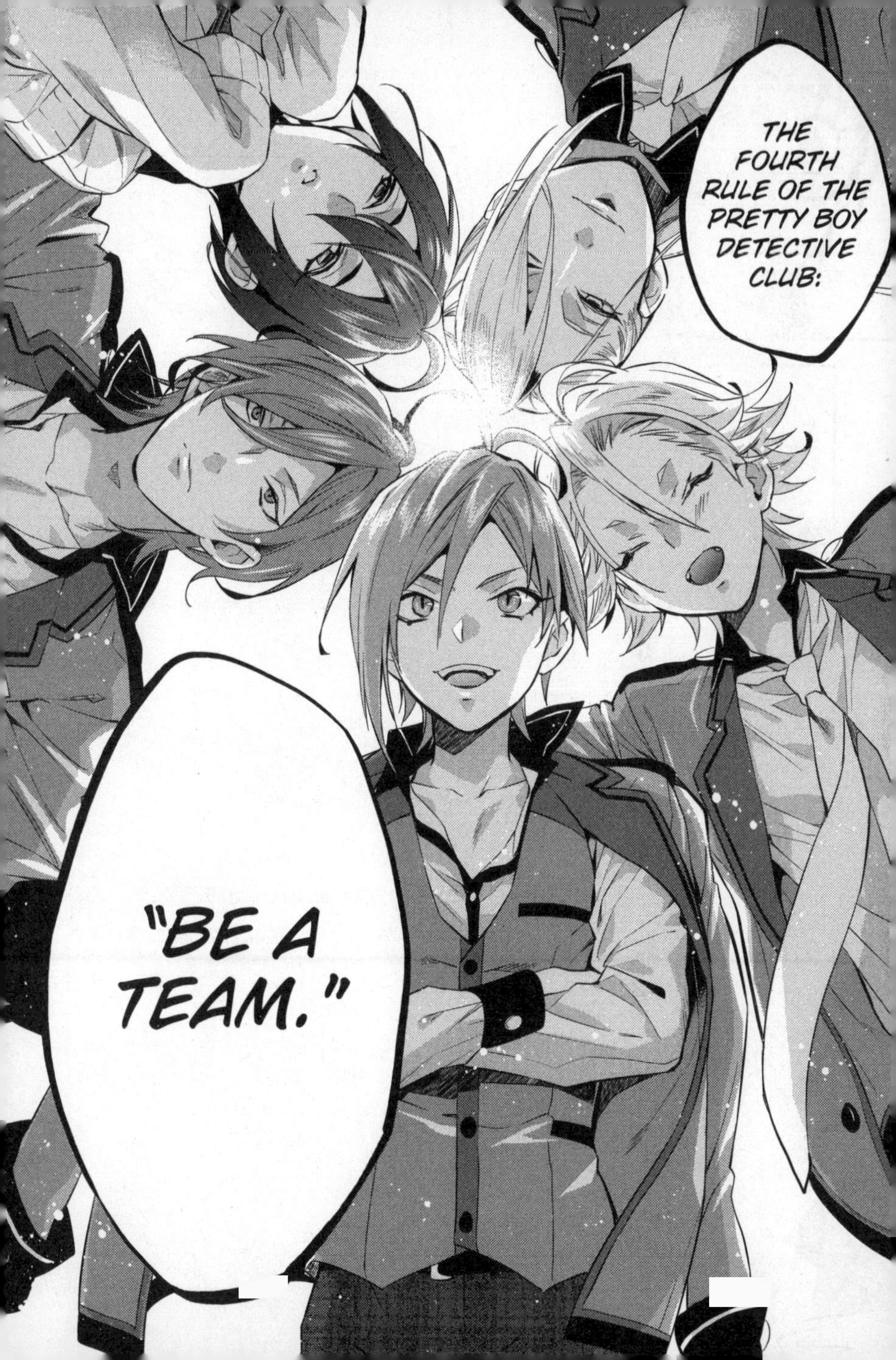
THE FOURTH RULE OF THE PRETTY BOY DETECTIVE CLUB:
"BE A TEAM."

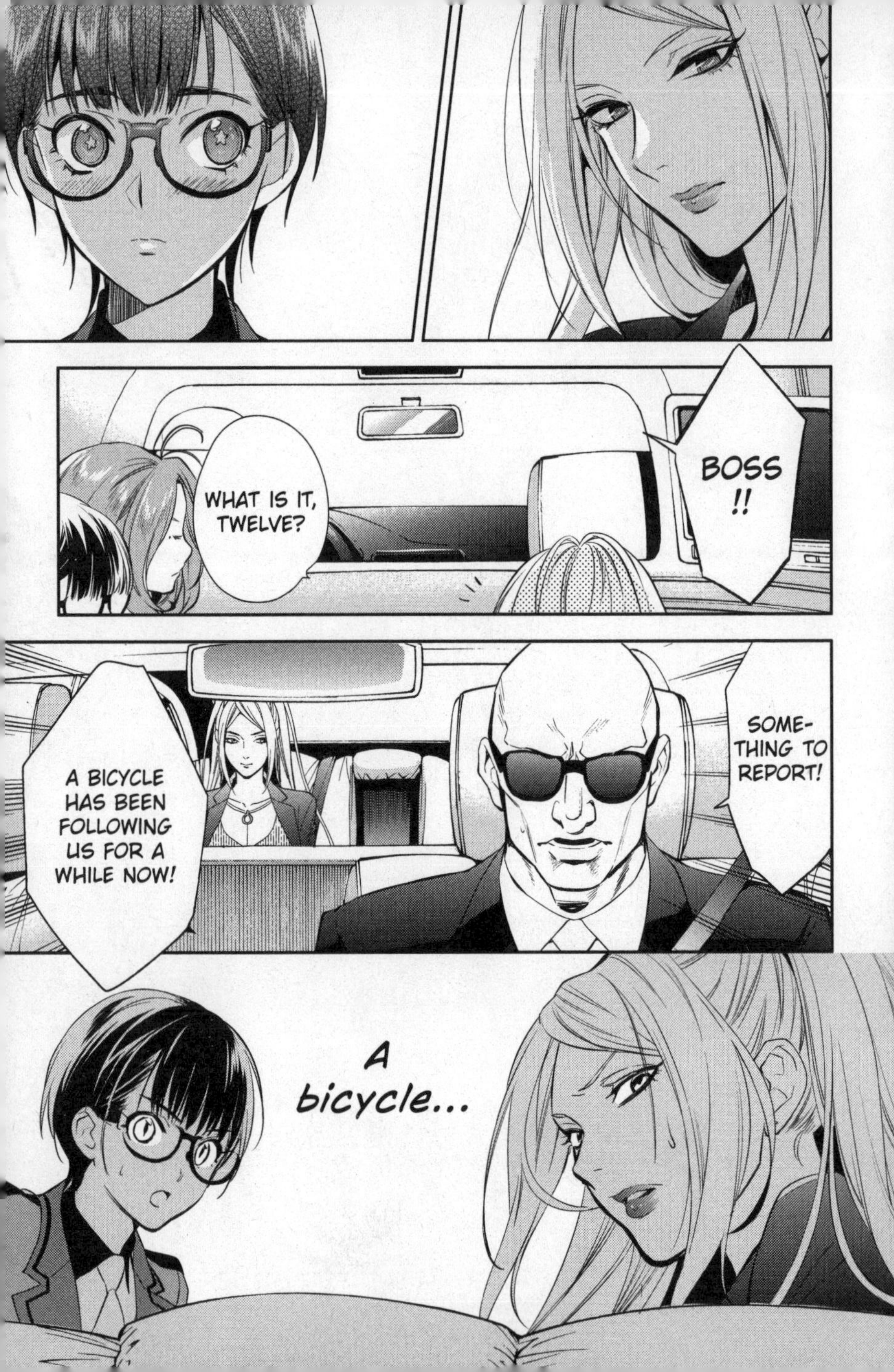
BOSS !!
WHAT IS IT, TWELVE?
SOME-THING TO REPORT!
A BICYCLE HAS BEEN FOLLOWING US FOR A WHILE NOW!
A bicycle...

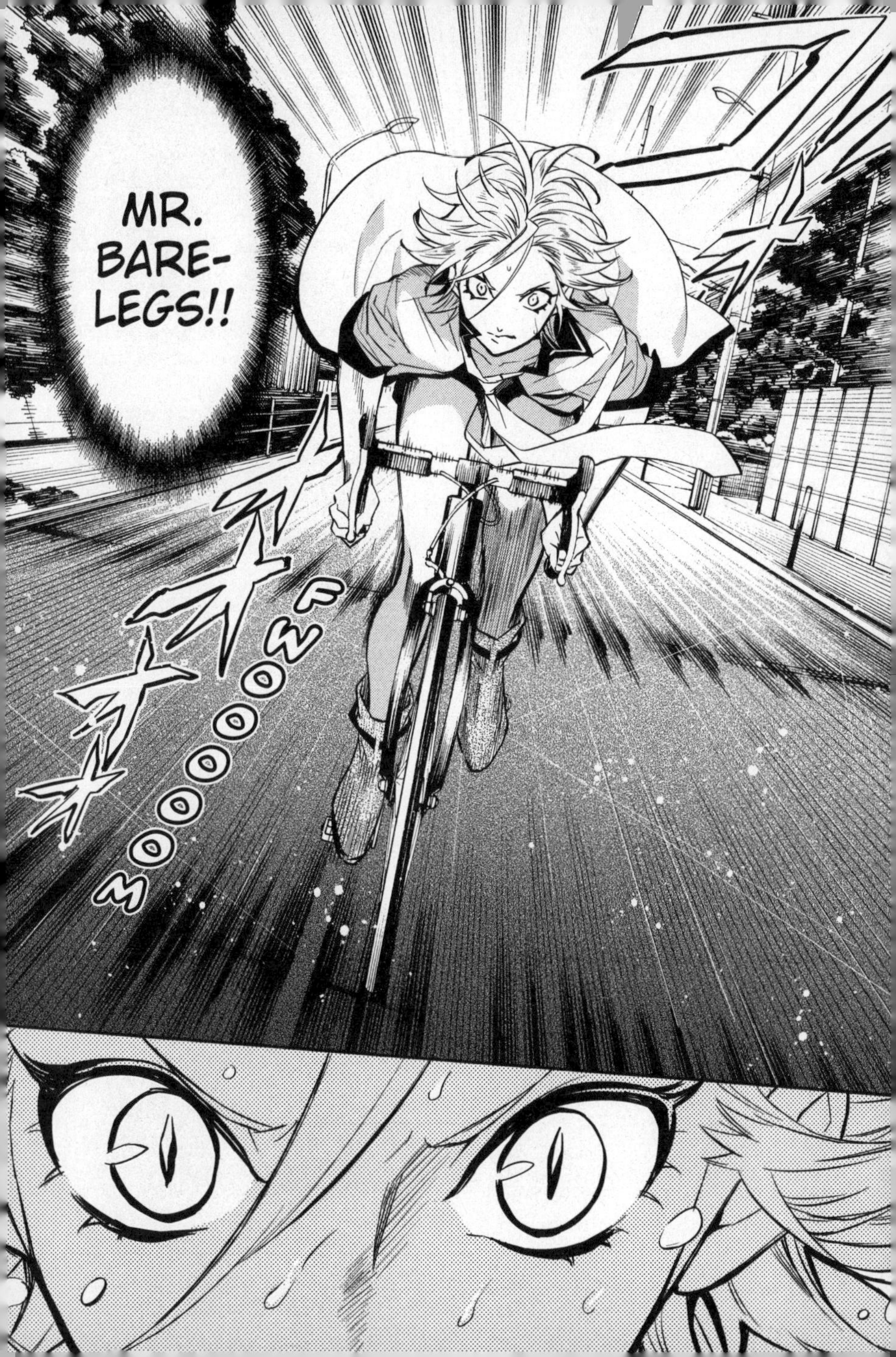
MR. BARE-LEGS!!
FWOOOOOM

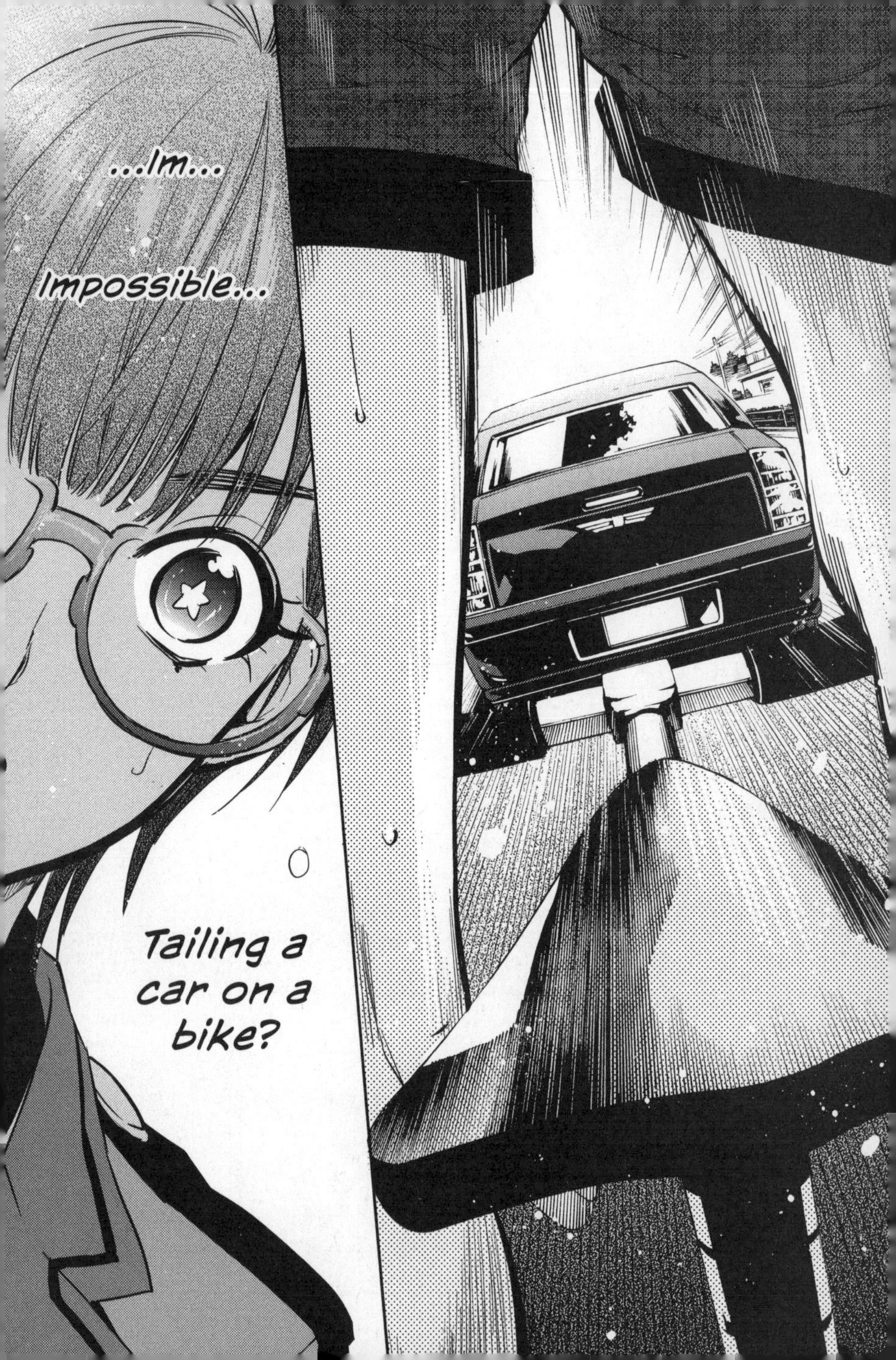
...Im...
Impossible...
Tailing a car on a bike?

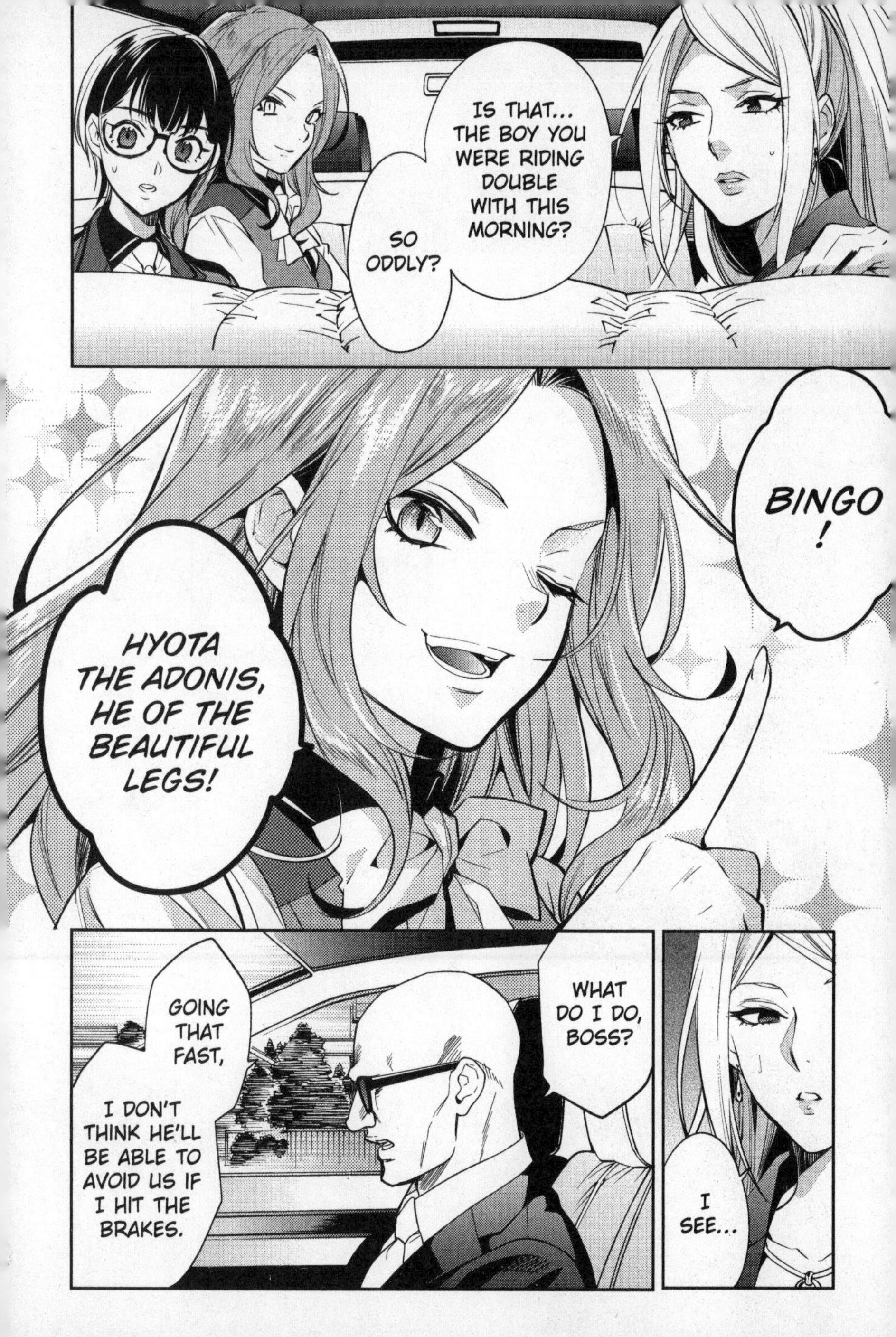
IS THAT... THE BOY YOU WERE RIDING DOUBLE WITH THIS MORNING?
SO ODDLY?
BINGO!
HYOTA THE ADONIS, HE OF THE BEAUTIFUL LEGS!
I SEE...
WHAT DO I DO, BOSS?
GOING THAT FAST,
I DON'T THINK HE'LL BE ABLE TO AVOID US IF I HIT THE BRAKES.

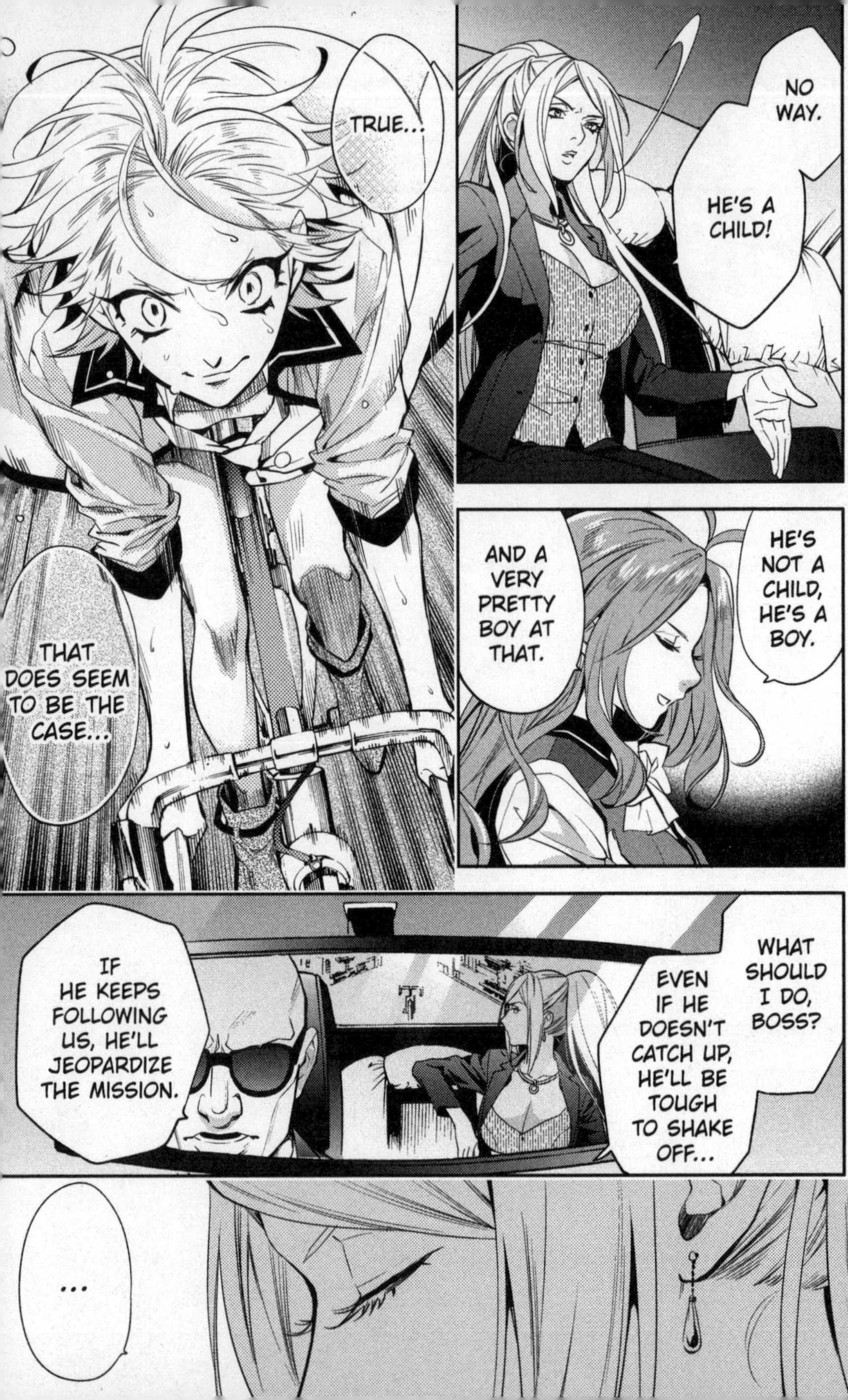
NO WAY.
HE'S A CHILD!
HE'S NOT A CHILD, HE'S A BOY.
AND A VERY PRETTY BOY AT THAT.
TRUE...
THAT DOES SEEM TO BE THE CASE...
WHAT SHOULD I DO, BOSS?
EVEN IF HE DOESN'T CATCH UP, HE'LL BE TOUGH TO SHAKE OFF...
IF HE KEEPS FOLLOWING US, HE'LL JEOPARDIZE THE MISSION.
...

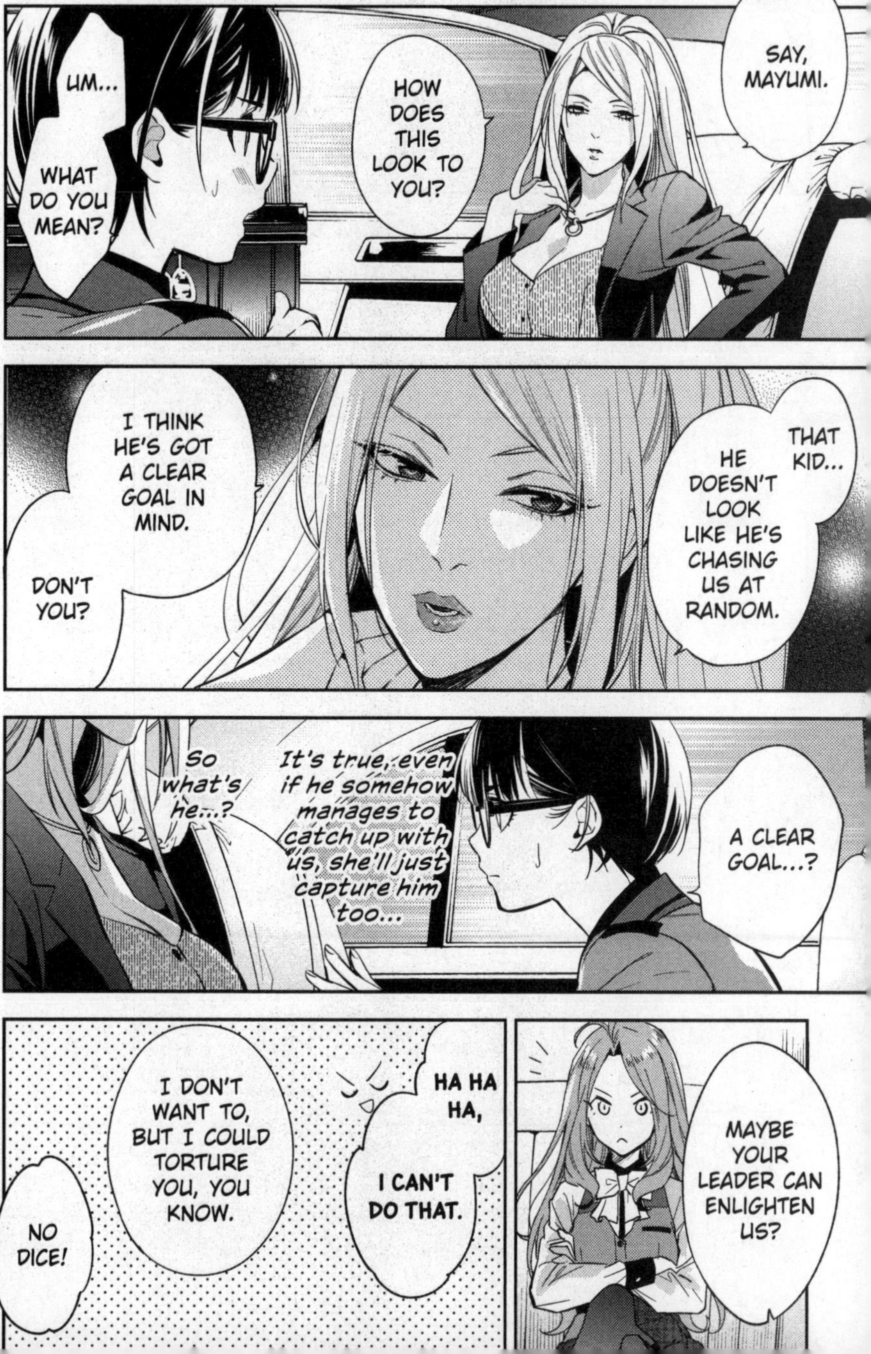
SAY, MAYUMI.
HOW DOES THIS LOOK TO YOU?
UM...
WHAT DO YOU MEAN?
THAT KID...
HE DOESN'T LOOK LIKE HE'S CHASING US AT RANDOM.
I THINK HE'S GOT A CLEAR GOAL IN MIND.
DON'T YOU?
A CLEAR GOAL...?
It's true, even if he somehow manages to catch up with us, she'll just capture him too...
So what's he...?
MAYBE YOUR LEADER CAN ENLIGHTEN US?
HA HA HA,
I CAN'T DO THAT.
I DON'T WANT TO, BUT I COULD TORTURE YOU, YOU KNOW.
NO DICE!

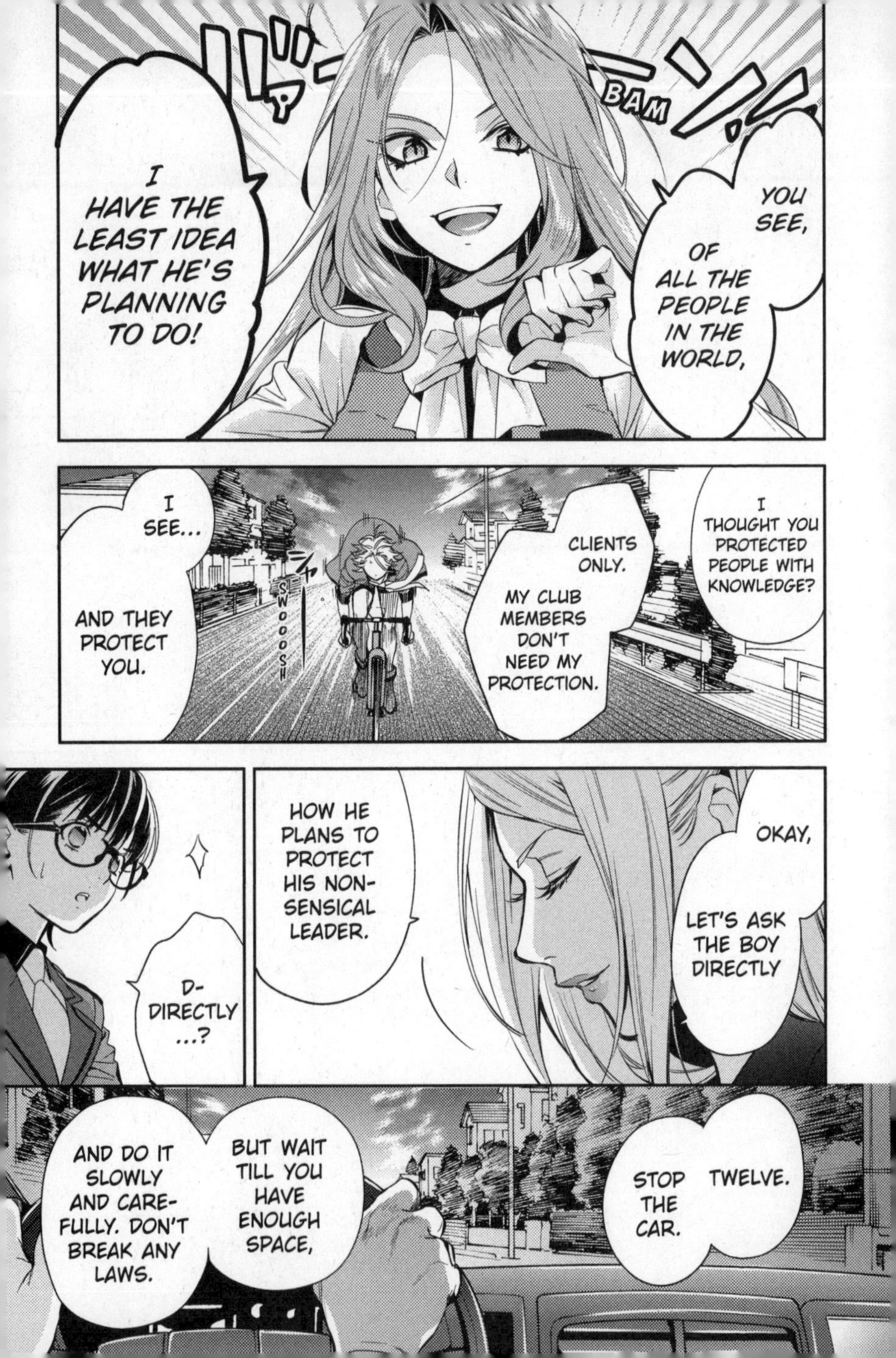
BAM
YOU SEE, OF ALL THE PEOPLE IN THE WORLD,
I HAVE THE LEAST IDEA WHAT HE'S PLANNING TO DO!
I THOUGHT YOU PROTECTED PEOPLE WITH KNOWLEDGE?
CLIENTS ONLY.
MY CLUB MEMBERS DON'T NEED MY PROTECTION.
SWOOOSH
I SEE...
AND THEY PROTECT YOU.
OKAY,
LET'S ASK THE BOY DIRECTLY
HOW HE PLANS TO PROTECT HIS NON-SENSICAL LEADER.
D-DIRECTLY...?
TWELVE.
STOP THE CAR.
BUT WAIT TILL YOU HAVE ENOUGH SPACE,
AND DO IT SLOWLY AND CAREFULLY. DON'T BREAK ANY LAWS.

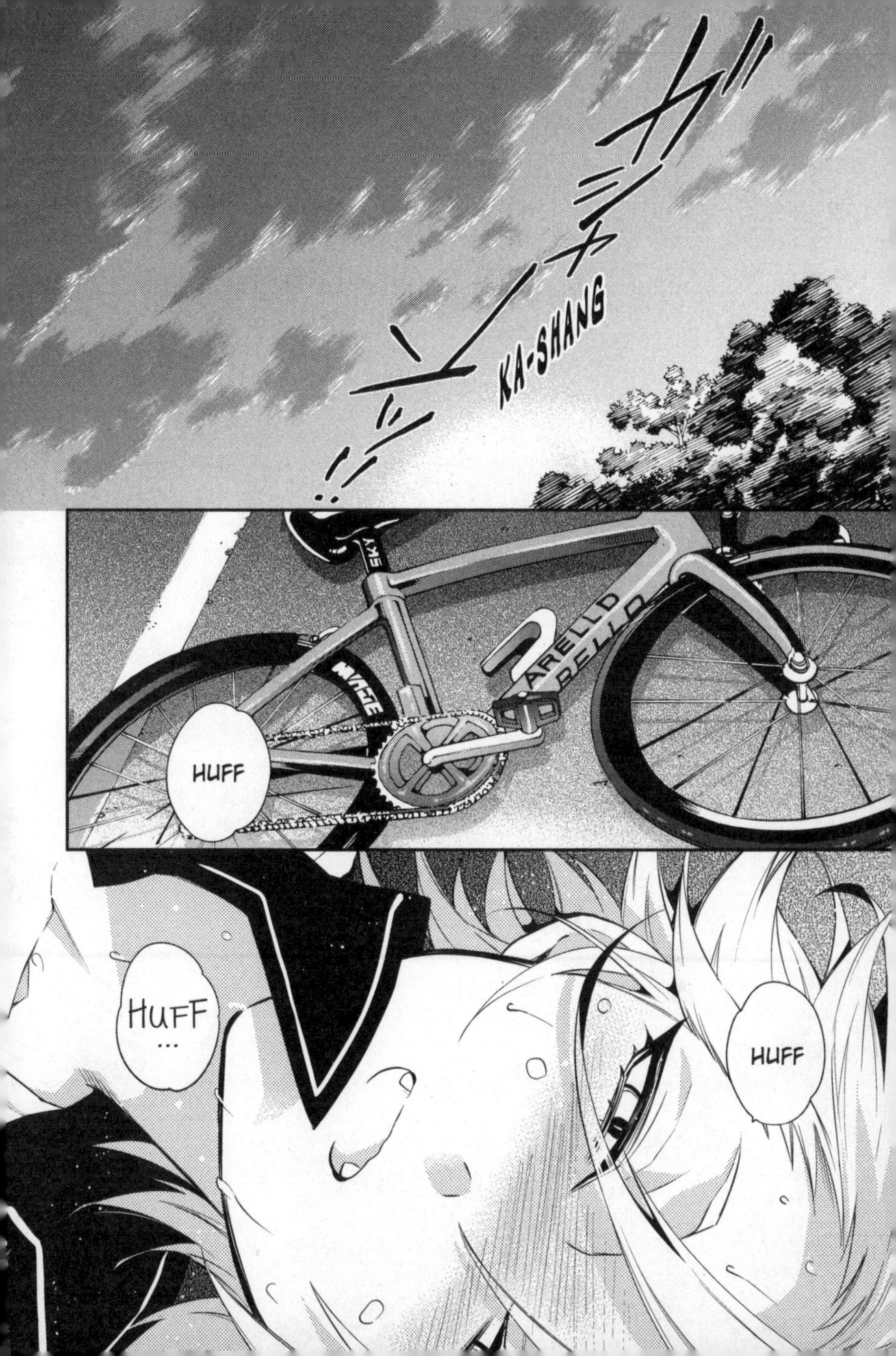
ガシャーン!!
KA-SHANG
HUFF
HUFF
HUFF
...

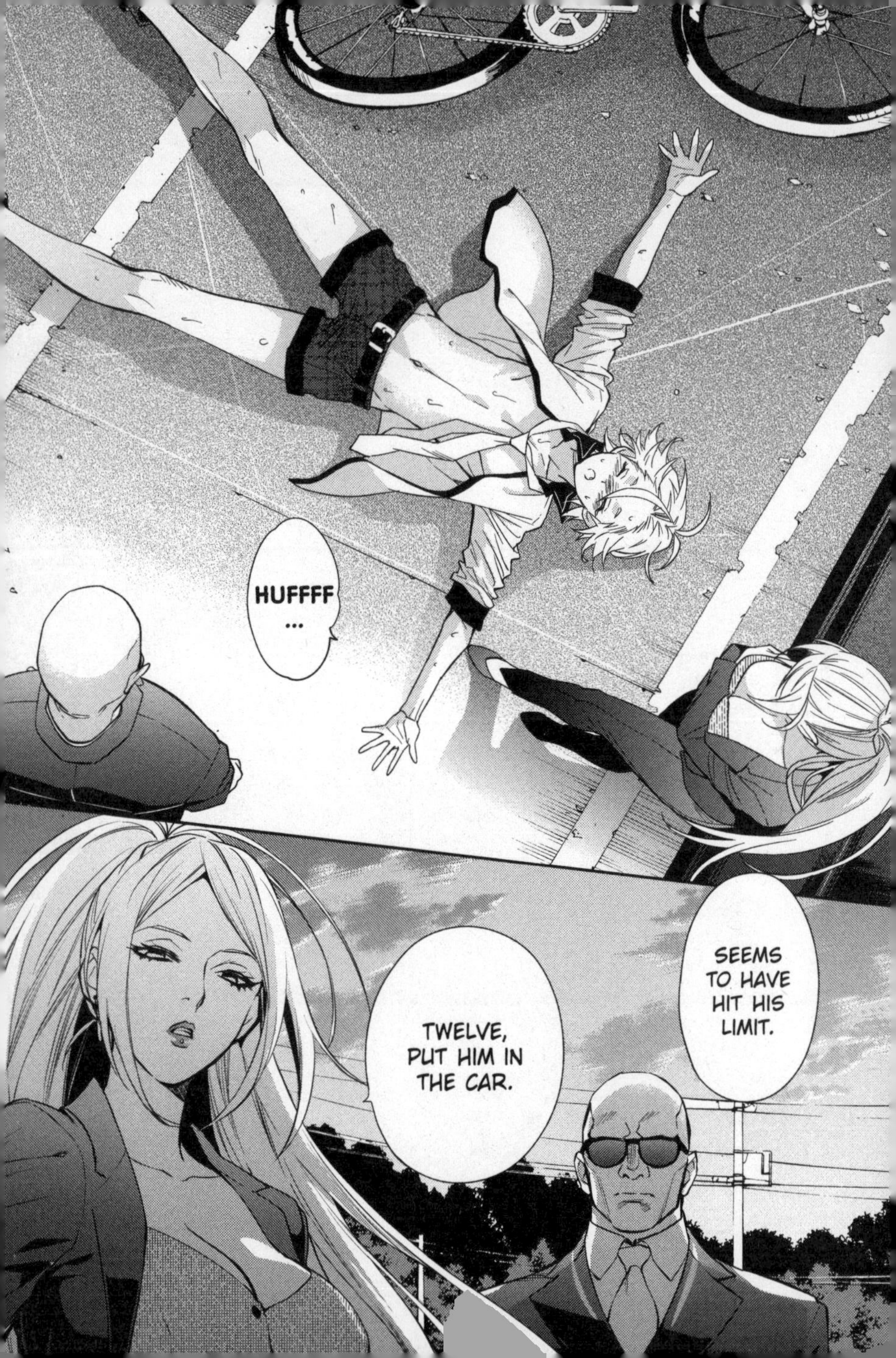
HUFFFF ...
SEEMS TO HAVE HIT HIS LIMIT.
TWELVE, PUT HIM IN THE CAR.

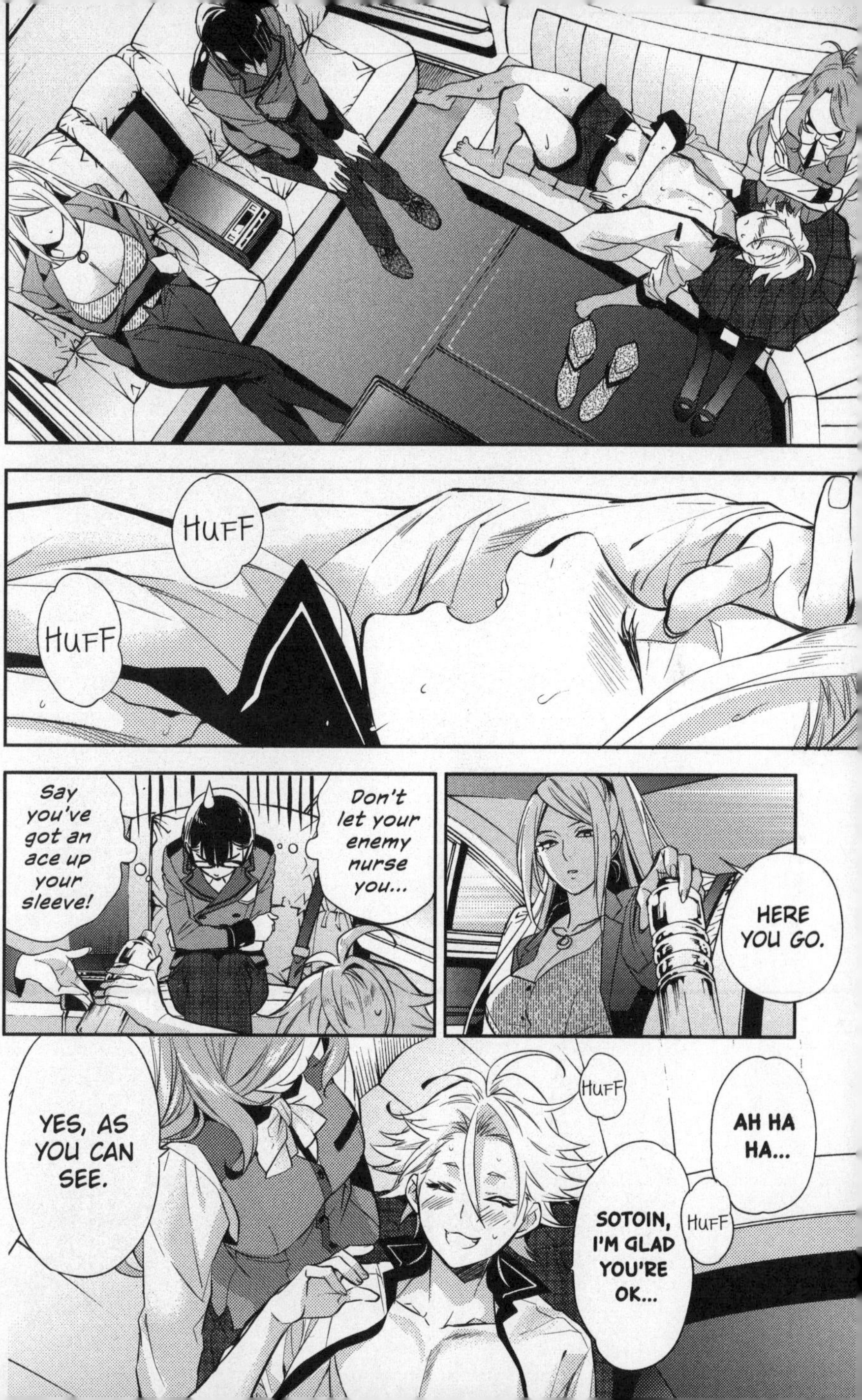
HUFF
HUFF
HERE YOU GO.
Don't let your enemy nurse you...
Say you've got an ace up your sleeve!
AH HA HA...
HUFF
HUFF
SOTOIN, I'M GLAD YOU'RE OK...
YES, AS YOU CAN SEE.

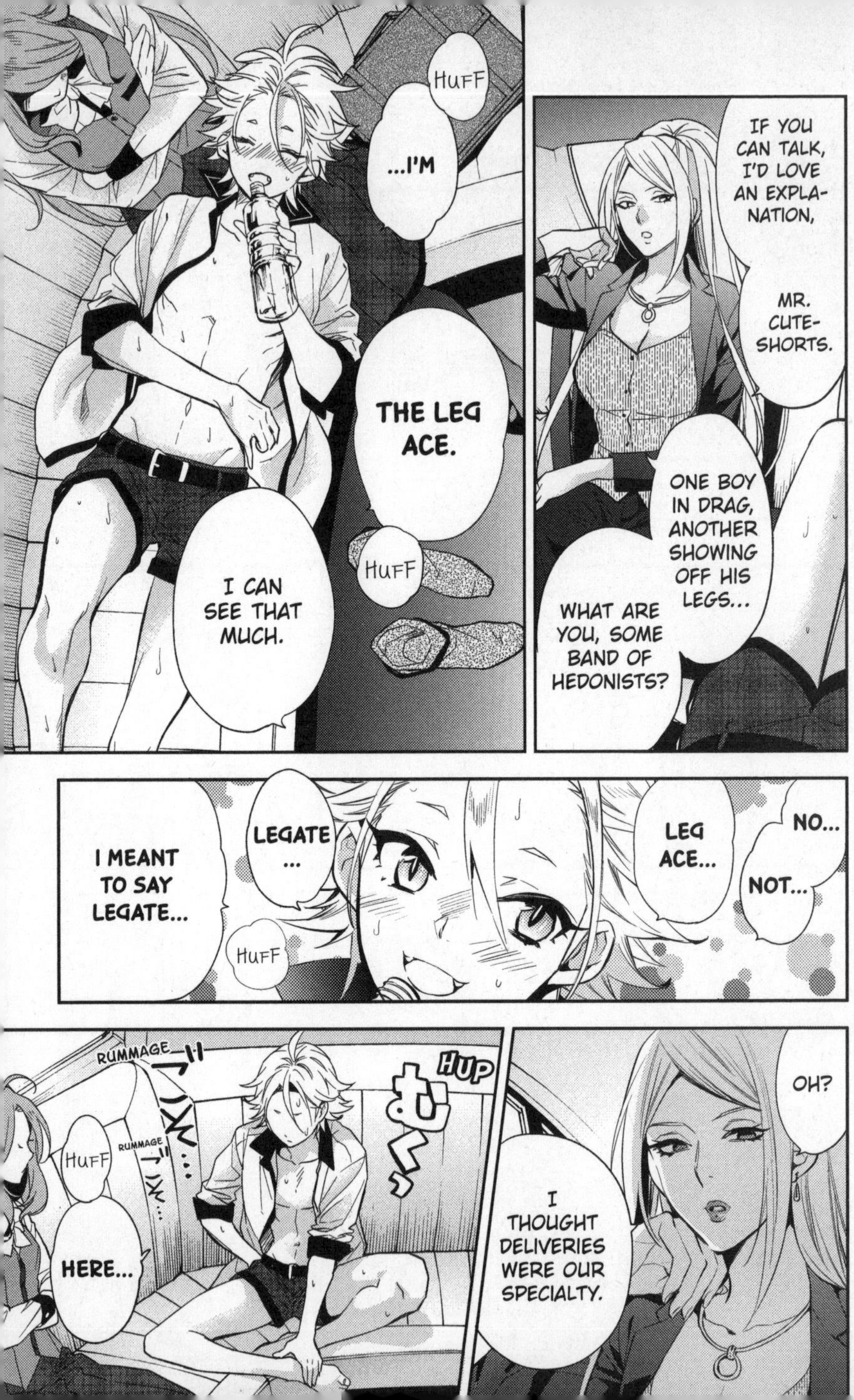
IF YOU CAN TALK, I'D LOVE AN EXPLANATION,
MR. CUTE-SHORTS.
ONE BOY IN DRAG, ANOTHER SHOWING OFF HIS LEGS...
WHAT ARE YOU, SOME BAND OF HEDONISTS?
HUFF
...I'M
THE LEG ACE.
HUFF
I CAN SEE THAT MUCH.
NO... NOT...
LEG ACE...
LEGATE...
HUFF
I MEANT TO SAY LEGATE...
OH?
I THOUGHT DELIVERIES WERE OUR SPECIALTY.
HUP
RUMMAGE
RUMMAGE
HUFF
HERE...

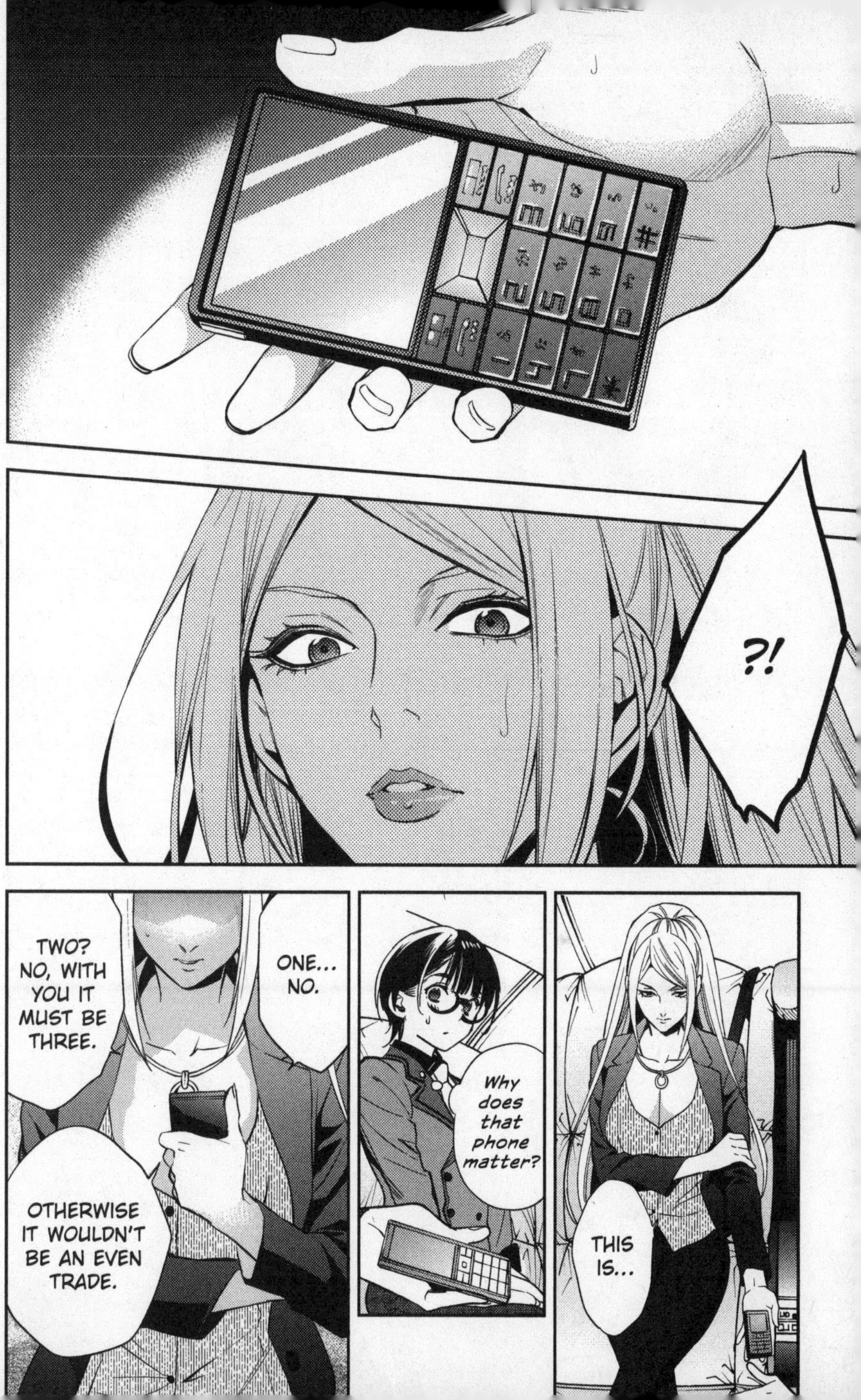
?!
THIS IS...
Why does that phone matter?
ONE... NO.
TWO? NO, WITH YOU IT MUST BE THREE.
OTHERWISE IT WOULDN'T BE AN EVEN TRADE.

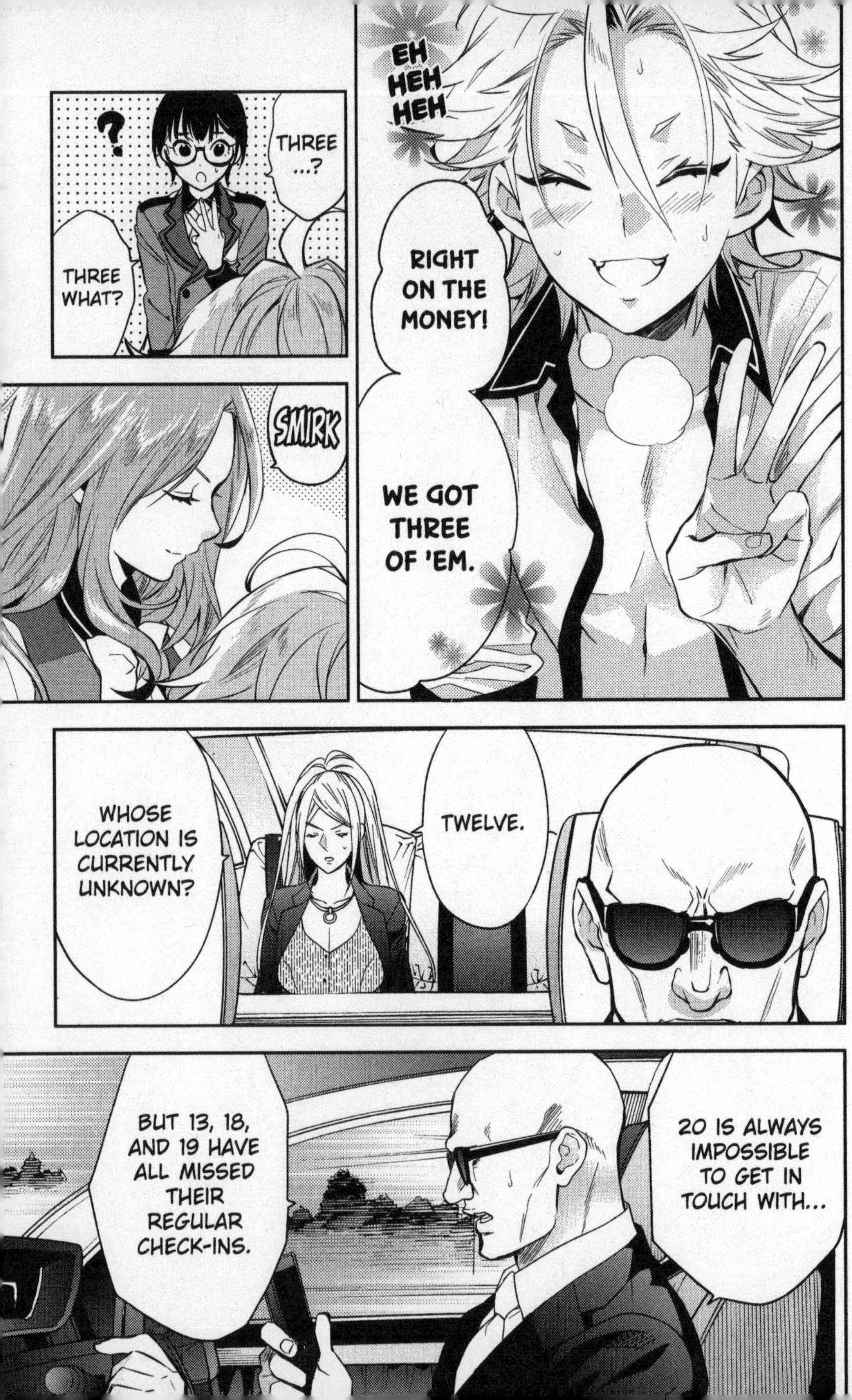
EH HEH HEH
RIGHT ON THE MONEY!
WE GOT THREE OF 'EM.
THREE ...?
?
THREE WHAT?
SMIRK
TWELVE.
WHOSE LOCATION IS CURRENTLY UNKNOWN?
20 IS ALWAYS IMPOSSIBLE TO GET IN TOUCH WITH...
BUT 13, 18, AND 19 HAVE ALL MISSED THEIR REGULAR CHECK-INS.

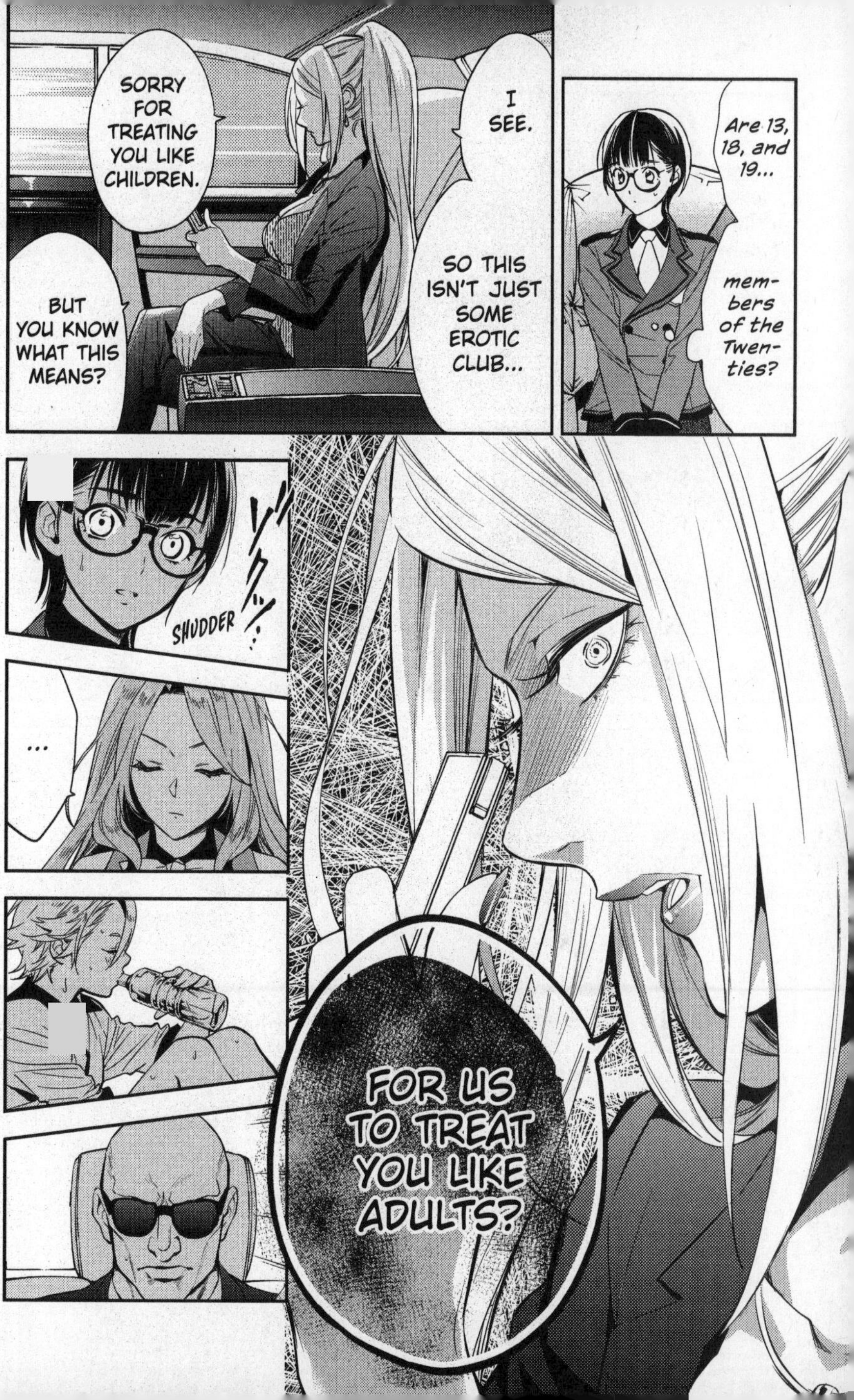
Are 13, 18, and 19...
members of the Twenties?
I SEE.
SO THIS ISN'T JUST SOME EROTIC CLUB...
SORRY FOR TREATING YOU LIKE CHILDREN.
BUT YOU KNOW WHAT THIS MEANS?
FOR US TO TREAT YOU LIKE ADULTS?
SHUDDER
...

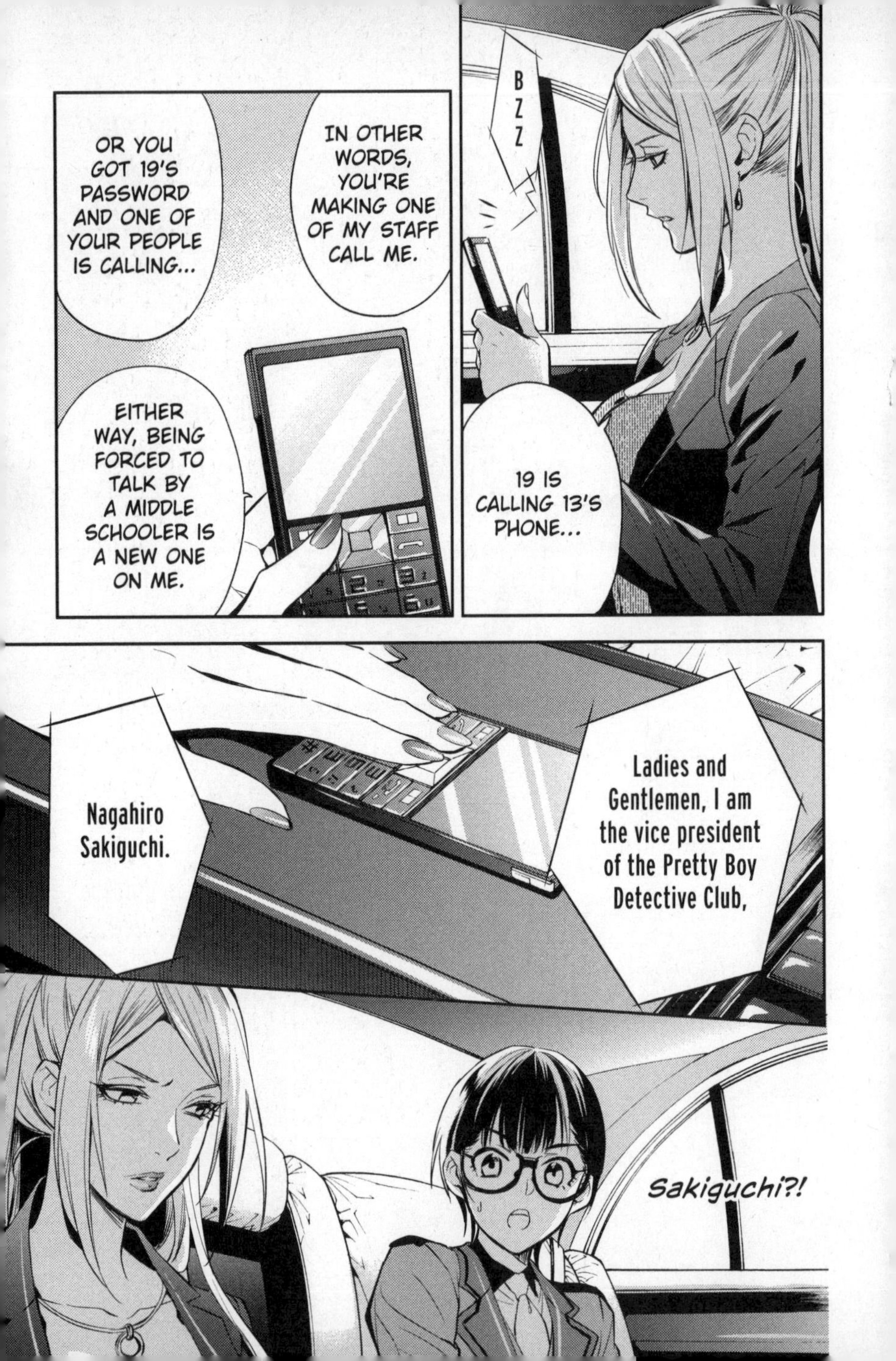
BZZ
19 IS CALLING 13'S PHONE...
IN OTHER WORDS, YOU'RE MAKING ONE OF MY STAFF CALL ME.
OR YOU GOT 19'S PASSWORD AND ONE OF YOUR PEOPLE IS CALLING...
EITHER WAY, BEING FORCED TO TALK BY A MIDDLE SCHOOLER IS A NEW ONE ON ME.
Ladies and Gentlemen, I am the vice president of the Pretty Boy Detective Club,
Nagahiro Sakiguchi.
Sakiguchi?!

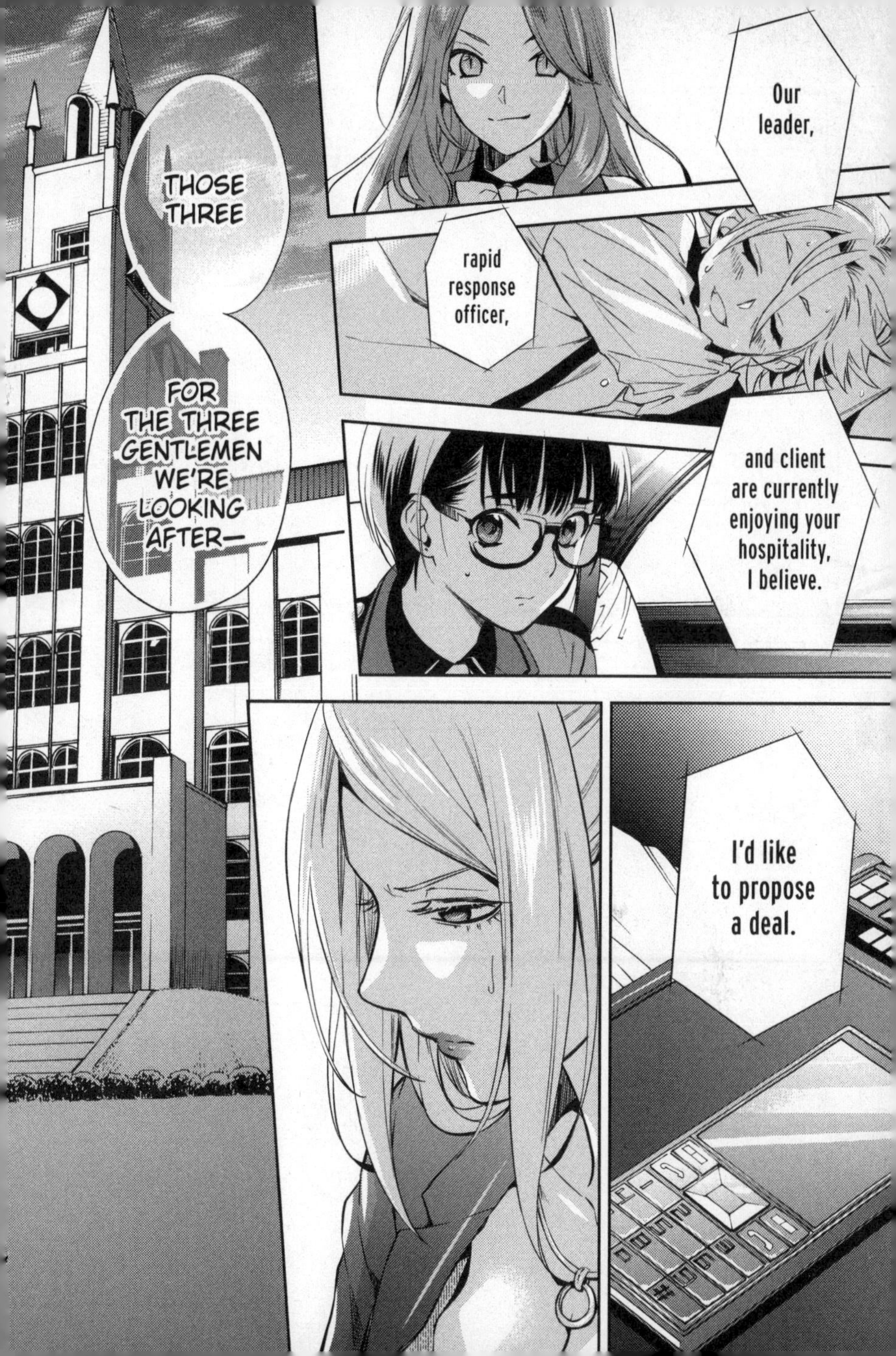
Our leader,
rapid response officer,
and client are currently enjoying your hospitality, I believe.
I'd like to propose a deal.
THOSE THREE
FOR THE THREE GENTLEMEN WE'RE LOOKING AFTER—

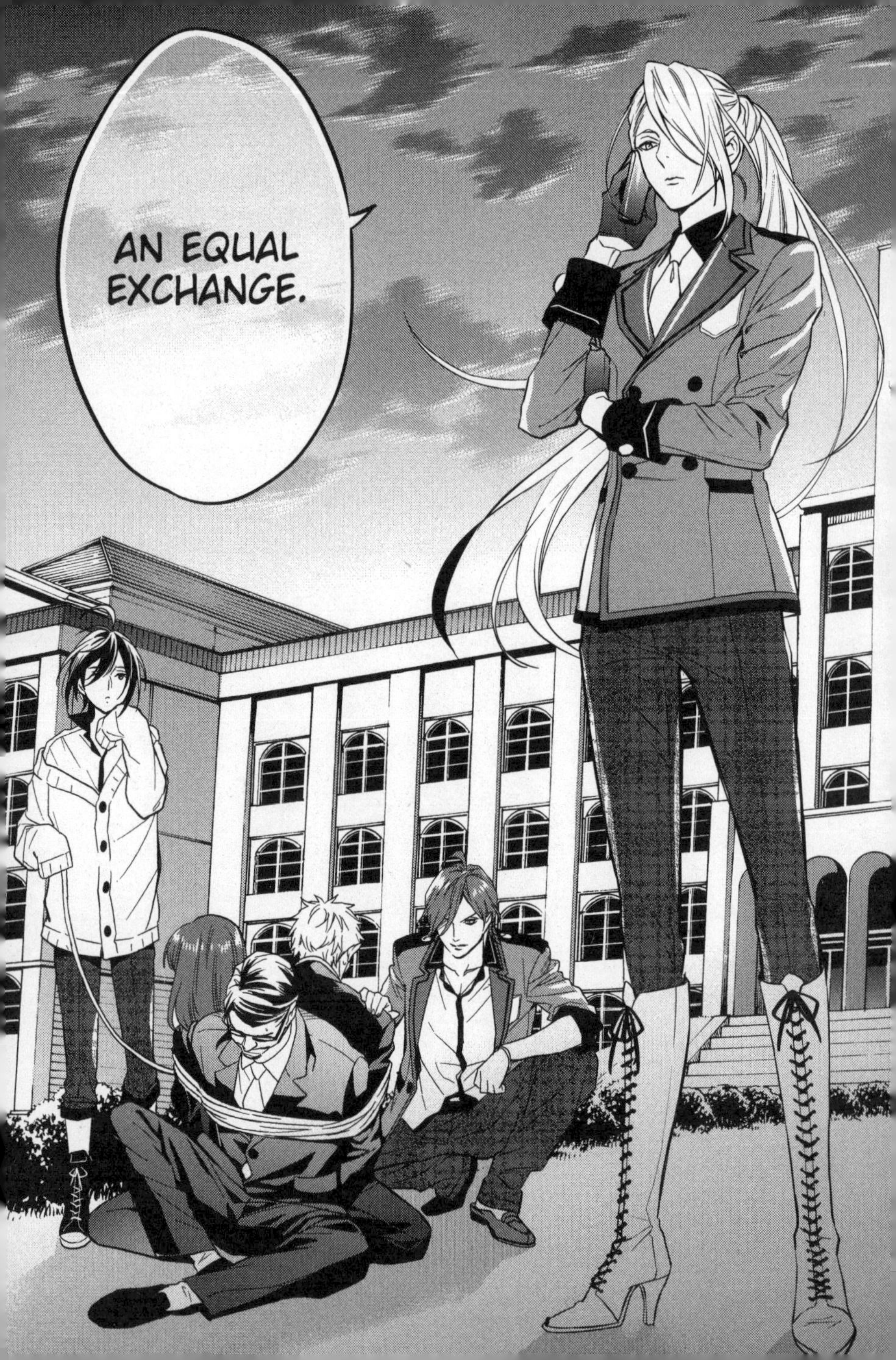
AN EQUAL EXCHANGE.

PRETTY BOY

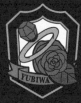

DETECTIVE CLUB!!

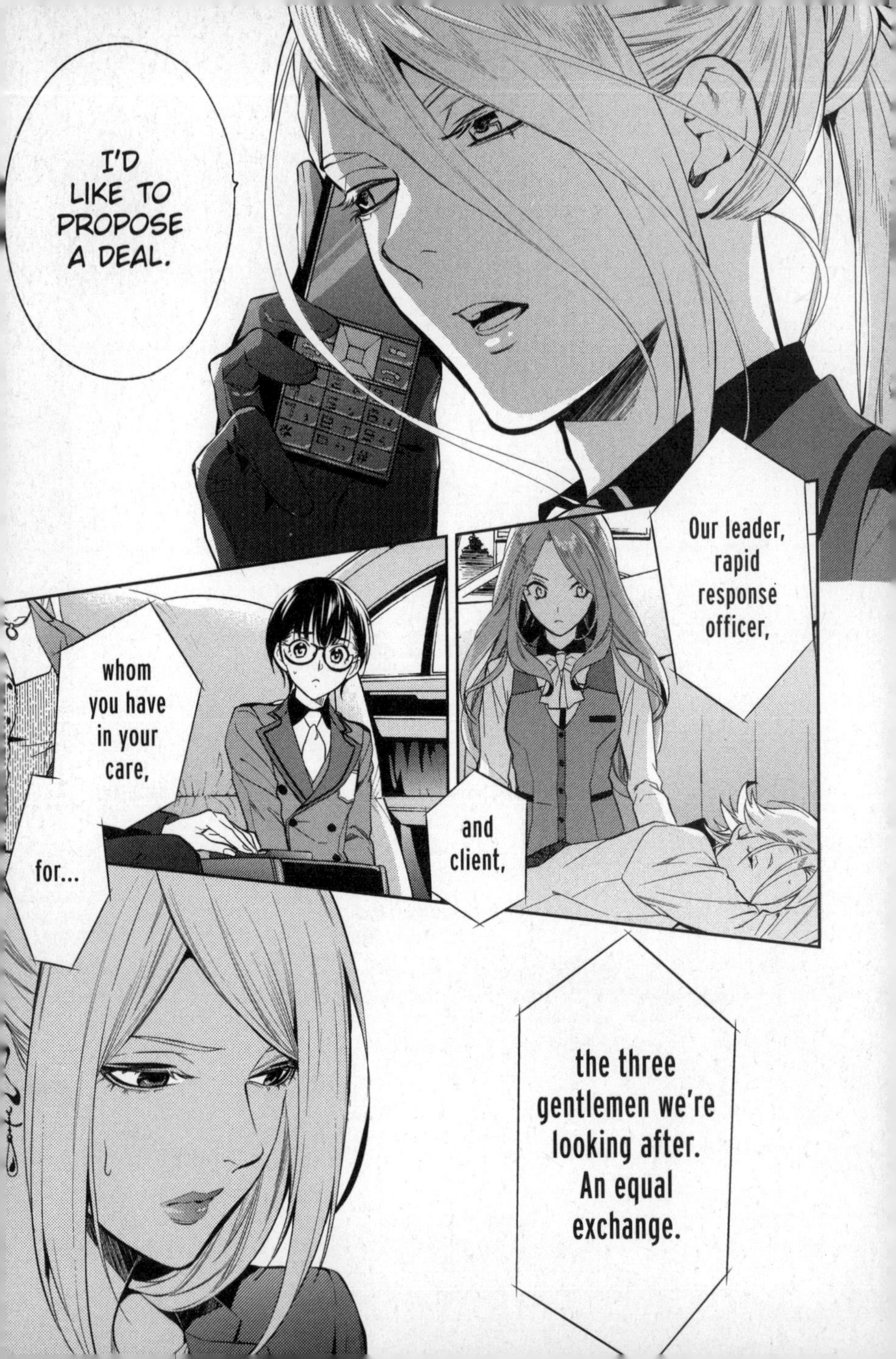
I'D LIKE TO PROPOSE A DEAL.
Our leader, rapid response officer,
and client,
whom you have in your care,
for...
the three gentlemen we're looking after. An equal exchange.

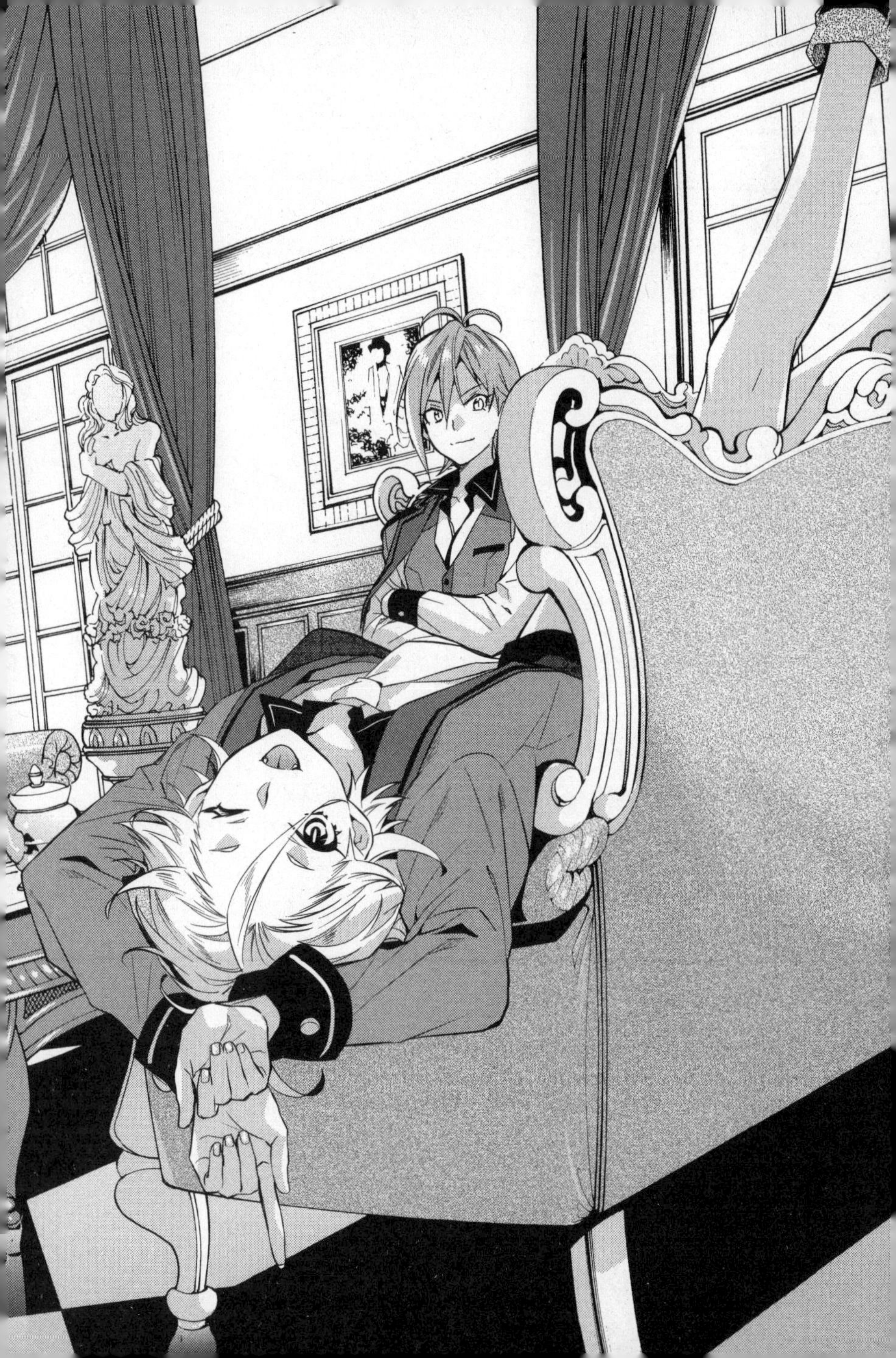

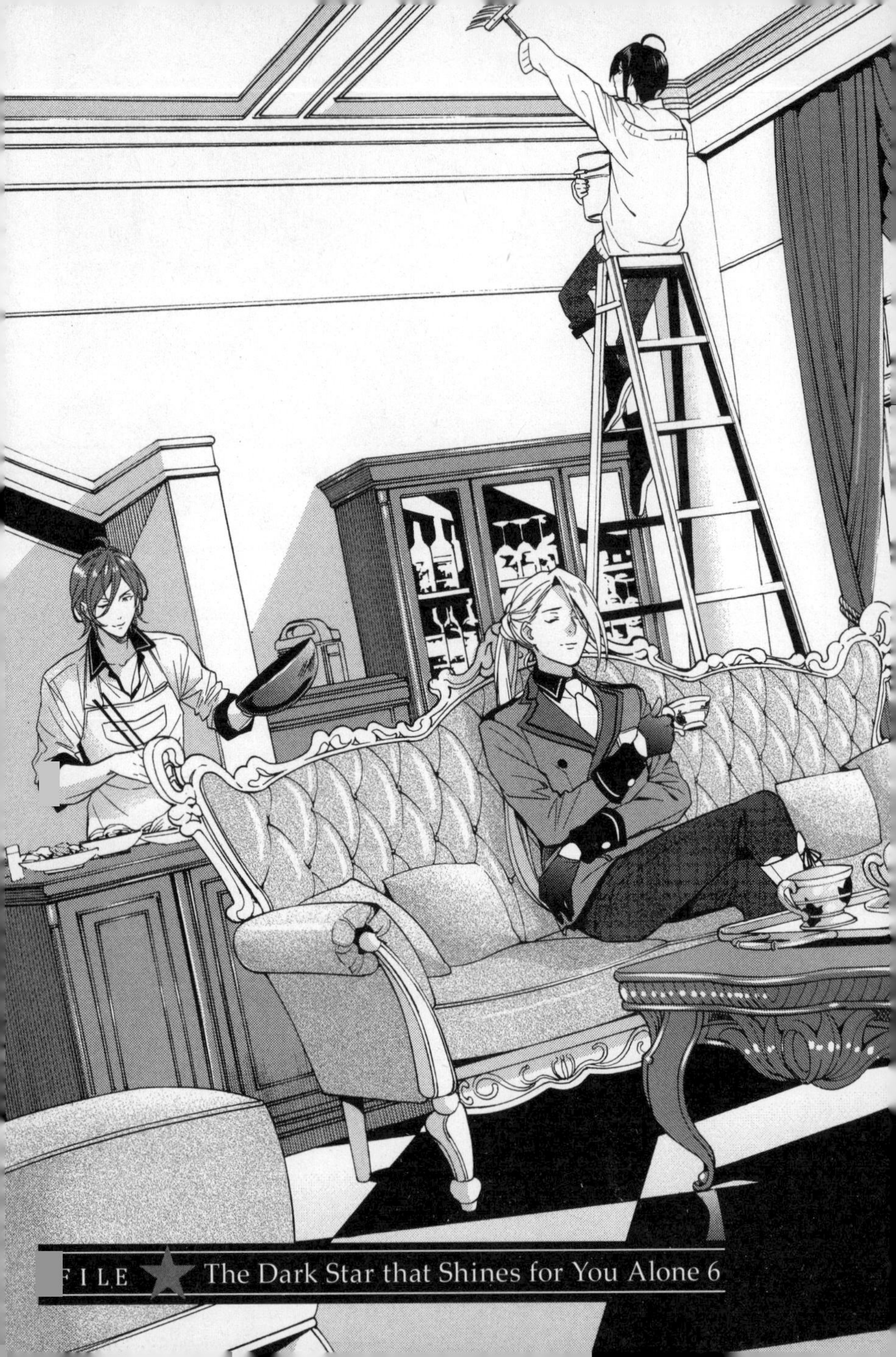

FILE ★ The Dark Star that Shines for You Alone 6

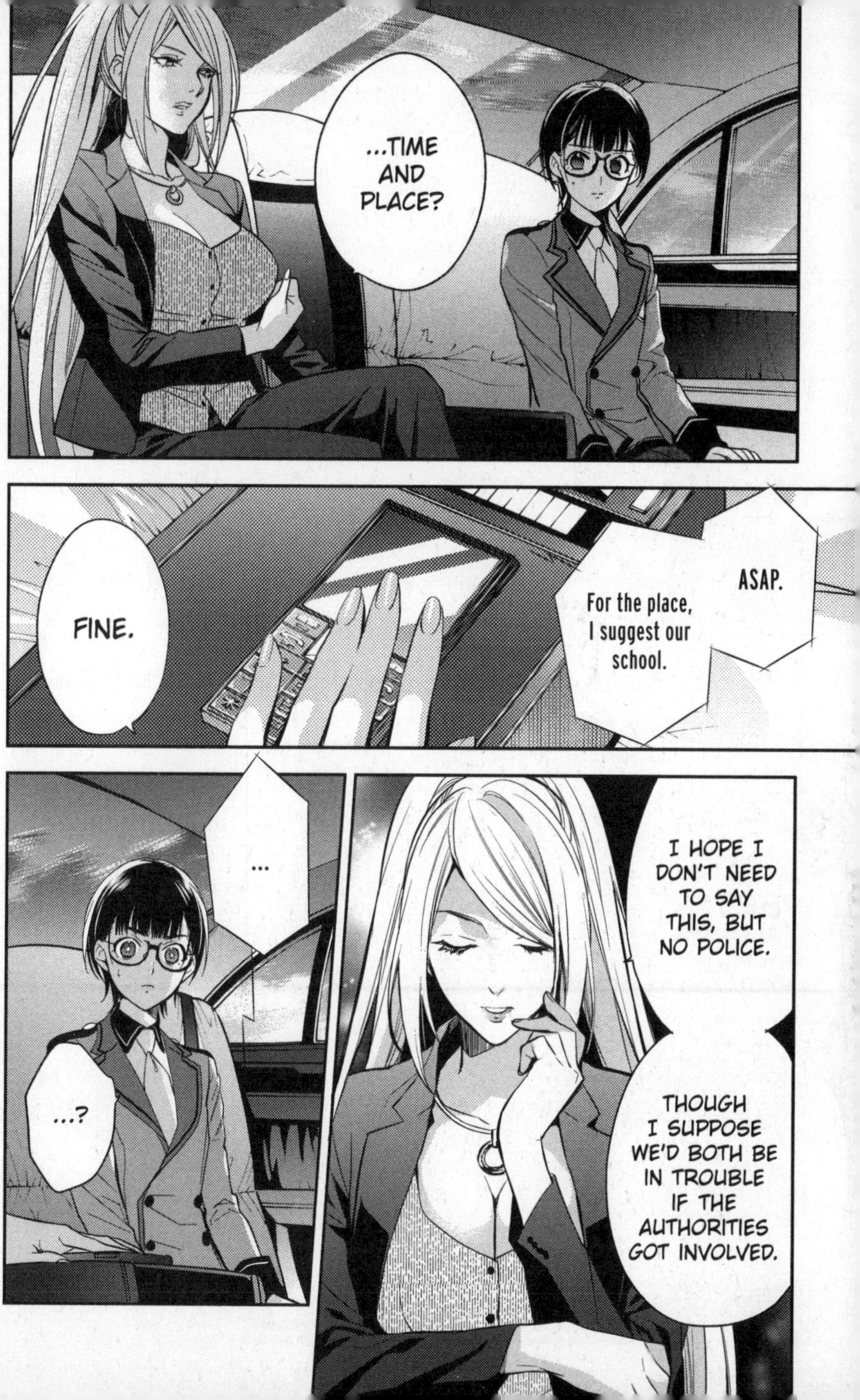
...TIME AND PLACE?
ASAP.
For the place, I suggest our school.
FINE.
I HOPE I DON'T NEED TO SAY THIS, BUT NO POLICE.
THOUGH I SUPPOSE WE'D BOTH BE IN TROUBLE IF THE AUTHORITIES GOT INVOLVED.
...
...?

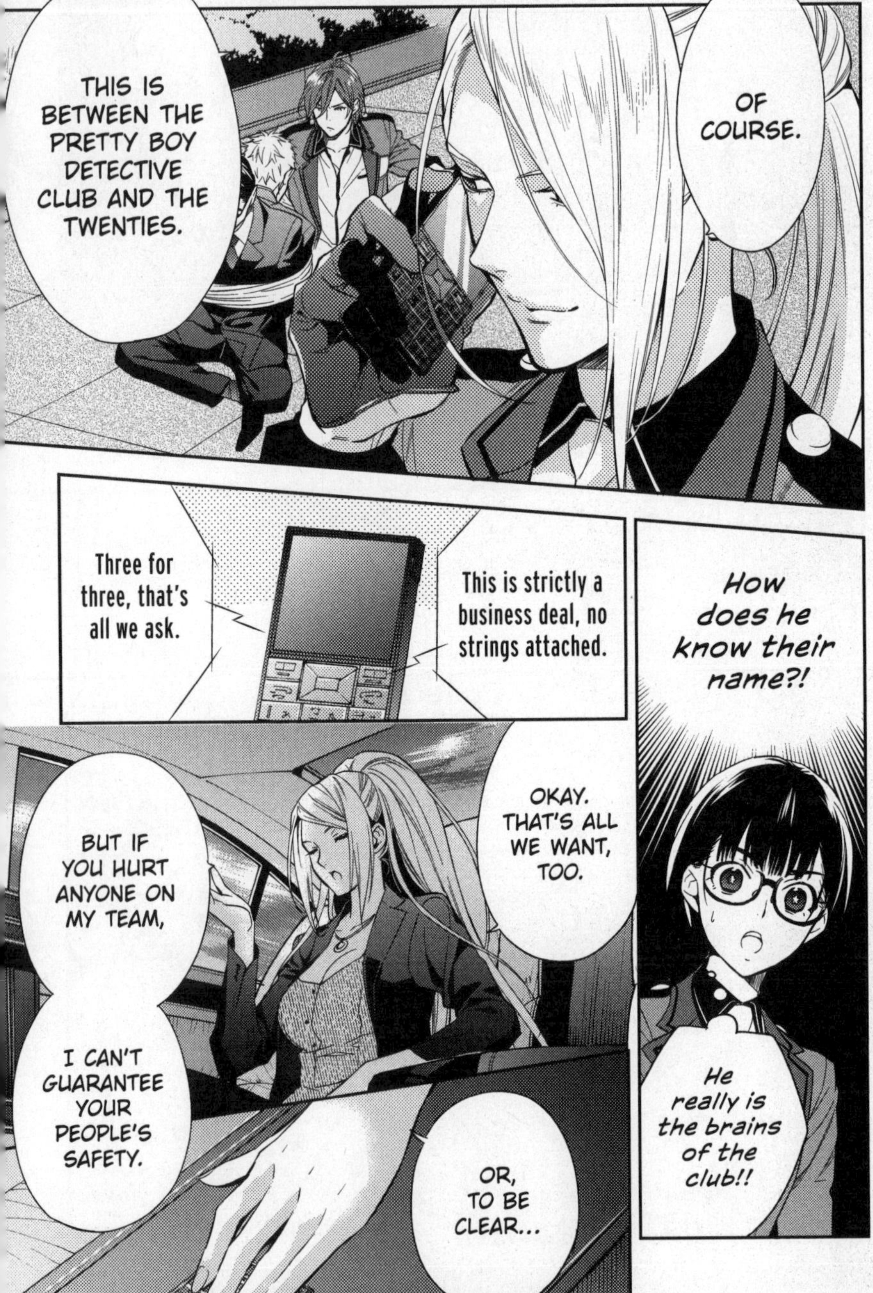
OF COURSE.
THIS IS BETWEEN THE PRETTY BOY DETECTIVE CLUB AND THE TWENTIES.
How does he know their name?!
He really is the brains of the club!!
This is strictly a business deal, no strings attached.
Three for three, that's all we ask.
OKAY. THAT'S ALL WE WANT, TOO.
BUT IF YOU HURT ANYONE ON MY TEAM,
I CAN'T GUARANTEE YOUR PEOPLE'S SAFETY.
OR, TO BE CLEAR...

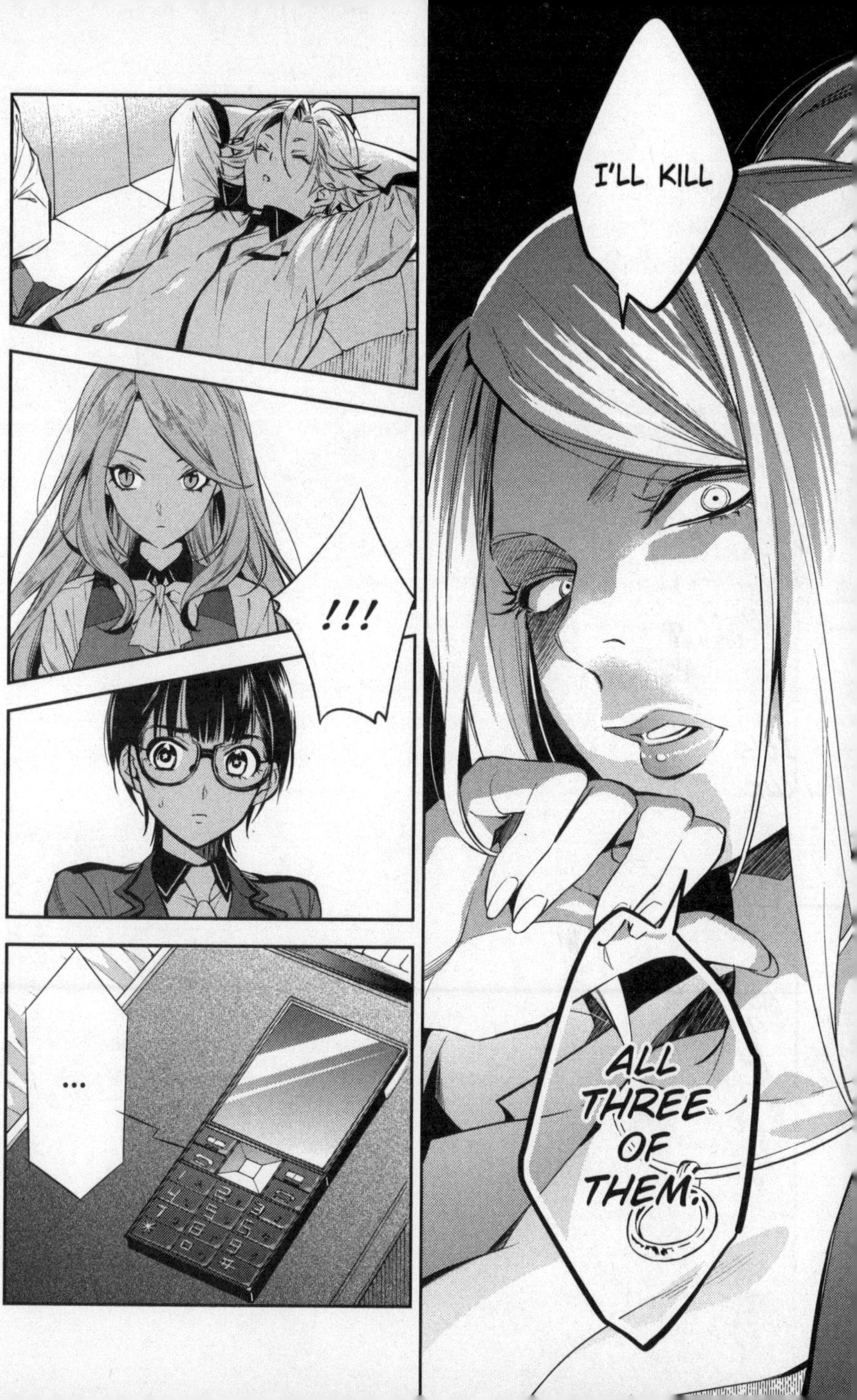
I'LL KILL
ALL THREE OF THEM.
!!!
...

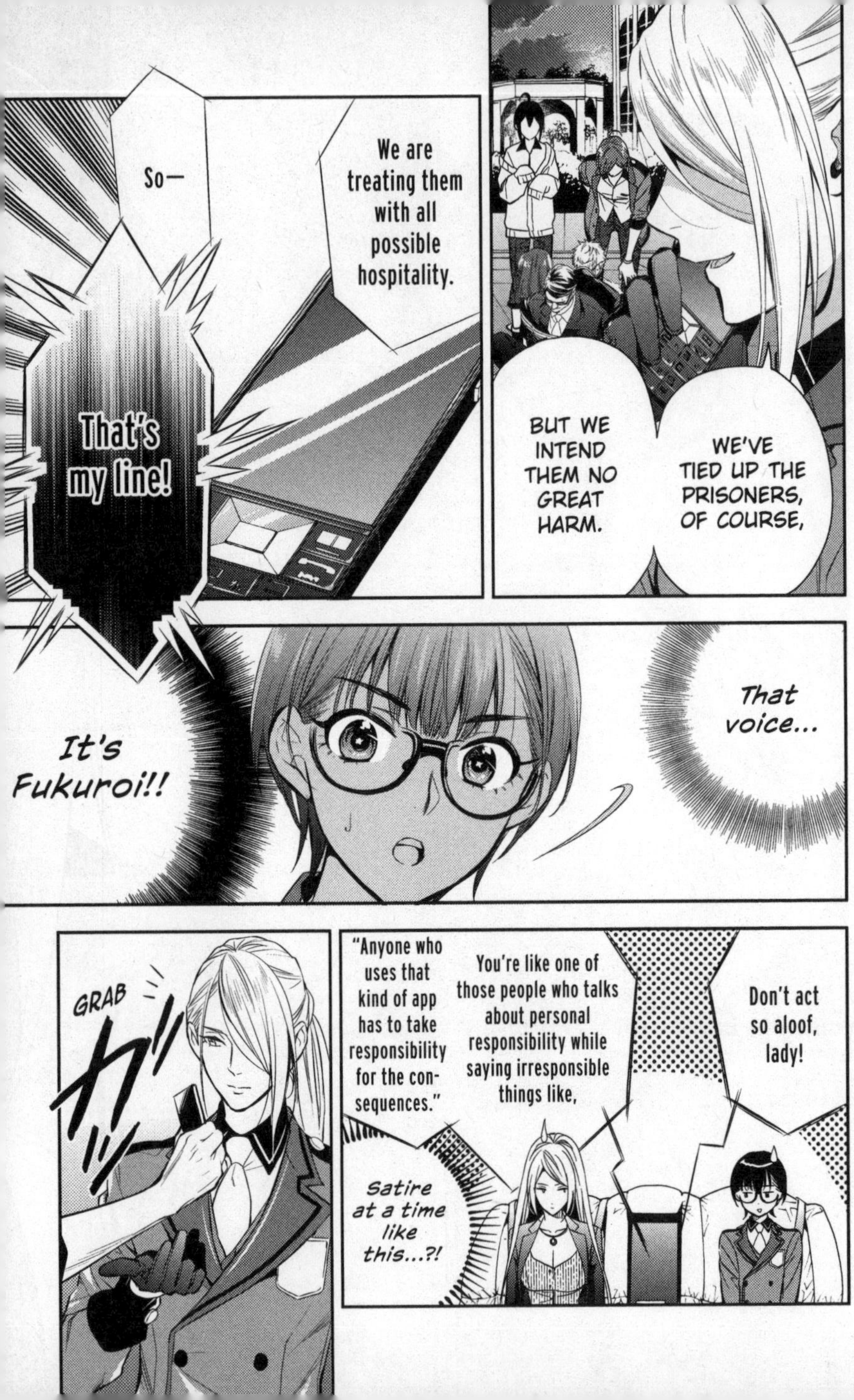
WE'VE TIED UP THE PRISONERS, OF COURSE,
BUT WE INTEND THEM NO GREAT HARM.
We are treating them with all possible hospitality.
So—
That's my line!
That voice...
It's Fukuroi!!
Don't act so aloof, lady!
You're like one of those people who talks about personal responsibility while saying irresponsible things like,
"Anyone who uses that kind of app has to take responsibility for the con-sequences."
Satire at a time like this...?!
GRAB

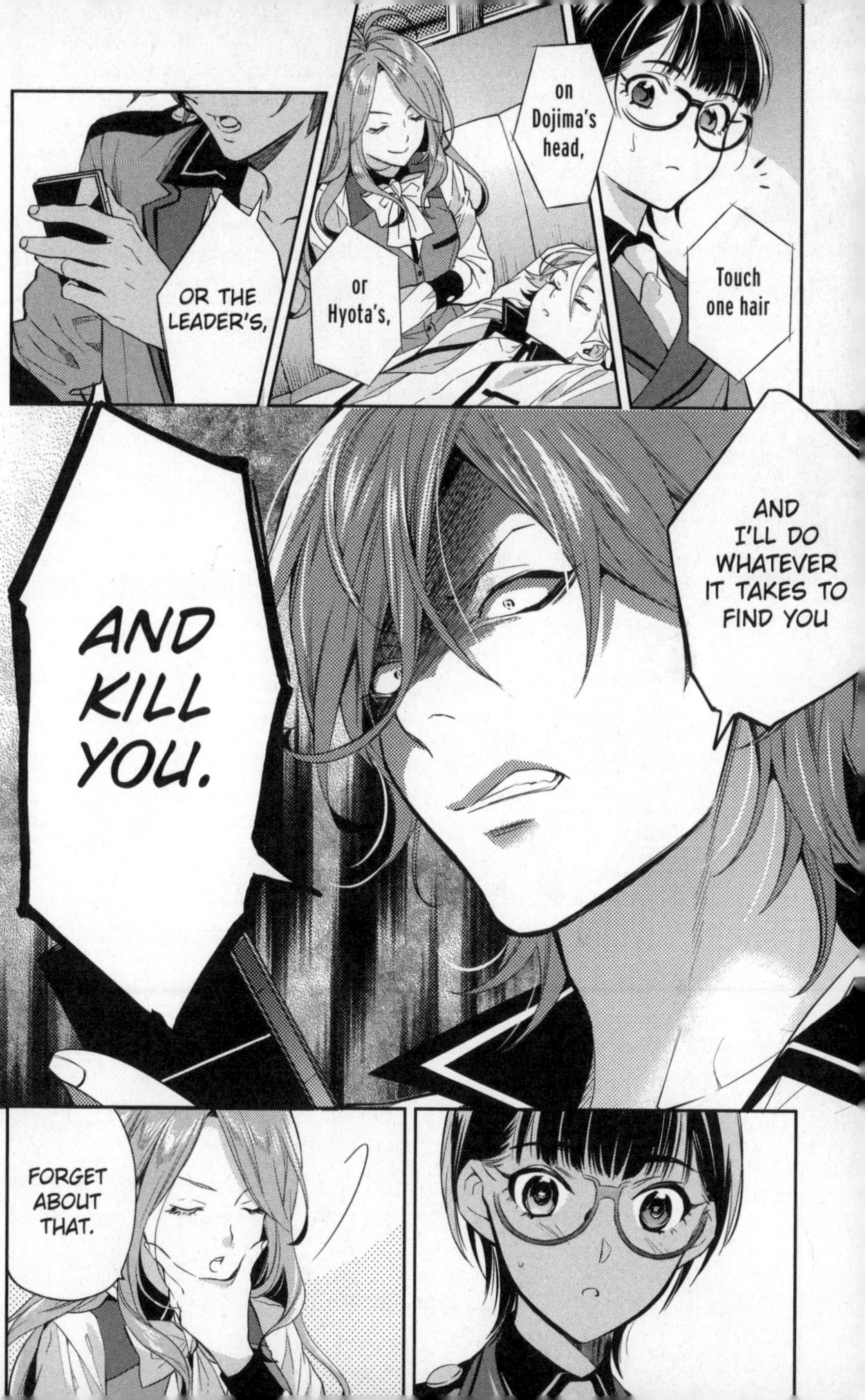
Touch one hair
on Dojima's head,
or Hyota's,
OR THE LEADER'S,
AND I'LL DO WHATEVER IT TAKES TO FIND YOU
AND KILL YOU.
FORGET ABOUT THAT.

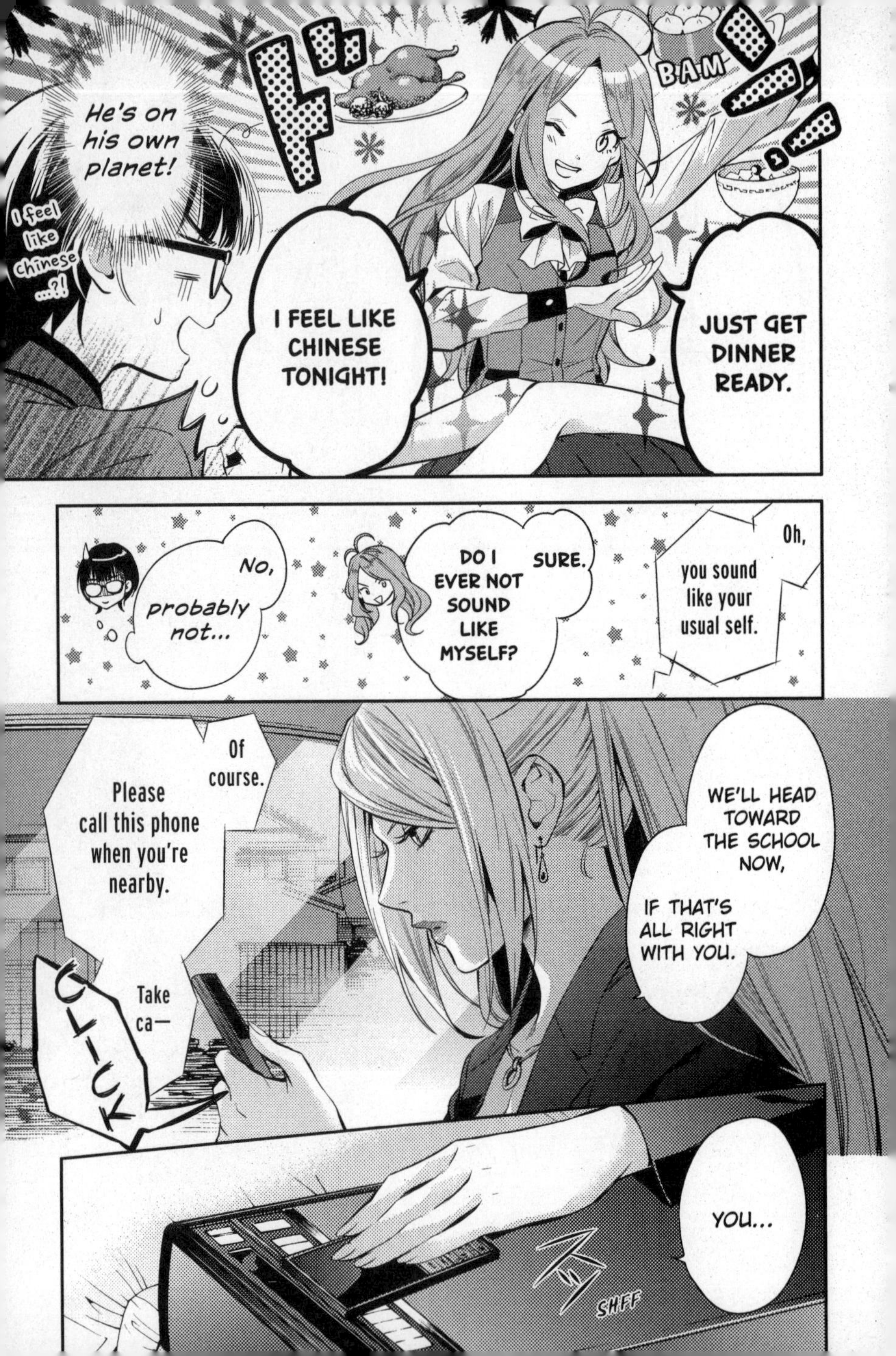
BAM
JUST GET DINNER READY.
I FEEL LIKE CHINESE TONIGHT!
He's on his own planet!
I feel like chinese ...?!
Oh, you sound like your usual self.
SURE. DO I EVER NOT SOUND LIKE MYSELF?
No, probably not...
WE'LL HEAD TOWARD THE SCHOOL NOW,
IF THAT'S ALL RIGHT WITH YOU.
Of course.
Please call this phone when you're nearby.
Take ca—
CLICK
YOU...
SHFF

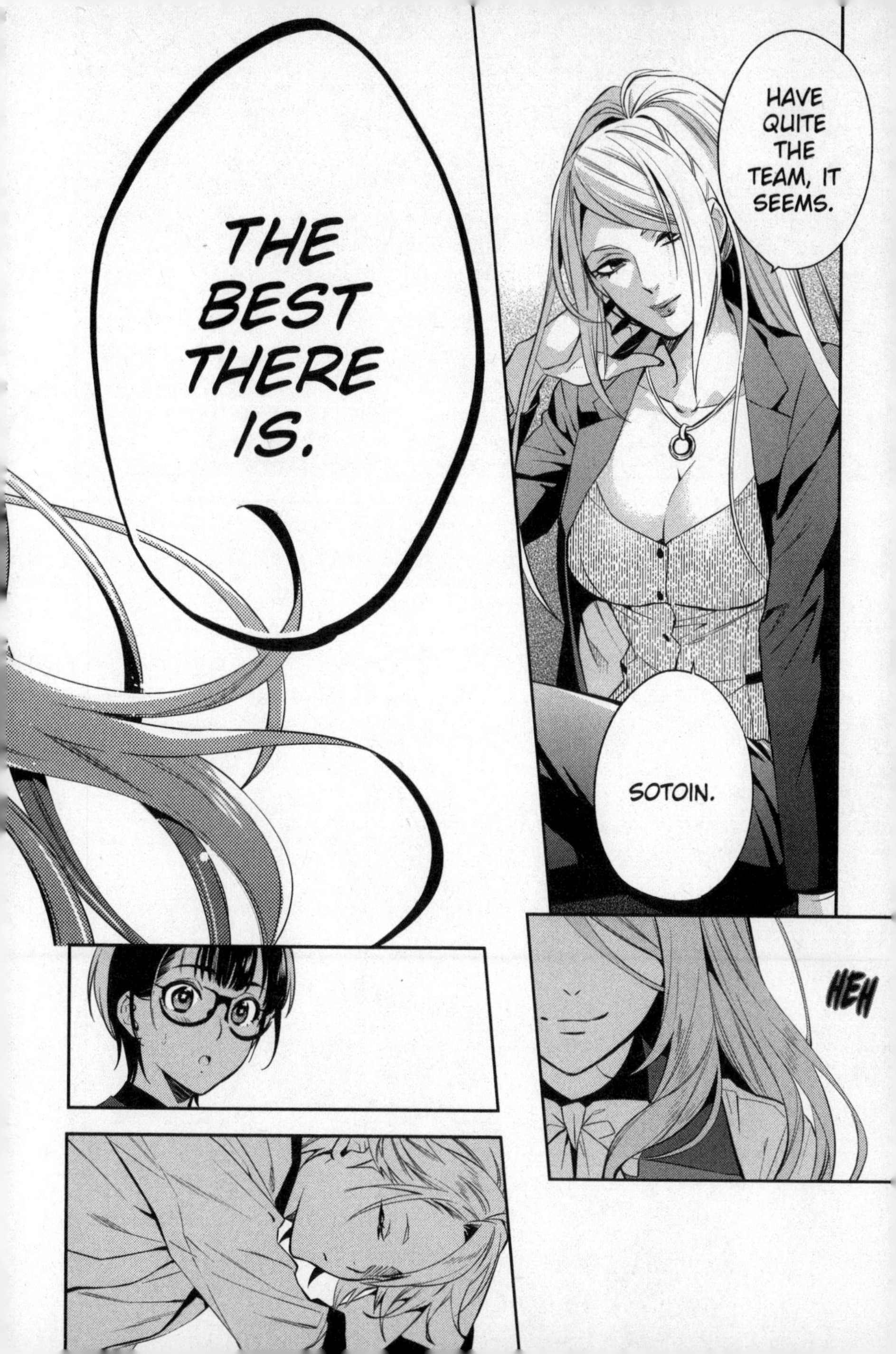
HAVE QUITE THE TEAM, IT SEEMS.
SOTOIN.
THE BEST THERE IS.
HEH

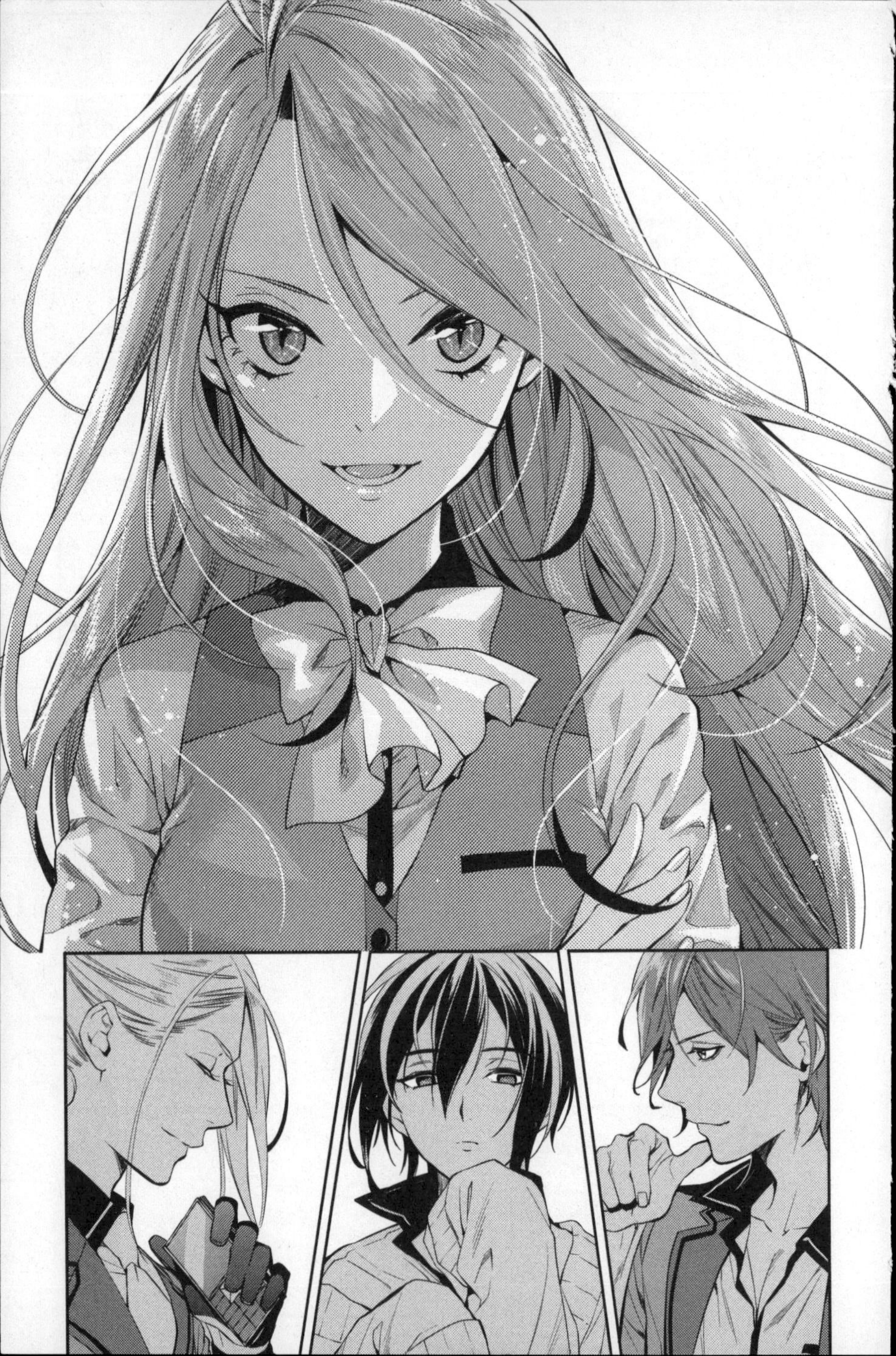

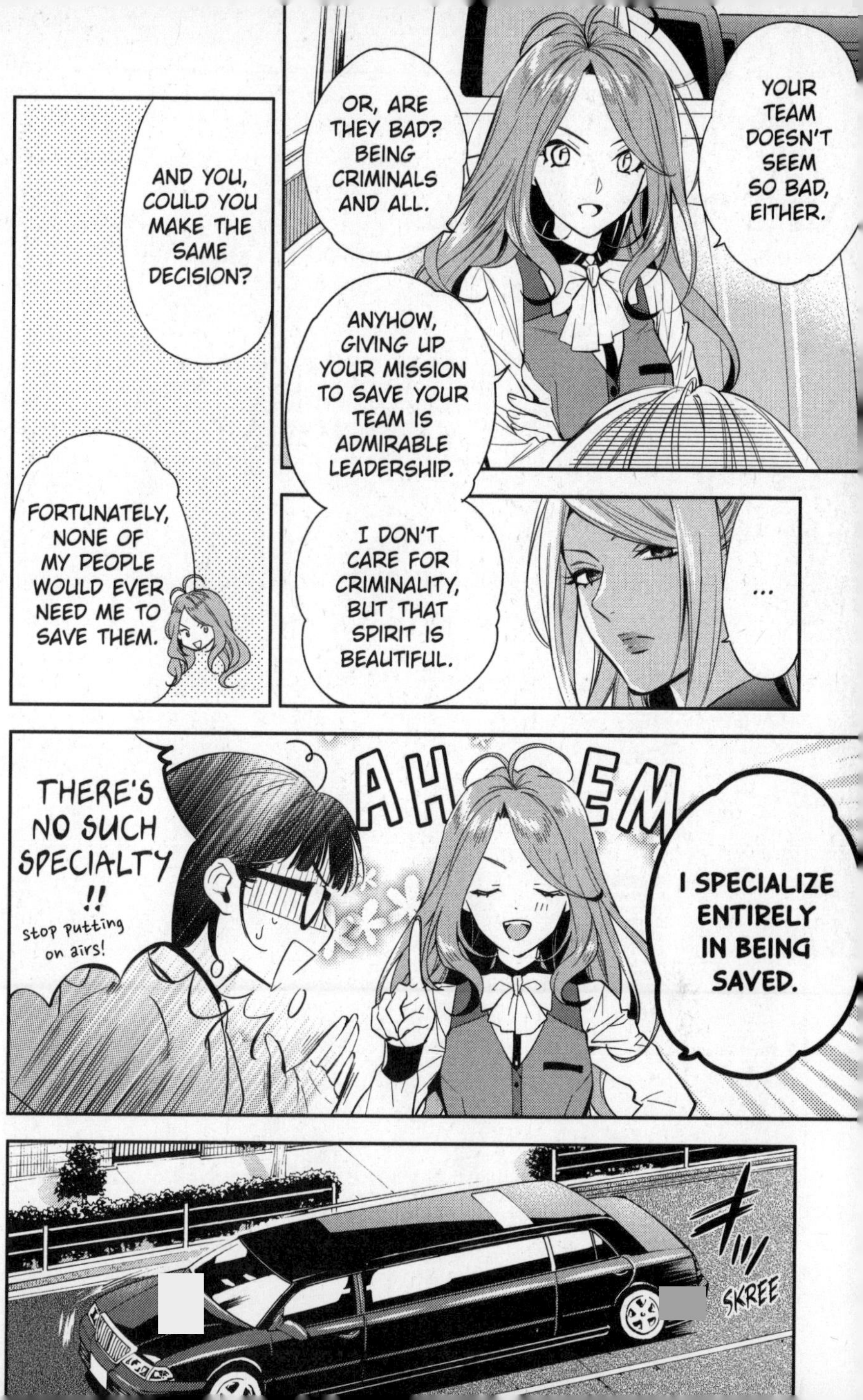
YOUR TEAM DOESN'T SEEM SO BAD, EITHER.
OR, ARE THEY BAD? BEING CRIMINALS AND ALL.
ANYHOW, GIVING UP YOUR MISSION TO SAVE YOUR TEAM IS ADMIRABLE LEADERSHIP.
...
I DON'T CARE FOR CRIMINALITY, BUT THAT SPIRIT IS BEAUTIFUL.
AND YOU, COULD YOU MAKE THE SAME DECISION?
FORTUNATELY, NONE OF MY PEOPLE WOULD EVER NEED ME TO SAVE THEM.
I SPECIALIZE ENTIRELY IN BEING SAVED.
AHEM
THERE'S NO SUCH SPECIALTY !!
stop putting on airs!
SKREE

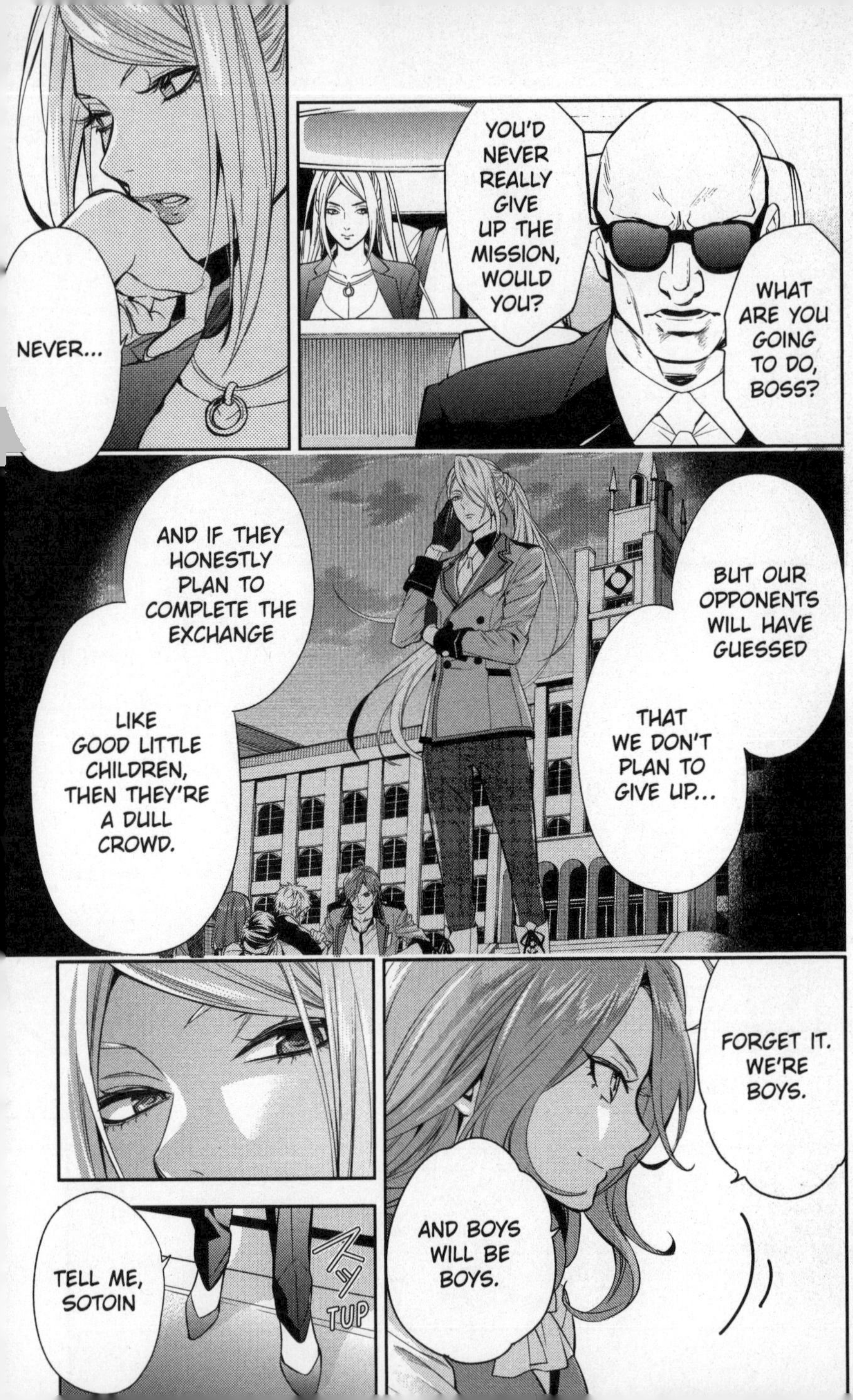
WHAT ARE YOU GOING TO DO, BOSS?
YOU'D NEVER REALLY GIVE UP THE MISSION, WOULD YOU?
NEVER...
BUT OUR OPPONENTS WILL HAVE GUESSED
THAT WE DON'T PLAN TO GIVE UP...
AND IF THEY HONESTLY PLAN TO COMPLETE THE EXCHANGE
LIKE GOOD LITTLE CHILDREN, THEN THEY'RE A DULL CROWD.
FORGET IT. WE'RE BOYS.
AND BOYS WILL BE BOYS.
TUP
TELL ME, SOTOIN

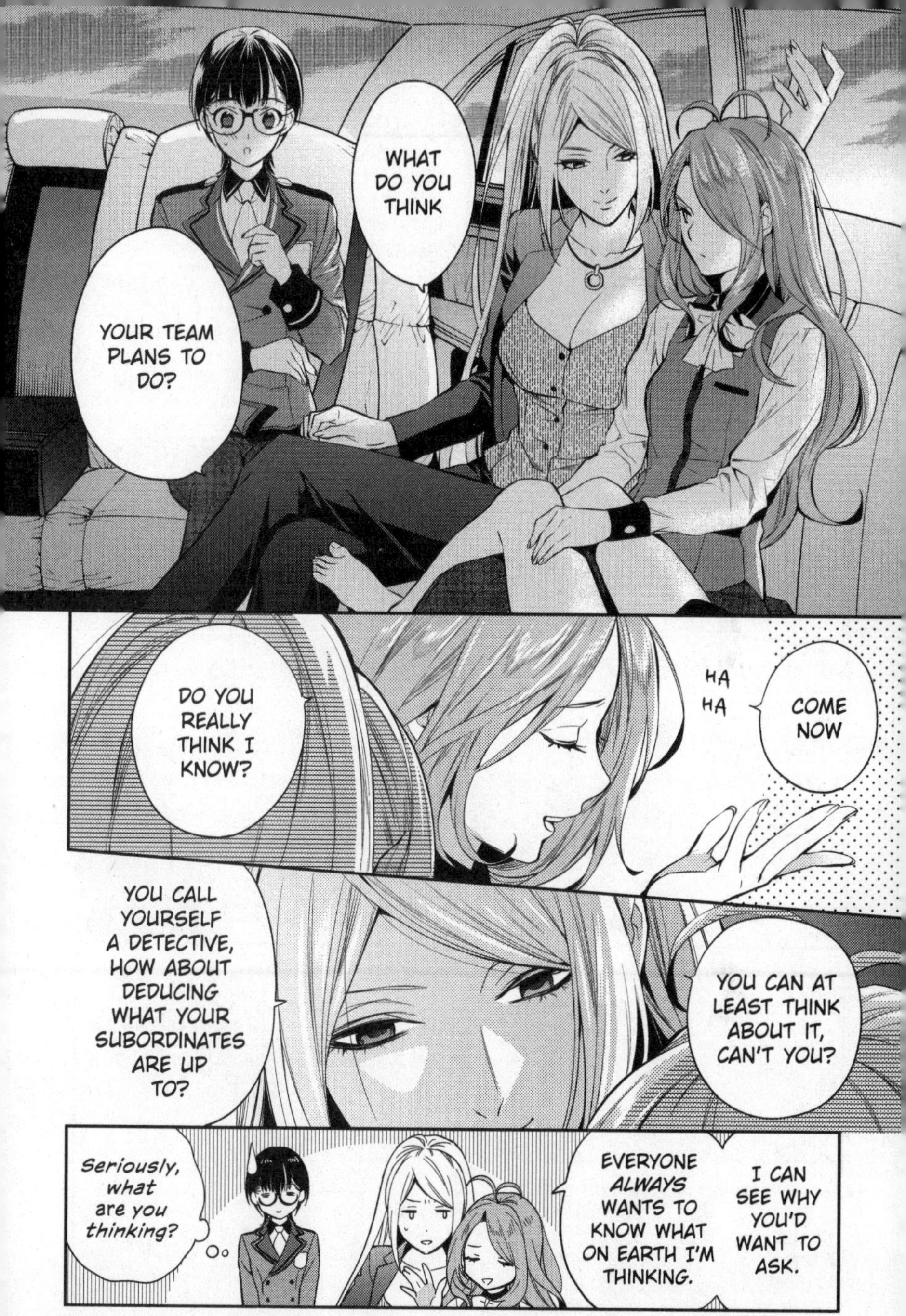
WHAT DO YOU THINK
YOUR TEAM PLANS TO DO?
COME NOW
HA HA
DO YOU REALLY THINK I KNOW?
YOU CAN AT LEAST THINK ABOUT IT, CAN'T YOU?
YOU CALL YOURSELF A DETECTIVE, HOW ABOUT DEDUCING WHAT YOUR SUBORDINATES ARE UP TO?
I CAN SEE WHY YOU'D WANT TO ASK.
EVERYONE *ALWAYS* WANTS TO KNOW WHAT ON EARTH I'M THINKING.
Seriously, what are you thinking?

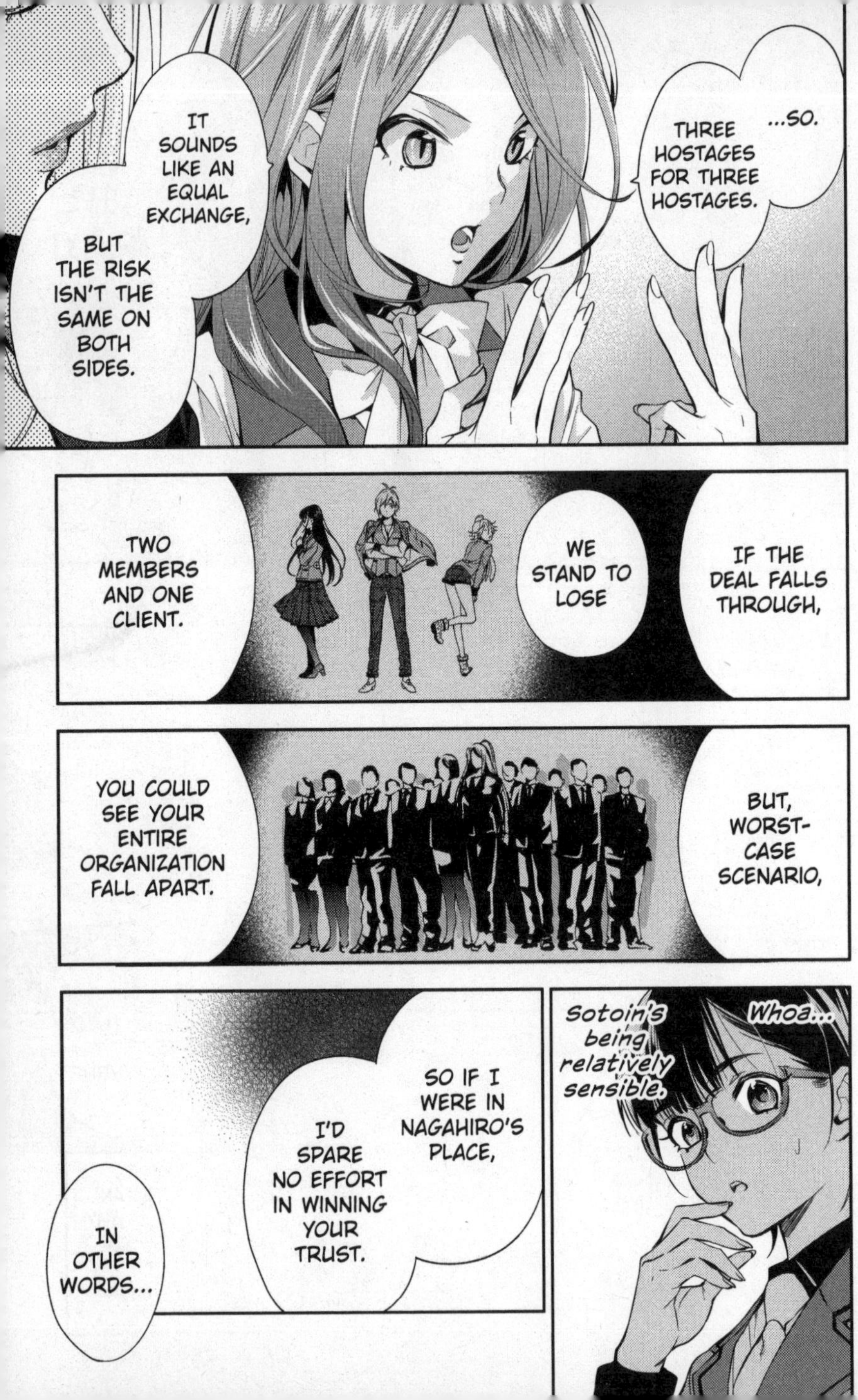
...SO.
THREE HOSTAGES FOR THREE HOSTAGES.
IT SOUNDS LIKE AN EQUAL EXCHANGE,
BUT THE RISK ISN'T THE SAME ON BOTH SIDES.
IF THE DEAL FALLS THROUGH,
WE STAND TO LOSE
TWO MEMBERS AND ONE CLIENT.
BUT, WORST-CASE SCENARIO,
YOU COULD SEE YOUR ENTIRE ORGANIZATION FALL APART.
Whoa...
Sotoin's being relatively sensible.
SO IF I WERE IN NAGAHIRO'S PLACE,
I'D SPARE NO EFFORT IN WINNING YOUR TRUST.
IN OTHER WORDS...

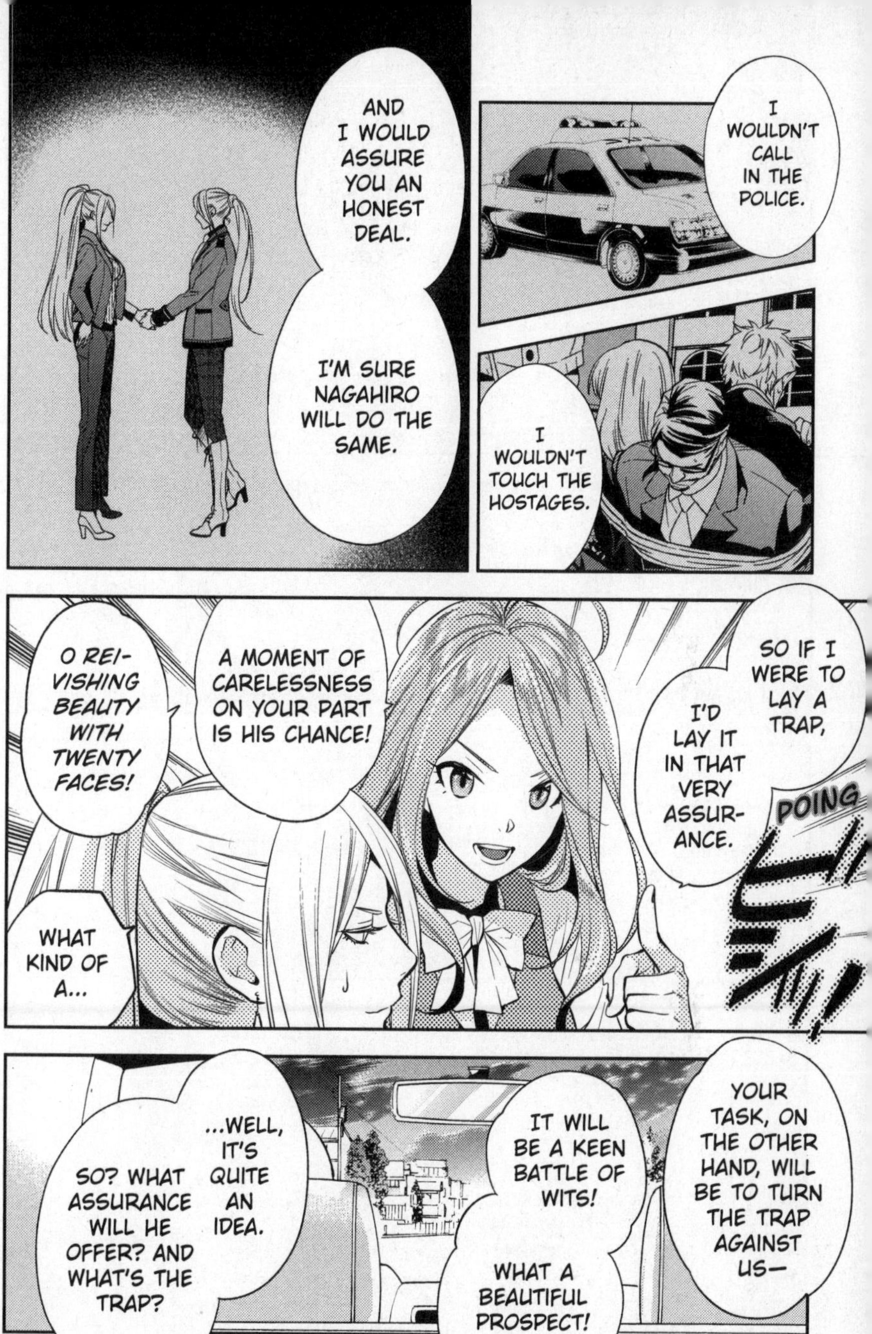

I WOULDN'T CALL IN THE POLICE.
I WOULDN'T TOUCH THE HOSTAGES.
AND I WOULD ASSURE YOU AN HONEST DEAL.
I'M SURE NAGAHIRO WILL DO THE SAME.
SO IF I WERE TO LAY A TRAP,
I'D LAY IT IN THAT VERY ASSURANCE.
POING
A MOMENT OF CARELESSNESS ON YOUR PART IS HIS CHANCE!
O REI-VISHING BEAUTY WITH TWENTY FACES!
WHAT KIND OF A...
YOUR TASK, ON THE OTHER HAND, WILL BE TO TURN THE TRAP AGAINST US—
IT WILL BE A KEEN BATTLE OF WITS!
WHAT A BEAUTIFUL PROSPECT!
...WELL, IT'S QUITE AN IDEA.
SO? WHAT ASSURANCE WILL HE OFFER? AND WHAT'S THE TRAP?

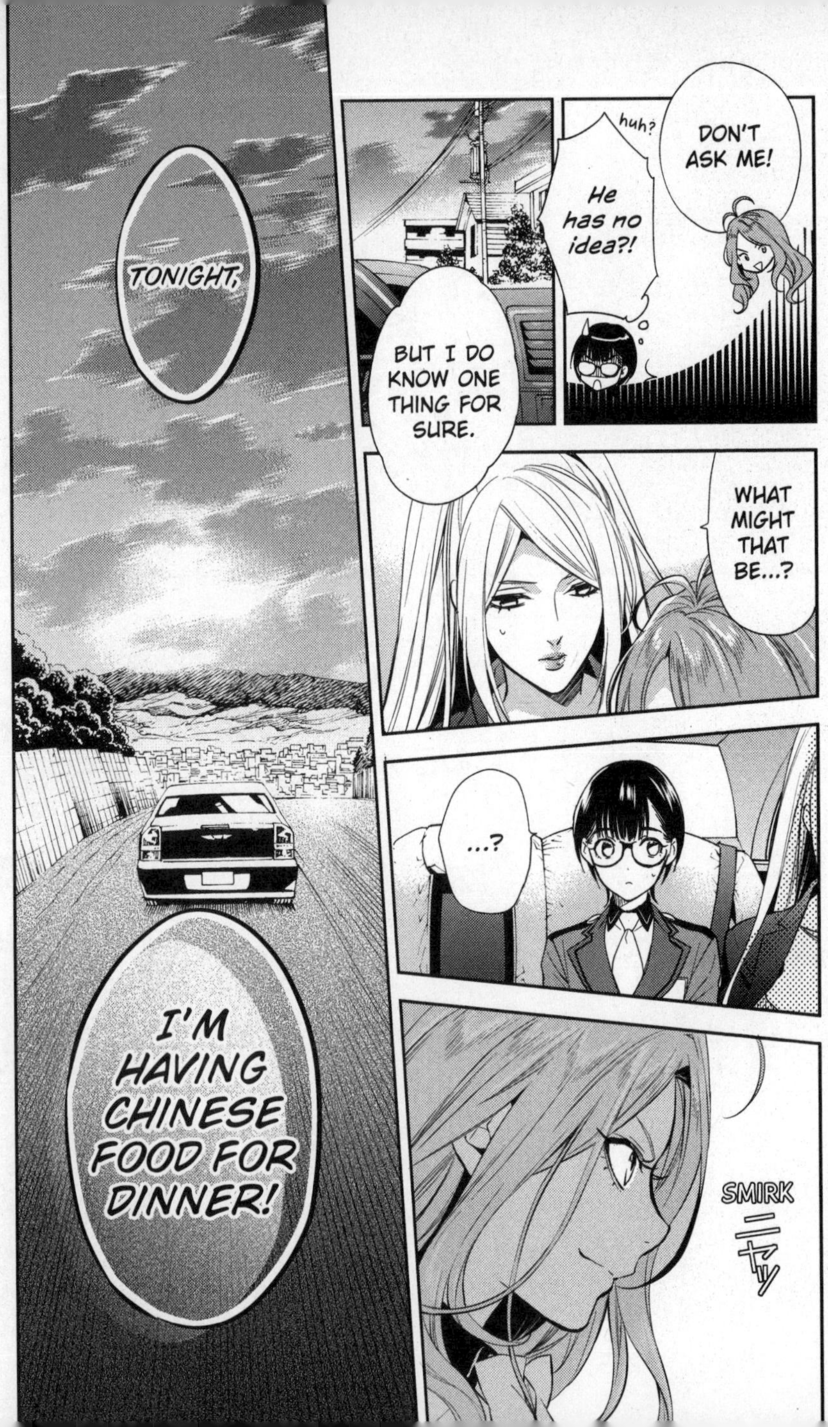
DON'T ASK ME!
huh?
He has no idea?!
BUT I DO KNOW ONE THING FOR SURE.
WHAT MIGHT THAT BE...?
...?
SMIRK
ニヤッ
TONIGHT,
I'M HAVING CHINESE FOOD FOR DINNER!

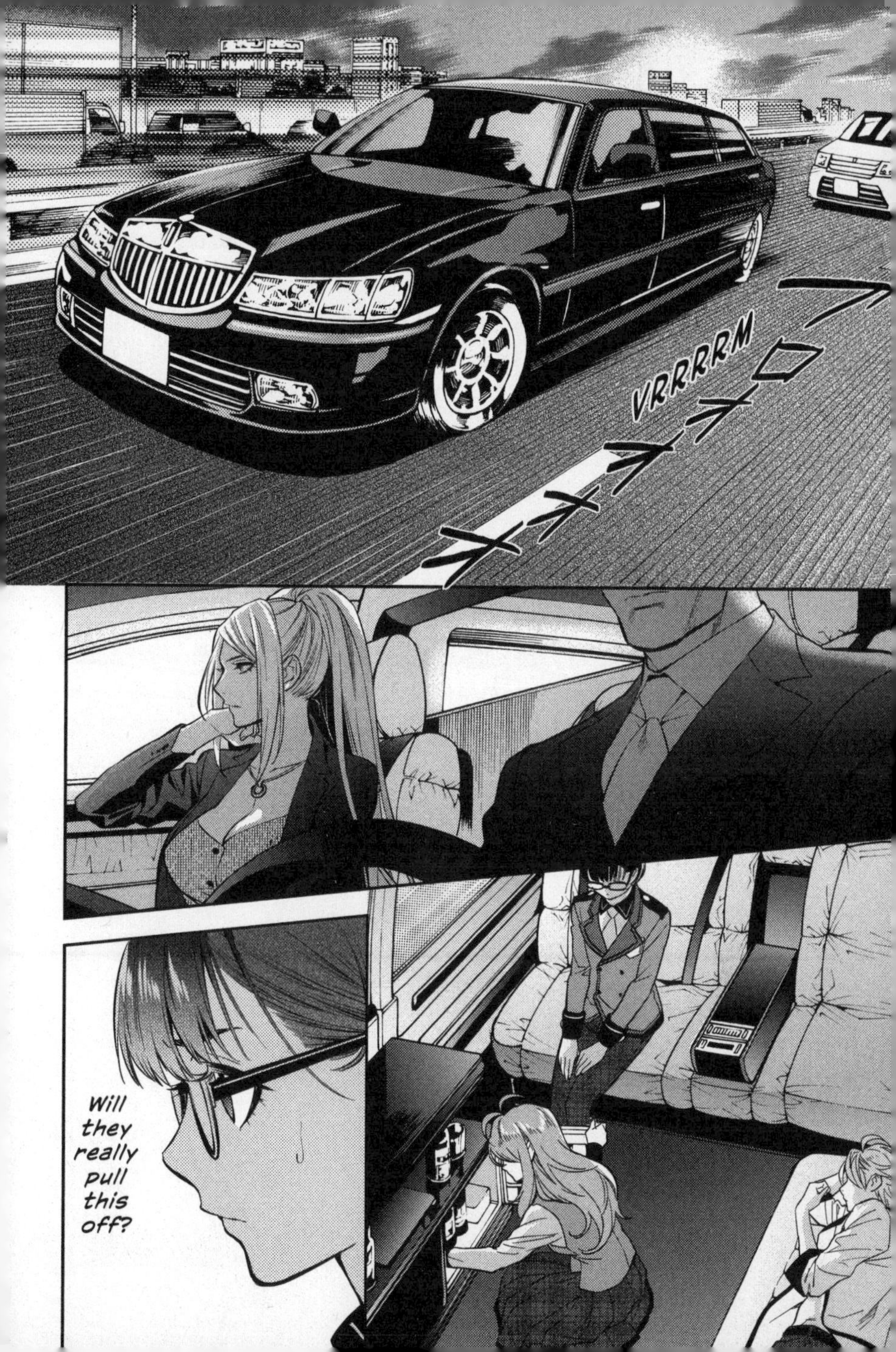
フロオオオオ
VRRRRM
Will they really pull this off?

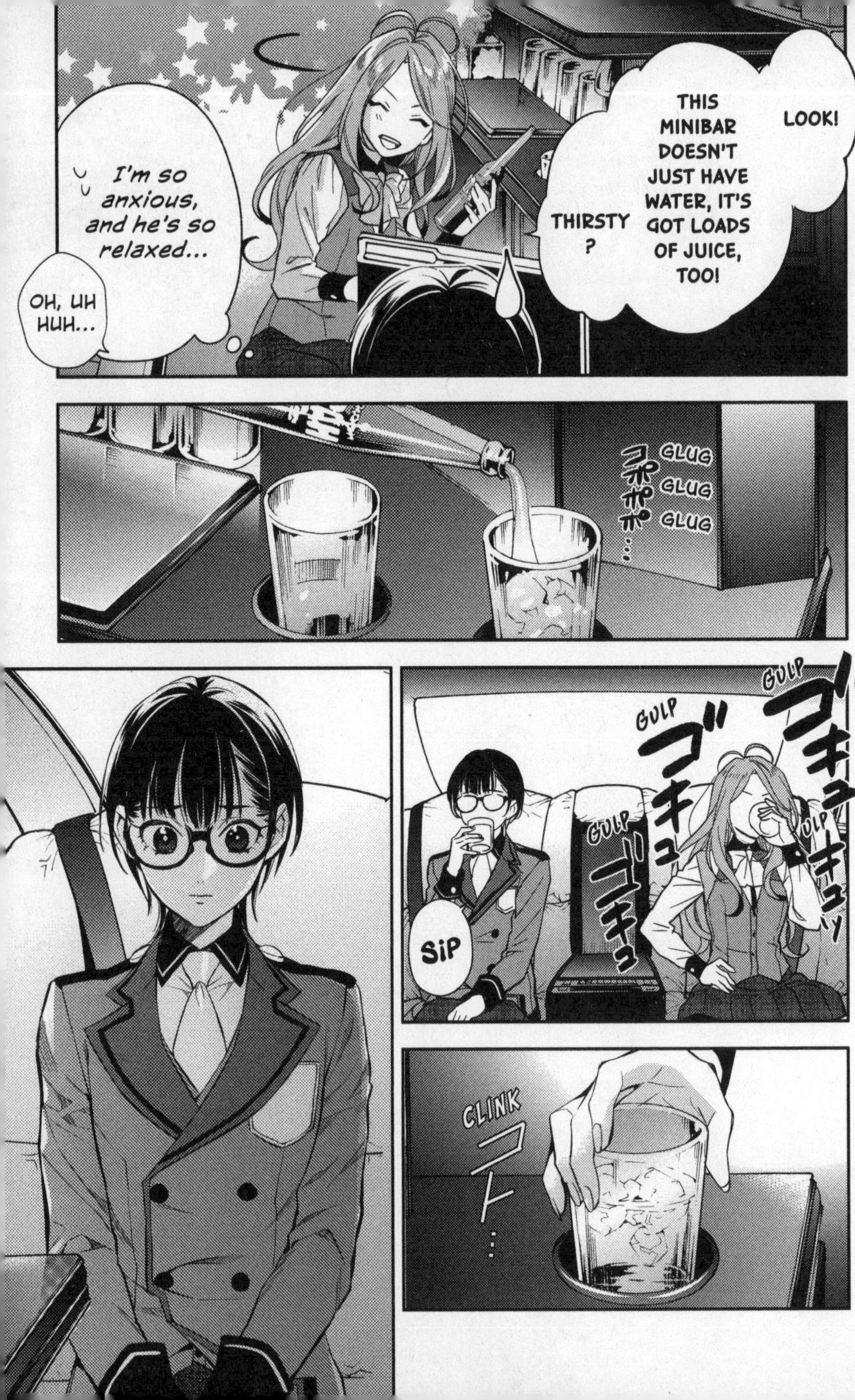
LOOK!
THIS MINIBAR DOESN'T JUST HAVE WATER, IT'S GOT LOADS OF JUICE, TOO!
THIRSTY?
I'm so anxious, and he's so relaxed...
OH, UH HUH...
GLUG GLUG GLUG
コポポポ…
GULP
GULP
GULP
GULP
ゴキュ
ゴキュ
ゴキュ
ゴキュッ
SIP
CLINK
コト…

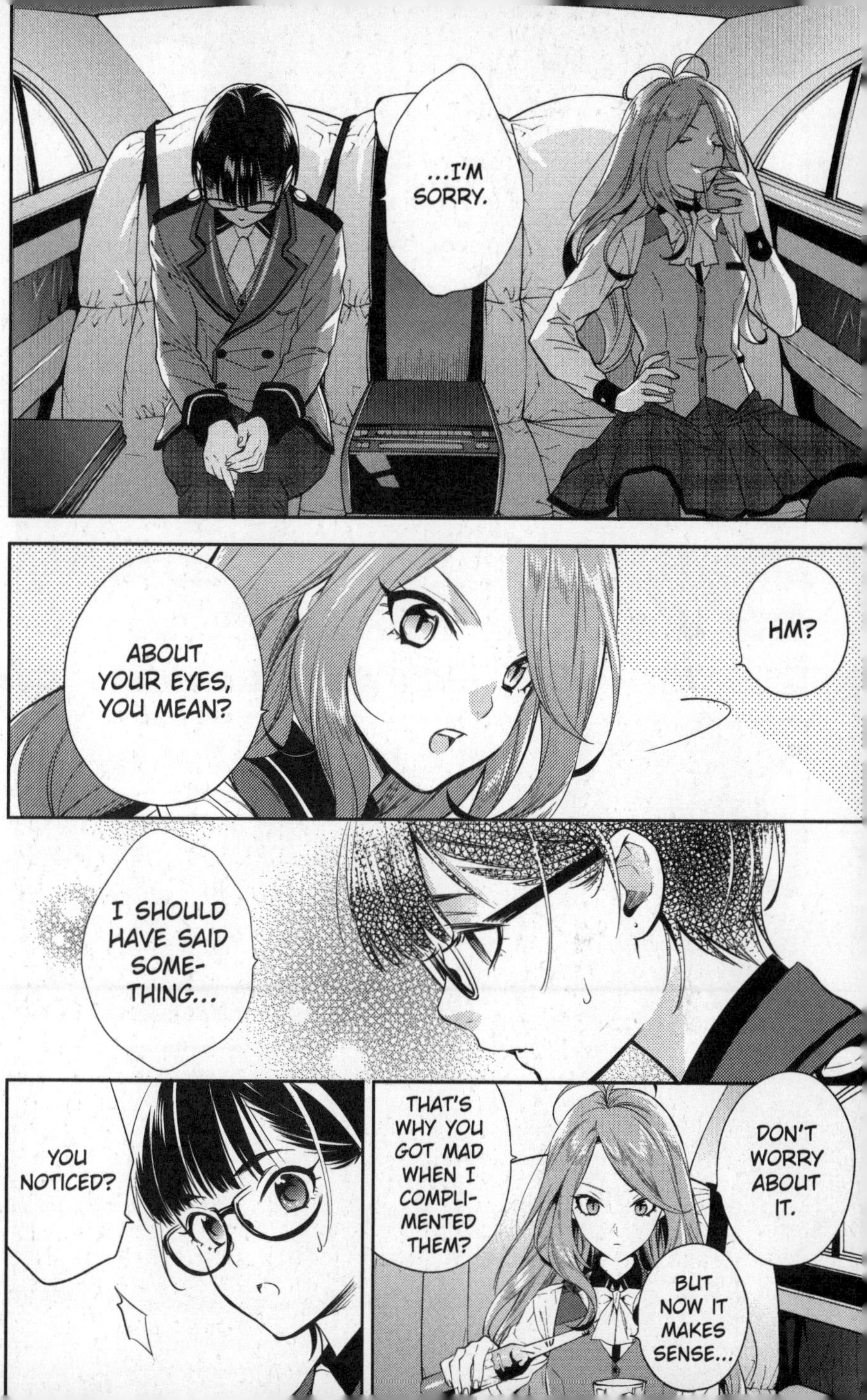
...I'M SORRY.
HM?
ABOUT YOUR EYES, YOU MEAN?
I SHOULD HAVE SAID SOME-THING...
DON'T WORRY ABOUT IT.
THAT'S WHY YOU GOT MAD WHEN I COMPLI-MENTED THEM?
BUT NOW IT MAKES SENSE...
YOU NOTICED?

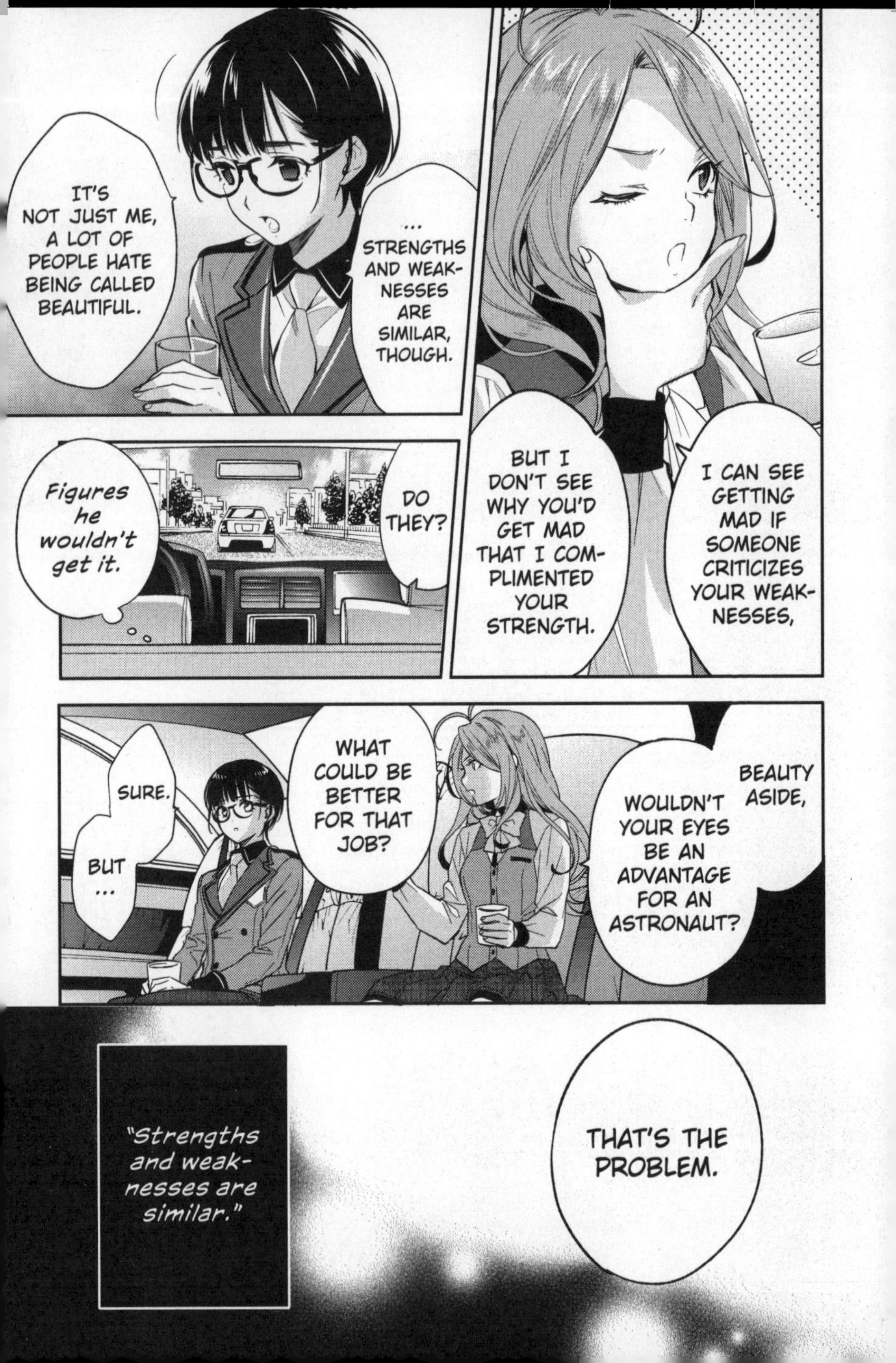
I CAN SEE GETTING MAD IF SOMEONE CRITICIZES YOUR WEAK-NESSES,
BUT I DON'T SEE WHY YOU'D GET MAD THAT I COM-PLIMENTED YOUR STRENGTH.
IT'S NOT JUST ME, A LOT OF PEOPLE HATE BEING CALLED BEAUTIFUL.
... STRENGTHS AND WEAK-NESSES ARE SIMILAR, THOUGH.
DO THEY?
Figures he wouldn't get it.
BEAUTY ASIDE,
WOULDN'T YOUR EYES BE AN ADVANTAGE FOR AN ASTRONAUT?
WHAT COULD BE BETTER FOR THAT JOB?
SURE.
BUT ...
THAT'S THE PROBLEM.
"Strengths and weak-nesses are similar."

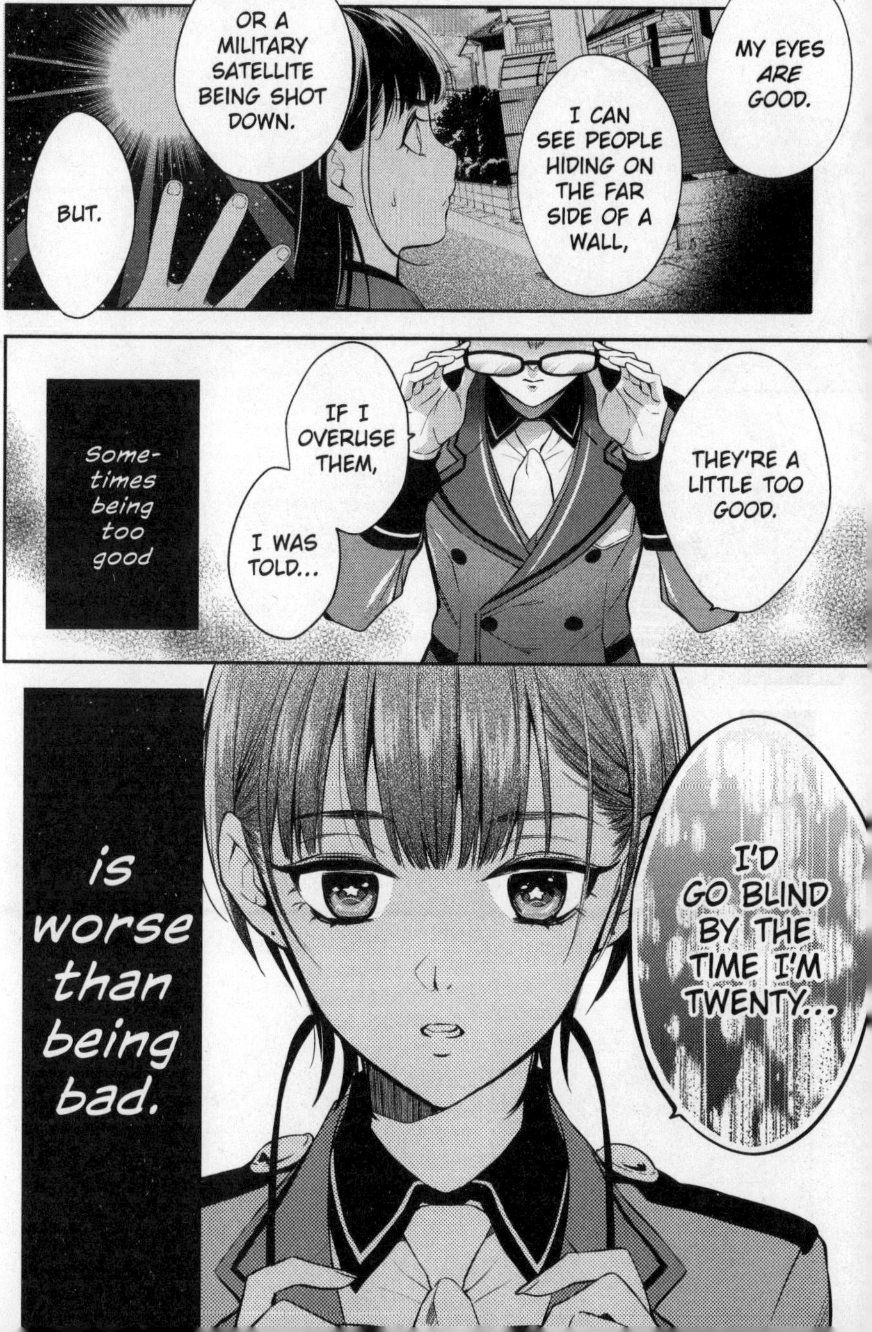
MY EYES ARE GOOD.
I CAN SEE PEOPLE HIDING ON THE FAR SIDE OF A WALL,
OR A MILITARY SATELLITE BEING SHOT DOWN.
BUT.
THEY'RE A LITTLE TOO GOOD.
IF I OVERUSE THEM,
I WAS TOLD...
Some-times being too good
I'D GO BLIND BY THE TIME I'M TWENTY...
is worse than being bad.

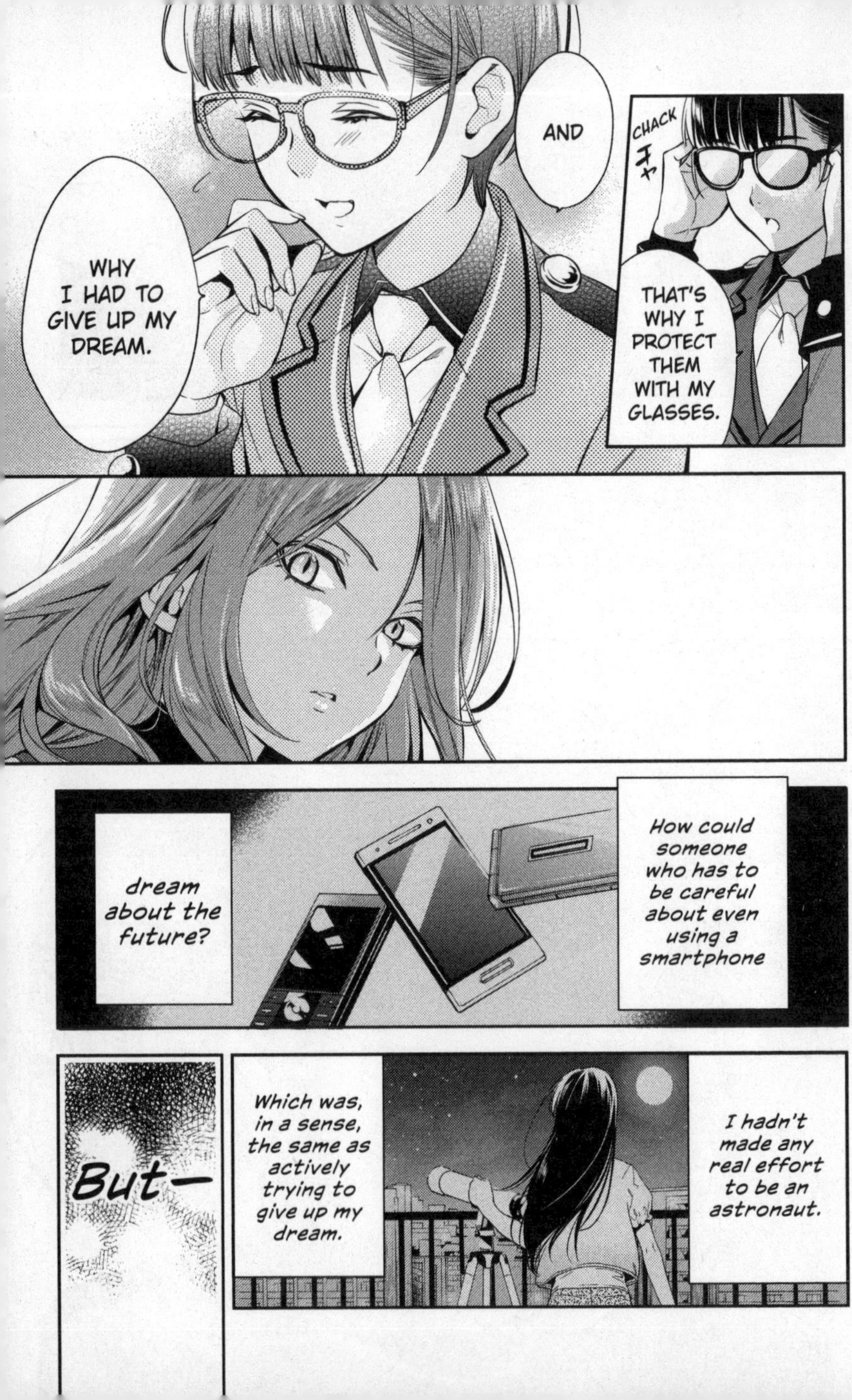
CHACK
THAT'S WHY I PROTECT THEM WITH MY GLASSES.
AND
WHY I HAD TO GIVE UP MY DREAM.
How could someone who has to be careful about even using a smartphone
dream about the future?
I hadn't made any real effort to be an astronaut.
Which was, in a sense, the same as actively trying to give up my dream.
But—

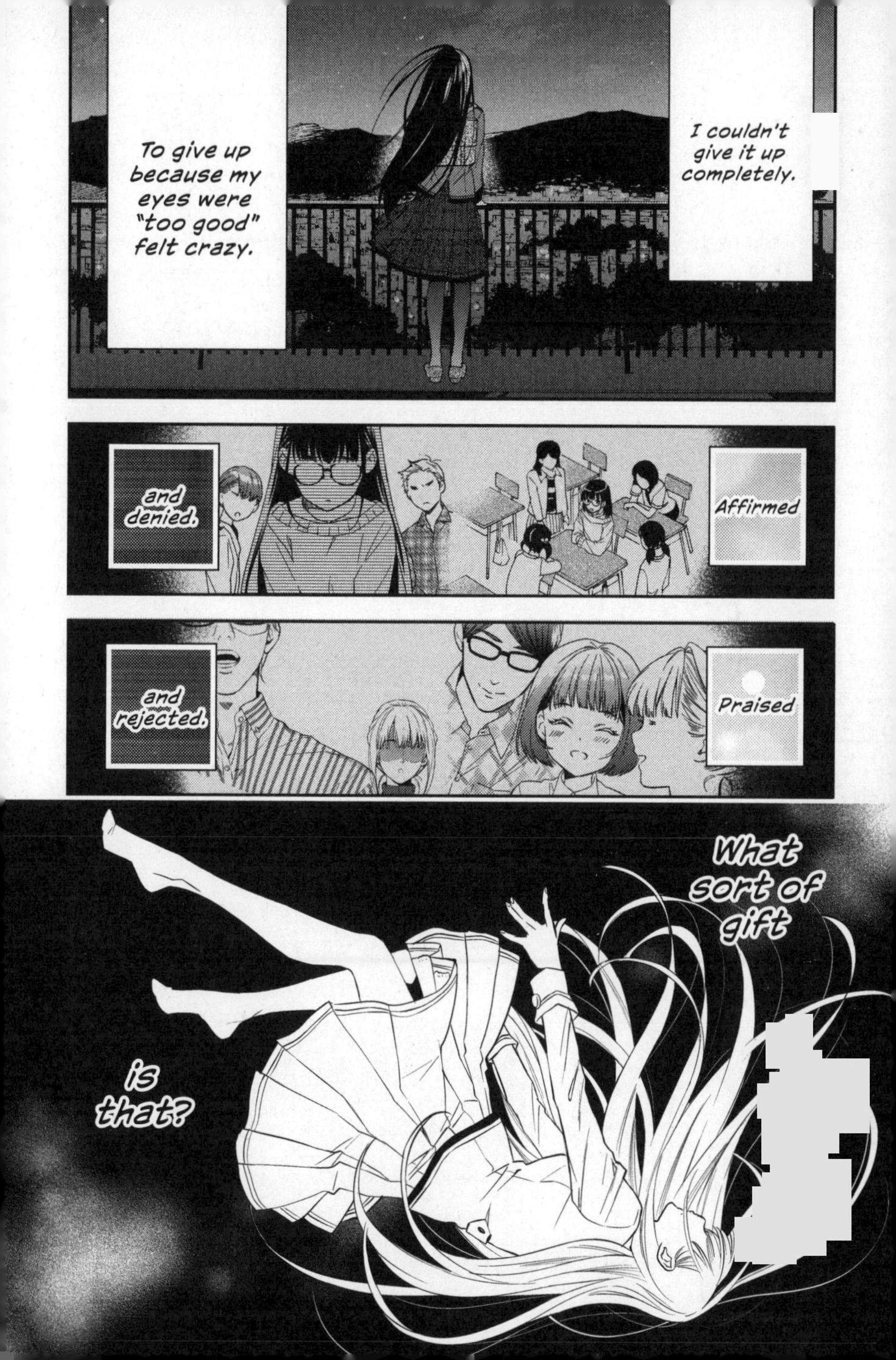
I couldn't give it up completely.
To give up because my eyes were "too good" felt crazy.
Affirmed
and denied.
Praised
and rejected.
What sort of gift
is that?

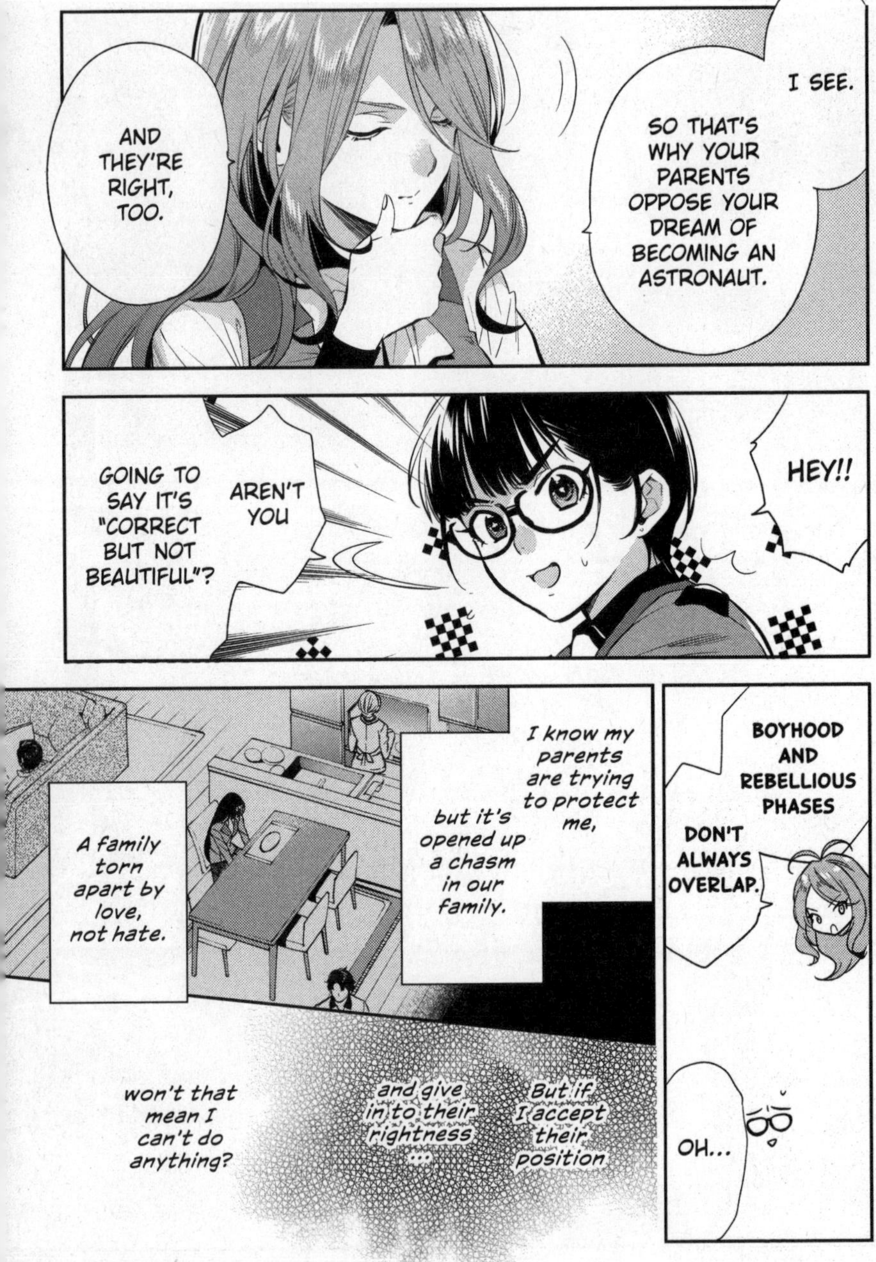
I SEE.
SO THAT'S WHY YOUR PARENTS OPPOSE YOUR DREAM OF BECOMING AN ASTRONAUT.
AND THEY'RE RIGHT, TOO.
HEY!!
AREN'T YOU
GOING TO SAY IT'S "CORRECT BUT NOT BEAUTIFUL"?
BOYHOOD AND REBELLIOUS PHASES
DON'T ALWAYS OVERLAP.
OH...
I know my parents are trying to protect me,
but it's opened up a chasm in our family.
A family torn apart by love, not hate.
But if I accept their position
and give in to their rightness...
won't that mean I can't do anything?

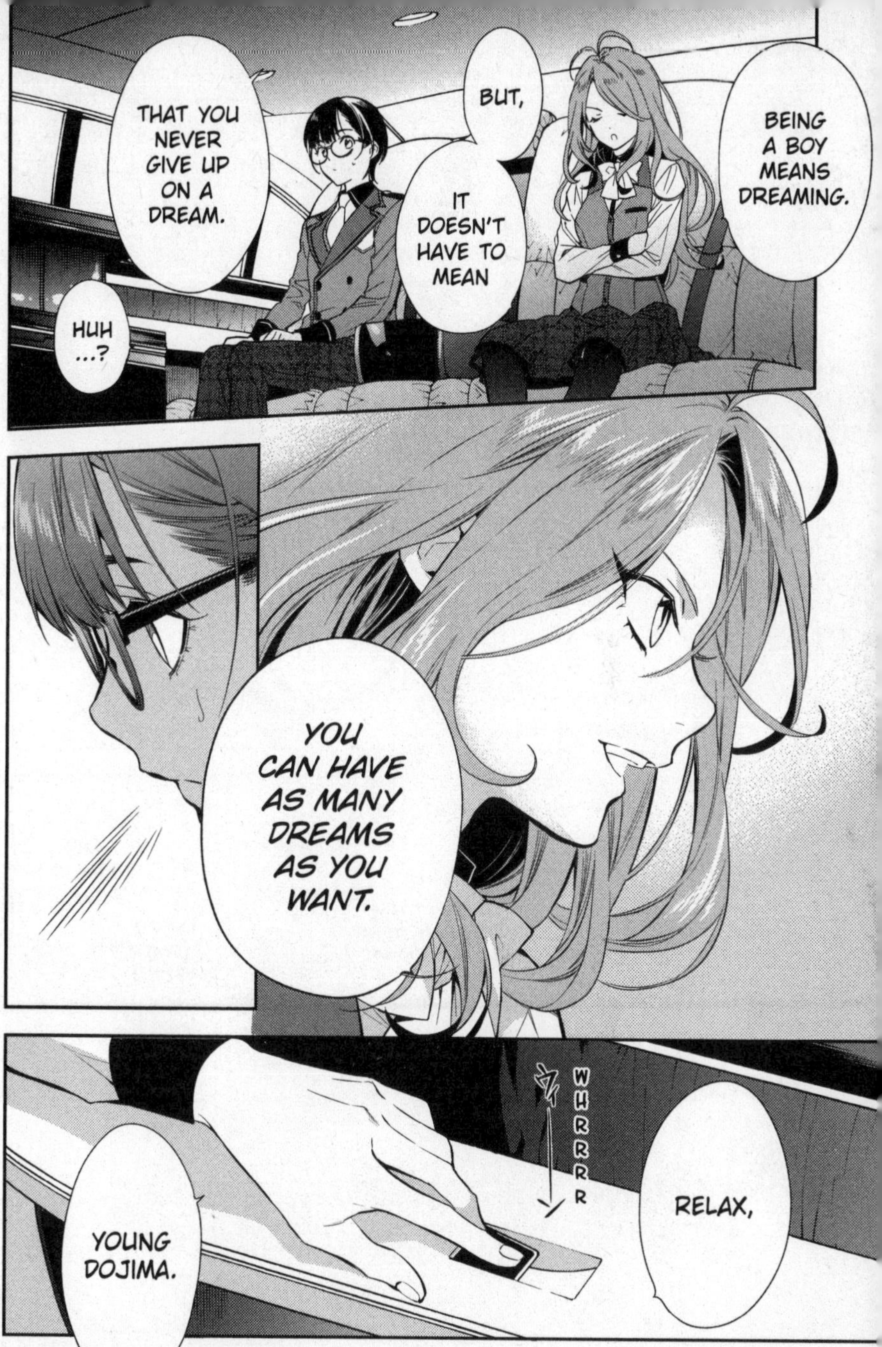
BEING A BOY MEANS DREAMING.
BUT,
IT DOESN'T HAVE TO MEAN
THAT YOU NEVER GIVE UP ON A DREAM.
HUH ...?
YOU CAN HAVE AS MANY DREAMS AS YOU WANT.
RELAX,
WHRRRR
YOUNG DOJIMA.

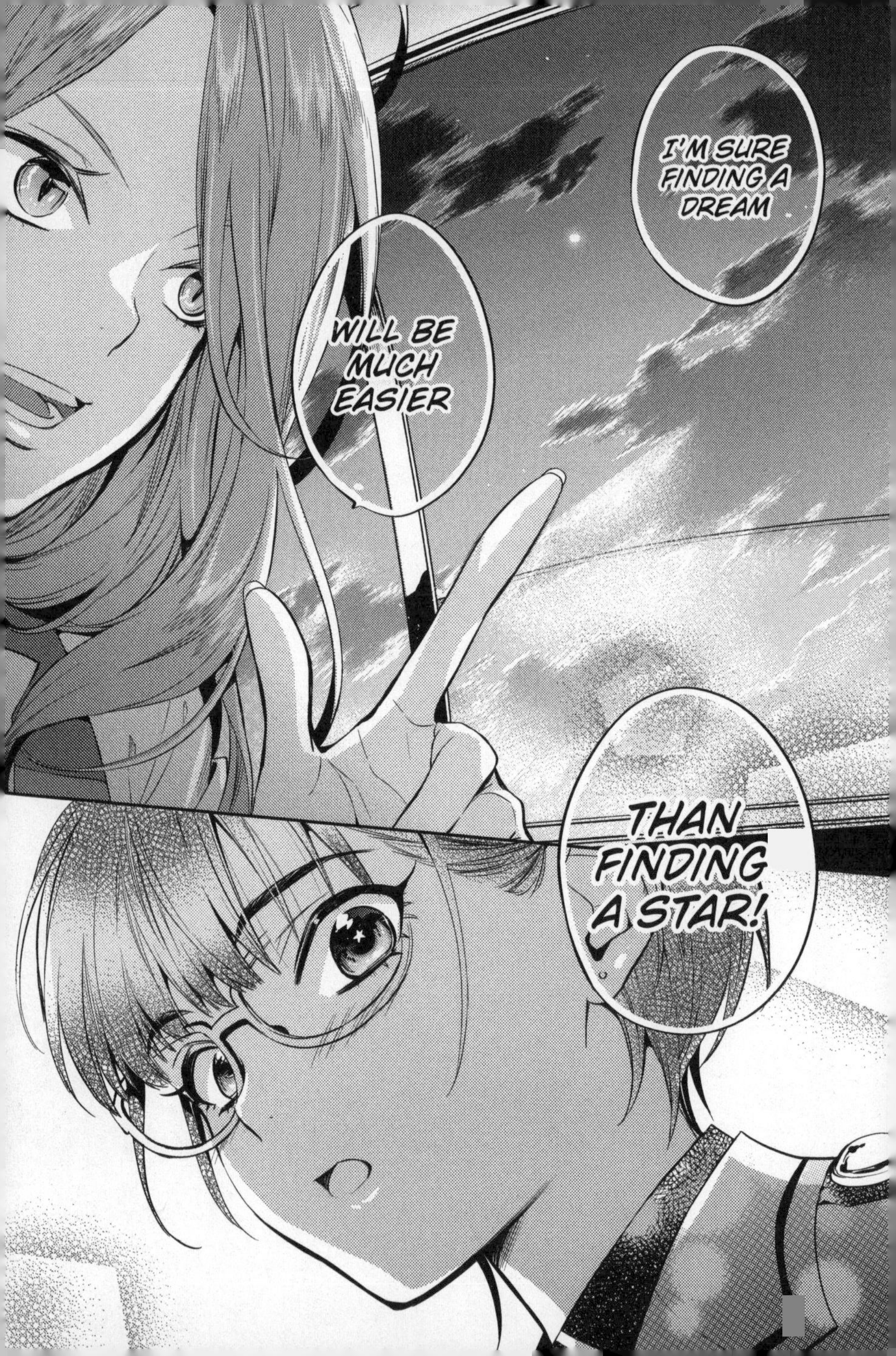
I'M SURE FINDING A DREAM
WILL BE MUCH EASIER
THAN FINDING A STAR!

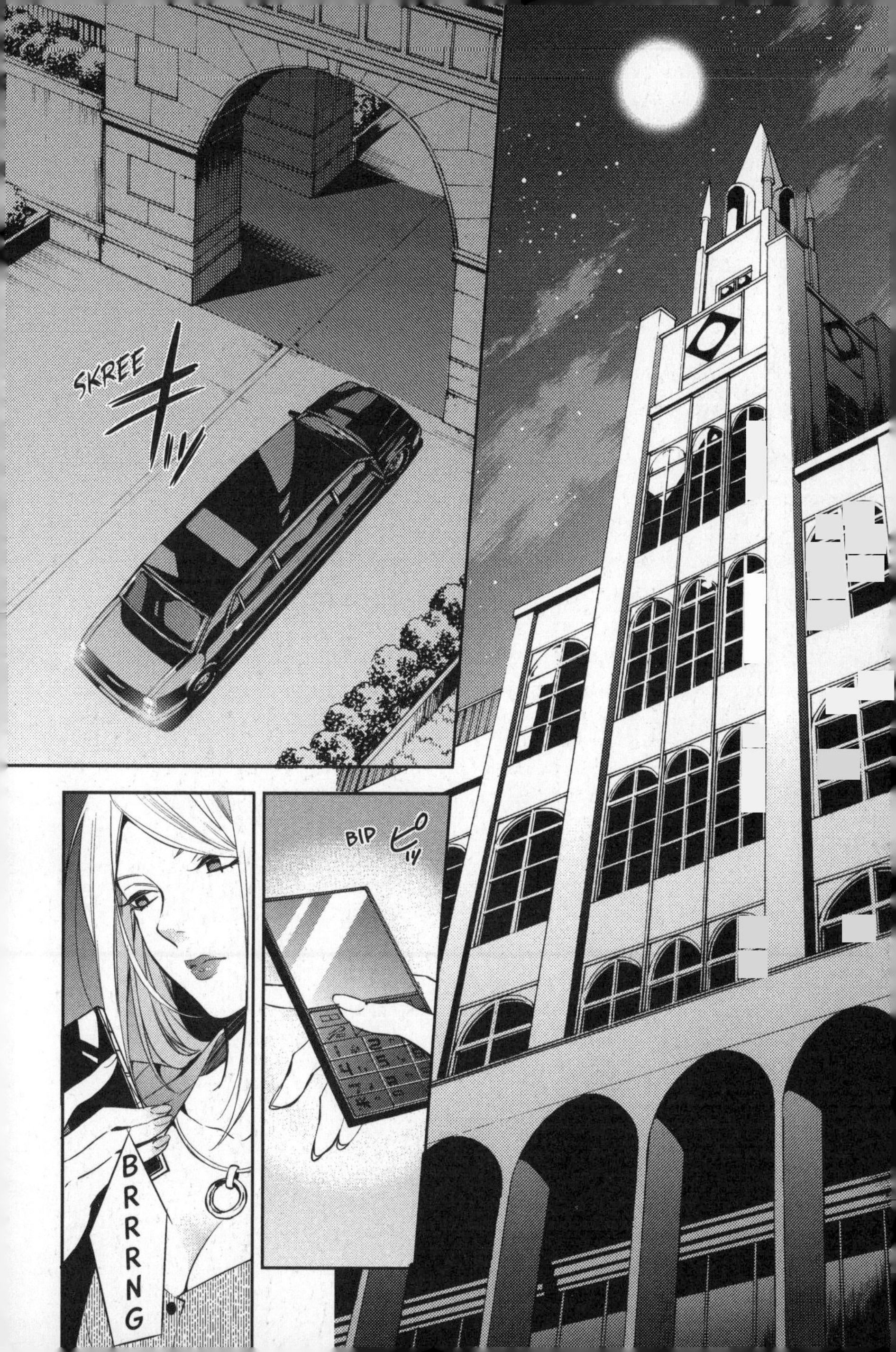
SKREE
ギッ
BIP
ピッ
BRRRNG

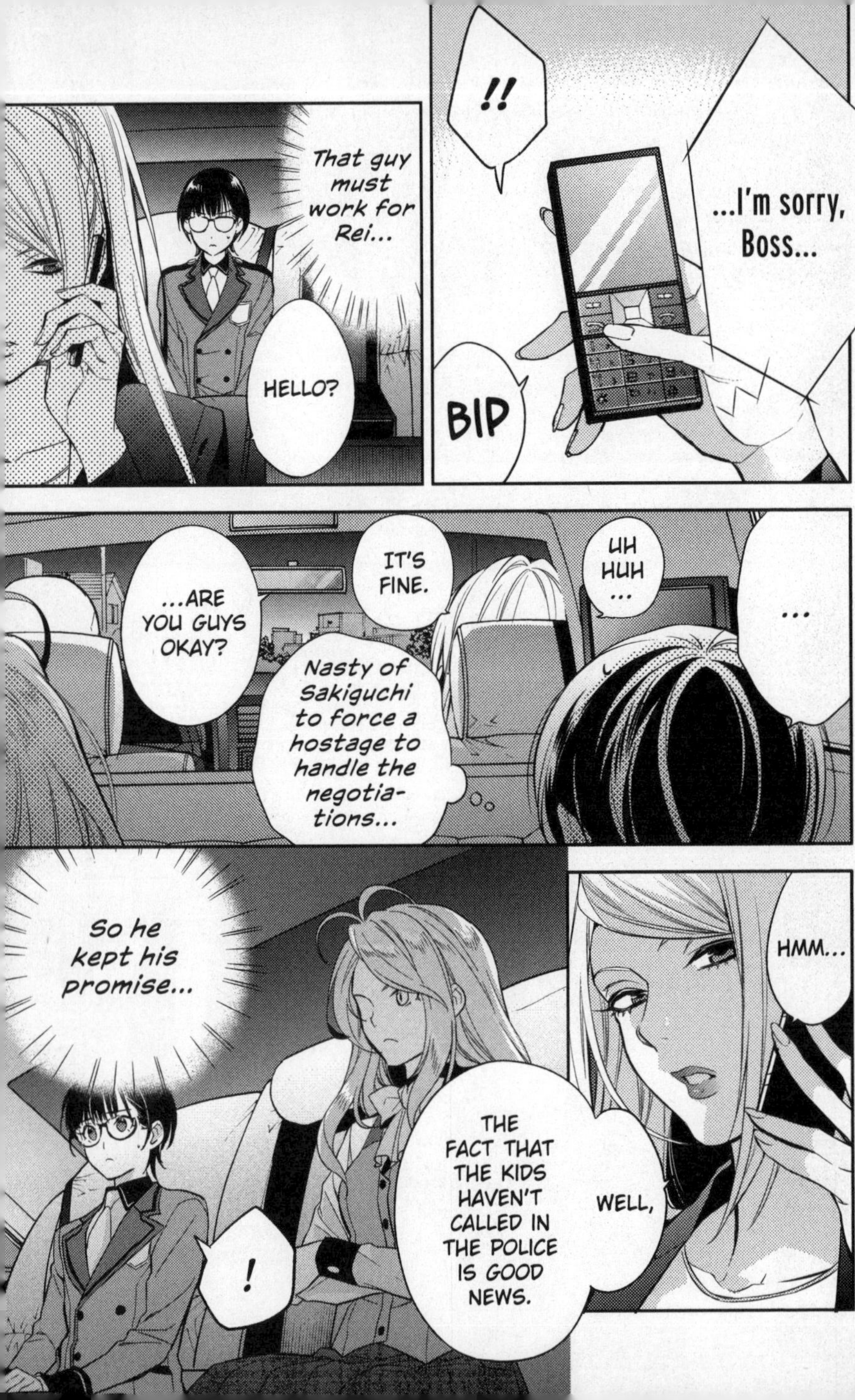
...I'm sorry, Boss...
!!
BIP
That guy must work for Rei...
HELLO?
...
UH HUH ...
IT'S FINE.
...ARE YOU GUYS OKAY?
Nasty of Sakiguchi to force a hostage to handle the negotia-tions...
HMM...
WELL,
THE FACT THAT THE KIDS HAVEN'T CALLED IN THE POLICE IS GOOD NEWS.
So he kept his promise...
!

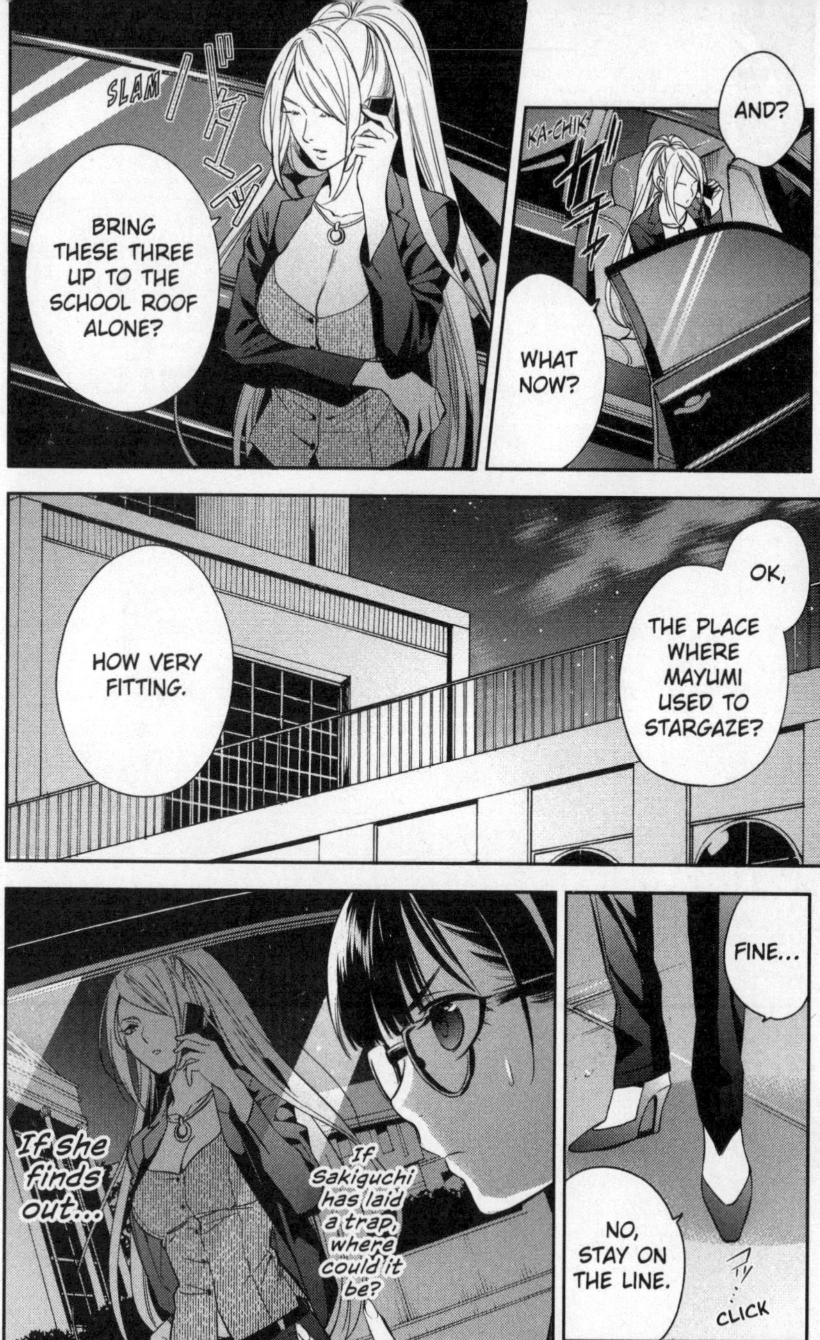
AND?
KA-CHIK
WHAT NOW?
SLAM
BRING THESE THREE UP TO THE SCHOOL ROOF ALONE?
OK, THE PLACE WHERE MAYUMI USED TO STARGAZE?
HOW VERY FITTING.
FINE...
NO, STAY ON THE LINE.
CLICK
If Sakiguchi has laid a trap, where could it be?
If she finds out...

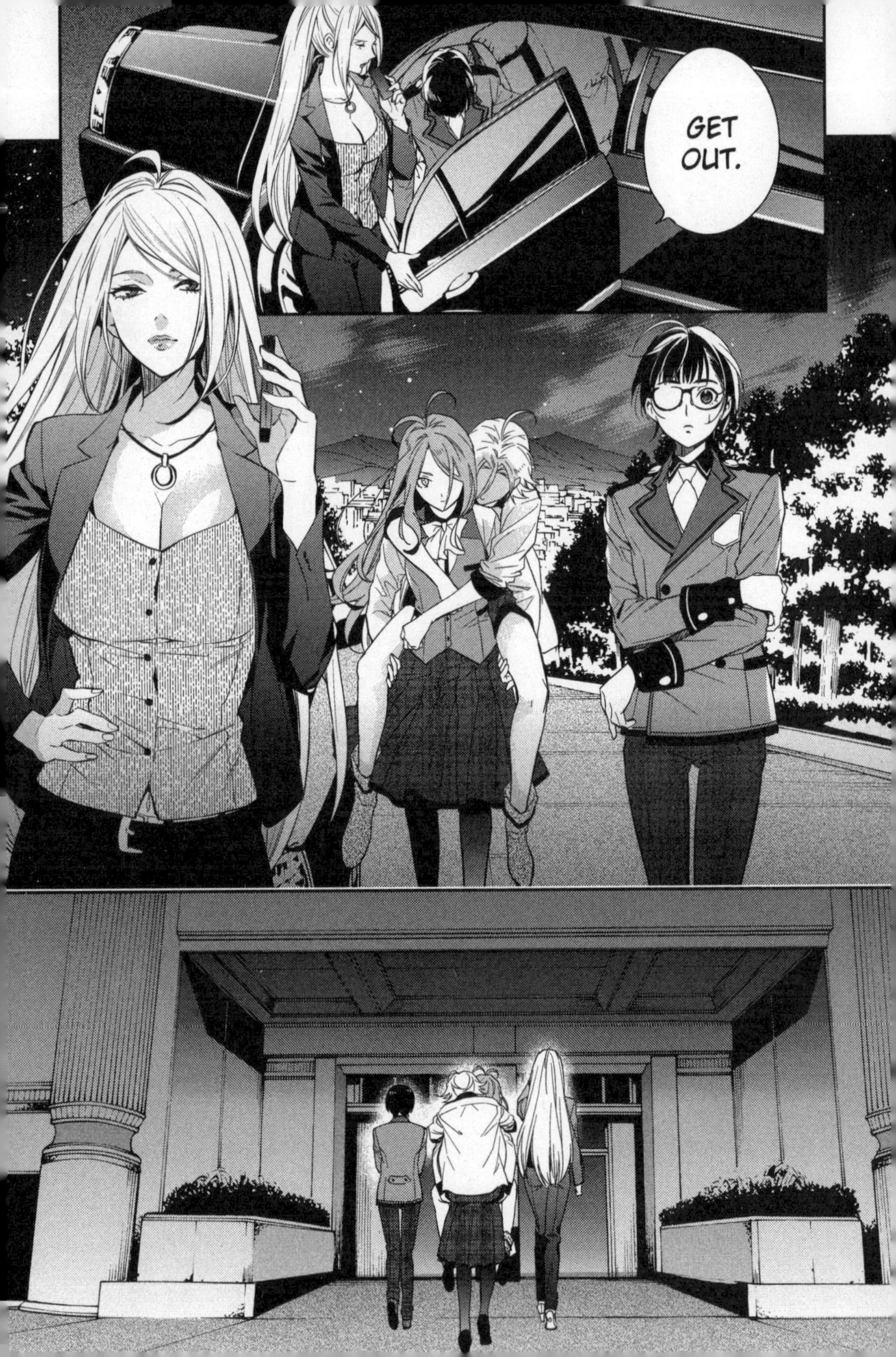
GET OUT.

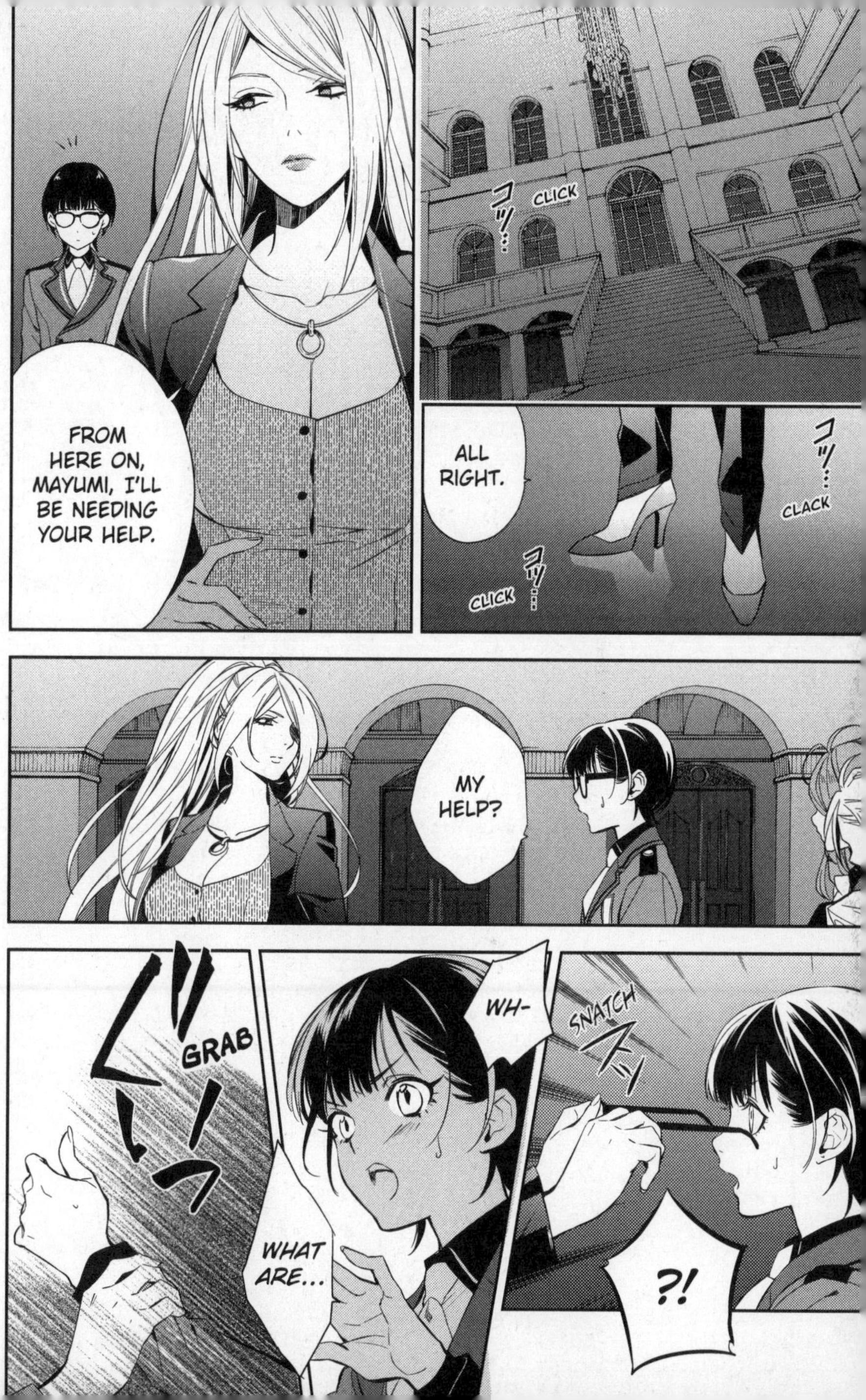

コッ…
CLICK
ALL RIGHT.
コッ…
CLACK
コッ…
CLICK
FROM HERE ON, MAYUMI, I'LL BE NEEDING YOUR HELP.
MY HELP?
SNATCH
?!
WH-
WHAT ARE...
GRAB

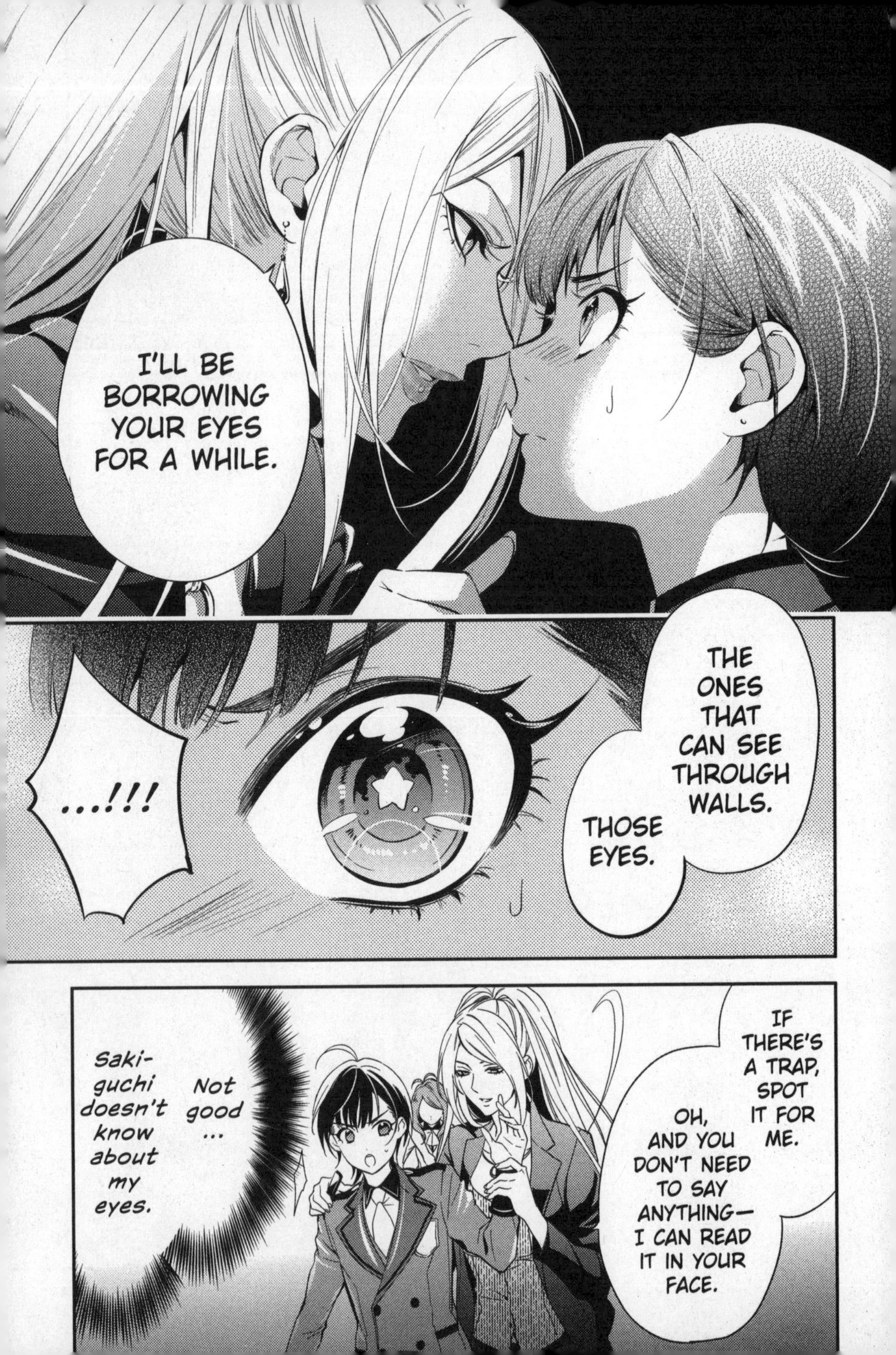
I'LL BE BORROWING YOUR EYES FOR A WHILE.
THE ONES THAT CAN SEE THROUGH WALLS.
THOSE EYES.
...!!!
IF THERE'S A TRAP, SPOT IT FOR ME.
OH, AND YOU DON'T NEED TO SAY ANYTHING—I CAN READ IT IN YOUR FACE.
Not good...
Saki-guchi doesn't know about my eyes.

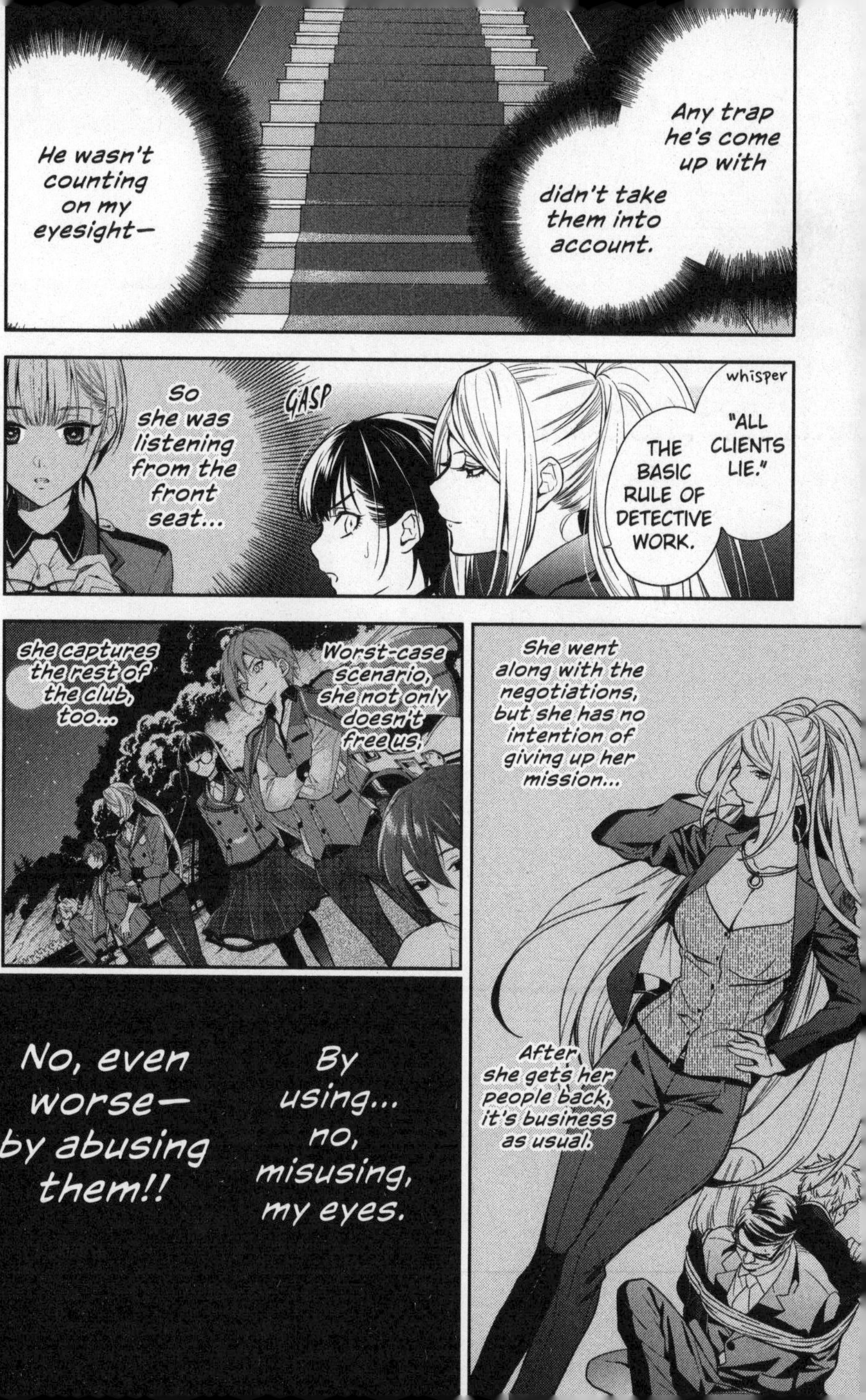

Any trap he's come up with
didn't take them into account.
He wasn't counting on my eyesight—
whisper
"ALL CLIENTS LIE."
THE BASIC RULE OF DETECTIVE WORK.
GASP
So she was listening from the front seat...
She went along with the negotiations, but she has no intention of giving up her mission...
After she gets her people back, it's business as usual.
Worst-case scenario, she not only doesn't free us,
she captures the rest of the club, too...
By using... no, misusing, my eyes.
No, even worse— by abusing them!!

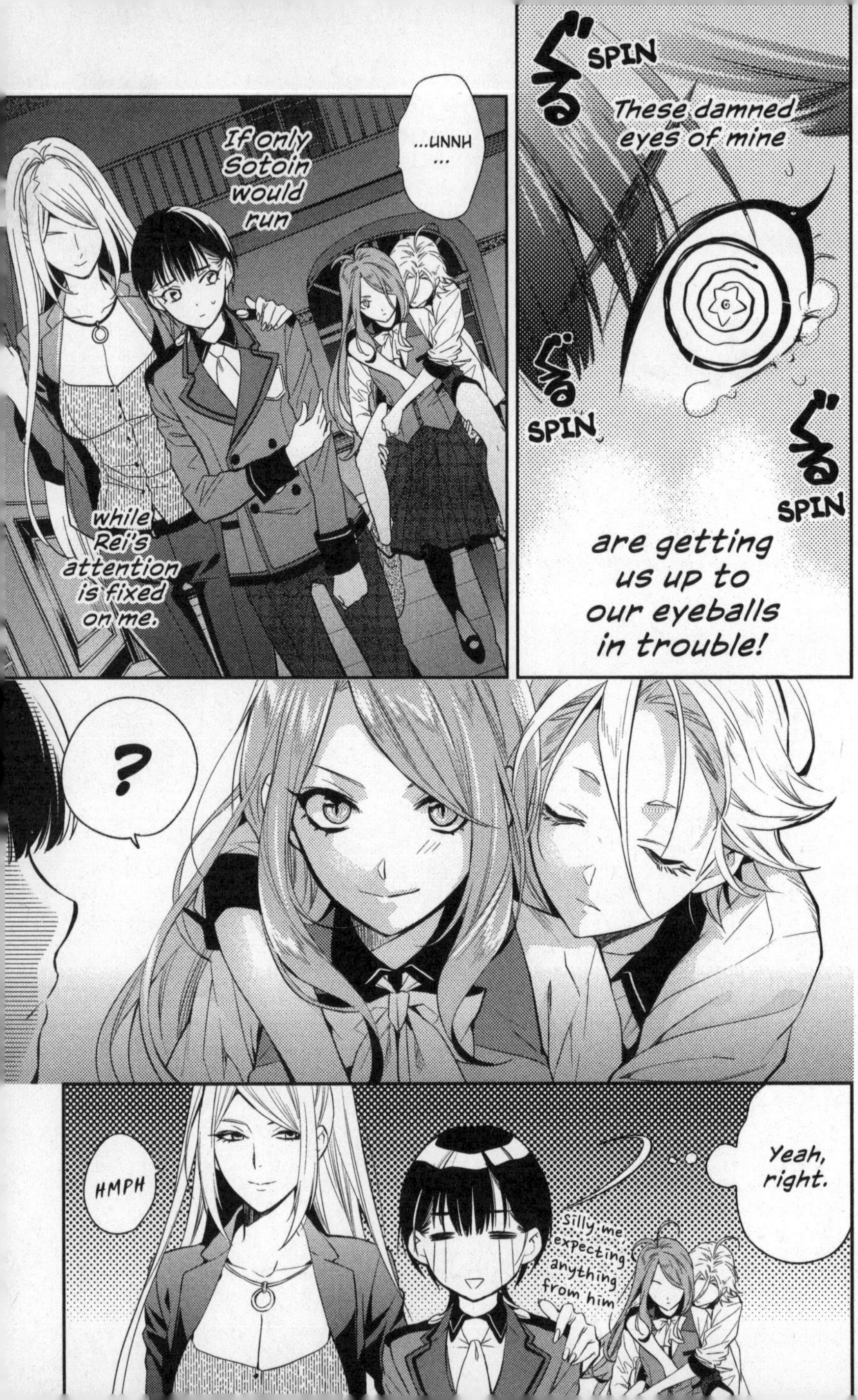
ぐる
SPIN
These damned eyes of mine
ぐる
SPIN
ぐる
SPIN
are getting us up to our eyeballs in trouble!
...UNNH ...
If only Sotoin would run
while Rei's attention is fixed on me.
?
Yeah, right.
Silly me, expecting anything from him
HMPH

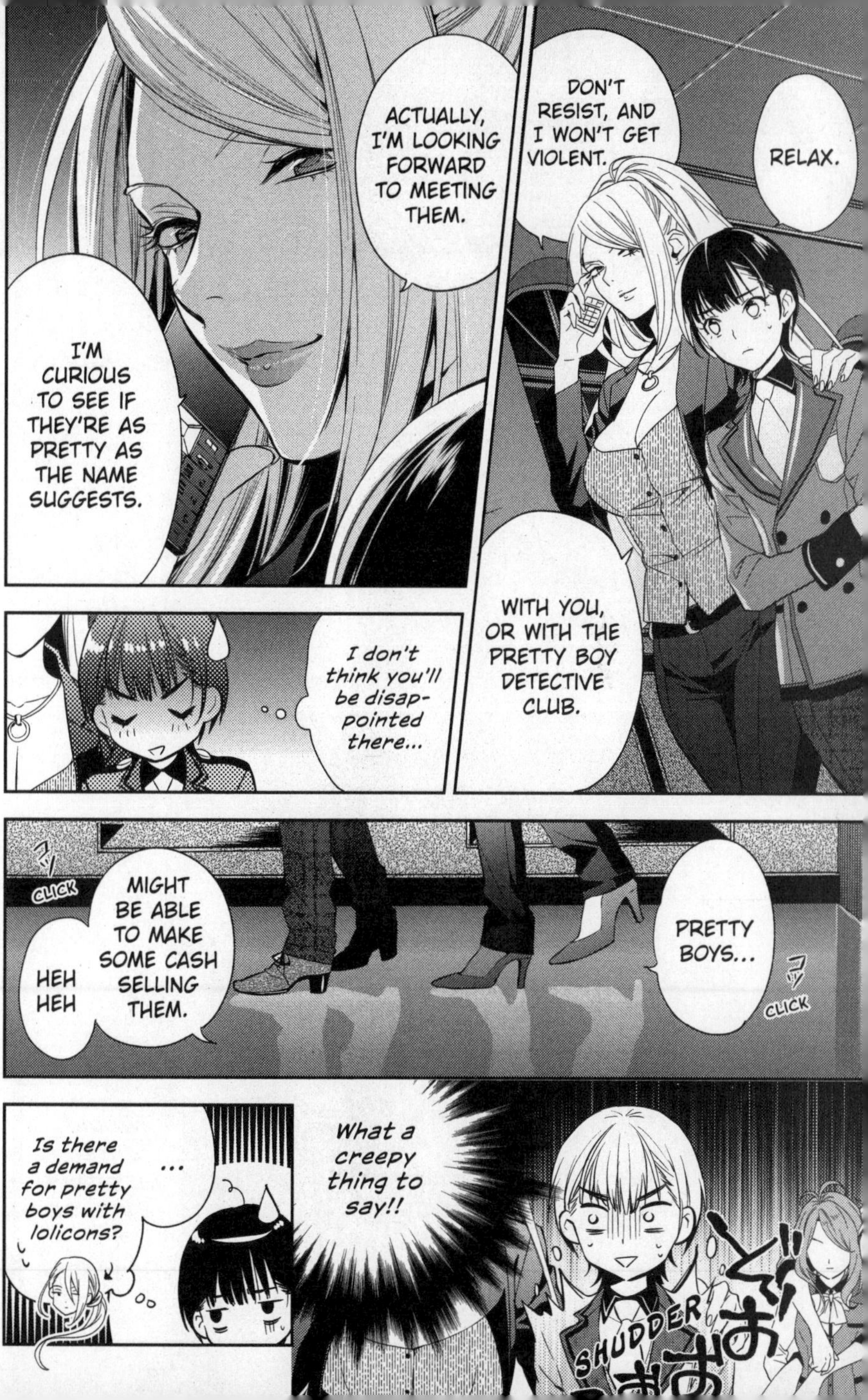
RELAX.
DON'T RESIST, AND I WON'T GET VIOLENT.
WITH YOU, OR WITH THE PRETTY BOY DETECTIVE CLUB.
ACTUALLY, I'M LOOKING FORWARD TO MEETING THEM.
I'M CURIOUS TO SEE IF THEY'RE AS PRETTY AS THE NAME SUGGESTS.
I don't think you'll be disap-pointed there...
PRETTY BOYS...
CLICK
MIGHT BE ABLE TO MAKE SOME CASH SELLING THEM.
HEH HEH
CLICK
SHUDDER
What a creepy thing to say!!
...
Is there a demand for pretty boys with lolicons?

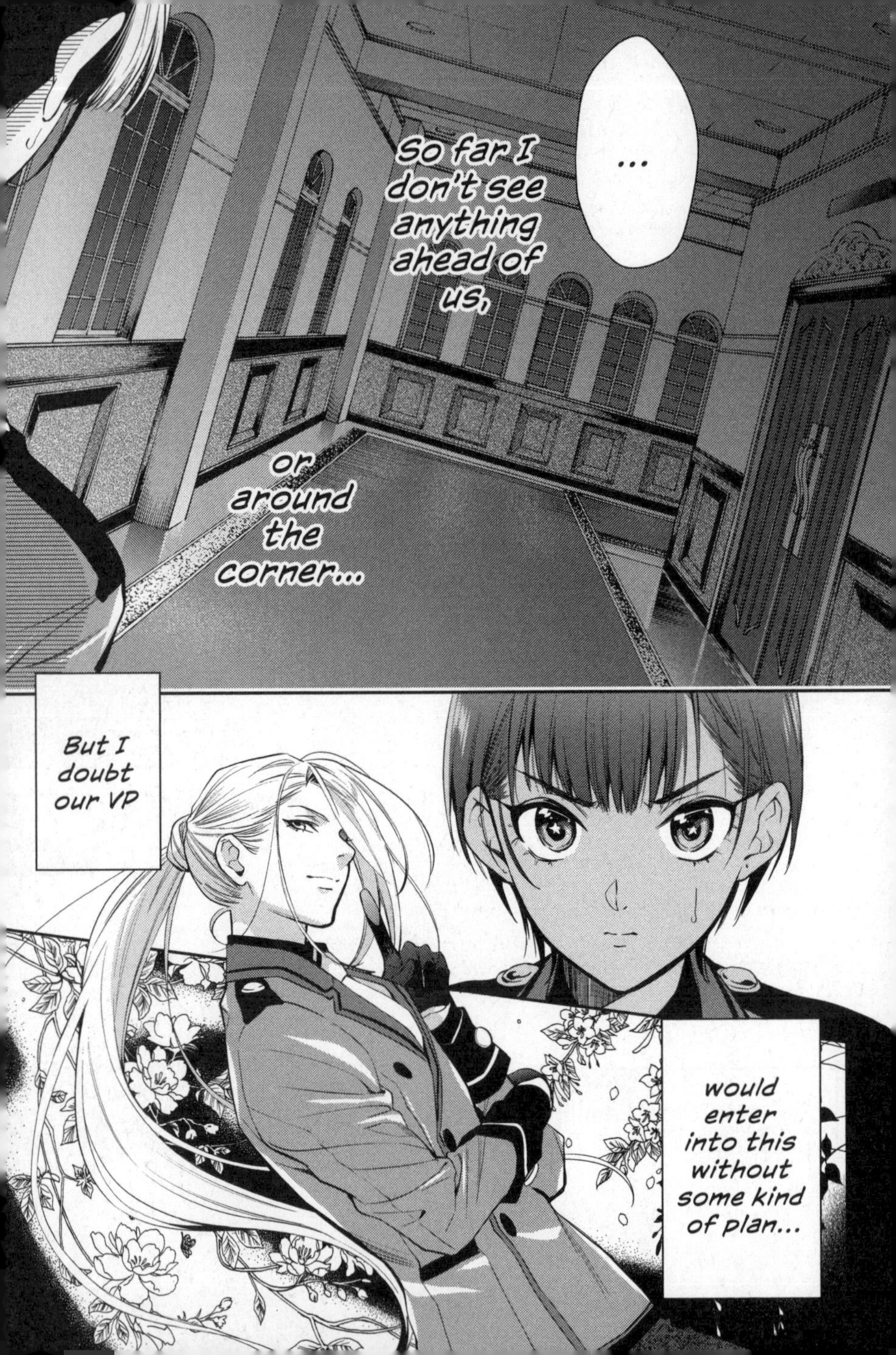
...
So far I don't see anything ahead of us,
or around the corner...
But I doubt our VP
would enter into this without some kind of plan...

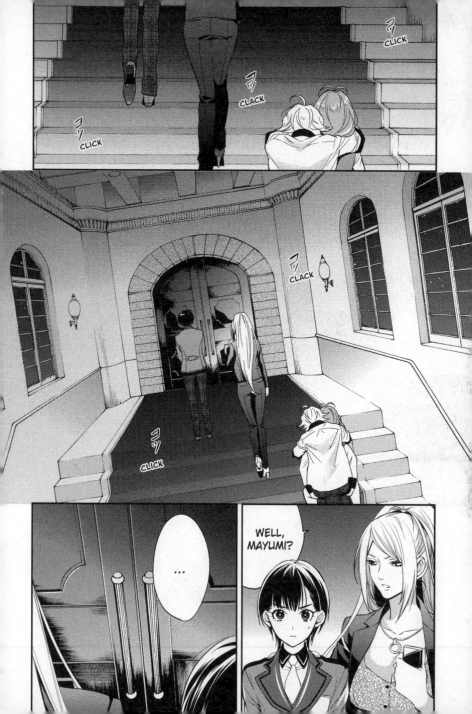

CLICK

CLACK

CLICK

CLACK

CLICK

...

WELL, MAYUMI?

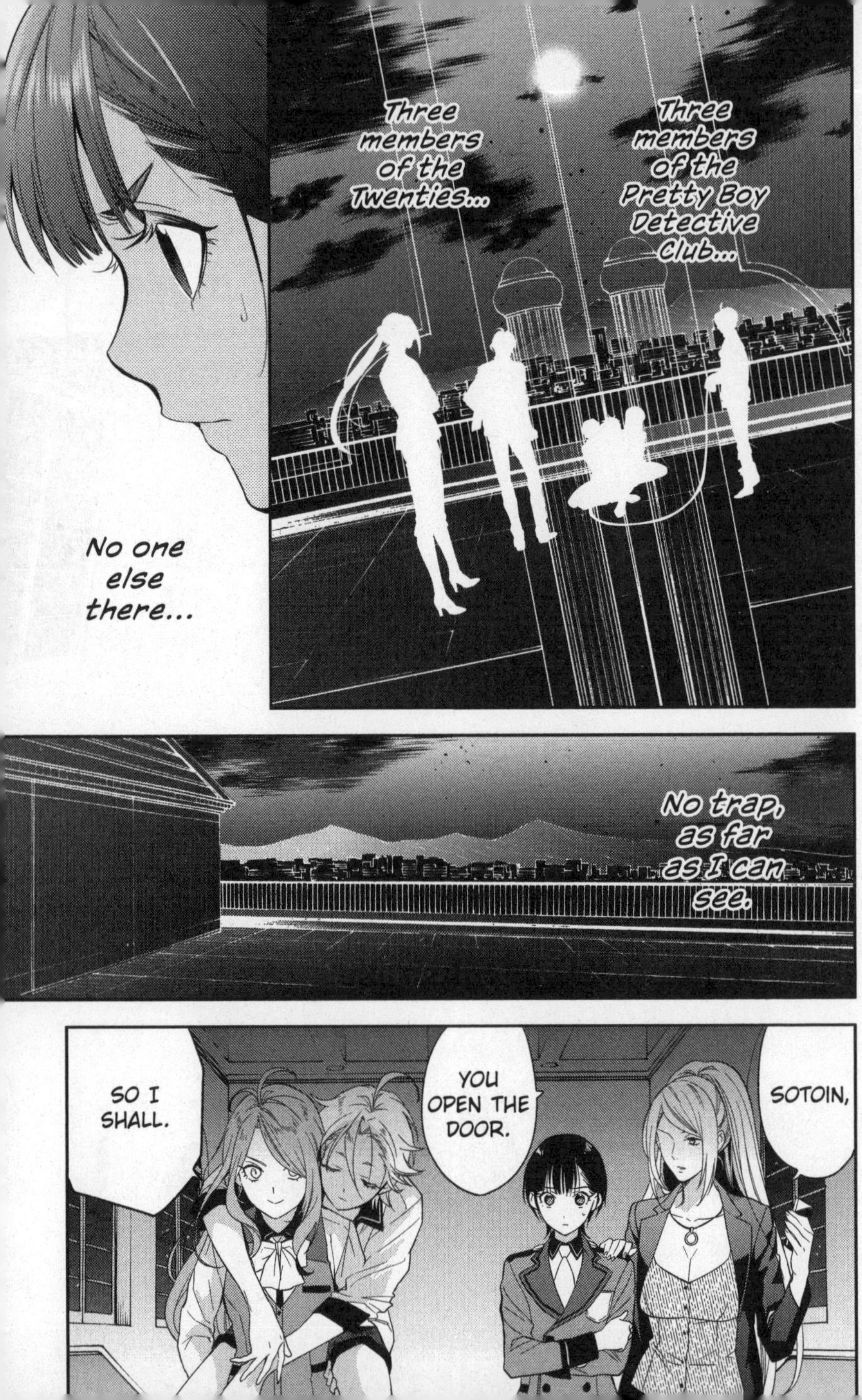
Three members of the Pretty Boy Detective Club...
Three members of the Twenties...
No one else there...
No trap, as far as I can see.
SOTOIN,
YOU OPEN THE DOOR.
SO I SHALL.

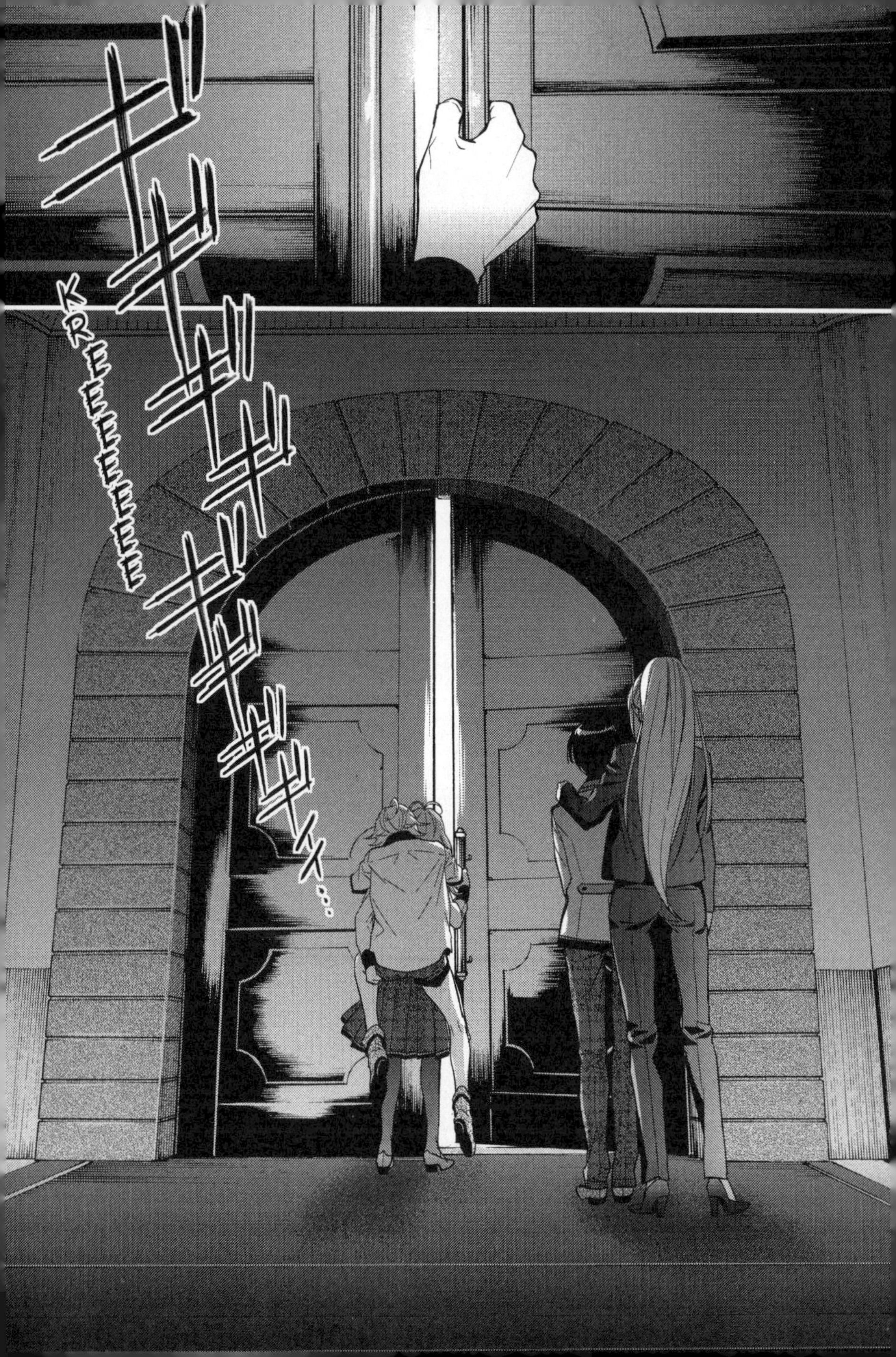
KREEEEEEEE

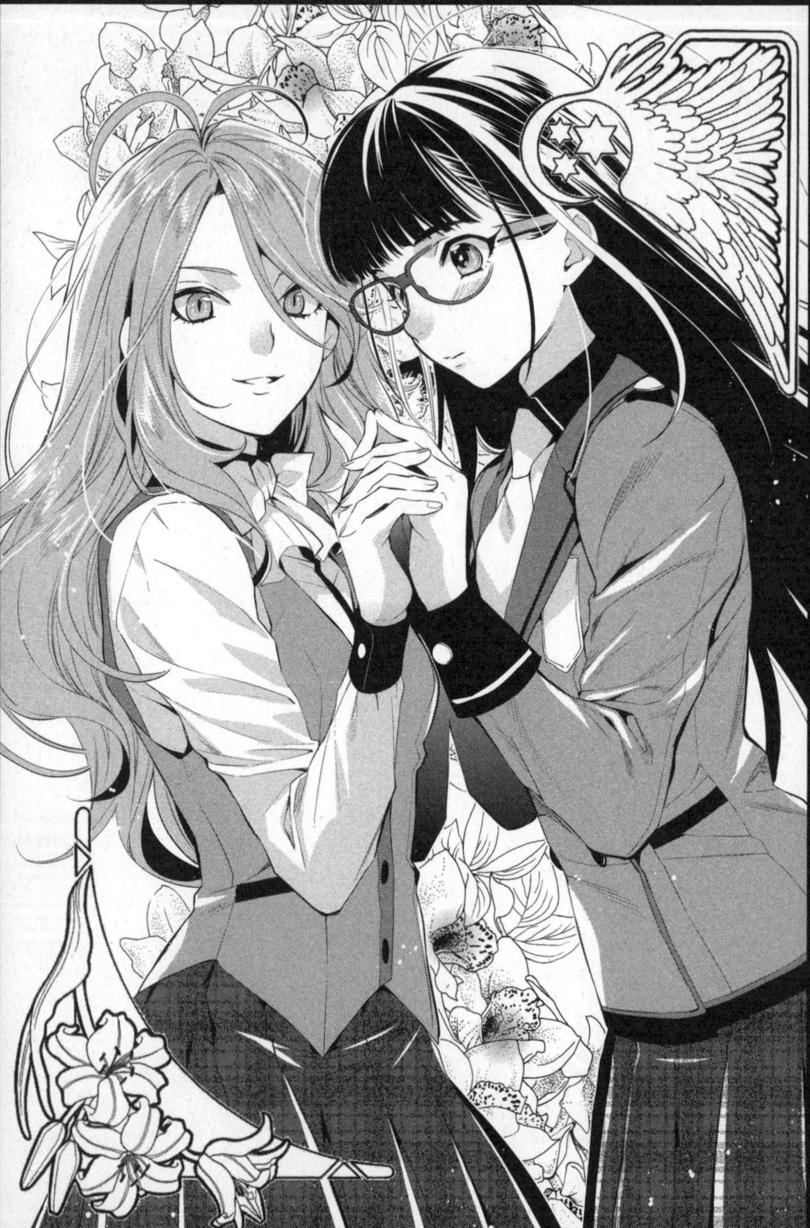

FILE ★ The Dark Star that Shines for You Alone 7

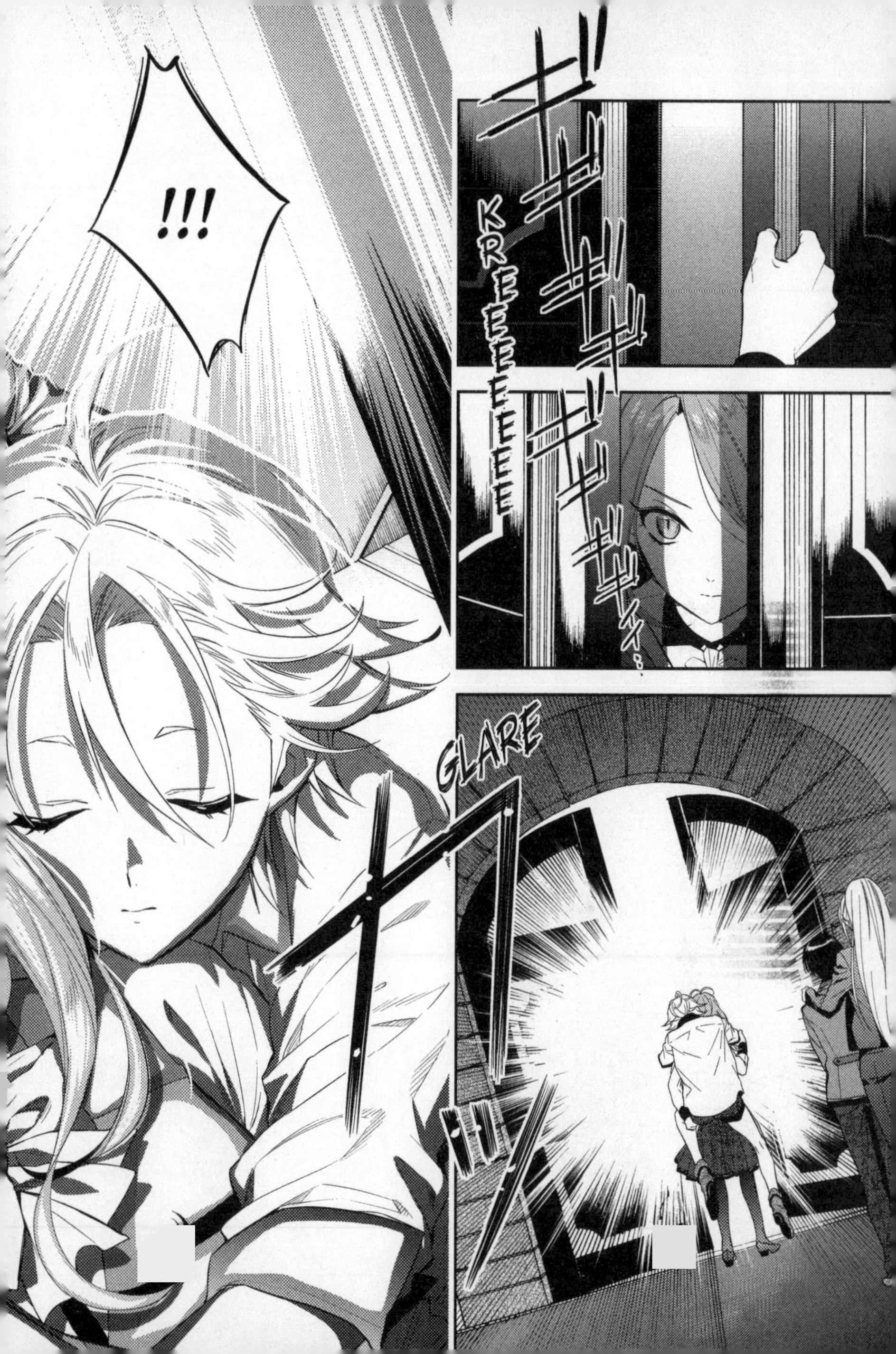
KREEEEEEEEE
GLARE
!!!

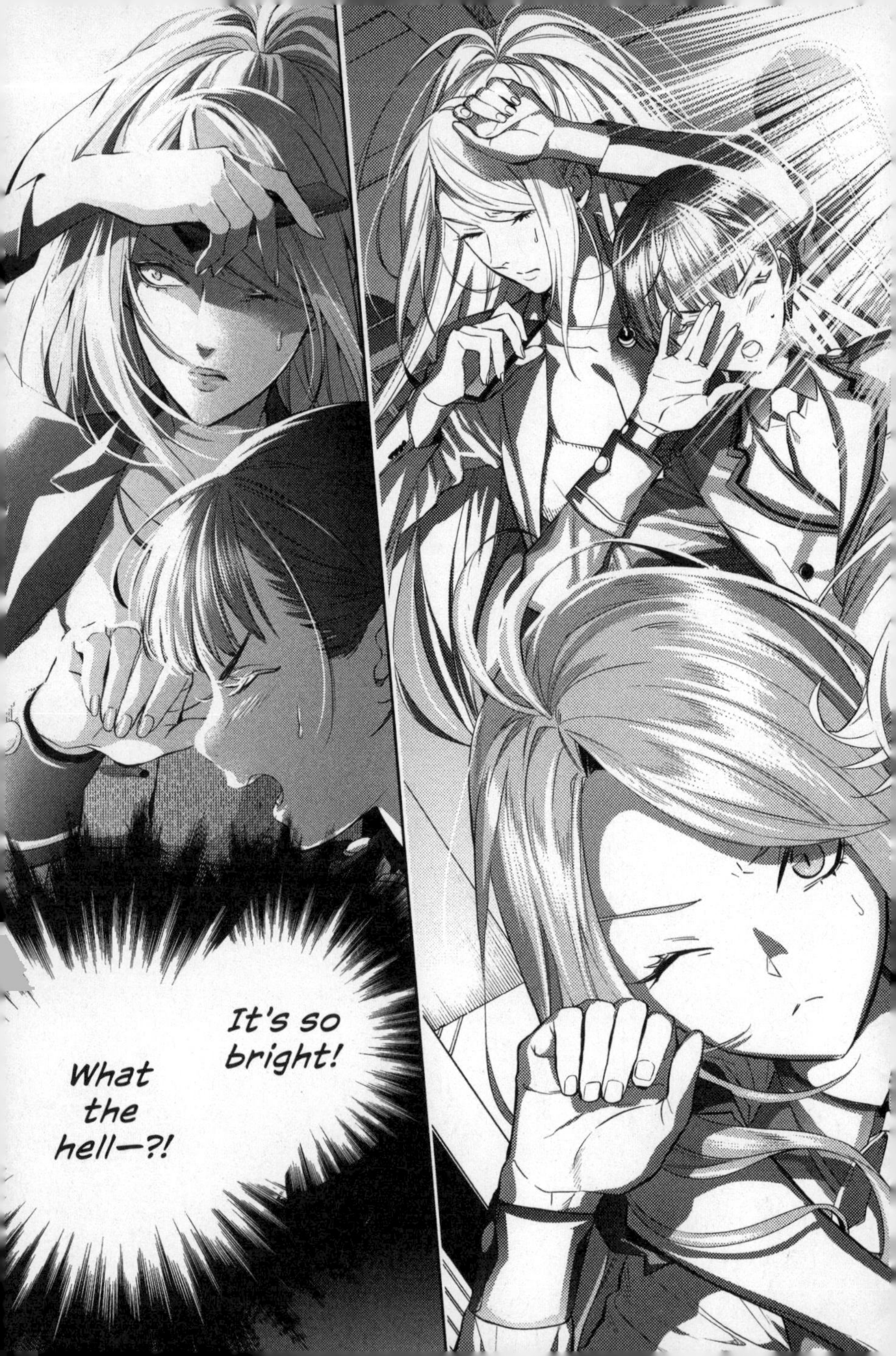
It's so bright!
What the hell—?!

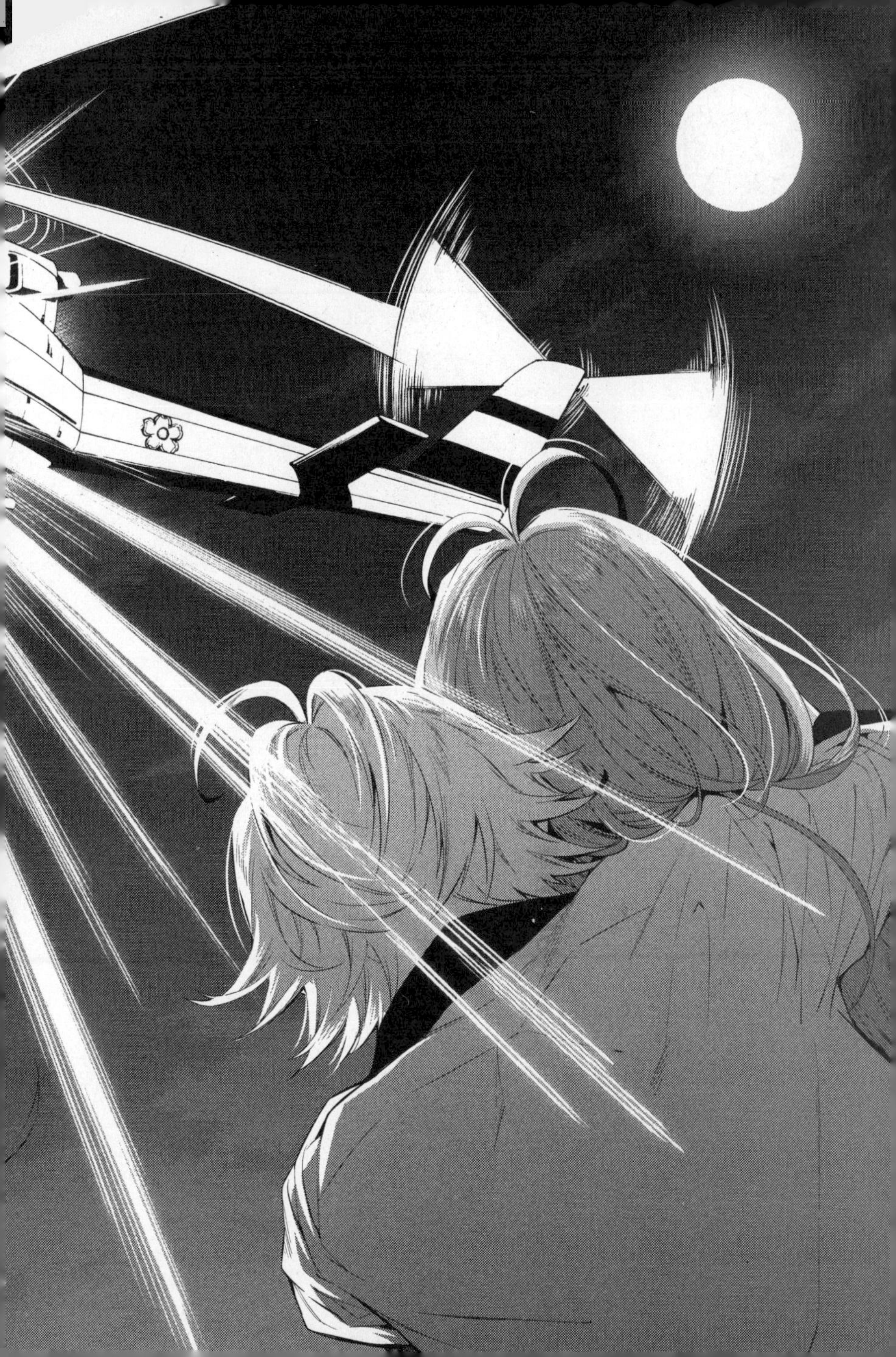

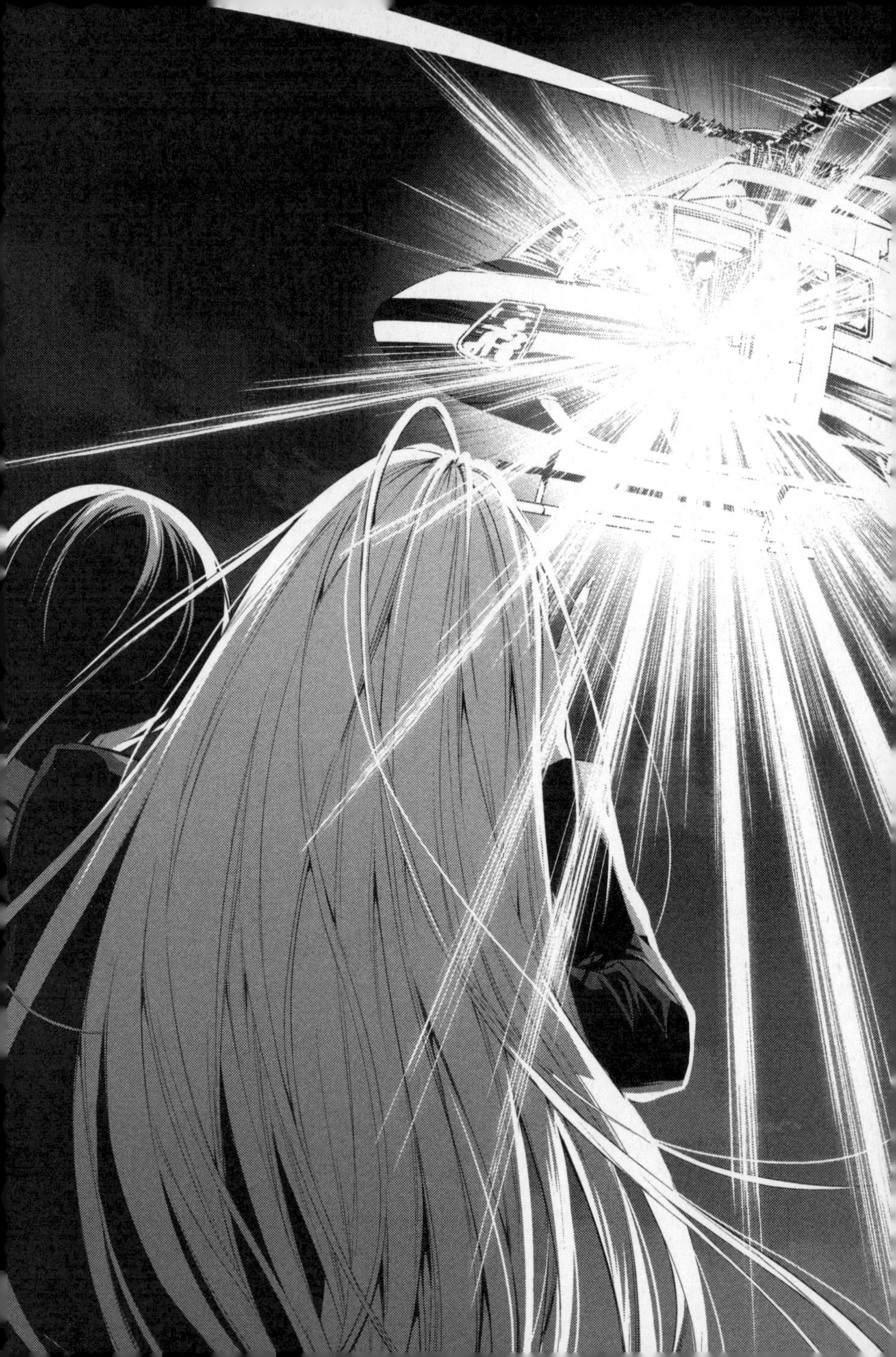

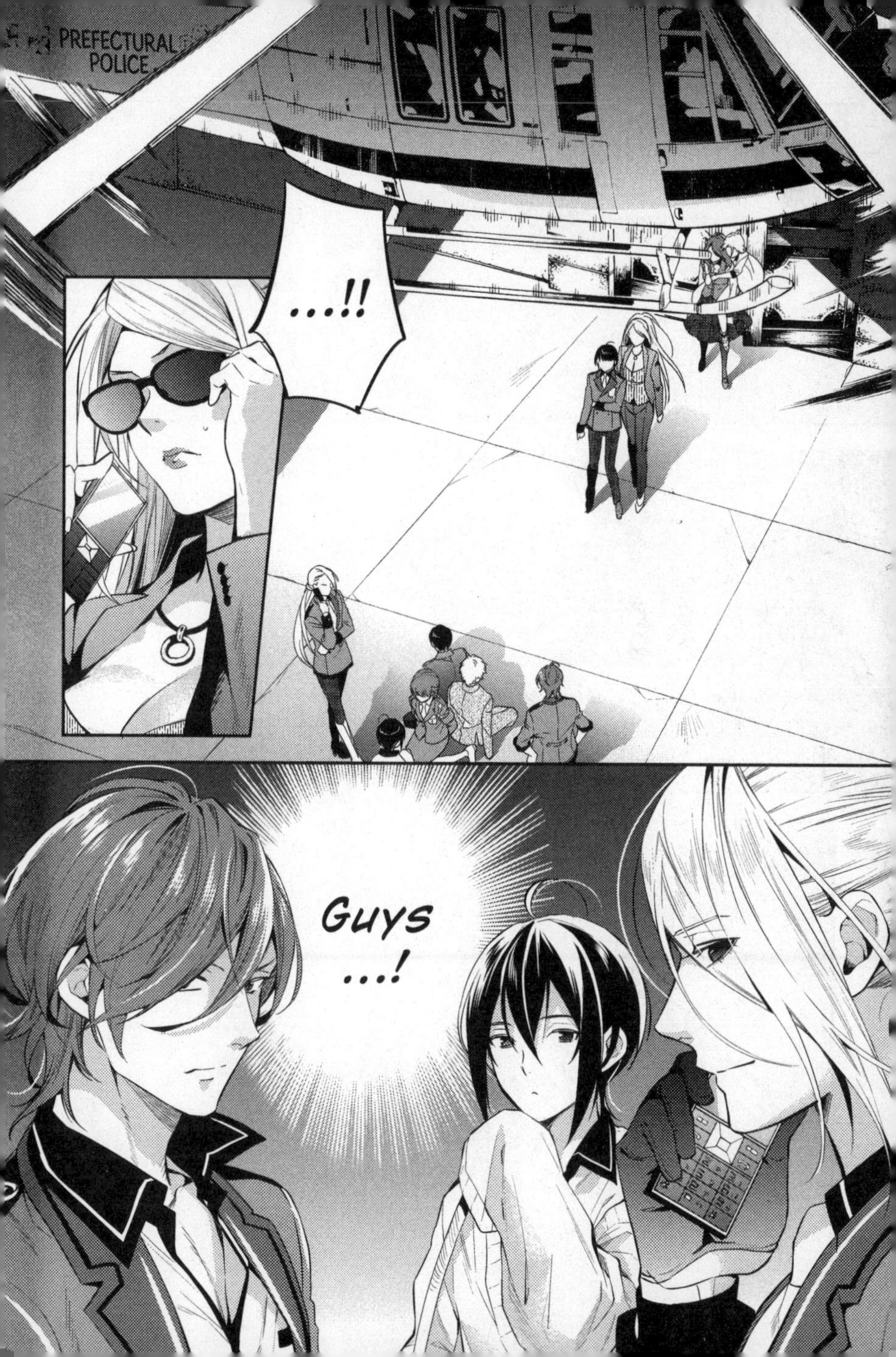
PREFECTURAL POLICE
...!!
Guys ...!

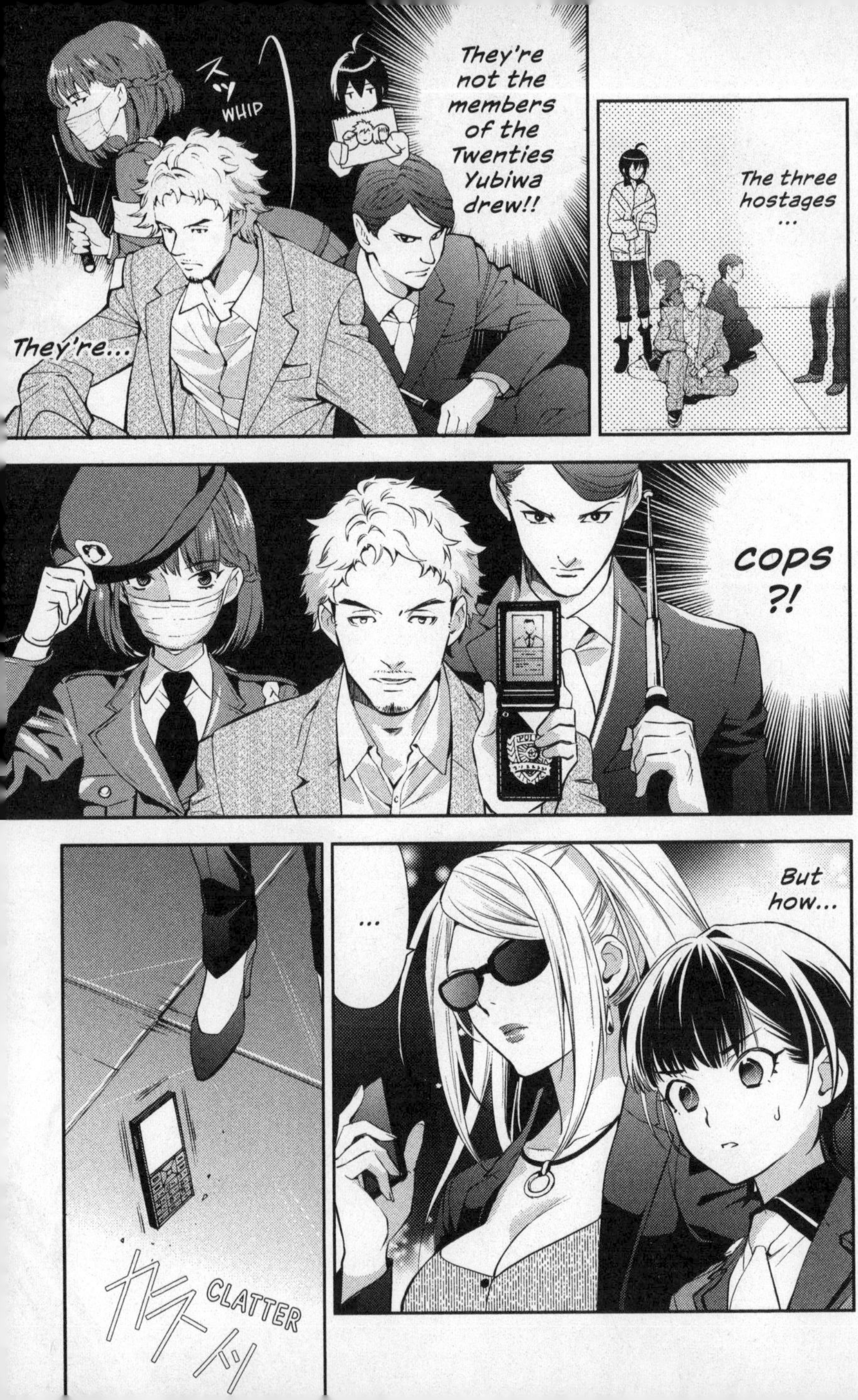
The three hostages ...
They're not the members of the Twenties Yubiwa drew!!
スッ
WHIP
They're...
COPS ?!
But how...
...
カラーッ
CLATTER

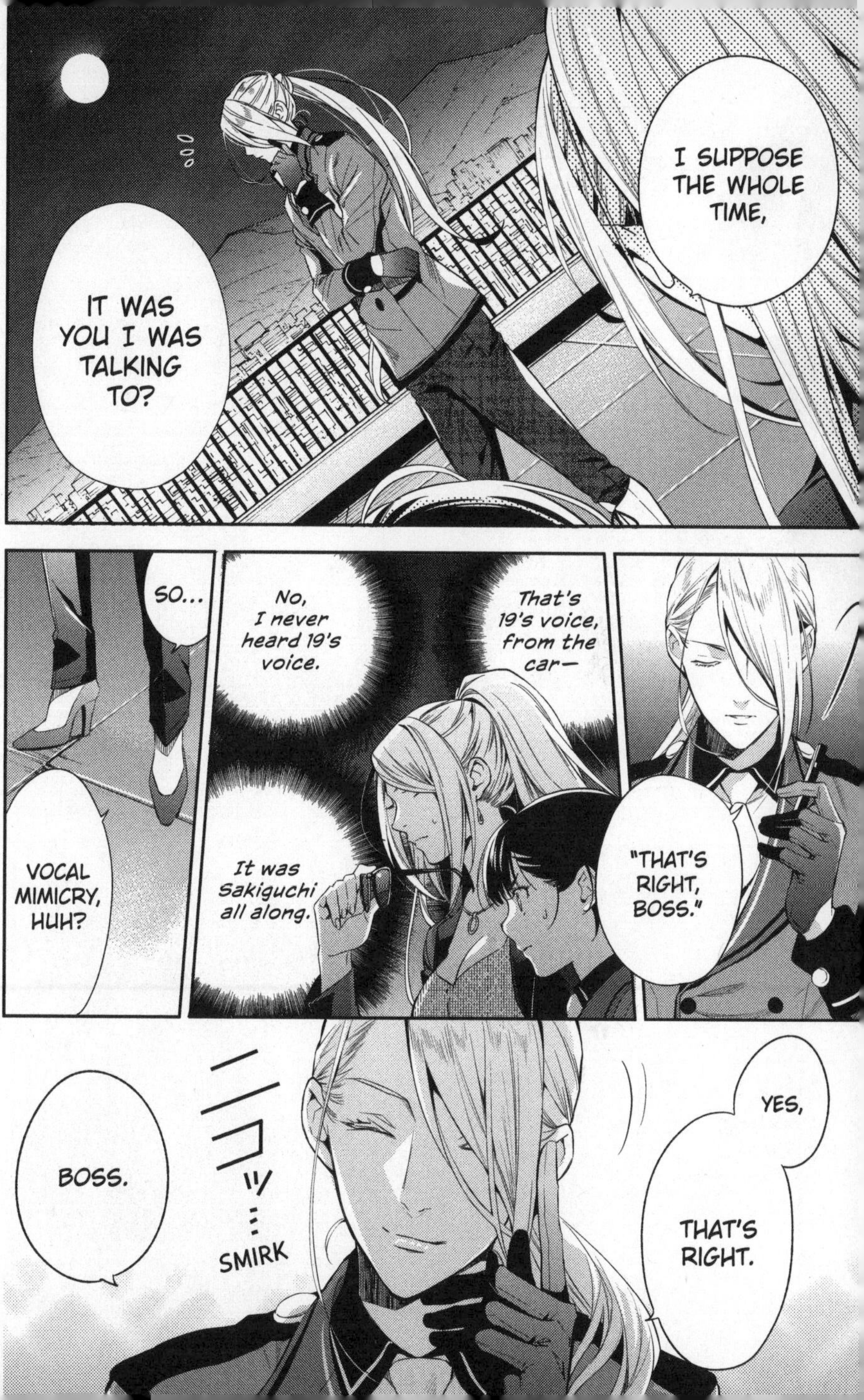
I SUPPOSE THE WHOLE TIME,
IT WAS YOU I WAS TALKING TO?
"THAT'S RIGHT, BOSS."
That's 19's voice, from the car—
No, I never heard 19's voice.
It was Sakiguchi all along.
SO...
VOCAL MIMICRY, HUH?
YES,
THAT'S RIGHT.
SMIRK
BOSS.

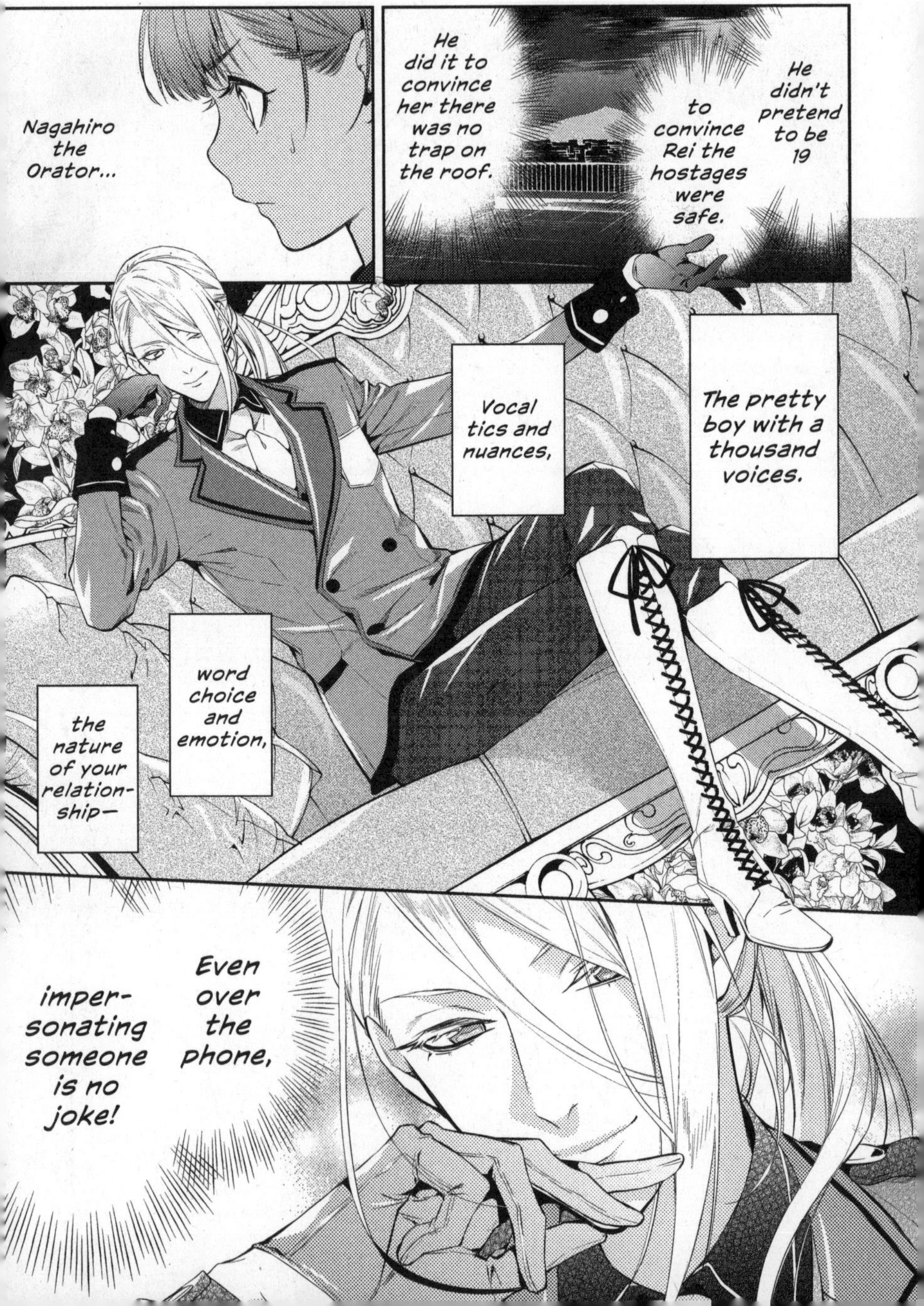
He didn't pretend to be 19
to convince Rei the hostages were safe.
He did it to convince her there was no trap on the roof.
Nagahiro the Orator...
The pretty boy with a thousand voices.
Vocal tics and nuances,
word choice and emotion,
the nature of your relation-ship—
Even over the phone,
imper-sonating someone is no joke!

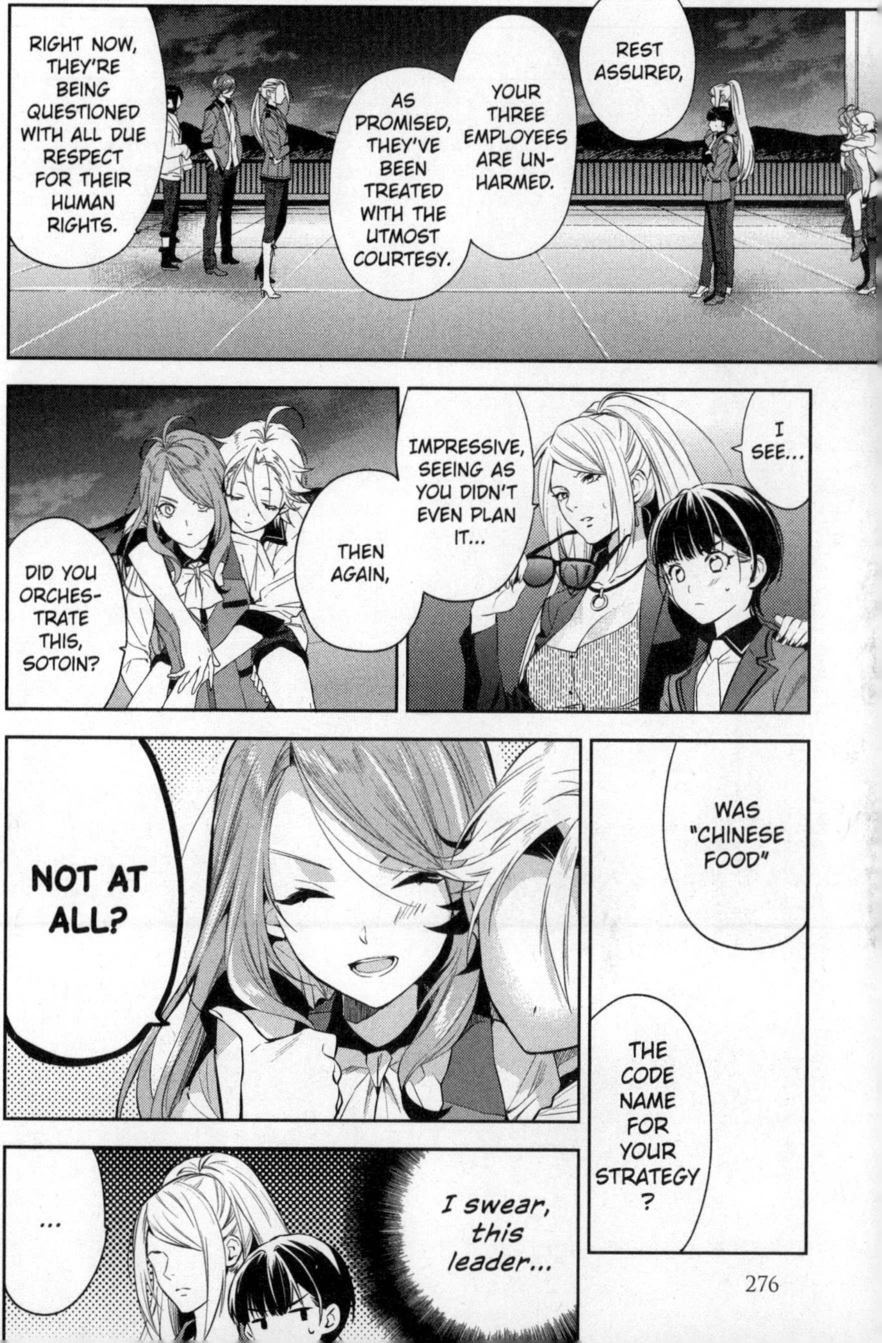
REST ASSURED,
YOUR THREE EMPLOYEES ARE UN-HARMED.
AS PROMISED, THEY'VE BEEN TREATED WITH THE UTMOST COURTESY.
RIGHT NOW, THEY'RE BEING QUESTIONED WITH ALL DUE RESPECT FOR THEIR HUMAN RIGHTS.
I SEE...
IMPRESSIVE, SEEING AS YOU DIDN'T EVEN PLAN IT...
THEN AGAIN,
DID YOU ORCHES-TRATE THIS, SOTOIN?
WAS "CHINESE FOOD"
THE CODE NAME FOR YOUR STRATEGY ?
NOT AT ALL?
I swear, this leader...
...

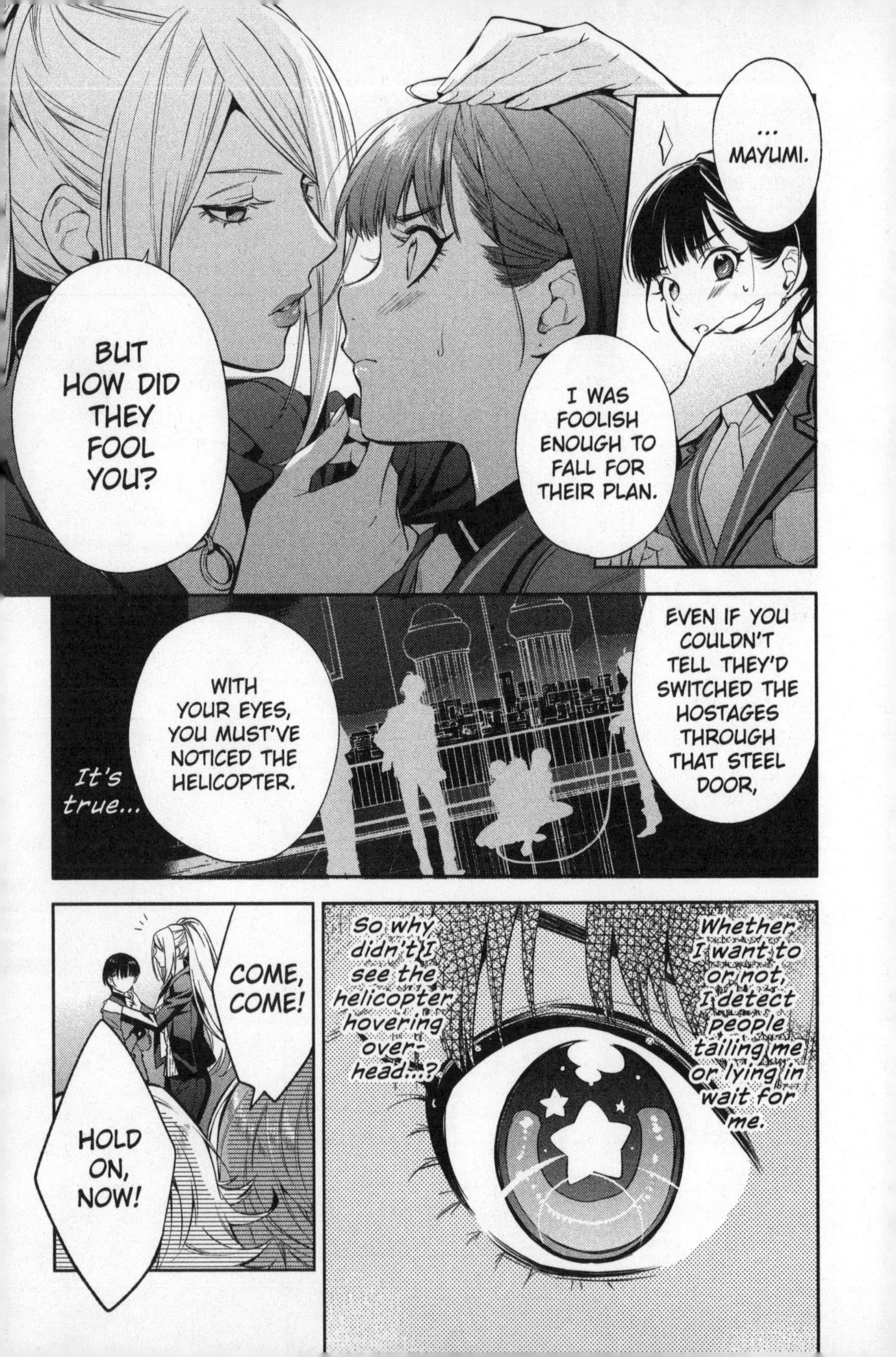
...MAYUMI.
I WAS FOOLISH ENOUGH TO FALL FOR THEIR PLAN.
BUT HOW DID THEY FOOL YOU?
EVEN IF YOU COULDN'T TELL THEY'D SWITCHED THE HOSTAGES THROUGH THAT STEEL DOOR,
WITH YOUR EYES, YOU MUST'VE NOTICED THE HELICOPTER.
It's true...
Whether I want to or not, I detect people tailing me or lying in wait for me.
So why didn't I see the helicopter hovering overhead...?
COME, COME!
HOLD ON, NOW!

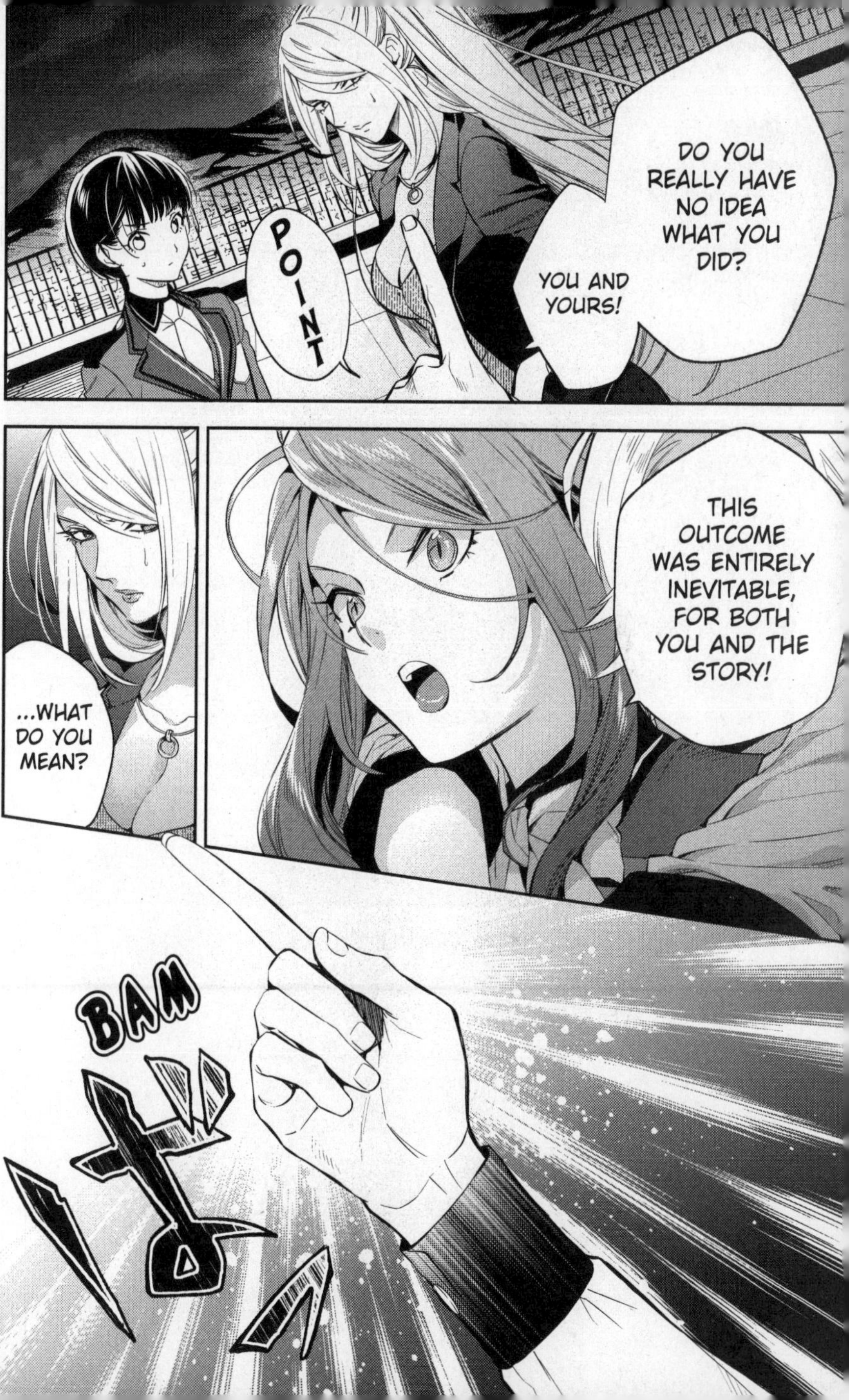
DO YOU REALLY HAVE NO IDEA WHAT YOU DID?
YOU AND YOURS!
POINT
THIS OUTCOME WAS ENTIRELY INEVITABLE, FOR BOTH YOU AND THE STORY!
...WHAT DO YOU MEAN?
BAM

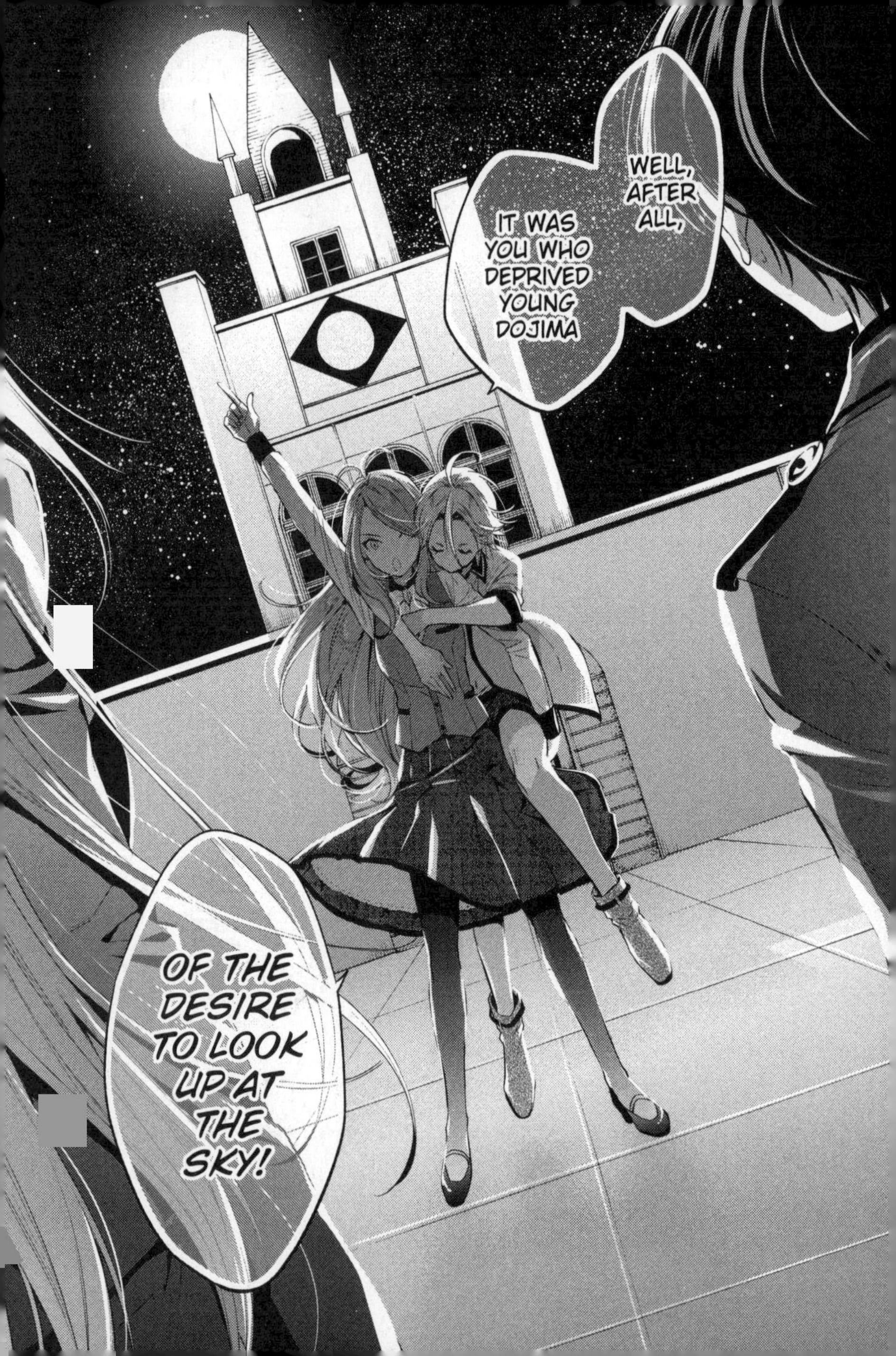
WELL, AFTER ALL,
IT WAS YOU WHO DEPRIVED YOUNG DOJIMA
OF THE DESIRE TO LOOK UP AT THE SKY!

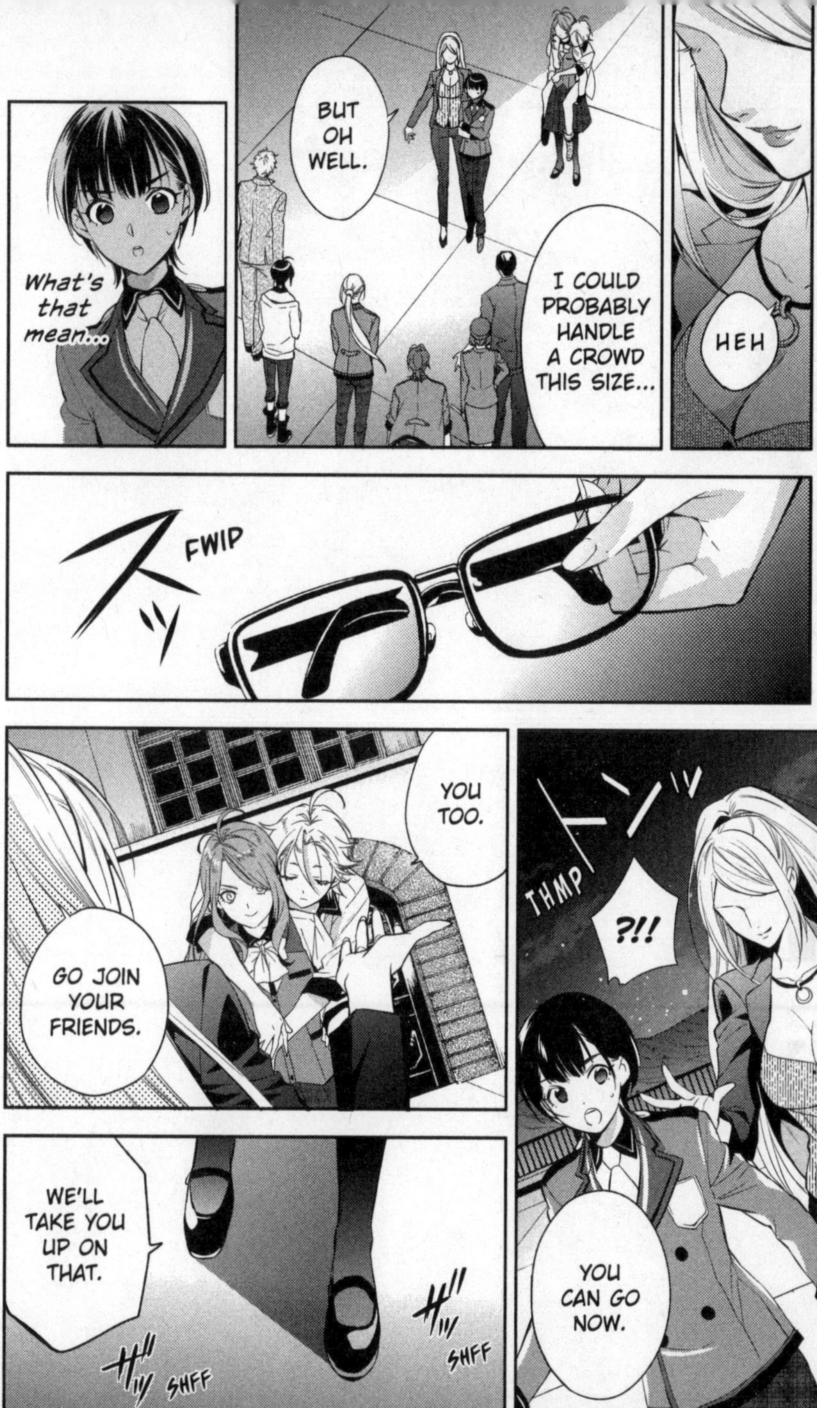
HEH
I COULD PROBABLY HANDLE A CROWD THIS SIZE...
BUT OH WELL.
What's that mean...
スッ
FWIP
THMP
?!!
YOU CAN GO NOW.
YOU TOO.
GO JOIN YOUR FRIENDS.
WE'LL TAKE YOU UP ON THAT.
SHFF
SHFF

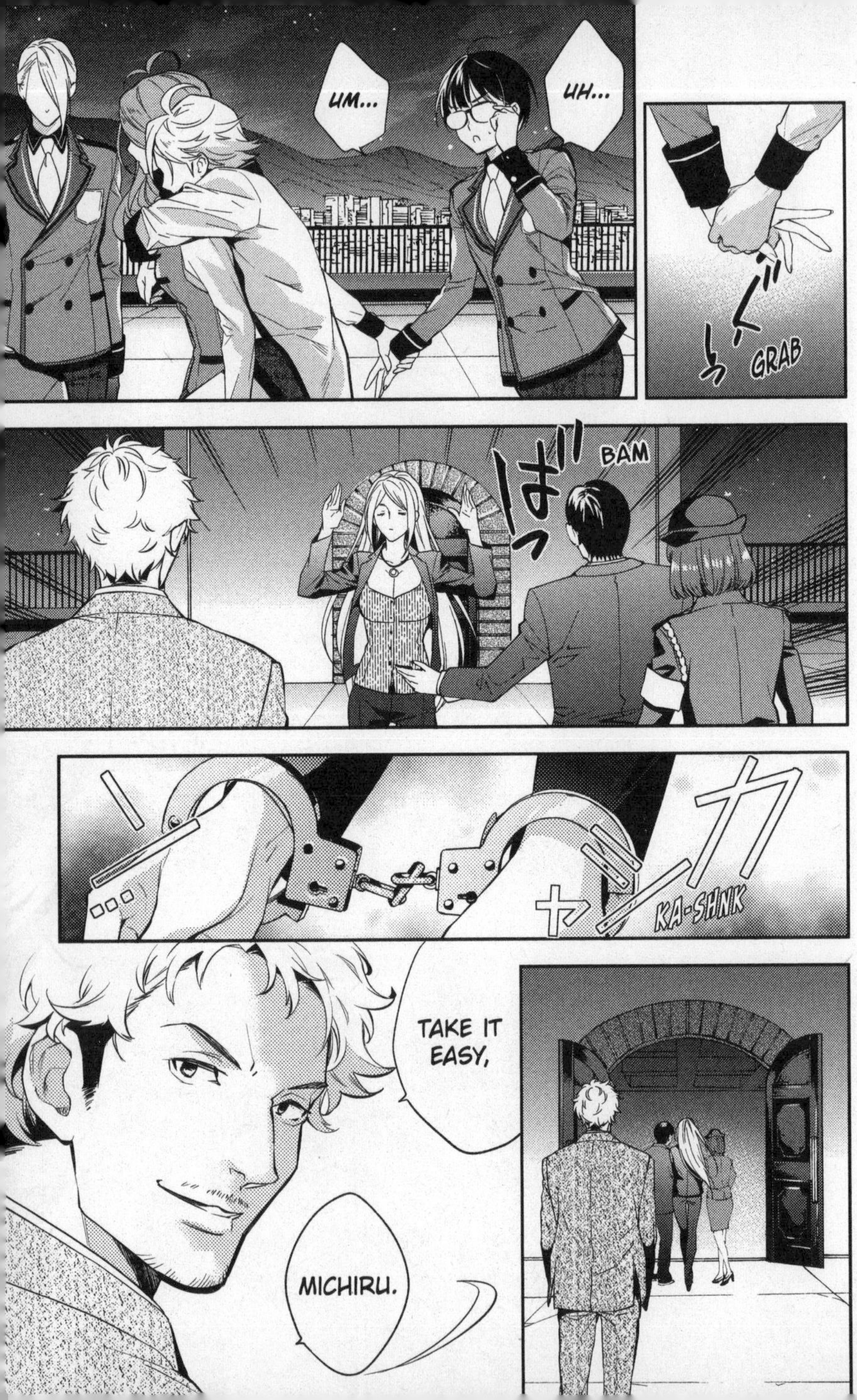
GRAB
UH...
UM...
BAM
KA-SHNK
TAKE IT EASY,
MICHIRU.

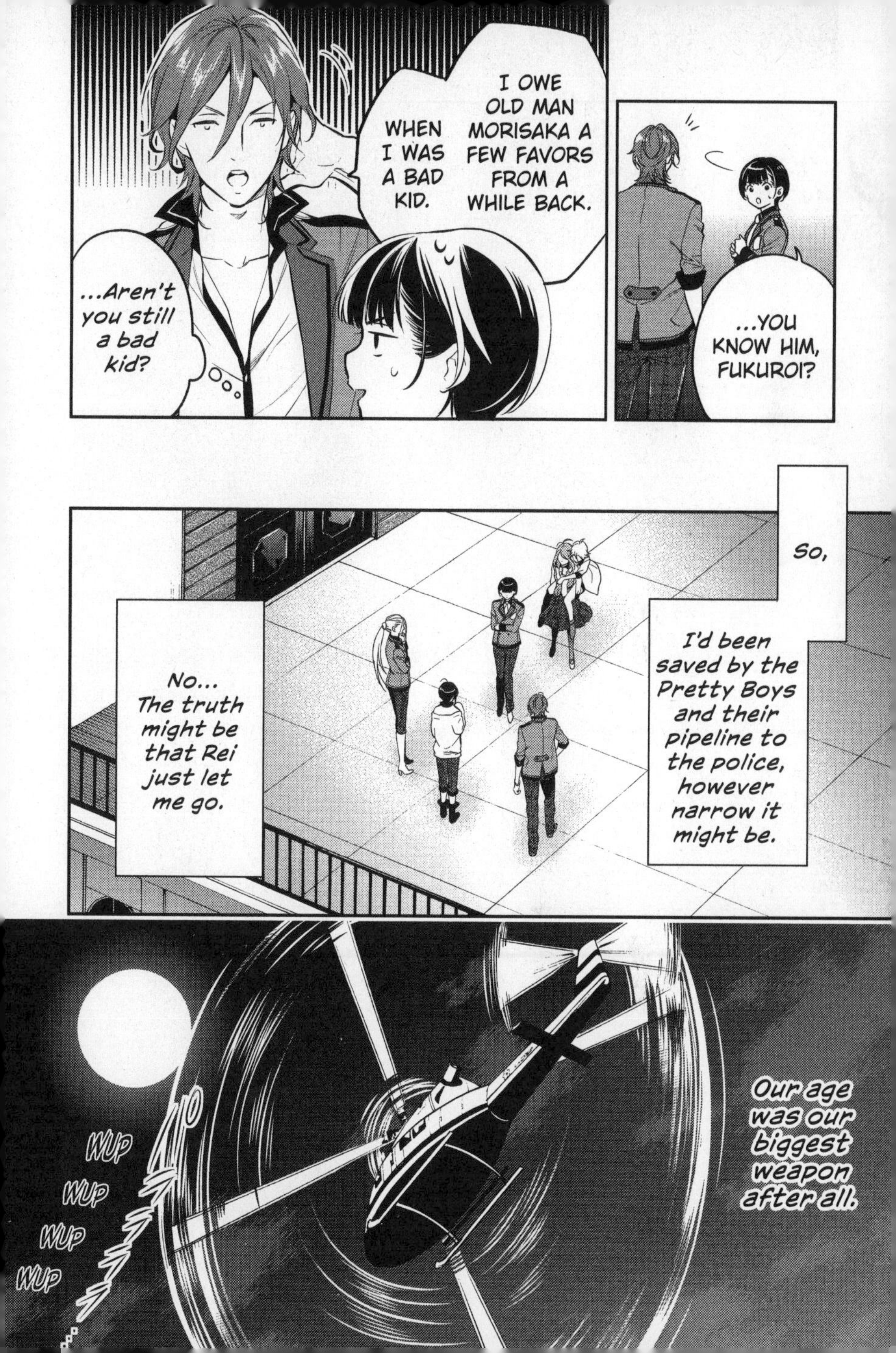
...YOU KNOW HIM, FUKUROI?
I OWE OLD MAN MORISAKA A FEW FAVORS FROM A WHILE BACK.
WHEN I WAS A BAD KID.
...Aren't you still a bad kid?
So,
I'd been saved by the Pretty Boys and their pipeline to the police, however narrow it might be.
No... The truth might be that Rei just let me go.
Our age was our biggest weapon after all.
WUP
WUP
WUP
WUP

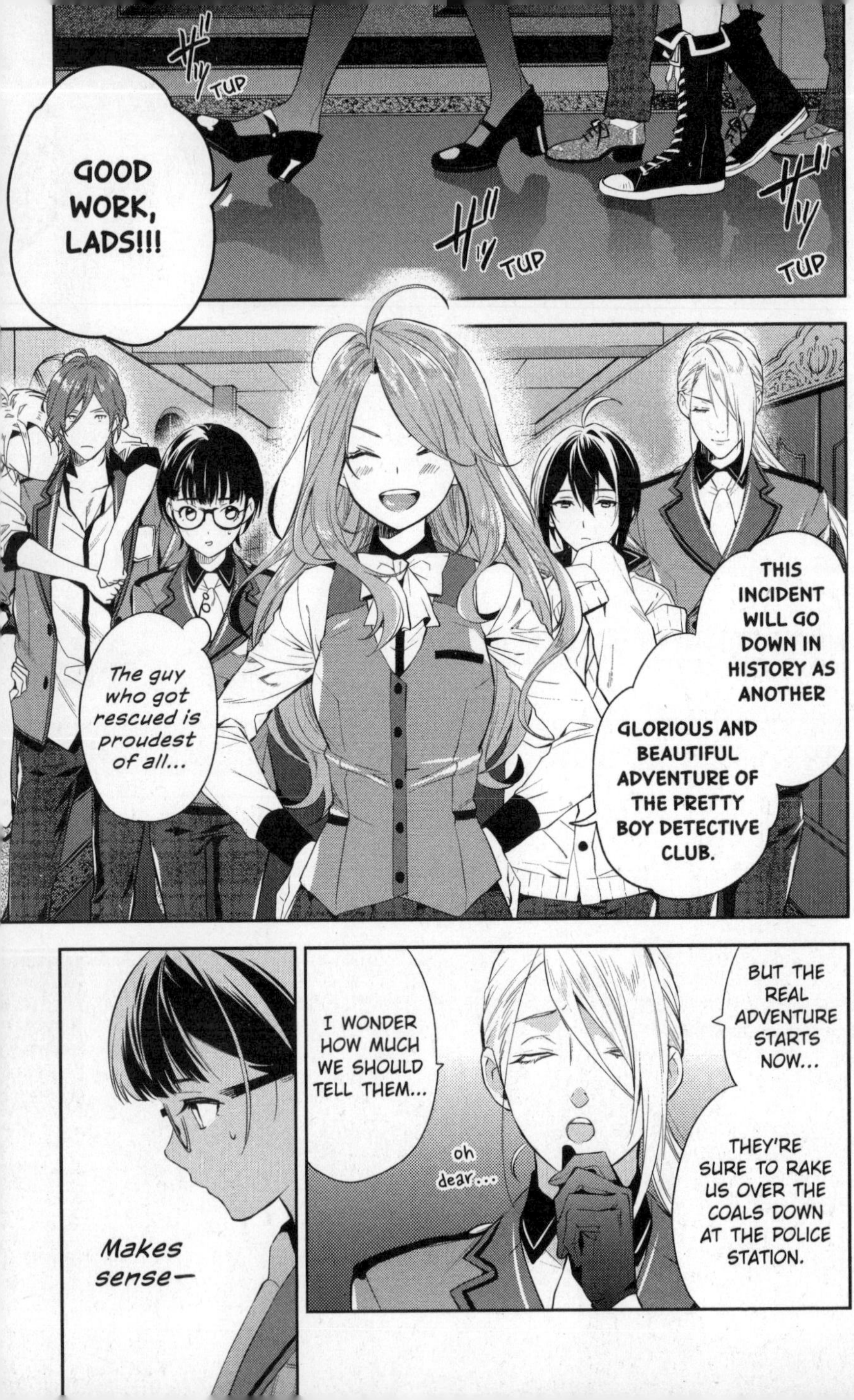
TUP
TUP
TUP
GOOD WORK, LADS!!!
THIS INCIDENT WILL GO DOWN IN HISTORY AS ANOTHER
GLORIOUS AND BEAUTIFUL ADVENTURE OF THE PRETTY BOY DETECTIVE CLUB.
The guy who got rescued is proudest of all...
BUT THE REAL ADVENTURE STARTS NOW...
THEY'RE SURE TO RAKE US OVER THE COALS DOWN AT THE POLICE STATION.
oh dear...
I WONDER HOW MUCH WE SHOULD TELL THEM...
Makes sense—

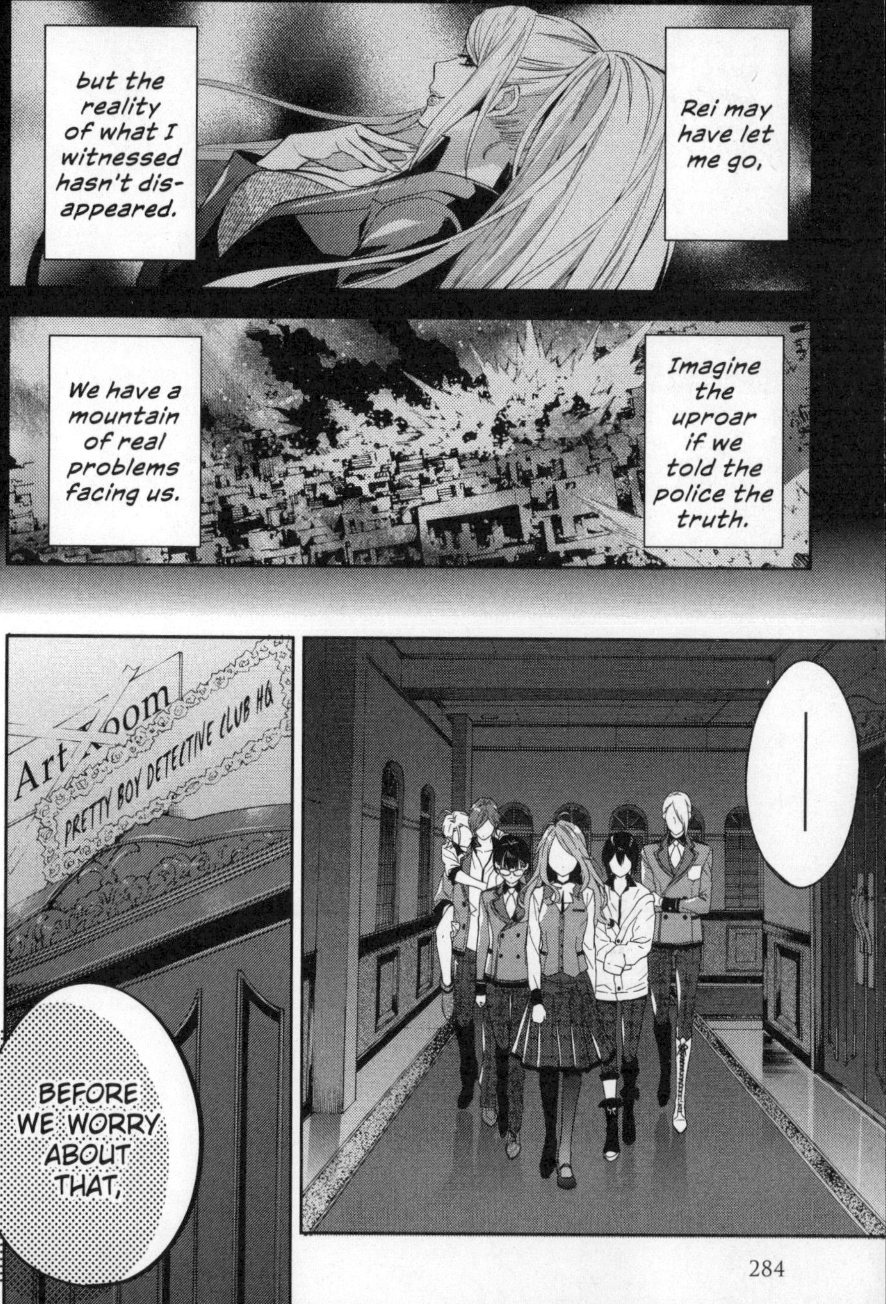
Rei may have let me go,
but the reality of what I witnessed hasn't disappeared.
Imagine the uproar if we told the police the truth.
We have a mountain of real problems facing us.
—
Art Room
PRETTY BOY DETECTIVE CLUB HQ
BEFORE WE WORRY ABOUT THAT,

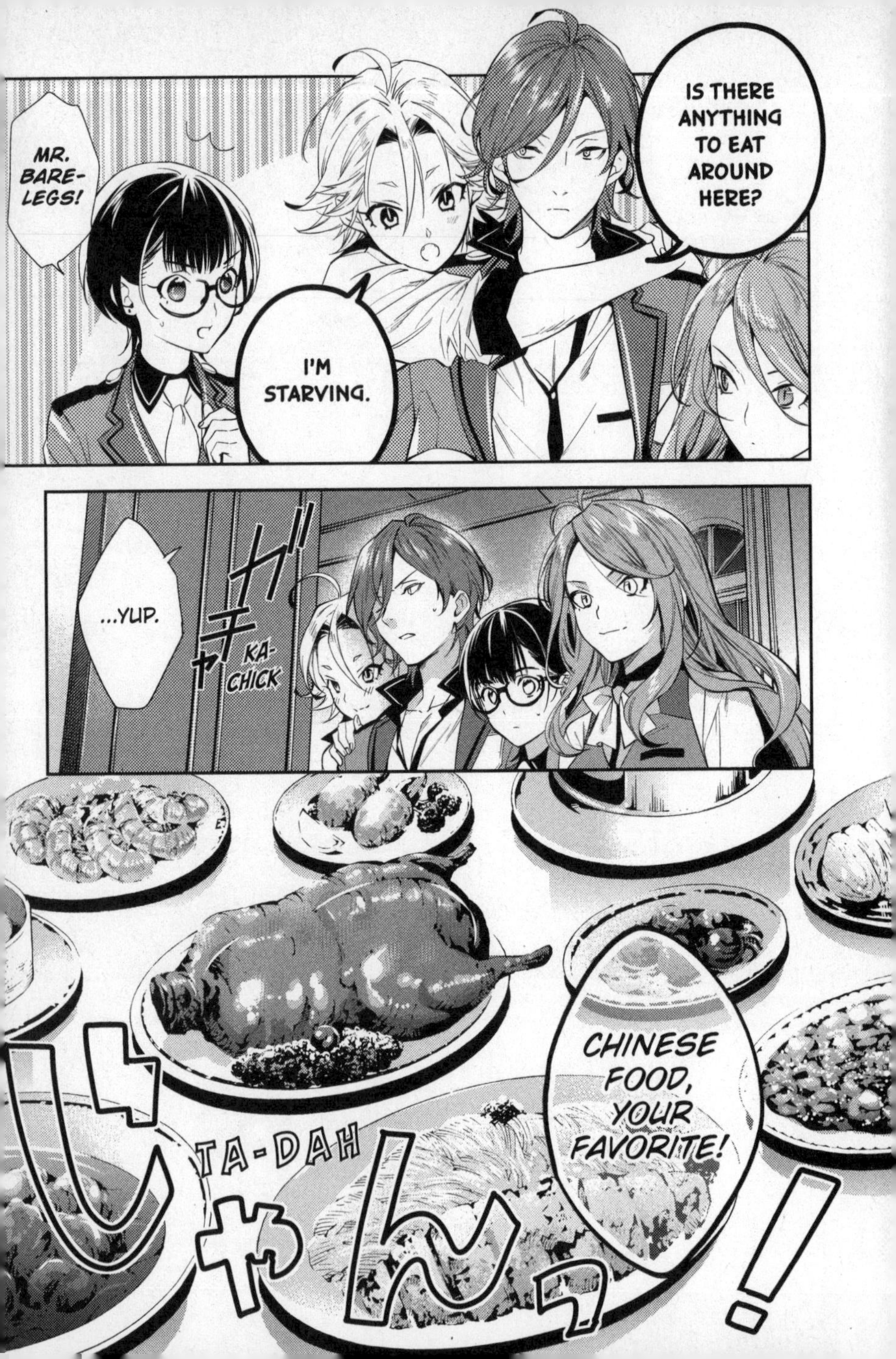
IS THERE ANYTHING TO EAT AROUND HERE?
I'M STARVING.
MR. BARE-LEGS!
...YUP.
ガチャ
KA-CHICK
じゃんっ!
TA-DAH
CHINESE FOOD, YOUR FAVORITE!

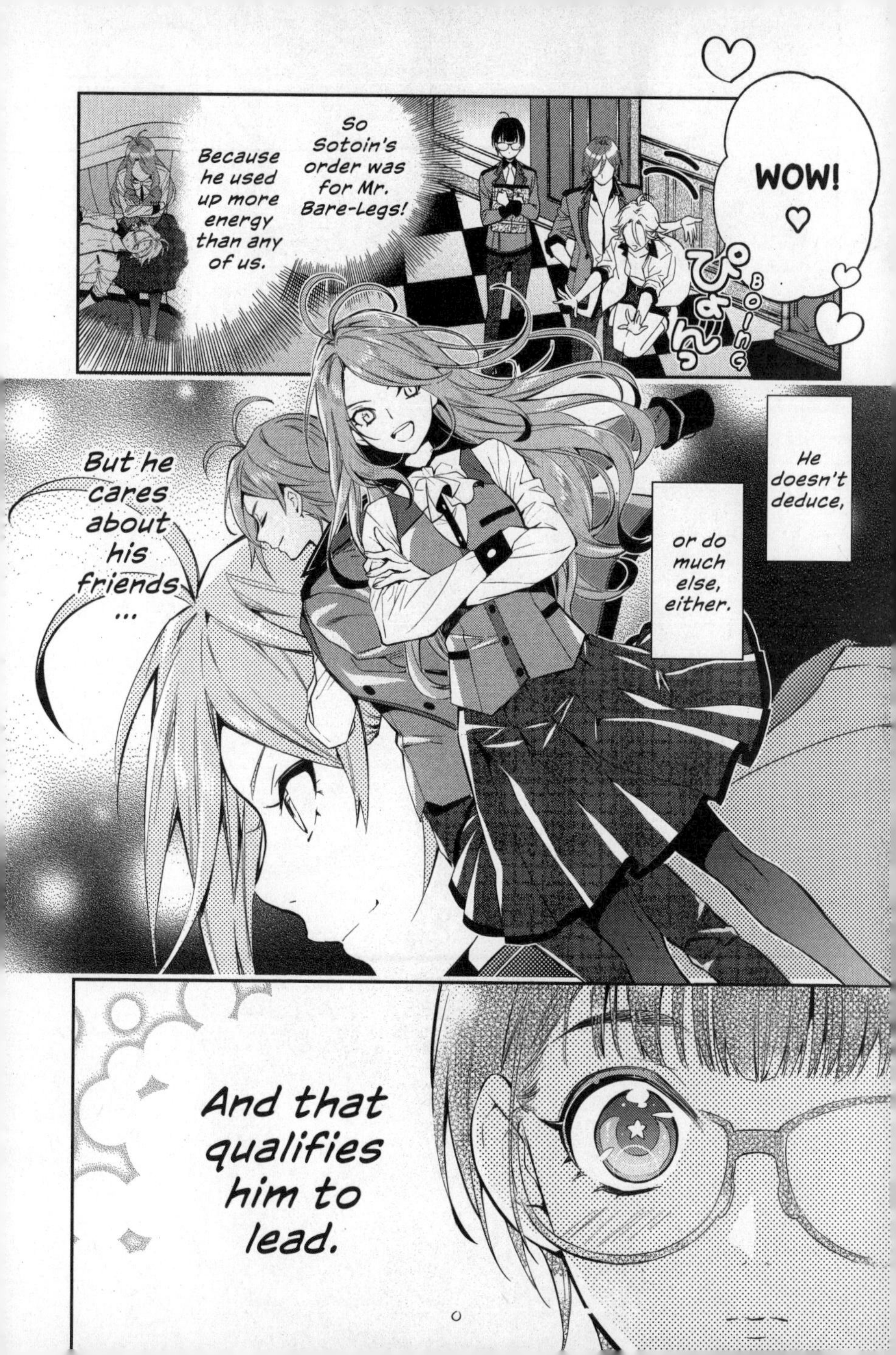
WOW! ♡
ぴょんっ
BOING
So Sotoin's order was for Mr. Bare-Legs!
Because he used up more energy than any of us.
He doesn't deduce,
or do much else, either.
But he cares about his friends...
And that qualifies him to lead.

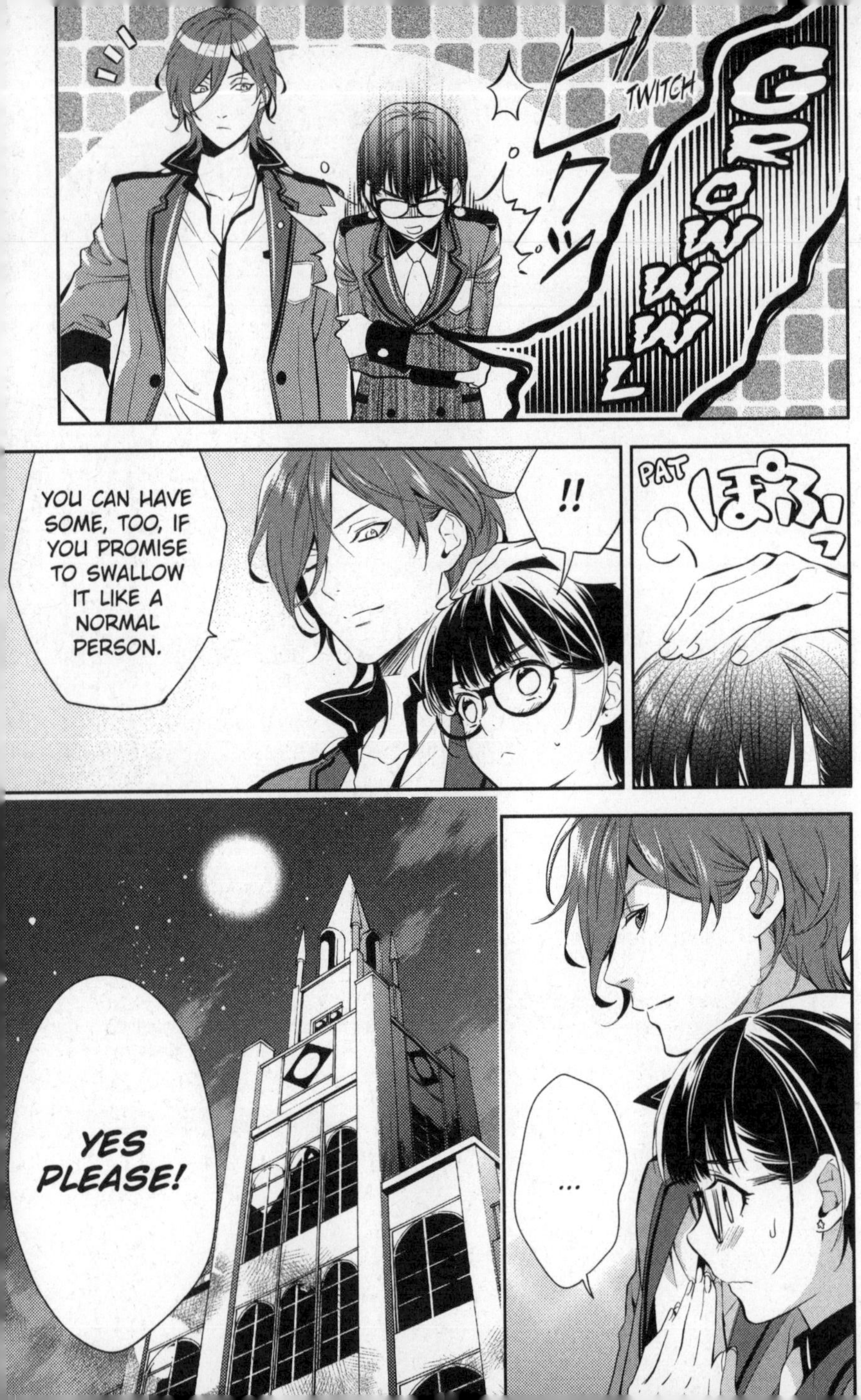
GROWWWWL
TWITCH
ビクッ
PAT
ぽふっ
!!
YOU CAN HAVE SOME, TOO, IF YOU PROMISE TO SWALLOW IT LIKE A NORMAL PERSON.
...
YES PLEASE!

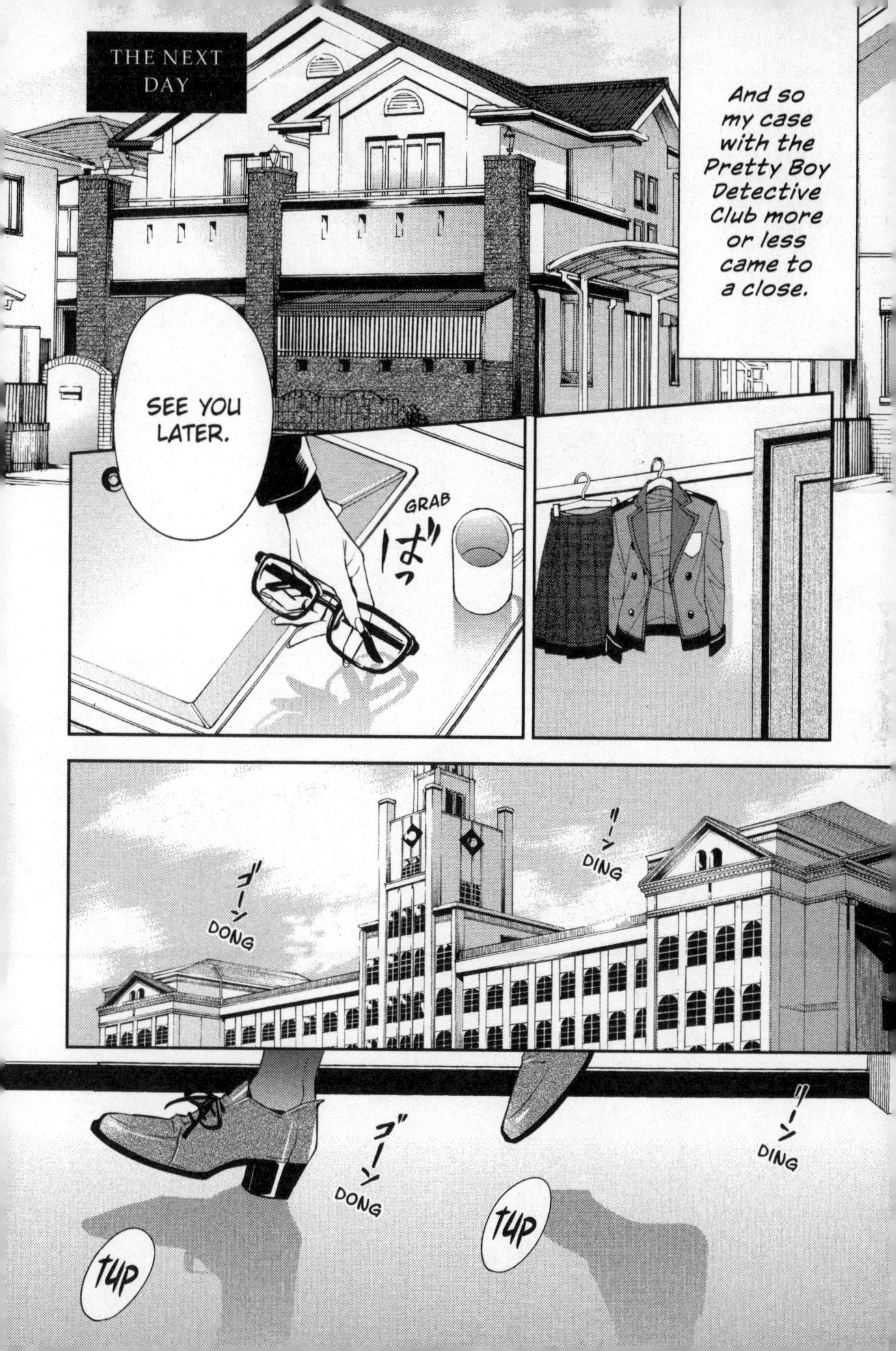
And so my case with the Pretty Boy Detective Club more or less came to a close.
THE NEXT DAY
SEE YOU LATER.
GRAB
ばっ
DING
ゴーン
DONG
DING
ゴーン
DONG
TUP
TUP

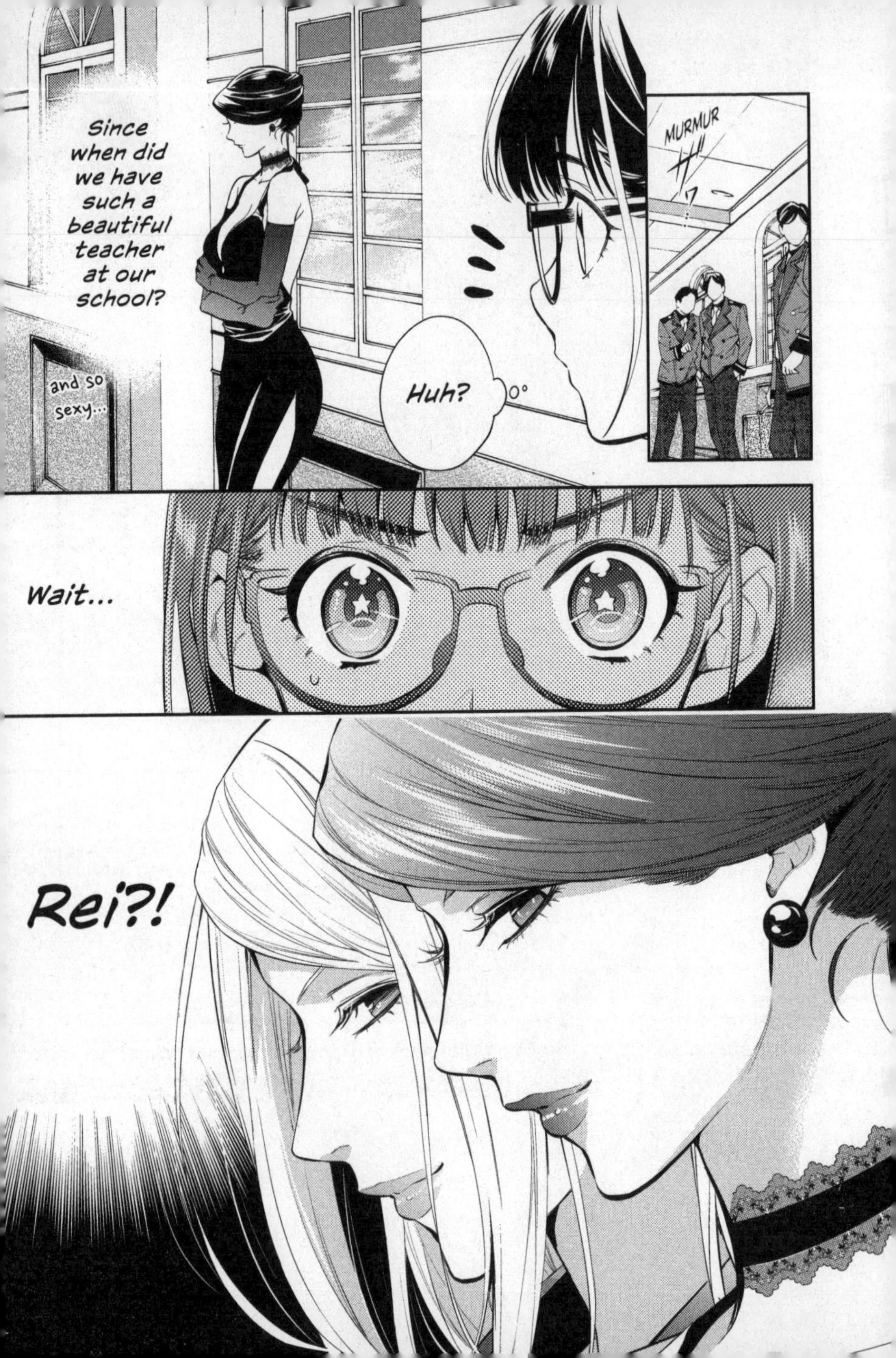
MURMUR
Huh?
Since when did we have such a beautiful teacher at our school?
and so sexy...
Wait...
Rei?!

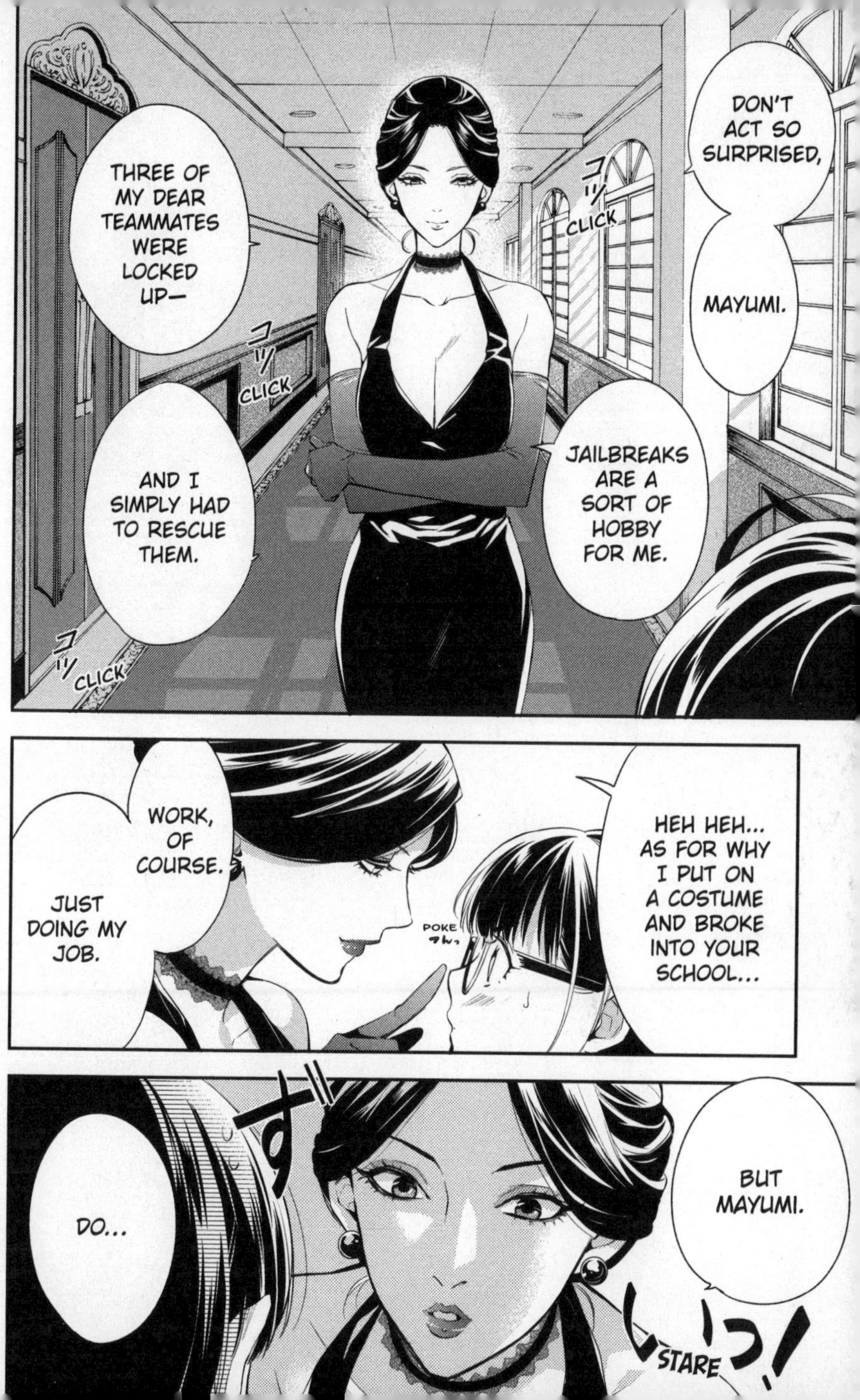
DON'T ACT SO SURPRISED,
MAYUMI.
CLICK
JAILBREAKS ARE A SORT OF HOBBY FOR ME.
THREE OF MY DEAR TEAMMATES WERE LOCKED UP—
CLICK
AND I SIMPLY HAD TO RESCUE THEM.
CLICK
HEH HEH... AS FOR WHY I PUT ON A COSTUME AND BROKE INTO YOUR SCHOOL...
POKE
WORK, OF COURSE.
JUST DOING MY JOB.
BUT MAYUMI.
STARE
DO...

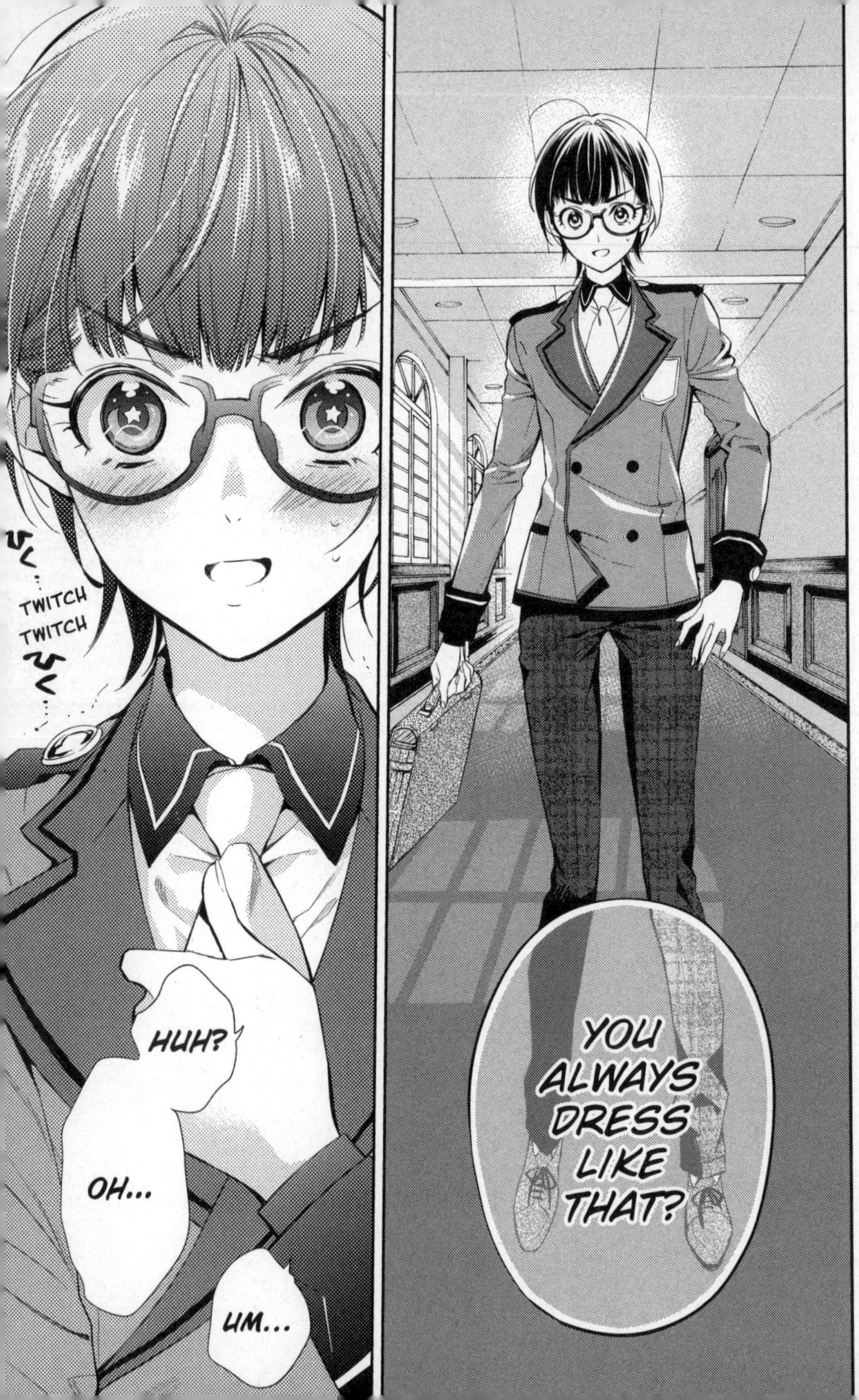
YOU ALWAYS DRESS LIKE THAT?
TWITCH TWITCH
HUH?
OH...
UM...

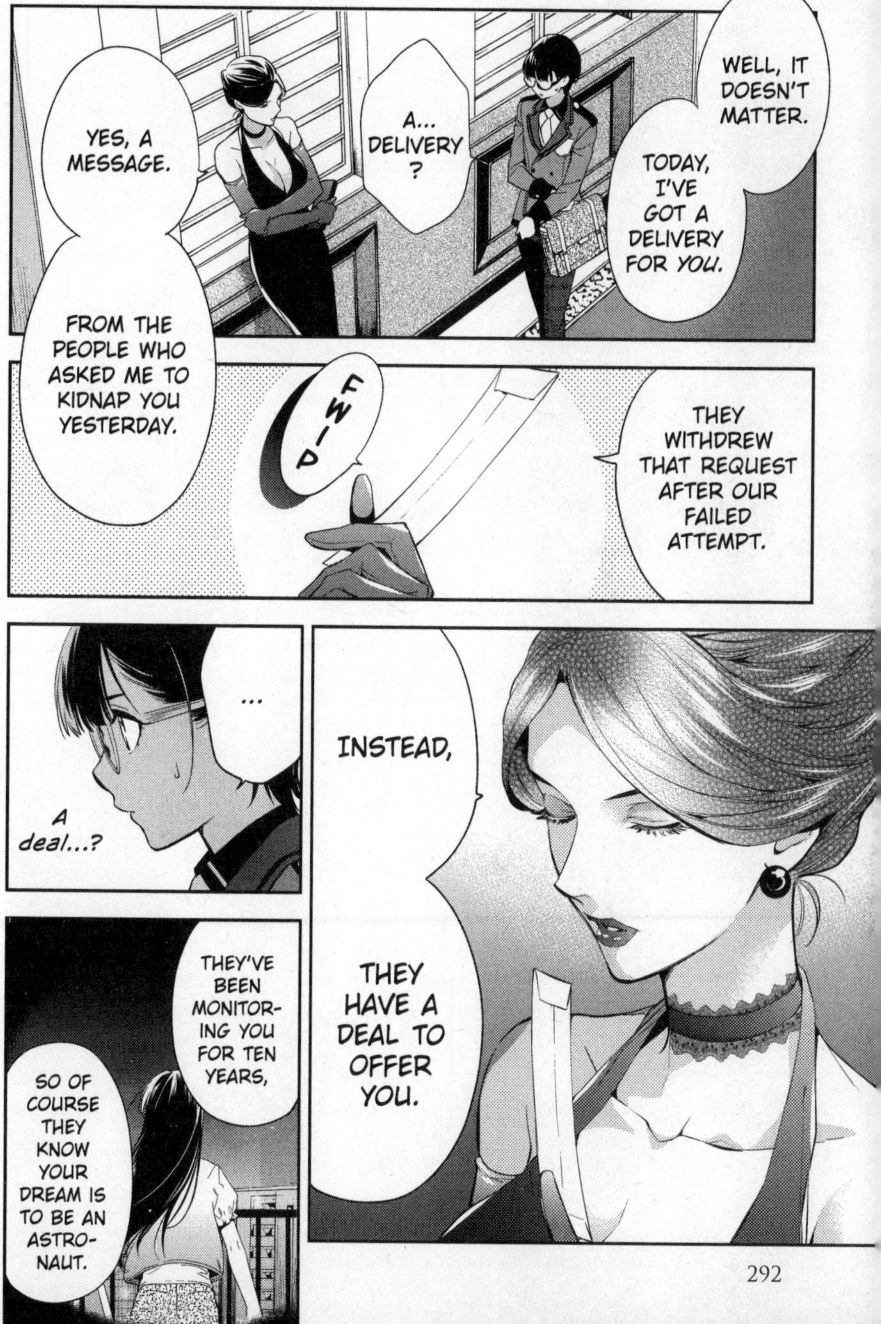
WELL, IT DOESN'T MATTER.
TODAY, I'VE GOT A DELIVERY FOR *YOU*.
A... DELIVERY?
YES, A MESSAGE.
FROM THE PEOPLE WHO ASKED ME TO KIDNAP YOU YESTERDAY.
THEY WITHDREW THAT REQUEST AFTER OUR FAILED ATTEMPT.
FWIP
INSTEAD,
THEY HAVE A DEAL TO OFFER YOU.
...
A deal...?
THEY'VE BEEN MONITORING YOU FOR TEN YEARS,
SO OF COURSE THEY KNOW YOUR DREAM IS TO BE AN ASTRONAUT.

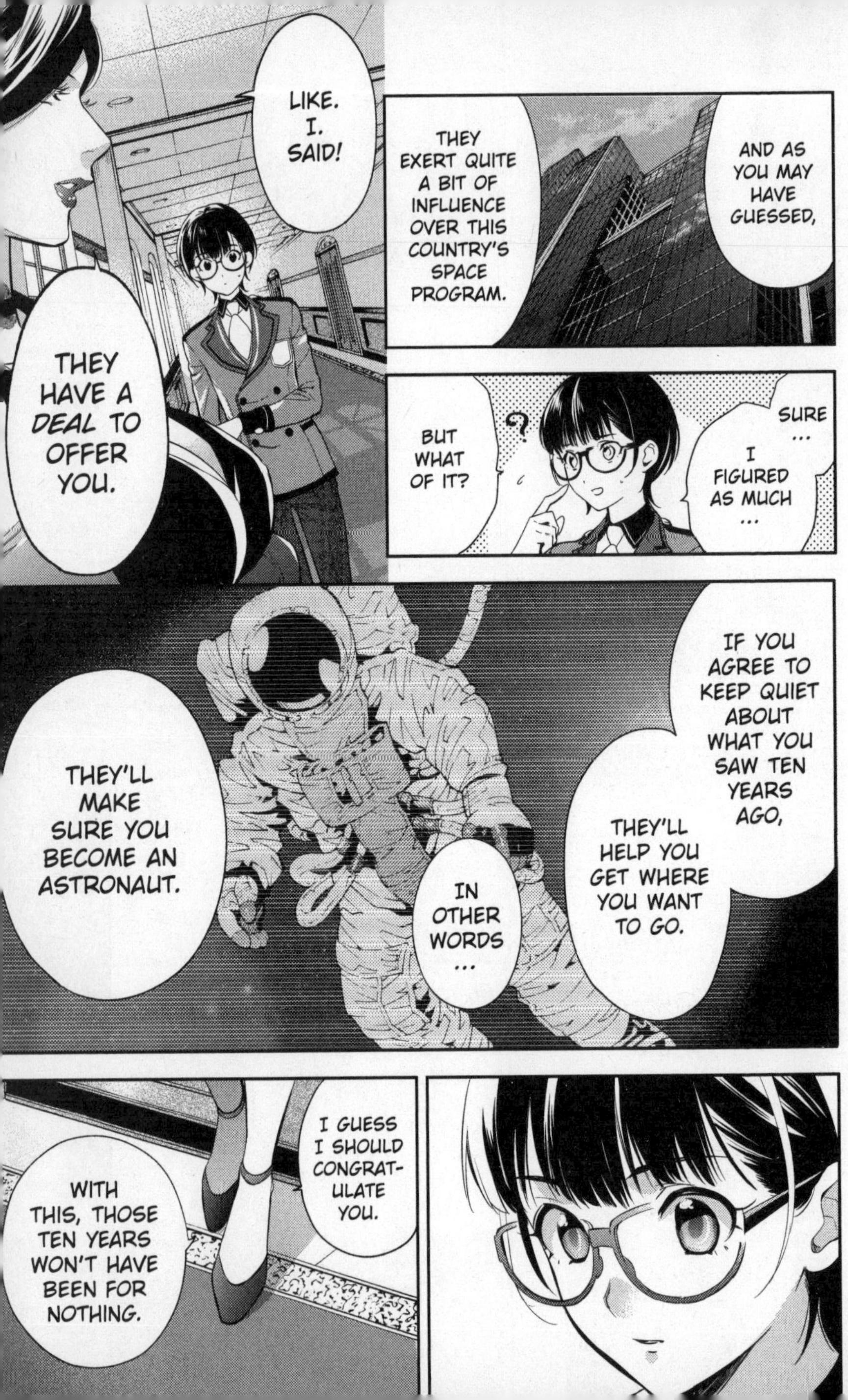
AND AS YOU MAY HAVE GUESSED,
THEY EXERT QUITE A BIT OF INFLUENCE OVER THIS COUNTRY'S SPACE PROGRAM.
SURE ... I FIGURED AS MUCH ...
BUT WHAT OF IT?
?
LIKE. I. SAID!
THEY HAVE A *DEAL* TO OFFER YOU.
IF YOU AGREE TO KEEP QUIET ABOUT WHAT YOU SAW TEN YEARS AGO,
THEY'LL HELP YOU GET WHERE YOU WANT TO GO.
IN OTHER WORDS ...
THEY'LL MAKE SURE YOU BECOME AN ASTRONAUT.
I GUESS I SHOULD CONGRAT-ULATE YOU.
WITH THIS, THOSE TEN YEARS WON'T HAVE BEEN FOR NOTHING.

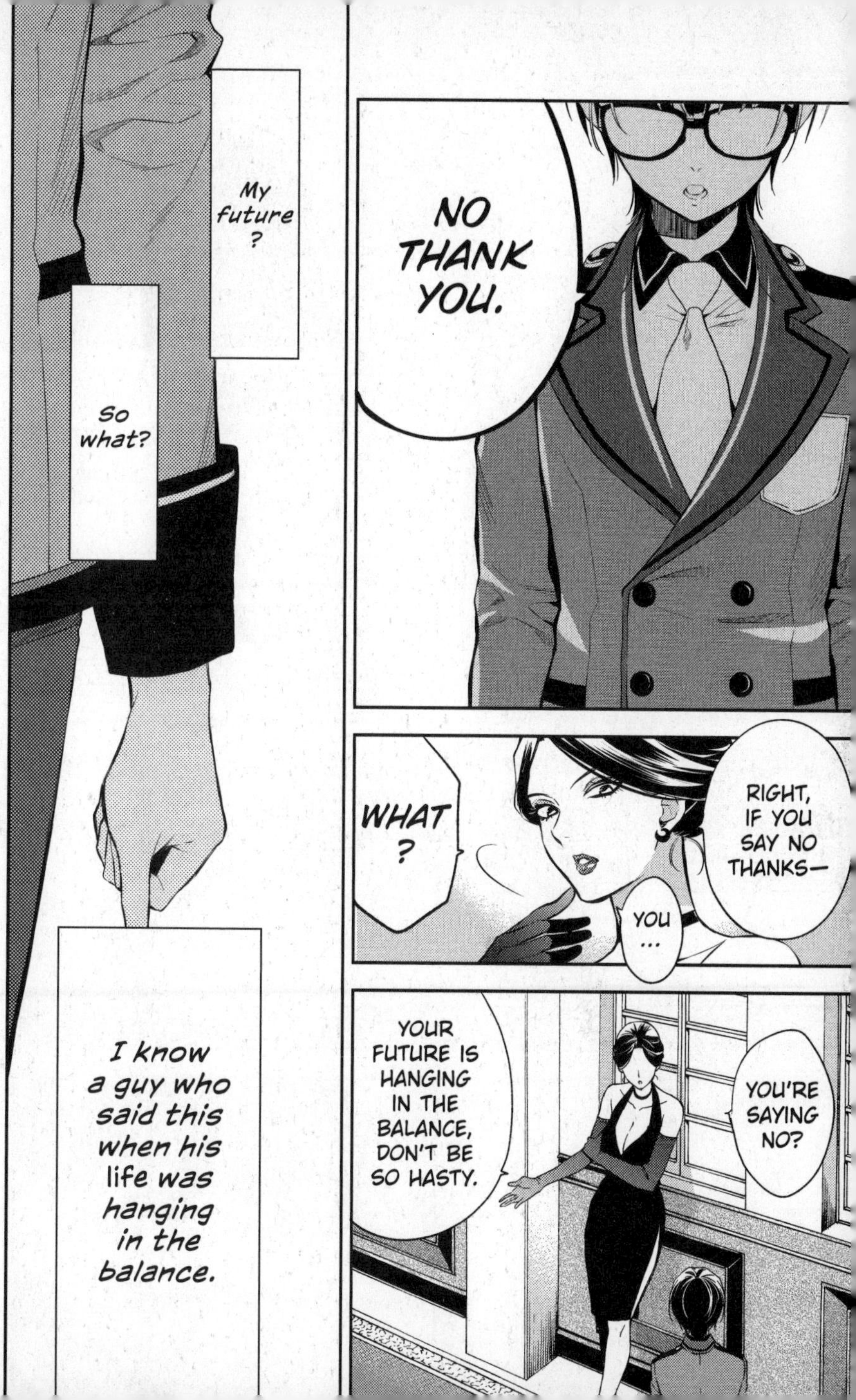
NO THANK YOU.
RIGHT, IF YOU SAY NO THANKS—
YOU ...
WHAT ?
YOU'RE SAYING NO?
YOUR FUTURE IS HANGING IN THE BALANCE, DON'T BE SO HASTY.
My future ?
So what?
I know a guy who said this when his life was hanging in the balance.

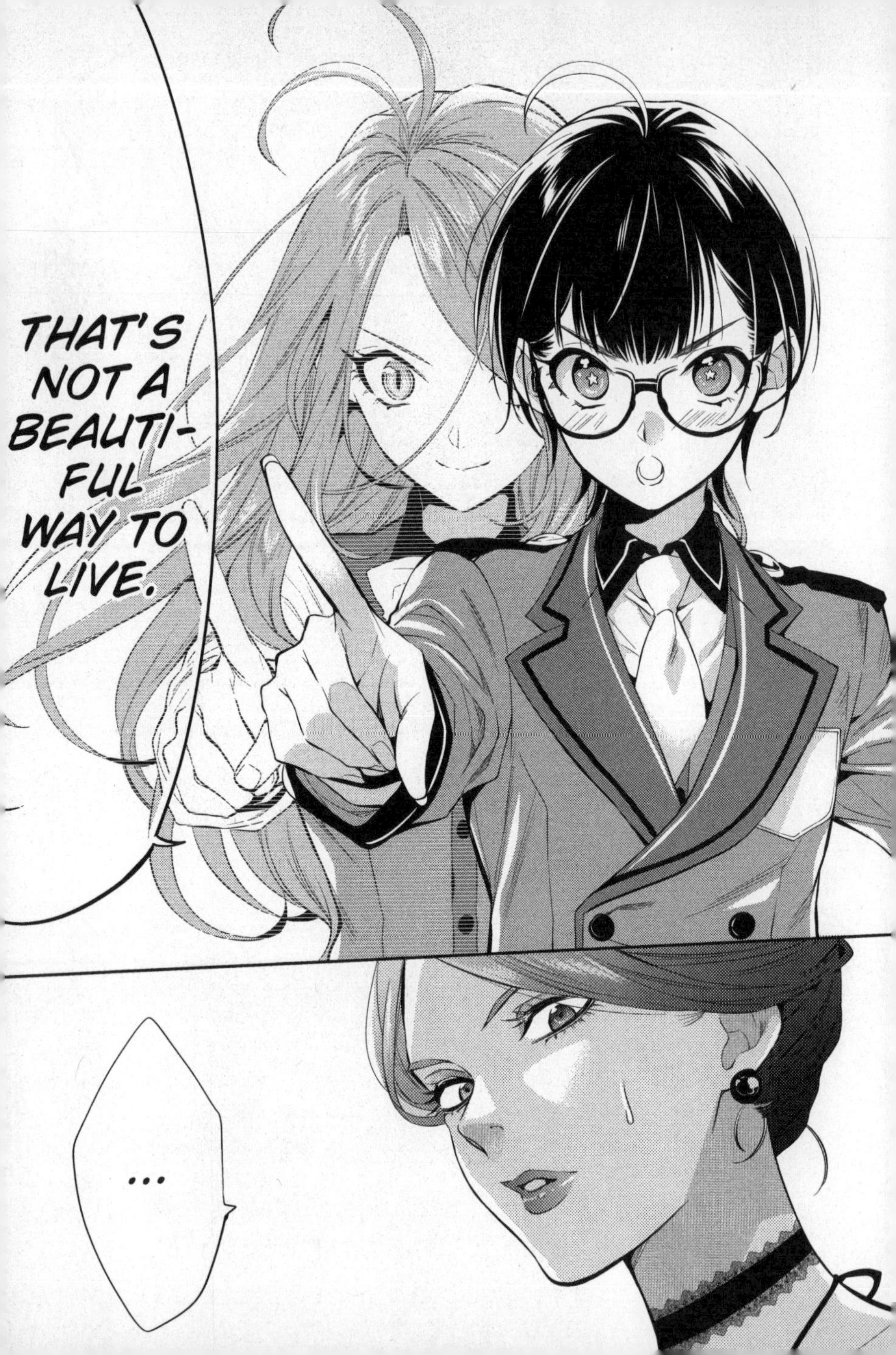
THAT'S NOT A BEAUTIFUL WAY TO LIVE.
...

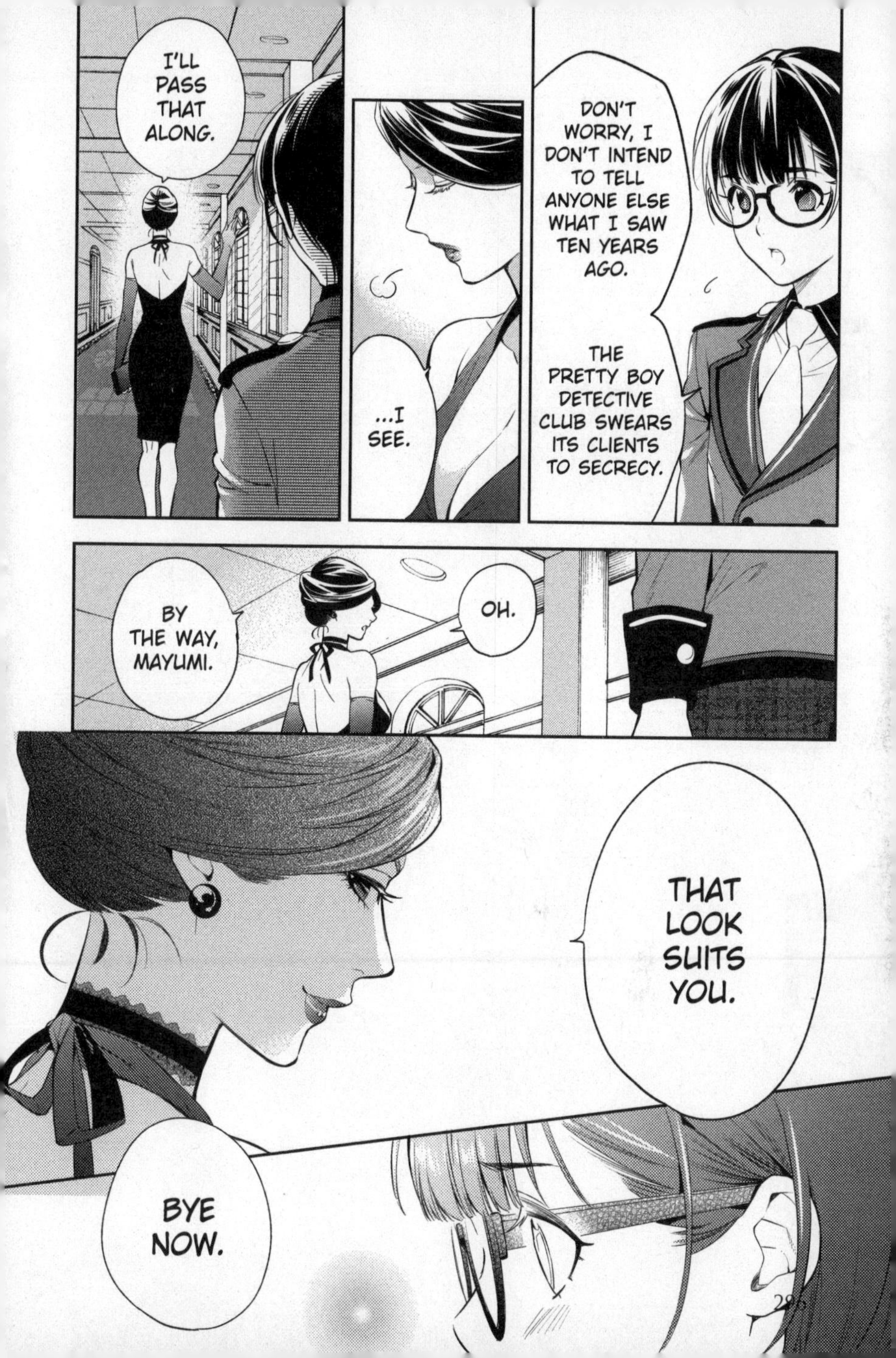
DON'T WORRY, I DON'T INTEND TO TELL ANYONE ELSE WHAT I SAW TEN YEARS AGO.
THE PRETTY BOY DETECTIVE CLUB SWEARS ITS CLIENTS TO SECRECY.
...I SEE.
I'LL PASS THAT ALONG.
OH.
BY THE WAY, MAYUMI.
THAT LOOK SUITS YOU.
BYE NOW.

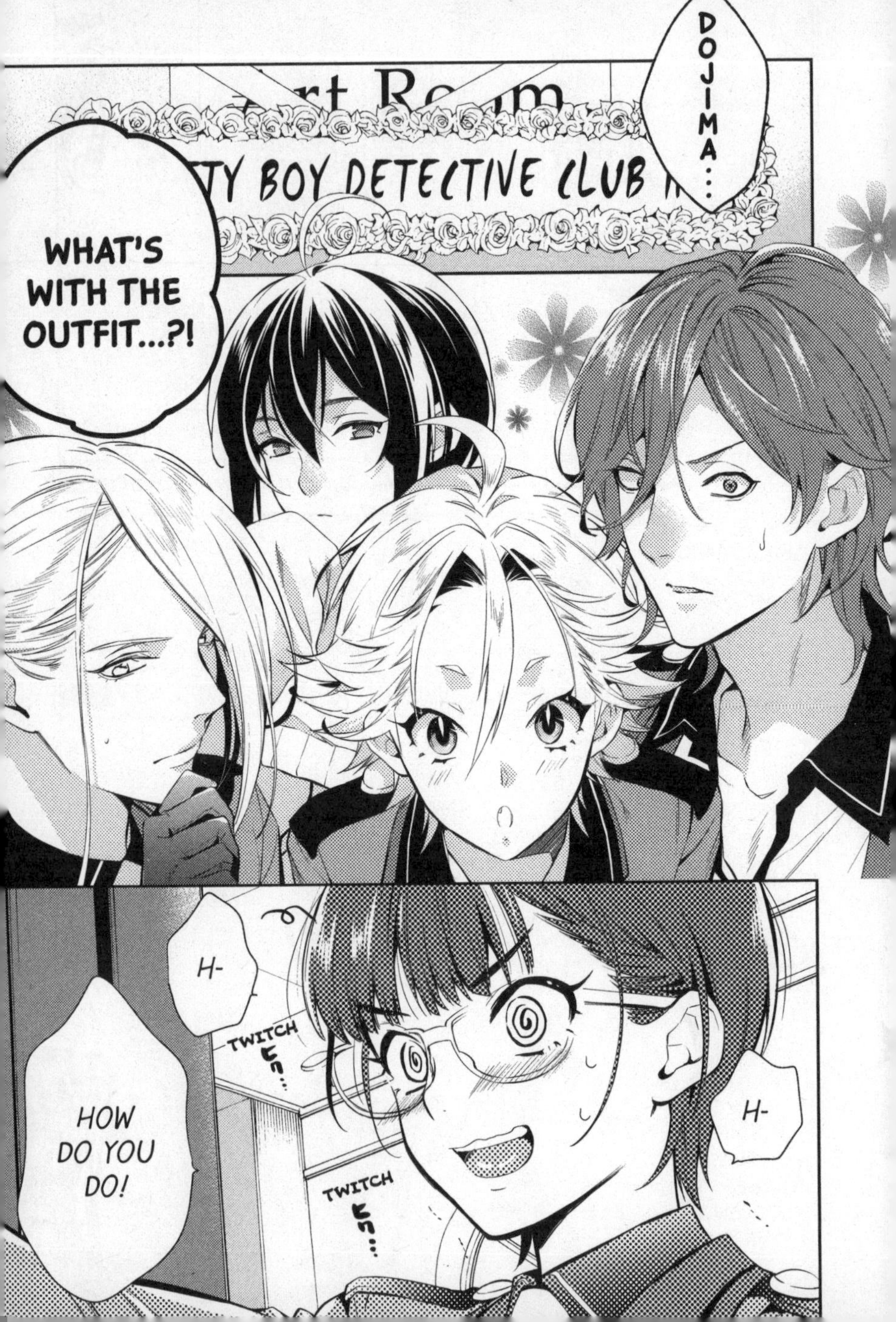
DOJIMA...
WHAT'S WITH THE OUTFIT...?!
BOY DETECTIVE CLUB
H-
H-
TWITCH
TWITCH
HOW DO YOU DO!

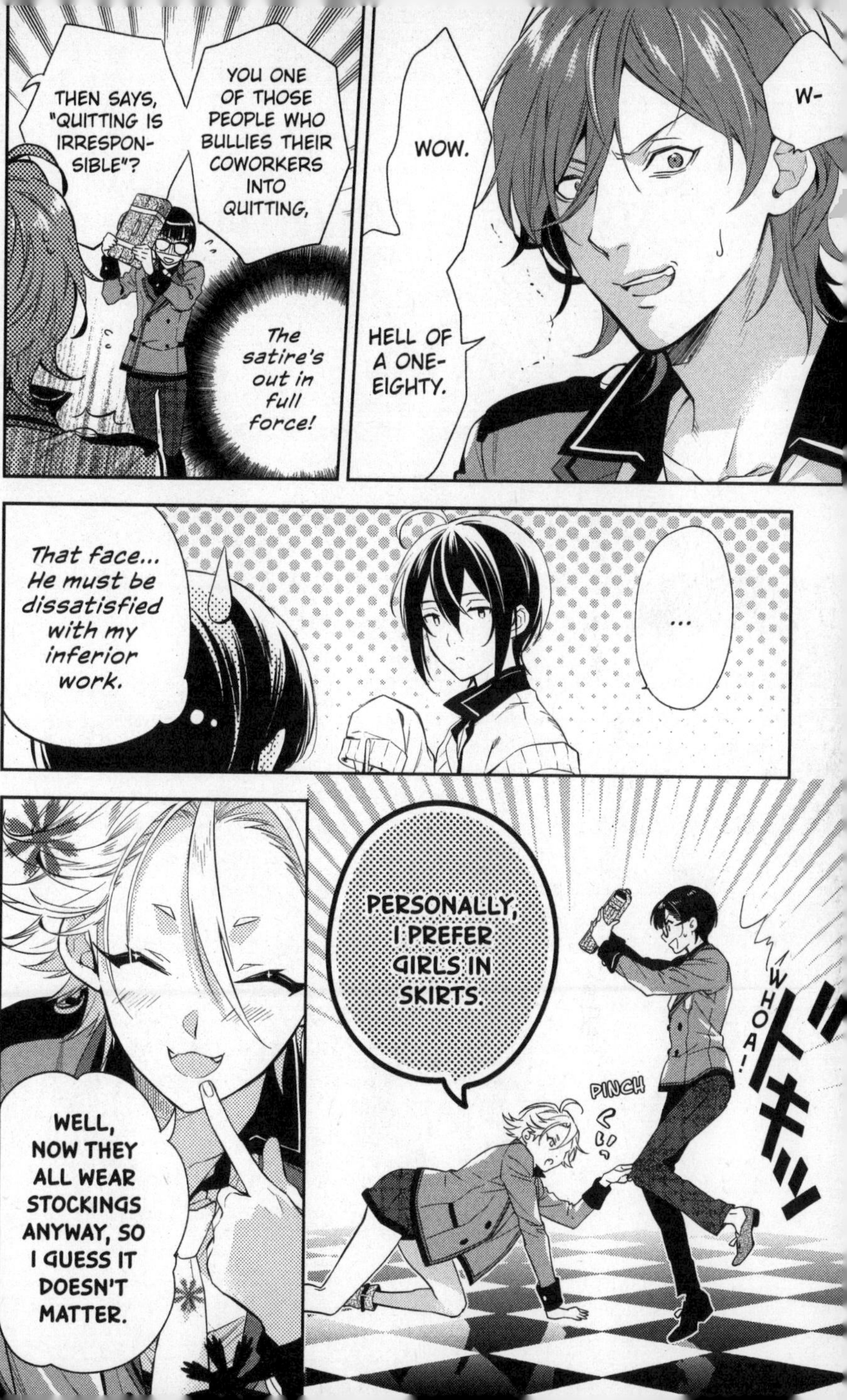
W-
WOW.
HELL OF A ONE-EIGHTY.
YOU ONE OF THOSE PEOPLE WHO BULLIES THEIR COWORKERS INTO QUITTING,
THEN SAYS, "QUITTING IS IRRESPON-SIBLE"?
The satire's out in full force!
...
That face... He must be dissatisfied with my inferior work.
WHOA!
ドキッ!
PINCH
PERSONALLY, I PREFER GIRLS IN SKIRTS.
WELL, NOW THEY ALL WEAR STOCKINGS ANYWAY, SO I GUESS IT DOESN'T MATTER.

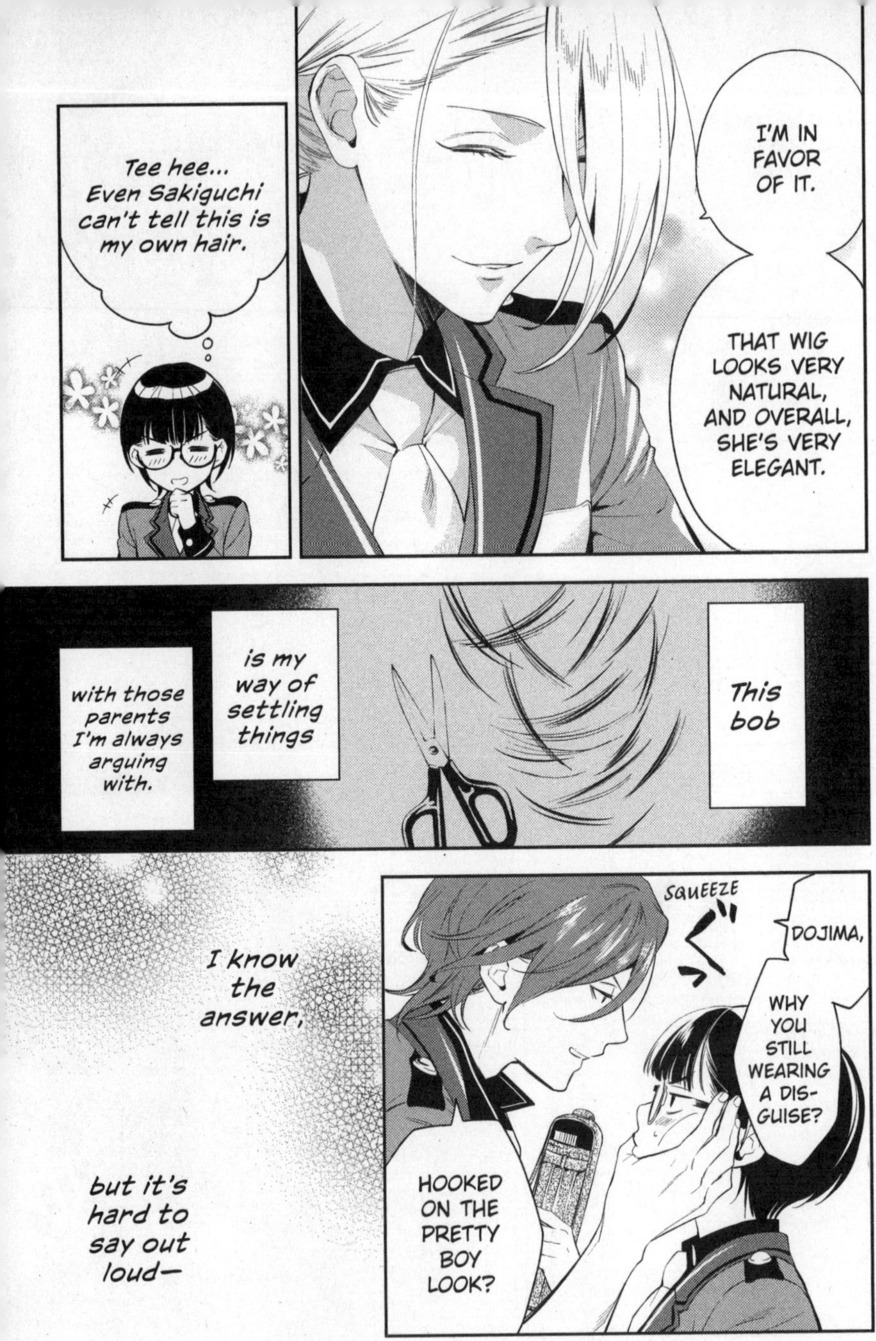
I'M IN FAVOR OF IT.
THAT WIG LOOKS VERY NATURAL, AND OVERALL, SHE'S VERY ELEGANT.
Tee hee... Even Sakiguchi can't tell this is my own hair.
This bob
is my way of settling things
with those parents I'm always arguing with.
SQUEEZE
DOJIMA,
WHY YOU STILL WEARING A DIS-GUISE?
HOOKED ON THE PRETTY BOY LOOK?
I know the answer,
but it's hard to say out loud—

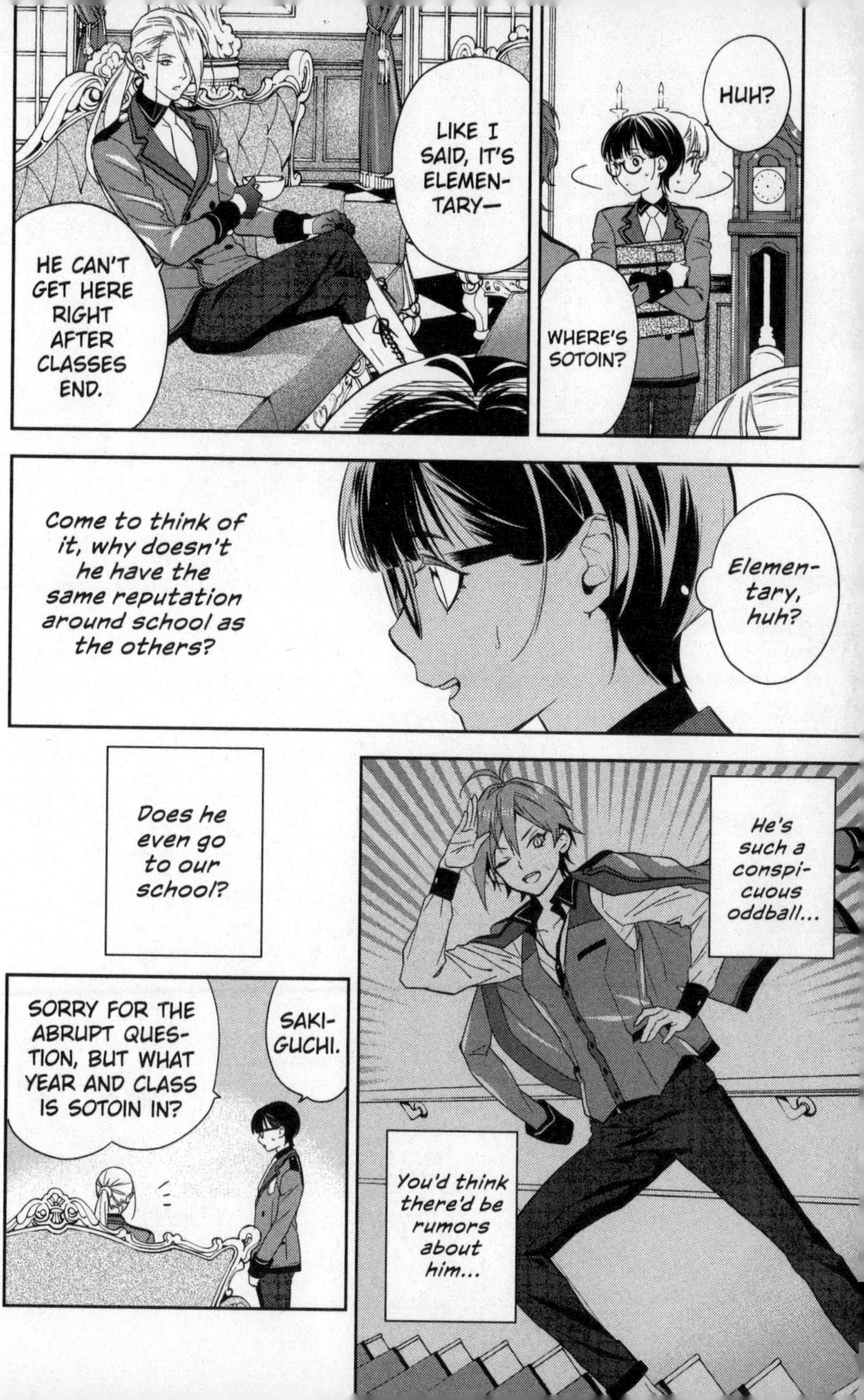
HUH?
WHERE'S SOTOIN?
LIKE I SAID, IT'S ELEMENTARY—
HE CAN'T GET HERE RIGHT AFTER CLASSES END.
Elementary, huh?
Come to think of it, why doesn't he have the same reputation around school as the others?
He's such a conspicuous oddball...
You'd think there'd be rumors about him...
Does he even go to our school?
SAKIGUCHI.
SORRY FOR THE ABRUPT QUESTION, BUT WHAT YEAR AND CLASS IS SOTOIN IN?

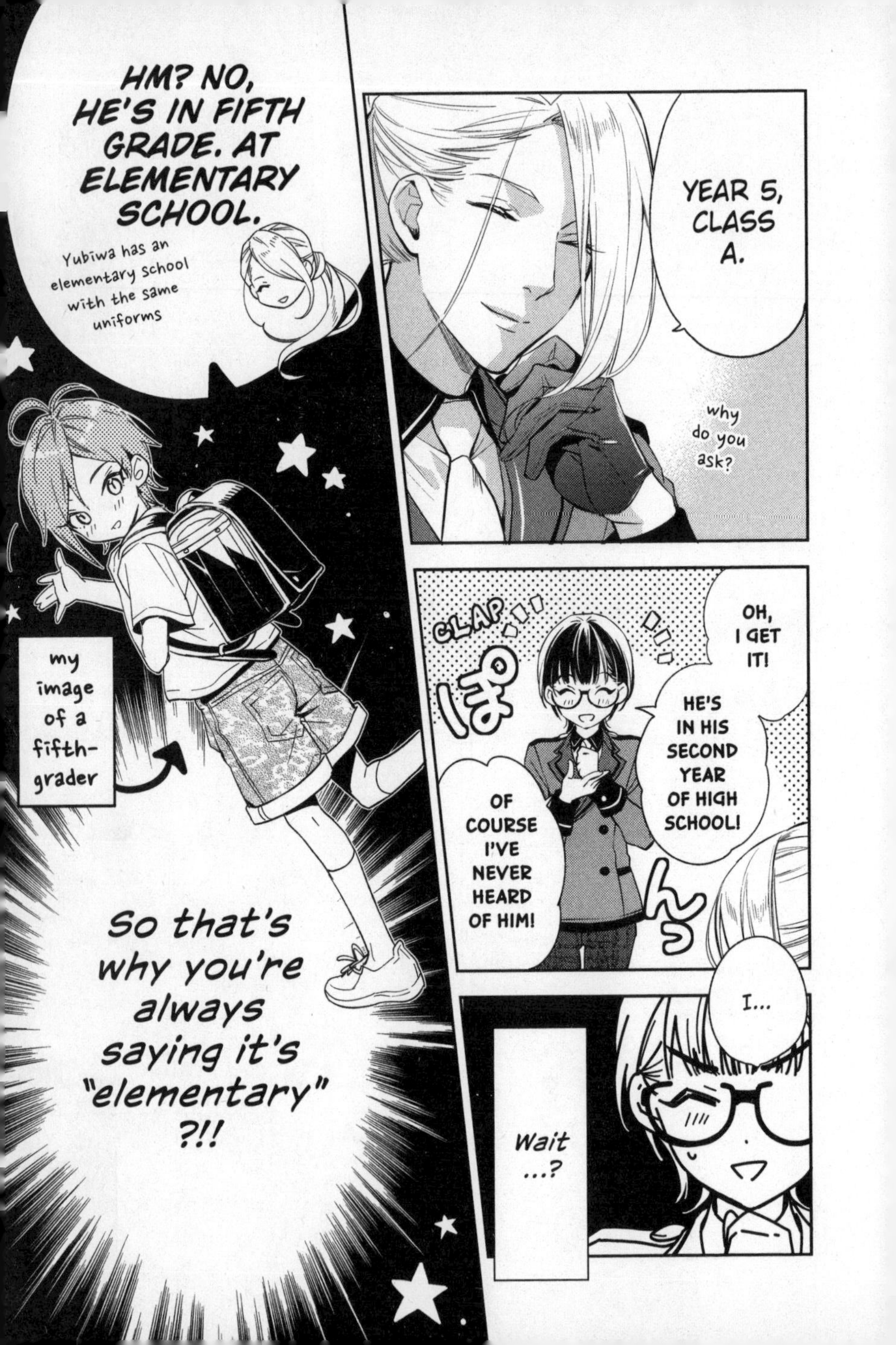
YEAR 5, CLASS A.
why do you ask?
OH, I GET IT!
HE'S IN HIS SECOND YEAR OF HIGH SCHOOL!
CLAP
ぽ
OF COURSE I'VE NEVER HEARD OF HIM!
ん
I...
Wait ...?
HM? NO, HE'S IN FIFTH GRADE. AT ELEMENTARY SCHOOL.
Yubiwa has an elementary school with the same uniforms
my image of a fifth-grader
So that's why you're always saying it's "elementary" ?!!

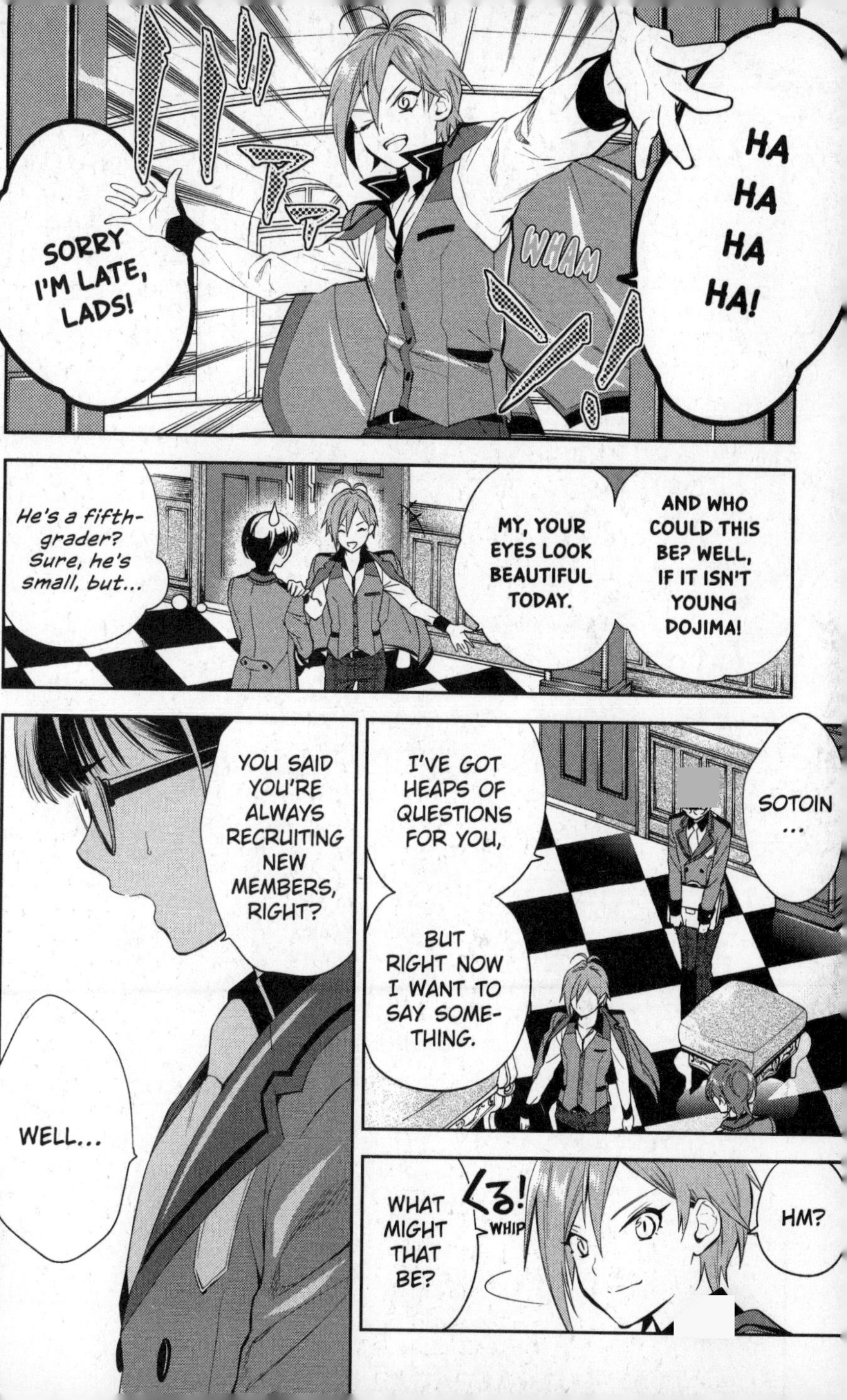
HA HA HA HA!
WHAM
SORRY I'M LATE, LADS!
AND WHO COULD THIS BE? WELL, IF IT ISN'T YOUNG DOJIMA!
MY, YOUR EYES LOOK BEAUTIFUL TODAY.
He's a fifth-grader? Sure, he's small, but...
SOTOIN ...
I'VE GOT HEAPS OF QUESTIONS FOR YOU,
BUT RIGHT NOW I WANT TO SAY SOME-THING.
HM?
くる!
WHIP
WHAT MIGHT THAT BE?
YOU SAID YOU'RE ALWAYS RECRUITING NEW MEMBERS, RIGHT?
WELL...

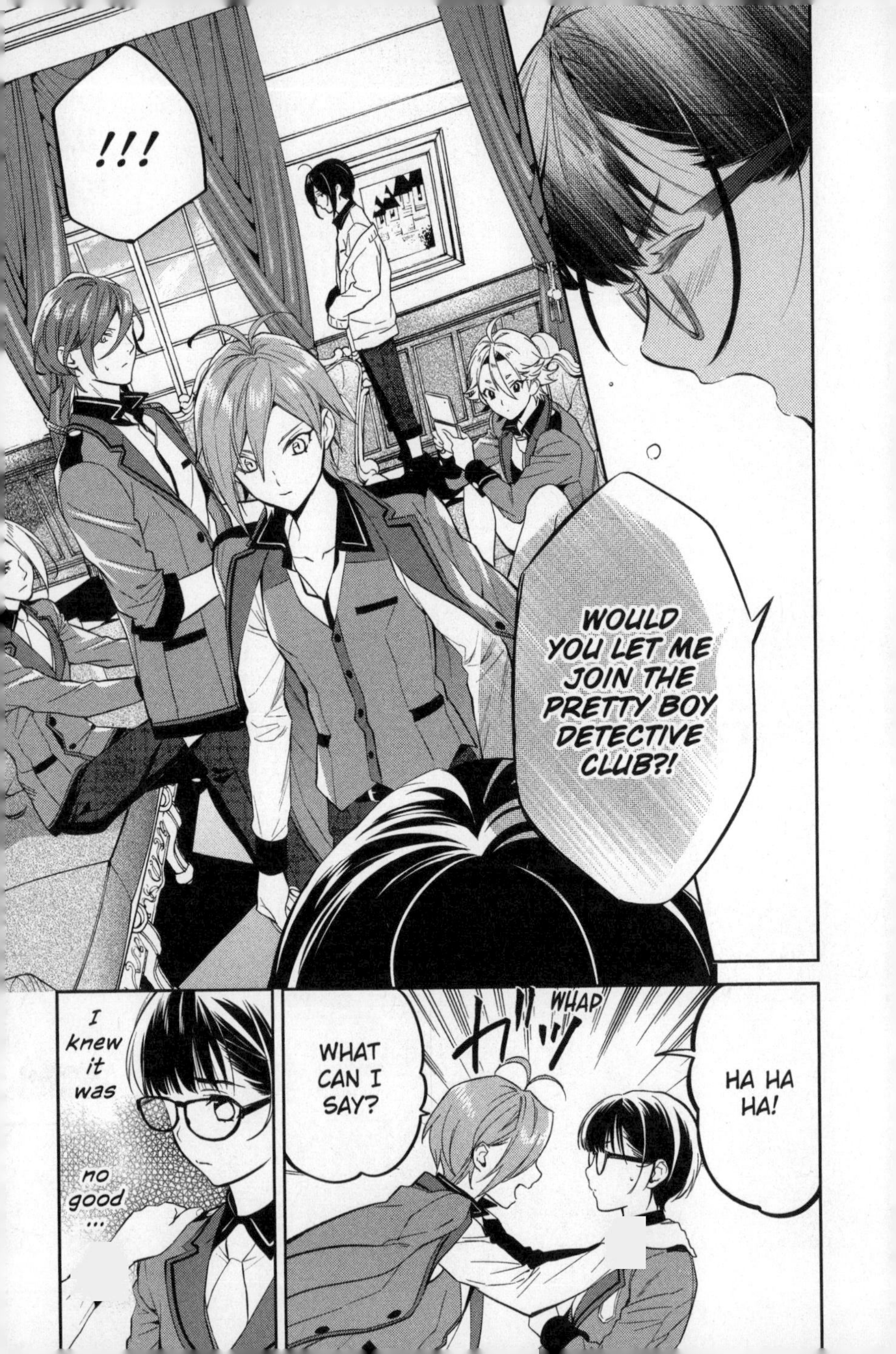
WOULD YOU LET ME JOIN THE PRETTY BOY DETECTIVE CLUB?!
!!!
HA HA HA!
WHAP
WHAT CAN I SAY?
I knew it was no good...

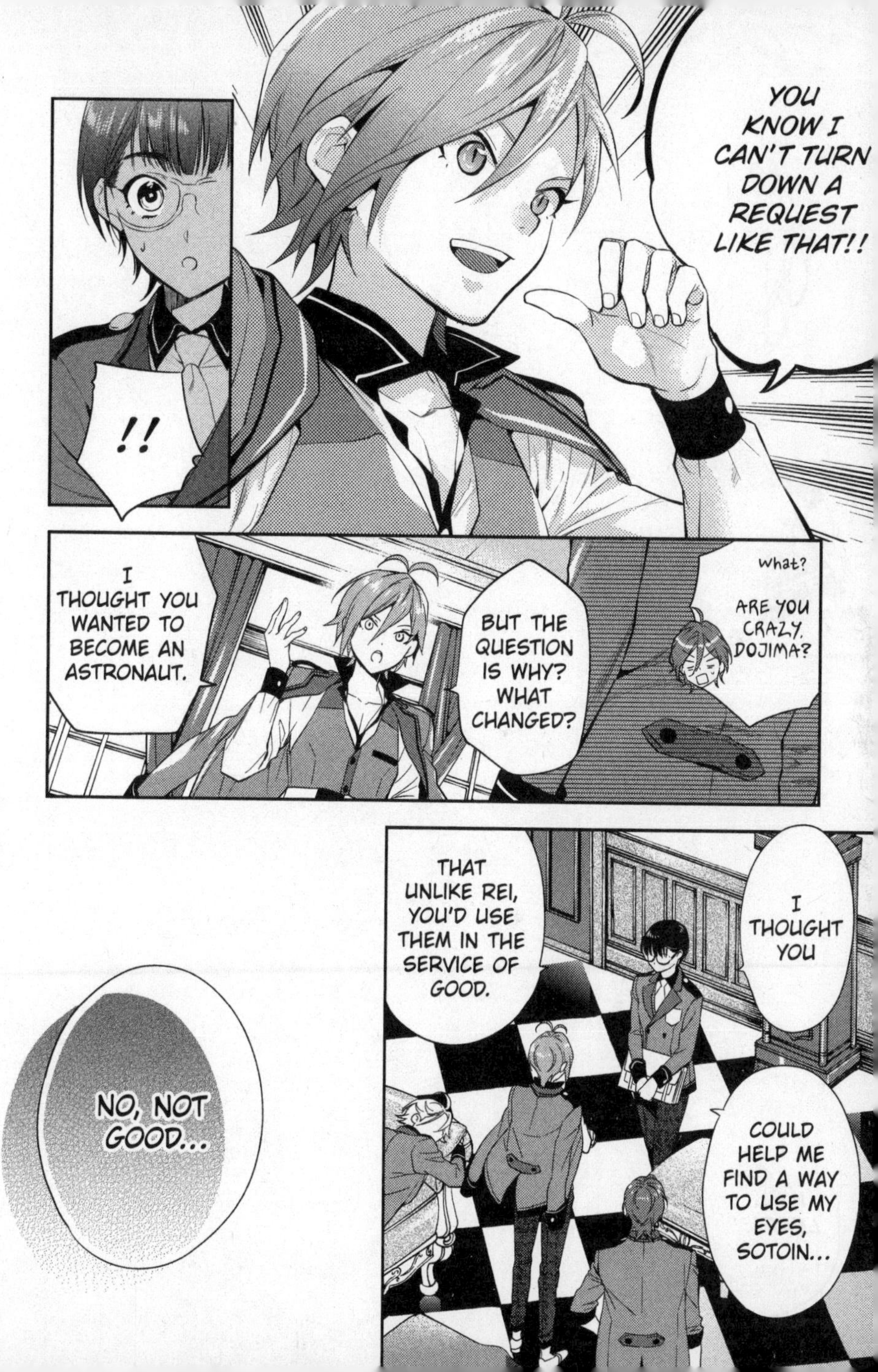
YOU KNOW I CAN'T TURN DOWN A REQUEST LIKE THAT!!
!!
What?
ARE YOU CRAZY, DOJIMA?
BUT THE QUESTION IS WHY? WHAT CHANGED?
I THOUGHT YOU WANTED TO BECOME AN ASTRONAUT.
I THOUGHT YOU
COULD HELP ME FIND A WAY TO USE MY EYES, SOTOIN...
THAT UNLIKE REI, YOU'D USE THEM IN THE SERVICE OF GOOD.
NO, NOT GOOD...

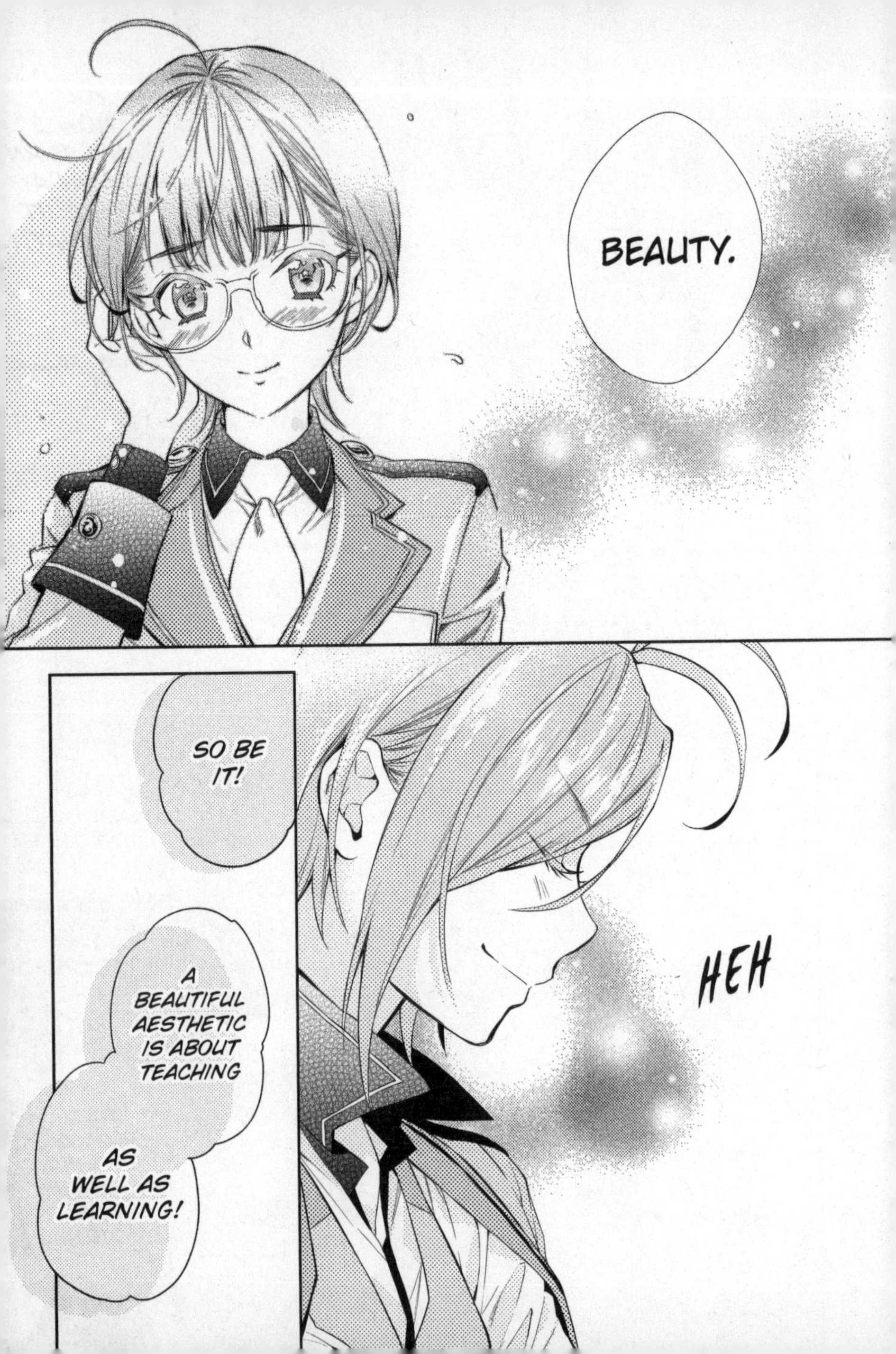
BEAUTY.
SO BE IT!
HEH
A BEAUTIFUL AESTHETIC IS ABOUT TEACHING
AS WELL AS LEARNING!

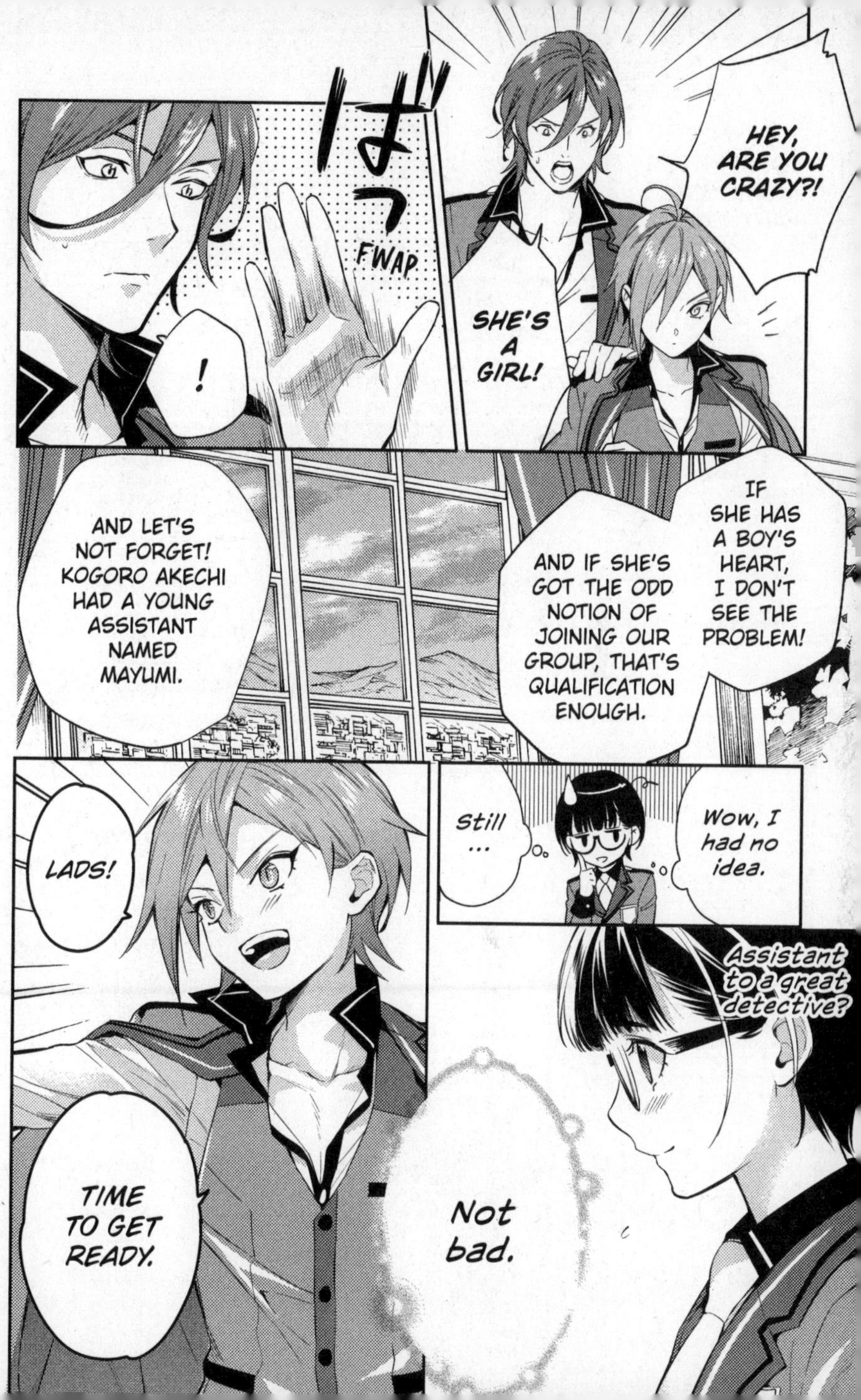
HEY, ARE YOU CRAZY?!
SHE'S A GIRL!
ばっ
FWAP
!
IF SHE HAS A BOY'S HEART, I DON'T SEE THE PROBLEM!
AND IF SHE'S GOT THE ODD NOTION OF JOINING OUR GROUP, THAT'S QUALIFICATION ENOUGH.
AND LET'S NOT FORGET! KOGORO AKECHI HAD A YOUNG ASSISTANT NAMED MAYUMI.
Wow, I had no idea.
Still ...
Assistant to a great detective?
Not bad.
LADS!
TIME TO GET READY.

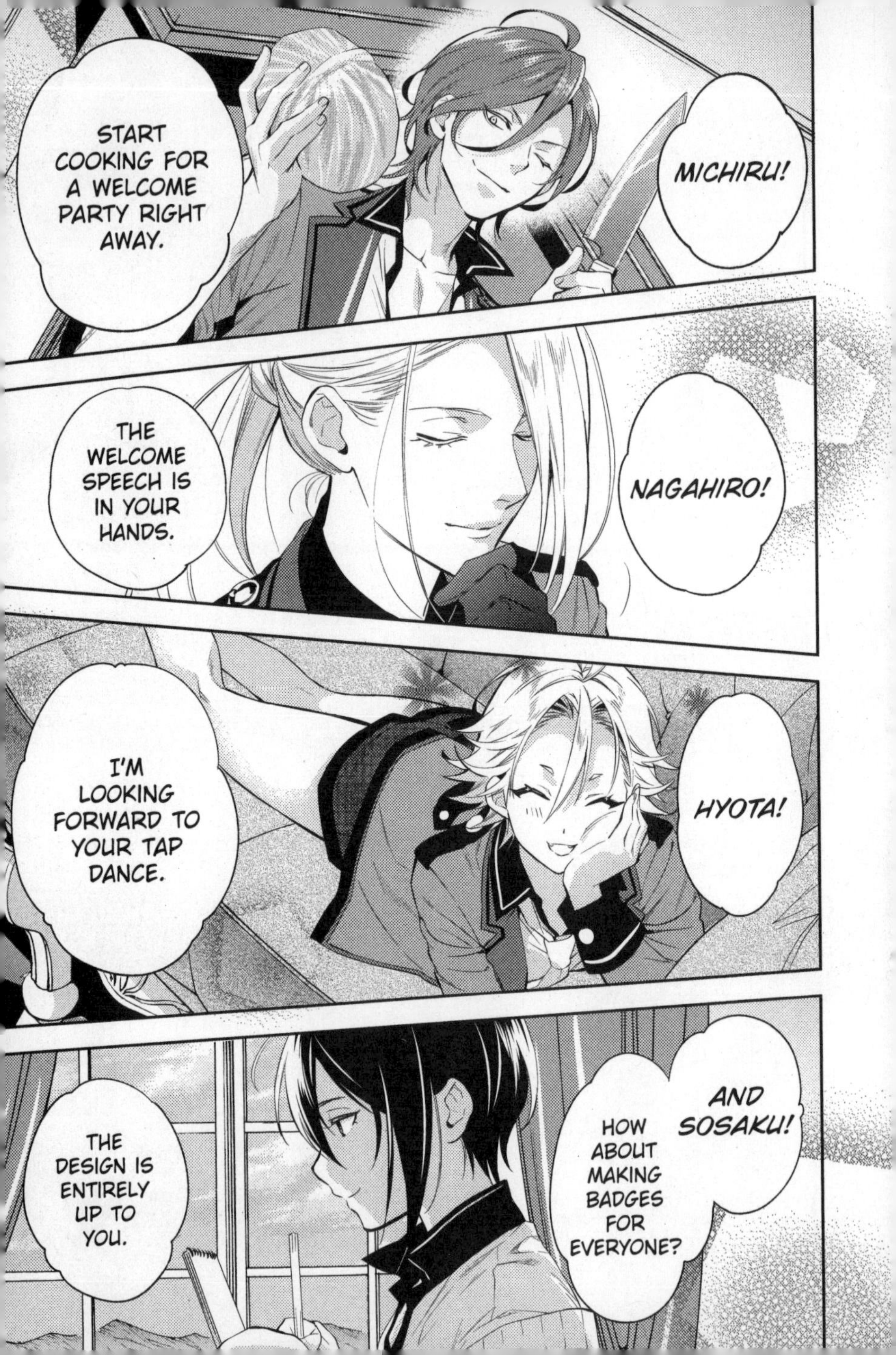
MICHIRU!
START COOKING FOR A WELCOME PARTY RIGHT AWAY.
NAGAHIRO!
THE WELCOME SPEECH IS IN YOUR HANDS.
HYOTA!
I'M LOOKING FORWARD TO YOUR TAP DANCE.
AND SOSAKU!
HOW ABOUT MAKING BADGES FOR EVERYONE?
THE DESIGN IS ENTIRELY UP TO YOU.

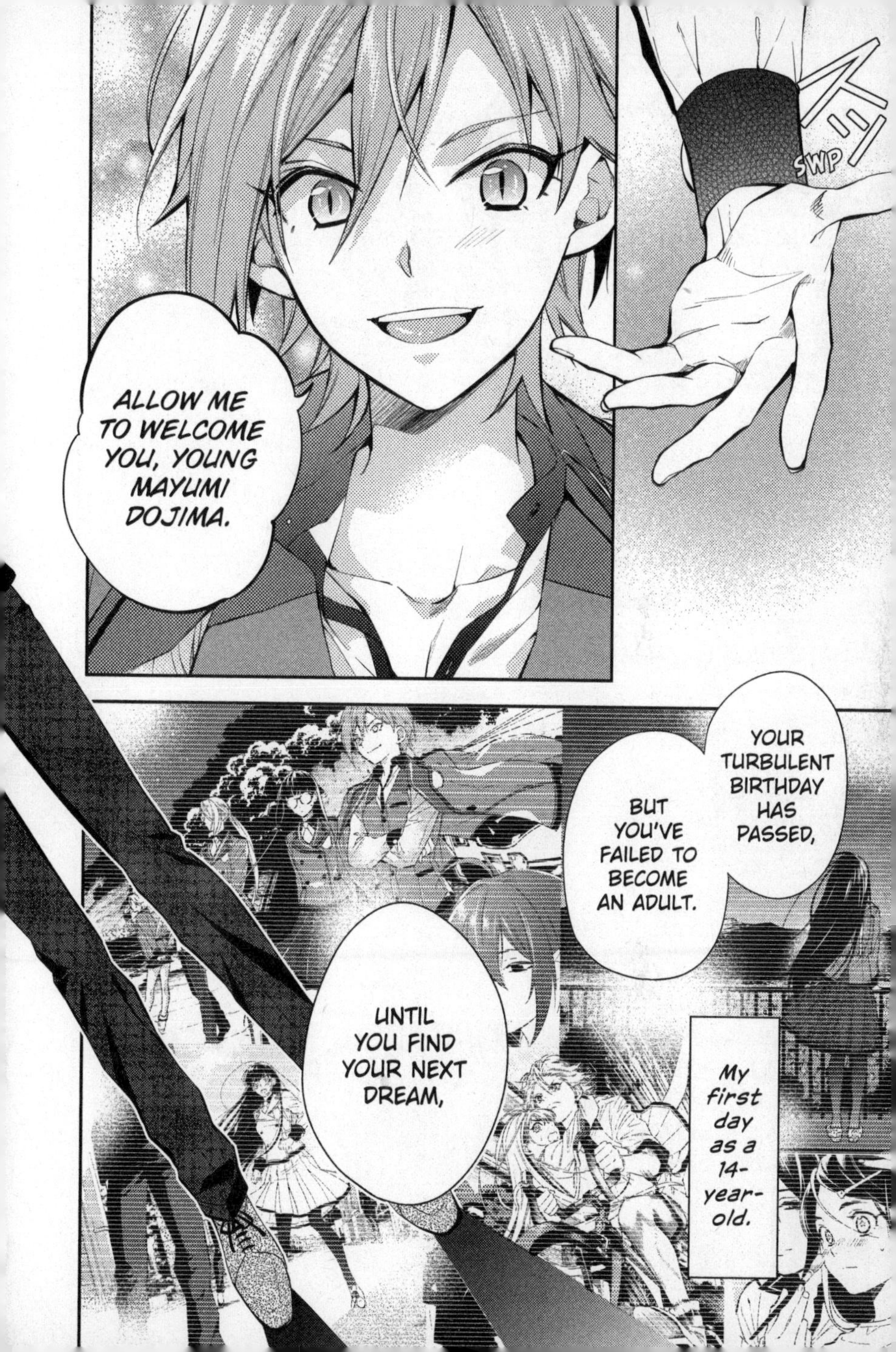
SWP
ALLOW ME TO WELCOME YOU, YOUNG MAYUMI DOJIMA.
YOUR TURBULENT BIRTHDAY HAS PASSED,
BUT YOU'VE FAILED TO BECOME AN ADULT.
UNTIL YOU FIND YOUR NEXT DREAM,
My first day as a 14-year-old.

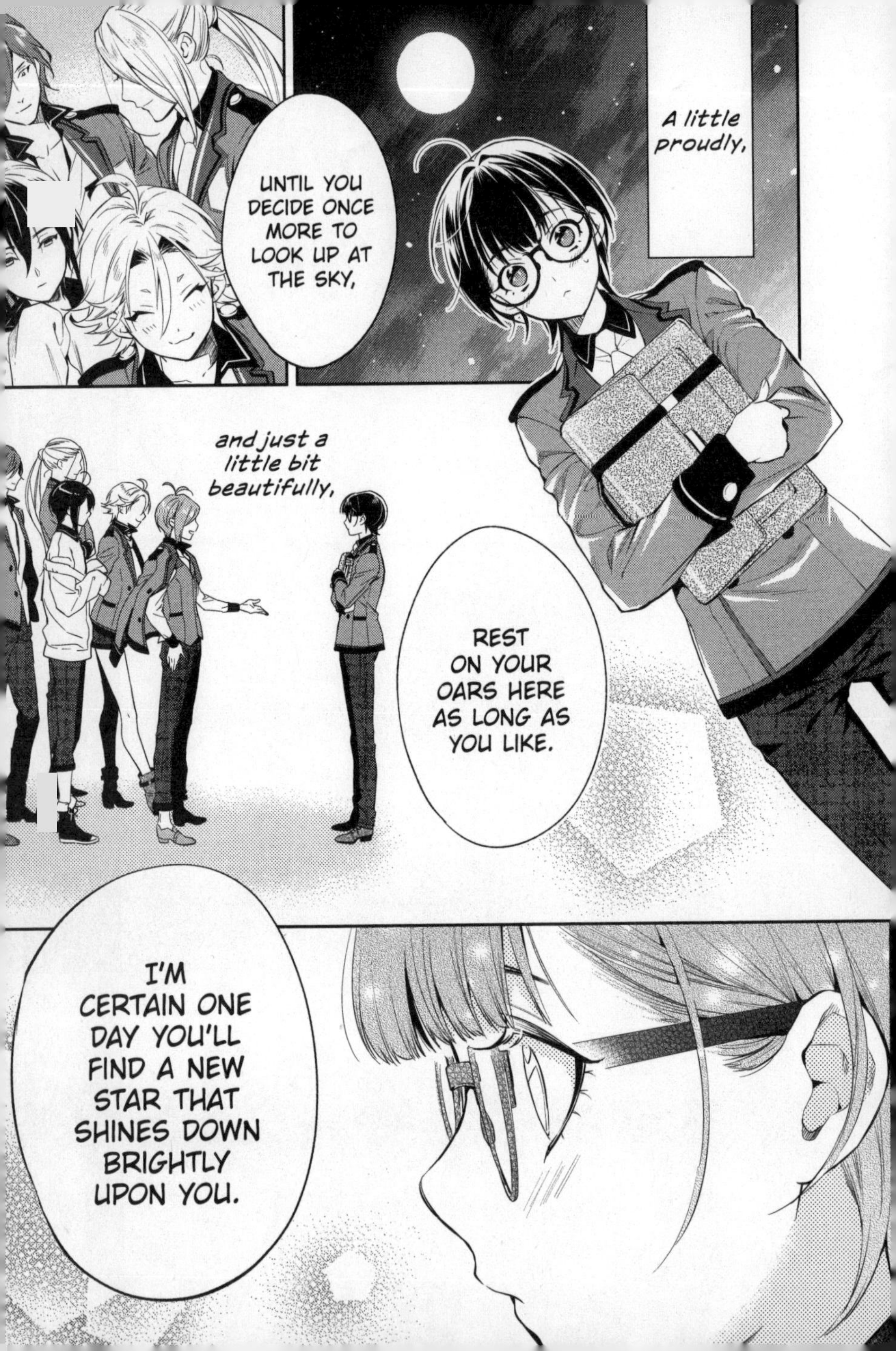
A little proudly,
REST ON YOUR OARS HERE AS LONG AS YOU LIKE.
UNTIL YOU DECIDE ONCE MORE TO LOOK UP AT THE SKY,
and just a little bit beautifully,
I'M CERTAIN ONE DAY YOU'LL FIND A NEW STAR THAT SHINES DOWN BRIGHTLY UPON YOU.

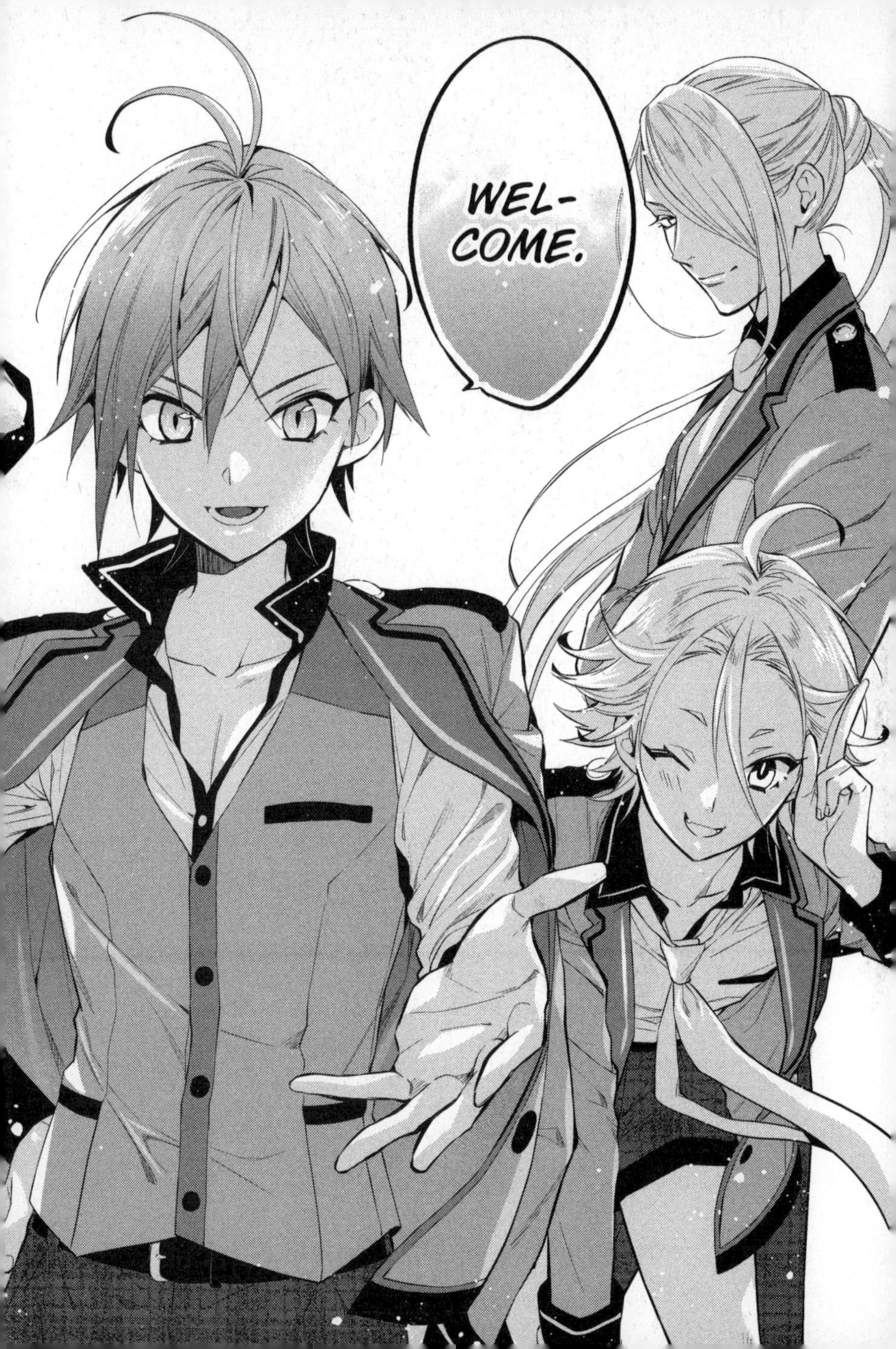
WEL-
COME.

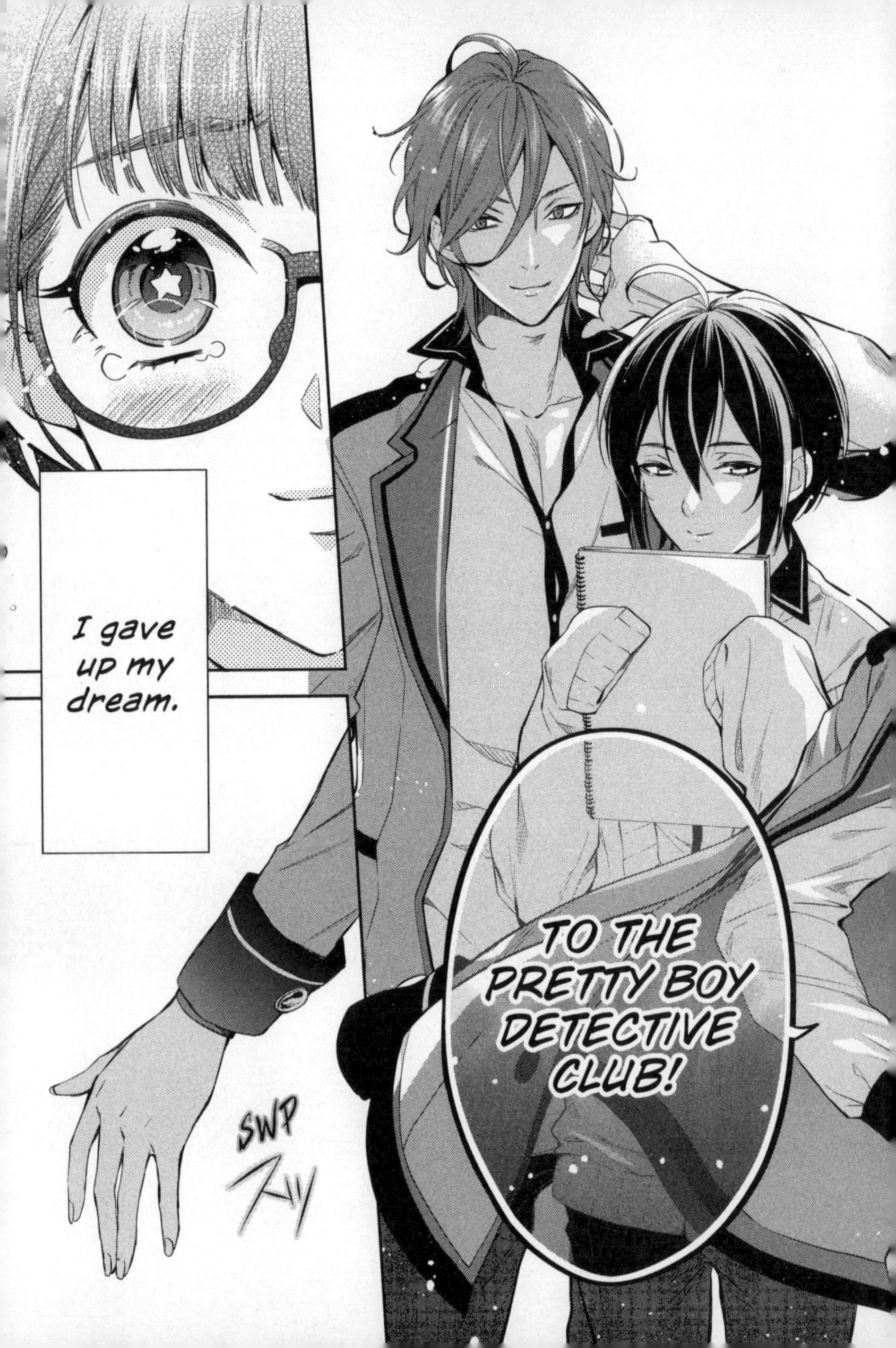

I gave up my dream.
TO THE PRETTY BOY DETECTIVE CLUB!
SWP

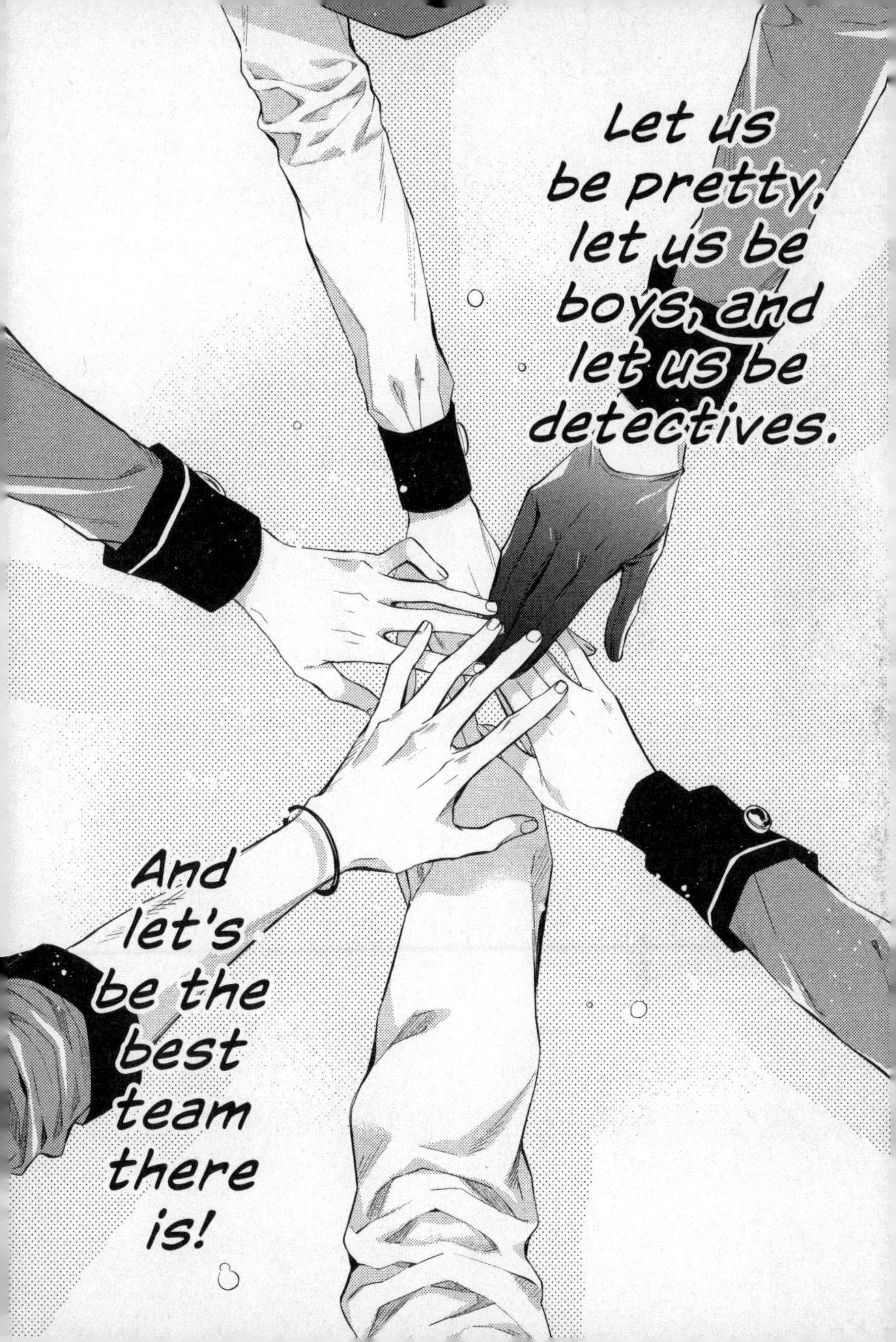
Let us be pretty, let us be boys, and let us be detectives.
And let's be the best team there is!

Continued in Volume 2

PRETTY BOY

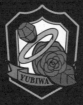

DETECTIVE CLUB!!

A note on the manga version of Pretty Boy Detective Club

NISIOISIN

I originally conceived of the individuals in the Pretty Boy Detective Club as characters (or rather, as a group of characters) for the Kyoko Okitegami series. Because Yakusuke Kakushidate, the narrator of that series (one of them, anyway), is constantly being falsely accused of crimes, he keeps the phone numbers of various detectives and detective agencies in his phone so he can commission them to solve cases at the drop of a hat. Kyoko Okitegami is one of them, and the Pretty Boy Detective Club are another. I intended at some point to write a sort of "Kyoko Okitegami vs. Pretty Boy Detective Club" novel, but as I thought more about it, I decided they were capable of standing on their own as detectives, which led to Kodansha Taiga's publication of *Pretty Boy Detective Club—The Dark Star that Shines for You Alone*. As the author of the original work, I'm all the more delighted to see it adapted as a comic. Now, because of the nature of the series (although for different reasons than pertain to Koyomi Araragi from the *Monogatari* series), Mayumi Dojima's ordinary look hasn't yet appeared on the cover of any of the novels in the series—but I'm glad to see her portrayed so charmingly in the manga. I hope you'll agree that's part of the unique appeal, and beauty, of the manga version.

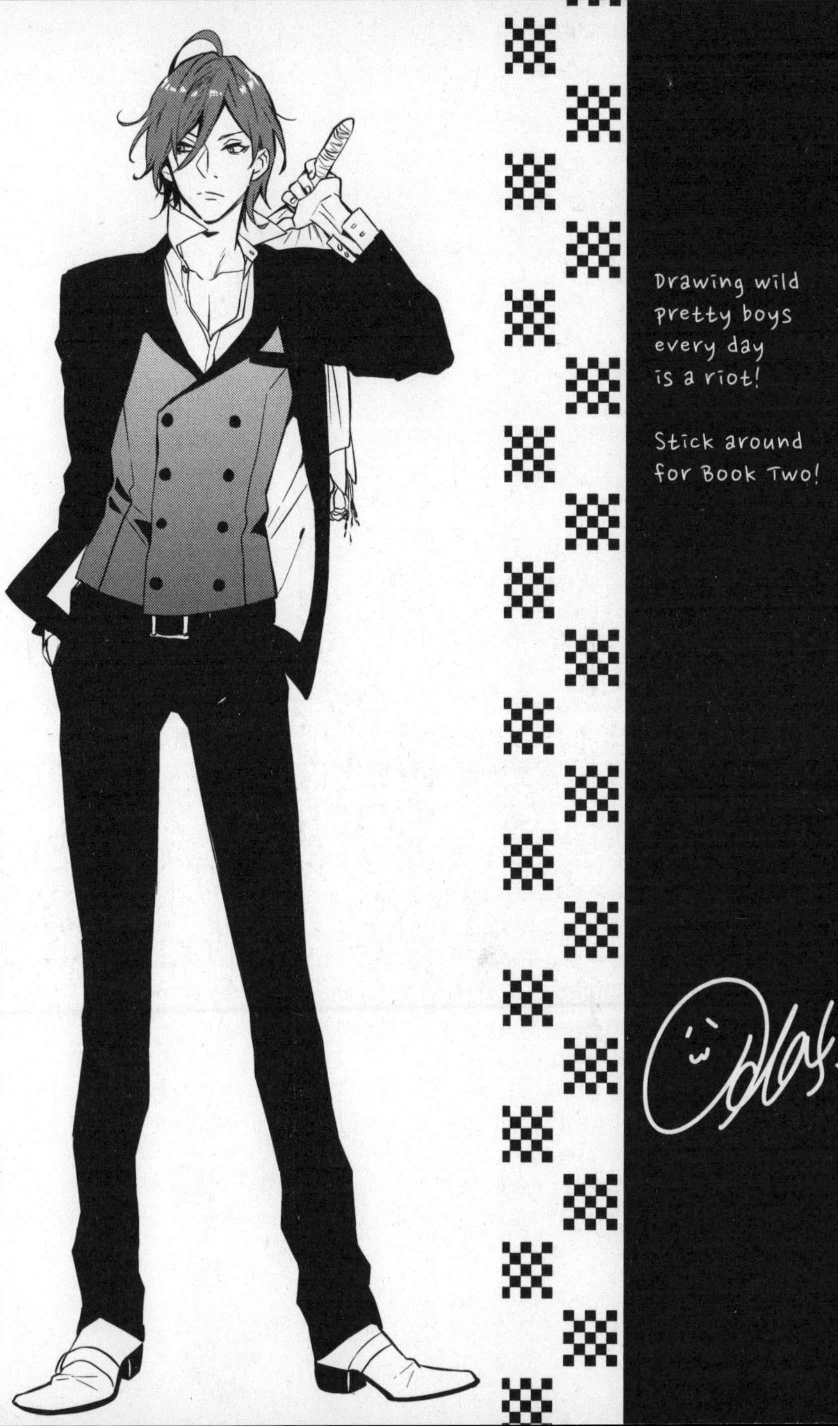

Drawing wild pretty boys every day is a riot!

Stick around for Book Two!

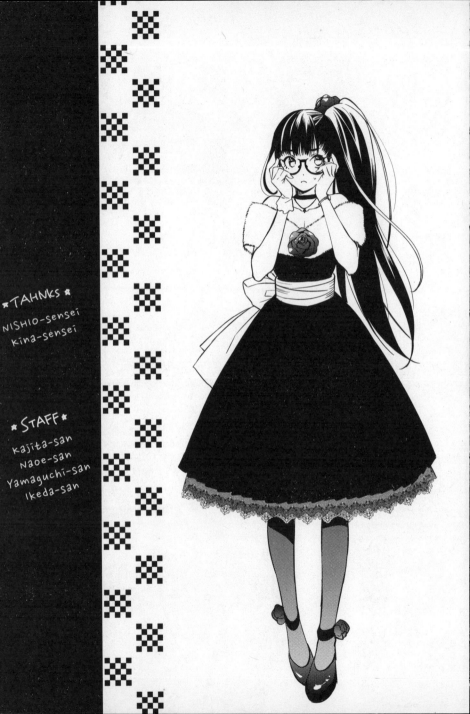

★TAHNKS★
NISHIO-sensei
Kina-sensei

★STAFF★
Kajita-san
Naoe-san
Yamaguchi-san
Ikeda-san

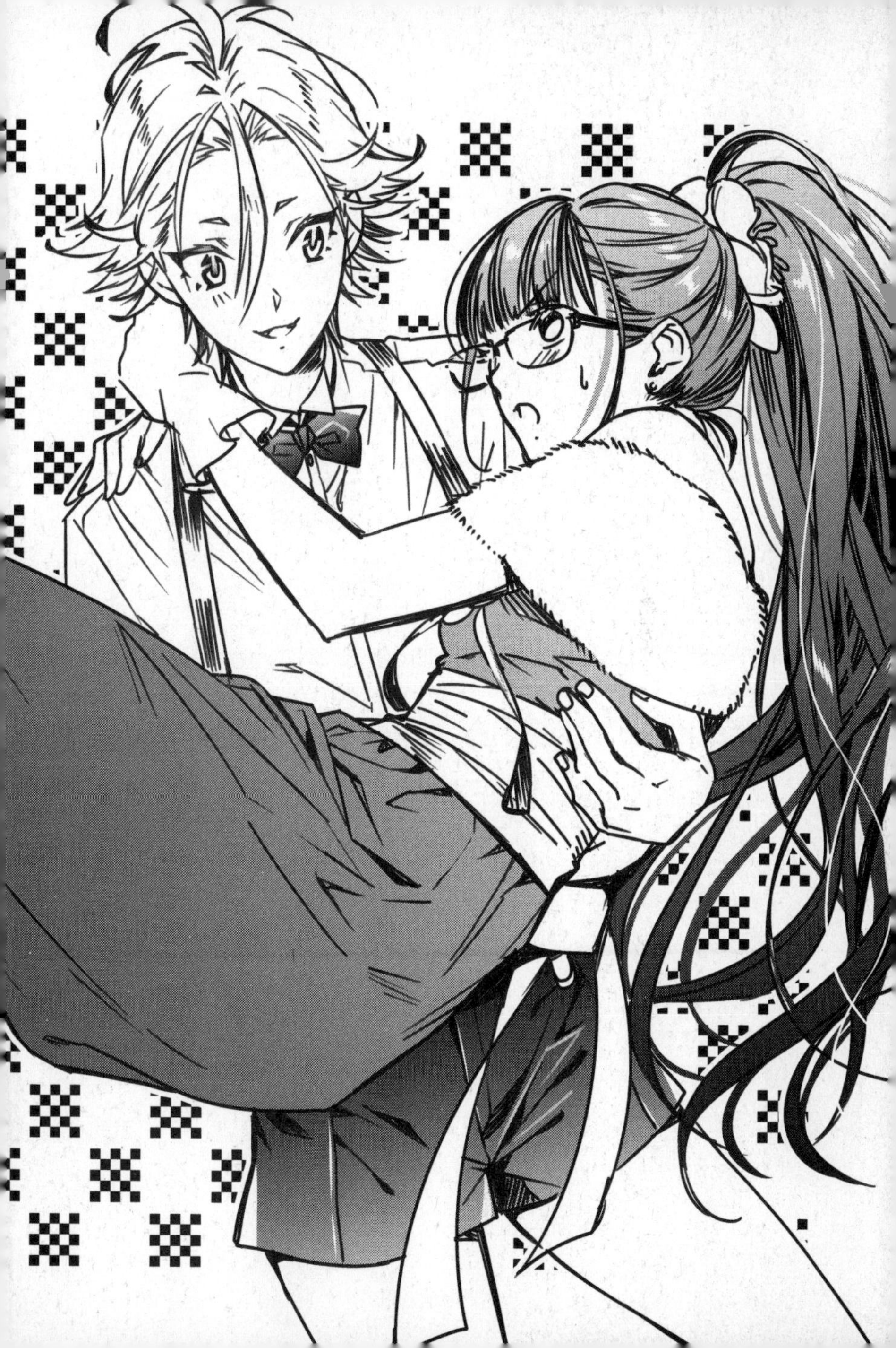

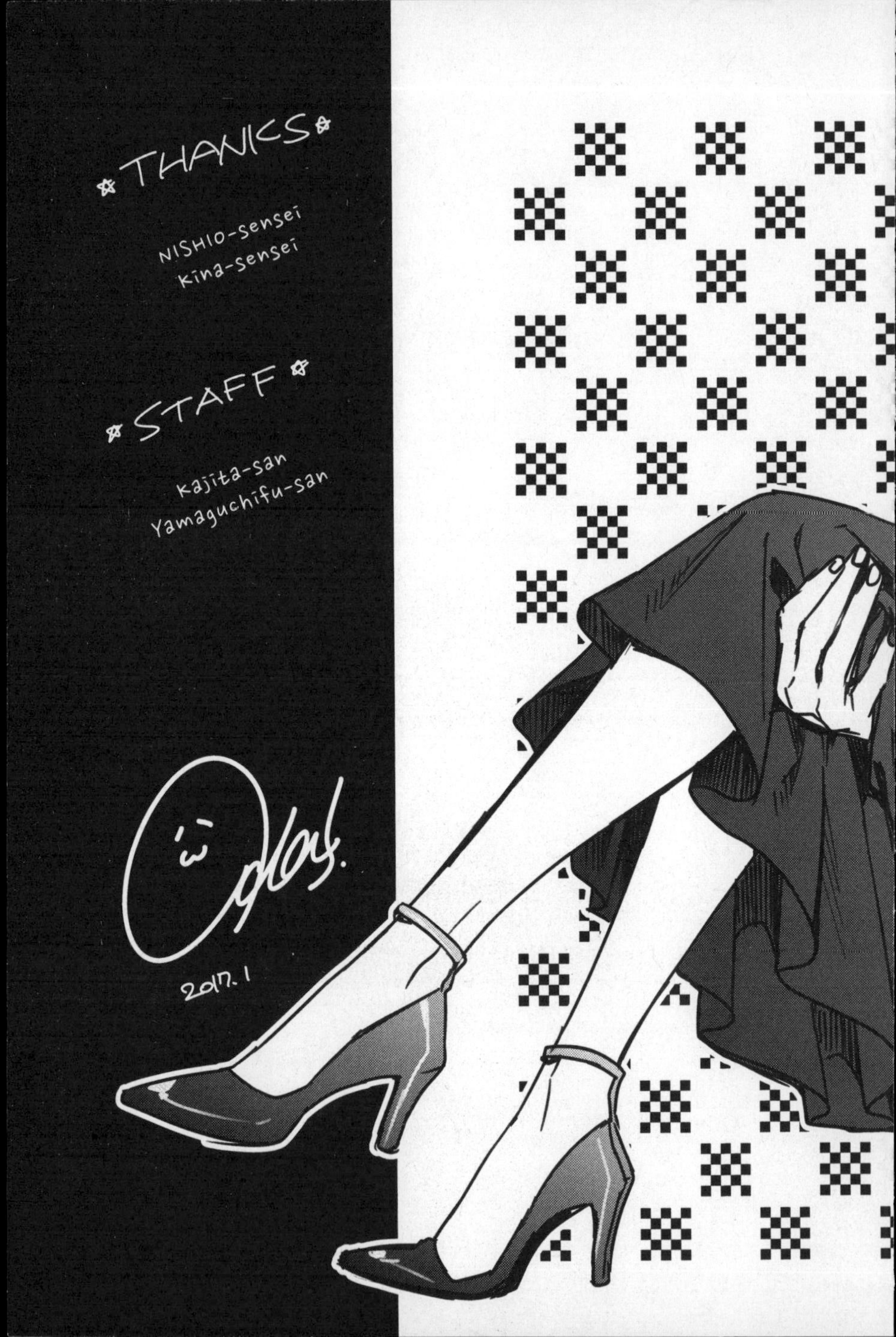
THANKS
NISHIO-sensei
Kina-sensei
STAFF
Kajita-san
Yamaguchifu-san
2017.1

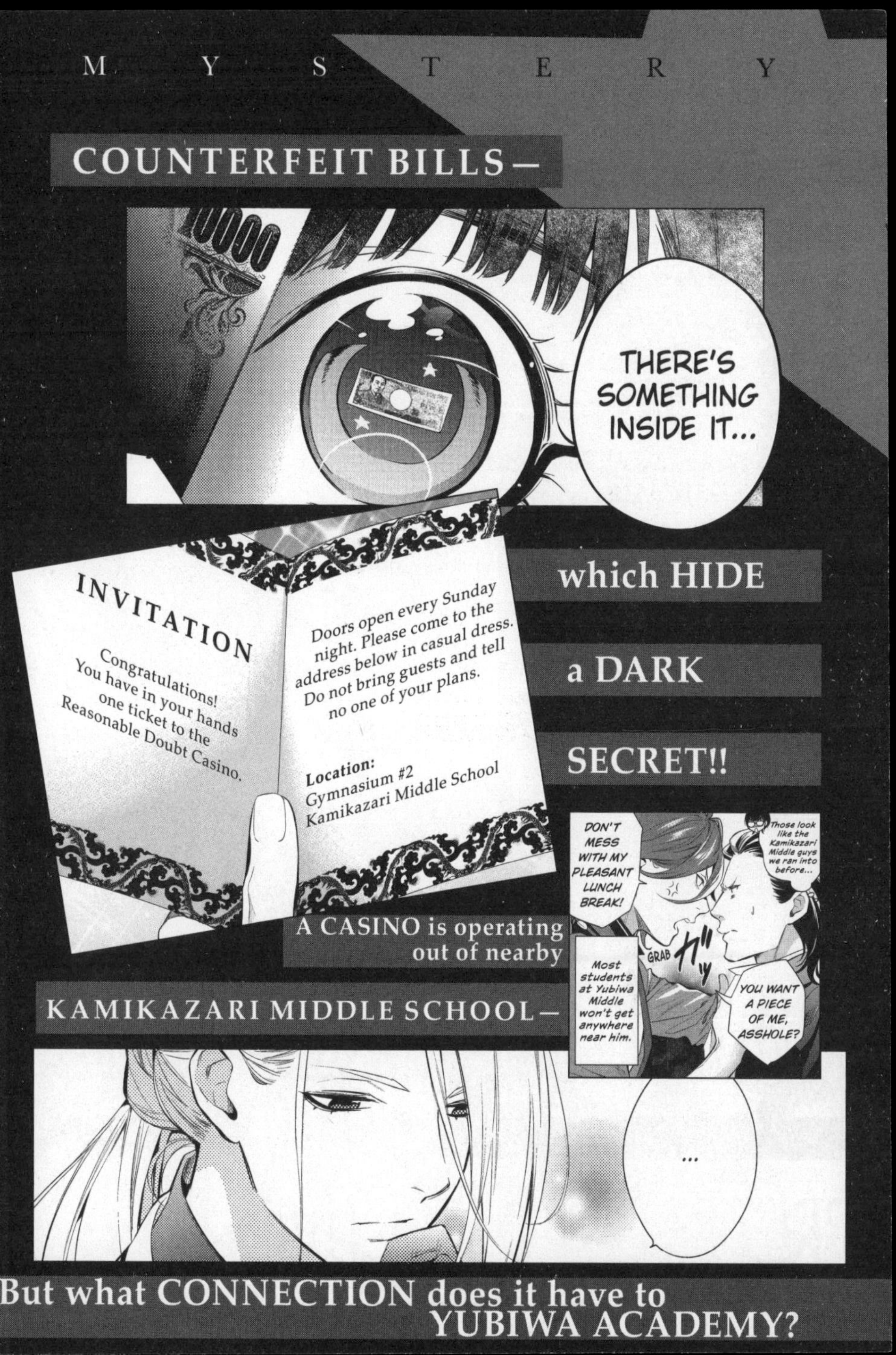
M Y S T E R Y
COUNTERFEIT BILLS—
THERE'S SOMETHING INSIDE IT...
INVITATION
Congratulations! You have in your hands one ticket to the Reasonable Doubt Casino.
Doors open every Sunday night. Please come to the address below in casual dress. Do not bring guests and tell no one of your plans.
Location:
Gymnasium #2
Kamikazari Middle School
which HIDE
a DARK
SECRET!!
Those look like the Kamikazari Middle guys we ran into before...
DON'T MESS WITH MY PLEASANT LUNCH BREAK!
GRAB
YOU WANT A PIECE OF ME, ASSHOLE?
Most students at Yubiwa Middle won't get anywhere near him.
A CASINO is operating out of nearby
KAMIKAZARI MIDDLE SCHOOL—
...
But what CONNECTION does it have to YUBIWA ACADEMY?

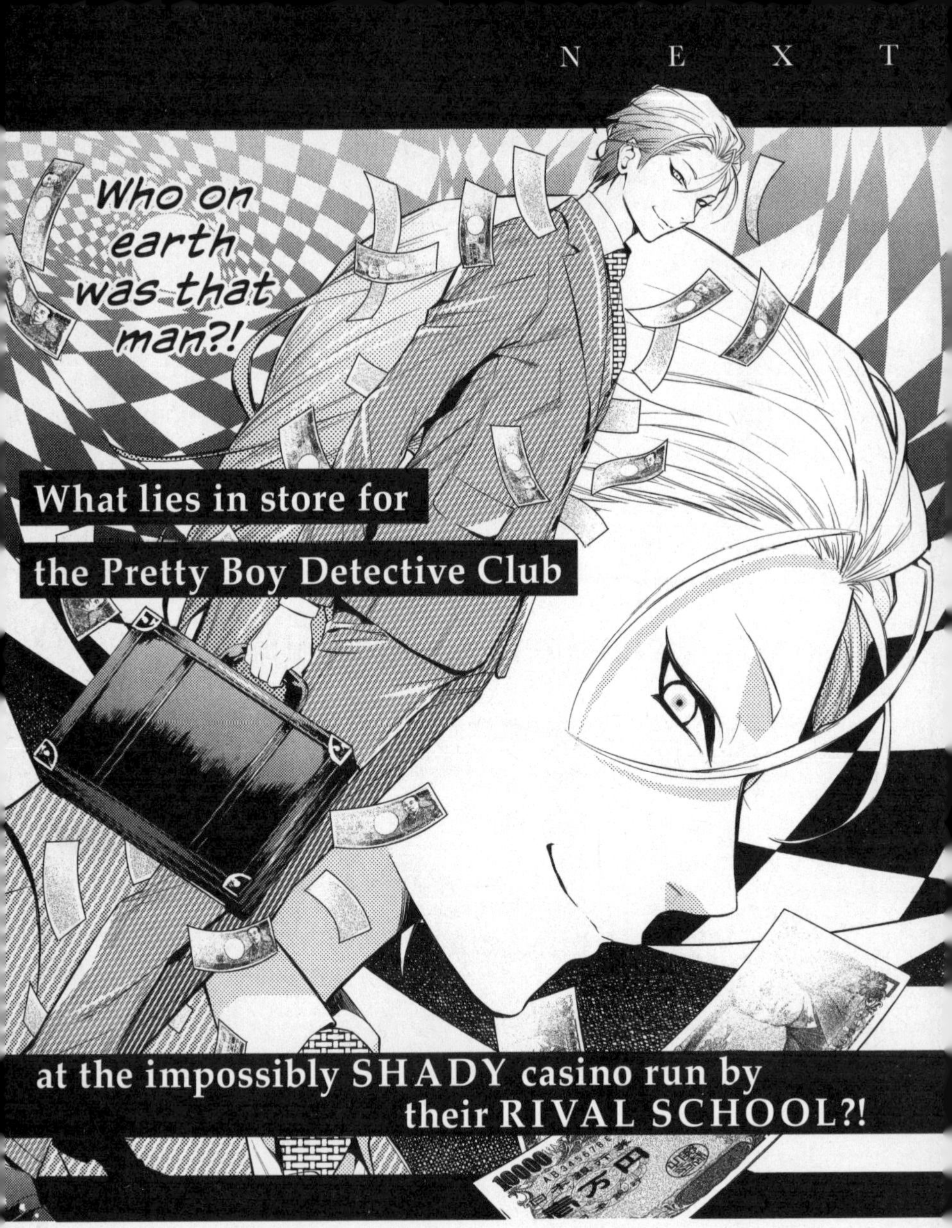
N E X T
Who on earth was that man?!
What lies in store for
the Pretty Boy Detective Club
at the impossibly SHADY casino run by
their RIVAL SCHOOL?!

PRETTY BOY DETECTIVE CLUB 2

COMING OCTOBER 2021!!

JOIN THE CLUB

Ten years ago, Mayumi Dojima saw a star...and she's been searching for it ever since. The mysterious organization that solves (and causes?) all the problems at Yubiwa Academy—the *Pretty Boy Detective Club* is on the case! Five beautiful youths, each more eccentric than the last, united only by their devotion to the aesthetics of mystery-solving. Together they find much, much more than they bargained for.

Read the original novels!

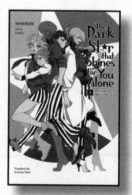

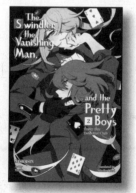

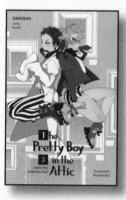

**The Dark Star
that Shines
for You Alone**

**The Swindler,
the Vanishing Man,
and the Pretty Boys**

**The Pretty Boy
in the Attic**

AVAILABLE NOW!

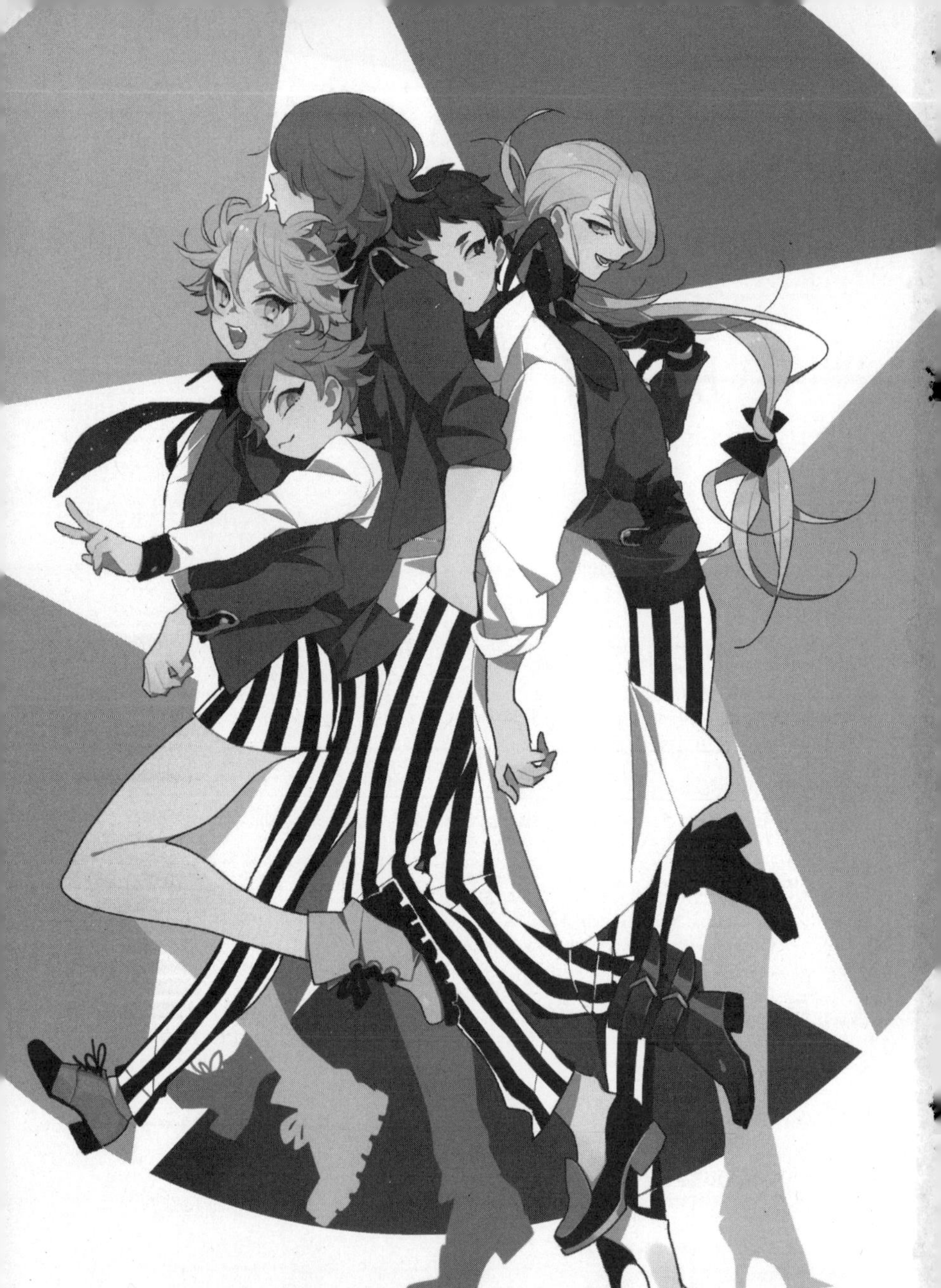

Pretty Boy Detective Club

PRETTY BOY DETECTIVE CLUB 1

A Vertical Comics Edition

Editor:	Daniel Joseph
Translation:	Winifred Bird
Production:	Risa Cho
	Lorina Mapa
Proofreading:	Micah Q. Allen

First published in Japan in 2016-2017 by Kodansha, Ltd., Tokyo
Publication rights for this English edition arranged through Kodansha, Ltd., Tokyo
English language version produced by Vertical Comics, an imprint of
Kodansha USA Publishing, LLC

Translation provided by Vertical Comics, 2021
Published by Kodansha USA Publishing, LLC, New York

Originally published in Japanese as *Bishounen Tanteidan* 1 & 2 by Kodansha, Ltd.,
2016, 2017
Bishounen Tanteidan serialized in *ARIA*, Kodansha, Ltd., 2016-

This is a work of fiction.

ISBN: 978-1-64729-047-4

Manufactured in the United States of America

First Edition

Kodansha USA Publishing, LLC
451 Park Avenue South
7th Floor
New York, NY 10016
www.kodansha.us

Vertical books are distributed through Penguin-Random House Publisher Services.